Algorithms for Decision Making

Algorithms for Decision Making

Mykel J. Kochenderfer
Tim A. Wheeler
Kyle H. Wray

The MIT Press
Cambridge, Massachusetts
London, England

The MIT Press would like to thank the anonymous peer reviewers who provided comments on drafts of this book. The generous work of academic experts is essential for establishing the authority and quality of our publications. We acknowledge with gratitude the contributions of these otherwise uncredited readers.

This book was set in TEX Gyre Pagella by the authors in LATEX.
Printed and bound in the United States of America.

Library of Congress Cataloging-in-Publication Data

Names: Kochenderfer, Mykel J., 1980– author. | Wheeler, Tim A. (Tim Allan), author. | Wray, Kyle H., author.
Title: Algorithms for decision making / Mykel J. Kochenderfer, Tim A. Wheeler, Kyle H. Wray.
Description: Cambridge : Massachusetts Institute of Technology, [2022] |
    Includes bibliographical references and index.
Identifiers: LCCN 2021038701 | ISBN 9780262047012 (hardcover)
Subjects: LCSH: Decision support systems–Mathematics. | Algorithms.
Classification: LCC T58.62 .K666 2022 | DDC 658.4/03—dc23
LC record available at https://lccn.loc.gov/2021038701

10   9   8   7   6   5   4   3   2   1

To our families

Contents

PART II   SEQUENTIAL PROBLEMS

PART III MODEL UNCERTAINTY

PART V MULTIAGENT SYSTEMS

APPENDICES

Preface

This book provides a broad introduction to algorithms for decision making under uncertainty. We cover a wide variety of topics related to decision making, introducing the underlying mathematical problem formulations and the algorithms for solving them. Figures, examples, and exercises are provided to convey the intuition behind the various approaches.

This book is intended for advanced undergraduates and graduate students, as well as professionals. It requires some mathematical maturity and assumes prior exposure to multivariable calculus, linear algebra, and probability concepts. Some review material is provided in the appendices. Disciplines where the book would be especially useful include mathematics, statistics, computer science, aerospace, electrical engineering, and operations research.

Fundamental to this textbook are the algorithms, which are all implemented in the Julia programming language. We have found this language to be ideal for specifying algorithms in human-readable form. The priority in the design of the algorithmic implementations was interpretability rather than efficiency. Industrial applications, for example, may benefit from alternative implementations. Permission is granted, free of charge, to use the code snippets associated with this book, subject to the condition that the source of the code is acknowledged.

Mykel J. Kochenderfer
Tim A. Wheeler
Kyle H. Wray
Stanford, California
February 28, 2022

Acknowledgments

This textbook has grown from a course on decision making under uncertainty taught at Stanford. We are grateful to the students and teaching assistants who have helped shape the course over the past six years.

The authors wish to thank the many individuals who have provided valuable feedback on early drafts of our manuscript, including Dylan Asmar, Drew Bagnell, Safa Bakhshi, Edward Balaban, Jean Betterton, Raunak Bhattacharyya, Kelsey Bing, Maxime Bouton, Austin Chan, Simon Chauvin, Shushman Choudhury, Jon Cox, Matthew Daly, Victoria Dax, Richard Dewey, Dea Dressel, Ben Duprey, Torstein Eliassen, Johannes Fischer, Rushil Goradia, Jayesh Gupta, Arec Jamgochian, Rohan Kapre, Mark Koren, Liam Kruse, Tor Lattimore, Bernard Lange, Ritchie Lee, Sheng Li, Michael Littman, Robert Moss, Joshua Ott, Oriana Peltzer, Francesco Piccoli, Jeffrey Sarnoff, Marc Schlichting, Ransalu Senanayake, Chelsea Sidrane, Chris Strong, Zach Sunberg, Abiy Teshome, Alexandros Tzikas, Kemal Ure, Josh Wolff, Anıl Yıldız, and Zongzhang Zhang. We also would like to thank Sydney Katz, Kunal Menda, and Ayan Mukhopadhyay for their contributions to the discussion in chapter 1. Ross Alexander produced many of the exercises throughout the book. It has been a pleasure working with Elizabeth Swayze from the MIT Press in preparing this manuscript for publication.

The style of this book was inspired by Edward Tufte. Among other stylistic elements, we adopted his wide margins and use of small multiples. The typesetting of this book is based on the Tufte-LaTeX package by Kevin Godby, Bil Kleb, and Bill Wood. The book's color scheme was adapted from the Monokai theme by Jon Skinner of Sublime Text (sublimetext.com) and a palette that better accommodates individuals with color blindness.[1] For plots, we use the viridis color map defined by Stéfan van der Walt and Nathaniel Smith.

[1] B. Wong, "Points of View: Color Blindness," *Nature Methods*, vol. 8, no. 6, pp. 441–442, 2011.

We have also benefited from the various open-source packages on which this textbook depends (see appendix G). The typesetting of the code was done with the help of pythontex, which is maintained by Geoffrey Poore. The typeface used for the algorithms is JuliaMono (github.com/cormullion/juliamono). The plotting was handled by pgfplots, which is maintained by Christian Feuersänger.

1 *Introduction*

Many important problems involve decision making under uncertainty, including aircraft collision avoidance, wildfire management, and disaster response. When designing automated decision-making systems or decision-support systems, it is important to account for various sources of uncertainty while carefully balancing multiple objectives. We will discuss these challenges from a computational perspective, aiming to provide the theory behind decision-making models and computational approaches. This chapter introduces the problem of decision making under uncertainty, provides some examples of applications, and outlines the space of computational approaches. It then summarizes how various disciplines have contributed to our understanding of intelligent decision making and highlights areas of potential societal impact. We conclude with an outline of the remainder of the book.

1.1 *Decision Making*

An *agent* is an entity that acts based on observations of its environment. Agents may be physical entities, like humans or robots, or they may be nonphysical entities, such as decision support systems that are implemented entirely in software. As shown in figure 1.1, the interaction between the agent and the environment follows an *observe-act cycle* or *loop*.

The agent at time t receives an *observation* of the environment, denoted as o_t. Observations may be made, for example, through a biological sensory process, as in humans, or by a sensor system, like radar in an air traffic control system. Observations are often incomplete or noisy; humans may not see an approaching aircraft or a radar system might miss a detection due to electromagnetic interference. The agent then chooses an action a_t through some decision-making process.

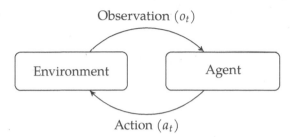

Figure 1.1. Interaction between an agent and its environment.

This action, such as sounding an alert, may have a nondeterministic effect on the environment.

Our focus is on agents that interact intelligently to achieve their objectives over time. Given the past sequence of observations, $o_1, \ldots, o_t$, and knowledge of the environment, the agent must choose an action a_t that best achieves its objectives in the presence of various sources of uncertainty,[1] including the following:

- *outcome uncertainty*, where the effects of our actions are uncertain,

- *model uncertainty*, where our model of the problem is uncertain,

- *state uncertainty*, where the true state of the environment is uncertain, and

- *interaction uncertainty*, where the behavior of the other agents interacting in the environment is uncertain.

This book is organized around these four sources of uncertainty. Making decisions in the presence of uncertainty is central to the field of *artificial intelligence*,[2] as well as many other fields, as outlined in section 1.4. We will discuss a variety of algorithms, or descriptions of computational processes, for making decisions that are robust to uncertainty.

1.2   Applications

The decision-making framework presented in the previous section can be applied to a wide variety of domains. This section discusses a few conceptual examples with real-world applications. Appendix F outlines additional notional problems that are used throughout this text to demonstrate the algorithms we discuss.

[1] We focus here on discrete time problems. Continuous time problems are studied in the field of *control theory*. See D. E. Kirk, *Optimal Control Theory: An Introduction*. Prentice-Hall, 1970.

[2] A comprehensive introduction to artificial intelligence is provided by S. Russell and P. Norvig, *Artificial Intelligence: A Modern Approach*, 4th ed. Pearson, 2021.

1.2.1 Aircraft Collision Avoidance

To help prevent midair collisions between aircraft, we want to design a system that can alert pilots to potential threats and direct them how to maneuver to avoid them.[3] The system communicates with the transponders of other aircraft to identify their positions with some degree of accuracy. Deciding what guidance to provide to the pilots is challenging. There is uncertainty in how quickly the pilots will respond and how aggressively they will comply with the guidance. In addition, there is uncertainty in the behavior of other aircraft. We want our system to alert sufficiently early to provide enough time for pilots to maneuver their aircraft to avoid collisions, but we do not want our system to issue alerts too early, which would result in many unnecessary maneuvers. Since this system is to be used continuously worldwide, we need the system to provide an exceptional level of safety.

[3] This application is discussed in a chapter titled ''Collision Avoidance'' by M. J. Kochenderfer, *Decision Making Under Uncertainty: Theory and Application*. MIT Press, 2015.

1.2.2 Automated Driving

We want to build an autonomous vehicle that can safely drive in urban environments.[4] The vehicle must rely on a suite of sensors to perceive its environment in order to make safe decisions. One type of sensor is lidar, which involves measuring laser reflections off the environment to determine distances to obstacles. Another type of sensor is a camera, which, through computer vision algorithms, can detect pedestrians and other vehicles. Both of these types of sensors are imperfect and susceptible to noise and occlusions. For example, a parked truck may occlude a pedestrian who may be trying to cross at a crosswalk. Our system must predict the intentions and future paths of other vehicles, pedestrians, and other road users from their observable behaviors in order to navigate safely to our destination.

[4] A similar application was explored by M. Bouton, A. Nakhaei, K. Fujimura, and M. J. Kochenderfer, ''Safe Reinforcement Learning with Scene Decomposition for Navigating Complex Urban Environments,'' in *IEEE Intelligent Vehicles Symposium (IV)*, 2019.

1.2.3 Breast Cancer Screening

Worldwide, breast cancer is the most common cancer in women. Detecting breast cancer early can help save lives, with mammography being the most effective screening tool available. However, mammography carries with it potential risks, including false positives, which can result in unnecessary and invasive diagnostic follow-up. Research over the years has resulted in various population-based screening schedules based on age to balance the benefits and risks of testing. Developing a system that can make recommendations based on personal risk characteristics and screening history has the potential to result in better health outcomes.[5] The success of such a system can be compared to populationwide screening schedules in terms of total expected quality-adjusted life years, the number of mammograms, the prevalence of false positives, and the risk of undetected, invasive cancer.

[5] Such a concept is proposed by T. Ayer, O. Alagoz, and N. K. Stout, "A POMDP Approach to Personalize Mammography Screening Decisions," *Operations Research*, vol. 60, no. 5, pp. 1019–1034, 2012.

1.2.4   *Financial Consumption and Portfolio Allocation*

Suppose that we want to build a system that recommends how much of an individual's wealth should be consumed that year and how much should be invested.[6] The investment portfolio may include stocks and bonds with different levels of risk and expected return. The evolution of wealth is stochastic due to uncertainty in both earned and investment income, often increasing until the investor is near retirement, and then steadily decreasing. The enjoyment that comes from the consumption of a unit of wealth in a year typically diminishes with the amount consumed, resulting in a desire to smooth consumption over the lifespan of the individual.

[6] A related problem was studied by R. C. Merton, "Optimum Consumption and Portfolio Rules in a Continuous-Time Model," *Journal of Economic Theory*, vol. 3, no. 4, pp. 373–413, 1971.

1.2.5   *Distributed Wildfire Surveillance*

Situational awareness is a major challenge when fighting wildfires. The state of a fire evolves over time, influenced by factors such as wind and the distribution of fuel in the environment. Many wildfires span large geographic regions. One concept for monitoring a wildfire is to use a team of drones equipped with sensors to fly above it.[7] The sensing range of individual drones is limited, but the information from the team can be fused to provide a unified snapshot of the situation to drive resource allocation decisions. We would like the team members to autonomously determine how to collaborate with each other to provide the best coverage of the fire. Effective monitoring requires deciding how to maneuver to cover areas where new sensor information is likely to be useful; spending time in areas where we are certain of whether the fire is burning or not would be wasteful. Identifying important areas to explore requires reasoning about the stochastic evolution of the fire, given only imperfect knowledge of its current state.

[7] This application was explored by K. D. Julian and M. J. Kochenderfer, "Distributed Wildfire Surveillance with Autonomous Aircraft Using Deep Reinforcement Learning," *AIAA Journal of Guidance, Control, and Dynamics*, vol. 42, no. 8, pp. 1768–1778, 2019.

1.2.6 Mars Science Exploration

Rovers have made important discoveries on and increased our understanding of Mars. However, a major bottleneck in scientific exploration has been the communication link between the rover and the operations team on Earth. It can take as much as half an hour for sensor information to be sent from Mars to Earth and for commands to be sent from Earth to Mars. In addition, guidance to rovers needs to be planned in advance because there are limited upload and download windows with Mars due to the positions of orbiters serving as information relays between the planets. Recent research has suggested that the efficiency of science exploration missions can be improved by a factor of five through the introduction of greater levels of autonomy.[8] Human operators would still provide high-level guidance on mission objectives, but the rover would have the flexibility to select its own science targets using the most up-to-date information. In addition, it would be desirable for rovers to respond appropriately to various hazards and system failures without human intervention.

[8] This concept is presented and evaluated by D. Gaines, G. Doran, M. Paton, B. Rothrock, J. Russino, R. Mackey, R. Anderson, R. Francis, C. Joswig, H. Justice, K. Kolcio, G. Rabideau, S. Schaffer, J. Sawoniewicz, A. Vasavada, V. Wong, K. Yu, and A.-a. Agha-mohammadi, "Self-Reliant Rovers for Increased Mission Productivity," *Journal of Field Robotics*, vol. 37, no. 7, pp. 1171–1196, 2020.

1.3 Methods

There are many methods for designing decision-making agents. Depending on the application, some may be more appropriate than others. They differ in the responsibilities of the designer and the tasks left to automation. This section briefly overviews a collection of these methods. The book will focus primarily on planning and reinforcement learning, but some of the techniques will involve elements of supervised learning and optimization.

1.3.1 Explicit Programming

The most direct method for designing a decision-making agent is to anticipate all the scenarios that the agent might find itself in and explicitly program what the agent should do in response to each one. The explicit programming approach may work well for simple problems, but it places a large burden on the designer to provide a complete strategy. Various agent programming languages and frameworks have been proposed to make programming agents easier.

1.3.2   Supervised Learning

With some problems, it may be easier to show an agent what to do rather than to write a program for the agent to follow. The designer provides a set of training examples, and an automated learning algorithm must generalize from these examples. This approach is known as *supervised learning* and has been widely applied to classification problems. This technique is sometimes called *behavioral cloning* when applied to learning mappings from observations to actions. Behavioral cloning works well when an expert designer actually knows the best course of action for a representative collection of situations. Although a wide variety of different learning algorithms exist, they generally cannot perform better than human designers in new situations.

1.3.3   Optimization

Another approach is for the designer to specify the space of possible decision strategies and a performance measure to be maximized. Evaluating the performance of a decision strategy generally involves running a batch of simulations. The optimization algorithm then performs a search in this space for the optimal strategy. If the space is relatively small and the performance measure does not have many local optima, then various local or global search methods may be appropriate. Although knowledge of a dynamic model is generally assumed to run the simulations, it is not otherwise used to guide the search, which can be important for complex problems.

1.3.4   Planning

Planning is a form of optimization that uses a model of the problem dynamics to help guide the search. A broad base of literature explores various planning problems, much of it focused on deterministic problems. For some problems, it may be acceptable to approximate the dynamics with a deterministic model. Assuming a deterministic model allows us to use methods that can more easily scale to high-dimensional problems. For other problems, accounting for future uncertainty is critical. This book focuses entirely on problems in which accounting for uncertainty is important.

1.3.5 Reinforcement Learning

Reinforcement learning relaxes the assumption in planning that a model is known ahead of time. Instead, the decision-making strategy is learned while the agent interacts with the environment. The designer only has to provide a performance measure; it is up to the learning algorithm to optimize the behavior of the agent. One of the interesting complexities that arises in reinforcement learning is that the choice of action affects not only the immediate success of the agent in achieving its objectives, but also the agent's ability to learn about the environment and identify the characteristics of the problem that it can exploit.

1.4 History

The theory of automating the process of decision making has its roots in the dreams of early philosophers, scientists, mathematicians, and writers. The ancient Greeks began incorporating automation into myths and stories as early as 800 BC. The word *automaton* was first used in Homer's *Iliad*, which contains references to the notion of automatic machines, including mechanical tripods used to serve dinner guests.[9] In the seventeenth century, philosophers proposed the use of logic rules to automatically settle disagreements. Their ideas created the foundation for mechanized reasoning.

Beginning in the late eighteenth century, inventors began creating automatic machines to perform labor. In particular, a series of innovations in the textile industry led to the development of the automatic loom, which in turn laid the foundation for the first factory robots.[10] In the early nineteenth century, the use of intelligent machines to automate labor began to make its way into science fiction novels. The word *robot* originated in the Czech writer Karel Čapek's play titled *R.U.R.*, short for *Rossum's Universal Robots*, about machines that could perform work that humans would prefer not to do. The play inspired other science fiction writers to incorporate robots into their writing. In the mid-twentieth century, the notable writer and professor Isaac Asimov laid out his vision for robotics in his famous *Robot* series.

A major challenge in practical implementations of automated decision making is accounting for uncertainty. Even at the end of the twentieth century, George Dantzig, most famous for developing the simplex algorithm, stated in 1991:

[9] S. Vasileiadou, D. Kalligeropoulos, and N. Karcanias, "Systems, Modelling and Control in Ancient Greece: Part 1: Mythical Automata," *Measurement and Control*, vol. 36, no. 3, pp. 76–80, 2003.

[10] N. J. Nilsson, *The Quest for Artificial Intelligence*. Cambridge University Press, 2009.

In retrospect it is interesting to note that the original problem that started my research is still outstanding—namely the problem of planning or scheduling dynamically over time, particularly planning dynamically under uncertainty. If such a problem could be successfully solved it could (eventually through better planning) contribute to the well-being and stability of the world.[11]

[11] G. B. Dantzig, "Linear Programming," *Operations Research*, vol. 50, no. 1, pp. 42–47, 2002.

While decision making under uncertainty still remains an active area of research, over the past few centuries, researchers and engineers have come closer to making the concepts posed by these early dreamers possible. Current state-of-the-art decision-making algorithms rely on a convergence of concepts developed in multiple disciplines, including economics, psychology, neuroscience, computer science, engineering, mathematics, and operations research. This section highlights some major contributions from these disciplines. The cross-pollination between disciplines has led to many recent advances and will likely continue to support growth in the future.

1.4.1 Economics

Economics requires models of human decision making. One approach to building such models involves utility theory, which was first introduced in the late eighteenth century.[12] Utility theory provides a means to model and compare the desirability of various outcomes. For example, utility can be used to compare the desirability of monetary quantities. In the *Theory of Legislation*, Jeremy Bentham summarized the nonlinearity in the utility of money:

[12] G. J. Stigler, "The Development of Utility Theory. I," *Journal of Political Economy*, vol. 58, no. 4, pp. 307–327, 1950.

1st. Each portion of wealth has a corresponding portion of happiness.
2nd. Of two individuals with unequal fortunes, he who has the most wealth has the most happiness.
3rd. The excess in happiness of the richer will not be so great as the excess of his wealth.[13]

[13] J. Bentham, *Theory of Legislation*. Trübner & Company, 1887.

By combining the concept of utility with the notion of rational decision making, economists in the mid-twentieth century established a basis for the maximum expected utility principle. This principle is a key concept behind the creation of autonomous decision-making agents. Utility theory also gave rise to the development of game theory, which attempts to understand the behavior of multiple agents acting in the presence of one another to maximize their interests.[14]

[14] O. Morgenstern and J. von Neumann, *Theory of Games and Economic Behavior*. Princeton University Press, 1953.

1.4.2 *Psychology*

Psychologists also study human decision making, typically from the perspective of human behavior. By studying the reactions of animals to stimuli, psychologists have been developing theories of trial-and-error learning since the nineteenth century. Researchers noticed that animals tend to make decisions based on the satisfaction or discomfort they experienced in previous similar situations. Russian psychologist Ivan Pavlov combined this idea with the concept of reinforcement after observing the salivation patterns of dogs when fed. Psychologists found that a pattern of behavior could be strengthened or weakened using continuous reinforcement of a particular stimulus. In the mid-twentieth century, the mathematician and computer scientist Alan Turing expressed the possibility of allowing machines to learn in the same manner:

> The organization of a machine into a universal machine would be most impressive if the arrangements of interference involve very few inputs. The training of a human child depends largely on a system of rewards and punishments, and this suggests that it ought to be possible to carry through the organising with only two interfering inputs, one for "pleasure" or "reward" (R) and the other for "pain" or "punishment" (P).[15]

The work of psychologists laid the foundation for the field of reinforcement learning, a critical technique used to teach agents to make decisions in uncertain environments.[16]

1.4.3 *Neuroscience*

While psychologists study human behavior as it happens, neuroscientists focus on the biological processes used to create the behavior. At the end of the nineteenth century, scientists found that the brain is composed of an interconnected network of neurons, which is responsible for its ability to perceive and reason about the world. Artificial intelligence pioneer Nils Nilsson describes the application of these findings to decision making as follows:

> Because it is the *brain* of an animal that is responsible for converting sensory information into action, it is to be expected that several good ideas can be found in the work of neurophysiologists and neuroanatomists who study brains and their fundamental components, neurons.[17]

[15] A. M. Turing, "Intelligent Machinery," National Physical Laboratory, Report, 1948.

[16] R. S. Sutton and A. G. Barto, *Reinforcement Learning: An Introduction*, 2nd ed. MIT Press, 2018.

[17] N. J. Nilsson, *The Quest for Artificial Intelligence*. Cambridge University Press, 2009.

In the 1940s, researchers first proposed that neurons could be considered as individual "logic units" capable of performing computational operations when pieced together into a network. This work served as a basis for neural networks, which are used in the field of artificial intelligence to perform a variety of complex tasks.

1.4.4   Computer Science

In the mid-twentieth century, computer scientists began formulating the problem of intelligent decision making as a problem of symbolic manipulation through formal logic. The computer program Logic Theorist, written in the mid-twentieth century to perform automated reasoning, used this way of thinking to prove mathematical theorems. Herbert Simon, one of its inventors, addressed the symbolic nature of the program by relating it to the human mind:

> We invented a computer program capable of thinking nonnumerically, and thereby solved the venerable mind/body problem, explaining how a system composed of matter can have the properties of mind.[18]

[18] Quoted by J. Agar, *Science in the 20th Century and Beyond.* Polity, 2012.

These symbolic systems relied heavily on human expertise. An alternative approach to intelligence, called *connectionism*, was inspired in part by developments in neuroscience and focuses on the use of artificial neural networks as a substrate for intelligence. With the knowledge that neural networks could be trained for pattern recognition, connectionists attempt to learn intelligent behavior from data or experience rather than the hard-coded knowledge of experts. The connectionist paradigm underpinned the success of AlphaGo, the autonomous program that beat a human professional at the game of Go, as well as much of the development of autonomous vehicles. Algorithms that combine both symbolic and connectionist paradigms remain an active area of research today.

1.4.5   Engineering

The field of engineering has focused on allowing physical systems, such as robots, to make intelligent decisions. World-renowned roboticist Sebastian Thrun describes the components of these systems as follows:

> Robotics systems have in common that they are situated in the physical world, perceive their environments through sensors, and manipulate their environment through things that move.[19]

[19] S. Thrun, "Probabilistic Robotics," *Communications of the ACM,* vol. 45, no. 3, pp. 52–57, 2002.

To design these systems, engineers must address perception, planning, and acting. Physical systems perceive the world by using their sensors to create a representation of the salient features of their environment. The field of state estimation has focused on using sensor measurements to construct a belief about the state of the world. Planning requires reasoning about the ways to execute the tasks they are designed to perform. The planning process has been enabled by advances in the semiconductor industry spanning many decades.[20] Once a plan has been devised, an autonomous agent must act on it in the real world. This task requires both hardware (in the form of actuators) and algorithms to control the actuators and reject disturbances. The field of control theory has focused on the stabilization of mechanical systems through feedback control.[21] Automatic control systems are widely used in industry, from the regulation of temperature in an oven to the navigation of aerospace systems.

1.4.6 Mathematics

An agent must be able to quantify its uncertainty to make informed decisions in uncertain environments. The field of decision making relies heavily on probability theory for this task. In particular, Bayesian statistics plays an important role in this text. In 1763, a paper of Thomas Bayes was published posthumously, containing what would later be known as Bayes' rule. His approach to probabilistic inference fell in and out of favor until the mid-twentieth century, when researchers began to find Bayesian methods useful in a number of settings.[22] Mathematician Bernard Koopman found practical use for the theory during World War II:

> Every operation involved in search is beset with uncertainties; it can be understood quantitatively only in terms of [...] probability. This may now be regarded as a truism, but it seems to have taken the developments in operational research of the Second World War to drive home its practical implications.[23]

Sampling-based methods (sometimes referred to as *Monte Carlo methods*) developed in the early twentieth century for large-scale calculations as part of the Manhattan Project, made some inference techniques possible that would previously have been intractable. These foundations serve as a basis for Bayesian networks, which increased in popularity later in the twentieth century in the field of artificial intelligence.

[20] G. E. Moore, "Cramming More Components onto Integrated Circuits," *Electronics*, vol. 38, no. 8, pp. 114–117, 1965.

[21] D. A. Mindell, *Between Human and Machine: Feedback, Control, and Computing Before Cybernetics*. JHU Press, 2002.

[22] W. M. Bolstad and J. M. Curran, *Introduction to Bayesian Statistics*. Wiley, 2016.

[23] B. O. Koopman, *Search and Screening: General Principles with Historical Applications*. Pergamon Press, 1980.

1.4.7   Operations Research

Operations research is concerned with finding optimal solutions to decision-making problems such as resource allocation, asset investment, and maintenance scheduling. In the late nineteenth century, researchers began to explore the application of mathematical and scientific analysis to the production of goods and services. The field was accelerated during the Industrial Revolution when companies began to subdivide their management into departments responsible for distinct aspects of overall decisions. During World War II, the optimization of decisions was applied to allocating resources to an army. Once the war came to an end, businesses began to notice that the same operations research concepts previously used to make military decisions could help them optimize business decisions. This realization led to the development of management science, as described by the organizational theorist Harold Koontz:

> The abiding belief of this group is that, if management, or organization, or planning, or decision making is a logical process, it can be expressed in terms of mathematical symbols and relationships. The central approach of this school is the model, for it is through these devices that the problem is expressed in its basic relationships and in terms of selected goals or objectives.[24]

This desire to be able to better model and understand business decisions sparked the development of a number of concepts used today, such as linear programming, dynamic programming, and queuing theory.[25]

1.5   Societal Impact

Algorithmic approaches to decision making have transformed society and will likely continue to in the future. This section briefly highlights a few ways that decision-making algorithms can contribute to society and introduces challenges that remain when attempting to ensure a broad benefit.[26]

Algorithmic approaches have contributed to environmental sustainability. In the context of energy management, for example, Bayesian optimization has been applied to automated home energy management systems. Algorithms from the field of multiagent systems are used to predict the operation of smart grids, design markets for trading energy, and predict rooftop solar-power adoption. Algorithms have also been developed to protect biodiversity. For example, neural networks are used to automate wildlife censuses, game-theoretic approaches are used to

[24] H. Koontz, "The Management Theory Jungle," *Academy of Management Journal*, vol. 4, no. 3, pp. 174–188, 1961.

[25] F. S. Hillier, *Introduction to Operations Research*. McGraw-Hill, 2012.

[26] A much more thorough discussion is provided by Z. R. Shi, C. Wang, and F. Fang, "Artificial Intelligence for Social Good: A Survey," 2020. arXiv: 2001.01818v1.

combat poaching in forests, and optimization techniques are employed to allocate resources for habitat management.

Decision-making algorithms have found success in the field of medicine for decades. Such algorithms have been used for matching residents to hospitals and organ donors to patients in need. An early application of Bayesian networks, which we will cover in the first part of this book, was disease diagnosis. Since then, Bayesian networks have been widely used in medicine for the diagnosis and prognosis of diseases. The field of medical image processing has been transformed by deep learning, and algorithmic ideas have recently played an important role in understanding the spread of disease.

Algorithms have enabled us to understand the growth of urban areas and facilitate their design. Data-driven algorithms have been widely used to improve public infrastructure. For example, stochastic processes have been used to predict failures in water pipelines, deep learning has improved traffic management, and Markov decision processes and Monte Carlo methods have been employed to improve emergency response. Ideas from decentralized multiagent systems have optimized travel routes, and path-planning techniques have been used to optimize the delivery of goods. Decision-making algorithms have been used for autonomous cars and improving aircraft safety.

Algorithms for optimizing decisions can amplify the impact of its users, regardless of their intention. If the objective of the user of these algorithms, for example, is to spread misinformation during a political election, then optimization processes can help facilitate this. However, similar algorithms can be used to monitor and counteract the spread of false information. Sometimes the implementation of these decision-making algorithms can lead to downstream consequences that their users did not intend.[27]

Although algorithms have the potential to bring significant benefits, there are also challenges associated with their implementation in society. Data-driven algorithms often suffer from inherent biases and blind spots due to the way that data is collected. As algorithms become part of our lives, it is important to understand how the risk of bias can be reduced and how the benefits of algorithmic progress can be distributed in a manner that is equitable and fair. Algorithms can also be vulnerable to adversarial manipulation, and it is critical that we design algorithms that are robust to such attacks. It is also important to extend moral and legal frameworks for preventing unintended consequences and assigning responsibility.

[27] For a general discussion, see B. Christian, *The Alignment Problem*. Norton & Company, 2020. See also the discussion by D. Amodei, C. Olah, J. Steinhardt, P. Christiano, J. Schulman, and D. Mané, "Concrete Problems in AI Safety," 2016. arXiv: 1606.06565v2.

1.6   Overview

This book is divided into five parts. The first part addresses the problem of reasoning about uncertainty and objectives in simple decisions at a single point in time. The second extends decision making to sequential problems, where we must make a sequence of decisions in response to information about the outcomes of our actions as we proceed. The third addresses model uncertainty, where we do not start with a known model and must learn how to act through interaction with the environment. The fourth addresses state uncertainty, where imperfect perceptual information prevents us from knowing the full environmental state. The final part discusses decision contexts involving multiple agents.

1.6.1   Probabilistic Reasoning

Rational decision making requires reasoning about our uncertainty and objectives. This part of the book begins by discussing how to represent uncertainty as a probability distribution. Real-world problems require reasoning about distributions over many variables. We will discuss how to construct these models, how to use them to make inferences, and how to learn their parameters and structure from data. We then introduce the foundations of *utility theory* and show how it forms the basis for rational decision making under uncertainty through the maximum expected utility principle. We then discuss how notions of utility theory can be incorporated into the probabilistic graphical models introduced earlier in this chapter to form what are called *decision networks*.

1.6.2   Sequential Problems

Many important problems require that we make a series of decisions. The same principle of maximum expected utility still applies, but optimal decision making in a sequential context requires reasoning about future sequences of actions and observations. This part of the book will discuss sequential decision problems in stochastic environments, where the outcomes of our actions are uncertain. We will focus on a general formulation of sequential decision problems under the assumption that the model is known and that the environment is fully observable. We will relax both of these assumptions later in the book. Our discussion will begin with the introduction of the *Markov decision process* (*MDP*), the standard mathematical model for sequential decision problems. We will discuss several approaches for finding exact solutions to these types of problems. Because large problems sometimes do not permit exact solutions to be found efficiently, we will discuss a collection of both offline and online approximate solution methods, along with a type of method that involves directly searching the space of parameterized decision policies. Finally, we will discuss approaches for validating that our decision strategies will perform as expected when deployed in the real world.

1.6.3 Model Uncertainty

In our discussion of sequential decision problems up to this point, we have assumed that the transition and reward models are known. In many problems, however, the dynamics and rewards are not known exactly, and the agent must learn to act through experience. By observing the outcomes of its actions in the form of state transitions and rewards, the agent is to choose actions that maximize its long-term accumulation of rewards. Solving such problems in which there is model uncertainty is the subject of the field of *reinforcement learning* and the focus of this part of the book. We will discuss several challenges in addressing model uncertainty. First, the agent must carefully balance the exploration of the environment with the exploitation of knowledge gained through experience. Second, rewards may be received long after the important decisions have been made, so credit for later rewards must be assigned to earlier decisions. Third, the agent must generalize from limited experience. We will review the theory and some of the key algorithms for addressing these challenges.

1.6.4 State Uncertainty

In this part, we extend uncertainty to include the state. Instead of observing the state exactly, we receive observations that have only a probabilistic relationship with the state. Such problems can be modeled as a *partially observable Markov decision process (POMDP)*. A common approach to solving POMDPs involves inferring a belief distribution over the underlying state at the current time step and then applying a policy that maps beliefs to actions. This part begins by discussing how to update our belief distribution, given a past sequence of observations and actions. It then discusses a variety of exact and approximate methods for solving POMDPs.

1.6.5   *Multiagent Systems*

Up to this point, there has only been one agent making decisions within the environment. This part expands the previous four parts to multiple agents, discussing the challenges that arise from interaction uncertainty. We begin by discussing simple games, where a group of agents simultaneously each select an action. The result is an individual reward for each agent based on the combined joint action. The *Markov game* (*MG*) represents a generalization of both simple games to multiple states and the MDP to multiple agents. Consequently, the agents select actions that can stochastically change the state of a shared environment. Algorithms for MGs rely on reinforcement learning due to uncertainty about the policies of the other agents. A *partially observable Markov game* (*POMG*) introduces state uncertainty, further generalizing MGs and POMDPs, as agents now receive only noisy local observations. The *decentralized partially observable Markov decision process* (*Dec-POMDP*) focuses the POMG on a collaborative, multiagent team where there is a shared reward among the agents. This part of the book presents these four categories of problems and discusses exact and approximate algorithms that solve them.

PART I

PROBABILISTIC REASONING

Rational decision making requires reasoning about our uncertainty and objectives. Uncertainty arises from practical and theoretical limitations on our ability to predict future events. For example, predicting exactly how a human operator will respond to advice from a decision support system would require, among other things, a detailed model of how the human brain works. Even the paths of satellites can be difficult to predict. Although Newtonian physics permit highly precise predictions of satellite trajectories, spontaneous failures in attitude thrusters can result in large deviations from the nominal path, and even small imprecisions can compound over time. To achieve its objectives, a robust decision-making system must account for various sources of uncertainty in the current state of the world and future events. This part of the book begins by discussing how to represent uncertainty using probability distributions. Real-world problems require reasoning about distributions over many variables. We will discuss how to construct these models, use them to make inferences, and learn their parameters and structure from data. We then introduce the foundations of utility theory and show how it forms the basis for rational decision making under uncertainty. Utility theory can be incorporated into the probabilistic graphical models introduced earlier to form what are called decision networks. We focus on single-step decisions, reserving discussion of sequential decision problems for the next part of the book.

2 Representation

Computationally accounting for uncertainty requires a formal representation. This chapter discusses how to represent uncertainty.[1] We begin by introducing the notion of degree of belief and show how a set of axioms results in our ability to use probability distributions to quantify our uncertainty.[2] We discuss several useful forms of distributions over both discrete and continuous variables. Because many important problems involve probability distributions over a large number of variables, we discuss a way to represent joint distributions efficiently that takes advantage of conditional independence between variables.

[1] A detailed discussion of a variety of approaches to representing uncertainty is provided by F. Cuzzolin, *The Geometry of Uncertainty*. Springer, 2021.

[2] For a more comprehensive elaboration, see E. T. Jaynes, *Probability Theory: The Logic of Science*. Cambridge University Press, 2003.

2.1 Degrees of Belief and Probability

In problems involving uncertainty, it is essential to be able to compare the plausibility of different statements. We would like to be able to represent, for example, that proposition A is more plausible than proposition B. If A represents "my actuator failed," and B represents "my sensor failed," then we would write $A \succ B$. Using this basic relation $\succ$, we can define several other relations:

$$A \prec B \text{ if and only if } B \succ A \tag{2.1}$$

$$A \sim B \text{ if and only if neither } A \succ B \text{ nor } B \succ A \tag{2.2}$$

$$A \succeq B \text{ if and only if } A \succ B \text{ or } A \sim B \tag{2.3}$$

$$A \preceq B \text{ if and only if } B \succ A \text{ or } A \sim B \tag{2.4}$$

We want to make certain assumptions about the relationships induced by the operators $\succ$, $\sim$, and $\prec$. The assumption of *universal comparability* requires exactly one of the following to hold: $A \succ B$, $A \sim B$, or $A \prec B$. The assumption of *transitivity* requires that if $A \succeq B$ and $B \succeq C$, then $A \succeq C$. Universal comparability and transitivity assumptions lead to an ability to represent plausibility by a real-valued function P that has the following two properties:[3]

$$P(A) > P(B) \text{ if and only if } A \succ B \qquad (2.5)$$

$$P(A) = P(B) \text{ if and only if } A \sim B \qquad (2.6)$$

If we make a set of additional assumptions[4] about the form of P, then we can show that P must satisfy the basic *axioms of probability* (see appendix A.2). If we are certain of A, then $P(A) = 1$. If we believe that A is impossible, then $P(A) = 0$. Uncertainty in the truth of A is represented by values between the two extrema. Hence, probability masses must lie between 0 and 1, with $0 \leq P(A) \leq 1$.

2.2   Probability Distributions

A *probability distribution* assigns probabilities to different outcomes.[5] There are different ways to represent probability distributions depending on whether they involve discrete or continuous outcomes.

2.2.1   Discrete Probability Distributions

A *discrete probability distribution* is a distribution over a discrete set of values. We can represent such a distribution as a *probability mass function*, which assigns a probability to every possible assignment of its input variable to a value. For example, suppose that we have a variable X that can take on one of n values: $1, \ldots, n$, or, using *colon notation*, $1:n$.[6] A distribution associated with X specifies the n probabilities of the various assignments of values to that variable, in particular $P(X = 1), \ldots, P(X = n)$. Figure 2.1 shows an example of a discrete distribution.

There are constraints on the probability masses associated with discrete distributions. The masses must sum to 1:

$$\sum_{i=1}^{n} P(X = i) = 1 \qquad (2.7)$$

and $0 \leq P(X = i) \leq 1$ for all i.

For notational convenience, we will use lowercase letters and superscripts as shorthand when discussing the assignment of values to variables. For example, $P(x^3)$ is shorthand for $P(X = 3)$. If X is a *binary variable*, it can take on the value of true or false.[7] We will use 0 to represent false and 1 to represent true. For example, we use $P(x^0)$ to represent the probability that X is false.

[3] See discussion in E. T. Jaynes, *Probability Theory: The Logic of Science*. Cambridge University Press, 2003.

[4] The axiomatization of subjective probability is given by P. C. Fishburn, "The Axioms of Subjective Probability," *Statistical Science*, vol. 1, no. 3, pp. 335–345, 1986. A more recent axiomatization is contained in M. J. Dupré and F. J. Tipler, "New Axioms for Rigorous Bayesian Probability," *Bayesian Analysis*, vol. 4, no. 3, pp. 599–606, 2009.

[5] For an introduction to probability theory, see D. P. Bertsekas and J. N. Tsitsiklis, *Introduction to Probability*. Athena Scientific, 2002.

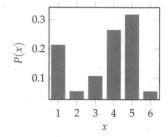

Figure 2.1.   A probability mass function for a distribution over $1:6$.

[6] We will often use this colon notation for compactness. Other texts sometimes use the notation $[1 \mathinner{.\,.} n]$ for integer intervals from 1 to n. We will also use this colon notation to index into vectors and matrices. For example $x_{1:n}$ represents $x_1, \ldots, x_n$. The colon notation is sometimes used in programming languages, such as Julia and MATLAB.

[7] Julia, like many other programming languages, similarly treats Boolean values as 0 and 1 in numerical operations.

The *parameters* of a distribution govern the probabilities associated with different assignments. For example, if we use X to represent the outcome of a roll of a six-sided die, then we would have $P(x^1) = \theta_1, \ldots, P(x^6) = \theta_6$, with $\theta_{1:6}$ being the six parameters of the distribution. However, we need only five *independent parameters* to uniquely specify the distribution over the outcomes of the roll because we know that the distribution must sum to 1.

2.2.2   Continuous Probability Distributions

A *continuous probability distribution* is a distribution over a continuous set of values. Representing a distribution over a continuous variable is a little less straightforward than for a discrete variable. For instance, in many continuous distributions, the probability that a variable takes on a particular value is infinitesimally small. One way to represent a continuous probability distribution is to use a *probability density function* (see figure 2.2), represented with lowercase letters. If $p(x)$ is a probability density function over X, then $p(x)dx$ is the probability that X falls within the interval $(x, x+dx)$ as $dx \to 0$. Similar to how the probability masses associated with a discrete distribution must sum to 1, a probability density function $p(x)$ must integrate to 1:

$$\int_{-\infty}^{\infty} p(x)\,\mathrm{d}x = 1 \qquad (2.8)$$

Another way to represent a continuous distribution is with a *cumulative distribution function* (see figure 2.3), which specifies the probability mass associated with values below some threshold. If we have a cumulative distribution function P associated with variable X, then $P(x)$ represents the probability mass associated with X taking on a value less than or equal to x. A cumulative distribution function can be defined in terms of a probability density function p as follows:

$$\mathrm{cdf}_X(x) = P(X \leq x) = \int_{-\infty}^{x} p(x')\,\mathrm{d}x' \qquad (2.9)$$

Related to the cumulative distribution function is the *quantile function*, also called the *inverse cumulative distribution function* (see figure 2.4). The value of $\mathrm{quantile}_X(\alpha)$ is the value x such that $P(X \leq x) = \alpha$. In other words, the quantile function returns the minimum value of x whose cumulative distribution value is greater than or equal to α. Of course, we have $0 \leq \alpha \leq 1$.

There are many different parameterized families of distributions. We outline several in appendix B. A simple distribution family is the *uniform distribution*

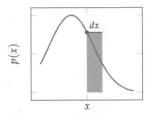

Figure 2.2. Probability density functions are used to represent continuous probability distributions. If $p(x)$ is a probability density, then $p(x)dx$ indicated by the area of the blue rectangle is the probability that a sample from the random variable falls within the interval $(x, x+dx)$ as $dx \to 0$.

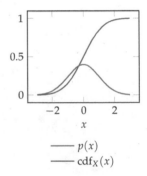

Figure 2.3. The probability density function and cumulative distribution function for a standard Gaussian distribution.

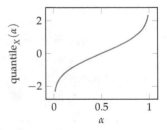

Figure 2.4. The quantile function for a standard Gaussian distribution.

$\mathcal{U}(a,b)$, which assigns probability density uniformly between a and b, and zero elsewhere. Hence, the probability density function is $p(x) = 1/(b-a)$ for x in the interval $[a, b]$. We can use $\mathcal{U}(x \mid a, b)$ to represent the density at x.[8] The *support* of a distribution is the set of values that are assigned nonzero density. In the case of $\mathcal{U}(a,b)$, the support is the interval $[a, b]$. See example 2.1.

[8] Some texts use a semicolon to separate the parameters of the distribution. For example, one can also write $\mathcal{U}(x; a, b)$.

The uniform distribution $\mathcal{U}(0, 10)$ assigns equal probability to all values in the range $[0, 10]$ with a probability density function:

$$\mathcal{U}(x \mid 0, 10) = \begin{cases} 1/10 & \text{if } 0 \leq x \leq 10 \\ 0 & \text{otherwise} \end{cases} \qquad (2.10)$$

The probability that a random sample from this distribution is equal to the constant π is essentially zero. However, we can define nonzero probabilities for samples being within some interval, such as $[3, 5]$. For example, the probability that a sample lies between 3 and 5 given the distribution plotted here is:

$$\int_3^5 \mathcal{U}(x \mid 0, 10) \, dx = \frac{5-3}{10} = \frac{1}{5} \qquad (2.11)$$

The support of this distribution is the interval $[0, 10]$.

Example 2.1.   An example of a uniform distribution with a lower bound of 0 and an upper bound of 10.

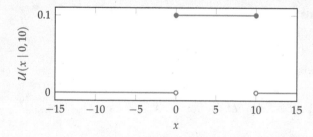

Another common distribution for continuous variables is the *Gaussian distribution* (also called the *normal distribution*). The Gaussian distribution is parameterized by a mean μ and variance σ^2:

$$p(x) = \mathcal{N}(x \mid \mu, \sigma^2) \qquad (2.12)$$

Here, σ is the *standard deviation*, which is the square root of the variance. The variance is also commonly denoted by v. We use $\mathcal{N}(\mu, \sigma^2)$ to represent a Gaussian distribution with parameters μ and σ^2 and $\mathcal{N}(x \mid \mu, \sigma^2)$ to represent the probability density at x, as given by

$$\mathcal{N}(x \mid \mu, \sigma^2) = \frac{1}{\sigma} \phi\left(\frac{x - \mu}{\sigma}\right) \tag{2.13}$$

where ϕ is the *standard normal density function*:

$$\phi(x) = \frac{1}{\sqrt{2\pi}} \exp\left(-\frac{x^2}{2}\right) \tag{2.14}$$

Appendix B shows plots of Gaussian density functions with different parameters.

Although a Gaussian distribution is often convenient because it is defined by only two parameters and makes computation and derivation easy, it has some limitations. It assigns nonzero probability to large positive and negative values, which may not be appropriate for the quantity we are trying to model. For example, we might not want to assign nonzero probabilities for aircraft flying below the ground or at infeasible altitudes. We can use a *truncated Gaussian distribution* (see figure 2.5) to bound the *support* of possible values; that is, the range of values assigned nonzero probabilities. The density function is given by

$$\mathcal{N}(x \mid \mu, \sigma^2, a, b) = \frac{\frac{1}{\sigma} \phi\left(\frac{x - \mu}{\sigma}\right)}{\Phi\left(\frac{b - \mu}{\sigma}\right) - \Phi\left(\frac{a - \mu}{\sigma}\right)} \tag{2.15}$$

when x is within the interval (a, b).

The function Φ is the *standard normal cumulative distribution function*, as given by

$$\Phi(x) = \int_{-\infty}^{x} \phi(x')\, dx' \tag{2.16}$$

The Gaussian distribution is *unimodal*, meaning that there is a point in the distribution at which the density increases on one side and decreases on the other side. There are different ways to represent continuous distributions that are *multimodal*. One way is to use a *mixture model*, which is a mixture of multiple distributions. We mix together a collection of unimodal distributions to obtain a multimodal distribution. A *Gaussian mixture model* is a mixture model that is simply a weighted average of various Gaussian distributions. The parameters of a Gaussian mixture model include the parameters of the Gaussian distribution components $\mu_{1:n}, \sigma^2_{1:n}$, as well as their weights $\rho_{1:n}$. The density is given by

$$p(x \mid \mu_{1:n}, \sigma^2_{1:n}, \rho_{1:n}) = \sum_{i=1}^{n} \rho_i \mathcal{N}(x \mid \mu_i, \sigma_i^2) \tag{2.17}$$

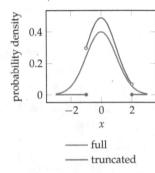

—— full
—— truncated

Figure 2.5. The probability density functions for a unit Gaussian distribution and the same distribution truncated between −1 and 2.

where the weights must sum to 1. Example 2.2 shows a Gaussian mixture model with two components.

We can create a Gaussian mixture model with components $\mu_1 = 5$, $\sigma_1 = 2$ and $\mu_2 = -5$, $\sigma_2 = 4$, weighted according to $\rho_1 = 0.6$ and $\rho_2 = 0.4$. Here we plot the density of two components scaled by their weights:

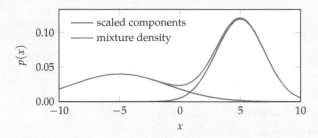

Example 2.2. An example of a Gaussian mixture model.

Another approach to representing multimodal continuous distributions is through discretization. For example, we can represent a distribution over a continuous variable as a *piecewise-uniform density*. The density is specified by the bin edges, and a probability mass is associated with each bin. Such a piecewise-uniform distribution is a type of mixture model where the components are uniform distributions.

2.3   *Joint Distributions*

A *joint distribution* is a probability distribution over multiple variables. A distribution over a single variable is called a *univariate distribution*, and a distribution over multiple variables is called a *multivariate distribution*. If we have a joint distribution over two discrete variables X and Y, then $P(x, y)$ denotes the probability that both $X = x$ and $Y = y$.

From a joint distribution, we can compute a *marginal* distribution of a variable or a set of variables by summing out all other variables using what is known as the *law of total probability*:[9]

$$P(x) = \sum_y P(x, y) \tag{2.18}$$

This property is used throughout this book.

[9] If our distribution is continuous, then we integrate out the other variables when marginalizing. For example:

$$p(x) = \int p(x, y)\, dy$$

Real-world decision making often requires reasoning about joint distributions involving many variables. Sometimes there are complex relationships between the variables that are important to represent. We may use different strategies to represent joint distributions depending on whether the variables involve discrete or continuous values.

2.3.1   Discrete Joint Distributions

If the variables are discrete, the joint distribution can be represented by a table like the one shown in table 2.1. That table lists all the possible assignments of values to three binary variables. Each variable can only be 0 or 1, resulting in $2^3 = 8$ possible assignments. As with other discrete distributions, the probabilities in the table must sum to 1. It follows that although there are eight entries in the table, only seven of them are *independent*. If θ_i represents the probability in the ith row in the table, then we only need the parameters $\theta_1, \ldots, \theta_7$ to represent the distribution because we know that $\theta_8 = 1 - (\theta_1 + \ldots + \theta_7)$.

If we have n binary variables, then we need as many as $2^n - 1$ independent parameters to specify the joint distribution. This exponential growth in the number of parameters makes storing the distribution in memory difficult. In some cases, we can assume that our variables are *independent*, which means that the realization of one does not affect the probability distribution of the other. If X and Y are independent, which is sometimes written as $X \perp Y$, then we know that $P(x, y) = P(x)P(y)$ for all x and y. Suppose we have binary variables $X_1, \ldots, X_n$ that are all independent of each other, resulting in $P(x_{1:n}) = \prod_i P(x_i)$. This factorization allows us to represent this joint distribution with only n independent parameters instead of the $2^n - 1$ required when we cannot assume independence (see table 2.2). Independence can result in an enormous savings in terms of representational complexity, but it is often a poor assumption.

We can represent joint distributions in terms of factors. A *factor* ϕ over a set of variables is a function from assignments of those variables to the real numbers. In order to represent a probability distribution, the real numbers in the factor must be nonnegative. A factor with nonnegative values can be normalized such that it represents a probability distribution. Algorithm 2.1 provides an implementation for discrete factors, and example 2.3 demonstrates how they work.

Another approach to reduce the storage required to represent joint distributions with repeated values is to use a *decision tree*. A decision tree involving three discrete

Table 2.1. Example of a joint distribution involving binary variables X, Y, and Z.

X	Y	Z	$P(X,Y,Z)$
0	0	0	0.08
0	0	1	0.31
0	1	0	0.09
0	1	1	0.37
1	0	0	0.01
1	0	1	0.05
1	1	0	0.02
1	1	1	0.07

Table 2.2. If we know the variables in table 2.1 are independent, we can represent $P(x, y, z)$ using the product $P(x)P(y)P(z)$. This representation requires only one parameter for each of the three univariate distributions.

X	$P(X)$	Y	$P(Y)$
0	0.85	0	0.45
1	0.15	1	0.55

Z	$P(Z)$
0	0.20
1	0.80

```
struct Variable
    name::Symbol
    r::Int # number of possible values
end

const Assignment = Dict{Symbol,Int}
const FactorTable = Dict{Assignment,Float64}

struct Factor
    vars::Vector{Variable}
    table::FactorTable
end

variablenames(φ::Factor) = [var.name for var in φ.vars]

select(a::Assignment, varnames::Vector{Symbol}) =
    Assignment(n⇒a[n] for n in varnames)

function assignments(vars::AbstractVector{Variable})
    names = [var.name for var in vars]
    return vec([Assignment(n⇒v for (n,v) in zip(names, values))
                    for values in product((1:v.r for v in vars)...)])
end

function normalize!(φ::Factor)
    z = sum(p for (a,p) in φ.table)
    for (a,p) in φ.table
        φ.table[a] = p/z
    end
    return φ
end
```

Algorithm 2.1. Types and functions relevant to working with factors over a set of discrete variables. A variable is given a name (represented as a symbol) and may take on an integer from 1 to m. An assignment is a mapping from variable names to values represented as integers. A factor is defined by a factor table, which assigns values to different assignments involving a set of variables and is a mapping from assignments to real values. This mapping is represented by a dictionary. Any assignments not contained in the dictionary are set to 0. Also included in this algorithm block are some utility functions for returning the variable names associated with a factor, selecting a subset of an assignment, enumerating possible assignments, and normalizing factors. As discussed in appendix G.3.3, product produces the Cartesian product of a set of collections. It is imported from Base.Iterators.

We can instantiate the table from table 2.1 using the Factor type using the following code:

```
# requires convenience functions from appendix G.5
X = Variable(:x, 2)
Y = Variable(:y, 2)
Z = Variable(:z, 2)
φ = Factor([X, Y, Z], FactorTable(
    (x=1, y=1, z=1) ⇒ 0.08, (x=1, y=1, z=2) ⇒ 0.31,
    (x=1, y=2, z=1) ⇒ 0.09, (x=1, y=2, z=2) ⇒ 0.37,
    (x=2, y=1, z=1) ⇒ 0.01, (x=2, y=1, z=2) ⇒ 0.05,
    (x=2, y=2, z=1) ⇒ 0.02, (x=2, y=2, z=2) ⇒ 0.07,
))
```

Example 2.3. Constructing a discrete factor. *The construction of the factor table using named tuples takes advantage of the utility functions defined in appendix G.5.*

variables is shown in example 2.4. Although the savings in this example in terms of the number of parameters may not be significant, it can become quite substantial when there are many variables and many repeated values.

Suppose we have the following table representing a joint probability distribution. We can use the decision tree to the right of it to more compactly represent the values in the table. Red arrows are followed when a variable is 0, and blue arrows are followed when a variable is 1. Instead of storing eight probabilities, we store only five, along with a representation of the tree.

Example 2.4. A decision tree can be a more efficient representation of a joint distribution than a table.

X	Y	Z	$P(X,Y,Z)$
0	0	0	0.01
0	0	1	0.01
0	1	0	0.50
0	1	1	0.38
1	0	0	0.02
1	0	1	0.03
1	1	0	0.02
1	1	1	0.03

2.3.2   Continuous Joint Distributions

We can also define joint distributions over continuous variables. A rather simple distribution is the *multivariate uniform distribution*, which assigns a constant probability density everywhere there is support. We can use $\mathcal{U}(\mathbf{a}, \mathbf{b})$ to represent a uniform distribution over a *box*, which is a Cartesian product of intervals, with the ith interval being $[a_i, b_i]$. This family of uniform distributions is a special type of *multivariate product distribution*, which is a distribution defined in terms of the product of univariate distributions. In this case,

$$\mathcal{U}(\mathbf{x} \mid \mathbf{a}, \mathbf{b}) = \prod_i \mathcal{U}(x_i \mid a_i, b_i) \qquad (2.19)$$

We can create a mixture model from a weighted collection of multivariate uniform distributions, just as we can with univariate distributions. If we have a joint distribution over n variables and k mixture components, we need to define $k(2n+1) - 1$ independent parameters. For each of the k components, we need to define the upper and lower bounds for each of the variables as well as their weights. We can subtract 1 because the weights must sum to 1. Figure 2.6 shows an example that can be represented by five components.

It is also common to represent piecewise constant density functions by discretizing each of the variables independently. The discretization is represented by a set of bin edges for each variable. These bin edges define a grid over the variables. We then associate a constant probability density with each grid cell. The bin edges do not have to be uniformly separated. In some cases, it may be desirable to have increased resolution around certain values. Different variables might have different bin edges associated with them. If there are n variables and m bins for each variable, then we need $m^n - 1$ independent parameters to define the distribution—in addition to the values that define the bin edges.

In some cases, it may be more memory efficient to represent a continuous joint distribution as a decision tree in a manner similar to what we discussed for discrete joint distributions. The internal nodes compare variables against thresholds and the leaf nodes are density values. Figure 2.7 shows a decision tree that represents the density function in figure 2.6.

Another useful distribution is the *multivariate Gaussian distribution* with the density function

$$\mathcal{N}(\mathbf{x} \mid \boldsymbol{\mu}, \boldsymbol{\Sigma}) = \frac{1}{(2\pi)^{n/2}|\boldsymbol{\Sigma}|^{1/2}} \exp\left(-\frac{1}{2}(\mathbf{x} - \boldsymbol{\mu})^\top \boldsymbol{\Sigma}^{-1}(\mathbf{x} - \boldsymbol{\mu})\right) \qquad (2.20)$$

where $\mathbf{x}$ is in $\mathbb{R}^n$, $\boldsymbol{\mu}$ is the *mean vector*, and $\boldsymbol{\Sigma}$ is the *covariance matrix*. The density function given here requires that $\boldsymbol{\Sigma}$ be *positive definite*.[10] The number of independent parameters is equal to $n + (n+1)n/2$, the number of components in $\boldsymbol{\mu}$ added to the number of components in the upper triangle of matrix $\boldsymbol{\Sigma}$.[11] Appendix B shows plots of different multivariate Gaussian density functions. We can also define *multivariate Gaussian mixture models*. Figure 2.8 shows an example of one with three components.

If we have a multivariate Gaussian with all the variables independent, then the covariance matrix $\boldsymbol{\Sigma}$ is diagonal with only n independent parameters. In fact,

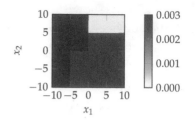

Figure 2.6. A density function for a mixture of multivariate uniform distributions.

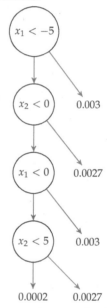

Figure 2.7. An example of a decision tree that represents a piecewise constant joint probability density defined over x_1 and x_2 over the interval $[-10, 10]^2$.

[10] This definition is reviewed in appendix A.5.

[11] If we know the parameters in the upper triangle of $\boldsymbol{\Sigma}$, we know the parameters in the lower triangle as well, because $\boldsymbol{\Sigma}$ is symmetric.

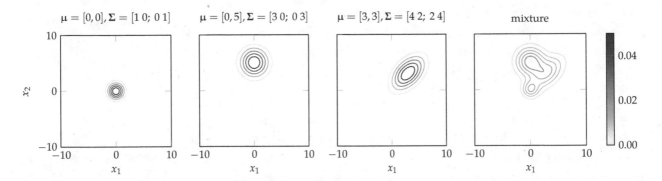

Figure 2.8. Multivariate Gaussian mixture model with three components. The components are mixed together with the weights 0.1, 0.5, and 0.4, respectively.

we can write the density function as a product of univariate Gaussian densities:

$$\mathcal{N}(\mathbf{x} \mid \boldsymbol{\mu}, \boldsymbol{\Sigma}) = \prod_i \mathcal{N}(x_i \mid \mu_i, \Sigma_{ii}) \tag{2.21}$$

2.4 Conditional Distributions

The previous section introduced the idea of independence, which can help reduce the number of parameters used to define a joint distribution. However, as was mentioned, independence can be too strong of an assumption. This section will introduce the idea of conditional independence, which can help reduce the number of independent parameters without making assumptions that are as strong. Before discussing conditional independence, we will first introduce the notion of a *conditional distribution*, which is a distribution over a variable given the value of one or more other ones.

The definition of *conditional probability* states that

$$P(x \mid y) = \frac{P(x,y)}{P(y)} \tag{2.22}$$

where $P(x \mid y)$ is read as "probability of x given y." In some contexts, it is common to refer to y as *evidence*.

Since a conditional probability distribution is a probability distribution over one or more variables given some evidence, we know that

$$\sum_x P(x \mid y) = 1 \tag{2.23}$$

for a discrete X. If X is continuous, it integrates to 1.

We can incorporate the definition of conditional probability into equation (2.18) to obtain a slightly different form of the law of total probability:

$$P(x) = \sum_y P(x \mid y)P(y) \qquad (2.24)$$

for a discrete distribution.

Another useful relationship that follows from the definition of conditional probability is *Bayes' rule*:[12]

$$P(x \mid y) = \frac{P(y \mid x)P(x)}{P(y)} \qquad (2.25)$$

If we have a representation of a conditional distribution $P(y \mid x)$, we can apply Bayes' rule to swap y and x to obtain the conditional distribution $P(x \mid y)$.

We will now discuss a variety of ways to represent conditional probability distributions over discrete and continuous variables.

2.4.1   Discrete Conditional Models

A conditional probability distribution over discrete variables can be represented using a table. In fact, we can use the same discrete factor representation that we used in section 2.3.1 for joint distributions. Table 2.3 shows an example of a table representing $P(X \mid Y, Z)$ with all binary variables. In contrast with a joint table (e.g., table 2.1), the column containing the probabilities need not sum to 1. However, if we sum over the probabilities that are consistent with what we are conditioning on, we must get 1. For example, conditioning on y^0 and z^0 (the evidence), we have

$$P(x^0 \mid y^0, z^0) + P(x^1 \mid y^0, z^0) = 0.08 + 0.92 = 1 \qquad (2.26)$$

Conditional probability tables can become quite large. If we were to create a table like table 2.3, in which all variables can take on m values and we are conditioning on n variables, there would be m^{n+1} rows. However, since the m values of the variable we are not conditioning on must sum to 1, there are only $(m-1)m^n$ independent parameters. There is still an exponential growth in the number of variables on which we condition. When there are many repeated values in the conditional probability table, a decision tree (introduced in section 2.3.1) may be a more efficient representation.

[12] Named for the English statistician and Presbyterian minister Thomas Bayes (c. 1701–1761) who provided a formulation of this theorem. A history is provided by S. B. McGrayne, *The Theory That Would Not Die*. Yale University Press, 2011.

Table 2.3. An example of a conditional distribution involving the binary variables X, Y, and Z.

X	Y	Z	$P(X \mid Y,Z)$
0	0	0	0.08
0	0	1	0.15
0	1	0	0.05
0	1	1	0.10
1	0	0	0.92
1	0	1	0.85
1	1	0	0.95
1	1	1	0.90

2.4.2   Conditional Gaussian Models

A *conditional Gaussian* model can be used to represent a distribution over a continuous variable given one or more discrete variables. For example, if we have a continuous variable X and a discrete variable Y with values $1:n$, we can define a conditional Gaussian model as follows:[13]

$$p(x \mid y) = \begin{cases} \mathcal{N}(x \mid \mu_1, \sigma_1^2) & \text{if } y^1 \\ \vdots \\ \mathcal{N}(x \mid \mu_n, \sigma_n^2) & \text{if } y^n \end{cases} \qquad (2.27)$$

with parameter vector $\theta = [\mu_{1:n}, \sigma_{1:n}]$. All $2n$ of those parameters can be varied independently. If we want to condition on multiple discrete variables, we just need to add more cases and associated parameters.

2.4.3   Linear Gaussian Models

The *linear Gaussian* model of $P(X \mid Y)$ represents the distribution over a continuous variable X as a Gaussian distribution with the mean being a linear function of the value of the continuous variable Y. The conditional density function is

$$p(x \mid y) = \mathcal{N}(x \mid my + b, \sigma^2) \qquad (2.28)$$

with parameters $\theta = [m, b, \sigma]$. The mean is a linear function of y defined by parameters m and b. The variance is constant. Figure 2.9 shows an example.

2.4.4   Conditional Linear Gaussian Models

The *conditional linear Gaussian* model combines the ideas of conditional Gaussian and linear Gaussian models to be able to condition a continuous variable on both discrete and continuous variables. Suppose that we want to represent $p(X \mid Y, Z)$, where X and Y are continuous and Z is discrete with values $1:n$. The conditional density function is then

$$p(x \mid y, z) = \begin{cases} \mathcal{N}(x \mid m_1 y + b_1, \sigma_1^2) & \text{if } z^1 \\ \vdots \\ \mathcal{N}(x \mid m_n y + b_n, \sigma_n^2) & \text{if } z^n \end{cases} \qquad (2.29)$$

Here, the parameter vector $\theta = [m_{1:n}, b_{1:n}, \sigma_{1:n}]$ has $3n$ components.

[13] This definition is for a mixture of univariate Gaussians, but the concept can be easily generalized to a mixture of multidimensional Gaussians.

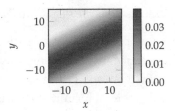

Figure 2.9. A linear Gaussian model with

$$p(x \mid y) = \mathcal{N}(x \mid 2y + 1, 10^2)$$

2.4.5   Sigmoid Models

We can use a *sigmoid*[14] model to represent a distribution over a binary variable conditioned on a continuous variable. For example, we may want to represent $P(x^1 \mid y)$, where x is binary and y is continuous. Of course, we could just set a threshold θ and say that $P(x^1 \mid y) = 0$ if $y < \theta$, and $P(x^1 \mid y) = 1$ otherwise. However, in many applications, we may not want to have such a hard threshold that results in assigning zero probability to x^1 for certain values of y.

Instead of a hard threshold, we could use a *soft threshold*, which assigns low probabilities when below a threshold and high probabilities when above a threshold. One way to represent a soft threshold is to use a *logit model*, which produces a sigmoid curve:

$$P(x^1 \mid y) = \frac{1}{1 + \exp\left(-2\frac{y - \theta_1}{\theta_2}\right)} \tag{2.30}$$

The parameter θ_1 governs the location of the threshold, and θ_2 controls the "softness" or spread of the probabilities. Figure 2.10 shows a plot of $P(x^1 \mid y)$ with a logit model.

2.4.6   Deterministic Variables

Some problems may involve a *deterministic variable*, whose value is fixed given evidence. In other words, we assign probability 1 to a value that is a deterministic function of its evidence. Using a conditional probability table to represent a discrete deterministic variable is possible, but it is wasteful. A single variable instantiation will have probability 1 for each parental instantiation, and the remaining entries will be 0. Our implementation can take advantage of this sparsity for a more compact representation. Algorithms in this text using discrete factors treat any assignments missing from the factor table as having value 0, making it so that we have to store only the assignments that have nonzero probability.

2.5   Bayesian Networks

A *Bayesian network* can be used to represent a joint probability distribution.[15] The structure of a Bayesian network is defined by a *directed acyclic graph* consisting of nodes and directed edges.[16] Each node corresponds to a variable. Directed edges connect pairs of nodes, with cycles in the graph being prohibited. The directed

[14] A sigmoid is an S-shaped curve. There are different ways to define such a curve mathematically, but we will focus on the logit model.

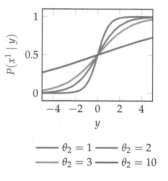

$$
\begin{array}{ll}
\text{---} \ \theta_2 = 1 & \text{---} \ \theta_2 = 2 \\
\text{---} \ \theta_2 = 3 & \text{---} \ \theta_2 = 10
\end{array}
$$

Figure 2.10. The logit model with $\theta_1 = 0$ and different values for θ_2.

[15] For an in-depth treatment of Bayesian networks and other forms of probabilistic graphical models, see D. Koller and N. Friedman, *Probabilistic Graphical Models: Principles and Techniques*. MIT Press, 2009.

[16] Appendix A.16 reviews common graph terminology.

edges indicate direct probabilistic relationships.[17] Associated with each node X_i is a conditional distribution $P(X_i \mid \mathrm{Pa}(X_i))$, where $\mathrm{Pa}(X_i)$ represents the parents of X_i in the graph. Algorithm 2.2 provides an implementation of a Bayesian network data structure. Example 2.5 illustrates the application of Bayesian networks to a satellite-monitoring problem.

```
struct BayesianNetwork
    vars::Vector{Variable}
    factors::Vector{Factor}
    graph::SimpleDiGraph{Int64}
end
```

[17] In *causal networks*, the direction of the edges indicate causal relationships between variables. However, causality is not required in general Bayesian networks. J. Pearl, *Causality: Models, Reasoning, and Inference*, 2nd ed. Cambridge University Press, 2009.

Algorithm 2.2. A discrete Bayesian network representation in terms of a set of variables, factors, and a graph. The graph data structure is provided by `Graphs.jl`.

The *chain rule* for Bayesian networks specifies how to construct a joint distribution from the local conditional probability distributions. Suppose that we have the variables $X_{1:n}$ and want to compute the probability of a particular assignment of all these variables to values $P(x_{1:n})$. The chain rule says

$$P(x_{1:n}) = \prod_{i=1}^{n} P(x_i \mid \mathrm{pa}(x_i)) \qquad (2.31)$$

where $\mathrm{pa}(x_i)$ is the particular assignment of the parents of X_i to their values. Algorithm 2.3 provides an implementation for Bayesian networks with conditional probability distributions represented as discrete factors.

```
function probability(bn::BayesianNetwork, assignment)
    subassignment(ϕ) = select(assignment, variablenames(ϕ))
    probability(ϕ) = get(ϕ.table, subassignment(ϕ), 0.0)
    return prod(probability(ϕ) for ϕ in bn.factors)
end
```

Algorithm 2.3. A function for evaluating the probability of an assignment given a Bayesian network bn. For example, if bn is as defined in example 2.5, then
a = (b=1,s=1,e=1,d=2,c=1)
probability(bn, Assignment(a))
returns 0.034228655999999996.

In the satellite example, suppose we want to compute the probability that nothing is wrong; that is, $P(b^0, s^0, e^0, d^0, c^0)$. From the chain rule,

$$P(b^0, s^0, e^0, d^0, c^0) = P(b^0)P(s^0)P(e^0 \mid b^0, s^0)P(d^0 \mid e^0)P(c^0 \mid e^0) \qquad (2.32)$$

If we had fully specified a joint distribution over the five variables $B, S, E, D,$ and C, then we would have needed $2^5 - 1 = 31$ independent parameters. The structure assumed in our Bayesian network allows us to specify the joint distribution using only $1 + 1 + 4 + 2 + 2 = 10$ independent parameters. The difference between

In the margin is a Bayesian network for a satellite-monitoring problem involving five binary variables. Fortunately, battery failure and solar panel failures are both rare, although solar panel failures are somewhat more likely than battery failures. Failures in either can lead to electrical system failure. There may be causes of electrical system failure other than battery or solar panel failure, such as a problem with the power management unit. An electrical system failure can result in trajectory deviation, which can be observed from the Earth by telescope, as well as a communication loss that interrupts the transmission of telemetry and mission data down to various ground stations. Other anomalies not involving the electrical system can result in trajectory deviation and communication loss.

Associated with each of the five variables are five conditional probability distributions. Because B and S have no parents, we only need to specify $P(B)$ and $P(S)$. The code here creates a Bayesian network structure with example values for the elements of the associated factor tables. The tuples in the factor tables index into the domains of the variables, which is $\{0, 1\}$ for all the variables. For example, (e=2,b=1,s=1) corresponds to (e^1, b^0, s^0).

```
# requires convenience functions from appendix G.5
B = Variable(:b, 2); S = Variable(:s, 2)
E = Variable(:e, 2)
D = Variable(:d, 2); C = Variable(:c, 2)
vars = [B, S, E, D, C]
factors = [
    Factor([B], FactorTable((b=1,) ⇒ 0.99, (b=2,) ⇒ 0.01)),
    Factor([S], FactorTable((s=1,) ⇒ 0.98, (s=2,) ⇒ 0.02)),
    Factor([E,B,S], FactorTable(
        (e=1,b=1,s=1) ⇒ 0.90, (e=1,b=1,s=2) ⇒ 0.04,
        (e=1,b=2,s=1) ⇒ 0.05, (e=1,b=2,s=2) ⇒ 0.01,
        (e=2,b=1,s=1) ⇒ 0.10, (e=2,b=1,s=2) ⇒ 0.96,
        (e=2,b=2,s=1) ⇒ 0.95, (e=2,b=2,s=2) ⇒ 0.99)),
    Factor([D, E], FactorTable(
        (d=1,e=1) ⇒ 0.96, (d=1,e=2) ⇒ 0.03,
        (d=2,e=1) ⇒ 0.04, (d=2,e=2) ⇒ 0.97)),
    Factor([C, E], FactorTable(
        (c=1,e=1) ⇒ 0.98, (c=1,e=2) ⇒ 0.01,
        (c=2,e=1) ⇒ 0.02, (c=2,e=2) ⇒ 0.99))
]
graph = SimpleDiGraph(5)
add_edge!(graph, 1, 3); add_edge!(graph, 2, 3)
add_edge!(graph, 3, 4); add_edge!(graph, 3, 5)
bn = BayesianNetwork(vars, factors, graph)
```

Example 2.5. A Bayesian network representing a satellite-monitoring problem. Here is the structure of the network represented as a directed acyclic graph. Associated with each node is a conditional probability distribution.

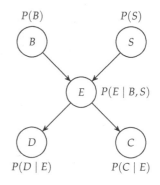

B battery failure
S solar panel failure
E electrical system failure
D trajectory deviation
C communication loss

10 and 31 does not represent an especially significant savings in the number of parameters, but the savings can become enormous in larger Bayesian networks. The power of Bayesian networks comes from their ability to reduce the number of parameters required to specify a joint probability distribution.

2.6 Conditional Independence

The reason that a Bayesian network can represent a joint distribution with fewer independent parameters than would normally be required is the *conditional independence* assumptions encoded in its graphical structure.[18] Conditional independence is a generalization of the notion of independence introduced in section 2.3.1. Variables X and Y are conditionally independent given Z if and only if $P(X, Y \mid Z) = P(X \mid Z)P(Y \mid Z)$. The assertion that X and Y are conditionally independent given Z is written as $(X \perp Y \mid Z)$. It is possible to show from this definition that $(X \perp Y \mid Z)$ if and only if $P(X \mid Z) = P(X \mid Y, Z)$. Given Z, information about Y provides no additional information about X, and vice versa. Example 2.6 shows an instance of this.

[18] If the conditional independence assumptions made by the Bayesian network are invalid, then we run the risk of not properly modeling the joint distribution, as will be discussed in chapter 5.

Suppose the presence of satellite trajectory deviation (D) is conditionally independent of whether we have a communication loss (C) given knowledge of whether we have an electrical system failure (E). We would write this $(D \perp C \mid E)$. If we know that we have an electrical system failure, then the fact that we observe a loss of communication has no impact on our belief that there is a trajectory deviation. We may have an elevated expectation that there is a trajectory deviation, but that is only because we know that an electrical system failure has occurred.

Example 2.6. Conditional independence in the satellite-tracking problem.

We can use a set of rules to determine whether the structure of a Bayesian network implies that two variables must be conditionally independent given a set of other evidence variables.[19] Suppose that we want to check whether $(A \perp B \mid C)$ is implied by the network structure, where C is a set of evidence variables. We have to check all possible undirected paths from A to B for what is called *d-separation*. A path between A and B is d-separated by C if any of the following is true:

[19] Even if the structure of a network does not imply conditional independence, there may still be conditional independence due to the choice of conditional probability distributions. See exercise 2.10.

1. The path contains a *chain* of nodes, $X \to Y \to Z$, such that Y is in C.

2. The path contains a *fork*, $X \leftarrow Y \rightarrow Z$, such that Y is in $\mathcal{C}$.

3. The path contains an *inverted fork* (also called a *v-structure*), $X \rightarrow Y \leftarrow Z$, such that Y is *not* in $\mathcal{C}$ and no descendant of Y is in $\mathcal{C}$. Example 2.7 provides some intuition for this rule.

We say that A and B are d-separated by $\mathcal{C}$ if all the paths between A and B are d-separated by $\mathcal{C}$. This d-separation implies that $(A \perp B \mid \mathcal{C})$.[20] Example 2.8 demonstrates this process for checking whether a graph implies a particular conditional independence assumption.

[20] An algorithm for efficiently determining d-separation is a bit complicated. See algorithm 3.1 in D. Koller and N. Friedman, *Probabilistic Graphical Models: Principles and Techniques*. MIT Press, 2009.

If we have $X \rightarrow Y \rightarrow Z$ (chain) or $X \leftarrow Y \rightarrow Z$ (fork) with evidence at Y, then X and Z are conditionally independent, meaning that $P(X \mid Y, Z) = P(X \mid Y)$. Interestingly, if the directions of the arrows were slightly different, with $X \rightarrow Y \leftarrow Z$ (inverted fork), then X and Z may no longer be conditionally independent given Y. In other words, it may be the case that $P(B \mid E) \neq P(B \mid S, E)$. To provide some intuition, consider the inverted fork path from battery failure B to solar panel failure S via electrical system failure E. Suppose we know that we have an electrical failure. If we know that we do not have a battery failure, then we are more inclined to believe that we have a solar panel failure because it is an alternative cause of the electrical failure. Conversely, if we found out that we do have a battery failure, then our belief that we have a solar panel failure decreases. This effect is referred to as *explaining away*. Observing a solar panel failure explains away the cause of the electrical system failure.

Example 2.7.   Intuition behind conditional independence assumptions implied (and not implied) in chains, forks, and inverted forks.

Sometimes the term *Markov blanket*[21] of node X is used to refer to the minimal set of nodes that, if their values were known, make X conditionally independent of all other nodes. A Markov blanket of a particular node turns out to consist of its parents, its children, and the other parents of its children.

[21] Named after the Russian mathematician Andrey Andreyevich Markov (1856–1922). J. Pearl, *Probabilistic Reasoning in Intelligent Systems: Networks of Plausible Inference*. Morgan Kaufmann, 1988.

2.7   Summary

- Representing uncertainty as a probability distribution is motivated by a set of axioms related to the comparison of the plausibility of different statements.

Suppose that we want to determine whether the network shown in the margin implies that $(D \perp B \mid F)$. There are two undirected paths from D to B. We need to check both paths for d-separation.

The path $D \leftarrow A \rightarrow C \leftarrow B$ involves the fork $D \leftarrow A \rightarrow C$, followed by an inverted fork, $A \rightarrow C \leftarrow B$. There is no evidence at A, so there is no d-separation from the fork. Since F is a descendant of C, there is no d-separation along the inverted fork. Hence, there is no d-separation along this path.

The second path, $D \rightarrow E \leftarrow C \leftarrow B$, involves the inverted fork $D \rightarrow E \leftarrow C$ and a chain, $E \leftarrow C \leftarrow B$. Since F is a descendant of E, there is no d-separation along the inverted fork. Because there is no d-separation along the chain part of this path either, there is no d-separation along this path from D to B.

For D and B to be conditionally independent given F, there must be d-separation along all undirected paths from D to B. In this case, neither of the two paths has d-separation. Hence, conditional independence is not implied by the network structure.

Example 2.8. Conditional independence assumptions implied by the graphical structure below.

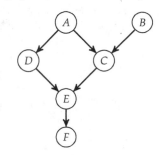

- There are many families of both discrete and continuous probability distributions.

- Continuous probability distributions can be represented by density functions.

- Probability distribution families can be combined in mixtures to create more flexible distributions.

- Joint distributions are distributions over multiple variables.

- Conditional distributions are distributions over one or more variables given the values of evidence variables.

- A Bayesian network is defined by a graphical structure and a set of conditional distributions.

- Depending on the structure of the Bayesian network, we can represent joint distributions with fewer parameters due to conditional independence assumptions.

2.8   Exercises

Exercise 2.1. Consider a continuous random variable X that follows the *exponential distribution* parameterized by λ with density $p(x \mid \lambda) = \lambda \exp(-\lambda x)$ with nonnegative support. Compute the cumulative distribution function of X.

Solution: We start with the definition of the cumulative distribution function. Since the support of the distribution is lower-bounded by $x = 0$, there is no probability mass in the interval $(-\infty, 0)$, allowing us to adjust the lower bound of the integral to 0. After computing the integral, we obtain $\text{cdf}_X(x)$:

$$\text{cdf}_X(x) = \int_{-\infty}^{x} p(x')\,dx'$$

$$\text{cdf}_X(x) = \int_{0}^{x} \lambda e^{-\lambda x'}\,dx'$$

$$\text{cdf}_X(x) = -e^{-\lambda x'}\Big|_{0}^{x}$$

$$\text{cdf}_X(x) = 1 - e^{-\lambda x}$$

Exercise 2.2. For the density function in figure 2.6, what are the five components of the mixture? (There are multiple valid solutions.)

Solution: One solution is $\mathcal{U}([-10, -10], [-5, 10])$, $\mathcal{U}([-5, 0], [0, 10])$, $\mathcal{U}([-5, -10], [0, 0])$, $\mathcal{U}([0, -10], [10, 5])$, and $\mathcal{U}([0, 5], [10, 10])$.

Exercise 2.3. Given the following table representation of $P(X, Y, Z)$, generate an equivalent compact decision tree representation:

X	Y	Z	$P(X,Y,Z)$
0	0	0	0.13
0	0	1	0.02
0	1	0	0.05
0	1	1	0.02
1	0	0	0.13
1	0	1	0.01
1	1	0	0.05
1	1	1	0.17
2	0	0	0.13
2	0	1	0.12
2	1	0	0.05
2	1	1	0.12

Solution: We start with the most common probabilities: 0.13, which occurs when $Z = 0$ and $Y = 0$, and 0.05, which occurs when $Z = 0$ and $Y = 1$. We choose to make Z the root of our decision tree, and when $Z = 0$, we continue to a Y node. Based on the value of Y, we branch to either 0.13 or 0.05. Next, we continue with cases when $Z = 1$. The most common probabilities are 0.02, which occurs when $Z = 1$ and $X = 0$, and 0.12, which occurs when $Z = 1$ and $X = 2$. So, when $Z = 1$, we choose to continue to an X node. Based on the whether X is 0, 1, or 2, we continue to 0.02, a Y node, or 0.12, respectively. Finally, based on the value of Y, we branch to either 0.01 or 0.17.

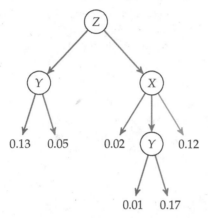

Exercise 2.4. Suppose that we want to specify a multivariate Gaussian mixture model with three components defined over four variables. We require that two of the three Gaussian distributions assume independence between the four variables, while the other Gaussian distribution is defined without any independence assumptions. How many independent parameters are required to specify this mixture model?

Solution: For a Gaussian distribution over four variables ($n = 4$) with independence assumptions, we need to specify $n + n = 2n = 8$ independent parameters; there are four parameters for the mean vector and four parameters for the covariance matrix (which is equivalent to the mean and variance parameters of four independent univariate Gaussian distributions). For a Gaussian distribution over four variables without independence assumptions, we need to specify $n + n(n+1)/2 = 14$ independent parameters; there are 4 parameters for the mean vector and 10 parameters for the covariance matrix. In addition, for our three mixture components ($k = 3$), we need to specify $k - 1 = 2$ independent parameters for the weights. Thus, we need $2(8) + 1(14) + 2 = 32$ independent parameters to specify this mixture distribution.

Exercise 2.5. We have three independent variables $X_{1:3}$ defined by piecewise-constant densities with 4, 7, and 3 bin edges, respectively. How many independent parameters are required to specify their joint distribution?

Solution: If we have a piecewise-constant density with m bin edges, then there are $m - 1$ bins and $m - 2$ independent parameters. For this problem, there will be $(4 - 2) + (7 - 2) + (3 - 2) = 8$ independent parameters.

Exercise 2.6. Suppose that we have four continuous random variables, X_1, X_2, Y_1, and Y_2, and we want to construct a linear Gaussian model of $X = X_{1:2}$ given $Y = Y_{1:2}$; that is, $p(X \mid Y)$. How many independent parameters are required for this model?

Solution: In this case, our mean vector for the Gaussian distribution is two-dimensional and requires four independent parameters for the transformation matrix $\mathbf{M}$ and two independent parameters for the bias vector $\mathbf{b}$. We also require three independent parameters for the covariance matrix $\mathbf{\Sigma}$. In total, we need $4 + 2 + 3 = 9$ independent parameters to specify this model:

$$p(\mathbf{x} \mid \mathbf{y}) = \mathcal{N}(\mathbf{x} \mid \mathbf{My} + \mathbf{b}, \mathbf{\Sigma})$$

Exercise 2.7. Given the following Bayesian network, in which each node can take on one of four values, how many independent parameters are there? What is the percent reduction in the number of independent parameters required when using the following Bayesian network compared to using a full joint probability table?

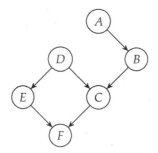

Solution: The number of independent parameters for each node is equal to $(k - 1)k^m$, where k is the number of values that the node can take on and m is the number of parents that the node has. Variable A has 3, B has 12, C has 48, D has 3, E has 12, and F has 48 independent parameters. There are 126 total independent parameters for this Bayesian network.

The number of independent parameters required to specify a joint probability table over n variables that can take on k values is equal to $k^n - 1$. Therefore, specifying a joint probability table would require $4^6 - 1 = 4096 - 1 = 4095$ independent parameters. The percent reduction in the number of independent parameters required is $(4095 - 126)/4095 \approx 96.9\%$.

Exercise 2.8. Given the following Bayesian network, is A d-separated from E, given C?

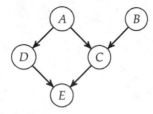

Solution: There are two paths from A to E: $A \rightarrow D \rightarrow E$ and $A \rightarrow C \rightarrow E$. There is d-separation along the second path, but not the first. Hence, A is not d-separated from E given C.

Exercise 2.9. Given the following Bayesian network, determine the Markov blanket of B:

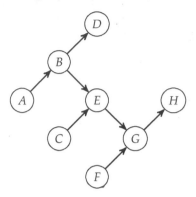

Solution: Paths from B to A can only be d-separated given A. Paths from B to D can only be d-separated given D. Paths from B to E, and simultaneously F, G, and H, can be efficiently d-separated given E. Paths from B to C are naturally d-separated due to a v-structure; however, since E must be contained in our Markov blanket, paths from B to C given E can only be d-separated given C. So, the Markov blanket of B is $\{A, C, D, E\}$.

Exercise 2.10. In a Bayesian network with structure $A \rightarrow B$, is it possible for A to be independent of B?

Solution: There is a direct arrow from A to B, which indicates that independence is not implied. However, this does not mean that they are not independent. Whether A and B are independent depends on the choice of conditional probability tables. We can choose the tables so that there is independence. For example, suppose that both variables are binary and $P(a) = 0.5$ is uniform and $P(b \mid a) = 0.5$. Clearly, $P(A)P(B \mid A) = P(A)P(B)$, which means they are independent.

3 Inference

The previous chapter explained how to represent probability distributions. This chapter will show how to use these probabilistic representations for *inference*, which involves determining the distribution over one or more unobserved variables given the values associated with a set of observed variables. It begins by introducing exact inference methods. Because exact inference can be computationally intractable depending on the structure of the network, we will also discuss several algorithms for approximate inference.

3.1 Inference in Bayesian Networks

In inference problems, we want to infer a distribution over *query variables* given some observed *evidence variables*. The other nodes are referred to as *hidden variables*. We often refer to the distribution over the query variables, given the evidence, as a *posterior distribution*.

To illustrate the computations involved in inference, recall the Bayesian network from example 2.5, the structure of which is reproduced in figure 3.1. Suppose we have B as a query variable and evidence $D = 1$ and $C = 1$. The inference task is to compute $P(b^1 \mid d^1, c^1)$, which corresponds to computing the probability that we have a battery failure given an observed trajectory deviation and communication loss.

From the definition of conditional probability introduced in equation (2.22), we know that

$$P(b^1 \mid d^1, c^1) = \frac{P(b^1, d^1, c^1)}{P(d^1, c^1)} \qquad (3.1)$$

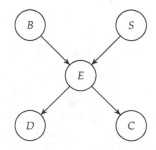

Figure 3.1. Bayesian network structure from example 2.5.

To compute the numerator, we must use a process known as *marginalization*, where we sum out variables that are not involved (in this case S and E):

$$P(b^1, d^1, c^1) = \sum_s \sum_e P(b^1, s, e, d^1, c^1) \tag{3.2}$$

We know from the chain rule for Bayesian networks introduced in equation (2.31) that

$$P(b^1, s, e, d^1, c^1) = P(b^1)P(s)P(e \mid b^1, s)P(d^1 \mid e)P(c^1 \mid e) \tag{3.3}$$

All the components on the right side are specified in the conditional probability distributions associated with the nodes in the Bayesian network. We can compute the denominator in equation (3.1) using the same approach, but with an additional summation over the values for B.

This process of using the definition of conditional probability, marginalization, and applying the chain rule can be used to perform exact inference in any Bayesian network. We can implement exact inference using factors. Recall that factors represent discrete multivariate distributions. We use the following three operations on factors to achieve this:

- We use the *factor product* (algorithm 3.1) to combine two factors to produce a larger factor whose scope is the combined scope of the input factors. If we have $\phi(X, Y)$ and $\psi(Y, Z)$, then $\phi \cdot \psi$ will be over X, Y, and Z with $(\phi \cdot \psi)(x, y, z) = \phi(x, y)\psi(y, z)$. The factor product is demonstrated in example 3.1.

- We use *factor marginalization* (algorithm 3.2) to sum out a particular variable from the entire factor table, removing it from the resulting scope. Example 3.2 illustrates this process.

- We use *factor conditioning* (algorithm 3.3) with respect to some evidence to remove any rows in the table inconsistent with that evidence. Example 3.3 demonstrates factor conditioning.

These three factor operations are used together in algorithm 3.4 to perform exact inference. It starts by computing the product of all the factors, conditioning on the evidence, marginalizing out the hidden variables, and normalizing. One potential issue with this approach is the size of the product of all the factors. The size of the factor product is equal to the product of the number of values each variable can assume. For the satellite example problem, there are only $2^5 = 32$ possible assignments, but many interesting problems would have a factor product that is too large to enumerate practically.

```
function Base.:*(φ::Factor, ψ::Factor)
    φnames = variablenames(φ)
    ψnames = variablenames(ψ)
    ψonly = setdiff(ψ.vars, φ.vars)
    table = FactorTable()
    for (φa,φp) in φ.table
        for a in assignments(ψonly)
            a = merge(φa, a)
            ψa = select(a, ψnames)
            table[a] = φp * get(ψ.table, ψa, 0.0)
        end
    end
    vars = vcat(φ.vars, ψonly)
    return Factor(vars, table)
end
```

Algorithm 3.1. An implementation of the factor product, which constructs the factor representing the joint distribution of two smaller factors φ and ψ. If we want to compute the factor product of φ and ψ, we simply write φ∗ψ.

The factor product of two factors produces a new factor over the union of their variables. Here, we produce a new factor from two factors that share a variable:

Example 3.1. An illustration of a factor product combining two factors representing $\phi_1(X, Y)$ and $\phi_2(Y, Z)$ to produce a factor representing $\phi_3(X, Y, Z)$.

X	Y	$\phi_1(X, Y)$
0	0	0.3
0	1	0.4
1	0	0.2
1	1	0.1

X	Y	Z	$\phi_3(X, Y, Z)$
0	0	0	0.06
0	0	1	0.00
0	1	0	0.12
0	1	1	0.20
1	0	0	0.04
1	0	1	0.00
1	1	0	0.03
1	1	1	0.05

Y	Z	$\phi_2(Y, Z)$
0	0	0.2
0	1	0.0
1	0	0.3
1	1	0.5

```
function marginalize(φ::Factor, name)
    table = FactorTable()
    for (a, p) in φ.table
        a′ = delete!(copy(a), name)
        table[a′] = get(table, a′, 0.0) + p
    end
    vars = filter(v → v.name != name, φ.vars)
    return Factor(vars, table)
end
```

Algorithm 3.2. A method for marginalizing a variable named name from a factor φ.

Recall the joint probability distribution $P(X, Y, Z)$ from table 2.1. We can marginalize out Y by summing the probabilities in each row that have matching assignments for X and Z:

Example 3.2. A demonstration of factor marginalization.

X	Y	Z	$\phi(X,Y,Z)$
0	0	0	0.08
0	0	1	0.31
0	1	0	0.09
0	1	1	0.37
1	0	0	0.01
1	0	1	0.05
1	1	0	0.02
1	1	1	0.07

X	Z	$\phi(X,Z)$
0	0	0.17
0	1	0.68
1	0	0.03
1	1	0.12

```
in_scope(name, φ) = any(name == v.name for v in φ.vars)

function condition(φ::Factor, name, value)
    if !in_scope(name, φ)
        return φ
    end
    table = FactorTable()
    for (a, p) in φ.table
        if a[name] == value
            table[delete!(copy(a), name)] = p
        end
    end
    vars = filter(v → v.name != name, φ.vars)
    return Factor(vars, table)
end

function condition(φ::Factor, evidence)
    for (name, value) in pairs(evidence)
        φ = condition(φ, name, value)
    end
    return φ
end
```

Algorithm 3.3. Two methods for factor conditioning given some evidence. The first takes a factor φ and returns a new factor whose table entries are consistent with the variable named name having the value value. The second takes a factor φ and applies evidence in the form of a named tuple. The in_scope method returns true if the variable named name is within the scope of the factor φ.

Factor conditioning involves dropping any rows inconsistent with the evidence. Here is the factor from table 2.1, and we condition on $Y = 1$. All rows for which $Y \neq 1$ are removed:

Example 3.3. An illustration of setting evidence, in this case for Y, in a factor. The resulting values must be renormalized.

X	Y	Z	$\phi(X,Y,Z)$
0	0	0	0.08
0	0	1	0.31
0	1	0	0.09
0	1	1	0.37
1	0	0	0.01
1	0	1	0.05
1	1	0	0.02
1	1	1	0.07

$Y = 1$

X	Z	$\phi(X,Z)$
0	0	0.09
0	1	0.37
1	0	0.02
1	1	0.07

```
struct ExactInference end

function infer(M::ExactInference, bn, query, evidence)
    φ = prod(bn.factors)
    φ = condition(φ, evidence)
    for name in setdiff(variablenames(φ), query)
        φ = marginalize(φ, name)
    end
    return normalize!(φ)
end
```

Algorithm 3.4. A naive exact inference algorithm for a discrete Bayesian network bn, which takes as input a set of query variable names query and evidence associating values with observed variables. The algorithm computes a joint distribution over the query variables in the form of a factor. We introduce the ExactInference type to allow infer to be called with different inference methods, as shall be seen in the rest of this chapter.

3.2   Inference in Naive Bayes Models

The previous section presented a general method for performing exact inference in any Bayesian network. This section discusses how this same method can be used to solve *classification* problems for a special kind of Bayesian network structure known as a *naive Bayes* model. This structure is given in figure 3.2. An equivalent but more compact representation is shown in figure 3.3 using a *plate*, shown here as a rounded box. The $i = 1 : n$ in the bottom of the box specifies that the i in the subscript of the variable name is repeated from 1 to n.

In the naive Bayes model, class C is the query variable, and the observed features $O_{1:n}$ are the evidence variables. The naive Bayes model is called naive because it assumes conditional independence between the evidence variables given the class. Using the notation introduced in section 2.6, we can say $(O_i \perp O_j \mid C)$ for all $i \neq j$. Of course, if these conditional independence assumptions do not hold, then we can add the necessary directed edges between the observed features.

We have to specify the *prior* $P(C)$ and the *class-conditional distributions* $P(O_i \mid C)$. As done in the previous section, we can apply the chain rule to compute the joint distribution:

$$P(c, o_{1:n}) = P(c) \prod_{i=1}^{n} P(o_i \mid c) \tag{3.4}$$

Our classification task involves computing the conditional probability $P(c \mid o_{1:n})$. From the definition of conditional probability, we have

$$P(c \mid o_{1:n}) = \frac{P(c, o_{1:n})}{P(o_{1:n})} \tag{3.5}$$

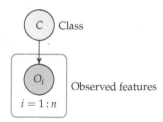

Figure 3.2.   A naive Bayes model.

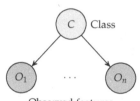

Figure 3.3.   Plate representation of a naive Bayes model.

We can compute the denominator by marginalizing the joint distribution:

$$P(o_{1:n}) = \sum_c P(c, o_{1:n}) \tag{3.6}$$

The denominator in equation (3.5) is not a function of C and can therefore be treated as a constant. Hence, we can write

$$P(c \mid o_{1:n}) = \kappa P(c, o_{1:n}) \tag{3.7}$$

where κ is a *normalization constant* such that $\sum_c P(c \mid o_{1:n}) = 1$. We often drop κ and write

$$P(c \mid o_{1:n}) \propto P(c, o_{1:n}) \tag{3.8}$$

where the *proportional to* symbol $\propto$ is used to represent that the left side is proportional to the right side. Example 3.4 illustrates how inference can be applied to classifying radar tracks.

We can use this method to infer a distribution over classes, but for many applications, we have to commit to a particular class. It is common to classify according to the class with the highest posterior probability, $\arg\max_c P(c \mid o_{1:n})$. However, choosing a class is really a decision problem that often should take into account the consequences of misclassification. For example, if we are interested in using our classifier to filter out targets that are not aircraft for the purpose of air traffic control, then we can afford to occasionally let a few birds and other clutter tracks through our filter. However, we would want to avoid filtering out any real aircraft because that could lead to a collision. In this case, we would probably want to classify a track as a bird only if the posterior probability were close to 1. Decision problems will be discussed in chapter 6.

3.3 Sum-Product Variable Elimination

A variety of methods can be used to perform efficient inference in more complicated Bayesian networks. One method is known as *sum-product variable elimination*, which interleaves eliminating hidden variables (summations) with applications of the chain rule (products). It is more efficient to marginalize variables out as early as possible to avoid generating large factors.

Suppose that we have a radar track and we want to determine whether it was generated by a bird or an aircraft. We base our inference on airspeed and the amount of heading fluctuation. The first represents our belief about whether a target is a bird or an aircraft in the absence of any information about the track. Here are example class-conditional distributions for airspeed v as estimated from radar data:

Example 3.4. Radar target classification in which we want to determine whether a radar track corresponds to a bird or an aircraft.

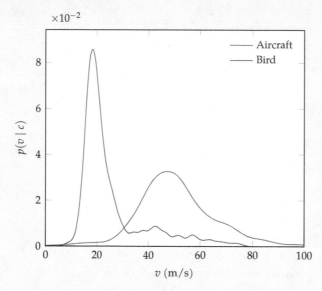

Suppose from the chain rule, we determine:

$$P(\text{bird, slow, little heading fluctuation}) = 0.03$$
$$P(\text{aircraft, slow, little heading fluctuation}) = 0.01$$

Of course, these probabilities do not sum to 1. If we want to determine the probability that a target is a bird given the evidence, then we would make the following calculation:

$$P(\text{bird} \mid \text{slow, little heading fluctuation}) = \frac{0.03}{0.03 + 0.01} = 0.75$$

We will illustrate the variable elimination algorithm by computing the distribution $P(B \mid d^1, c^1)$ for the Bayesian network in figure 3.1. The conditional probability distributions associated with the nodes in the network can be represented by the following factors:

$$\phi_1(B), \phi_2(S), \phi_3(E, B, S), \phi_4(D, E), \phi_5(C, E) \tag{3.9}$$

Because D and C are observed variables, the last two factors can be replaced with $\phi_6(E)$ and $\phi_7(E)$ by setting the evidence $D = 1$ and $C = 1$.

We then proceed by eliminating the hidden variables in sequence. Different strategies can be used for choosing an ordering, but for this example, we arbitrarily choose the ordering E and then S. To eliminate E, we take the product of all the factors involving E and then marginalize out E to get a new factor:

$$\phi_8(B, S) = \sum_e \phi_3(e, B, S)\phi_6(e)\phi_7(e) \tag{3.10}$$

We can now discard ϕ_3, ϕ_6, and ϕ_7 because all the information we need from them is contained in ϕ_8.

Next, we eliminate S. Again, we gather all remaining factors that involve S and marginalize out S from the product of these factors:

$$\phi_9(B) = \sum_s \phi_2(s)\phi_8(B, s) \tag{3.11}$$

We discard ϕ_2 and ϕ_8 and are left with $\phi_1(B)$ and $\phi_9(B)$. Finally, we take the product of these two factors and normalize the result to obtain a factor representing $P(B \mid d^1, c^1)$.

This procedure is equivalent to computing the following:

$$P(B \mid d^1, c^1) \propto \phi_1(B) \sum_s \left(\phi_2(s) \sum_e \left(\phi_3(e \mid B, s)\phi_4(d^1 \mid e)\phi_5(c^1 \mid e) \right) \right) \tag{3.12}$$

This produces the same result as, but is more efficient than, the naive procedure of taking the product of all the factors and then marginalizing:

$$P(B \mid d^1, c^1) \propto \sum_s \sum_e \phi_1(B)\phi_2(s)\phi_3(e \mid B, s)\phi_4(d^1 \mid e)\phi_5(c^1 \mid e) \tag{3.13}$$

The sum-product variable elimination algorithm is implemented in algorithm 3.5. It takes as input a Bayesian network, a set of query variables, a list of observed values, and an ordering of the variables. We first set all observed values. Then, for each variable, we multiply all factors containing it and then marginalize that variable out. This new factor replaces the consumed factors, and we repeat the process for the next variable.

For many networks, variable elimination allows inference to be done in an amount of time that scales linearly with the size of the network, but it has exponential time complexity in the worst case. What influences the amount of computation is the variable elimination order. Choosing the optimal elimination order is *NP-hard*,[1] meaning that it cannot be done in polynomial time in the worst case (section 3.5). Even if we found the optimal elimination order, variable elimination can still require an exponential number of computations. Variable elimination heuristics generally try to minimize the number of variables involved in the intermediate factors generated by the algorithm.

[1] S. Arnborg, D. G. Corneil, and A. Proskurowski, "Complexity of Finding Embeddings in a *k*-Tree," *SIAM Journal on Algebraic Discrete Methods*, vol. 8, no. 2, pp. 277–284, 1987.

```
struct VariableElimination
    ordering # array of variable indices
end

function infer(M::VariableElimination, bn, query, evidence)
    Φ = [condition(ϕ, evidence) for ϕ in bn.factors]
    for i in M.ordering
        name = bn.vars[i].name
        if name ∉ query
            inds = findall(ϕ→in_scope(name, ϕ), Φ)
            if !isempty(inds)
                ϕ = prod(Φ[inds])
                deleteat!(Φ, inds)
                ϕ = marginalize(ϕ, name)
                push!(Φ, ϕ)
            end
        end
    end
    return normalize!(prod(Φ))
end
```

Algorithm 3.5. An implementation of the sum-product variable elimination algorithm, which takes in a Bayesian network bn, a list of query variables query, and evidence evidence. The variables are processed in the order given by ordering.

3.4   Belief Propagation

An approach to inference known as *belief propagation* works by propagating "messages" through the network using the *sum-product algorithm* in order to compute the marginal distributions of the query variables.[2] Belief propagation requires linear time but provides an exact answer only if the network does not have undirected cycles. If the network has undirected cycles, then it can be converted to a tree by combining multiple variables into single nodes by using what is known as the *junction tree algorithm*. If the number of variables that have to be combined into any one node in the resulting network is small, then inference can be done efficiently. A variation of belief propagation known as *loopy belief propagation* can provide approximate solutions in networks with undirected cycles. Although this approach does not provide any guarantees and may not converge, it can work well in practice.[3]

3.5   Computational Complexity

We can show that inference in Bayesian networks is NP-hard by using an NP-complete problem called 3SAT.[4] It is easy to construct a Bayesian network from an arbitrary 3SAT problem. For example, consider the following 3SAT formula:[5]

$$F(x_1, x_2, x_3, x_4) = \begin{array}{c} (\quad x_1 \quad \lor \quad x_2 \quad \lor \quad x_3 \quad) \quad \land \\ (\quad \neg x_1 \quad \lor \quad \neg x_2 \quad \lor \quad x_3 \quad) \quad \land \\ (\quad x_2 \quad \lor \quad \neg x_3 \quad \lor \quad x_4 \quad) \end{array} \qquad (3.14)$$

where $\neg$ represents *logical negation* ("not"), $\land$ represents *logical conjunction* ("and"), and $\lor$ represents *logical disjunction* ("or"). The formula consists of a conjunction of *clauses*, which are disjunctions of what are called *literals*. A literal is simply a variable or its negation.

Figure 3.4 shows the corresponding Bayesian network representation. The variables are represented by $X_{1:4}$, and the clauses are represented by $C_{1:3}$. The distributions over the variables are uniform. The nodes representing clauses have as parents the participating variables. Because this is a 3SAT problem, each clause node has exactly three parents. Each clause node assigns probability 0 to assignments that do not satisfy the clause and probability 1 to all satisfying assignments. The remaining nodes assign probability 1 to true if all their parents

[2] A tutorial on the sum-product algorithm with a discussion of its connections to many other algorithms developed in separate communities is provided by F. Kschischang, B. Frey, and H.-A. Loeliger, "Factor Graphs and the Sum-Product Algorithm," *IEEE Transactions on Information Theory*, vol. 47, no. 2, pp. 498–519, 2001.

[3] Belief propagation and related algorithms are covered in detail by D. Barber, *Bayesian Reasoning and Machine Learning*. Cambridge University Press, 2012.

[4] G. F. Cooper, "The Computational Complexity of Probabilistic Inference Using Bayesian Belief Networks," *Artificial Intelligence*, vol. 42, no. 2–3, pp. 393–405, 1990. The Bayesian network construction in this section follows that text. See appendix C for a brief review of complexity classes.

[5] This formula also appears in example C.3 in appendix C.

are true. The original problem is satisfiable if and only if $P(y^1) > 0$. Hence, inference in Bayesian networks is at least as hard as 3SAT.

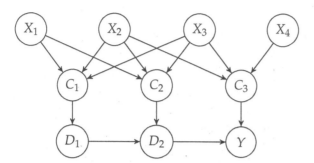

Figure 3.4. Bayesian network representing a 3SAT problem.

The reason we go to the effort of showing that inference in Bayesian networks is NP-hard is so that we know to avoid wasting time looking for an efficient, exact inference algorithm that works on all Bayesian networks. Therefore, research over the past couple of decades has focused on approximate inference methods, which are discussed next.

3.6   Direct Sampling

Motivated by the fact that exact inference is computationally intractable, many approximation methods have been developed. One of the simplest methods for inference is based on *direct sampling*, where random samples from the joint distribution are used to arrive at a probability estimate.[6] To illustrate this point, suppose that we want to infer $P(b^1 \mid d^1, c^1)$ from a set of n samples from the joint distribution $P(b, s, e, d, c)$. We use parenthetical superscripts to indicate the index of a sample, where we write $(b^{(i)}, s^{(i)}, e^{(i)}, d^{(i)}, c^{(i)})$ for the ith sample. The direct sample estimate is

$$P(b^1 \mid d^1, c^1) \approx \frac{\sum_i (b^{(i)} = 1 \land d^{(i)} = 1 \land c^{(i)} = 1)}{\sum_i (d^{(i)} = 1 \land c^{(i)} = 1)} \qquad (3.15)$$

We use the convention where a logical statement in parentheses is treated numerically as 1 when true and 0 when false. The numerator is the number of samples consistent with b, d, and c all set to 1, and the denominator is the number of samples consistent with d and c all set to 1.

[6] Sometimes approaches involving random sampling are referred to as *Monte Carlo methods*. The name comes from the Monte Carlo Casino in Monaco. An introduction to randomized algorithms and their application to a variety of problem domains is provided by R. Motwani and P. Raghavan, *Randomized Algorithms*. Cambridge University Press, 1995.

Sampling from the joint distribution represented by a Bayesian network is straightforward. The first step involves finding a *topological sort* of the nodes in the Bayesian network. A topological sort of the nodes in a directed acyclic graph is an ordered list such that if there is an edge $A \rightarrow B$, then A comes before B in the list.[7] For example, a topological sort for the network in figure 3.1 is B, S, E, D, C. A topological sort always exists, but it may not be unique. Another topological sort for the network is S, B, E, C, D.

Once we have a topological sort, we can begin sampling from the conditional probability distributions. Algorithm 3.6 shows how to sample from a Bayesian network given an ordering $X_{1:n}$ that represents a topological sort. We draw a sample from the conditional distribution associated with X_i given the values of the parents that have already been assigned. Because $X_{1:n}$ is a topological sort, we know that all the parents of X_i have already been instantiated, allowing this sampling to be done. Direct sampling is implemented in algorithm 3.7 and is demonstrated in example 3.5.

[7] A. B. Kahn, "Topological Sorting of Large Networks," *Communications of the ACM*, vol. 5, no. 11, pp. 558–562, 1962. An implementation of topological sorting is provided by the Graphs.jl package.

```
function Base.rand(φ::Factor)
    tot, p, w = 0.0, rand(), sum(values(φ.table))
    for (a,v) in φ.table
        tot += v/w
        if tot >= p
            return a
        end
    end
    return Assignment()
end

function Base.rand(bn::BayesianNetwork)
    a = Assignment()
    for i in topological_sort(bn.graph)
        name, φ = bn.vars[i].name, bn.factors[i]
        a[name] = rand(condition(φ, a))[name]
    end
    return a
end
```

Algorithm 3.6. A method for sampling an assignment from a Bayesian network bn. We also provide a method for sampling an assignment from a factor φ.

Suppose we draw 10 random samples from the network in figure 3.1. We are interested in inferring $P(b^1 \mid d^1, c^1)$. Only 2 of the 10 samples (pointed to in the table) are consistent with observations d^1 and c^1. One sample has $b = 1$, and the other sample has $b = 0$. From these samples, we infer that $P(b^1 \mid d^1, c^1) = 0.5$. Of course, we would want to use more than just 2 samples to accurately estimate $P(b^1 \mid d^1, c^1)$.

B	S	E	D	C	
0	0	1	1	0	
0	0	0	0	0	
1	0	1	0	0	
1	0	1	1	1	←
0	0	0	0	0	
0	0	0	1	0	
0	0	0	0	1	
0	1	1	1	1	←
0	0	0	0	0	
0	0	0	1	0	

Example 3.5. An example of how direct samples from a Bayesian network can be used for inference.

```
struct DirectSampling
    m # number of samples
end

function infer(M::DirectSampling, bn, query, evidence)
    table = FactorTable()
    for i in 1:(M.m)
        a = rand(bn)
        if all(a[k] == v for (k,v) in pairs(evidence))
            b = select(a, query)
            table[b] = get(table, b, 0) + 1
        end
    end
    vars = filter(v→v.name ∈ query, bn.vars)
    return normalize!(Factor(vars, table))
end
```

Algorithm 3.7. The direct sampling inference method, which takes a Bayesian network bn, a list of query variables query, and evidence evidence. The method draws m samples from the Bayesian network and retains those samples that are consistent with the evidence. A factor over the query variables is returned. This method can fail if no samples that satisfy the evidence are found.

3.7   Likelihood Weighted Sampling

The problem with direct sampling is that we may waste time generating samples that are inconsistent with the observations, especially if the observations are unlikely. An alternative approach is called *likelihood weighted sampling*, which involves generating weighted samples that are consistent with the observations.

To illustrate, we will again attempt to infer $P(b^1 \mid d^1, c^1)$. We have a set of n samples, where the ith sample is again denoted $(b^{(i)}, s^{(i)}, e^{(i)}, d^{(i)}, c^{(i)})$. The weight of the ith sample is w_i. The weighted estimate is

$$P(b^1 \mid d^1, c^1) \approx \frac{\sum_i w_i (b^{(i)} = 1 \wedge d^{(i)} = 1 \wedge c^{(i)} = 1)}{\sum_i w_i (d^{(i)} = 1 \wedge c^{(i)} = 1)} \tag{3.16}$$

$$= \frac{\sum_i w_i (b^{(i)} = 1)}{\sum_i w_i} \tag{3.17}$$

To generate these weighted samples, we begin with a topological sort and sample from the conditional distributions in sequence. The only difference in likelihood weighting is how we handle observed variables. Instead of sampling their values from a conditional distribution, we assign variables to their observed values and adjust the weight of the sample appropriately. The weight of a sample is simply the product of the conditional probabilities at the observed nodes. Likelihood weighted sampling is implemented in algorithm 3.8. Example 3.6 demonstrates inference with likelihood weighted sampling.

```
struct LikelihoodWeightedSampling
    m # number of samples
end

function infer(M::LikelihoodWeightedSampling, bn, query, evidence)
    table = FactorTable()
    ordering = topological_sort(bn.graph)
    for i in 1:(M.m)
        a, w = Assignment(), 1.0
        for j in ordering
            name, ϕ = bn.vars[j].name, bn.factors[j]
            if haskey(evidence, name)
                a[name] = evidence[name]
                w *= ϕ.table[select(a, variablenames(ϕ))]
            else
                a[name] = rand(condition(ϕ, a))[name]
            end
        end
        b = select(a, query)
        table[b] = get(table, b, 0) + w
    end
    vars = filter(v→v.name ∈ query, bn.vars)
    return normalize!(Factor(vars, table))
end
```

Algorithm 3.8. The likelihood weighted sampling inference method, which takes a Bayesian network bn, a list of query variables query, and evidence evidence. The method draws m samples from the Bayesian network but sets values from evidence when possible, keeping track of the conditional probability when doing so. These probabilities are used to weight the samples such that the final inference estimate is accurate. A factor over the query variables is returned.

The table here shows five likelihood weighted samples from the network in figure 3.1. We sample from $P(B)$, $P(S)$, and $P(E \mid B, S)$, as we would with direct sampling. When we come to D and C, we assign $D = 1$ and $C = 1$. If the sample has $E = 1$, then the weight is $P(d^1 \mid e^1)P(c^1 \mid e^1)$; otherwise, the weight is $P(d^1 \mid e^0)P(c^1 \mid e^0)$. If we assume

$$P(d^1 \mid e^1)P(c^1 \mid e^1) = 0.95$$
$$P(d^1 \mid e^0)P(c^1 \mid e^0) = 0.01$$

then we may approximate from the samples in the table:

$$P(b^1 \mid d^1, c^1) = \frac{0.95}{0.95 + 0.95 + 0.01 + 0.01 + 0.95} \approx 0.331$$

B	S	E	D	C	Weight
1	0	1	1	1	$P(d^1 \mid e^1)P(c^1 \mid e^1)$
0	1	1	1	1	$P(d^1 \mid e^1)P(c^1 \mid e^1)$
0	0	0	1	1	$P(d^1 \mid e^0)P(c^1 \mid e^0)$
0	0	0	1	1	$P(d^1 \mid e^0)P(c^1 \mid e^0)$
0	0	1	1	1	$P(d^1 \mid e^1)P(c^1 \mid e^1)$

Example 3.6. Likelihood weighted samples from a Bayesian network.

Although likelihood weighting makes it so that all samples are consistent with the observations, it can still be wasteful. Consider the simple chemical detection Bayesian network shown in figure 3.5, and assume that we detected a chemical of interest. We want to infer $P(c^1 \mid d^1)$. Because this network is small, we can easily compute this probability exactly by using Bayes' rule:

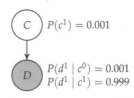

$$P(c^1 \mid d^1) = \frac{P(d^1 \mid c^1)P(c^1)}{P(d^1 \mid c^1)P(c^1) + P(d^1 \mid c^0)P(c^0)} \tag{3.18}$$

$$= \frac{0.999 \times 0.001}{0.999 \times 0.001 + 0.001 \times 0.999} \tag{3.19}$$

$$= 0.5 \tag{3.20}$$

Figure 3.5.   Chemical detection Bayesian network, with C indicating whether the chemical is present and D indicating whether the chemical is detected.

If we use likelihood weighting, then 99.9 % of the samples will have $C = 0$, with a weight of 0.001. Until we get a sample of $C = 1$, which has an associated weight of 0.999, our estimate of $P(c^1 \mid d^1)$ will be 0.

3.8   Gibbs Sampling

An alternative approach to inference is to use *Gibbs sampling*,[8] which is a kind of *Markov chain Monte Carlo* technique. Gibbs sampling involves drawing samples consistent with the evidence in a way that does not involve weighting. From these samples, we can infer the distribution over the query variables.

Gibbs sampling involves generating a sequence of samples, starting with an initial sample, $x_{1:n}^{(1)}$, generated randomly with the evidence variables set to their observed values. The kth sample $x_{1:n}^{(k)}$ depends probabilistically on the previous sample, $x_{1:n}^{(k-1)}$. We modify $x_{1:n}^{(k-1)}$ in place to obtain $x_{1:n}^{(k)}$ as follows. Using any ordering of the unobserved variables, which need not be a topological sort, $x_i^{(k)}$ is sampled from the distribution represented by $P(X_i \mid x_{-i}^{(k)})$. Here, $x_{-i}^{(k)}$ represents the values of all other variables except X_i in sample k. Sampling from $P(X_i \mid x_{-i}^{(k)})$ can be done efficiently because we only need to consider the Markov blanket of variable X_i (see section 2.6).

Unlike the other sampling methods discussed so far, the samples produced by this method are not independent. However, it can be proven that, in the limit, samples are drawn exactly from the joint distribution over the unobserved

[8] Named for the American scientist Josiah Willard Gibbs (1839–1903), who, with James Clerk Maxwell and Ludwig Boltzman, created the field of statistical mechanics.

variables given the observations. Algorithm 3.9 shows how to compute a factor for $P(X_i \mid x_{-i})$. Gibbs sampling is implemented in algorithm 3.10.

```julia
function blanket(bn, a, i)
    name = bn.vars[i].name
    val = a[name]
    a = delete!(copy(a), name)
    Φ = filter(ϕ → in_scope(name, ϕ), bn.factors)
    ϕ = prod(condition(ϕ, a) for ϕ in Φ)
    return normalize!(ϕ)
end
```

Algorithm 3.9. A method for obtaining $P(X_i \mid x_{-i})$ for a Bayesian network bn given a current assignment a.

Gibbs sampling can be applied to our running example. We can use our m samples to estimate

$$P(b^1 \mid d^1, c^1) \approx \frac{1}{m} \sum_i (b^{(i)} = 1) \tag{3.21}$$

Figure 3.6 compares the convergence of the estimate of $P(c^1 \mid d^1)$ in the chemical detection network using direct, likelihood weighted, and Gibbs sampling. Direct sampling takes the longest to converge. The direct sampling curve has long periods during which the estimate does not change because samples are inconsistent with the observations. Likelihood weighted sampling converges faster in this example. Spikes occur when a sample is generated with $C = 1$, and then gradually decrease. Gibbs sampling, in this example, quickly converges to the true value of 0.5.

As mentioned earlier, Gibbs sampling, like other Markov chain Monte Carlo methods, produces samples from the desired distribution in the limit. In practice, we have to run Gibbs for some amount of time, called the *burn-in period*, before converging to a steady-state distribution. The samples produced during burn-in are normally discarded. If many samples are to be used from a single Gibbs sampling series, it is common to *thin* the samples by keeping only every hth sample because of potential correlation between samples.

```
function update_gibbs_sample!(a, bn, evidence, ordering)
    for i in ordering
        name = bn.vars[i].name
        if !haskey(evidence, name)
            b = blanket(bn, a, i)
            a[name] = rand(b)[name]
        end
    end
end

function gibbs_sample!(a, bn, evidence, ordering, m)
    for j in 1:m
        update_gibbs_sample!(a, bn, evidence, ordering)
    end
end

struct GibbsSampling
    m_samples # number of samples to use
    m_burnin  # number of samples to discard during burn-in
    m_skip    # number of samples to skip for thinning
    ordering  # array of variable indices
end

function infer(M::GibbsSampling, bn, query, evidence)
    table = FactorTable()
    a = merge(rand(bn), evidence)
    gibbs_sample!(a, bn, evidence, M.ordering, M.m_burnin)
    for i in 1:(M.m_samples)
        gibbs_sample!(a, bn, evidence, M.ordering, M.m_skip)
        b = select(a, query)
        table[b] = get(table, b, 0) + 1
    end
    vars = filter(v→v.name ∈ query, bn.vars)
    return normalize!(Factor(vars, table))
end
```

Algorithm 3.10. Gibbs sampling implemented for a Bayesian network bn with evidence evidence and an ordering ordering. The method iteratively updates the assignment a for m iterations.

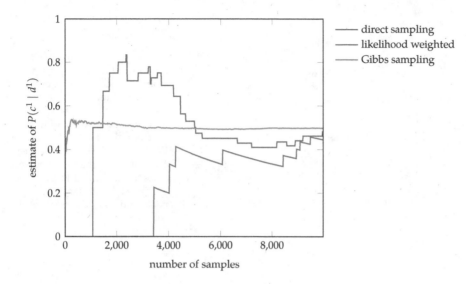

Figure 3.6.   A comparison of sampling-based inference methods on the chemical detection network. Both likelihood weighted and direct sampling have poor convergence due to the rarity of events, whereas Gibbs sampling is able to converge to the true value efficiently, even with no burn-in period or thinning.

3.9   Inference in Gaussian Models

If the joint distribution is Gaussian, we can perform exact inference analytically. Two jointly Gaussian random variables $\mathbf{a}$ and $\mathbf{b}$ can be written

$$\begin{bmatrix} \mathbf{a} \\ \mathbf{b} \end{bmatrix} \sim \mathcal{N}\left(\begin{bmatrix} \boldsymbol{\mu}_\mathbf{a} \\ \boldsymbol{\mu}_\mathbf{b} \end{bmatrix}, \begin{bmatrix} \mathbf{A} & \mathbf{C} \\ \mathbf{C}^\top & \mathbf{B} \end{bmatrix} \right) \tag{3.22}$$

The marginal distribution of a multivariate Gaussian is also Gaussian:

$$\mathbf{a} \sim \mathcal{N}(\boldsymbol{\mu}_\mathbf{a}, \mathbf{A}) \qquad \mathbf{b} \sim \mathcal{N}(\boldsymbol{\mu}_\mathbf{b}, \mathbf{B}) \tag{3.23}$$

The conditional distribution of a multivariate Gaussian is also Gaussian, with a convenient closed-form solution:

$$p(\mathbf{a} \mid \mathbf{b}) = \mathcal{N}\left(\mathbf{a} \mid \boldsymbol{\mu}_{\mathbf{a}\mid\mathbf{b}}, \boldsymbol{\Sigma}_{\mathbf{a}\mid\mathbf{b}} \right) \tag{3.24}$$

$$\boldsymbol{\mu}_{\mathbf{a}\mid\mathbf{b}} = \boldsymbol{\mu}_\mathbf{a} + \mathbf{C}\mathbf{B}^{-1}(\mathbf{b} - \boldsymbol{\mu}_\mathbf{b}) \tag{3.25}$$

$$\boldsymbol{\Sigma}_{\mathbf{a}\mid\mathbf{b}} = \mathbf{A} - \mathbf{C}\mathbf{B}^{-1}\mathbf{C}^\top \tag{3.26}$$

Algorithm 3.11 shows how to use these equations to infer a distribution over a set of query variables given evidence. Example 3.7 illustrates how to extract the marginal and conditional distributions from a multivariate Gaussian.

```
function infer(D::MvNormal, query, evidencevars, evidence)
    μ, Σ = D.μ, D.Σ.mat
    b, μa, μb = evidence, μ[query], μ[evidencevars]
    A = Σ[query,query]
    B = Σ[evidencevars,evidencevars]
    C = Σ[query,evidencevars]
    μ = μ[query] + C * (B\(b - μb))
    Σ = A - C * (B \ C')
    return MvNormal(μ, Σ)
end
```

Algorithm 3.11. Inference in a multivariate Gaussian distribution D. A vector of integers specifies the query variables in the query argument, and a vector of integers specifies the evidence variables in the evidencevars argument. The values of the evidence variables are contained in the vector evidence. The Distributions.jl package defines the MvNormal distribution.

Consider

$$\begin{bmatrix} x_1 \\ x_2 \end{bmatrix} \sim \mathcal{N}\left(\begin{bmatrix} 0 \\ 1 \end{bmatrix}, \begin{bmatrix} 3 & 1 \\ 1 & 2 \end{bmatrix}\right)$$

Example 3.7. Marginal and conditional distributions for a multivariate Gaussian.

The marginal distribution for x_1 is $\mathcal{N}(0,3)$, and the marginal distribution for x_2 is $\mathcal{N}(1,2)$.

The conditional distribution for x_1 given $x_2 = 2$ is

$$\mu_{x_1|x_2=2} = 0 + 1 \cdot 2^{-1} \cdot (2-1) = 0.5$$
$$\Sigma_{x_1|x_2=2} = 3 - 1 \cdot 2^{-1} \cdot 1 = 2.5$$
$$x_1 \mid (x_2 = 2) \sim \mathcal{N}(0.5, 2.5)$$

We can perform this inference calculation using algorithm 3.11 by constructing the joint distribution

D = MvNormal([0.0,1.0],[3.0 1.0; 1.0 2.0])

and then calling infer(D, [1], [2], [2.0]).

3.10 Summary

- Inference involves determining the probability of query variables given some evidence.

- Exact inference can be done by computing the joint distribution over the variables, setting evidence, and marginalizing out any hidden variables.

- Inference can be done efficiently in naive Bayes models, in which a single parent variable affects many conditionally independent children.

- The variable elimination algorithm can make exact inference more efficient by marginalizing variables in sequence.

- Belief propagation represents another method for inference, in which information is iteratively passed between factors to arrive at a result.

- Inference in a Bayesian network can be shown to be NP-hard through a reduction to the 3SAT problem, motivating the development of approximate inference methods.

- Approximate inference can be done by directly sampling from the joint distribution represented by a Bayesian network, but it may involve discarding many samples that are inconsistent with the evidence.

- Likelihood weighted sampling can reduce computation required for approximate inference by only generating samples that are consistent with the evidence and weighting each sample accordingly.

- Gibbs sampling generates a series of unweighted samples that are consistent with the evidence and can greatly speed approximate inference.

- Exact inference can be done efficiently through matrix operations when the joint distribution is Gaussian.

3.11   *Exercises*

Exercise 3.1. Given the following Bayesian network and its associated conditional probability distributions, write the equation required to perform exact inference for the query
$P(a^1 \mid d^1)$.

Solution: We first expand the inference expression using the definition of conditional
probability.

$$P(a^1 \mid d^1) = \frac{P(a^1, d^1)}{P(d^1)}$$

We can rewrite the numerator as a marginalization over the hidden variables and we can
rewrite the denominator as a marginalization over both the hidden and query variables:

$$P(a^1 \mid d^1) = \frac{\sum_b \sum_c P(a^1, b, c, d^1)}{\sum_a \sum_b \sum_c P(a, b, c, d^1)}$$

The definition of the joint probability in both the numerator and the denominator can be
rewritten using the chain rule for Bayesian networks and the resulting equation can be
simplified by removing constants from inside the summations:

$$\begin{aligned}
P(a^1 \mid d^1) &= \frac{\sum_b \sum_c P(a^1) P(b \mid a^1) P(c \mid b) P(d^1 \mid c)}{\sum_a \sum_b \sum_c P(a) P(b \mid a) P(c \mid b) P(d^1 \mid c)} \\
&= \frac{P(a^1) \sum_b \sum_c P(b \mid a^1) P(c \mid b) P(d^1 \mid c)}{\sum_a \sum_b \sum_c P(a) P(b \mid a) P(c \mid b) P(d^1 \mid c)} \\
&= \frac{P(a^1) \sum_b P(b \mid a^1) \sum_c P(c \mid b) P(d^1 \mid c)}{\sum_a P(a) \sum_b P(b \mid a) \sum_c P(c \mid b) P(d^1 \mid c)}
\end{aligned}$$

Exercise 3.2. Given the following Bayesian network and its associated conditional probability distributions, write the equation required to perform an exact inference for the query
$P(c^1, d^1 \mid a^0, f^1)$.

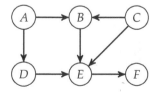

Solution: We first expand the inference expression using the definition of conditional
probability:

$$P(c^1, d^1 \mid a^0, f^1) = \frac{P(a^0, c^1, d^1, f^1)}{P(a^0, f^1)}$$

We can rewrite the numerator as a marginalization over the hidden variables, and we can rewrite the denominator as a marginalization over both the hidden and query variables:

$$P(c^1, d^1 \mid a^0, f^1) = \frac{\sum_b \sum_e P(a^0, b, c^1, d^1, e, f^1)}{\sum_b \sum_c \sum_d \sum_e P(a^0, b, c, d, e, f^1)}$$

The definition of the joint probability in both the numerator and the denominator can be rewritten using the chain rule for Bayesian networks, and the resulting equation can be simplified by removing constants from inside the summations. Note that there are multiple possible orderings of the summations in the final equation:

$$P(c^1, d^1 \mid a^0, f^1) = \frac{\sum_b \sum_e P(a^0)P(b \mid a^0, c^1)P(c^1)P(d^1 \mid a^0)P(e \mid b, c^1, d^1)P(f^1 \mid e)}{\sum_b \sum_c \sum_d \sum_e P(a^0)P(b \mid a^0, c)P(c)P(d \mid a^0)P(e \mid b, c, d)P(f^1 \mid e)}$$

$$= \frac{P(a^0)P(c^1)P(d^1 \mid a^0) \sum_b \sum_e P(b \mid a^0, c^1)P(e \mid b, c^1, d^1)P(f^1 \mid e)}{P(a^0) \sum_b \sum_c \sum_d \sum_e P(b \mid a^0, c)P(c)P(d \mid a^0)P(e \mid b, c, d)P(f^1 \mid e)}$$

$$= \frac{P(c^1)P(d^1 \mid a^0) \sum_b P(b \mid a^0, c^1) \sum_e P(e \mid b, c^1, d^1)P(f^1 \mid e)}{\sum_c P(c) \sum_b P(b \mid a^0, c) \sum_d P(d \mid a^0) \sum_e P(e \mid b, c, d)P(f^1 \mid e)}$$

Exercise 3.3. Suppose that we are developing an object detection system for an autonomous vehicle driving in a city. Our vehicle's perception system reports an object's size S (either small, medium, or large) and speed V (either slow, moderate, or fast). We want to design a model that will determine the class C of an object—either a vehicle, pedestrian, or a ball—given observations of the object's size and speed. Assuming a naive Bayes model with the following class prior and class-conditional distributions, what is the detected class given observations S = medium and V = slow?

C	P(C)
vehicle	0.80
pedestrian	0.19
ball	0.01

C	S	P(S | C)
vehicle	small	0.001
vehicle	medium	0.009
vehicle	large	0.990
pedestrian	small	0.200
pedestrian	medium	0.750
pedestrian	large	0.050
ball	small	0.800
ball	medium	0.199
ball	large	0.001

C	V	P(V | C)
vehicle	slow	0.2
vehicle	moderate	0.2
vehicle	fast	0.6
pedestrian	slow	0.5
pedestrian	moderate	0.4
pedestrian	fast	0.1
ball	slow	0.4
ball	moderate	0.4
ball	fast	0.2

Solution: To compute the posterior distribution $P(c \mid o_{1:n})$, we use the definition of the joint distribution for a naive Bayes model in equation (3.4):

$$P(c \mid o_{1:n}) \propto P(c) \prod_{i=1}^{n} P(o_i \mid c)$$

$P(\text{vehicle} \mid \text{medium}, \text{slow}) \propto P(\text{vehicle}) P(S = \text{medium} \mid \text{vehicle}) P(V = \text{slow} \mid \text{vehicle})$

$P(\text{vehicle} \mid \text{medium}, \text{slow}) \propto (0.80)(0.009)(0.2) = 0.00144$

$P(\text{pedestrian} \mid \text{medium}, \text{slow}) \propto P(\text{pedestrian}) P(S = \text{medium} \mid \text{pedestrian}) P(V = \text{slow} \mid \text{pedestrian})$

$P(\text{pedestrian} \mid \text{medium}, \text{slow}) \propto (0.19)(0.75)(0.5) = 0.07125$

$P(\text{ball} \mid \text{medium}, \text{slow}) \propto P(\text{ball}) P(S = \text{medium} \mid \text{ball}) P(V = \text{slow} \mid \text{ball})$

$P(\text{ball} \mid \text{medium}, \text{slow}) \propto (0.01)(0.199)(0.4) = 0.000796$

Since $P(\text{pedestrian} \mid \text{medium}, \text{slow})$ has the largest probability, the object is classified as a pedestrian.

Exercise 3.4. Given the 3SAT formula in equation (3.14) and the Bayesian network structure in figure 3.4, what are the values of $P(c_3^1 \mid x_2^1, x_3^0, x_4^1)$ and $P(y^1 \mid d_2^1, c_3^0)$?

Solution: We have $P(c_3^1 \mid x_2^1, x_3^0, x_4^1) = 1$ because x_2^1, x_3^0, x_4^1 makes the third clause true, and $P(y^1 \mid d_2^1, c_3^0) = 0$, because $Y = 1$ requires that both D_2 and C_3 be true.

Exercise 3.5. Give a topological sort for each of the following directed graphs:

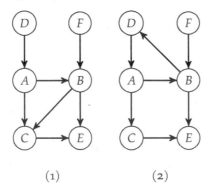

(1)   (2)

Solution: There are three valid topological sorts for the first directed graph (Bayesian network): (F, D, A, B, C, E), (D, A, F, B, C, E), and (D, F, A, B, C, E). There are no valid topological sorts for the second directed graph since it is cyclic.

Exercise 3.6. Suppose that we have the following Bayesian network and we are interested in generating an approximation of the inference query $P(e^1 \mid b^0, d^1)$ using likelihood weighted sampling. Given the following samples, write the expressions for each of the sample weights. In addition, write the equation for estimating $P(e^1 \mid b^0, d^1)$ in terms of the sample weights w_i.

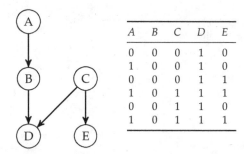

A	B	C	D	E
0	0	0	1	0
1	0	0	1	0
0	0	0	1	1
1	0	1	1	1
0	0	1	1	0
1	0	1	1	1

Solution: For likelihood weighted sampling, the sample weights are the product of the distributions over evidence variables conditioned on the values of their parents. Thus, the general form for our weights is $P(b^0 \mid a)P(d^1 \mid b^0, c)$. We then match each of the values for each sample from the joint distribution:

A	B	C	D	E	Weight
0	0	0	1	0	$P(b^0 \mid a^0)P(d^1 \mid b^0, c^0)$
1	0	0	1	0	$P(b^0 \mid a^1)P(d^1 \mid b^0, c^0)$
0	0	0	1	1	$P(b^0 \mid a^0)P(d^1 \mid b^0, c^0)$
1	0	1	1	1	$P(b^0 \mid a^1)P(d^1 \mid b^0, c^1)$
0	0	1	1	0	$P(b^0 \mid a^0)P(d^1 \mid b^0, c^1)$
1	0	1	1	1	$P(b^0 \mid a^1)P(d^1 \mid b^0, c^1)$

To estimate $P(e^1 \mid b^0, d^1)$, we simply need to sum the weights of samples consistent with the query variable and divide this by the sum of all the weights:

$$P(e^1 \mid b^0, d^1) = \frac{\sum_i w_i(e^{(i)} = 1)}{\sum_i w_i} = \frac{w_3 + w_4 + w_6}{w_1 + w_2 + w_3 + w_4 + w_5 + w_6}$$

Exercise 3.7. Each year, we receive student scores on standardized mathematics M, reading R, and writing W exams. Using data from prior years, we create the following distribution:

$$\begin{bmatrix} M \\ R \\ W \end{bmatrix} \sim \mathcal{N}\left(\begin{bmatrix} 81 \\ 82 \\ 80 \end{bmatrix}, \begin{bmatrix} 25 & -9 & -16 \\ -9 & 36 & 16 \\ -16 & 16 & 36 \end{bmatrix} \right)$$

Compute the parameters of the conditional distribution over a student's math and reading test scores, given a writing score of 90.

Solution: If we let **a** represent the vector of math and reading scores and **b** represent the writing score, the joint and conditional distributions are as follows:

$$\begin{bmatrix} a \\ b \end{bmatrix} \sim \mathcal{N}\left(\begin{bmatrix} \mu_a \\ \mu_b \end{bmatrix}, \begin{bmatrix} A & C \\ C^\top & B \end{bmatrix} \right)$$

$$p(a \mid b) = \mathcal{N}\left(a \mid \mu_{a|b}, \Sigma_{a|b} \right)$$

$$\mu_{a|b} = \mu_a + CB^{-1}(b - \mu_b)$$

$$\Sigma_{a|b} = A - CB^{-1}C^\top$$

In the example, we have the following definitions:

$$\mu_a = \begin{bmatrix} 81 \\ 82 \end{bmatrix} \qquad \mu_b = \begin{bmatrix} 80 \end{bmatrix} \qquad A = \begin{bmatrix} 25 & -9 \\ -9 & 36 \end{bmatrix} \qquad B = \begin{bmatrix} 36 \end{bmatrix} \qquad C = \begin{bmatrix} -16 \\ 16 \end{bmatrix}$$

Thus, the parameters of our conditional distribution given $b = W = 90$ are

$$\mu_{M,R|W=90} = \begin{bmatrix} 81 \\ 82 \end{bmatrix} + \begin{bmatrix} -16 \\ 16 \end{bmatrix} \frac{1}{36}(90 - 80) \approx \begin{bmatrix} 76.5 \\ 86.4 \end{bmatrix}$$

$$\Sigma_{M,R|W=90} = \begin{bmatrix} 25 & -9 \\ -9 & 36 \end{bmatrix} - \begin{bmatrix} -16 \\ 16 \end{bmatrix} \frac{1}{36} \begin{bmatrix} -16 & 16 \end{bmatrix} \approx \begin{bmatrix} 25 & -9 \\ -9 & 36 \end{bmatrix} - \begin{bmatrix} 7.1 & -7.1 \\ -7.1 & 7.1 \end{bmatrix} = \begin{bmatrix} 17.9 & -1.9 \\ -1.9 & 28.9 \end{bmatrix}$$

Given that the student scores a 90 on the writing test, based on our conditional distribution, we expect the student to earn a 76.5 on the math test, with a standard deviation of $\sqrt{17.9}$, and an 86.4 on the reading test, with a standard deviation of $\sqrt{28.9}$.

4 Parameter Learning

We have assumed so far that the parameters and structure of our probabilistic models were known. This chapter addresses the problem of *learning* or *fitting* model parameters from data.[1] We begin by introducing an approach where we identify the parameters of a model that maximize the likelihood of observing the data. After discussing the limitations of such an approach, we introduce an alternative Bayesian approach, in which we start with a probability distribution over the unknown parameters and then update that distribution based on the observed data using the laws of probability. We then discuss probabilistic models that avoid committing to a fixed number of parameters.

[1] This chapter focuses on learning model parameters from data, which is an important component of the field of *machine learning*. A broad introduction to the field is provided by K. P. Murphy, *Probabilistic Machine Learning: An Introduction*. MIT Press, 2022.

4.1 Maximum Likelihood Parameter Learning

In *maximum likelihood parameter learning*, we attempt to find the parameters of a distribution that maximize the likelihood of observing the data. If θ represents the parameters of a distribution, then the *maximum likelihood estimate* is

$$\hat{\theta} = \arg\max_{\theta} P(D \mid \theta) \tag{4.1}$$

where $P(D \mid \theta)$ is the likelihood that our probability model assigns to the data D occurring when the model parameters are set to θ.[2] We often use the "hat" accent ("ˆ") to indicate an estimate of a parameter.

There are two challenges associated with maximum likelihood parameter learning. One is to choose an appropriate probability model by which we define $P(D \mid \theta)$. We often assume that the samples in our data D are *independently and identically distributed*, which means that our samples $D = o_{1:m}$ are drawn from a

[2] Here, we write $P(D \mid \theta)$ as if it is a probability mass associated with a discrete distribution. However, our probability model may be continuous, in which case we are working with densities.

distribution $o_i \sim P(\cdot \mid \theta)$ with

$$P(D \mid \theta) = \prod_i P(o_i \mid \theta) \tag{4.2}$$

Probability models could include, for example, the categorical distributions or Gaussian distributions mentioned in earlier chapters.

The other challenge is performing the maximization in equation (4.3). For many common probability models, we can perform this optimization analytically. Others may be difficult. A common approach is to maximize the *log-likelihood*, often denoted as $\ell(\theta)$. Since the log-transformation is monotonically increasing, maximizing the log-likelihood is equivalent to maximizing the likelihood:[3]

$$\hat{\theta} = \arg\max_\theta \sum_i \log P(o_i \mid \theta) \tag{4.3}$$

Computing the sum of log-likelihoods is typically much more numerically stable compared to computing the product of many small probability masses or densities. The remainder of this section will demonstrate how to optimize equation (4.3) for different types of distributions.

4.1.1   Maximum Likelihood Estimates for Categorical Distributions

Suppose that the random variable C represents whether a flight will result in a midair collision, and we are interested in estimating the distribution $P(C)$. Because C is either 0 or 1, it is sufficient to estimate the parameter $\theta = P(c^1)$. What we want to do is infer θ from data D. We have a historical database spanning a decade consisting of m flights with n midair collisions. Our intuition, of course, tells us that a good estimate for θ, given the data D, is n/m. Under the assumption of independence of outcomes between flights, the probability of a sequence of m outcomes in D with n midair collisions is:

$$P(D \mid \theta) = \theta^n (1-\theta)^{m-n} \tag{4.4}$$

The maximum likelihood estimate $\hat{\theta}$ is the value for θ that maximizes equation (4.4), which is equivalent to maximizing the logarithm of the likelihood:

$$\ell(\theta) = \log\big(\theta^n (1-\theta)^{m-n}\big) \tag{4.5}$$
$$= n \log \theta + (m-n)\log(1-\theta) \tag{4.6}$$

[3] Although it does not matter whether we maximize the natural logarithm (base e) or the common logarithm (base 10) in this equation, throughout this book we will use $\log(x)$ to mean the logarithm of x with base e.

We can use the standard technique for finding the maximum of a function by setting the first derivative of ℓ to 0 and then solving for θ. The derivative is given by

$$\frac{\partial}{\partial \theta} \ell(\theta) = \frac{n}{\theta} - \frac{m-n}{1-\theta} \tag{4.7}$$

We can solve for $\hat{\theta}$ by setting the derivative to 0:

$$\frac{n}{\hat{\theta}} - \frac{m-n}{1-\hat{\theta}} = 0 \tag{4.8}$$

After a few algebraic steps, we see that, indeed, $\hat{\theta} = n/m$.

Computing the maximum likelihood estimate for a variable X that can assume k values is also straightforward. If $n_{1:k}$ are the observed counts for the k different values, then the maximum likelihood estimate for $P(x^i \mid n_{1:k})$ is given by

$$\hat{\theta}_i = \frac{n_i}{\sum_{j=1}^{k} n_j} \tag{4.9}$$

4.1.2   *Maximum Likelihood Estimates for Gaussian Distributions*

In a Gaussian distribution, the log-likelihood of the mean μ and variance σ^2 with m samples is given by

$$\ell(\mu, \sigma^2) \propto -m \log \sigma - \frac{\sum_i (o_i - \mu)^2}{2\sigma^2} \tag{4.10}$$

Again, we can set the derivative to 0 with respect to the parameters and solve for the maximum likelihood estimate:

$$\frac{\partial}{\partial \mu} \ell(\mu, \sigma^2) = \frac{\sum_i (o_i - \hat{\mu})}{\hat{\sigma}^2} = 0 \tag{4.11}$$

$$\frac{\partial}{\partial \sigma} \ell(\mu, \sigma^2) = -\frac{m}{\hat{\sigma}} + \frac{\sum_i (o_i - \hat{\mu})^2}{\hat{\sigma}^3} = 0 \tag{4.12}$$

After some algebraic manipulation, we get

$$\hat{\mu} = \frac{\sum_i o_i}{m} \qquad \hat{\sigma}^2 = \frac{\sum_i (o_i - \hat{\mu})^2}{m} \tag{4.13}$$

Figure 4.1 provides an example of fitting a Gaussian to data.

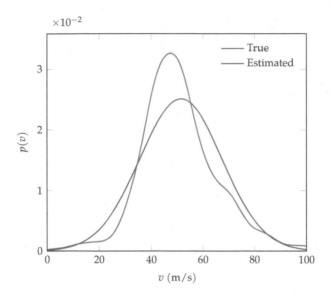

Figure 4.1. Suppose that we have airspeed measurements $o_{1:m}$ from m aircraft tracks, and we want to fit a Gaussian model. This figure shows a Gaussian with the maximum likelihood estimates $\hat{\mu} = 51.5\,\text{m/s}$ and $\hat{\sigma} = 15.9\,\text{m/s}$. The "true" distribution is shown for comparison. In this case, the Gaussian is a fairly reasonable approximation of the true distribution.

4.1.3   Maximum Likelihood Estimates for Bayesian Networks

We can apply maximum likelihood parameter learning to Bayesian networks. Here, we will assume that our network is composed of a set of n discrete variables that we denote as $X_{1:n}$. Our data $D = \{\mathbf{o}_1, \ldots, \mathbf{o}_m\}$ consists of observed samples from those variables. In our network with structure G, r_i is the number of instantiations of X_i, and q_i is the number of instantiations of the parents of X_i. If X_i has no parents, then $q_i = 1$. The jth instantiation of the parents of X_i is denoted as π_{ij}.

The factor table for X_i thus has $r_i q_i$ entries, resulting in a total of $\sum_{i=1}^{n} r_i q_i$ parameters in our Bayesian network. Each parameter is written as θ_{ijk} and determines

$$P(X_i = k \mid \pi_{ij}) = \theta_{ijk} \tag{4.14}$$

Although there are $\sum_{i=1}^{n} r_i q_i$ parameters, only $\sum_{i=1}^{n} (r_i - 1) q_i$ are independent. We use θ to represent the set of all parameters.

We use m_{ijk} to represent the number of times $X_i = k$ given parental instantiation j in the data set. Algorithm 4.1 provides an implementation of a function for extracting these counts or statistics from a data set. The likelihood is given in terms of m_{ijk}:

$$P(D \mid \boldsymbol{\theta}, G) = \prod_{i=1}^{n} \prod_{j=1}^{q_i} \prod_{k=1}^{r_i} \theta_{ijk}^{m_{ijk}} \tag{4.15}$$

Similar to the maximum likelihood estimate for the univariate distribution in equation (4.9), the maximum likelihood estimate in our discrete Bayesian network model is

$$\hat{\theta}_{ijk} = \frac{m_{ijk}}{\sum_{k'} m_{ijk'}} \tag{4.16}$$

Example 4.1 illustrates this process.

```
function sub2ind(siz, x)
    k = vcat(1, cumprod(siz[1:end-1]))
    return dot(k, x .- 1) + 1
end

function statistics(vars, G, D::Matrix{Int})
    n = size(D, 1)
    r = [vars[i].r for i in 1:n]
    q = [prod([r[j] for j in inneighbors(G,i)]) for i in 1:n]
    M = [zeros(q[i], r[i]) for i in 1:n]
    for o in eachcol(D)
        for i in 1:n
            k = o[i]
            parents = inneighbors(G,i)
            j = 1
            if !isempty(parents)
                j = sub2ind(r[parents], o[parents])
            end
            M[i][j,k] += 1.0
        end
    end
    return M
end
```

Algorithm 4.1. A function for extracting the statistics, or counts, from a discrete data set D, assuming a Bayesian network with variables vars and structure G. The data set is an $n \times m$ matrix, where n is the number of variables and m is the number of data points. This function returns an array M of length n. The ith component consists of a $q_i \times r_i$ matrix of counts. The sub2ind(siz, x) function returns a linear index into an array with dimensions specified by siz given coordinates x. It is used to identify which parental instantiation is relevant to a particular data point and variable.

4.2 Bayesian Parameter Learning

Bayesian parameter learning addresses some of the drawbacks of maximum likelihood estimation, especially when the amount of data is limited. For example, suppose that our aviation safety database was limited to the events of the past week, and we found no recorded midair collisions. If θ is the probability that a flight results in a midair collision, then the maximum likelihood estimate would

Suppose that we have a small network, $A \rightarrow B \leftarrow C$, and we want to extract the statistics from data matrix D. We can use the following code:

```
G = SimpleDiGraph(3)
add_edge!(G, 1, 2)
add_edge!(G, 3, 2)
vars = [Variable(:A,2), Variable(:B,2), Variable(:C,2)]
D = [1 2 2 1; 1 2 2 1; 2 2 2 2]
M = statistics(vars, G, D)
```

Example 4.1.   Using the statistics function for extracting the statistics from a data set. Bayesian parameter learning can be used to avoid NAN values, but we must specify a prior.

The output is an array M consisting of these three count matrices, each of size $q_i \times r_i$:

$$\begin{bmatrix} 2 & 2 \end{bmatrix} \qquad \begin{bmatrix} 0 & 0 \\ 0 & 0 \\ 2 & 0 \\ 0 & 2 \end{bmatrix} \qquad \begin{bmatrix} 0 & 4 \end{bmatrix}$$

We can compute the maximum likelihood estimate by normalizing the rows in the matrices in M:

```
θ = [mapslices(x→normalize(x,1), Mi, dims=2) for Mi in M]
```

which produces

$$\begin{bmatrix} 0.5 & 0.5 \end{bmatrix} \qquad \begin{bmatrix} \text{NAN} & \text{NAN} \\ \text{NAN} & \text{NAN} \\ 1 & 0 \\ 0 & 1 \end{bmatrix} \qquad \begin{bmatrix} 0 & 1 \end{bmatrix}$$

As we can see, the first and second parental instantiations of the second variable B leads to NAN ("not a number") estimates. Because there are no observations of those two parental instantiations in the data, the denominator of equation (4.16) equals zero, making the parameter estimate undefined. Most of the other parameters are not NAN. For example, the parameter $\theta_{112} = 0.5$ means that the maximum likelihood estimate of $P(a^2)$ is 0.5.

be $\hat{\theta} = 0$. Believing that there is zero chance of a midair collision is not a reasonable conclusion unless our prior hypothesis was, for example, that all flights were perfectly safe.

The Bayesian approach to parameter learning involves estimating $p(\theta \mid D)$, the posterior distribution over θ given our data D. Instead of obtaining a point estimate $\hat{\theta}$ as in maximum likelihood estimation, we obtain a distribution. This distribution can help us quantify our uncertainty about the true value of θ. We can convert this distribution into a point estimate by computing the expectation:

$$\hat{\theta} = \mathbb{E}_{\theta \sim p(\cdot \mid D)}[\theta] = \int \theta p(\theta \mid D) \, d\theta \tag{4.17}$$

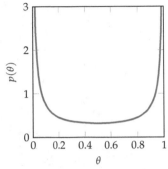

In some cases, however, the expectation may not be an acceptable estimate, as illustrated in figure 4.2. An alternative is to use the *maximum a posteriori* estimate:

$$\hat{\theta} = \arg\max_{\theta} p(\theta \mid D) \tag{4.18}$$

Figure 4.2. An example of a distribution where the expected value of θ is not a good estimate. The expected value of 0.5 has a lower density than occurs at the extreme values of 0 or 1. This distribution happens to be a beta distribution, a type of distribution we will discuss shortly, with parameters $(0.2, 0.2)$.

This estimate corresponds to a value of θ that is assigned the greatest density. This is often referred to as the *mode* of the distribution. As shown in figure 4.2, the mode may not be unique.

Bayesian parameter learning can be viewed as inference in a Bayesian network with the structure in figure 4.3, which makes the assumption that the observed variables are conditionally independent of each other. As with any Bayesian network, we must specify $p(\theta)$ and $P(O_i \mid \theta)$. We often use a uniform prior $p(\theta)$. The remainder of this section discusses how to apply Bayesian parameter learning to different models of $P(O_i \mid \theta)$.

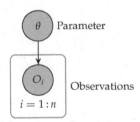

Figure 4.3. Bayesian network representing parameter learning.

4.2.1 Bayesian Learning for Binary Distributions

Suppose we want to learn the parameters of a binary distribution. Here, we will use $P(o^1 \mid \theta) = \theta$. To infer the distribution over θ in the Bayesian network in figure 4.3, we can proceed with the standard method for performing inference discussed in chapter 3. Here, we will assume a uniform prior:

$$p(\theta \mid o_{1:m}) \propto p(\theta, o_{1:m}) \qquad (4.19)$$

$$= p(\theta) \prod_{i=1}^{m} P(o_i \mid \theta) \qquad (4.20)$$

$$= \prod_{i=1}^{m} P(o_i \mid \theta) \qquad (4.21)$$

$$= \prod_{i=1}^{m} \theta^{o_i} (1-\theta)^{1-o_i} \qquad (4.22)$$

$$= \theta^n (1-\theta)^{m-n} \qquad (4.23)$$

The posterior is proportional to $\theta^n (1-\theta)^{m-n}$, where n is the number of times $O_i = 1$. To find the normalization constant, we integrate

$$\int_0^1 \theta^n (1-\theta)^{m-n} \, d\theta = \frac{\Gamma(n+1)\Gamma(m-n+1)}{\Gamma(m+2)} \qquad (4.24)$$

where Γ is the *gamma function*. The gamma function is a real-valued generalization of the factorial. If m is an integer, then $\Gamma(m) = (m-1)!$. Taking normalization into account, we have

$$p(\theta \mid o_{1:m}) = \frac{\Gamma(m+2)}{\Gamma(n+1)\Gamma(m-n+1)} \theta^n (1-\theta)^{m-n} \qquad (4.25)$$

$$= \text{Beta}(\theta \mid n+1, m-n+1) \qquad (4.26)$$

The *beta distribution* $\text{Beta}(\alpha, \beta)$ is defined by parameters α and β, and curves for this distribution are shown in figure 4.4. The distribution $\text{Beta}(1,1)$ corresponds to the uniform distribution spanning 0 to 1.

The distribution $\text{Beta}(\alpha, \beta)$ has mean

$$\frac{\alpha}{\alpha + \beta} \qquad (4.27)$$

When α and β are both greater than 1, the mode is

$$\frac{\alpha - 1}{\alpha + \beta - 2} \qquad (4.28)$$

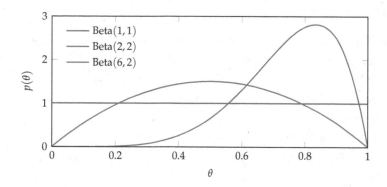

Figure 4.4. An overlay of several beta probability densities.

Conveniently, if a beta distribution is used as a prior over a parameter of a binary distribution, then the posterior is also a beta distribution. In particular, if the prior is given by $\text{Beta}(\alpha, \beta)$ and we make an observation o_i, then we get a posterior of $\text{Beta}(\alpha + 1, \beta)$ if $o_i = 1$ and $\text{Beta}(\alpha, \beta + 1)$ if $o_i = 0$. Hence, if we started with a prior given by $\text{Beta}(\alpha, \beta)$ and our data showed that there were n collisions out of m flights, then the posterior would be given by $\text{Beta}(\alpha + n, \beta + m - n)$. The α and β parameters in the prior are sometimes called *pseudocounts* because they are treated similarly to the observed counts of the two outcome classes in the posterior, although the pseudocounts need not be integers.

Choosing the prior, in principle, should be done without knowledge of the data used to compute the posterior. Uniform priors often work well in practice, although if expert knowledge is available, then it can be encoded into the prior. For example, suppose that we had a slightly bent coin and we wanted to estimate θ, the probability that the coin would land heads. Before we collected any data by flipping the coin, we would start with a belief θ that is likely to be around 0.5. Instead of starting with a uniform prior $\text{Beta}(1, 1)$, we might use $\text{Beta}(2, 2)$ (shown in figure 4.4), which gives more weight to values near 0.5. If we were more confident in an estimate near 0.5, then we could reduce the variance of the prior by increasing the pseudocounts. The prior $\text{Beta}(10, 10)$ is much more peaked than $\text{Beta}(2, 2)$. In general, however, the importance of the prior diminishes with the amount of data used to compute the posterior. If we observe m flips and n were heads, then the difference between $\text{Beta}(1 + n, 1 + m - n)$ and $\text{Beta}(10 + n, 10 + m - n)$ is negligible if we observe thousands of coin flips.

4.2.2   Bayesian Learning for Categorical Distributions

The *Dirichlet distribution*[4] is a generalization of the beta distribution and can be used to estimate the parameters of categorical distributions. Suppose that X is a discrete random variable that takes integer values from 1 to n. We define the parameters of the distribution to be $\theta_{1:n}$, where $P(x^i) = \theta_i$. Of course, the parameters must sum to 1, and so only the first $n-1$ parameters are independent. The Dirichlet distribution can be used to represent both the prior and the posterior distribution and is parameterized by $\alpha_{1:n}$. The density is given by

$$\text{Dir}(\theta_{1:n} \mid \alpha_{1:n}) = \frac{\Gamma(\alpha_0)}{\prod_{i=1}^{n} \Gamma(\alpha_i)} \prod_{i=1}^{n} \theta_i^{\alpha_i - 1} \tag{4.29}$$

where α_0 is used to denote the summation of the parameters $\alpha_{1:n}$.[5] If $n = 2$, then it is easy to see that equation (4.29) is equivalent to the beta distribution.

It is common to use a uniform prior where all the Dirichlet parameters $\alpha_{1:n}$ are set to 1. As with the beta distribution, the parameters in the Dirichlet are often referred to as *pseudocounts*. If the prior over $\theta_{1:n}$ is given by $\text{Dir}(\alpha_{1:n})$ and there are m_i observations of $X = i$, then the posterior is given by

$$p(\theta_{1:n} \mid \alpha_{1:n}, m_{1:n}) = \text{Dir}(\theta_{1:n} \mid \alpha_1 + m_1, \ldots, \alpha_n + m_n) \tag{4.30}$$

The distribution $\text{Dir}(\alpha_{1:n})$ has a mean vector whose ith component is

$$\frac{\alpha_i}{\sum_{j=1}^{n} \alpha_j} \tag{4.31}$$

When $\alpha_i > 1$, the ith component of the mode is

$$\frac{\alpha_i - 1}{\sum_{j=1}^{n} \alpha_j - n} \tag{4.32}$$

As we have seen, Bayesian parameter estimation is straightforward for binary and discrete random variables because it involves simply counting the various outcomes in the data. Bayes' rule can be used to infer the distribution over the parameters for other parametric distributions. Depending on the choice of prior and the form of the parametric distribution, calculating the posterior over the space of parameters also might be done analytically.

[4] This distribution is named after the German mathematician Johann Peter Gustav Lejeune Dirichlet (1805–1859).

[5] See appendix B for plots of Dirichlet distribution densities for different parameters.

4.2.3   Bayesian Learning for Bayesian Networks

We can apply Bayesian parameter learning to discrete Bayesian networks. The prior over the Bayesian network parameters θ can be factorized as follows:

$$p(\theta \mid G) = \prod_{i=1}^{n}\prod_{j=1}^{q_i} p(\theta_{ij}) \qquad (4.33)$$

where $\theta_{ij} = (\theta_{ij1}, \ldots, \theta_{ijr_i})$. The prior $p(\theta_{ij})$, under some weak assumptions, can be shown to follow a Dirichlet distribution $\mathrm{Dir}(\alpha_{ij1}, \ldots, \alpha_{ijr_i})$. Algorithm 4.2 provides an implementation for creating a data structure holding α_{ijk}, where all entries are 1, corresponding to a uniform prior.

After observing data in the form of m_{ijk} counts (as introduced in section 4.1.3), the posterior is then

$$p(\theta_{ij} \mid \alpha_{ij}, m_{ij}) = \mathrm{Dir}(\theta_{ij} \mid \alpha_{ij1} + m_{ij1}, \ldots, \alpha_{ijr_i} + m_{ijr_i}) \qquad (4.34)$$

similar to equation (4.30). Example 4.2 demonstrates this process.

```
function prior(vars, G)
    n = length(vars)
    r = [vars[i].r for i in 1:n]
    q = [prod([r[j] for j in inneighbors(G,i)]) for i in 1:n]
    return [ones(q[i], r[i]) for i in 1:n]
end
```

Algorithm 4.2. A function for generating a prior α_{ijk} where all entries are 1. The array of matrices that this function returns takes the same form as the statistics generated by algorithm 4.1. To determine the appropriate dimensions, the function takes as input the list of variables vars and structure G.

We can compute the parameters of the posterior associated with a Bayesian network through simple addition of the prior parameters and counts (equation (4.34)). If we use the matrix of counts M obtained in example 4.1, we can add it to the matrices of prior parameters α = prior(vars, G) to obtain the set of posterior parameters M + α:

Example 4.2. Computing the posterior parameters in a Bayesian network. Note that unlike example 4.1, here we do not have NAN values.

$$\begin{bmatrix} 3 & 3 \end{bmatrix} \qquad \begin{bmatrix} 1 & 1 \\ 1 & 1 \\ 3 & 1 \\ 1 & 3 \end{bmatrix} \qquad \begin{bmatrix} 1 & 5 \end{bmatrix}$$

4.3   Nonparametric Learning

The previous two sections assumed that the probabilistic model was of a fixed form and that a fixed set of parameters were to be learned from the data. An alternative approach is based on *nonparametric* methods in which the number of parameters scales with the amount of data. A common nonparametric method is *kernel density estimation* (algorithm 4.3). Given observations $o_{1:m}$, kernel density estimation represents the density as follows:

$$p(x) = \frac{1}{m}\sum_{i=1}^{m}\phi(x - o_i) \tag{4.35}$$

where ϕ is a *kernel function*, which integrates to 1. The kernel function is used to assign greater density to values near the observed data points. A kernel function is generally symmetric, meaning that $\phi(x) = \phi(-x)$. A common kernel is the zero-mean Gaussian distribution. When such a kernel is used, the standard deviation is often referred to as the *bandwidth*, which can be tuned to control the smoothness of the density function. Larger bandwidths generally lead to smoother densities. Bayesian methods can be applied to the selection of the appropriate bandwidth based on the data. The effect of the bandwidth choice is shown in figure 4.5.

```
gaussian_kernel(b) = x→pdf(Normal(0,b), x)

function kernel_density_estimate(ϕ, O)
    return x → sum([ϕ(x - o) for o in O])/length(O)
end
```

Algorithm 4.3.   The method gaussian_kernel returns a zero-mean Gaussian kernel $\phi(x)$ with bandwidth b. Kernel density estimation is also implemented for a kernel ϕ and list of observations O.

4.4   Learning with Missing Data

When learning the parameters of our probabilistic model we may have *missing* entries in our data.[6] For example, if we are conducting a survey, some respondents may decide to skip a question. Table 4.1 shows an example of a data set with missing entries involving three binary variables: *A*, *B*, and *C*. One approach to handling missing data is to discard all the instances that are *incomplete*, where there are one or more missing entries. Depending on how much of the data is missing, we might have to discard much of it. In table 4.1, we would have to discard all but one of the rows, which can be wasteful.

[6] Learning with missing data is the subject of a large body of literature. A comprehensive introduction and review is provided by G. Molenberghs, G. Fitzmaurice, M. G. Kenward, A. Tsiatis, and G. Verbeke, eds., *Handbook of Missing Data Methodology*. CRC Press, 2014.

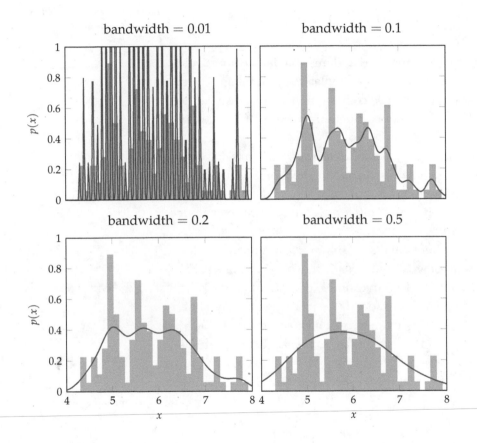

Figure 4.5. Kernel density estimation applied to the same data set using zero-mean Gaussian kernels with different bandwidths. The histogram in blue shows the underlying data set frequencies, and the black lines indicate the probability density from kernel density estimation. Larger bandwidths smooth out the estimate, whereas smaller bandwidths can overfit to specific samples.

We can learn model parameters from missing data using either a maximum likelihood or a Bayesian approach. If taking a Bayesian maximum a posteriori approach, we want to find the estimate

$$\hat{\theta} = \arg\max_{\theta} p(\theta \mid D_{\text{obs}}) \tag{4.36}$$

$$= \arg\max_{\theta} \sum_{D_{\text{mis}}} p(\theta \mid D_{\text{obs}}, D_{\text{mis}}) P(D_{\text{mis}} \mid D_{\text{obs}}) \tag{4.37}$$

A	B	C
1	1	0
?	1	1
1	?	?
?	?	?

Table 4.1. Example of data consisting of four instances with six missing entries.

where D_{obs} and D_{mis} consist of all the observed and missing data, respectively. If the data is continuous, then the sum would be replaced by an integral. The marginalization over the missing data can be computationally expensive. The same marginalization also affects the computational tractability of a Bayesian approach.

This section discusses two general approaches for learning with missing data without having to enumerate over all the possible combinations of missing values. The first involves learning the distribution parameters using predicted values of the missing entries. The second involves an iterative approach for improving our parameter estimates.

We will focus on the context where data is *missing at random*, meaning that the probability that an entry is missing is conditionally independent of its value, given the values of the observed variables. An example of a situation that does not adhere to this assumption might include radar data containing measurements of the distance to a target, but the measurement may be missing either due to noise or because the target is beyond the sensing range. The fact that an entry is missing is an indication that the value is more likely to be high. Accounting for this form of missingness requires different models and algorithms from what we discuss here.[7]

[7] Different *missingness mechanisms* and associated inference techniques are reviewed by R.J.A. Little and D.B. Rubin, *Statistical Analysis with Missing Data*, 3rd ed. Wiley, 2020.

4.4.1   Data Imputation

An alternative to discarding incomplete instances is to impute the values of missing entries. *Data imputation* is the process of inferring values for missing entries. One way to view imputation is as an approximation of equation (4.37), where we find

$$\hat{D}_{\text{mis}} = \arg\max_{D_{\text{mis}}} p(D_{\text{mis}} \mid D_{\text{obs}}) \tag{4.38}$$

Once we have the imputed missing values, we can use that data to produce a maximum posteriori estimate:

$$\hat{\theta} = \arg\max_{\theta} p(\theta \mid D_{\text{obs}}) \approx \arg\max_{\theta} p(\theta \mid D_{\text{obs}}, \hat{D}_{\text{mis}}) \qquad (4.39)$$

or, alternatively, we can take a maximum likelihood approach.

Solving equation (4.38) may still be computationally challenging. One simple approach for discrete data sets is to replace missing entries with the most commonly observed value, called the *marginal mode*. For example, in table 4.1, we might replace all the missing values for A with its marginal mode of 1.

Continuous data often lacks duplicates. However, we can fit a distribution to continuous values and then use the mode of the resulting distribution. For example, we might fit a Gaussian distribution to the data in table 4.2, and then fill in the missing entries with the mean of the observed values associated with each variable. The top-left plot in figure 4.6 illustrates the effect of this approach on two-dimensional data. The red lines show how values with missing first or second components are paired with their imputed counterparts. We can then use the observed and imputed data to arrive at a maximum likelihood estimate of the parameters of a joint Gaussian distribution. As we can see, this method of imputation does not always produce sensible predictions and the learned model is quite poor.

We can often do better if we account for the probabilistic relationships between the observed and unobserved variables. In figure 4.6, there is clearly correlation between the two variables; hence, knowing the value of one variable can help predict the value of the other variable. A common approach to imputation, called *nearest-neighbor imputation*, is to use the values associated with the instance that is nearest with respect to a distance measure defined on the observed variables. The top-right plot in figure 4.6 uses the Euclidean distance for imputation. This approach tends to lead to better imputations and learned distributions.

An alternative approach is to fit a distribution to the fully observed data and then use that distribution to infer the missing values. We can use the inference algorithms from the previous chapter to perform this inference. For example, if our data is discrete and we can assume a Bayesian network structure, we can use variable elimination or Gibbs sampling to produce a distribution over the missing variables for an instance from the observed variables. From this distribution, we might use the mean or mode to impute the missing values. Alternatively, we can

A	B	C
−6.5	0.9	4.2
?	4.4	9.2
7.8	?	?
?	?	?

Table 4.2. Example of data with continuous values.

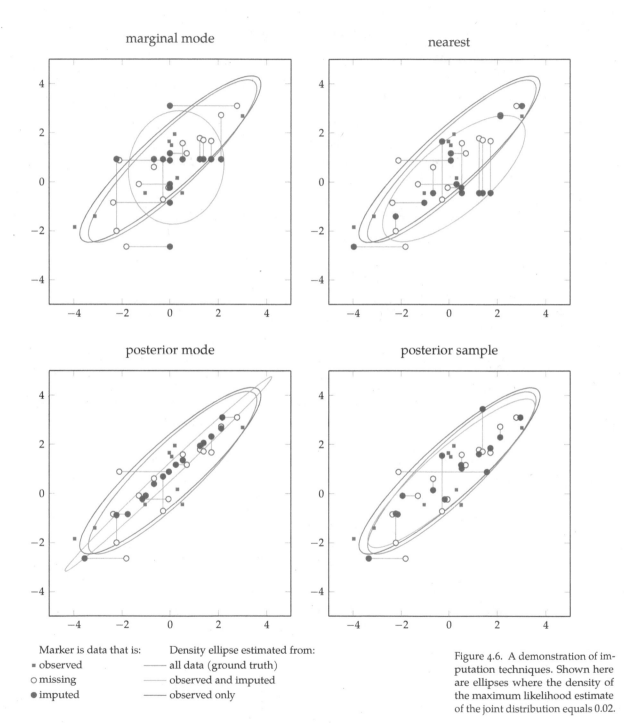

Marker is data that is:
- observed
- missing
- imputed

Density ellipse estimated from:
—— all data (ground truth)
—— observed and imputed
—— observed only

Figure 4.6. A demonstration of imputation techniques. Shown here are ellipses where the density of the maximum likelihood estimate of the joint distribution equals 0.02.

pull a sample from this distribution. If our data is continuous and we can assume that the data is jointly Gaussian, we can use algorithm 3.11 to infer the posterior distribution. The bottom plots in figure 4.6 demonstrate imputation using these posterior mode and posterior sampling approaches.

4.4.2 Expectation-Maximization

The *expectation-maximization (EM)* category of approaches involves iterative improvement of the distribution parameter estimate $\hat{\theta}$.[8] We begin with an initial $\hat{\theta}$, which may be a guess, randomly sampled from a prior distribution over distribution parameters, or estimated using one of the methods discussed in section 4.4.1. At each iteration, we perform a two-step process to update $\hat{\theta}$.

The first step is called the *expectation step (E-step)*, where we use the current estimate of θ to infer completions of the data. For example, if we are modeling our data using a discrete Bayesian network, we can use one of our inference algorithms to infer a distribution over the missing entries for each instance. When extracting the counts, we apply a weighting proportional to the likelihood of the completions as shown in example 4.3. In cases where there are many missing variables, there may be too many possible completions to practically enumerate, making a sampling-based approach attractive. We may also want to use sampling as an approximation method when our variables are continuous.

The second step is called the *maximization step (M-step)*, where we attempt to find a new $\hat{\theta}$ that maximizes the likelihood of the completed data. If we have a discrete Bayesian network with the weighted counts in the form shown in example 4.3, then we can perform the same maximum likelihood estimate as discussed earlier in this chapter. Alternatively, we can use a maximum a posteriori estimate if we want to incorporate a prior.

This approach is not guaranteed to converge to model parameters that maximize the likelihood of the observed data, but it can work well in practice. To reduce the risk of the algorithm converging to only a local optimum, we can run the algorithm to convergence from many different initial points in the parameter space. We simply choose the resulting parameter estimate in the end that maximizes likelihood.

Expectation-maximization can even be used to impute values for variables that are not observed at all in the data. Such variables are called *latent variables*. To illustrate, suppose we have a Bayesian network $Z \rightarrow X$, where X is continuous

[8] Expectation-maximization was introduced by A. P. Dempster, N. M. Laird, and D. B. Rubin, "Maximum Likelihood from Incomplete Data via the EM Algorithm," *Journal of the Royal Statistical Society, Series B (Methodological)*, vol. 39, no. 1, pp. 1–38, 1977.

Suppose that we have a binary Bayesian network with $A \to B$. We start by assuming that $\hat{\theta}$ implies

$$P(a^1) = 0.5 \qquad P(b^1 \mid a^0) = 0.2 \qquad P(b^1 \mid a^1) = 0.6$$

Using these parameters, we can expand the data set with missing values (left) to a weighted data set with all possible individual completions (right):

A	B		A	B	weight
1	1		1	1	1
0	1		0	1	1
0	?		0	0	$1 - P(b^1 \mid a^0) = 0.8$
?	0		0	1	$P(b^1 \mid a^0) = 0.2$
			0	0	$\alpha P(a^0)P(b^0 \mid a^0) = \alpha 0.4 = 2/3$
			1	0	$\alpha P(a^1)P(b^0 \mid a^1) = \alpha 0.2 = 1/3$

The α in the calculation here is a normalization constant, which enforces that each instance is expanded to instances whose weights sum to 1. The count matrices are then

$$\begin{bmatrix} (2 + 2/3) & (1 + 1/3) \end{bmatrix} \qquad \begin{bmatrix} (0.8 + 2/3) & 1.2 \\ 1/3 & 1 \end{bmatrix}$$

Example 4.3. Expanding an incomplete data set using assumed model parameters.

and Z is discrete and can take on one of three values. Our model assumes $p(x \mid z)$ is conditional Gaussian. Our data set contains only values for X, but none for Z. We start with an initial $\hat{\theta}$ and use it to infer a probability distribution over the values of Z, given the value of X for each instance. The distribution over entry completions are then used to update our estimate of the parameters of $P(Z)$ and $P(X \mid Z)$ as illustrated in example 4.4. We iterate to convergence, which often occurs very quickly. The parameters that we obtain in this example define a Gaussian mixture model, which was introduced in section 2.2.2.

4.5 Summary

- Parameter learning involves inferring the parameters of a probabilistic model from data.

- A maximum likelihood approach to parameter learning involves maximizing a likelihood function, which can be done analytically for some models.

- A Bayesian approach to parameter learning involves inferring a probability distribution over the underlying parameter using Bayes' rule.

- The beta and Dirichlet distributions are examples of Bayesian priors that are easily updated with evidence.

- In contrast with parametric learning, which assumes a fixed parameterization of a probability model, nonparametric learning uses representations that grow with the amount of data.

- We can approach the problem of learning parameters from missing data using methods such as data imputation or expectation-maximization, where we make inferences based on observed values.

4.6 Exercises

Exercise 4.1. Suppose that Anna is shooting basketball free throws. Before we see her play, we start with an independent uniform prior over the probability that she successfully makes a basket per shot. We observe her take three shots, with two of them resulting in successful baskets. What is the probability that we assign to her making the next basket?

We have a Bayesian network $Z \to X$, where Z is a discrete latent variable with three values and X is continuous with $p(x \mid z)$ modeled as a conditional Gaussian. Hence, we have parameters defining $P(z^1)$, $P(z^2)$, and $P(z^3)$, as well as μ_i and σ_i for each of the three Gaussian distributions associated with different values of Z. In this example, we use an initial parameter vector $\hat{\theta}$ that specifies $P(z^i) = 1/3$ and $\sigma_i = 1$ for all i. We spread out the means with $\mu_1 = -4$, $\mu_2 = 0$, and $\mu_3 = 4$.

Suppose our first instance in our data has $X = 4.2$. We want to infer the distribution over Z for that instance:

$$P(z^i \mid X = 4.2) = \frac{P(z^i)\,\mathcal{N}(4.2 \mid \mu_i, \sigma_i^2)}{\sum_j P(z^j)\,\mathcal{N}(4.2 \mid \mu_j, \sigma_j^2)}$$

We compute this distribution for all the instances in our data set. For the weighted completions, we can obtain a new estimate for $\hat{\theta}$. We estimate $P(z^i)$ by taking the mean across the instances in our data set. To estimate μ_i and σ_i, we use the mean and standard deviation of the values for X over the instances in our data set, weighted by the probability of z^i associated with the various instances.

We repeat the process until convergence occurs. The plot here shows three iterations. The histogram was generated from the values of X. The dark blue function indicates the inferred density. By the third iteration, our parameters of the Gaussian mixture model closely represent the data distribution.

Example 4.4. Expectation maximization applied to learning the parameters of a Gaussian mixture model.

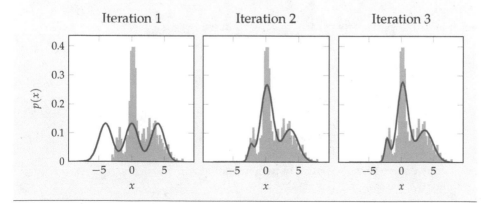

Solution: We denote the probability of making a basket as θ. Since we start with a uniform prior Beta$(1,1)$ and observe two baskets and one miss, our posterior is then Beta$(1+2,1+1) =$ Beta$(3,2)$. We want to compute the probability of a basket as follows:

$$P(\text{basket}) = \int P(\text{basket} \mid \theta)\,\text{Beta}(\theta \mid 3,2)\,d\theta = \int \theta\,\text{Beta}(\theta \mid 3,2)\,d\theta$$

This expression is just the expectation (or mean) of a beta distribution, which gives us $P(\text{basket}) = 3/5$.

Exercise 4.2. Consider a continuous random variable X that follows the *Laplace distribution* parameterized by μ and b, with density

$$p(x \mid \mu, b) = \frac{1}{2b}\exp\left(-\frac{|x-\mu|}{b}\right)$$

Compute the maximum likelihood estimates of the parameters of a Laplace distribution given a data set D of m independent observations $x_{1:m}$. Note that $\partial|u|/\partial x = \text{sign}(u)\partial u/\partial x$, where the sign function returns the sign of its argument.

Solution: Since the observations are independent, we can write the log-likelihood function as the summation:

$$\ell(\mu, b) = \sum_{i=1}^{m} \log\left[\frac{1}{2b}\exp\left(-\frac{|x_i-\mu|}{b}\right)\right]$$

$$= -\sum_{i=1}^{m}\log 2b - \sum_{i=1}^{m}\frac{|x_i-\mu|}{b}$$

$$= -m\log 2b - \frac{1}{b}\sum_{i=1}^{m}|x_i-\mu|$$

To obtain the maximum likelihood estimates of the true parameters μ and b, we take the partial derivatives of the log-likelihood with respect to each of the parameters, set them to zero, and solve for each parameter. First, we solve for $\hat{\mu}$:

$$\frac{\partial}{\partial \mu}\ell(\mu, b) = \frac{1}{b}\sum_{i=1}^{m}\text{sign}(x_i-\mu)$$

$$0 = \frac{1}{b}\sum_{i=1}^{m}\text{sign}(x_i-\hat{\mu})$$

$$0 = \sum_{i=1}^{m}\text{sign}(x_i-\hat{\mu})$$

$$\hat{\mu} = \text{median}(x_{1:m})$$

Now, solving for $\hat{b}$:

$$\frac{\partial}{\partial b}\ell(\mu, b) = -\frac{m}{b} + \frac{1}{b^2}\sum_{i=1}^{m}|x_i - \hat{\mu}|$$

$$0 = -\frac{m}{\hat{b}} + \frac{1}{\hat{b}^2}\sum_{i=1}^{m}|x_i - \hat{\mu}|$$

$$\frac{m}{\hat{b}} = \frac{1}{\hat{b}^2}\sum_{i=1}^{m}|x_i - \hat{\mu}|$$

$$\hat{b} = \frac{1}{m}\sum_{i=1}^{m}|x_i - \hat{\mu}|$$

Thus, the maximum likelihood estimates for the parameters of a Laplace distribution are $\hat{\mu}$, the median of the observations, and $\hat{b}$, the mean of absolute deviations from the median.

Exercise 4.3. This question explores the application of maximum likelihood estimation to *censored data*, where some measurements are only partially known. Suppose that we are building electric motors for a quadcopter drone, and we want to produce a model of how long they last until failure. Although there may be more suitable distributions for modeling the reliability of components,[9] we will use an *exponential distribution* parameterized by λ with probability density function $\lambda \exp(-\lambda x)$ and cumulative distribution function $1 - \exp(-\lambda x)$. We fly five drones. Three have motor failures after 132 hours, 42 hours, and 89 hours. We stopped testing the other two after 200 hours without failure; we do not know their failure times; we just know that they are greater than 200 hours. What is the maximum likelihood estimate for λ given this data?

[9] K. S. Trivedi and A. Bobbio, *Reliability and Availability Engineering*. Cambridge University Press, 2017.

Solution: This problem has $n = 3$ fully observed measurements and $m = 2$ censored measurements. We use t_i to represent the ith fully observed measurement and $\underline{t}_j$ to represent the jth censored measurement. The likelihood of a single measurement above $\underline{t}_j$ is the complement of the cumulative distribution function, which is simply $\exp(-\lambda \underline{t}_j)$. Hence, the likelihood of the data is

$$\left(\prod_{i=1}^{n}\lambda e^{-\lambda t_i}\right)\left(\prod_{j=1}^{m}e^{-\lambda \underline{t}_j}\right)$$

We use our standard approach of maximizing the log-likelihood, which is given by

$$\ell(\lambda) = \sum_{i=1}^{n}(\log\lambda - \lambda t_i) + \sum_{j=1}^{m}-\lambda\underline{t}_j$$

The derivative with respect to λ is

$$\frac{\partial\ell}{\partial\lambda} = \frac{n}{\lambda} - \sum_{i=1}^{n}t_i - \sum_{j=1}^{m}\underline{t}_j$$

Setting this derivative to 0, we can solve for λ to obtain the maximum likelihood estimate:

$$\hat{\lambda} = \frac{n}{\sum_{i=1}^{n} t_i + \sum_{j=1}^{m} t_j} = \frac{3}{132 + 42 + 89 + 200 + 200} \approx 0.00452$$

The mean of the exponential distribution is $1/\lambda$, making the mean in our problem 221 hours.

Exercise 4.4. We have a Bayesian network where the variables $X_{1:3}$ can take on values in $\{1,2\}$ and X_4 can take on values in $\{1,2,3\}$. Given the data set D of observations $o_{1:m}$, as illustrated here, generate the maximum likelihood estimates of the associated conditional distribution parameters θ.

$$D = \begin{bmatrix} 1 & 2 & 1 & 1 & 1 & 2 & 1 & 2 & 1 & 1 \\ 2 & 2 & 2 & 1 & 2 & 1 & 1 & 1 & 2 & 1 \\ 2 & 2 & 2 & 1 & 1 & 1 & 1 & 1 & 2 & 1 \\ 3 & 2 & 1 & 1 & 1 & 3 & 3 & 1 & 1 & 1 \end{bmatrix}$$

Solution: We can generate count matrices $\mathbf{M}_i$ of size $q_i \times r_i$ for each node by iterating through the data set and storing the counts. We then normalize each row in the count matrices to yield the matrices containing the maximum likelihood estimates of the parameters:

$$\mathbf{M}_1 = \begin{bmatrix} 7 & 3 \end{bmatrix} \quad \mathbf{M}_2 = \begin{bmatrix} 3 & 1 \\ 0 & 0 \\ 2 & 0 \\ 0 & 2 \\ 0 & 1 \\ 0 & 1 \end{bmatrix} \quad \mathbf{M}_3 = \begin{bmatrix} 6 & 4 \end{bmatrix} \quad \mathbf{M}_4 = \begin{bmatrix} 5 & 0 & 2 \\ 1 & 1 & 1 \end{bmatrix}$$

$$\hat{\theta}_1 = \begin{bmatrix} 0.7 & 0.3 \end{bmatrix} \quad \hat{\theta}_2 = \begin{bmatrix} 0.75 & 0.25 \\ \text{NAN} & \text{NAN} \\ 1.0 & 0.0 \\ 0.0 & 1.0 \\ 0.0 & 1.0 \\ 0.0 & 1.0 \end{bmatrix} \quad \hat{\theta}_3 = \begin{bmatrix} 0.6 & 0.4 \end{bmatrix} \quad \hat{\theta}_4 \approx \begin{bmatrix} 0.71 & 0.0 & 0.29 \\ 0.33 & 0.33 & 0.34 \end{bmatrix}$$

Exercise 4.5. We have a biased coin, and we want to estimate the Bernoulli parameter ϕ that specifies the probability the coin lands on heads. If the first toss lands on heads ($o_1 = 1$), answer the following questions:

- What is the maximum likelihood estimate of ϕ?

- Using a uniform prior, what is the maximum a posteriori estimate of ϕ?
- Using a uniform prior, what is the expectation of our posterior distribution over ϕ?

Solution: Since our first toss lands on heads, we have $n = 1$ successes and $m = 1$ trials.

- The maximum likelihood estimate of ϕ is $n/m = 1$.
- Using a uniform Beta$(1,1)$ prior, the posterior distribution is Beta$(1 + n, 1 + m - n) =$ Beta$(2,1)$. The maximum a posteriori estimate of ϕ or mode of the posterior distribution is

$$\frac{\alpha - 1}{\alpha + \beta - 2} = \frac{2 - 1}{2 + 1 - 2} = 1$$

- The mean of the posterior distribution is

$$\frac{\alpha}{\alpha + \beta} = \frac{2}{2 + 1} = \frac{2}{3}$$

Exercise 4.6. Suppose we are given the following data set, with one missing value. What is the value that will be imputed using marginal mode imputation, assuming that the marginal distribution is a Gaussian? What is the value that will be imputed using nearest-neighbor imputation?

X_1	X_2
0.5	1.0
?	0.3
−0.6	−0.3
0.1	0.2

Solution: Assuming that the marginal distribution over X_1 is a Gaussian, we can compute the marginal mode, which is the mean parameter of the Gaussian distribution:

$$\mu = \frac{1}{m}\sum_{i=1}^{m} x_i = \frac{0.5 - 0.6 + 0.1}{3} = 0$$

Thus, for marginal mode imputation, the missing value will be set to 0. For nearest-neighbor imputation, the nearest sample to $X_2 = 0.3$ is the fourth sample, so the missing value will be set to 0.1.

Exercise 4.7. Suppose we are given a data set over two variables $X_{1:2}$, with several missing values. We assume that $X_{1:2}$ are jointly Gaussian and use the fully-observed samples to fit the following distribution:

$$\begin{bmatrix} X_1 \\ X_2 \end{bmatrix} \sim \mathcal{N}\left(\begin{bmatrix} 5 \\ 2 \end{bmatrix}, \begin{bmatrix} 4 & 1 \\ 1 & 2 \end{bmatrix} \right)$$

What is the value that will be imputed for X_1 for the sample $X_2 = 1.5$ using posterior mode imputation? What distribution do we need to sample from for posterior sample imputation?

Solution: Since we assumed that $X_{1:2}$ are jointly Gaussian, the posterior distribution over X_1 given X_2 is also Gaussian, and its mode is the mean parameter of the posterior distribution. We can compute the mean of the posterior distribution as follows:

$$p(x_1 \mid x_2) = \mathcal{N}\left(x_1 \mid \mu_{x_1 \mid x_2}, \sigma^2_{x_1 \mid x_2}\right)$$

$$\mu_{x_1 \mid x_2 = 1.5} = 5 + (1)(2)^{-1}(1.5 - 2) = 4.75$$

Thus, for posterior mode imputation, the missing value will be set to 4.75. For posterior sample imputation, we will sample a value $X_1 \sim \mathcal{N}(4.75, 3.5)$.

5 Structure Learning

The previous chapters of this book assumed that the structures of our probabilistic models were known. This chapter discusses methods for learning the structure of models from data.[1] We begin by explaining how to compute the probability of a graphical structure, given the data. Generally, we want to maximize this probability. Because the space of possible graphical structures is usually too large to enumerate, we also discuss ways to search this space efficiently.

5.1 Bayesian Network Scoring

We want to be able to score a network structure G based on how well it models the data. A maximum a posteriori approach to structure learning involves finding a G that maximizes $P(G \mid D)$. We first explain how to compute a Bayesian score based on $P(G \mid D)$ to measure how well G models the data. We then explain how to go about searching the space of networks for the highest-scoring network. Like inference in Bayesian networks, it can be shown that for general graphs and input data, learning the structure of a Bayesian network is NP-hard.[2]

We compute $P(G \mid D)$ using Bayes' rule and the law of total probability:

$$P(G \mid D) \propto P(G)P(D \mid G) \tag{5.1}$$

$$= P(G) \int P(D \mid \theta, G) p(\theta \mid G) \, d\theta \tag{5.2}$$

where θ contains the network parameters as introduced in the previous chapter. Integrating with respect to θ results in[3]

$$P(G \mid D) = P(G) \prod_{i=1}^{n} \prod_{j=1}^{q_i} \frac{\Gamma(\alpha_{ij0})}{\Gamma(\alpha_{ij0} + m_{ij0})} \prod_{k=1}^{r_i} \frac{\Gamma(\alpha_{ijk} + m_{ijk})}{\Gamma(\alpha_{ijk})} \tag{5.3}$$

[1] Overviews of Bayesian network structure learning can be found in the following textbooks: D. Koller and N. Friedman, *Probabilistic Graphical Models: Principles and Techniques*. MIT Press, 2009. R. E. Neapolitan, *Learning Bayesian Networks*. Prentice Hall, 2003.

[2] See D. M. Chickering, "Learning Bayesian Networks is NP-Complete," in *Learning from Data: Artificial Intelligence and Statistics V*, D. Fisher and H.-J. Lenz, eds., Springer, 1996, pp. 121–130. D. M. Chickering, D. Heckerman, and C. Meek, "Large-Sample Learning of Bayesian Networks is NP-Hard," *Journal of Machine Learning Research*, vol. 5, pp. 1287–1330, 2004.

[3] For the derivation, see the appendix of G. F. Cooper and E. Herskovits, "A Bayesian Method for the Induction of Probabilistic Networks from Data," *Machine Learning*, vol. 4, no. 9, pp. 309–347, 1992.

where the values for α_{ijk} are the pseudocounts and m_{ijk} are the counts, as introduced in the previous chapter. We also define

$$\alpha_{ij0} = \sum_{k=1}^{r_i} \alpha_{ijk} \qquad m_{ij0} = \sum_{k=1}^{r_i} m_{ijk} \qquad (5.4)$$

Finding the G that maximizes equation (5.2) is the same as finding the G that maximizes what is called the *Bayesian score*:

$$\log P(G \mid D) = \log P(G) + \sum_{i=1}^{n} \sum_{j=1}^{q_i} \left(\log \left(\frac{\Gamma(\alpha_{ij0})}{\Gamma(\alpha_{ij0} + m_{ij0})} \right) + \sum_{k=1}^{r_i} \log \left(\frac{\Gamma(\alpha_{ijk} + m_{ijk})}{\Gamma(\alpha_{ijk})} \right) \right) \qquad (5.5)$$

The Bayesian score is more convenient to compute numerically because it is easier to add the logarithm of small numbers together than to multiply small numbers together. Many software libraries can compute the logarithm of the gamma function directly.

A variety of graph priors have been explored in the literature, although a uniform prior is often used in practice, in which case $\log P(G)$ can be dropped from the computation of the Bayesian score in equation (5.5). Algorithm 5.1 provides an implementation.

```
function bayesian_score_component(M, α)
    p =  sum(loggamma.(α + M))
    p -= sum(loggamma.(α))
    p += sum(loggamma.(sum(α,dims=2)))
    p -= sum(loggamma.(sum(α,dims=2) + sum(M,dims=2)))
    return p
end

function bayesian_score(vars, G, D)
    n = length(vars)
    M = statistics(vars, G, D)
    α = prior(vars, G)
    return sum(bayesian_score_component(M[i], α[i]) for i in 1:n)
end
```

Algorithm 5.1. An algorithm for computing the Bayesian score for a list of variables vars and a graph G given data D. This method uses a uniform prior $\alpha_{ijk} = 1$ for all i, j, and k as generated by algorithm 4.2. The loggamma function is provided by SpecialFunctions.jl. Chapter 4 introduced the statistics and prior functions. Note that $\log(\Gamma(\alpha)/\Gamma(\alpha + m)) = \log\Gamma(\alpha) - \log\Gamma(\alpha + m)$, and that $\log\Gamma(1) = 0$.

A by-product of optimizing the structure with respect to the Bayesian score is that we are able to find the right balance in the model complexity, given the available data. We do not want a model that misses out on capturing important relationships between variables, but we also do not want a model that has too many parameters to be adequately learned from limited data.

To illustrate how the Bayesian score helps us balance model complexity, consider the network in figure 5.1. The value of A weakly influences the value of B, and C is independent of the other variables. We sample from this "true" model to generate data D, and then try to learn the model structure. There are 25 possible network structures involving three variables, but we will focus on the scores for the models in figure 5.2.

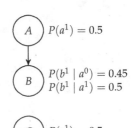

Figure 5.1. A simple Bayesian network to illustrate how the Bayesian score helps us balance model complexity.

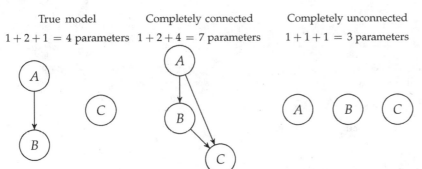

Figure 5.2. Three Bayesian network structures with varying levels of complexity.

Figure 5.3 shows how the Bayesian scores of the completely connected and unconnected models compare to the true model as the amount of data increases. In the plot, we subtract the score of the true model, so values above 0 indicate that the model provides a better representation than the true model, given the available data. The plot shows that the unconnected model does better than the true model when there are fewer than 5×10^3 samples. The completely connected model never does better than the true model, but it starts to do better than the unconnected model at about 10^4 samples because there are sufficient data to adequately estimate its seven independent parameters.

5.2   Directed Graph Search

In a *directed graph search*, we search the space of directed acyclic graphs for one that maximizes the Bayesian score. The space of possible Bayesian network structures grows superexponentially.[4] With 10 nodes, there are 4.2×10^{18} possible directed acyclic graphs. With 20 nodes, there are 2.4×10^{72}. Except for Bayesian networks with few nodes, we cannot enumerate the space of possible structures to find the highest-scoring network. Therefore, we have to rely on a search strategy.

[4] R. W. Robinson, "Counting Labeled Acyclic Digraphs," in *Ann Arbor Conference on Graph Theory*, 1973.

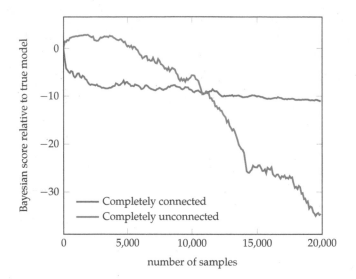

Figure 5.3. Bayesian network structure learning balances model complexity with the available data. The completely connected model never outperforms the true model, whereas the completely unconnected model eventually underperforms when more than about 5×10^3 samples have been drawn. This result indicates that simpler models can outperform complicated models when data is scarce—even when a more complicated model generated the samples.

Fortunately, search is a general problem, and a wide variety of generic search algorithms have been studied over the years.

One of the most common search strategies is called $K2$.[5] The search (algorithm 5.2) runs in polynomial time but does not guarantee finding a globally optimal network structure. It can use any scoring function, but it is often used with the Bayesian score because of its ability to balance the complexity of the model with the amount of data available. K2 begins with a graph with no directed edges and then iterates over the variables according to a provided ordering, greedily adding parents to the nodes in a way that maximally increases the score. It is common for K2 to impose an upper bound on the number of parents for any one node to reduce the required computation. The original K2 algorithm assumed a unit uniform Dirichlet prior with $\alpha_{ijk} = 1$ for all i, j, and k, but any prior can be used in principle.

A general search strategy is *local search*, which is sometimes called *hill climbing*. Algorithm 5.3 provides an implementation of this concept. We start with an initial graph and then move to the highest-scoring neighbor. The neighborhood of a graph consists of the graphs that are only one basic graph operation away, where the basic graph operations include introducing an edge, removing an edge, and reversing an edge. Of course, not all operations are possible from a particular

[5] The name comes from the fact that it is an evolution of a system called Kutató. The algorithm was introduced by G. F. Cooper and E. Herskovits, "A Bayesian Method for the Induction of Probabilistic Networks from Data," *Machine Learning*, vol. 4, no. 9, pp. 309–347, 1992.

```
struct K2Search
    ordering::Vector{Int} # variable ordering
end

function fit(method::K2Search, vars, D)
    G = SimpleDiGraph(length(vars))
    for (k,i) in enumerate(method.ordering[2:end])
        y = bayesian_score(vars, G, D)
        while true
            y_best, j_best = -Inf, 0
            for j in method.ordering[1:k]
                if !has_edge(G, j, i)
                    add_edge!(G, j, i)
                    y′ = bayesian_score(vars, G, D)
                    if y′ > y_best
                        y_best, j_best = y′, j
                    end
                    rem_edge!(G, j, i)
                end
            end
            if y_best > y
                y = y_best
                add_edge!(G, j_best, i)
            else
                break
            end
        end
    end
    return G
end
```

Algorithm 5.2. K2 search of the space of directed acyclic graphs using a specified variable ordering. This variable ordering imposes a topological ordering in the resulting graph. The fit function takes an ordered list variables vars and a data set D. The method starts with an empty graph and iteratively adds the next parent that maximally improves the Bayesian score.

graph, and operations that introduce cycles into the graph are invalid. The search continues until the current graph scores no lower than any of its neighbors.

An *opportunistic* version of local search is implemented in algorithm 5.3. Rather than generating all graph neighbors at every iteration, this method generates a single random neighbor and accepts it if its Bayesian score is greater than that of the current graph.

```
struct LocalDirectedGraphSearch
    G     # initial graph
    k_max # number of iterations
end

function rand_graph_neighbor(G)
    n = nv(G)
    i = rand(1:n)
    j = mod1(i + rand(2:n)-1, n)
    G′ = copy(G)
    has_edge(G, i, j) ? rem_edge!(G′, i, j) : add_edge!(G′, i, j)
    return G′
end

function fit(method::LocalDirectedGraphSearch, vars, D)
    G = method.G
    y = bayesian_score(vars, G, D)
    for k in 1:method.k_max
        G′ = rand_graph_neighbor(G)
        y′ = is_cyclic(G′) ? -Inf : bayesian_score(vars, G′, D)
        if y′ > y
            y, G = y′, G′
        end
    end
    return G
end
```

Algorithm 5.3. Local directed graph search, which starts with an initial directed graph G and opportunistically moves to a random graph neighbor whenever its Bayesian score is greater. It repeats this process for k_max iterations. Random graph neighbors are generated by either adding or removing a single edge. This algorithm can be extended to include reversing the direction of an edge. Edge addition can result in a graph with cycles, in which case we assign a score of $-\infty$.

Local search can get stuck in *local optima*, preventing it from finding the globally optimal network structure. Various strategies have been proposed for addressing local optima, including the following:[6]

- *Randomized restart*. Once a local optima has been found, simply restart the search at a random point in the search space.

- *Simulated annealing*. Instead of always moving to the neighbor with greatest fitness, the search can visit neighbors with lower fitness according to some randomized exploration strategy. As the search progresses, the randomness in

[6] The field of optimization is quite vast, and many methods have been developed for addressing local optima. This textbook provides an overview: M. J. Kochenderfer and T. A. Wheeler, *Algorithms for Optimization*. MIT Press, 2019.

the exploration decreases according to a particular schedule. This approach is called simulated annealing because of its inspiration from annealing in metallurgy.

- *Genetic algorithms.* The procedure begins with an initial random population of points in the search space represented as binary strings. Each bit in a string indicates the presence or absence of an arrow between two nodes. String manipulation thus allows for searching the space of directed graphs. The individuals in the population reproduce at a rate proportional to their score. Individuals selected for reproduction have their strings recombined randomly through genetic crossover, which involves selecting a crossover point on two randomly selected individuals and then swapping the strings after that point. Mutations are also introduced randomly into the population by randomly flipping bits in the strings. The process of evolution continues until a satisfactory point in the search space is found.

- *Memetic algorithms.* This approach, sometimes called *genetic local search*, is simply a combination of genetic algorithms and local search. After genetic recombination, local search is applied to the individuals.

- *Tabu search.* Previous methods can be augmented to maintain a *tabu list* containing recently visited points in the search space. The search algorithm avoids neighbors in the tabu list.

Some search strategies may work better than others on certain data sets, but in general, finding the global optima remains NP-hard. Many applications, however, do not require the globally optimal network structure. A locally optimal structure is often acceptable.

5.3   Markov Equivalence Classes

As discussed earlier, the structure of a Bayesian network encodes a set of conditional independence assumptions. An important observation to make when trying to learn the structure of a Bayesian network is that two different graphs can encode the same independence assumptions. As a simple example, the two-variable network $A \rightarrow B$ has the same independence assumptions as $A \leftarrow B$. Solely on the basis of the data, we cannot justify the direction of the edge between A and B.

If two networks encode the same conditional independence assumptions, we say that they are *Markov equivalent*. It can be proven that two graphs are Markov equivalent if and only if they have (1) the same edges, without regard to direction; and (2) the same set of immoral v-structures. An *immoral v-structure* is a v-structure $X \rightarrow Y \leftarrow Z$, with X and Z not directly connected, as shown in figure 5.4. A *Markov equivalence class* is a set containing all the directed acyclic graphs that are Markov equivalent to each other. A method for checking Markov equivalence is given in algorithm 5.4.

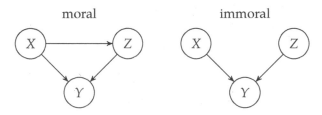

Figure 5.4. Moral and immoral v-structures.

In general, two structures belonging to the same Markov equivalence class may be given different scores. However, if the Bayesian score is used with Dirichlet priors such that $\kappa = \sum_j \sum_k \alpha_{ijk}$ is constant for all i, then two Markov equivalent structures are assigned the same score.[7] Such priors are called *BDe*, and a special case is the *BDeu* prior,[8] which assigns $\alpha_{ijk} = \kappa/(q_i r_i)$. Although the commonly used uniform prior $\alpha_{ijk} = 1$ does not always result in identical scores being assigned to structures in the same equivalence class, they are often fairly close. A scoring function that assigns the same score to all structures in the same class is called *score equivalent*.

5.4   Partially Directed Graph Search

A Markov equivalence class can be represented as a *partially directed graph*, sometimes called an *essential graph* or a *directed acyclic graph pattern*. A partially directed graph can contain both directed edges and undirected edges. An example of a partially directed graph that encodes a Markov equivalence class is shown in figure 5.5. A directed acyclic graph G is a member of the Markov equivalence class encoded by a partially directed graph G' if and only if G has the same edges as G' without regard to direction and has the same immoral v-structures as G'.

[7] This was shown by D. Heckerman, D. Geiger, and D. M. Chickering, "Learning Bayesian Networks: The Combination of Knowledge and Statistical Data," *Machine Learning*, vol. 20, no. 3, pp. 197–243, 1995.

[8] W. L. Buntine, "Theory Refinement on Bayesian Networks," in *Conference on Uncertainty in Artificial Intelligence (UAI)*, 1991.

```
function are_markov_equivalent(G, H)
    if nv(G) != nv(H) || ne(G) != ne(H) ||
        !all(has_edge(H, e) || has_edge(H, reverse(e))
                                    for e in edges(G))
        return false
    end
    for (I, J) in [(G,H), (H,G)]
        for c in 1:nv(I)
            parents = inneighbors(I, c)
            for (a, b) in subsets(parents, 2)
                if !has_edge(I, a, b) && !has_edge(I, b, a) &&
                    !(has_edge(J, a, c) && has_edge(J, b, c))
                    return false
                end
            end
        end
    end

    return true
end
```

Algorithm 5.4. A method for determining whether the directed acyclic graphs G and H are Markov equivalent. The subsets function from IterTools.jl returns all subsets of a given set and a specified size.

Markov equivalence class

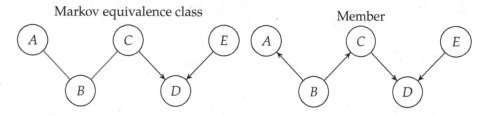

Member

Member   Nonmember

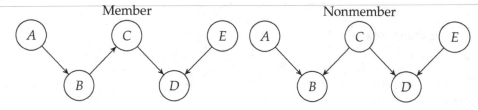

Figure 5.5. A Markov equivalence class and examples of members and a nonmember. The nonmember does not belong to the Markov equivalence class because it introduces an immoral v-structure, $A \to B \leftarrow C$, which is not indicated in the partially directed graph.

Instead of searching the space of directed acyclic graphs, we can search the space of Markov equivalence classes represented by partially directed graphs.[9] Although the space of Markov equivalence classes is, of course, smaller than the space of directed acyclic graphs, it is not significantly smaller; the ratio of directed acyclic graphs to equivalence classes asymptotes to around 3.7 fairly quickly.[10] A problem with hill climbing in the space of directed acyclic graphs is that the neighborhood may consist of other graphs that are in the same equivalence class with the same score, which can lead to the search becoming stuck in a local optimum. Searching the space of equivalence classes allows us to jump to different directed acyclic graphs outside the current equivalence class.

Any of the general search strategies presented in section 5.2 can be used. If a form of local search is used, then we need to define the local graph operations that define the neighborhood of the graph. Examples of local graph operations include:

- If an edge between X and Y does not exist, add either $X - Y$ or $X \rightarrow Y$.

- If $X - Y$ or $X \rightarrow Y$, then remove the edge between X and Y.

- If $X \rightarrow Y$, then reverse the direction of the edge to get $X \leftarrow Y$.

- If $X - Y - Z$, then add $X \rightarrow Y \leftarrow Z$.

To score a partially directed graph, we generate a member of its Markov equivalence class and compute its score.

5.5   Summary

- Fitting a Bayesian network to data requires selecting the Bayesian network structure that dictates the conditional dependencies between variables.

- Bayesian approaches to structure learning maximize the Bayesian score, which is related to the probability of the graph structure given a data set.

- The Bayesian score promotes simpler structures for smaller data sets and supports more complicated structures for larger data sets.

- The number of possible structures is superexponential in the number of variables, and finding a structure that maximizes the Bayesian score is NP-hard.

[9] Details of how to search this space are provided by D. M. Chickering, "Learning Equivalence Classes of Bayesian-Network Structures," *Journal of Machine Learning Research*, vol. 2, pp. 445–498, 2002.

[10] S. B. Gillispie and M. D. Perlman, "The Size Distribution for Markov Equivalence Classes of Acyclic Digraph Models," *Artificial Intelligence*, vol. 141, no. 1–2, pp. 137–155, 2002.

- Directed graph search algorithms like K2 and local search can be efficient but do not guarantee optimality.

- Methods like partially directed graph search traverse the space of Markov equivalence classes, which may be more efficient than searching the larger space of directed acyclic graphs.

5.6 Exercises

Exercise 5.1. How many neighbors does an edgeless directed acyclic graph with m nodes have?

Solution: Of the three basic graph operations, we can only add edges. We can add any edge to an edgeless directed acyclic graph and it will remain acyclic. There are $m(m-1) = m^2 - m$ node pairs, and therefore that many neighbors.

Exercise 5.2. How many networks are in the neighborhood of the following Bayesian network?

Solution: We can perform the following graph operations:

- Add $A \rightarrow D, D \rightarrow A, D \rightarrow C$
- Remove $A \rightarrow B, A \rightarrow C, B \rightarrow C, D \rightarrow B$
- Flip $A \rightarrow B, B \rightarrow C, D \rightarrow B$

Thus, there are 10 Bayesian networks in the neighborhood.

Exercise 5.3. Suppose we start local search with a Bayesian network G. What is the fewest number of iterations of local search that could be performed to converge to the optimal Bayesian network G^*?

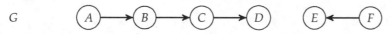

Solution: At each iteration, local search can move from the original network to a network in its neighborhood, which is at most one edge operation from the original network. Since there are three differences between the edges of G and G^*, performing local search from G would require a minimum of three iterations to arrive at G^*. One potential minimal sequence of local search iterations could be flipping $A \rightarrow B$, removing $B \rightarrow C$, and adding $E \rightarrow D$. We assume that the graphs formed with these edge operations yielded the highest Bayesian scores of all graphs in the considered neighborhood.

Exercise 5.4. Draw the partially directed acyclic graph representing the Markov equivalence class of the following Bayesian network. How many graphs are in this Markov equivalence class?

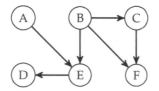

Solution: The Markov equivalence class can be represented by the following partially directed acyclic graph:

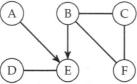

There are six networks in this Markov equivalence class, which are shown here:

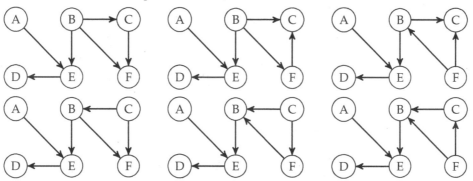

Exercise 5.5. Give an example of a partially directed acyclic graph with four nodes that does not define a nonempty Markov equivalence class.

Solution: Consider the following partially directed acyclic graph:

We cannot replace the undirected edge with a directed edge because doing so would introduce a new v-structure.

6   Simple Decisions

This chapter introduces the notion of *simple decisions*, where we make a single decision under uncertainty.[1] We will study the problem of decision making from the perspective of *utility theory*, which involves modeling the preferences of an agent as a real-valued function over uncertain outcomes.[2] This chapter begins by discussing how a small set of constraints on rational preferences can lead to the existence of a utility function. This utility function can be inferred from a sequence of preference queries. We then introduce the maximum expected utility principle as a definition of rationality, a central concept in *decision theory* that will be used as a driving principle for decision making in this book.[3] We show how decision problems can be represented as decision networks and show an algorithm for solving for an optimal decision. The concept of value of information is introduced, which measures the utility gained through observing additional variables. The chapter concludes with a brief discussion of how human decision making is not always consistent with the maximum expected utility principle.

6.1   Constraints on Rational Preferences

We began our discussion on uncertainty in chapter 2 by identifying the need to compare our degree of belief in different statements. This chapter requires the ability to compare the degree of desirability of two different outcomes. We state our preferences using the following operators:

- $A \succ B$ if we prefer A over B.

- $A \sim B$ if we are indifferent between A and B.

- $A \succeq B$ if we prefer A over B or are indifferent.

[1] Simple decisions are simple compared to sequential problems, which are the focus of the rest of the book. Simple decisions are not necessarily simple to solve, though.

[2] Schoemaker provides an overview of the development of utility theory. See P. J. H. Schoemaker, "The Expected Utility Model: Its Variants, Purposes, Evidence and Limitations," *Journal of Economic Literature*, vol. 20, no. 2, pp. 529–563, 1982. Fishburn surveys the field. See P. C. Fishburn, "Utility Theory," *Management Science*, vol. 14, no. 5, pp. 335–378, 1968.

[3] A survey of the field of decision theory is provided by M. Peterson, *An Introduction to Decision Theory*. Cambridge University Press, 2009.

Just as beliefs can be subjective, so can preferences.

In addition to comparing events, our preference operators can be used to compare preferences over uncertain outcomes. A *lottery* is a set of probabilities associated with a set of outcomes. For example, if $S_{1:n}$ is a set of outcomes and $p_{1:n}$ are their associated probabilities, then the lottery involving these outcomes and probabilities is written as

$$[S_1 : p_1; \ \ldots; \ S_n : p_n] \tag{6.1}$$

The existence of a real-valued measure of utility emerges from a set of assumptions about preferences.[4] From this utility function, it is possible to define what it means to make rational decisions under uncertainty. Just as we imposed a set of constraints on beliefs, we will impose some constraints on preferences:[5]

- *Completeness.* Exactly one of the following holds: $A \succ B$, $B \succ A$, or $A \sim B$.

- *Transitivity.* If $A \succeq B$ and $B \succeq C$, then $A \succeq C$.

- *Continuity.* If $A \succeq C \succeq B$, then there exists a probability p such that $[A : p; B : 1 - p] \sim C$.

- *Independence.* If $A \succ B$, then for any C and probability p, $[A : p; C : 1 - p] \succeq [B : p; C : 1 - p]$.

These are constraints on *rational preferences*. They say nothing about the preferences of actual human beings; in fact, there is strong evidence that humans are not always rational (a point discussed further in section 6.7). Our objective in this book is to understand rational decision making from a computational perspective so that we can build useful systems. The possible extension of this theory to understanding human decision making is only of secondary interest.

6.2   Utility Functions

Just as constraints on the comparison of the plausibility of different statements lead to the existence of a real-valued probability measure, constraints on rational preferences lead to the existence of a real-valued *utility* measure. It follows from our constraints on rational preferences that there exists a real-valued utility function U such that

[4] The theory of expected utility was introduced by the Swiss mathematician and physicist Daniel Bernoulli (1700–1782) in 1738. See D. Bernoulli, "Exposition of a New Theory on the Measurement of Risk," *Econometrica*, vol. 22, no. 1, pp. 23–36, 1954.

[5] These constraints are sometimes called the *von Neumann–Morgenstern axioms*, named after the Hungarian-American mathematician and physicist John von Neumann (1903–1957) and the Austrian-American economist Oskar Morgenstern (1902–1977). They formulated a variation of these axioms. See J. von Neumann and O. Morgenstern, *Theory of Games and Economic Behavior*. Princeton University Press, 1944. Critiques of these axioms are discussed by P. Anand, "Are the Preference Axioms Really Rational?" *Theory and Decision*, vol. 23, no. 2, pp. 189–214, 1987.

- $U(A) > U(B)$ if and only if $A \succ B$, and

- $U(A) = U(B)$ if and only if $A \sim B$.

The utility function is unique up to a *positive affine transformation*. In other words, for any constants $m > 0$ and b, $U'(S) = mU(S) + b$ if and only if the preferences induced by U' are the same as U. Utilities are like temperatures: you can compare temperatures using Kelvin, Celsius, or Fahrenheit, all of which are affine transformations of each other.

It follows from the constraints on rational preferences that the utility of a lottery is given by

$$U([S_1 : p_1; \ \ldots; \ S_n : p_n]) = \sum_{i=1}^{n} p_i U(S_i) \tag{6.2}$$

Example 6.1 applies this equation to compute the utility of outcomes involving a collision avoidance system.

Suppose that we are building a collision avoidance system. The outcome of an encounter of an aircraft is defined by whether the system alerts (A) and whether a collision occurs (C). Because A and C are binary, there are four possible outcomes. So long as our preferences are rational, we can write our utility function over the space of possible lotteries in terms of four parameters: $U(a^0, c^0)$, $U(a^1, c^0)$, $U(a^0, c^1)$, and $U(a^1, c^1)$. For example,

$$U([a^0, c^0 : 0.5; \quad a^1, c^0 : 0.3; \quad a^0, c^1 : 0.1; \quad a^1, c^1 : 0.1])$$

is equal to

$$0.5U(a^0, c^0) + 0.3U(a^1, c^0) + 0.1U(a^0, c^1) + 0.1U(a^1, c^1)$$

Example 6.1. A lottery involving the outcomes of a collision avoidance system.

If the utility function is bounded, then we can define a *normalized utility function*, where the best possible outcome is assigned utility 1 and the worst possible outcome is assigned utility 0. The utility of each of the other outcomes is scaled and translated as necessary.

6.3   Utility Elicitation

In building a decision-making or decision support system, it is often helpful to infer the utility function from a human or a group of humans. This approach is called *utility elicitation* or *preference elicitation*.[6] One way to go about doing this is to fix the utility of the worst outcome $\underline{S}$ to 0 and the best outcome $\overline{S}$ to 1. So long as the utilities of the outcomes are bounded, we can translate and scale the utilities without altering our preferences. If we want to determine the utility of outcome S, then we determine probability p such that $S \sim [\overline{S} : p; \underline{S} : 1 - p]$. It then follows that $U(S) = p$. Example 6.2 applies this process to determine the utility function associated with a collision avoidance problem.

[6] A variety of methods for utility elicitation are surveyed by P. H. Farquhar, "Utility Assessment Methods," *Management Science*, vol. 30, no. 11, pp. 1283–1300, 1984.

In our collision avoidance example, the best possible event is to not alert and not have a collision, and so we set $U(a^0, c^0) = 1$. The worst possible event is to alert and have a collision, and so we set $U(a^1, c^1) = 0$. We define the lottery $L(p)$ to be $[a^0, c^0 : p;\ a^1, c^1 : 1 - p]$. To determine $U(a^1, c^0)$, we must find p such that $(a^1, c^0) \sim L(p)$. Similarly, to determine $U(a^0, c^1)$, we find p such that $(a^0, c^1) \sim L(p)$.

Example 6.2.   Utility elicitation applied to collision avoidance.

It may be tempting to use monetary values to infer utility functions. For example, if we are building a decision support system for managing wildfires, it may be tempting to define a utility function in terms of the monetary cost incurred by property damage and the monetary cost for deploying fire suppression resources. However, it is well known in economics that the utility of wealth, in general, is not linear.[7] If there were a linear relationship between utility and wealth, then decisions should be made in terms of maximizing expected monetary value. Someone who tries to maximize expected monetary value would have no use for insurance because the expected monetary values of insurance policies are generally negative.

[7] H. Markowitz, "The Utility of Wealth," *Journal of Political Economy*, vol. 60, no. 2, pp. 151–158, 1952.

Instead of trying to maximize expected wealth, we generally want to maximize the expected utility of wealth. Of course, different people have different utility functions. Figure 6.1 shows an example of a utility function. For small amounts of wealth, the curve is roughly linear, where $100 is about twice as good at $50. For larger amounts of wealth, however, the curve tends to flatten out; after all,

$1000 is worth less to a billionaire than it is to the average person. The flattening of the curve is sometimes referred to as *diminishing marginal utility*.

When discussing monetary utility functions, the three terms listed here are often used. To illustrate this, assume that A represents being given $50 and B represents a 50 % chance of winning $100.

- *Risk neutral.* The utility function is linear. There is no preference between $50 and the 50 % chance of winning $100 ($A \sim B$).

- *Risk seeking.* The utility function is convex. There is a preference for the 50 % chance of winning $100 ($A \prec B$).

- *Risk averse.* The utility function is concave. There is a preference for the $50 ($A \succ B$).

There are several common functional forms for modeling risk aversion of scalar quantities,[8] such as wealth or the availability of hospital beds. One is *quadratic utility*:

$$U(x) = \lambda x - x^2 \tag{6.3}$$

where the parameter $\lambda > 0$ controls the risk aversion. Since we generally want this utility function to be monotonically increasing when modeling the utility of quantities like wealth, we would cap this function at $x = \lambda/2$. After that point, the utility starts decreasing. Another simple form is *exponential utility*:

$$U(x) = 1 - e^{-\lambda x} \tag{6.4}$$

with $\lambda > 0$. Although it has a convenient mathematical form, it is generally not viewed as a plausible model of the utility of wealth. An alternative is the *power utility*:

$$U(x) = \frac{x^{1-\lambda} - 1}{1 - \lambda} \tag{6.5}$$

with $\lambda \geq 0$ and $\lambda \neq 1$. The *logarithmic utility*

$$U(x) = \log x \tag{6.6}$$

with $x > 0$ can be viewed as a special case of the power utility where $\lambda \to 1$. Figure 6.2 shows a plot of the power utility function with the logarithmic utility as a special case.

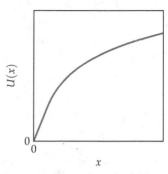

Figure 6.1. The utility of wealth x is often modeled as linear for small values and then concave for larger values, exhibiting risk aversion.

[8] These functional forms have been well studied within economics and finance. J. E. Ingersoll, *Theory of Financial Decision Making*. Rowman and Littlefield Publishers, 1987.

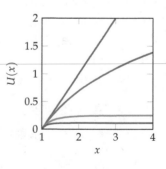

$\lambda = 0$ —— $\lambda \to 1$
$\lambda = 5$ —— $\lambda = 10$

Figure 6.2. Power utility functions.

6.4   Maximum Expected Utility Principle

We are interested in the problem of making rational decisions with imperfect knowledge of the state of the world. Suppose that we have a probabilistic model $P(s' \mid o, a)$, which represents the probability that the state of the world becomes s', given that we observe o and take action a. We have a utility function $U(s')$ that encodes our preferences over the space of outcomes. Our *expected utility* of taking action a, given observation o, is given by

$$EU(a \mid o) = \sum_{s'} P(s' \mid a, o) U(s') \tag{6.7}$$

The *principle of maximum expected utility* says that a rational agent should choose the action that maximizes expected utility:

$$a^* = \arg\max_a EU(a \mid o) \tag{6.8}$$

Because we are interested in building rational agents, equation (6.8) plays a central role in this book.[9] Example 6.3 applies this principle to a simple decision problem.

6.5   Decision Networks

A *decision network*, sometimes called an *influence diagram*, is a generalization of a Bayesian network to include action and utility nodes so that we may compactly represent the probability and utility models defining a decision problem.[10] The state, action, and observation spaces in the previous section may be factored, and the structure of a decision network captures the relationships between the various components.

Decision networks are composed of three types of nodes:

- A *chance node* corresponds to a random variable (indicated by a circle).

- An *action node* corresponds to a decision variable (indicated by a square).

- A *utility node* corresponds to a utility variable (indicated by a diamond) and cannot have children.

[9] The importance of the maximum expected utility principle to the field of artificial intelligence is discussed by S. Russell and P. Norvig, *Artificial Intelligence: A Modern Approach*, 4th ed. Pearson, 2021.

[10] An extensive discussion of decision networks can be found in F. V. Jensen and T. D. Nielsen, *Bayesian Networks and Decision Graphs*, 2nd ed. Springer, 2007.

Suppose that we are trying to decide whether to bring an umbrella on our vacation given the weather forecast for our destination. We observe the forecast o, which may be either rain or sun. Our action a is either to bring our umbrella or leave our umbrella. The resulting state s' is a combination of whether we brought our umbrella and whether there is sun or rain at our destination. Our probabilistic model is as follows:

Example 6.3. Applying the principle of maximum expected utility to the simple decision of whether to bring an umbrella.

o	a	s'	$P(s' \mid a,o)$
forecast rain	bring umbrella	rain with umbrella	0.9
forecast rain	leave umbrella	rain without umbrella	0.9
forecast rain	bring umbrella	sun with umbrella	0.1
forecast rain	leave umbrella	sun without umbrella	0.1
forecast sun	bring umbrella	rain with umbrella	0.2
forecast sun	leave umbrella	rain without umbrella	0.2
forecast sun	bring umbrella	sun with umbrella	0.8
forecast sun	leave umbrella	sun without umbrella	0.8

As shown in the table, we assume that our forecast is imperfect; rain forecasts are right 90 % of the time and sun forecasts are right 80 % of the time. In addition, we assume that bringing an umbrella does not affect the weather, though some may question this assumption. The utility function is as follows:

s'	$U(s')$
rain with umbrella	−0.1
rain without umbrella	−1
sun with umbrella	0.9
sun without umbrella	1

We can compute the expected utility of bringing our umbrella if we forecast rain using equation (6.7):

$$EU(\text{bring umbrella} \mid \text{forecast rain}) = 0.9 \times -0.1 + 0.1 \times 0.9 = 0$$

Likewise, we can compute the expected utility of leaving our umbrella if we forecast rain using equation (6.7):

$$EU(\text{leave umbrella} \mid \text{forecast rain}) = 0.9 \times -1 + 0.1 \times 1 = -0.8$$

Hence, we will want to bring our umbrella.

There are three kinds of directed edges:

- A *conditional edge* ends in a chance node and indicates that the uncertainty in that chance node is conditioned on the values of all its parents.

- An *informational edge* ends in an action node and indicates that the decision associated with that node is made with knowledge of the values of its parents. (These edges are often drawn with dashed lines and are sometimes omitted from diagrams for simplicity.)

- A *functional edge* ends in a utility node and indicates that the utility node is determined by the outcomes of its parents.

Like Bayesian networks, decision networks cannot have cycles. The utility associated with an action is equal to the sum of the values at all the utility nodes. Example 6.4 illustrates how a decision network can model the problem of whether to treat a disease, given the results of diagnostic tests.

We have a set of results from diagnostic tests that may indicate the presence of a particular disease. Given what is known about the tests, we need to decide whether to apply a treatment. The utility is a function of whether a treatment is applied and whether the disease is actually present. Conditional edges connect D to O_1, O_2, and O_3. Informational edges are not explicitly shown in the illustration, but they would connect the observations to T. Functional edges connect T and D to U.

T	D	$U(T,D)$
0	0	0
0	1	−10
1	0	−1
1	1	−1

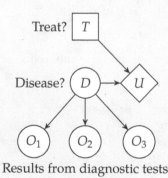

Example 6.4. An example of a decision network used to model whether to treat a disease, given information from diagnostic tests.

Solving a simple problem (algorithm 6.1) requires iterating over all possible decision instantiations to find a decision that maximizes expected utility. For each instantiation, we evaluate the associated expected utility. We begin by instantiating the action nodes and observed chance nodes. We can then apply any inference algorithm to compute the posterior over the inputs to the utility function. The expected utility is the sum of the values at the utility nodes. Example 6.5 shows how this process can be applied to our running example.

```
struct SimpleProblem
    bn::BayesianNetwork
    chance_vars::Vector{Variable}
    decision_vars::Vector{Variable}
    utility_vars::Vector{Variable}
    utilities::Dict{Symbol, Vector{Float64}}
end

function solve(𝒫::SimpleProblem, evidence, M)
    query = [var.name for var in 𝒫.utility_vars]
    U(a) = sum(𝒫.utilities[uname][a[uname]] for uname in query)
    best = (a=nothing, u=-Inf)
    for assignment in assignments(𝒫.decision_vars)
        evidence = merge(evidence, assignment)
        ϕ = infer(M, 𝒫.bn, query, evidence)
        u = sum(p*U(a) for (a, p) in ϕ.table)
        if u > best.u
            best = (a=assignment, u=u)
        end
    end
    return best
end
```

Algorithm 6.1. A simple problem as a decision network. A decision network is a Bayesian network with chance, decision, and utility variables. Utility variables are treated as deterministic. Because variables in our Bayesian network take values from $1:r_i$, the utility variables are mapped to real values by the utilities field. For example, if we have a utility variable :u1, the ith utility associated with that variable is utilities[:u1][i]. The solve function takes as input the problem, evidence, and an inference method. It returns the best assignment to the decision variables and its associated expected utility.

A variety of methods have been developed to make evaluating decision networks more efficient.[11] One method involves removing action and chance nodes from decision networks if they have no children, as defined by conditional, informational, or functional edges. In example 6.5, we can remove O_2 and O_3 because they have no children. We cannot remove O_1 because we treated it as observed, indicating that there is an informational edge from O_1 to T (although it is not drawn explicitly).

6.6   Value of Information

We make decisions based on what we observe. In many applications, it is natural to want to quantify the *value of information*, which is how much observing additional variables is expected to increase our utility.[12] For example, in the disease treatment

[11] R. D. Shachter, "Evaluating Influence Diagrams," *Operations Research*, vol. 34, no. 6, pp. 871–882, 1986. R. D. Shachter, "Probabilistic Inference and Influence Diagrams," *Operations Research*, vol. 36, no. 4, pp. 589–604, 1988.

[12] R. A. Howard, "Information Value Theory," *IEEE Transactions on Systems Science and Cybernetics*, vol. 2, no. 1, pp. 22–26, 1966. Applications to decision networks can be found in: S. L. Dittmer and F. V. Jensen, "Myopic Value of Information in Influence Diagrams," in *Conference on Uncertainty in Artificial Intelligence (UAI)*, 1997. R. D. Shachter, "Efficient Value of Information Computation," in *Conference on Uncertainty in Artificial Intelligence (UAI)*, 1999.

We can use equation (6.7) to compute the expected utility of treating a disease for the decision network in example 6.4. For now, we will assume that we have the result from only the first diagnostic test and it came back positive. If we wanted to make the knowledge of the first diagnostic test explicit in the diagram, then we would draw an informational edge from O_1 to T, and we would have

$$EU(t^1 \mid o_1^1) = \sum_{o_3}\sum_{o_2}\sum_{d} P(d, o_2, o_3 \mid t^1, o_1^1) U(t^1, d, o_1^1, o_2, o_3)$$

We can use the chain rule for Bayesian networks and the definition of conditional probability to compute $P(d, o_2, o_3 \mid t^1, o_1^1)$. Because the utility node depends only on whether the disease is present and whether we treat it, we can simplify $U(t^1, d, o_1^1, o_2, o_3)$ to $U(t^1, d)$. Hence,

$$EU(t^1 \mid o_1^1) = \sum_{d} P(d \mid t^1, o_1^1) U(t^1, d)$$

Any of the exact or approximate inference methods introduced in the previous chapter can be used to evaluate $P(d \mid t^1, o_1^1)$. To decide whether to apply a treatment, we compute $EU(t^1 \mid o_1^1)$ and $EU(t^0 \mid o_1^1)$ and make the decision that provides the highest expected utility.

Example 6.5. Decision network evaluation of the diagnostic test problem.

application in example 6.5, we assumed that we have only observed o_1^1. Given the positive result from that one diagnostic test alone, we may decide against treatment. However, it may be beneficial to administer additional diagnostic tests to reduce the risk of not treating a disease that is really present.

In computing the value of information, we will use $EU^*(o)$ to denote the expected utility of an optimal action, given observation o. The value of information about variable O', given o, is

$$VOI(O' \mid o) = \left(\sum_{o'} P(o' \mid o)EU^*(o,o') \right) - EU^*(o) \qquad (6.9)$$

In other words, the value of information about a variable is the increase in expected utility if that variable is observed. Algorithm 6.2 provides an implementation of this.

```
function value_of_information(𝒫, query, evidence, M)
    ϕ = infer(M, 𝒫.bn, query, evidence)
    voi = -solve(𝒫, evidence, M).u
    query_vars = filter(v→v.name ∈ query, 𝒫.chance_vars)
    for o′ in assignments(query_vars)
        oo′ = merge(evidence, o′)
        p = ϕ.table[o′]
        voi += p*solve(𝒫, oo′, M).u
    end
    return voi
end
```

Algorithm 6.2. A method for decision network evaluation, which takes a simple problem 𝒫, a list of query variables query, a dictionary containing observed chance variables and their values evidence, and an inference strategy M. The method returns an assignment of decision values that maximizes the expected utility, given the evidence.

The value of information is never negative. The expected utility can increase only if additional observations can lead to different optimal decisions. If observing a new variable O' makes no difference in the choice of action, then $EU^*(o,o') = EU^*(o)$ for all o', in which case equation (6.9) evaluates to 0. For example, if the optimal decision is to treat the disease regardless of the outcome of the *diagnostic test*, then the value of observing the outcome of the test is 0.

The value of information only captures the increase in expected utility from making an observation. A cost may be associated with making a particular observation. Some diagnostic tests may be inexpensive, such as a temperature reading; other diagnostic tests are more costly and invasive, such as a lumbar puncture. The value of information obtained by a lumbar puncture may be much greater than that of a temperature reading, but the costs of the tests should be taken into consideration.

Value of information is an important and often-used metric for choosing what to observe. Sometimes the value of information metric is used to determine an appropriate sequence of observations. After each observation, the value of information is determined for the remaining unobserved variables. The unobserved variable with the greatest value of information is then selected for observation. If there are costs associated with making different observations, then these costs are subtracted from the value of information when determining which variable to observe. The process continues until it is no longer beneficial to observe any more variables. The optimal action is then chosen. This greedy selection of observations is only a heuristic; it may not represent the truly optimal sequence of observations. The optimal selection of observations can be determined by using the techniques for sequential decision making introduced in later chapters.

6.7   Irrationality

Decision theory is a *normative theory*, which is prescriptive, not a *descriptive theory*, which is predictive of human behavior. Human judgment and preference often do not follow the rules of rationality outlined in section 6.1.[13] Even human experts may have an inconsistent set of preferences, which can be problematic when designing a decision support system that attempts to maximize expected utility.

Example 6.6 shows that certainty often exaggerates losses that are certain compared to losses that are merely probable. This *certainty effect* works with gains as well. A smaller gain that is certain is often preferred over a much greater gain that is only probable, in a way that the axioms of rationality are necessarily violated.

Example 6.7 demonstrates the *framing effect*, where people decide on options based on whether they are presented as a loss or as a gain. Many other cognitive biases can lead to deviations from what is prescribed by utility theory.[14] Special care must be given when trying to elicit utility functions from human experts to build decision support systems. Although the recommendations of the decision support system may be rational, they may not exactly reflect human preferences in certain situations.

[13] Kahneman and Tversky provide a critique of expected utility theory and introduce an alternative model called *prospect theory*, which appears to be more consistent with human behavior. D. Kahneman and A. Tversky, "Prospect Theory: An Analysis of Decision Under Risk," *Econometrica*, vol. 47, no. 2, pp. 263–292, 1979.

[14] Several recent books discuss apparent human irrationality. D. Ariely, *Predictably Irrational: The Hidden Forces That Shape Our Decisions*. Harper, 2008. J. Lehrer, *How We Decide*. Houghton Mifflin, 2009.

Tversky and Kahneman studied the preferences of university students who answered questionnaires in a classroom setting. They presented students with questions dealing with the response to an epidemic. The students were to reveal their preference between the following two outcomes:

- A: 100 % chance of losing 75 lives

- B: 80 % chance of losing 100 lives

Most preferred B over A. From equation (6.2), we know

$$U(\text{lose } 75) < 0.8U(\text{lose } 100) \tag{6.10}$$

They were then asked to choose between the following two outcomes:

- C: 10 % chance of losing 75 lives

- D: 8 % chance of losing 100 lives

Most preferred C over D. Hence, $0.1U(\text{lose } 75) > 0.08U(\text{lose } 100)$. We multiply both sides by 10 and get

$$U(\text{lose } 75) > 0.8U(\text{lose } 100) \tag{6.11}$$

Of course, equations (6.10) and (6.11) result in a contradiction. We have made no assumption about the actual value of $U(\text{lose } 75)$ and $U(\text{lose } 100)$—we did not even assume that losing 100 lives was worse than losing 75 lives. Because equation (6.2) follows directly from the von Neumann–Morgenstern axioms given in section 6.1, there must be a violation of at least one of the axioms, even though many people who select B and C seem to find the axioms agreeable.

Example 6.6. An experiment demonstrating that certainty often exaggerates losses that are certain relative to losses that are merely probable. A. Tversky and D. Kahneman, "The Framing of Decisions and the Psychology of Choice," *Science*, vol. 211, no. 4481, pp. 453–458, 1981.

Tversky and Kahneman demonstrated the *framing effect* using a hypothetical scenario in which an epidemic is expected to kill 600 people. They presented students with the following two outcomes:

- *E*: 200 people will be saved.

- *F*: 1/3 chance that 600 people will be saved and 2/3 chance that no people will be saved.

The majority of students chose *E* over *F*. They then asked them to choose between the following:

- *G*: 400 people will die.

- *H*: 1/3 chance that nobody will die and 2/3 chance that 600 people will die.

The majority of students chose *H* over *G*, even though *E* is equivalent to *G* and *F* is equivalent to *H*. This inconsistency is due to how the question is framed.

Example 6.7.   An experiment demonstrating the framing effect. A. Tversky and D. Kahneman, "The Framing of Decisions and the Psychology of Choice," *Science*, vol. 211, no. 4481, pp. 453–458, 1981.

6.8 Summary

- Rational decision making combines probability and utility theory.

- The existence of a utility function follows from constraints on rational preferences.

- A rational decision is one that maximizes expected utility.

- Decision problems can be modeled using decision networks, which are extensions of Bayesian networks that include actions and utilities.

- Solving a simple decision involves inference in Bayesian networks and is thus NP-hard.

- The value of information measures the gain in expected utility should a new variable be observed.

- Humans are not always rational.

6.9 Exercises

Exercise 6.1. Suppose that we have a utility function $U(s)$ with a finite maximum value $\overline{U}$ and a finite minimum value $\underline{U}$. What is the corresponding normalized utility function $\hat{U}(s)$ that preserves the same preferences?

Solution: A normalized utility function has a maximum value of 1 and a minimum value of 0. Preferences are preserved under affine transforms, so we determine the affine transform of $U(s)$ that matches the unit bounds. This transform is

$$\hat{U}(s) = \frac{U(s) - \underline{U}}{\overline{U} - \underline{U}} = \frac{1}{\overline{U} - \underline{U}} U(s) - \frac{\underline{U}}{\overline{U} - \underline{U}}$$

Exercise 6.2. If $A \succeq C \succeq B$ and the utilities of each outcome are $U(A) = 450$, $U(B) = -150$, and $U(C) = 60$, what is the lottery over A and B that will make us indifferent between the lottery and C?

Solution: A lottery over A and B is defined as $[A:p;B:1-p]$. To satisfy indifference between the lottery and C ($[A:p;B:1-p] \sim C$), we must have $U([A:p;B:1-p]) = U(C)$. Thus, we must compute p that satisfies the equality

$$U([A:p;B:1-p]) = U(C)$$
$$pU(A) + (1-p)U(B) = U(C)$$
$$p = \frac{U(C) - U(B)}{U(A) - U(B)}$$
$$p = \frac{60 - (-150)}{450 - (-150)} = 0.35$$

This implies that the lottery $[A:0.35;B:0.65]$ is equally as desired as C.

Exercise 6.3. Suppose that for a utility function U over three outcomes A, B, and C, that $U(A) = 5$, $U(B) = 20$, and $U(C) = 0$. We are given a choice between a lottery that gives us a 50 % probability of B and a 50 % probability of C and a lottery that guarantees A. Compute the preferred lottery and show that, under the positive affine transformation with $m = 2$ and $b = 30$, that we maintain a preference for the same lottery.

Solution: The first lottery is given by $[A:0.0;B:0.5;C:0.5]$, and the second lottery is given by $[A:1.0;B:0.0;C:0.0]$. The original utilities for each lottery are given by

$$U([A:0.0;B:0.5;C:0.5]) = 0.0U(A) + 0.5U(B) + 0.5U(C) = 10$$
$$U([A:1.0;B:0.0;C:0.0]) = 1.0U(A) + 0.0U(B) + 0.0U(C) = 5$$

Thus, since $U([A:0.0;B:0.5;C:0.5]) > U([A:1.0;B:0.0;C:0.0])$, we prefer the first lottery. Under the positive affine transformation $m = 2$ and $b = 30$, our new utilities can be computed as $U' = 2U + 30$. The new utilities are then $U'(A) = 40$, $U'(B) = 70$, and $U'(C) = 30$. The new utilities for each lottery are

$$U'([A:0.0;B:0.5;C:0.5]) = 0.0U'(A) + 0.5U'(B) + 0.5U'(C) = 50$$
$$U'([A:1.0;B:0.0;C:0.0]) = 1.0U'(A) + 0.0U'(B) + 0.0U'(C) = 40$$

Since $U'([A:0.0;B:0.5;C:0.5]) > U'([A:1.0;B:0.0;C:0.0])$, we maintain a preference for the first lottery.

Exercise 6.4. Prove that the power utility function in equation (6.5) is risk averse for all $x > 0$ and $\lambda > 0$ with $\lambda \neq 1$.

Solution: Risk aversion implies that the utility function is concave, which requires that the second derivative of the utility function is negative. The utility function and its derivatives are computed as follows:

$$U(x) = \frac{x^{1-\lambda} - 1}{1 - \lambda}$$

$$\frac{dU}{dx} = \frac{1}{x^{\lambda}}$$

$$\frac{d^2U}{dx^2} = \frac{-\lambda}{x^{\lambda+1}}$$

For $x > 0$ and $\lambda > 0$, $\lambda \neq 1$, $x^{\lambda+1}$ is a positive number raised to a positive exponent, which is guaranteed to be positive. Multiplying this by $-\lambda$ guarantees that the second derivative is negative. Thus, for all $x > 0$ and $\lambda > 0$, $\lambda \neq 1$, the power utility function is risk averse.

Exercise 6.5. Using the parameters given in example 6.3, compute the expected utility of bringing our umbrella if we forecast sun and the expected utility of leaving our umbrella behind if we forecast sun. What is the action that maximizes our expected utility, given that we forecast sun?

Solution:

$$EU(\text{bring umbrella} \mid \text{forecast sun}) = 0.2 \times -0.1 + 0.8 \times 0.9 = 0.7$$
$$EU(\text{leave umbrella} \mid \text{forecast sun}) = 0.2 \times -1.0 + 0.8 \times 1.0 = 0.6$$

The action that maximizes our expected utility if we forecast sun is to bring our umbrella!

Exercise 6.6. Suppose that we are trying to optimally decide whether or not to feed (F) our new puppy based on the likelihood that the puppy is hungry (H). We can observe whether the puppy is whining (W) and whether someone else has recently fed the puppy (R). The utilities of each combination of feeding and hunger and the decision network representation are provided here:

F	H	U(F,H)
0	0	0.0
0	1	−1.0
1	0	−0.5
1	1	−0.1

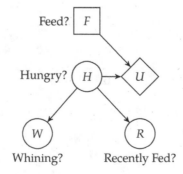

Given that $P(h^1 \mid w^1) = 0.78$, if we observe the puppy whining (w^1), what are the expected utilities of not feeding the puppy (f^0) and feeding the puppy (f^1)? What is the optimal action?

Solution: We start with the definition of expected utility and recognize that the utility depends only on H and F:

$$EU(f^0 \mid w^1) = \sum_h P(h \mid w^1)U(f^0, h)$$

Now, we can compute the expected utility of feeding the puppy given that it is whining and, in a similar fashion as before, the expected utility of not feeding the puppy given that it is whining:

$$EU(f^0 \mid w^1) = 0.22 \times 0.0 + 0.78 \times -1.0 = -0.78$$
$$EU(f^1 \mid w^1) = 0.22 \times -0.5 + 0.78 \times -0.1 = -0.188$$

Thus, the optimal action is to feed the puppy (f^1) since this maximizes our expected utility $EU^*(w^1) = -0.188$.

Exercise 6.7. Using the results from exercise 6.6, if $P(r^1 \mid w^1) = 0.2$, $P(h^1 \mid w^1, r^0) = 0.9$, and $P(h^1 \mid w^1, r^1) = 0.3$, what is the value of information of asking someone else if the puppy has recently been fed, given that we observe the puppy to be whining (w^1)?

Solution: We are interested in computing

$$\text{VOI}(R \mid w^1) = \left(\sum_r P(r \mid w^1)EU^*(w^1, r) \right) - EU^*(w^1)$$

We start by computing $EU(f \mid w^1, r)$ for all f and r. Following a similar derivation as in exercise 6.6, we have

$$EU(f^0 \mid w^1, r^0) = \sum_h P(h \mid w^1, r^0)U(f^0, h)$$

So, for each combination of F and R, we have the following expected utilities:

$$EU(f^0 \mid w^1, r^0) = \sum_h P(h \mid w^1, r^0)U(f^0, h) = 0.1 \times 0.0 + 0.9 \times -1.0 = -0.9$$
$$EU(f^1 \mid w^1, r^0) = \sum_h P(h \mid w^1, r^0)U(f^1, h) = 0.1 \times -0.5 + 0.9 \times -0.1 = -0.14$$
$$EU(f^0 \mid w^1, r^1) = \sum_h P(h \mid w^1, r^1)U(f^0, h) = 0.7 \times 0.0 + 0.3 \times -1.0 = -0.3$$
$$EU(f^1 \mid w^1, r^1) = \sum_h P(h \mid w^1, r^1)U(f^1, h) = 0.7 \times -0.5 + 0.3 \times -0.1 = -0.38$$

The optimal expected utilities are

$$EU^*(w^1, r^0) = -0.14$$
$$EU^*(w^1, r^1) = -0.3$$

Now, we can compute the value of information:

$$\text{VOI}(R \mid w^1) = 0.8(-0.14) + 0.2(-0.3) - (-0.188) = 0.016$$

PART II

SEQUENTIAL PROBLEMS

Up to this point, we have assumed that we make a single decision at one point in time, but many important problems require that we make a series of decisions. The same principle of maximum expected utility still applies, but optimal decision making in a sequential context requires reasoning about future sequences of actions and observations. This part of the book will discuss sequential decision problems in stochastic environments. We will focus on a general formulation of sequential decision problems under the assumption that the model is known and that the environment is fully observable. We will relax both of these assumptions later. Our discussion will begin with the introduction of the *Markov decision process* (*MDP*), the standard mathematical model for sequential decision problems. We will discuss several approaches for finding exact solutions. Because large problems sometimes do not permit exact solutions to be efficiently found, we will discuss a collection of both offline and online approximate solution methods, along with a type of method that involves directly searching the space of parameterized decision policies. Finally, we will discuss approaches for validating that our decision strategies will perform as expected when deployed in the real world.

7 Exact Solution Methods

This chapter introduces a model known as a *Markov decision process (MDP)* to represent sequential decision problems where the effects of our actions are uncertain.[1] We begin with a description of the model, which specifies both the stochastic dynamics of the system as well as the utility associated with its evolution. Different algorithms can be used to compute the utility associated with a decision strategy and to search for an optimal strategy. Under certain assumptions, we can find exact solutions to MDPs. Later chapters will discuss approximation methods that tend to scale better to larger problems.

[1] Such models were originally studied in the 1950s. R. E. Bellman, *Dynamic Programming*. Princeton University Press, 1957. A modern treatment can be found in M. L. Puterman, *Markov Decision Processes: Discrete Stochastic Dynamic Programming*. Wiley, 2005.

7.1 Markov Decision Processes

In an MDP (algorithm 7.1), we choose action a_t at time t based on observing state s_t. We then receive a reward r_t. The *action space* $\mathcal{A}$ is the set of possible actions, and the *state space* $\mathcal{S}$ is the set of possible states. Some of the algorithms assume that these sets are finite, but this is not required in general. The state evolves probabilistically based on the current state and action we take. The assumption that the next state depends only on the current state and action and not on any prior state or action is known as the *Markov assumption*.

An MDP can be represented using a decision network as shown in figure 7.1. There are informational edges (not shown here) from $A_{1:t-1}$ and $S_{1:t}$ to A_t. The utility function is decomposed into rewards $R_{1:t}$. We focus on *stationary* MDPs in which $P(S_{t+1} \mid S_t, A_t)$ and $P(R_t \mid S_t, A_t)$ do not vary with time. Stationary MDPs can be compactly represented by a dynamic decision diagram as shown in figure 7.2. The *state transition model* $T(s' \mid s, a)$ represents the probability of transitioning from state s to s' after executing action a. The *reward function* $R(s, a)$ represents the expected reward received when executing action a from state s.

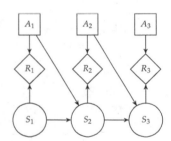

Figure 7.1. MDP decision network diagram.

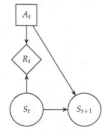

Figure 7.2. Stationary MDP decision network diagram. All MDPs have this general structure.

The reward function is a deterministic function of *s* and *a* because it represents an expectation, but rewards may be generated stochastically in the environment or even depend on the resulting next state.[2] Example 7.1 shows how to frame a collision avoidance problem as an MDP.

The problem of aircraft collision avoidance can be formulated as an MDP. The states represent the positions and velocities of our aircraft and the intruder aircraft, and the actions represent whether we climb, descend, or stay level. We receive a large negative reward for colliding with the other aircraft and a small negative reward for climbing or descending.

Given knowledge of the current state, we must decide whether an avoidance maneuver is required. The problem is challenging because the positions of the aircraft evolve probabilistically, and we want to make sure that we start our maneuver early enough to avoid collision, but late enough so that we avoid unnecessary maneuvering.

---

[2] For example, if the reward depends on the next state as given by $R(s, a, s')$, then the expected reward function would be

$$R(s,a) = \sum_{s'} T(s' \mid s,a)R(s,a,s')$$

Example 7.1. Aircraft collision avoidance framed as an MDP. Many other real-world applications are discussed in D. J. White, "A Survey of Applications of Markov Decision Processes," *Journal of the Operational Research Society*, vol. 44, no. 11, pp. 1073–1096, 1993.

```
struct MDP
    γ  # discount factor
    S  # state space
    A  # action space
    T  # transition function
    R  # reward function
    TR # sample transition and reward
end
```

Algorithm 7.1. Data structure for an MDP. We will use the TR field later to sample the next state and reward given the current state and action: s', r = TR(s, a). In mathematical writing, MDPs are sometimes defined in terms of a tuple consisting of the various components of the MDP, written (S, A, T, R, γ).

The rewards in an MDP are treated as components in an additively decomposed utility function. In a *finite horizon* problem with *n* decisions, the utility associated with a sequence of rewards $r_{1:n}$ is simply

$$\sum_{t=1}^{n} r_t \qquad (7.1)$$

The sum of rewards is sometimes called the *return*.

In an *infinite horizon* problem in which the number of decisions is unbounded, the sum of rewards can become infinite.[3] There are several ways to define utility in terms of individual rewards in infinite horizon problems. One way is to impose

[3] Suppose that strategy *A* results in a reward of 1 per time step and strategy *B* results in a reward of 100 per time step. Intuitively, a rational agent should prefer strategy *B* over strategy *A*, but both provide the same infinite expected utility.

a *discount factor* γ between 0 and 1. The utility is then given by

$$\sum_{t=1}^{\infty} \gamma^{t-1} r_t \qquad (7.2)$$

This value is sometimes called the *discounted return*. So long as $0 \leq \gamma < 1$ and the rewards are finite, the utility will be finite. The discount factor makes it so that rewards in the present are worth more than rewards in the future, a concept that also appears in economics.

Another way to define utility in infinite horizon problems is to use the *average reward*, also called the *average return*, given by

$$\lim_{n \to \infty} \frac{1}{n} \sum_{t=1}^{n} r_t \qquad (7.3)$$

This formulation can be attractive because we do not have to choose a discount factor, but there is often no practical difference between this formulation and a discounted return with a discount factor close to 1. Because the discounted return is often computationally simpler to work with, we will focus on the discounted formulation.

A *policy* tells us what action to select given the past history of states and actions. The action to select at time t, given the *history* $h_t = (s_{1:t}, a_{1:t-1})$, is written $\pi_t(h_t)$. Because the future states and rewards depend only on the current state and action (as made apparent in the conditional independence assumptions in figure 7.1), we can restrict our attention to policies that depend only on the current state. In addition, we will primarily focus on *deterministic policies* because there is guaranteed to exist in MDPs an optimal policy that is deterministic. Later chapters discuss *stochastic policies*, where $\pi_t(a_t \mid s_t)$ denotes the probability that the policy assigns to taking action a_t in state s_t at time t.

In infinite horizon problems with stationary transitions and rewards, we can further restrict our attention to *stationary policies*, which do not depend on time. We will write the action associated with stationary policy π in state s as $\pi(s)$, without the temporal subscript. In finite horizon problems, however, it may be beneficial to select a different action depending on how many time steps are remaining. For example, when playing basketball, it is generally not a good strategy to attempt a half-court shot unless there are only a couple of seconds remaining in the game. We can make stationary policies account for time by incorporating time as a state variable.

The expected utility of executing π from state s is denoted as $U^{\pi}(s)$. In the context of MDPs, U^{π} is often referred to as the *value function*. An *optimal policy* π^* is a policy that maximizes expected utility:[4]

$$\pi^*(s) = \arg\max_{\pi} U^{\pi}(s) \qquad (7.4)$$

[4] Doing so is consistent with the maximum expected utility principle introduced in section 6.4.

for all states s. Depending on the model, there may be multiple policies that are optimal. The value function associated with an optimal policy π^* is called the *optimal value function* and is denoted as U^*.

An optimal policy can be found by using a computational technique called *dynamic programming*,[5] which involves simplifying a complicated problem by breaking it down into simpler subproblems in a recursive manner. Although we will focus on dynamic programming algorithms for MDPs, dynamic programming is a general technique that can be applied to a wide variety of other problems. For example, dynamic programming can be used in computing a Fibonacci sequence and finding the longest common subsequence between two strings.[6] In general, algorithms that use dynamic programming for solving MDPs are much more efficient than brute force methods.

[5] The term "dynamic programming" was coined by the American mathematician Richard Ernest Bellman (1920–1984). Dynamic refers to the fact that the problem is time-varying and programming refers to a methodology to find an optimal program or decision strategy. R. Bellman, *Eye of the Hurricane: An Autobiography*. World Scientific, 1984.

[6] T. H. Cormen, C. E. Leiserson, R. L. Rivest, and C. Stein, *Introduction to Algorithms*, 3rd ed. MIT Press, 2009.

7.2   Policy Evaluation

Before we discuss how to go about computing an optimal policy, we will discuss *policy evaluation*, where we compute the value function U^{π}. Policy evaluation can be done iteratively. If the policy is executed for a single step, the utility is $U_1^{\pi}(s) = R(s, \pi(s))$. Further steps can be obtained from the *lookahead* equation:

$$U_{k+1}^{\pi}(s) = R(s, \pi(s)) + \gamma \sum_{s'} T(s' \mid s, \pi(s)) U_k^{\pi}(s') \qquad (7.5)$$

This equation is implemented in algorithm 7.2. Iterative policy evaluation is implemented in algorithm 7.3. Several iterations are shown in figure 7.3.

The value function U^{π} can be computed to an arbitrary precision given sufficient iterations of the lookahead equation. Convergence is guaranteed because the update in equation (7.5) is a *contraction mapping* (reviewed in appendix A.15).[7] At convergence, the following equality holds:

[7] See exercise 7.12.

$$U^{\pi}(s) = R(s, \pi(s)) + \gamma \sum_{s'} T(s' \mid s, \pi(s)) U^{\pi}(s') \qquad (7.6)$$

```
function lookahead(𝒫::MDP, U, s, a)
    𝒮, T, R, γ = 𝒫.𝒮, 𝒫.T, 𝒫.R, 𝒫.γ
    return R(s,a) + γ*sum(T(s,a,s′)*U(s′) for s′ in 𝒮)
end
function lookahead(𝒫::MDP, U::Vector, s, a)
    𝒮, T, R, γ = 𝒫.𝒮, 𝒫.T, 𝒫.R, 𝒫.γ
    return R(s,a) + γ*sum(T(s,a,s′)*U[i] for (i,s′) in enumerate(𝒮))
end
```

Algorithm 7.2. Functions for computing the lookahead state-action value from a state s given an action a using an estimate of the value function U for the MDP 𝒫. The second version handles the case when U is a vector.

```
function iterative_policy_evaluation(𝒫::MDP, π, k_max)
    𝒮, T, R, γ = 𝒫.𝒮, 𝒫.T, 𝒫.R, 𝒫.γ
    U = [0.0 for s in 𝒮]
    for k in 1:k_max
        U = [lookahead(𝒫, U, s, π(s)) for s in 𝒮]
    end
    return U
end
```

Algorithm 7.3. Iterative policy evaluation, which iteratively computes the value function for a policy π for MDP 𝒫 with discrete state and action spaces using k_max iterations.

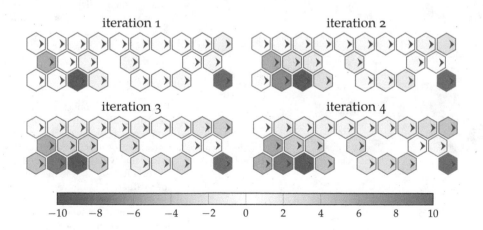

Figure 7.3. Iterative policy evaluation used to evaluate an east-moving policy on the hex world problem (see appendix F.1). The arrows indicate the direction recommended by the policy (i.e., always move east), and the colors indicate the values associated with the states. The values change with each iteration.

This equality is called the *Bellman expectation equation*.[8]

Policy evaluation can be done without iteration by solving the system of equations in the Bellman expectation equation directly. Equation (7.6) defines a set of $|S|$ linear equations with $|S|$ unknowns corresponding to the values at each state. One way to solve this system of equations is to first convert it into matrix form:

$$\mathbf{U}^\pi = \mathbf{R}^\pi + \gamma \mathbf{T}^\pi \mathbf{U}^\pi \tag{7.7}$$

where $\mathbf{U}^\pi$ and $\mathbf{R}^\pi$ are the utility and reward functions represented in vector form with $|S|$ components. The $|\mathcal{S}| \times |\mathcal{S}|$ matrix $\mathbf{T}^\pi$ contains state transition probabilities where T_{ij}^π is the probability of transitioning from the ith state to the jth state.

The value function is obtained as follows:

$$\mathbf{U}^\pi - \gamma \mathbf{T}^\pi \mathbf{U}^\pi = \mathbf{R}^\pi \tag{7.8}$$

$$(\mathbf{I} - \gamma \mathbf{T}^\pi)\mathbf{U}^\pi = \mathbf{R}^\pi \tag{7.9}$$

$$\mathbf{U}^\pi = (\mathbf{I} - \gamma \mathbf{T}^\pi)^{-1}\mathbf{R}^\pi \tag{7.10}$$

This method is implemented in algorithm 7.4. Solving for $\mathbf{U}^\pi$ in this way requires $O(|\mathcal{S}|^3)$ time. The method is used to evaluate a policy in figure 7.4.

[8] This equation is named for Richard E. Bellman, one of the pioneers of dynamic programming. R. E. Bellman, *Dynamic Programming*. Princeton University Press, 1957.

```
function policy_evaluation(𝒫::MDP, π)
    S, R, T, γ = 𝒫.S, 𝒫.R, 𝒫.T, 𝒫.γ
    R′ = [R(s, π(s)) for s in S]
    T′ = [T(s, π(s), s′) for s in S, s′ in S]
    return (I - γ*T′)\R′
end
```

Algorithm 7.4. Exact policy evaluation, which computes the value function for a policy π for an MDP 𝒫 with discrete state and action spaces.

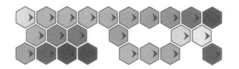

Figure 7.4. Exact policy evaluation used to evaluate an east-moving policy for the hex world problem. The exact solution contains lower values than what was contained in the first few steps of iterative policy evaluation in figure 7.3. If we ran iterative policy evaluation for more iterations, it would converge to the same value function.

7.3 Value Function Policies

The previous section showed how to compute a value function associated with a policy. This section shows how to extract a policy from a value function, which we later use when generating optimal policies. Given a value function U, which may or may not correspond to the optimal value function, we can construct a policy π that maximizes the lookahead equation introduced in equation (7.5):

$$\pi(s) = \arg\max_a \left(R(s,a) + \gamma \sum_{s'} T(s' \mid s,a) U(s') \right) \tag{7.11}$$

We refer to this policy as a *greedy policy* with respect to U. If U is the optimal value function, then the extracted policy is optimal. Algorithm 7.5 implements this idea.

An alternative way to represent a policy is to use the *action value function*, sometimes called the *Q-function*. The action value function represents the expected return when starting in state s, taking action a, and then continuing with the greedy policy with respect to Q:

$$Q(s,a) = R(s,a) + \gamma \sum_{s'} T(s' \mid s,a) U(s') \tag{7.12}$$

From this action value function, we can obtain the value function,

$$U(s) = \max_a Q(s,a) \tag{7.13}$$

as well as the policy,

$$\pi(s) = \arg\max_a Q(s,a) \tag{7.14}$$

Storing Q explicitly for discrete problems requires $O(|\mathcal{S}| \times |\mathcal{A}|)$ storage instead of $O(|\mathcal{S}|)$ storage for U, but we do not have to use R and T to extract the policy.

Policies can also be represented using the *advantage function*, which quantifies the advantage of taking an action in comparison to the greedy action. It is defined in terms of the difference between Q and U:

$$A(s,a) = Q(s,a) - U(s) \tag{7.15}$$

Greedy actions have zero advantage, and nongreedy actions have negative advantage. Some algorithms that we will discuss later in the book use U representations, but others will use Q or A.

```
struct ValueFunctionPolicy
    𝒫 # problem
    U # utility function
end

function greedy(𝒫::MDP, U, s)
    u, a = findmax(a→lookahead(𝒫, U, s, a), 𝒫.𝒜)
    return (a=a, u=u)
end

(π::ValueFunctionPolicy)(s) = greedy(π.𝒫, π.U, s).a
```

Algorithm 7.5. A value function policy extracted from a value function U for an MDP 𝒫. The greedy function will be used in other algorithms.

7.4   Policy Iteration

Policy iteration (algorithm 7.6) is one way to compute an optimal policy. It involves iterating between policy evaluation (section 7.2) and policy improvement through a greedy policy (algorithm 7.5). Policy iteration is guaranteed to converge given any initial policy. It converges in a finite number of iterations because there are finitely many policies and every iteration improves the policy if it can be improved. Although the number of possible policies is exponential in the number of states, policy iteration often converges quickly. Figure 7.5 demonstrates policy iteration on the hex world problem.

```
struct PolicyIteration
    π # initial policy
    k_max # maximum number of iterations
end

function solve(M::PolicyIteration, 𝒫::MDP)
    π, S = M.π, 𝒫.S
    for k = 1:M.k_max
        U = policy_evaluation(𝒫, π)
        π′ = ValueFunctionPolicy(𝒫, U)
        if all(π(s) == π′(s) for s in S)
            break
        end
        π = π′
    end
    return π
end
```

Algorithm 7.6. Policy iteration, which iteratively improves an initial policy π to obtain an optimal policy for an MDP 𝒫 with discrete state and action spaces.

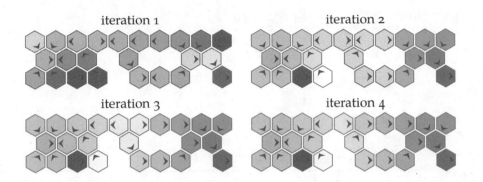

iteration 1   iteration 2

iteration 3   iteration 4

Figure 7.5. Policy iteration used to iteratively improve an initially east-moving policy in the hex world problem to obtain an optimal policy. In the first iteration, we see the value function associated with the east-moving policy and arrows indicating the policy that is greedy with respect to that value function. Policy iteration converges in four iterations; if we ran for a fifth or more iterations, we would get the same policy.

Policy iteration tends to be expensive because we must evaluate the policy in each iteration. A variation of policy iteration called *modified policy iteration*[9] approximates the value function using iterative policy evaluation instead of exact policy evaluation. We can choose the number of policy evaluation iterations between steps of policy improvement. If we use only one iteration between steps, then this approach is identical to value iteration.

[9] M. L. Puterman and M. C. Shin, "Modified Policy Iteration Algorithms for Discounted Markov Decision Problems," *Management Science*, vol. 24, no. 11, pp. 1127–1137, 1978.

7.5   Value Iteration

Value iteration is an alternative to policy iteration that is often used because of its simplicity. Unlike policy improvement, value iteration updates the value function directly. It begins with any bounded value function U, meaning that $|U(s)| < \infty$ for all s. One common initialization is $U(s) = 0$ for all s.

The value function can be improved by applying the *Bellman backup*, also called the *Bellman update*:[10]

$$U_{k+1}(s) = \max_a \left(R(s,a) + \gamma \sum_{s'} T(s' \mid s,a) U_k(s') \right) \tag{7.16}$$

This backup procedure is implemented in algorithm 7.7.

[10] It is referred to as a backup operation because it transfers information back to a state from its future states.

```
function backup(𝒫::MDP, U, s)
    return maximum(lookahead(𝒫, U, s, a) for a in 𝒫.𝒜)
end
```

Algorithm 7.7. The backup procedure applied to an MDP 𝒫, which improves a value function U at state s.

Repeated application of this update is guaranteed to converge to the optimal value function. Like iterative policy evaluation, we can use the fact that the update is a contraction mapping to prove convergence.[11] This optimal policy is guaranteed to satisfy the *Bellman optimality equation*:

$$U^*(s) = \max_a \left(R(s,a) + \gamma \sum_{s'} T(s' \mid s,a) U^*(s') \right) \quad (7.17)$$

[11] See exercise 7.13.

Further applications of the Bellman backup once this equality holds do not change the value function. An optimal policy can be extracted from U^* using equation (7.11). Value iteration is implemented in algorithm 7.8 and is applied to the hex world problem in figure 7.6.

The implementation in algorithm 7.8 stops after a fixed number of iterations, but it is also common to terminate the iterations early based on the maximum change in value $\|U_{k+1} - U_k\|_\infty$, called the *Bellman residual*. If the Bellman residual drops below a threshold δ, then the iterations terminate. A Bellman residual of δ guarantees that the optimal value function obtained by value iteration is within $\epsilon = \delta\gamma/(1-\gamma)$ of U^*.[12] Discount factors closer to 1 significantly inflate this error, leading to slower convergence. If we heavily discount future reward (γ closer to 0), then we do not need to iterate as much into the future. This effect is demonstrated in example 7.2.

[12] See exercise 7.8.

Knowing the maximum deviation of the estimated value function from the optimal value function, $\|U_k - U^*\|_\infty < \epsilon$, allows us to bound the maximum deviation of reward obtained under the extracted policy π from an optimal policy π^*. This *policy loss* $\|U^\pi - U^*\|_\infty$ is bounded by $2\epsilon\gamma/(1-\gamma)$.[13]

[13] S. P. Singh and R. C. Yee, "An Upper Bound on the Loss from Approximate Optimal-Value Functions," *Machine Learning*, vol. 16, no. 3, pp. 227–233, 1994.

```
struct ValueIteration
    k_max # maximum number of iterations
end

function solve(M::ValueIteration, P::MDP)
    U = [0.0 for s in P.S]
    for k = 1:M.k_max
        U = [backup(P, U, s) for s in P.S]
    end
    return ValueFunctionPolicy(P, U)
end
```

Algorithm 7.8. Value iteration, which iteratively improves a value function U to obtain an optimal policy for an MDP P with discrete state and action spaces. The method terminates after k_max iterations.

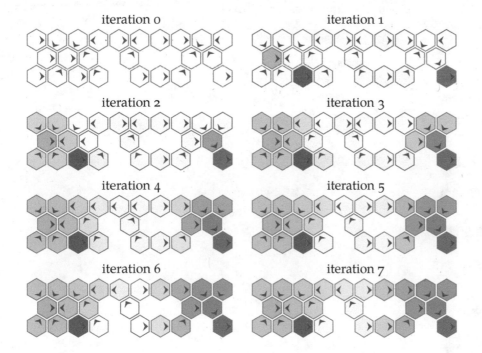

Figure 7.6. Value iteration in the hex world problem to obtain an optimal policy. Each hex is colored according to the value function, and arrows indicate the policy that is greedy with respect to that value function.

Consider a simple variation of the hex world problem, consisting of a straight line of tiles with a single consuming tile at the end producing a reward of 10. The discount factor directly affects the rate at which reward from the consuming tile propagates down the line to the other tiles, and thus how quickly value iteration converges.

Example 7.2. The effect of the discount factor on convergence of value iteration. In each case, value iteration was run until the Bellman residual was less than 1.

$\gamma = 0.9$ $\qquad\qquad\qquad$ $\gamma = 0.5$

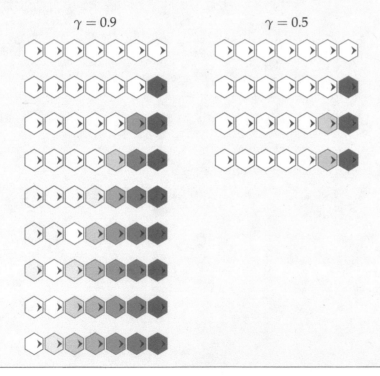

7.6   Asynchronous Value Iteration

Value iteration tends to be computationally intensive, as every entry in the value function U_k is updated in each iteration to obtain U_{k+1}. In *asynchronous value iteration*, only a subset of the states are updated with each iteration. Asynchronous value iteration is still guaranteed to converge on the optimal value function, provided that each state is updated an infinite number of times.

One common asynchronous value iteration method, *Gauss-Seidel value iteration* (algorithm 7.9), sweeps through an ordering of the states and applies the Bellman update in place:

$$U(s) \leftarrow \max_a \left(R(s,a) + \gamma \sum_{s'} T(s' \mid s,a)U(s') \right) \qquad (7.18)$$

The computational savings lies in not having to construct a second value function in memory with each iteration. Gauss-Seidel value iteration can converge more quickly than standard value iteration, depending on the ordering chosen.[14] In some problems, the state contains a time index that increments deterministically forward in time. If we apply Gauss-Seidel value iteration starting at the last time index and work our way backward, this process is sometimes called *backward induction value iteration*. An example of the impact of the state ordering is given in example 7.3.

[14] A poor ordering in Gauss-Seidel value iteration cannot cause the algorithm to be slower than standard value iteration.

```
struct GaussSeidelValueIteration
    k_max # maximum number of iterations
end

function solve(M::GaussSeidelValueIteration, 𝒫::MDP)
    U = [0.0 for s in 𝒫.𝒮]
    for k = 1:M.k_max
        for (i, s) in enumerate(𝒫.𝒮)
            U[i] = backup(𝒫, U, s)
        end
    end
    return ValueFunctionPolicy(𝒫, U)
end
```

Algorithm 7.9.   Asynchronous value iteration, which updates states in a different manner than value iteration, often saving computation time. The method terminates after k_max iterations.

Consider the linear variation of the hex world problem from example 7.2. We can solve the same problem using asynchronous value iteration. The ordering of the states directly affects the rate at which reward from the consuming tile propagates down the line to the other tiles, and thus how quickly the method converges.

Example 7.3. The effect of the state ordering on convergence of asynchronous value iteration. In this case, evaluating right to left allows convergence to occur in far fewer iterations.

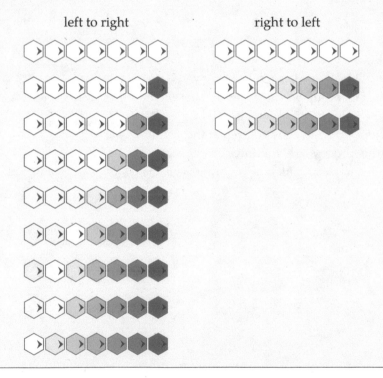

7.7 Linear Program Formulation

The problem of finding an optimal policy can be formulated as a *linear program*, which is an optimization problem with a linear objective function and a set of linear equality or inequality constraints. Once a problem is represented as a linear program, we can use one of many linear programming solvers.[15]

To show how we can convert the Bellman optimality equation into a linear program, we begin by replacing the equality in the Bellman optimality equation with a set of inequality constraints while minimizing $U(s)$ at each state s:[16]

$$\text{minimize} \sum_s U(s)$$
$$\text{subject to } U(s) \geq \max_a \left(R(s,a) + \gamma \sum_{s'} T(s' \mid s,a)U(s') \right) \text{ for all } s \quad (7.19)$$

The variables in the optimization are the utilities at each state. Once we know those utilities, we can extract an optimal policy using equation (7.11).

The maximization in the inequality constraints can be replaced by a set of linear constraints, making it a linear program:

$$\text{minimize} \sum_s U(s)$$
$$\text{subject to } U(s) \geq R(s,a) + \gamma \sum_{s'} T(s' \mid s,a)U(s') \text{ for all } s \text{ and } a \quad (7.20)$$

In the linear program shown in equation (7.20), the number of variables is equal to the number of states and the number of constraints is equal to the number of states times the number of actions. Because linear programs can be solved in polynomial time,[17] MDPs can be solved in polynomial time as well. Although a linear programming approach provides this asymptotic complexity guarantee, it is often more efficient in practice to simply use value iteration. Algorithm 7.10 provides an implementation of this.

7.8 Linear Systems with Quadratic Reward

So far, we have assumed discrete state and action spaces. This section relaxes this assumption, allowing for continuous, vector-valued states and actions. The Bellman optimality equation for discrete problems can be modified as follows:[18]

[15] For an overview of linear programming, see R. Vanderbei, *Linear Programming, Foundations and Extensions*, 4th ed. Springer, 2014.

[16] Intuitively, we want to push the value $U(s)$ at all states s down in order to convert the inequality constraints into equality constraints. Hence, we minimize the sum of all utilities.

[17] This was proved by L.G. Khachiyan, "Polynomial Algorithms in Linear Programming," *USSR Computational Mathematics and Mathematical Physics*, vol. 20, no. 1, pp. 53–72, 1980. Modern algorithms tend to be more efficient in practice.

[18] This section assumes that the problem is undiscounted and finite horizon, but these equations can be easily generalized.

```
struct LinearProgramFormulation end

function tensorform(𝒫::MDP)
    𝒮, 𝒜, R, T = 𝒫.𝒮, 𝒫.𝒜, 𝒫.R, 𝒫.T
    𝒮′ = eachindex(𝒮)
    𝒜′ = eachindex(𝒜)
    R′ = [R(s,a) for s in 𝒮, a in 𝒜]
    T′ = [T(s,a,s′) for s in 𝒮, a in 𝒜, s′ in 𝒮]
    return 𝒮′, 𝒜′, R′, T′
end

solve(𝒫::MDP) = solve(LinearProgramFormulation(), 𝒫)

function solve(M::LinearProgramFormulation, 𝒫::MDP)
    𝒮, 𝒜, R, T = tensorform(𝒫)
    model = Model(GLPK.Optimizer)
    @variable(model, U[𝒮])
    @objective(model, Min, sum(U))
    @constraint(model, [s=𝒮,a=𝒜], U[s] ≥ R[s,a] + 𝒫.γ*T[s,a,:]⋅U)
    optimize!(model)
    return ValueFunctionPolicy(𝒫, value.(U))
end
```

Algorithm 7.10. A method for solving a discrete MDP using a linear program formulation. For convenience in specifying the linear program, we define a function for converting an MDP into its tensor form, where the states and actions consist of integer indices, the reward function is a matrix, and the transition function is a three-dimensional tensor. It uses the JuMP.jl package for mathematical programming. The optimizer is set to use GLPK.jl, but others can be used instead. We also define the default solve behavior for MDPs to use this formulation.

$$U_{h+1}(\mathbf{s}) = \max_{\mathbf{a}} \left(R(\mathbf{s}, \mathbf{a}) + \int T(\mathbf{s}' \mid \mathbf{s}, \mathbf{a}) U_h(\mathbf{s}') \, d\mathbf{s}' \right) \tag{7.21}$$

where s and a in equation (7.16) are replaced with their vector equivalents, the summation is replaced with an integral, and T provides a probability density rather than a probability mass. Computing equation (7.21) is not straightforward for an arbitrary continuous transition distribution and reward function.

In some cases, exact solution methods do exist for MDPs with continuous state and action spaces.[19] In particular, if a problem has *linear dynamics* and has *quadratic reward*, then the optimal policy can be efficiently found in closed form. Such a system is known in control theory as a *linear quadratic regulator (LQR)* and has been well studied.[20]

A problem has linear dynamics if the transition function has the form:

$$T(\mathbf{s}' \mid \mathbf{s}, \mathbf{a}) = \mathbf{T}_s \mathbf{s} + \mathbf{T}_a \mathbf{a} + \mathbf{w} \tag{7.22}$$

where $\mathbf{T}_s$ and $\mathbf{T}_a$ are matrices that determine the mean of the next state $\mathbf{s}'$, given $\mathbf{s}$; and $\mathbf{a}$, and $\mathbf{w}$ is a random disturbance drawn from a zero mean, finite variance distribution that does not depend on $\mathbf{s}$ and $\mathbf{a}$. One common choice is the multivariate Gaussian.

[19] For a detailed overview, see chapter 4 of volume I of D. P. Bertsekas, *Dynamic Programming and Optimal Control*. Athena Scientific, 2007.

[20] For a compact summary of LQR and other related control problems, see A. Shaiju and I. R. Petersen, "Formulas for Discrete Time LQR, LQG, LEQG and Minimax LQG Optimal Control Problems," *IFAC Proceedings Volumes*, vol. 41, no. 2, pp. 8773–8778, 2008.

A reward function is quadratic if it can be written in the form:[21]

$$R(\mathbf{s}, \mathbf{a}) = \mathbf{s}^\top \mathbf{R}_s \mathbf{s} + \mathbf{a}^\top \mathbf{R}_a \mathbf{a} \qquad (7.23)$$

where $\mathbf{R}_s$ and $\mathbf{R}_a$ are matrices that determine how state and action component combinations contribute reward. We additionally require that $\mathbf{R}_s$ be negative semidefinite and $\mathbf{R}_a$ be negative definite. Such a reward function penalizes states and actions that deviate from $\mathbf{0}$.

Problems with linear dynamics and quadratic reward are common in control theory where one often seeks to regulate a process such that it does not deviate far from a desired value. The quadratic cost assigns a much higher cost to states far from the origin than to those near it. The optimal policy for a problem with linear dynamics and quadratic reward has an analytic, closed-form solution. Many MDPs can be approximated with linear quadratic MDPs and solved, often yielding reasonable policies for the original problem.

Substituting the transition and reward functions into equation (7.21) produces

$$U_{h+1}(\mathbf{s}) = \max_{\mathbf{a}} \left(\mathbf{s}^\top \mathbf{R}_s \mathbf{s} + \mathbf{a}^\top \mathbf{R}_a \mathbf{a} + \int p(\mathbf{w}) U_h(\mathbf{T}_s \mathbf{s} + \mathbf{T}_a \mathbf{a} + \mathbf{w})\, d\mathbf{w} \right) \qquad (7.24)$$

where $p(\mathbf{w})$ is the probability density of the random, zero-mean disturbance $\mathbf{w}$.

The optimal one-step value function is

$$U_1(\mathbf{s}) = \max_{\mathbf{a}} \left(\mathbf{s}^\top \mathbf{R}_s \mathbf{s} + \mathbf{a}^\top \mathbf{R}_a \mathbf{a} \right) = \mathbf{s}^\top \mathbf{R}_s \mathbf{s} \qquad (7.25)$$

for which the optimal action is $\mathbf{a} = \mathbf{0}$.

We will show through induction that $U_h(\mathbf{s})$ has a quadratic form, $\mathbf{s}^\top \mathbf{V}_h \mathbf{s} + q_h$, with symmetric matrices $\mathbf{V}_h$. For the one-step value function, $\mathbf{V}_1 = \mathbf{R}_s$ and $q_1 = 0$. Substituting this quadratic form into equation (7.24) yields

$$U_{h+1}(\mathbf{s}) = \mathbf{s}^\top \mathbf{R}_s \mathbf{s} + \max_{\mathbf{a}} \left(\mathbf{a}^\top \mathbf{R}_a \mathbf{a} + \int p(\mathbf{w}) \left((\mathbf{T}_s \mathbf{s} + \mathbf{T}_a \mathbf{a} + \mathbf{w})^\top \mathbf{V}_h (\mathbf{T}_s \mathbf{s} + \mathbf{T}_a \mathbf{a} + \mathbf{w}) + q_h \right) d\mathbf{w} \right) \qquad (7.26)$$

This can be simplified by expanding and using the fact that $\int p(\mathbf{w})\, d\mathbf{w} = 1$ and $\int \mathbf{w} p(\mathbf{w})\, d\mathbf{w} = 0$:

$$\begin{aligned} U_{h+1}(\mathbf{s}) = {}& \mathbf{s}^\top \mathbf{R}_s \mathbf{s} + \mathbf{s}^\top \mathbf{T}_s^\top \mathbf{V}_h \mathbf{T}_s \mathbf{s} \\ & + \max_{\mathbf{a}} \left(\mathbf{a}^\top \mathbf{R}_a \mathbf{a} + 2\mathbf{s}^\top \mathbf{T}_s^\top \mathbf{V}_h \mathbf{T}_a \mathbf{a} + \mathbf{a}^\top \mathbf{T}_a^\top \mathbf{V}_h \mathbf{T}_a \mathbf{a} \right) \\ & + \int p(\mathbf{w}) \left(\mathbf{w}^\top \mathbf{V}_h \mathbf{w} \right) d\mathbf{w} + q_h \end{aligned} \qquad (7.27)$$

[21] A third term, $2\mathbf{s}^\top \mathbf{R}_{sa} \mathbf{a}$, can also be included. For an example, see Shaiju and Petersen (2008).

We can obtain the optimal action by differentiating with respect to $\mathbf{a}$ and setting it to $\mathbf{0}$:[22]

$$
\begin{aligned}
\mathbf{0} &= \left(\mathbf{R}_a + \mathbf{R}_a^\top\right)\mathbf{a} + 2\mathbf{T}_a^\top \mathbf{V}_h \mathbf{T}_s \mathbf{s} + \left(\mathbf{T}_a^\top \mathbf{V}_h \mathbf{T}_a + \left(\mathbf{T}_a^\top \mathbf{V}_h \mathbf{T}_a\right)^\top\right)\mathbf{a} \\
&= 2\mathbf{R}_a \mathbf{a} + 2\mathbf{T}_a^\top \mathbf{V}_h \mathbf{T}_s \mathbf{s} + 2\mathbf{T}_a^\top \mathbf{V}_h \mathbf{T}_a \mathbf{a}
\end{aligned}
\tag{7.28}
$$

[22] Recall that
$$
\nabla_{\mathbf{x}} \mathbf{A}\mathbf{x} = \mathbf{A}^\top
$$
$$
\nabla_{\mathbf{x}} \mathbf{x}^\top \mathbf{A}\mathbf{x} = (\mathbf{A} + \mathbf{A}^\top)\mathbf{x}
$$

Solving for the optimal action yields[23]

$$
\mathbf{a} = -\left(\mathbf{R}_a + \mathbf{T}_a^\top \mathbf{V}_h \mathbf{T}_a\right)^{-1} \mathbf{T}_a^\top \mathbf{V}_h \mathbf{T}_s \mathbf{s}
\tag{7.29}
$$

[23] The matrix $\mathbf{R}_a + \mathbf{T}_a^\top \mathbf{V}_h \mathbf{T}_a$ is negative definite, and thus invertible.

Substituting the optimal action into $U_{h+1}(\mathbf{s})$ yields the quadratic form that we were seeking, $U_{h+1}(\mathbf{s}) = \mathbf{s}^\top \mathbf{V}_{h+1} \mathbf{s} + q_{h+1}$, with[24]

$$
\mathbf{V}_{h+1} = \mathbf{R}_s + \mathbf{T}_s^\top \mathbf{V}_h^\top \mathbf{T}_s - \left(\mathbf{T}_a^\top \mathbf{V}_h \mathbf{T}_s\right)^\top \left(\mathbf{R}_a + \mathbf{T}_a^\top \mathbf{V}_h \mathbf{T}_a\right)^{-1} \left(\mathbf{T}_a^\top \mathbf{V}_h \mathbf{T}_s\right)
\tag{7.30}
$$

and

[24] This equation is sometimes referred to as the *discrete-time Riccati equation*, named after the Venetian mathematician Jacopo Riccati (1676–1754).

$$
q_{h+1} = \sum_{i=1}^{h} \mathbb{E}_{\mathbf{w}} \left[\mathbf{w}^\top \mathbf{V}_i \mathbf{w} \right]
\tag{7.31}
$$

If $\mathbf{w} \sim \mathcal{N}(\mathbf{0}, \mathbf{\Sigma})$, then

$$
q_{h+1} = \sum_{i=1}^{h} \mathrm{Tr}(\mathbf{\Sigma} \mathbf{V}_i)
\tag{7.32}
$$

We can compute $\mathbf{V}_h$ and q_h up to any horizon h starting from $\mathbf{V}_1 = \mathbf{R}_s$ and $q_1 = 0$ and iterating using equations (7.30) and (7.31). The optimal action for an h-step policy comes directly from equation (7.29):

$$
\pi_h(\mathbf{s}) = -\left(\mathbf{T}_a^\top \mathbf{V}_{h-1} \mathbf{T}_a + \mathbf{R}_a\right)^{-1} \mathbf{T}_a^\top \mathbf{V}_{h-1} \mathbf{T}_s \mathbf{s}
\tag{7.33}
$$

Note that the optimal action is independent of the zero-mean disturbance distribution.[25] The variance of the disturbance, however, does affect the expected utility. Algorithm 7.11 provides an implementation. Example 7.4 demonstrates this process on a simple problem with linear Gaussian dynamics.

[25] In this case, we can replace the random disturbances with its expected value without changing the optimal policy. This property is known as *certainty equivalence*.

7.9   Summary

- Discrete MDPs with bounded rewards can be solved exactly through dynamic programming.

```
struct LinearQuadraticProblem
    Ts # transition matrix with respect to state
    Ta # transition matrix with respect to action
    Rs # reward matrix with respect to state (negative semidefinite)
    Ra # reward matrix with respect to action (negative definite)
    h_max # horizon
end

function solve(𝒫::LinearQuadraticProblem)
    Ts, Ta, Rs, Ra, h_max = 𝒫.Ts, 𝒫.Ta, 𝒫.Rs, 𝒫.Ra, 𝒫.h_max
    V = zeros(size(Rs))
    πs = Any[s → zeros(size(Ta, 2))]
    for h in 2:h_max
        V = Ts'*(V - V*Ta*((Ta'*V*Ta + Ra) \ Ta'*V))*Ts + Rs
        L = -(Ta'*V*Ta + Ra) \ Ta' * V * Ts
        push!(πs, s → L*s)
    end
    return πs
end
```

Algorithm 7.11. A method that computes an optimal policy for an h_max-step horizon MDP with stochastic linear dynamics parameterized by matrices Ts and Ta and quadratic reward parameterized by matrices Rs and Ra. The method returns a vector of policies where entry h produces the optimal first action in an h-step policy.

- Policy evaluation for such problems can be done exactly through matrix inversion or can be approximated by an iterative algorithm.

- Policy iteration can be used to solve for optimal policies by iterating between policy evaluation and policy improvement.

- Value iteration and asynchronous value iteration save computation by directly iterating the value function.

- The problem of finding an optimal policy can be framed as a linear program and solved in polynomial time.

- Continuous problems with linear transition functions and quadratic rewards can be solved exactly.

7.10   Exercises

Exercise 7.1. Show that for an infinite sequence of constant rewards ($r_t = r$ for all t), the infinite horizon discounted return converges to $r/(1 - \gamma)$.

Consider a continuous MDP where the state is composed of a scalar position and velocity $s = [x, v]$. Actions are scalar accelerations a that are each executed over a time step $\Delta t = 1$. Find an optimal five-step policy from $s_0 = [-10, 0]$, given a quadratic reward:

$$R(\mathbf{s}, a) = -x^2 - v^2 - 0.5a^2$$

such that the system tends toward rest at $s = \mathbf{0}$.

The transition dynamics are

$$\begin{bmatrix} x' \\ v' \end{bmatrix} = \begin{bmatrix} x + v\Delta t + \frac{1}{2}a\Delta t^2 + w_1 \\ v + a\Delta t + w_2 \end{bmatrix} = \begin{bmatrix} 1 & \Delta t \\ 0 & 1 \end{bmatrix} \begin{bmatrix} x \\ v \end{bmatrix} + \begin{bmatrix} 0.5\Delta t^2 \\ \Delta t \end{bmatrix} [a] + \mathbf{w}$$

where $\mathbf{w}$ is drawn from a zero-mean multivariate Gaussian distribution with covariance $0.1\mathbf{I}$.

The reward matrices are $\mathbf{R}_s = -\mathbf{I}$ and $\mathbf{R}_a = -[0.5]$.

The resulting optimal policies are:

$$\pi_1(\mathbf{s}) = \begin{bmatrix} 0 & 0 \end{bmatrix} \mathbf{s}$$

$$\pi_2(\mathbf{s}) = \begin{bmatrix} -0.286 & -0.857 \end{bmatrix} \mathbf{s}$$

$$\pi_3(\mathbf{s}) = \begin{bmatrix} -0.462 & -1.077 \end{bmatrix} \mathbf{s}$$

$$\pi_4(\mathbf{s}) = \begin{bmatrix} -0.499 & -1.118 \end{bmatrix} \mathbf{s}$$

$$\pi_5(\mathbf{s}) = \begin{bmatrix} -0.504 & -1.124 \end{bmatrix} \mathbf{s}$$

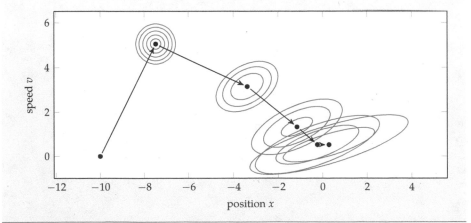

Example 7.4. Solving a finite horizon MDP with a linear transition function and quadratic reward. The illustration shows the progression of the system from $[-10, 0]$. The blue contour lines show the Gaussian distributions over the state at each iteration. The initial belief is circular, but it gets distorted to a noncircular shape as we propagate the belief forward using the Kalman filter.

Solution: We can prove that the infinite sequence of discounted constant rewards converges to $r/(1-\gamma)$ in the following steps:

$$\sum_{t=1}^{\infty} \gamma^{t-1} r_t = r + \gamma^1 r + \gamma^2 r + \cdots$$

$$= r + \gamma \sum_{t=1}^{\infty} \gamma^{t-1} r_t$$

We can move the summation to the left side and factor out $(1-\gamma)$:

$$(1-\gamma) \sum_{t=1}^{\infty} \gamma^{t-1} r = r$$

$$\sum_{t=1}^{\infty} \gamma^{t-1} r = \frac{r}{1-\gamma}$$

Exercise 7.2. Suppose we have an MDP consisting of five states, $s_{1:5}$, and two actions, to stay (a_S) and continue (a_C). We have the following:

$$T(s_i \mid s_i, a_S) = 1 \text{ for } i \in \{1,2,3,4\}$$
$$T(s_{i+1} \mid s_i, a_C) = 1 \text{ for } i \in \{1,2,3,4\}$$
$$T(s_5 \mid s_5, a) = 1 \text{ for all actions } a$$
$$R(s_i, a) = 0 \text{ for } i \in \{1,2,3,5\} \text{ and for all actions } a$$
$$R(s_4, a_S) = 0$$
$$R(s_4, a_C) = 10$$

What is the discount factor γ if the optimal value $U^*(s_1) = 1$?

Solution: The optimal value of $U^*(s_1)$ is associated with following the optimal policy π^* starting from s_1. Given the transition model, the optimal policy from s_1 is to continue until reaching s_5, which is a terminal state where we can no longer transition to another state or accumulate additional reward. Thus, the optimal value of s_1 can be computed as

$$U^*(s_1) = \sum_{t=1}^{\infty} \gamma^{t-1} r_t$$
$$U^*(s_1) = R(s_1, a_C) + \gamma^1 R(s_2, a_C) + \gamma^2 R(s_3, a_C) + \gamma^3 R(s_4, a_C) + \gamma^4 R(s_5, a_C) + \cdots$$
$$U^*(s_1) = 0 + \gamma^1 \times 0 + \gamma^2 \times 0 + \gamma^3 \times 10 + \gamma^4 \times 0 + 0$$
$$1 = 10\gamma^3$$

Thus, the discount factor is $\gamma = 0.1^{1/3} \approx 0.464$.

Exercise 7.3. What is the time complexity of performing k steps of iterative policy evaluation?

Solution: Iterative policy evaluation requires computing the lookahead equation:

$$U_{k+1}^\pi(s) = R(s, \pi(s)) + \gamma \sum_{s'} T(s' \mid s, \pi(s)) U_k^\pi(s')$$

Updating the value at a single state requires summing over all $|\mathcal{S}|$ states. For a single iteration over all states, we must do this operation $|\mathcal{S}|$ times. Thus, the time complexity of k steps of iterative policy evaluation is $O(k|\mathcal{S}|^2)$.

Exercise 7.4. Suppose that we have an MDP with six states, $s_{1:6}$, and four actions, $a_{1:4}$. Using the following tabular form of the action value function $Q(s, a)$, compute $U(s), \pi(s)$, and $A(s, a)$.

$Q(s, a)$	a_1	a_2	a_3	a_4
s_1	0.41	0.46	0.37	0.37
s_2	0.50	0.55	0.46	0.37
s_3	0.60	0.50	0.38	0.44
s_4	0.41	0.50	0.33	0.41
s_5	0.50	0.60	0.41	0.39
s_6	0.71	0.70	0.61	0.59

Solution: We can compute $U(s), \pi(s)$, and $A(s, a)$ using the following equations:

$$U(s) = \max_a Q(s, a) \qquad \pi(s) = \arg\max_a Q(s, a) \qquad A(s, a) = Q(s, a) - U(s)$$

s	$U(s)$	$\pi(s)$	$A(s, a_1)$	$A(s, a_2)$	$A(s, a_3)$	$A(s, a_4)$
s_1	0.46	a_2	−0.05	0.00	−0.09	−0.09
s_2	0.55	a_2	−0.05	0.00	−0.09	−0.18
s_3	0.60	a_1	0.00	−0.10	−0.22	−0.16
s_4	0.50	a_2	−0.09	0.00	−0.17	−0.09
s_5	0.60	a_2	−0.10	0.00	−0.19	−0.21
s_6	0.71	a_1	0.00	−0.01	−0.10	−0.12

Exercise 7.5. Suppose that we have a three-tile, straight-line hex world (appendix F.1) where the rightmost tile is an absorbing state. When we take any action in the rightmost state, we get a reward of 10 and we are transported to a fourth terminal state where we no longer receive any reward. Use a discount factor of $\gamma = 0.9$, and perform a single step of policy iteration where the initial policy π has us move east in the first tile, northeast in the second tile, and southwest in the third tile. For the policy evaluation step, write out the transition matrix $\mathbf{T}^\pi$ and the reward vector $\mathbf{R}^\pi$, and then solve the infinite horizon value function $\mathbf{U}^\pi$ directly using matrix inversion. For the policy improvement step, compute the updated policy π' by maximizing the lookahead equation.

Solution: For the policy evaluation step, we use equation (7.10), repeated here:

$$\mathbf{U}^\pi = (\mathbf{I} - \gamma \mathbf{T}^\pi)^{-1} \mathbf{R}^\pi$$

Forming the transition matrix $\mathbf{T}^\pi$ and reward vector $\mathbf{R}^\pi$ with an additional state for the terminal state, we can solve for the infinite horizon value function $\mathbf{U}^\pi$:[26]

$$\mathbf{U}^\pi = \left(\begin{bmatrix} 1 & 0 & 0 & 0 \\ 0 & 1 & 0 & 0 \\ 0 & 0 & 1 & 0 \\ 0 & 0 & 0 & 1 \end{bmatrix} - (0.9) \begin{bmatrix} 0.3 & 0.7 & 0 & 0 \\ 0 & 0.85 & 0.15 & 0 \\ 0 & 0 & 0 & 1 \\ 0 & 0 & 0 & 1 \end{bmatrix} \right)^{-1} \begin{bmatrix} -0.3 \\ -0.85 \\ 10 \\ 0 \end{bmatrix} \approx \begin{bmatrix} 1.425 \\ 2.128 \\ 10 \\ 0 \end{bmatrix}$$

For the policy improvement step, we apply equation (7.11) using the updated value function. The actions in the arg max term correspond to $a_E, a_{NE}, a_{NW}, a_W, a_{SW},$ and a_{SE}:

$$\pi(s_1) = \arg\max(1.425, 0.527, 0.283, 0.283, 0.283, 0.527) = a_E$$
$$\pi(s_2) = \arg\max(6.575, 2.128, 0.970, 1.172, 0.970, 2.128) = a_E$$
$$\pi(s_3) = \arg\max(10, 10, 10, 10, 10, 10) \text{ (all actions are equally desirable)}$$

Exercise 7.6. Perform two steps of value iteration to the problem in exercise 7.5, starting with an initial value function $U_0(s) = 0$ for all s.

Solution: We need to use the Bellman backup (equation (7.16)) to iteratively update the value function. The actions in the max term correspond to $a_E, a_{NE}, a_{NW}, a_W, a_{SW},$ and a_{SE}. For our first iteration, the value function is zero for all states, so we only need to consider the reward component:

$$U_1(s_1) = \max(-0.3, -0.85, -1, -1, -1, -0.85) = -0.3$$
$$U_1(s_2) = \max(-0.3, -0.85, -0.85, -0.3, -0.85, -0.85) = -0.3$$
$$U_1(s_3) = \max(10, 10, 10, 10, 10, 10) = 10$$

For the second iteration,

$$U_2(s_1) = \max(-0.57, -1.12, -1.27, -1.27, -1.27, -1.12) = -0.57$$
$$U_2(s_2) = \max(5.919, 0.271, -1.12, -0.57, -1.12, 0.271) = 5.919$$
$$U_2(s_3) = \max(10, 10, 10, 10, 10, 10) = 10$$

Exercise 7.7. Apply one sweep of asynchronous value iteration to the problem in exercise 7.5, starting with an initial value function $U_0(s) = 0$ for all s. Update the states from right to left.

The hex world problem defines $R(s, a, s')$, so in order to produce entries for $\mathbf{R}^\pi$, we must compute

$$R(s, a) = \sum_{s'} T(s' \mid s, a) R(s, a, s')$$

For example, -0.3 comes from the 30% chance that moving east causes a collision with the border, with cost -1.

Solution: We use the Bellman backup (equation (7.16)) to iteratively update the value function over each state following our ordering. The actions in the max term correspond to $a_E, a_{NE}, a_{NW}, a_W, a_{SW},$ and a_{SE}:

$$U(s_3) = \max(10, 10, 10, 10, 10, 10) = 10$$
$$U(s_2) = \max(6, 0.5, -0.85, -0.3, -0.85, 0.5) = 6$$
$$U(s_1) = \max(3.48, -0.04, -1, -1, -1, -0.04) = 3.48$$

Exercise 7.8. Prove that a Bellman residual of δ guarantees that the value function obtained by value iteration is within $\delta\gamma/(1-\gamma)$ of $U^*(s)$ at every state s.

Solution: For a given U_k, suppose we know that $\|U_k - U_{k-1}\|_\infty < \delta$. Then we bound the improvement in the next iteration:

$$U_{k+1}(s) - U_k(s) = \max_a\left(R(s,a) + \gamma\sum_{s'} T(s' \mid s,a)U_k(s')\right)$$
$$- \max_a\left(R(s,a) + \gamma\sum_{s'} T(s' \mid s,a)U_{k-1}(s')\right)$$
$$< \max_a\left(R(s,a) + \gamma\sum_{s'} T(s' \mid s,a)U_k(s')\right)$$
$$- \max_a\left(R(s,a) + \gamma\sum_{s'} T(s' \mid s,a)(U_k(s') - \delta)\right)$$
$$= \delta\gamma$$

Similarly,

$$U_{k+1}(s) - U_k(s) > \max_a\left(R(s,a) + \gamma\sum_{s'} T(s' \mid s,a)U_k(s')\right)$$
$$- \max_a\left(R(s,a) + \gamma\sum_{s'} T(s' \mid s,a)(U_k(s') + \delta)\right)$$
$$= -\delta\gamma$$

The accumulated improvement after infinite iterations is thus bounded by

$$\|U^*(s) - U_k(s)\|_\infty < \sum_{i=1}^\infty \delta\gamma^i = \frac{\delta\gamma}{1-\gamma}$$

A Bellman residual of δ thus guarantees that the optimal value function obtained by value iteration is within $\delta\gamma/(1-\gamma)$ of U^*.

Exercise 7.9. Suppose that we run policy evaluation on an expert policy to obtain a value function. If acting greedily with respect to that value function is equivalent to the expert policy, what can we deduce about the expert policy?

Solution: We know from the Bellman optimality equation that greedy lookahead on an optimal value function is stationary. If the greedy policy matches the expert policy, then the greedy policy is optimal.

Exercise 7.10. Show how an LQR problem with a quadratic reward function $R(\mathbf{s}, \mathbf{a}) = \mathbf{s}^\top \mathbf{R}_s \mathbf{s} + \mathbf{a}^\top \mathbf{R}_a \mathbf{a}$ can be reformulated so that the reward function includes linear terms in $\mathbf{s}$ and $\mathbf{a}$.

Solution: We can introduce an additional state dimension that is always equal to 1, yielding a new system with linear dynamics:

$$\begin{bmatrix} \mathbf{s}' \\ 1 \end{bmatrix} = \begin{bmatrix} \mathbf{T}_s & \mathbf{0} \\ \mathbf{0}^\top & 1 \end{bmatrix} \begin{bmatrix} \mathbf{s} \\ 1 \end{bmatrix} + \mathbf{T}_a \mathbf{a}$$

The reward function of the augmented system can now have linear state reward terms:

$$\begin{bmatrix} \mathbf{s} \\ 1 \end{bmatrix}^\top \mathbf{R}_{\text{augmented}} \begin{bmatrix} \mathbf{s} \\ 1 \end{bmatrix} = \mathbf{s}^\top \mathbf{R}_s \mathbf{s} + 2 \mathbf{r}_{s,\text{linear}}^\top \mathbf{s} + r_{s,\text{scalar}}$$

Similarly, we can include an additional action dimension that is always 1 in order to obtain linear action reward terms.

Exercise 7.11. Why does the optimal policy obtained in example 7.4 produce actions with greater magnitude when the horizon is greater?

Solution: The problem in example 7.4 has quadratic reward that penalizes deviations from the origin. The longer the horizon, the greater the negative reward that can be accumulated, making it more worthwhile to reach the origin sooner.

Exercise 7.12. Prove that iterative policy evaluation converges to the solution of equation (7.6).

Solution: Consider iterative policy evaluation applied to a policy π as given in equation (7.5):

$$U_{k+1}^\pi(s) = R(s, \pi(s)) + \gamma \sum_{s'} T(s' \mid s, \pi(s)) U_k^\pi(s')$$

Let us define an operator B_π and rewrite this as $U_{k+1}^\pi = B_\pi U_k^\pi$. We can show that B_π is a contraction mapping:

$$B_\pi U^\pi(s) = R(s, \pi(s)) + \gamma \sum_{s'} T(s' \mid s, \pi(s)) U^\pi(s')$$

$$= R(s, \pi(s)) + \gamma \sum_{s'} T(s' \mid s, \pi(s))(U^\pi(s') - \hat{U}^\pi(s') + \hat{U}^\pi(s'))$$

$$= B_\pi \hat{U}^\pi(s) + \gamma \sum_{s'} T(s' \mid s, \pi(s))(U^\pi(s') - \hat{U}^\pi(s'))$$

$$\leq B_\pi \hat{U}^\pi(s) + \gamma \| U^\pi - \hat{U}^\pi \|_\infty$$

Hence, $\| B_\pi U^\pi - B_\pi \hat{U}^\pi \|_\infty \leq \alpha \| U^\pi - \hat{U}^\pi \|_\infty$ for $\alpha = \gamma$, implying that B_π is a contraction mapping. As discussed in appendix A.15, $\lim_{t \to \infty} B_\pi^t U_1^\pi$ converges to a unique fixed point U^π, for which $U^\pi = B_\pi U^\pi$.

Exercise 7.13. Prove that value iteration converges to a unique solution.

Solution: The value iteration update (equation (7.16)) is

$$U^{k+1}(s) = \max_a \left(R(s, a) + \gamma \sum_{s'} T(s' \mid s, a) U_k(s') \right)$$

We will denote the Bellman operator as B and rewrite an application of the Bellman backup as $U_{k+1} = BU_k$. As with the previous problem, if B is a contraction mapping, then repeated application of B to U will converge to a unique fixed point.

We can show that B is a contraction mapping:

$$BU(s) = \max_a \left(R(s, a) + \gamma \sum_{s'} T(s' \mid s, a) U(s') \right)$$

$$= \max_a \left(R(s, a) + \gamma \sum_{s'} T(s' \mid s, a)(U(s') - \hat{U}(s') + \hat{U}(s')) \right)$$

$$\leq B\hat{U}(s) + \gamma \max_a \sum_{s'} T(s' \mid s, a)(U(s') - \hat{U}(s'))$$

$$\leq B\hat{U}(s) + \alpha \| U - \hat{U} \|_\infty$$

for $\alpha = \gamma \max_s \max_a \sum_{s'} T(s' \mid s, a)$, with $0 \leq \alpha < 1$. Hence, $\| BU - B\hat{U} \|_\infty \leq \alpha \| U - \hat{U} \|_\infty$, which implies that B is a contraction mapping.

Exercise 7.14. Show that the point to which value iteration converges corresponds to the optimal value function.

Solution: Let U be the value function produced by value iteration. We want to show that $U = U^*$. At convergence, we have $BU = U$. Let U_0 be a value function that maps all states to 0. For any policy π, it follows from the definition of B_π that $B_\pi U_0 \leq BU_0$. Similarly, $B_\pi^t U_0 \leq B^t U_0$. Because $B_{\pi^*}^t U_0 \to U^*$ and $B^t U_0 \to U$ as $t \to \infty$, it follows that $U^* \leq U$, which can be the case only if $U = U^*$.

Exercise 7.15. Suppose that we have a linear Gaussian problem with disturbance $\mathbf{w} \sim \mathcal{N}(\mathbf{0}, \boldsymbol{\Sigma})$ and quadratic reward. Show that the scalar term in the utility function has the form:

$$q_{h+1} = \sum_{i=1}^{h} \mathbb{E}_{\mathbf{w}}\left[\mathbf{w}^{\top} \mathbf{V}_i \mathbf{w}\right] = \sum_{i=1}^{\cdot h} \mathrm{Tr}(\boldsymbol{\Sigma} \mathbf{V}_i)$$

You may want to use the *trace trick*:

$$\mathbf{x}^{\top} \mathbf{A} \mathbf{x} = \mathrm{Tr}\left(\mathbf{x}^{\top} \mathbf{A} \mathbf{x}\right) = \mathrm{Tr}\left(\mathbf{A} \mathbf{x} \mathbf{x}^{\top}\right)$$

Solution: This equation is true if $\mathbb{E}_{\mathbf{w}}\left[\mathbf{w}^{\top} \mathbf{V}_i \mathbf{w}\right] = \mathrm{Tr}(\boldsymbol{\Sigma} \mathbf{V}_i)$. Our derivation is

$$\begin{aligned}
\mathbb{E}_{\mathbf{w}\sim\mathcal{N}(0,\boldsymbol{\Sigma})}\left[\mathbf{w}^{\top} \mathbf{V}_i \mathbf{w}\right] &= \mathbb{E}_{\mathbf{w}\sim\mathcal{N}(0,\boldsymbol{\Sigma})}\left[\mathrm{Tr}\left(\mathbf{w}^{\top} \mathbf{V}_i \mathbf{w}\right)\right] \\
&= \mathbb{E}_{\mathbf{w}\sim\mathcal{N}(0,\boldsymbol{\Sigma})}\left[\mathrm{Tr}\left(\mathbf{V}_i \mathbf{w} \mathbf{w}^{\top}\right)\right] \\
&= \mathrm{Tr}\left(\mathbb{E}_{\mathbf{w}\sim\mathcal{N}(0,\boldsymbol{\Sigma})}\left[\mathbf{V}_i \mathbf{w} \mathbf{w}^{\top}\right]\right) \\
&= \mathrm{Tr}\left(\mathbf{V}_i \mathbb{E}_{\mathbf{w}\sim\mathcal{N}(0,\boldsymbol{\Sigma})}\left[\mathbf{w} \mathbf{w}^{\top}\right]\right) \\
&= \mathrm{Tr}(\mathbf{V}_i \boldsymbol{\Sigma}) \\
&= \mathrm{Tr}(\boldsymbol{\Sigma} \mathbf{V}_i)
\end{aligned}$$

Exercise 7.16. What is the role of the scalar term q in the LQR optimal value function, as given in equation (7.31)?

$$q_{h+1} = \sum_{i=1}^{h} \mathbb{E}_{\mathbf{w}}\left[\mathbf{w}^{\top} \mathbf{V}_i \mathbf{w}\right]$$

Solution: A matrix $\mathbf{M}$ is positive definite if, for all nonzero $\mathbf{x}$, $\mathbf{x}^{\top} \mathbf{M} \mathbf{x} > 0$. In equation (7.31), every $\mathbf{V}_i$ is negative semidefinite, so $\mathbf{w}^{\top} \mathbf{V} \mathbf{w} \leq 0$ for all $\mathbf{w}$. Thus, these q terms are guaranteed to be nonpositive. This should be expected, as it is impossible to obtain positive reward in LQR problems, and we seek instead to minimize cost.

The q scalars are offsets in the quadratic optimal value function:

$$U(\mathbf{s}) = \mathbf{s}^{\top} \mathbf{V} \mathbf{s} + q$$

Each q represents the baseline reward around which the $\mathbf{s}^{\top} \mathbf{V} \mathbf{s}$ term fluctuates. We know that $\mathbf{V}$ is negative definite, so $\mathbf{s}^{\top} \mathbf{V} \mathbf{s} \leq 0$, and q thus represents the expected reward that one could obtain if one were at the origin, $\mathbf{s} = \mathbf{0}$.

8   Approximate Value Functions

Up to this point, we have assumed that the value function can be represented as a table. Tables are useful representations only for small, discrete problems. Problems with larger state spaces may require an infeasible amount of memory, and the exact methods discussed in the previous chapter may require an infeasible amount of computation. For such problems, we often have to resort to *approximate dynamic programming*, where the solution may not be exact.[1] One way to approximate solutions is to use *value function approximation*, which is the subject of this chapter. We will discuss different approaches to approximating the value function and how to incorporate dynamic programming to derive approximately optimal policies.

[1] A deeper treatment of this topic is provided by W. B. Powell, *Approximate Dynamic Programming: Solving the Curses of Dimensionality*, 2nd ed. Wiley, 2011. Relevant insights can be drawn from a variety of fields as discussed by W. B. Powell, *Reinforcement Learning and Stochastic Optimization*. Wiley, 2022.

8.1   Parametric Representations

We will use $U_\theta(s)$ to denote our *parametric representation* of the value function, where θ is the vector of *parameters*. There are many ways to represent $U_\theta(s)$, several of which will be mentioned later in this chapter. Assuming that we have such an approximation, we can extract an action according to

$$\pi(s) = \arg\max_a \left(R(s,a) + \gamma \sum_{s'} T(s' \mid s, a) U_\theta(s') \right) \qquad (8.1)$$

Value function approximations are often used in problems with continuous state spaces, in which case the summation above may be replaced with an integral. The integral can be approximated using transition model samples.

An alternative to the computation in equation (8.1) is to approximate the action value function $Q(s,a)$. If we use $Q_\theta(s,a)$ to represent our parametric approximation, we can obtain an action according to

$$\pi(s) = \arg\max_a Q_\theta(s,a) \qquad (8.2)$$

This chapter discusses how we can apply dynamic programming at a finite set of states $S = s_{1:m}$ to arrive at a parametric approximation of the value function over the full state space. Different schemes can be used to generate this set. If the state space is relatively low-dimensional, we can define a grid. Another approach is to use random sampling from the state space. However, some states are more likely to be encountered than others and are therefore more important in constructing the value function. We can bias the sampling toward more important states by running simulations with some policy (perhaps initially random), from a plausible set of initial states.

An iterative approach can be used to enhance our approximation of the value function at the states in S. We alternate between improving our value estimates at S through dynamic programming and refitting our approximation at those states. Algorithm 8.1 provides an implementation where the dynamic programming step consists of Bellman backups as done in value iteration (see section 7.5). A similar algorithm can be created for action value approximations Q_θ.[2]

[2] Several other categories of approaches for optimizing value function approximations are surveyed by A. Geramifard, T. J. Walsh, S. Tellex, G. Chowdhary, N. Roy, and J. P. How, "A Tutorial on Linear Function Approximators for Dynamic Programming and Reinforcement Learning," *Foundations and Trends in Machine Learning*, vol. 6, no. 4, pp. 375–451, 2013.

```
struct ApproximateValueIteration
    Uθ      # initial parameterized value function that supports fit!
    S       # set of discrete states for performing backups
    k_max   # maximum number of iterations
end

function solve(M::ApproximateValueIteration, 𝒫::MDP)
    Uθ, S, k_max = M.Uθ, M.S, M.k_max
    for k in 1:k_max
        U = [backup(𝒫, Uθ, s) for s in S]
        fit!(Uθ, S, U)
    end
    return ValueFunctionPolicy(𝒫, Uθ)
end
```

Algorithm 8.1. Approximate value iteration for an MDP with the parameterized value function approximation Uθ. We perform backups (defined in algorithm 7.7) at the states in S to obtain a vector of utilities U. We then call fit!(Uθ, S, U), which modifies the parametric representation Uθ to better match the value of the states in S to the utilities in U. Different parametric approximations have different implementations for fit!.

All of the parametric representations discussed in this chapter can be used with algorithm 8.1. To be used with that algorithm, a representation needs to support the evaluation of U_θ and the fitting of U_θ to estimates of the utilities at the points in S.

We can group the parametric representations into two categories. The first category includes *local approximation* methods, where θ corresponds to the values at the states in S. To evaluate $U_\theta(s)$ at an arbitrary state s, we take a weighted sum of the values stored in S. The second category includes *global approximation* methods, where θ is not directly related to the values at the states in S. In fact, θ may have far fewer or even far more components than there are states in S.

Both local approximation and many global approximations can be viewed as a *linear function approximation* $U_\theta(s) = \theta^\top \beta(s)$, where methods differ in how they define the vector function β. In local approximation methods, $\beta(s)$ determines how to weight the utilities of the states in S to approximate the utility at state s. The weights are generally nonnegative and sum to 1. In many global approximation methods, $\beta(s)$ is viewed as a set of basis functions that are combined in a linear fashion to obtain an approximation for an arbitrary s.

We can also approximate the action value function using a linear function, $Q_\theta(s, a) = \theta^\top \beta(s, a)$. In the context of local approximations, we can provide approximations over continuous action spaces by choosing a finite set of actions $A \subset \mathcal{A}$. Our parameter vector θ would then consist of $|S| \times |A|$ components, each corresponding to a state-action value. Our function $\beta(s, a)$ would return a vector with the same number of components that specifies how to weight together our finite set of state-action values to obtain an estimate of the utility associated with state s and action a.

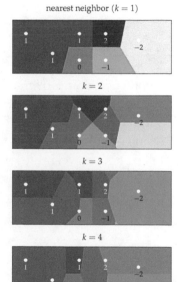

nearest neighbor ($k = 1$)

$k = 2$

$k = 3$

$k = 4$

8.2   Nearest Neighbor

A simple approach to local approximation is to use the value of the state in S that is the *nearest neighbor* of s. In order to use this approach, we need a *distance metric* (see appendix A.3). We use $d(s, s')$ to denote the distance between two states s and s'. The approximate value function is then $U_\theta(s) = \theta_i$, where $i = \arg\min_{j \in 1:m} d(s_j, s)$. Figure 8.1 shows an example of a value function represented using the nearest neighbor scheme.

We can generalize this approach to average together the values of the *k-nearest neighbors*. This approach still results in piecewise constant value functions, but different values for k can result in better approximations. Figure 8.1 shows examples of value functions approximated with different values for k. Algorithm 8.2 provides an implementation of this.

Figure 8.1. Approximating the values of states in a two-dimensional, continuous state space using the mean of the utility values of their k-nearest neighbors according to Euclidean distance. The resulting value function is piecewise constant.

```
mutable struct NearestNeighborValueFunction
    k # number of neighbors
    d # distance function d(s, s')
    S # set of discrete states
    θ # vector of values at states in S
end

function (Uθ::NearestNeighborValueFunction)(s)
    dists = [Uθ.d(s,s') for s' in Uθ.S]
    ind = sortperm(dists)[1:Uθ.k]
    return mean(Uθ.θ[i] for i in ind)
end

function fit!(Uθ::NearestNeighborValueFunction, S, U)
    Uθ.θ = U
    return Uθ
end
```

Algorithm 8.2.   The k-nearest neighbors method, which approximates the value of a state s based on the k closest states in S, as determined by a distance function d. The vector θ contains the values of the states in S. Greater efficiency can be achieved by using specialized data structures, such as kd-trees, implemented in `NearestNeighbors.jl`.

8.3   Kernel Smoothing

Another local approximation method is *kernel smoothing,* where the utilities of the states in S are smoothed over the entire state space. This method requires defining a *kernel function* $k(s, s')$ that relates pairs of states s and s'. We generally want $k(s, s')$ to be higher for states that are closer together because those values tell us how to weight together the utilities associated with the states in S. This method results in the following linear approximation:

$$U_\theta(s) = \sum_{i=1}^{m} \theta_i \beta_i(s) = \theta^\top \beta(s) \tag{8.3}$$

where

$$\beta_i(s) = \frac{k(s, s_i)}{\sum_{j=1}^{m} k(s, s_j)} \tag{8.4}$$

Algorithm 8.3 provides an implementation of this.

There are many ways that we can define a kernel function. We can define our kernel to simply be the inverse of the distance between states:

$$k(s, s') = \max(d(s, s'), \epsilon)^{-1} \tag{8.5}$$

where ϵ is a small positive constant in order to avoid dividing by zero when $s = s'$. Figure 8.2 shows value approximations using several distance functions. As we can see, kernel smoothing can result in smooth value function approximations, in contrast with k-nearest neighbors. Figure 8.3 applies this kernel to a discrete hex world problem and shows the outcome of a few iterations of approximate value iteration (algorithm 8.1). Figure 8.4 shows a value function and policy learned for the mountain car problem (appendix F.4) with a continuous state space.

Another common kernel is the *Gaussian kernel*:

$$k(s, s') = \exp\left(-\frac{d(s, s')^2}{2\sigma^2}\right) \tag{8.6}$$

where σ controls the degree of smoothing.

$d(\mathbf{s}, \mathbf{s}') = \|\mathbf{s} - \mathbf{s}'\|_1$

$d(\mathbf{s}, \mathbf{s}') = \|\mathbf{s} - \mathbf{s}'\|_2^2$

$d(\mathbf{s}, \mathbf{s}') = \exp(\|\mathbf{s} - \mathbf{s}'\|_2^2)$

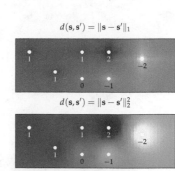

Figure 8.2. Approximating the values of states in a two-dimensional continuous state space by assigning values based on proximity to several states with known values. Approximations are constructed using several distance functions.

```
mutable struct LocallyWeightedValueFunction
    k # kernel function k(s, s')
    S # set of discrete states
    θ # vector of values at states in S
end

function (Uθ::LocallyWeightedValueFunction)(s)
    w = normalize([Uθ.k(s,s') for s' in Uθ.S], 1)
    return Uθ.θ · w
end

function fit!(Uθ::LocallyWeightedValueFunction, S, U)
    Uθ.θ = U
    return Uθ
end
```

Algorithm 8.3. Locally weighted value function approximation defined by a kernel function k and a vector of utilities θ at states in S.

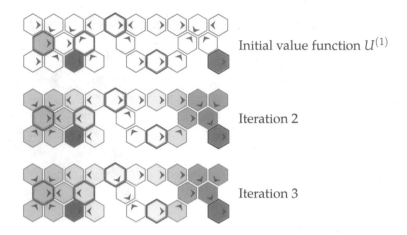

Initial value function $U^{(1)}$

Iteration 2

Iteration 3

Figure 8.3. Local approximation value iteration used to iteratively improve an approximate value function on the hex world problem. The five outlined states are used to approximate the value function. The value of the remaining states are approximated using the distance function $\|\mathbf{s} - \mathbf{s}'\|_2^2$. The resulting policy is reasonable but nevertheless suboptimal. Positive reward is shown in blue, and negative reward is shown in red.

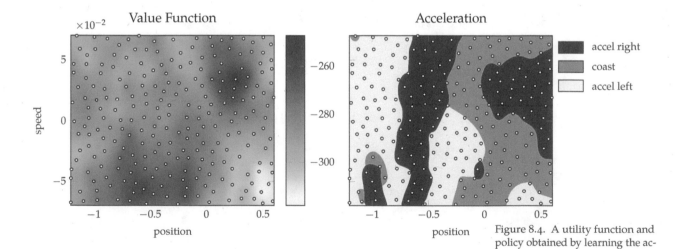

Figure 8.4. A utility function and policy obtained by learning the action values for a finite set of states (white) in the mountain car problem using the distance function $\|\mathbf{s} - \mathbf{s}'\|_2 + 0.1$.

8.4   Linear Interpolation

Linear interpolation is another common approach to local approximation. The one-dimensional case is straightforward, in which the approximated value for a state s between two states s_1 and s_2 is

$$U_\theta(s) = \alpha\theta_1 + (1 - \alpha)\theta_2 \tag{8.7}$$

with $\alpha = (s_2 - s)/(s_2 - s_1)$. This case is shown in figures 8.5 and 8.6.

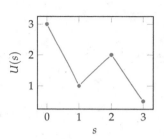

Figure 8.5. One-dimensional linear interpolation produces interpolated values along the line segment connecting two points.

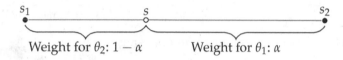

Figure 8.6. The weight assigned to each point in one dimension is proportional to the length of the segment on the opposite side of the interpolation state.

Linear interpolation can be extended to a multidimensional grid. In the two-dimensional case, called *bilinear interpolation*, we interpolate among four vertices. Bilinear interpolation is done through single-dimensional linear interpolation, once in each axis, requiring the utility of four states at the grid vertices. This interpolation is shown in figure 8.7.

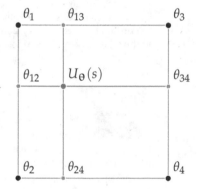

$\theta_{12} = $ 1D interpolation between θ_1 and θ_2 along the vertical axis
$\theta_{24} = $ 1D interpolation between θ_2 and θ_4 along the horizontal axis
$\theta_{13} = $ 1D interpolation between θ_1 and θ_3 along the horizontal axis
$\theta_{34} = $ 1D interpolation between θ_3 and θ_4 along the vertical axis

$$U_\theta(s) = \begin{cases} \text{1D interpolation between } \theta_{12} \text{ and } \theta_{34} \text{ along the horizontal axis} \\ \qquad\qquad\qquad\qquad\qquad \text{or} \\ \text{1D interpolation between } \theta_{13} \text{ and } \theta_{24} \text{ along the vertical axis} \end{cases}$$

Figure 8.7. Linear interpolation on a two-dimensional grid is achieved through linear interpolation on each axis in turn, in either order.

Given four vertices with coordinates $s_1 = [x_1, y_1]$, $s_2 = [x_1, y_2]$, $s_3 = [x_2, y_1]$, and $s_4 = [x_2, y_2]$, and a sample state $s = [x, y]$, the interpolated value is

$$U_\theta(s) = \alpha\theta_{12} + (1-\alpha)\theta_{34} \tag{8.8}$$

$$= \frac{x_2 - x}{x_2 - x_1}\theta_{12} + \frac{x - x_1}{x_2 - x_1}\theta_{34} \tag{8.9}$$

$$= \frac{x_2 - x}{x_2 - x_1}(\alpha\theta_1 + (1-\alpha)\theta_2) + \frac{x - x_1}{x_2 - x_1}(\alpha\theta_3 + (1-\alpha)\theta_4) \tag{8.10}$$

$$= \frac{x_2 - x}{x_2 - x_1}\left(\frac{y_2 - y}{y_2 - y_1}\theta_1 + \frac{y - y_1}{y_2 - y_1}\theta_2\right) + \frac{x - x_1}{x_2 - x_1}\left(\frac{y_2 - y}{y_2 - y_1}\theta_3 + \frac{y - y_1}{y_2 - y_1}\theta_4\right) \tag{8.11}$$

$$= \frac{(x_2 - x)(y_2 - y)}{(x_2 - x_1)(y_2 - y_1)}\theta_1 + \frac{(x_2 - x)(y - y_1)}{(x_2 - x_1)(y_2 - y_1)}\theta_2 + \frac{(x - x_1)(y_2 - y)}{(x_2 - x_1)(y_2 - y_1)}\theta_3 + \frac{(x - x_1)(y - y_1)}{(x_2 - x_1)(y_2 - y_1)}\theta_4 \tag{8.12}$$

The resulting interpolation weighs each vertex according to the area of its opposing quadrant, as shown in figure 8.8.

Multilinear interpolation in d dimensions is similarly achieved by linearly interpolating along each axis, requiring 2^d vertices. Here too, the utility of each vertex is weighted according to the volume of the opposing hyperrectangle. Multilinear interpolation is implemented in algorithm 8.4. Figure 8.9 demonstrates this approach on a two-dimensional state space.

8.5   Simplex Interpolation

Multilinear interpolation can be inefficient in high dimensions. Rather than weighting the contributions of 2^d points, *simplex interpolation* considers only $d + 1$ points in the neighborhood of a given state to produce a continuous surface that matches the known sample points.

We start with a multidimensional grid and divide each cell into $d!$ *simplexes*, which are multidimensional generalizations of triangles defined by the *convex hull* of $d + 1$ vertices. This process is known as *Coxeter-Freudenthal-Kuhn triangulation*,[3] and it ensures that any two simplexes that share a face will produce equivalent values across the face, thus producing continuity when interpolating, as shown in figure 8.10.

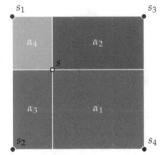

Figure 8.8. Linear interpolation on a two-dimensional grid results in a contribution of each vertex equal to the relative area of its opposing quadrant: $U_\theta(s) = \alpha_1\theta_1 + \alpha_2\theta_2 + \alpha_3\theta_3 + \alpha_4\theta_4$.

Figure 8.9. Two-dimensional linear interpolation over a 3×7 grid.

[3] A. W. Moore, "Simplicial Mesh Generation with Applications," Ph.D. dissertation, Cornell University, 1992.

```julia
mutable struct MultilinearValueFunction
    o # position of lower-left corner
    δ # vector of widths
    θ # vector of values at states in S
end

function (Uθ::MultilinearValueFunction)(s)
    o, δ, θ = Uθ.o, Uθ.δ, Uθ.θ
    Δ = (s - o)./δ
    # Multidimensional index of lower-left cell
    i = min.(floor.(Int, Δ) .+ 1, size(θ) .- 1)
    vertex_index = similar(i)
    d = length(s)
    u = 0.0
    for vertex in 0:2^d-1
        weight = 1.0
        for j in 1:d
            # Check whether jth bit is set
            if vertex & (1 << (j-1)) > 0
                vertex_index[j] = i[j] + 1
                weight *= Δ[j] - i[j] + 1
            else
                vertex_index[j] = i[j]
                weight *= i[j] - Δ[j]
            end
        end
        u += θ[vertex_index...]*weight
    end
    return u
end

function fit!(Uθ::MultilinearValueFunction, S, U)
    Uθ.θ = U
    return Uθ
end
```

Algorithm 8.4. A method for conducting multilinear interpolation to estimate the value of state vector s for known state values θ over a grid defined by a lower-left vertex o and vector of widths δ. Vertices of the grid can all be written o + δ.*i for some nonnegative integral vector i. The package `Interpolations.jl` also provides multilinear and other interpolation methods.

To illustrate, suppose that we have translated and scaled the cell containing a state such that the lowest vertex is **0** and the diagonally opposite vertex is **1**. There is a simplex for each permutation of $1:d$. The simplex given by permutation **p** is the set of points **x** satisfying

$$0 \leq x_{p_1} \leq x_{p_2} \leq \cdots \leq x_{p_d} \leq 1 \tag{8.13}$$

Figure 8.11 shows the simplexes obtained for the unit cube.

Simplex interpolation first translates and scales a state vector **s** to the unit hypercube of its corresponding cell to obtain **s'**. It then sorts the entries in **s'** to determine which simplex contains **s'**. The utility at **s'** can then be expressed by a unique linear combination of the vertices of that simplex.

Example 8.1 provides an example of simplex interpolation. The process is implemented in algorithm 8.5.

Consider a three-dimensional simplex given by the permutation $\mathbf{p} = [3, 1, 2]$ such that points within the simplex satisfy $0 \leq x_3 \leq x_1 \leq x_2 \leq 1$. This simplex has vertices $(0,0,0)$, $(0,1,0)$, $(1,1,0)$, and $(1,1,1)$.

Any point **s** belonging to the simplex can thus be expressed by a weighting of the vertices:

$$\begin{bmatrix} s_1 \\ s_2 \\ s_3 \end{bmatrix} = w_1 \begin{bmatrix} 0 \\ 0 \\ 0 \end{bmatrix} + w_2 \begin{bmatrix} 0 \\ 1 \\ 0 \end{bmatrix} + w_3 \begin{bmatrix} 1 \\ 1 \\ 0 \end{bmatrix} + w_4 \begin{bmatrix} 1 \\ 1 \\ 1 \end{bmatrix}$$

We can determine the values of the last three weights in succession:

$$w_4 = s_3 \qquad w_3 = s_1 - w_4 \qquad w_2 = s_2 - w_3 - w_4$$

We obtain w_1 by enforcing that the weights sum to 1.
If $\mathbf{s} = [0.3, 0.7, 0.2]$, then the weights are

$$w_4 = 0.2 \qquad w_3 = 0.1 \qquad w_2 = 0.4 \qquad w_1 = 0.3$$

Figure 8.10. Two-dimensional simplex interpolation over a 3×7 grid.

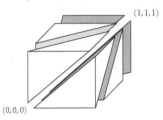

Figure 8.11. A triangulation of a unit cube. Based on figure 2.1 of A. W. Moore, "Simplicial Mesh Generation with Applications," Ph.D. dissertation, Cornell University, 1992.

Example 8.1. Simplex interpolation in three dimensions.

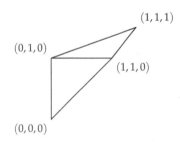

```julia
mutable struct SimplexValueFunction
    o # position of lower-left corner
    δ # vector of widths
    θ # vector of values at states in S
end

function (Uθ::SimplexValueFunction)(s)
    Δ = (s - Uθ.o)./Uθ.δ
    # Multidimensional index of upper-right cell
    i = min.(floor.(Int, Δ) .+ 1, size(Uθ.θ) .- 1) .+ 1
    u = 0.0
    s′ = (s - (Uθ.o + Uθ.δ.*(i.-2))) ./ Uθ.δ
    p = sortperm(s′) # increasing order
    w_tot = 0.0
    for j in p
        w = s′[j] - w_tot
        u += w*Uθ.θ[i...]
        i[j] -= 1
        w_tot += w
    end
    u += (1 - w_tot)*Uθ.θ[i...]
    return u
end

function fit!(Uθ::SimplexValueFunction, S, U)
    Uθ.θ = U
    return Uθ
end
```

Algorithm 8.5. A method for conducting simplex interpolation to estimate the value of state vector s for known state values θ over a grid defined by a lower-left vertex o and a vector of widths δ. Vertices of the grid can all be written o + δ.*i for some nonnegative integral vector i. Simplex interpolation is also implemented in the general `GridInterpolations.jl` package.

8.6   Linear Regression

A simple global approximation approach is *linear regression*, where $U_\theta(s)$ is a linear combination of *basis functions*, also commonly referred to as *features*. These basis functions are generally a nonlinear function of the state s and are combined into a vector function $\beta(s)$ or $\beta(s,a)$, resulting in the approximations

$$U_\theta(s) = \theta^\top \beta(s) \qquad Q_\theta(s,a) = \theta^\top \beta(s,a) \qquad (8.14)$$

Although our approximation is linear with respect to the basis functions, the resulting approximation may be nonlinear with respect to the underlying state variables. Figure 8.12 illustrates this concept. Example 8.2 provides an example of global linear value approximation using polynomial basis functions for the continuous mountain car problem, resulting in a nonlinear value function approximation with respect to the state variables.

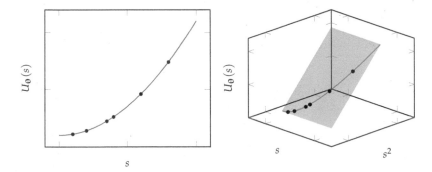

Figure 8.12. Linear regression with nonlinear basis functions is linear in higher dimensions. Here, polynomial regression can be seen as linear in a three-dimensional space. The function exists in the plane formed from its bases, but it does not occupy the entire plane because the terms are not independent.

Adding more basis functions generally improves the ability to match the target utilities at the states in S, but too many basis functions can lead to poor approximations at other states. Principled methods exist for choosing an appropriate set of basis functions for our regression model.[4]

Fitting linear models involves determining the vector θ that minimizes the squared error of the predictions at the states in $S = s_{1:m}$. If the utilities associated with those states are denoted as $u_{1:m}$, then we want to find the θ that minimizes

$$\sum_{i=1}^{m}(\hat{U}_\theta(s_i) - u_i)^2 = \sum_{i=1}^{m}(\theta^\top \beta(s_i) - u_i)^2 \qquad (8.15)$$

[4] See chapter 14 of M. J. Kochenderfer and T. A. Wheeler, *Algorithms for Optimization*. MIT Press, 2019. or chapter 7 of T. Hastie, R. Tibshirani, and J. Friedman, *The Elements of Statistical Learning: Data Mining, Inference, and Prediction*, 2nd ed. Springer Series in Statistics, 2001.

We can approximate the value function for the mountain car problem using a linear approximation. The problem has a continuous state space with two dimensions consisting of position x and speed v. Here are the basis functions up to degree six:

$$\beta(s) = \begin{matrix} [1, \\ x, & v, \\ x^2, & xv, & v^2, \\ x^3, & x^2v, & xv^2, & v^3, \\ x^4, & x^3v, & x^2v^2, & xv^3, & v^4, \\ x^5, & x^4v, & x^3v^2, & x^2v^3, & xv^4, & v^5, \\ x^6, & x^5v, & x^4v^2, & x^3v^3, & x^2v^4, & xv^5, & v^6] \end{matrix}$$

Here is a plot of an approximate value function fit to state-value pairs from an expert policy:

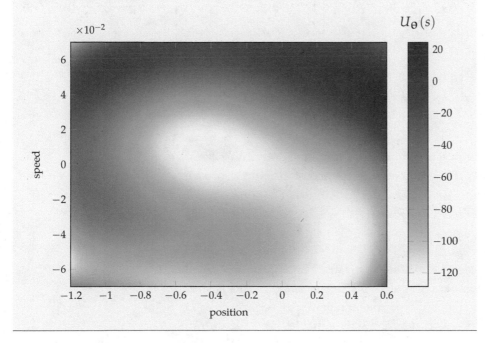

Example 8.2. Using a linear approximation to the mountain car value function. The choice of basis functions makes a big difference. The optimal value function for the mountain car is nonlinear, with a spiral shape and discontinuities. Even sixth-degree polynomials do not produce a perfect fit.

The optimal θ can be computed through some simple matrix operations. We first construct a matrix $\mathbf{X}$ where each of the m rows $\mathbf{X}_{i,:}$ contains $\beta(s_i)^\top$.[5] It can be shown that the value of θ that minimizes the squared error is

$$\theta = \left(\mathbf{X}^\top\mathbf{X}\right)^{-1}\mathbf{X}^\top u_{1:m} = \mathbf{X}^+ u_{1:m} \tag{8.16}$$

where $\mathbf{X}^+$ is the *Moore-Penrose pseudoinverse* of matrix $\mathbf{X}$. The pseudoinverse is often implemented by first computing the *singular value decomposition*, $\mathbf{X} = \mathbf{U}\Sigma\mathbf{U}^*$. We then have

$$\mathbf{X}^+ = \mathbf{U}\Sigma^+\mathbf{U}^* \tag{8.17}$$

The pseudoinverse of the diagonal matrix Σ is obtained by taking the reciprocal of each nonzero element of the diagonal and then transposing the result.

Figure 8.13 shows how the utilities of states in S are fit with several basis function families. Different choices of basis functions result in different errors.

[5] For an overview of the mathematics involved in linear regression as well as more advanced techniques, see T. Hastie, R. Tibshirani, and J. Friedman, *The Elements of Statistical Learning: Data Mining, Inference, and Prediction,* 2nd ed. Springer Series in Statistics, 2001.

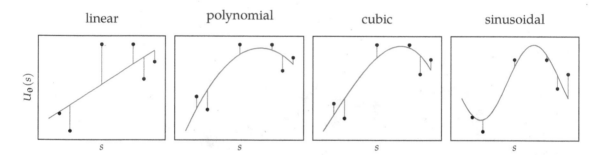

Figure 8.13. Linear regression with different basis function families.

Algorithm 8.6 provides an implementation for evaluating and fitting linear regression models of the value function. Example 8.3 demonstrates this approach with the mountain car problem.

8.7   Neural Network Regression

Neural network regression relieves us of having to construct an appropriate set of basis functions as required in linear regression. Instead, a *neural network* is used to represent our value function. For a review of neural networks, see appendix D. The input to the neural network would be the state variables, and the output would be the utility estimate. The parameters θ would correspond to the *weights* in the neural network.

```
mutable struct LinearRegressionValueFunction
    β # basis vector function
    θ # vector of parameters
end

function (Uθ::LinearRegressionValueFunction)(s)
    return Uθ.β(s) ⋅ Uθ.θ
end

function fit!(Uθ::LinearRegressionValueFunction, S, U)
    X = hcat([Uθ.β(s) for s in S]...)'
    Uθ.θ = pinv(X)*U
    return Uθ
end
```

Algorithm 8.6. Linear regression value function approximation, defined by a basis vector function β and a vector of parameters θ. The function `pinv` implements the psuedoinverse. Julia and other languages support the *backslash* operator, which allows us to write `X \ U` in place of `pinv(X)*U` in the `fit!` function.

As discussed in appendix D, we can optimize the network weights to achieve a particular objective. In the context of approximate dynamic programming, we would want to minimize the error of our predictions, just as we did in the previous section. However, minimizing the squared error cannot be done through simple matrix operations. Instead, we generally have to rely on optimization techniques such as gradient descent. Fortunately, computing the gradient of neural networks can be done exactly through straightforward application of the derivative chain rule.

8.8 Summary

- For large or continuous problems, we can attempt to find approximate policies represented by parameterized models of the value function.

- The approaches taken in this chapter involve iteratively applying steps of dynamic programming at a finite set of states and refining our parametric approximation.

- Local approximation techniques approximate the value function based on the values of nearby states with known values.

- A variety of local approximation techniques include nearest neighbor, kernel smoothing, linear interpolation, and simplex interpolation.

- Global approximation techniques include linear regression and neural network regression.

We can apply linear regression to learn a value function for the mountain car problem. The optimal value function has the form of a spiral, which can be difficult to approximate with polynomial basis functions (see example 8.2). We use Fourier basis functions whose components take the following form:

$$b_0(x) = 1/2$$
$$b_{s,i}(x) = \sin(2\pi i x/T) \text{ for } i = 1, 2, \dots$$
$$b_{c,i}(x) = \cos(2\pi i x/T) \text{ for } i = 1, 2, \dots$$

where T is the width of the component's domain. The multidimensional Fourier basis functions are all combinations of the one-dimensional components across the state-space axes. Here we use an eighth-order approximation, so i ranges up to 8. The expert policy is to accelerate in the direction of motion.

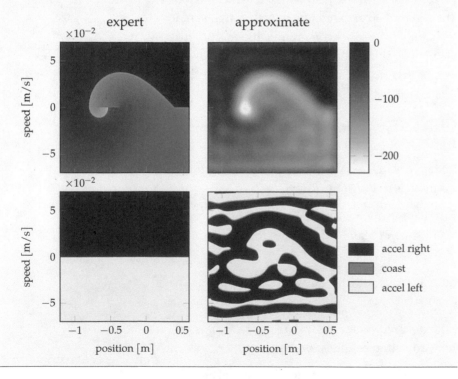

Example 8.3.   Linear regression using Fourier bases used to approximate the value function for the mountain car problem (appendix F.4). Value functions (top row) and resulting policies (bottom row) are shown. The globally approximated value function is a poor fit despite using eighth-order Fourier basis functions. The resulting approximate policy is not a close approximation to the expert policy. The small time step in the mountain car problem causes even small changes in the value function landscape to affect the policy. Optimal utility functions often have complex geometries that can be difficult to capture with global basis functions.

- Nonlinear utility functions can be obtained when using linear regression when combined with an appropriate selection of nonlinear basis functions.

- Neural network regression relieves us of having to specify basis functions, but fitting them is more complex and generally requires us to use gradient descent to tune our parametric approximation of the value function.

8.9 Exercises

Exercise 8.1. The value function approximation methods presented in this chapter have mostly assumed continuous state spaces. The hex world problem, appendix F.1, is discrete, but most of its states can be mapped to two-dimensional locations. It does, however, have an additional terminal state that produces zero reward, which does not have a two-dimensional location. How can one modify the continuous value function approximation methods in this chapter to handle such a state?

Solution: The hex world problem has the agent navigate through a two-dimensional hexagonal grid. However, the agent can enter a single terminal state from one of several grid hexes. This single terminal state presents a challenge for value function approximation methods, which often rely on proximity to infer a state's value.

While the terminal state could be projected to the same state space as the other states, perhaps far away, this hack would nevertheless force a form of proximity into the terminal state's value calculation. Selecting a single position for a state that should be equidistant to multiple predecessor states introduces bias.

One alternative is to treat the terminal state as a special case. The kernel function could be modified to produce infinite distance between the terminal state and any other states.

Another option is to adjust the problem to have a terminal state for every hex that produces a terminal reward. Each terminal state can be coincident with its predecessor state, but offset in an additional dimension. This transformation maintains proximity at the expense of additional states.

Exercise 8.2. A tabular representation is a special case of linear approximate value functions. Show how, for any discrete problem, a tabular representation can be framed as a linear approximate value function.

Solution: Consider a discrete MDP with m states $s_{1:m}$ and n actions $a_{1:n}$. A tabular representation associates a value with each state or state-action pair. We can recover the same behavior using a linear approximate value function. We associate an indicator function with each state or state-action pair, whose value is 1 when the input is the given state or state-action pair and 0 otherwise:

$$\beta_i(s) = (s = s_i) = \begin{cases} 1 & \text{if } s = s_i \\ 0 & \text{otherwise} \end{cases}$$

or

$$\beta_{ij}(s,a) - ((s,a) = (s_i,a_j)) = \begin{cases} 1 & \text{if } (s,a) = (s_i,a_j) \\ 0 & \text{otherwise} \end{cases}$$

Exercise 8.3. Suppose that we have a problem with continuous state and action spaces and we would like to construct both a local approximation and a global approximation of the action value function $Q(s,a) = \theta^\top \beta(s,a)$. For global approximation, we choose the basis functions

$$\beta(s,a) = \left[1, s, a, s^2, sa, a^2\right]$$

Given a set of 100 states $S = s_{1:100}$ and a set of five actions $A = a_{1:5}$, how many parameters are in θ for a local approximation method? How many parameters are in θ for the specified global approximation method?

Solution: In local approximation methods, the state-action values are the parameters. We will have $|S| \times |A| = 100 \times 5 = 500$ parameters in θ. In global approximation methods, the coefficients of the basis functions are the parameters. Since there are six components in $\beta(s,a)$, we will have six parameters in θ.

Exercise 8.4. We are given the states $s_1 = (4,5)$, $s_2 = (2,6)$, and $s_3 = (-1,-1)$, and their corresponding values, $U(s_1) = 2$, $U(s_2) = 10$, and $U(s_3) = 30$. Compute the value at state $s = (1,2)$ using 2-nearest neighbor local approximation with an L_1 distance metric, with an L_2 distance metric, and with an L_∞ distance metric.

Solution: We tabulate the distances from s to the points $s' \in S$ as given here:

$s' \in S$	L_1	L_2	L_∞
$s_1 = (4,5)$	6	$\sqrt{18}$	3
$s_2 = (2,6)$	5	$\sqrt{17}$	4
$s_3 = (-1,-1)$	5	$\sqrt{13}$	3

Using the L_1 norm, we estimate $U(s) = (10+30)/2 = 20$. Using the L_2 norm, we estimate $U(s) = (10+30)/2 = 20$. Using the L_∞ norm, we estimate $U(s) = (2+30)/2 = 16$.

Exercise 8.5. We would like to estimate the value at a state s given the values at a set of two states $S = \{s_1,s_2\}$. If we want to use local approximation value iteration, which of the following weighting functions are valid? If they are invalid, how could the weighting functions be modified to make them valid?

- $\beta(s) = [1,1]$
- $\beta(s) = [1-\lambda,\lambda]$ where $\lambda \in [0,1]$
- $\beta(s) = \left[e^{(s-s_1)^2}, e^{(s-s_2)^2}\right]$

Solution: The first set of weighting functions is not valid, as it violates the constraint $\sum_i \beta_i(s) = 1$. We can modify the weighting functions by normalizing them by their sum:

$$\beta(s) = \left[\tfrac{1}{1+1}, \tfrac{1}{1+1}\right] = \left[\tfrac{1}{2}, \tfrac{1}{2}\right]$$

The second set of weighting functions is valid. The third set of weighting functions is not valid, as it violates the constraint $\sum_i \beta_i(s) = 1$. We can modify the weighting functions by normalizing them by their sum:

$$\beta(s) = \left[\frac{e^{(s-s_1)^2}}{e^{(s-s_1)^2}+e^{(s-s_2)^2}}, \frac{e^{(s-s_2)^2}}{e^{(s-s_1)^2}+e^{(s-s_2)^2}}\right]$$

Exercise 8.6. Prove that bilinear interpolation is invariant under (nonzero) linear grid scaling.

Solution: It is straightforward to show that the interpolated value is invariant to a linear scaling on one or both axes, such as, $\tilde{U}_\theta(\tilde{s}) = U_\theta(s)$. We show this by substituting all x- and y-values by their scaled versions $\tilde{x} = \beta x$ and $\tilde{y} = \gamma y$, and showing that the grid scalings cancel out:

$$\tilde{U}_\theta(\tilde{s}) = \frac{(\tilde{x}_2 - \tilde{x})(\tilde{y}_2 - \tilde{y})}{(\tilde{x}_2 - \tilde{x}_1)(\tilde{y}_2 - \tilde{y}_1)}\theta_1 + \frac{(\tilde{x}_2 - \tilde{x})(\tilde{y} - \tilde{y}_1)}{(\tilde{x}_2 - \tilde{x}_1)(\tilde{y}_2 - \tilde{y}_1)}\theta_2 + \frac{(\tilde{x} - \tilde{x}_1)(\tilde{y}_2 - \tilde{y})}{(\tilde{x}_2 - \tilde{x}_1)(\tilde{y}_2 - \tilde{y}_1)}\theta_3 + \frac{(\tilde{x} - \tilde{x}_1)(\tilde{y} - \tilde{y}_1)}{(\tilde{x}_2 - \tilde{x}_1)(\tilde{y}_2 - \tilde{y}_1)}\theta_4$$

$$\tilde{U}_\theta(\tilde{s}) = \frac{\beta(x_2 - x)\gamma(y_2 - y)}{\beta(x_2 - x_1)\gamma(y_2 - y_1)}\theta_1 + \frac{\beta(x_2 - x)\gamma(y - y_1)}{\beta(x_2 - x_1)\gamma(y_2 - y_1)}\theta_2 + \frac{\beta(x - x_1)\gamma(y_2 - y)}{\beta(x_2 - x_1)\gamma(y_2 - y_1)}\theta_3 + \frac{\beta(x - x_1)\gamma(y - y_1)}{\beta(x_2 - x_1)\gamma(y_2 - y_1)}\theta_4$$

$$\tilde{U}_\theta(\tilde{s}) = \frac{(x_2 - x)(y_2 - y)}{(x_2 - x_1)(y_2 - y_1)}\theta_1 + \frac{(x_2 - x)(y - y_1)}{(x_2 - x_1)(y_2 - y_1)}\theta_2 + \frac{(x - x_1)(y_2 - y)}{(x_2 - x_1)(y_2 - y_1)}\theta_3 + \frac{(x - x_1)(y - y_1)}{(x_2 - x_1)(y_2 - y_1)}\theta_4$$

$$\tilde{U}_\theta(\tilde{s}) = U_\theta(s)$$

Exercise 8.7. Given the four states $s_1 = [0,5]$, $s_2 = [0,25]$, $s_3 = [1,5]$, and $s_4 = [1,25]$, and a sample state $s = [0.7, 10]$, generate the interpolant equation $U_\theta(s)$ for arbitrary θ.

Solution: The general form for bilinear interpolation is given in equation (8.12) and reproduced here. To generate the interpolant, we substitute our values into the equation and simplify:

$$U_\theta(s) = \frac{(x_2 - x)(y_2 - y)}{(x_2 - x_1)(y_2 - y_1)}\theta_1 + \frac{(x_2 - x)(y - y_1)}{(x_2 - x_1)(y_2 - y_1)}\theta_2 + \frac{(x - x_1)(y_2 - y)}{(x_2 - x_1)(y_2 - y_1)}\theta_3 + \frac{(x - x_1)(y - y_1)}{(x_2 - x_1)(y_2 - y_1)}\theta_4$$

$$U_\theta(s) = \frac{(1 - 0.7)(25 - 10)}{(1 - 0)(25 - 5)}\theta_1 + \frac{(1 - 0.7)(10 - 5)}{(1 - 0)(25 - 5)}\theta_2 + \frac{(0.7 - 0)(25 - 10)}{(1 - 0)(25 - 5)}\theta_3 + \frac{(0.7 - 0)(10 - 5)}{(1 - 0)(25 - 5)}\theta_4$$

$$U_\theta(s) = \frac{9}{40}\theta_1 + \frac{3}{40}\theta_2 + \frac{21}{40}\theta_3 + \frac{7}{40}\theta_4$$

Exercise 8.8. Following example 8.1, what are the simplex interpolant weights for a state $s = [0.4, 0.95, 0.6]$?

Solution: For the given state $\mathbf{s}$, we have $0 \leq x_1 \leq x_3 \leq x_2 \leq 1$, and so our permutation vector is $\mathbf{p} = [1, 3, 2]$. The vertices of our simplex can be generated by starting from $(0, 0, 0)$ and changing each 0 to a 1 in reverse order of the permutation vector. Thus, the vertices of the simplex are $(0, 0, 0)$, $(0, 1, 0)$, $(0, 1, 1)$, and $(1, 1, 1)$.

Any point $\mathbf{s}$ belonging to the simplex can thus be expressed by a weighting of the vertices:

$$\begin{bmatrix} s_1 \\ s_2 \\ s_3 \end{bmatrix} = w_1 \begin{bmatrix} 0 \\ 0 \\ 0 \end{bmatrix} + w_2 \begin{bmatrix} 0 \\ 1 \\ 0 \end{bmatrix} + w_3 \begin{bmatrix} 0 \\ 1 \\ 1 \end{bmatrix} + w_4 \begin{bmatrix} 1 \\ 1 \\ 1 \end{bmatrix}$$

We can determine the values of the weights in reverse order, finally solving for w_1 by applying the constraint that the weights must sum to 1. We can then compute the weights for $\mathbf{s} = [0.4, 0.95, 0.6]$:

$w_4 = s_1$	$w_3 = s_3 - w_4$	$w_2 = s_2 - w_3 - w_4$	$w_1 = 1 - w_2 - w_3 - w_4$
$w_4 = 0.4$	$w_3 = 0.2$	$w_2 = 0.35$	$w_1 = 0.05$

9 *Online Planning*

The solution methods we have discussed so far compute policies offline, before any actions are executed in the real problem. Even offline approximation methods can be intractable in many high-dimensional problems. This chapter discusses *online planning* methods that find actions based on reasoning about states that are reachable from the current state. The *reachable state space* is often orders of magnitude smaller than the full state space, which can significantly reduce storage and computational requirements compared to offline methods. We will discuss a variety of algorithms that aim to make online planning efficient, including pruning the state space, sampling, and planning more deeply along trajectories that appear more promising.

9.1 *Receding Horizon Planning*

In *receding horizon planning*, we plan from the current state to a maximum fixed horizon or depth d. We then execute the action from our current state, transition to the next state, and replan. The online planning methods discussed in this chapter follow this receding horizon planning scheme. They differ in how they explore different courses of action.

A challenge in applying receding horizon planning is determining the appropriate depth. Deeper planning generally requires more computation. For some problems, a shallow depth can be quite effective; the fact that we replan at each step can compensate for our lack of longer-term modeling. In other problems, greater planning depths may be necessary so that our planner can be driven toward goals or away from unsafe states, as illustrated in example 9.1.

Suppose we want to apply receding horizon planning to aircraft collision avoidance. The objective is to provide descend or climb advisories when necessary to avoid collision. A collision occurs when our altitude relative to the intruder h is within $\pm 50\,$m and the time to potential collision t_{col} is zero. We want to plan deeply enough so that we can provide an advisory sufficiently early to avoid collision with a high degree of confidence. The plots here show the actions that would be taken by a receding horizon planner with different depths.

Example 9.1.   Receding horizon planning for collision avoidance to different planning depths. In this problem, there are four state variables. These plots show slices of the state space under the assumption that the aircraft is currently level and there has not yet been an advisory. The horizontal axis is the time to collision t_{col}, and the vertical axis is our altitude h relative to the intruder. Appendix F.6 provides additional details about this problem.

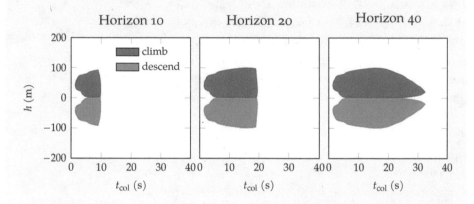

If the depth is $d = 10$, we provide advisories only within 10 s of collision. Due to the limitations of the vehicle dynamics and the uncertainty of the behavior of the other aircraft, providing advisories this late compromises safety. With $d = 20$, we can do better, but there are cases where we would want to alert a little earlier to further reduce collision risk. There is no motivation to plan deeper than $d = 40$ because we do not need to advise any maneuvers that far ahead of potential collision.

9.2   Lookahead with Rollouts

Chapter 8 involved extracting policies that are greedy with respect to an approximate value function U through the use of one-step lookahead.[1] A simple online strategy involves acting greedily with respect to values estimated through simulation to depth d. To run a simulation, we need a policy to simulate. Of course, we do not know the optimal policy, but we can use what is called a *rollout policy* instead. Rollout policies are typically stochastic, with actions drawn from a distribution $a \sim \pi(s)$. To produce these rollout simulations, we use a *generative model* $s' \sim T(s, a)$ to generate successor states s' from the distribution $T(s' \mid s, a)$. This generative model can be implemented through draws from a random number generator, which can be easier to implement in practice compared to explicitly representing the distribution $T(s' \mid s, a)$.

Algorithm 9.1 combines one-step lookahead with values estimated through rollout. This approach often results in better behavior than that of the original rollout policy, but optimality is not guaranteed. It can be viewed as an approximate form of policy improvement used in the policy iteration algorithm (section 7.4). A simple variation of this algorithm is to use multiple rollouts to arrive at a better estimate of the expected discounted return. If we run m simulations for each action and resulting state, the time complexity is $O(m \times |\mathcal{A}| \times |\mathcal{S}| \times d)$.

> [1] The lookahead strategy was originally introduced in algorithm 7.2 as part of our discussion of exact solution methods.

9.3   Forward Search

Forward search determines the best action to take from an initial state s by expanding all possible transitions up to depth d. These expansions form a *search tree*.[2] Such search trees have a worst-case branching factor of $|\mathcal{S}| \times |\mathcal{A}|$, yielding a computational complexity of $O((|\mathcal{S}| \times |\mathcal{A}|)^d)$. Figure 9.1 shows a search tree applied to a problem with three states and two actions. Figure 9.2 visualizes the states visited during forward search on the hex world problem.

Algorithm 9.2 calls itself recursively to the specified depth. Once reaching the specified depth, it uses an estimate of the utility provided by the function U. If we simply want to plan to the specified horizon, we set $U(s) = 0$. If our problem requires planning beyond the depth that we can afford to compute online, we can use an estimate of the value function obtained offline using, for example, one of the value function approximations described in the previous chapter. Combining

> [2] The exploration of the tree occurs as a *depth-first search*. Appendix E reviews depth-first search and other standard search algorithms in the deterministic context.

```
struct RolloutLookahead
    𝒫 # problem
    π # rollout policy
    d # depth
end

randstep(𝒫::MDP, s, a) = 𝒫.TR(s, a)

function rollout(𝒫, s, π, d)
    ret = 0.0
    for t in 1:d
        a = π(s)
        s, r = randstep(𝒫, s, a)
        ret += 𝒫.γ^(t-1) * r
    end
    return ret
end

function (π::RolloutLookahead)(s)
    U(s) = rollout(π.𝒫, s, π.π, π.d)
    return greedy(π.𝒫, U, s).a
end
```

Algorithm 9.1. A function that runs a rollout of policy π in problem 𝒫 from state s to depth d. It returns the total discounted reward. This function can be used with the greedy function (introduced in algorithm 7.5) to generate an action that is likely to be an improvement over the original rollout policy. We will use this algorithm later for problems other than MDPs, requiring us to only have to modify randstep appropriately.

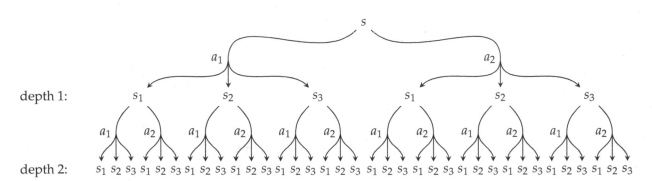

Figure 9.1. A forward search tree for a problem with three states and two actions.

online and offline approaches in this way is sometimes referred to as *hybrid planning*.

```
struct ForwardSearch
    𝒫 # problem
    d # depth
    U # value function at depth d
end

function forward_search(𝒫, s, d, U)
    if d ≤ 0
        return (a=nothing, u=U(s))
    end
    best = (a=nothing, u=-Inf)
    U′(s) = forward_search(𝒫, s, d-1, U).u
    for a in 𝒫.𝒜
        u = lookahead(𝒫, U′, s, a)
        if u > best.u
            best = (a=a, u=u)
        end
    end
    return best
end

(π::ForwardSearch)(s) = forward_search(π.𝒫, s, π.d, π.U).a
```

Algorithm 9.2. The forward search algorithm for finding an approximately optimal action online for a problem 𝒫 from a current state s. The search is performed to depth d, at which point the terminal value is estimated with an approximate value function U. The returned named tuple consists of the best action a and its finite-horizon expected value u. The problem type is not constrained to be an MDP; section 22.2 uses this same algorithm in the context of partially observable problems with a different implementation for lookahead.

9.4 Branch and Bound

Branch and bound (algorithm 9.3) attempts to avoid the exponential computational complexity of forward search. It prunes branches by reasoning about bounds on the value function. The algorithm requires knowing a lower bound on the value function $\underline{U}(s)$ and an upper bound on the action value function $\overline{Q}(s, a)$. The lower bound is used to evaluate the states at the maximum depth. This lower bound is propagated upward through the tree through Bellman updates. If we find that the upper bound of an action at a state is lower than the lower bound of a previously explored action from that state, then we need not explore that action, allowing us to *prune* the associated subtree from consideration.

Branch and bound will give the same result as forward search, but it can be more efficient depending on how many branches are pruned. The worst-case complexity of branch and bound is still the same as forward search. To facilitate

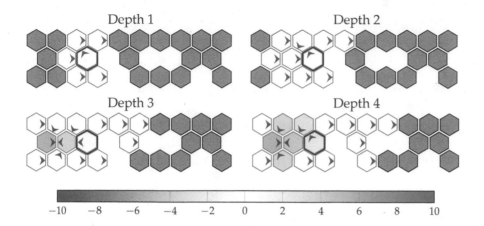

Figure 9.2. Forward search applied to the hex world problem with four maximum depths. The search can visit a node multiple times. The actions and colors for visited states were chosen according to the shallowest, highest-value node in the search tree for that state. The initial state has an additional black border.

```
struct BranchAndBound
    𝒫   # problem
    d   # depth
    Ulo # lower bound on value function at depth d
    Qhi # upper bound on action value function
end

function branch_and_bound(𝒫, s, d, Ulo, Qhi)
    if d ≤ 0
        return (a=nothing, u=Ulo(s))
    end
    U'(s) = branch_and_bound(𝒫, s, d-1, Ulo, Qhi).u
    best = (a=nothing, u=-Inf)
    for a in sort(𝒫.𝒜, by=a→Qhi(s,a), rev=true)
        if Qhi(s, a) < best.u
            return best # safe to prune
        end
        u = lookahead(𝒫, U', s, a)
        if u > best.u
            best = (a=a, u=u)
        end
    end
    return best
end

(π::BranchAndBound)(s) = branch_and_bound(π.𝒫, s, π.d, π.Ulo, π.Qhi).a
```

Algorithm 9.3. The branch and bound algorithm for finding an approximately optimal action online for a discrete MDP 𝒫 from a current state s. The search is performed to depth d with value function lower bound Ulo and action value function upper bound Qhi. The returned named tuple consists of the best action a and its finite-horizon expected value u. This algorithm is also used for POMDPs.

pruning, actions are traversed in descending order by upper bound. Tighter bounds will generally result in more pruning, as shown in example 9.2.

Consider applying branch and bound to the mountain car problem. We can use the value function of a heuristic policy for the lower bound $\underline{U}(s)$, such as a heuristic policy that always accelerates in the direction of motion. For our upper bound $\overline{Q}([x,v],a)$, we can use the return expected when accelerating toward the goal with no hill. Branch and bound visits about a third as many states as forward search.

Example 9.2. Branch and bound applied to the mountain car problem (appendix F.4). Branch and bound can achieve a significant speedup over forward search.

9.5 Sparse Sampling

A method known as *sparse sampling*[3] (algorithm 9.4) attempts to reduce the branching factor of forward search and branch and bound. Instead of branching on all possible next states, we consider only a limited number of samples of the next state. Although the sampling of the next state results in an approximation, this method can work well in practice and can significantly reduce computation. If we draw m samples of the next state for each action node in the search tree, the computational complexity is $O\left((m \times |\mathcal{A}|)^d\right)$, which is still exponential in the depth but no longer depends on the size of the state space. Figure 9.3 shows an example.

[3] M. J. Kearns, Y. Mansour, and A. Y. Ng, "A Sparse Sampling Algorithm for Near-Optimal Planning in Large Markov Decision Processes," *Machine Learning*, vol. 49, no. 2–3, pp. 193–208, 2002.

9.6 Monte Carlo Tree Search

Monte Carlo tree search (algorithm 9.5) avoids the exponential complexity in the horizon by running m simulations from the current state.[4] During these simulations, the algorithm updates estimates of the action value function $Q(s,a)$ and a record of the number of times a particular state-action pair has been selected, $N(s,a)$. After running these m simulations from our current state s, we simply choose the action that maximizes our estimate of $Q(s,a)$.

A simulation (algorithm 9.6) begins by traversing the explored state space, consisting of the states for which we have estimates of Q and N. We follow an exploration strategy to choose actions from the various states. A common approach is to select the action that maximizes the *UCB1 exploration heuristic*:[5]

[4] For a survey, see C. B. Browne, E. Powley, D. Whitehouse, S. M. Lucas, P. I. Cowling, P. Rohlfshagen, S. Tavener, D. Perez, S. Samothrakis, and S. Colton, "A Survey of Monte Carlo Tree Search Methods," *IEEE Transactions on Computational Intelligence and AI in Games*, vol. 4, no. 1, pp. 1–43, 2012.

[5] UCB stands for upper confidence bound. This is one of many strategies discussed by P. Auer, N. Cesa-Bianchi, and P. Fischer, "Finite-Time Analysis of the Multiarmed Bandit Problem," *Machine Learning*, vol. 47, no. 2–3, pp. 235–256, 2002. The equation is derived from the Chernoff-Hoeffding bound.

```
struct SparseSampling
    𝒫 # problem
    d # depth
    m # number of samples
    U # value function at depth d
end

function sparse_sampling(𝒫, s, d, m, U)
    if d ≤ 0
        return (a=nothing, u=U(s))
    end
    best = (a=nothing, u=-Inf)
    for a in 𝒫.𝒜
        u = 0.0
        for i in 1:m
            s′, r = randstep(𝒫, s, a)
            a′, u′ = sparse_sampling(𝒫, s′, d-1, m, U)
            u += (r + 𝒫.γ*u′) / m
        end
        if u > best.u
            best = (a=a, u=u)
        end
    end
    return best
end

(π::SparseSampling)(s) = sparse_sampling(π.𝒫, s, π.d, π.m, π.U).a
```

Algorithm 9.4. The sparse sampling algorithm for finding an approximately optimal action online for a discrete problem 𝒫 from a current state s to depth d with m samples per action. The returned named tuple consists of the best action a and its finite-horizon expected value u.

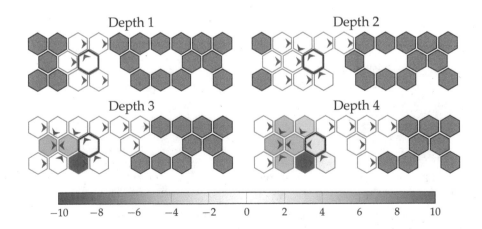

Figure 9.3. Sparse sampling with $m = 10$ applied to the hex world problem. Visited tiles are colored according to their estimated value. The bordered tile is the initial state. Compare to forward search in figure 9.2.

```
struct MonteCarloTreeSearch
    𝒫 # problem
    N # visit counts
    Q # action value estimates
    d # depth
    m # number of simulations
    c # exploration constant
    U # value function estimate
end

function (π::MonteCarloTreeSearch)(s)
    for k in 1:π.m
        simulate!(π, s)
    end
    return argmax(a→π.Q[(s,a)], π.𝒫.𝒜)
end
```

Algorithm 9.5. The Monte Carlo tree search policy for finding an approximately optimal action from a current state s.

$$Q(s,a) + c \sqrt{\frac{\log N(s)}{N(s,a)}} \qquad (9.1)$$

where $N(s) = \sum_a N(s,a)$ is the total visit count to s and c is an exploration parameter that scales the value of unexplored actions. The second term corresponds to an *exploration bonus*. If $N(s,a) = 0$, the bonus is defined to be infinity. With $N(s,a)$ in the denominator, the exploration bonus is higher for actions that have not been tried as frequently. Algorithm 9.7 implements this exploration strategy. We will discuss many other exploration strategies later in chapter 15.

As we take actions specified by algorithm 9.7, we step into new states sampled from the generative model $T(s,a)$, similar to the sparse sampling method. We increment the visit count $N(s,a)$ and update $Q(s,a)$ to maintain the mean value.

At some point, we will either reach the maximum depth or a state that we have not yet explored. If we reach an unexplored state s, we initialize $N(s,a)$ and $Q(s,a)$ to zero for each action a. We may modify algorithm 9.6 to initialize these counts and value estimates to some other values based on prior expert knowledge of the problem. After initializing N and Q, we then return a value estimate at the state s. It is common to estimate this value through a rollout of some policy using the process outlined in section 9.2.

Examples 9.3 to 9.7 work through an illustration of Monte Carlo tree search applied to the 2048 problem. Figure 9.4 shows a search tree generated by running Monte Carlo tree search on 2048. Example 9.8 discusses the impact of using different strategies for estimating values.

```
function simulate!(π::MonteCarloTreeSearch, s, d=π.d)
    if d ≤ 0
        return π.U(s)
    end
    𝒫, N, Q, c = π.𝒫, π.N, π.Q, π.c
    𝒜, TR, γ = 𝒫.𝒜, 𝒫.TR, 𝒫.γ
    if !haskey(N, (s, first(𝒜)))
        for a in 𝒜
            N[(s,a)] = 0
            Q[(s,a)] = 0.0
        end
        return π.U(s)
    end
    a = explore(π, s)
    s', r = TR(s,a)
    q = r + γ*simulate!(π, s', d-1)
    N[(s,a)] += 1
    Q[(s,a)] += (q-Q[(s,a)])/N[(s,a)]
    return q
end
```

Algorithm 9.6. A method for running a Monte Carlo tree search simulation starting from state s to depth d.

```
bonus(Nsa, Ns) = Nsa == 0 ? Inf : sqrt(log(Ns)/Nsa)

function explore(π::MonteCarloTreeSearch, s)
    𝒜, N, Q, c = π.𝒫.𝒜, π.N, π.Q, π.c
    Ns = sum(N[(s,a)] for a in 𝒜)
    return argmax(a→Q[(s,a)] + c*bonus(N[(s,a)], Ns), 𝒜)
end
```

Algorithm 9.7. An exploration policy used in Monte Carlo tree search when determining which nodes to traverse through the search tree. The policy is determined by a dictionary of state-action visitation counts N and values Q, as well as an exploration parameter c. When N[(s,a)] = 0, the policy returns infinity.

Example 9.3. An example of solving 2048 with Monte Carlo tree search.

Consider using Monte Carlo tree search to play 2048 (appendix F.2) with a maximum depth $d = 10$, an exploration parameter $c = 100$, and a 10-step random rollout to estimate $U(s)$. Our first simulation expands the starting state. The count and value are initialized for each action from the initial state:

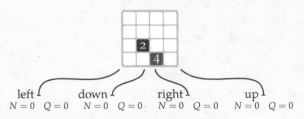

The second simulation begins by selecting the best action from the initial state according to our exploration strategy in equation (9.1). Because all states have the same value, we arbitrarily choose the first action, left. We then sample a new successor state and expand it, initializing the associated counts and value estimates. A rollout is run from the successor state and its value is used to update the value of left:

Example 9.4. A (continued) example of solving 2048 with Monte Carlo tree search.

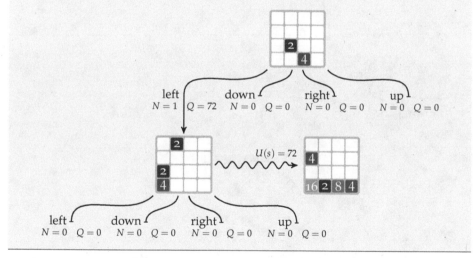

The third simulation begins by selecting the second action, down, because it has infinite value due to the exploration bonus given for unexplored actions. The first action has finite value:

Example 9.5. A (continued) example of solving 2048 with Monte Carlo tree search.

$$Q(s_0, \texttt{left}) + c\sqrt{\frac{\log N(s_0)}{N(s_0, \texttt{left})}} = 72 + 100\sqrt{\frac{\log 2}{1}} \approx 155.255$$

We take the down action and sample a new successor state, which is expanded. A rollout is run from the successor state and its value is used to update the value of down:

The next two simulations select `right` and `up`, respectively. This results in the following:

Example 9.6. A (continued) example of solving 2048 with Monte Carlo tree search.

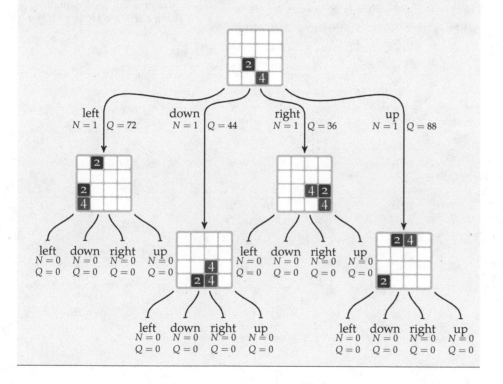

In the fifth simulation, **up** has the highest value. The successor state after taking **up** in the source state will not necessarily be the same as the first time up was selected. We evaluate $U(s) = 44$ and update our visitation count to 2 and our estimated value to $Q \leftarrow 88 + (44 - 88)/2 = 66$. A new successor node is created:

Example 9.7. A (continued) example of solving 2048 with Monte Carlo tree search.

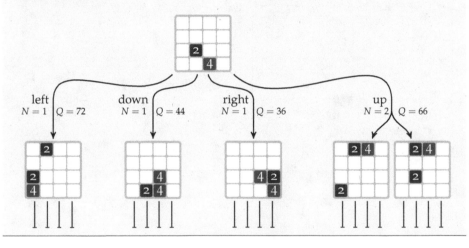

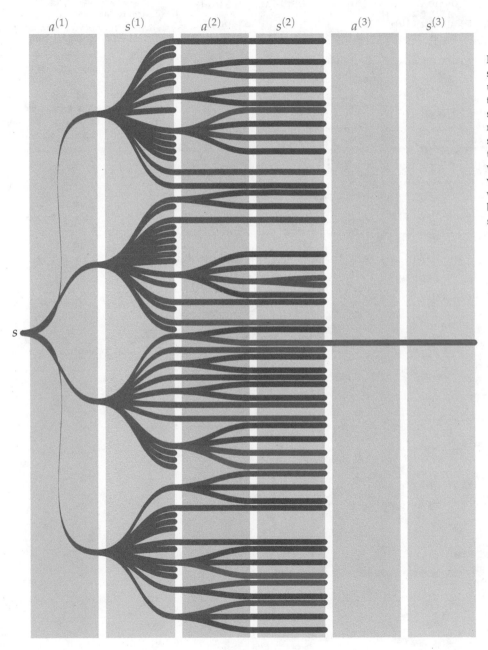

Figure 9.4. A Monte Carlo tree search tree on 2048 after 100 simulations. In general, Monte Carlo tree search for MDPs produces a search graph because there can be multiple ways to reach the same state. The colors in the tree indicate the estimated values at the nodes, with high values in blue and low values in red. The tree is shallow, with a fairly high branching factor, because 2048 has many reachable states for each action.

Rollouts are not the only means by which we can estimate utilities in Monte Carlo tree search. Custom evaluation functions can often be crafted for specific problems to help guide the algorithm. For example, we can encourage Monte Carlo tree search to order its tiles in 2048 using evaluation functions that return the weighted sum across tile values:

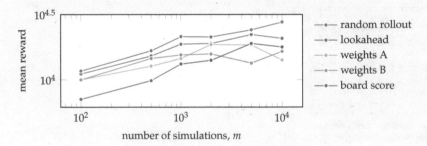

heuristic A weights   heuristic B weights

The plot here compares Monte Carlo tree search on 2048 using rollouts with a uniform random policy, rollouts with a one-step lookahead policy, the two evaluation functions, and using the current board score:

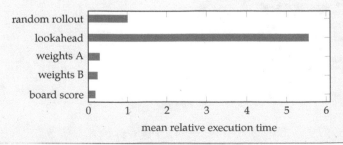

Rollouts perform well but require more execution time. Here we plot the average execution time relative to random rollouts for $m = 100$ from a starting state:

Example 9.8. The performance of Monte Carlo tree search varies with the number of simulations and as the board evaluation method is changed. Heuristic board evaluations tend to be efficient and can more effectively guide the search when run counts are low. Lookahead rollout evaluations take about 18 times longer than heuristic evaluations.

There are variations of this basic Monte Carlo tree search algorithm that can better handle large action and state spaces. Instead of expanding all the actions, we can use *progressive widening*. The number of actions considered from state s is limited to $\theta_1 N(s)^{\theta_2}$, where θ_1 and θ_2 are hyperparameters. Similarly, we can limit the number of states that result from taking action a from state s in the same way, using what is called *double progressive widening*. If the number of states that have been simulated from state s after action a is below $\theta_3 N(s,a)^{\theta_4}$, then we sample a new state; otherwise, we sample one of the previously sampled states with probability proportional to the number of times it has been visited. This strategy can be used to handle large as well as continuous action and state spaces.[6]

[6] A. Couëtoux, J.-B. Hoock, N. Sokolovska, O. Teytaud, and N. Bonnard, "Continuous Upper Confidence Trees," in *Learning and Intelligent Optimization (LION)*, 2011.

[7] A. G. Barto, S. J. Bradtke, and S. P. Singh, "Learning to Act Using Real-Time Dynamic Programming," *Artificial Intelligence*, vol. 72, no. 1–2, pp. 81–138, 1995. Other forms of heuristic search are discussed by Mausam and A. Kolobov, *Planning with Markov Decision Processes: An AI Perspective*. Morgan & Claypool, 2012.

9.7 Heuristic Search

Heuristic search (algorithm 9.8) uses m simulations of a greedy policy with respect to a value function U from the current state s.[7] The value function U is initialized to an upper bound of the value function $\overline{U}$, which is referred to as a *heuristic*. As we run these simulations, we update our estimate of U through lookahead. After running these simulations, we simply select the greedy action from s with respect to U. Figure 9.5 shows how U and the greedy policy changes with the number of simulations.

Heuristic search is guaranteed to converge to the optimal utility function so long as the heuristic $\overline{U}$ is indeed an upper bound on the value function.[8] The efficiency of the search depends on the tightness of the upper bound. Unfortunately, tight bounds can be difficult to obtain in practice. While a heuristic that is not a true upper bound may not converge to the optimal policy, it may still converge to a policy that performs well. The time complexity is $O(m \times d \times |S| \times |A|)$.

[8] Such a heuristic is referred to as an *admissible heuristic*.

9.8 Labeled Heuristic Search

Labeled heuristic search (algorithm 9.9) is a variation of heuristic search that runs simulations with value updates while labeling states based on whether their value is solved.[9] We say that a state s is solved if its utility residual falls below a threshold $\delta > 0$:

$$|U_{k+1}(s) - U_k(s)| < \delta \tag{9.2}$$

[9] B. Bonet and H. Geffner, "Labeled RTDP: Improving the Convergence of Real-Time Dynamic Programming," in *International Conference on Automated Planning and Scheduling (ICAPS)*, 2003.

```
struct HeuristicSearch
    𝒫    # problem
    Uhi  # upper bound on value function
    d    # depth
    m    # number of simulations
end

function simulate!(π::HeuristicSearch, U, s)
    𝒫 = π.𝒫
    for d in 1:π.d
        a, u = greedy(𝒫, U, s)
        U[s] = u
        s = rand(𝒫.T(s, a))
    end
end

function (π::HeuristicSearch)(s)
    U = [π.Uhi(s) for s in π.𝒫.𝒮]
    for i in 1:π.m
        simulate!(π, U, s)
    end
    return greedy(π.𝒫, U, s).a
end
```

Algorithm 9.8. Heuristic search runs m simulations starting from an initial state s to a depth d. The search is guided by a heuristic initial value function Uhi, which leads to optimality in the limit of simulations if it is an upper bound on the optimal value function.

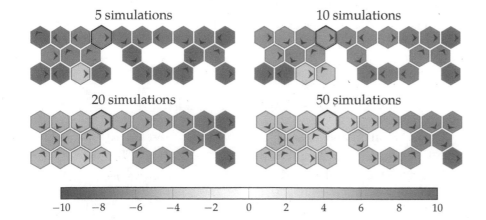

5 simulations

10 simulations

20 simulations

50 simulations

−10 −8 −6 −4 −2 0 2 4 6 8 10

Figure 9.5. Heuristic search runs simulations with Bellman updates to improve a value function on the hex world problem to obtain a policy from an initial state, shown here with an additional black border. These simulations are run to depth 8 with heuristic $\overline{U}(s) = 10$. Each hex is colored according to the utility function value in that iteration. We see that the algorithm eventually finds an optimal policy.

We run simulations with value updates until the current state is solved. In contrast with the heuristic search in the previous section, which runs a fixed number of iterations, this labeling process focuses computational effort on the most important areas of the state space.

```
struct LabeledHeuristicSearch
    𝒫        # problem
    Uhi      # upper bound on value function
    d        # depth
    δ        # gap threshold
end

function (π::LabeledHeuristicSearch)(s)
    U, solved = [π.Uhi(s) for s in 𝒫.S], Set()
    while s ∉ solved
        simulate!(π, U, solved, s)
    end
    return greedy(π.𝒫, U, s).a
end
```

Algorithm 9.9. Labeled heuristic search, which runs simulations starting from the current state to depth d until the current state is solved. The search is guided by a heuristic upper bound on the value function Uhi and maintains a growing set of solved states. States are considered solved when their utility residuals fall below δ. A value function policy is returned.

Simulations in labeled heuristic search (algorithm 9.10) begin by running to a maximum depth of *d* by following a policy that is greedy with respect to our estimated value function *U*, similar to the heuristic search in the previous section. We may stop a simulation before a depth of *d* if we reach a state that has been labeled as solved in a prior simulation.

```
function simulate!(π::LabeledHeuristicSearch, U, solved, s)
    visited = []
    for d in 1:π.d
        if s ∈ solved
            break
        end
        push!(visited, s)
        a, u = greedy(π.𝒫, U, s)
        U[s] = u
        s = rand(π.𝒫.T(s, a))
    end
    while !isempty(visited)
        if label!(π, U, solved, pop!(visited))
            break
        end
    end
end
```

Algorithm 9.10. Simulations are run from the current state to a maximum depth d. We stop a simulation at depth d or if we encounter a state that is in the set solved. After a simulation, we call label! on the states we visited in reverse order.

After each simulation, we iterate over the states we visited during that simulation in reverse order, performing a labeling routine on each state and stopping if a state is found that is not solved. The labeling routine (algorithm 9.11) searches the states in the *greedy envelope* of s, which is defined to be the states reachable from s under a greedy policy with respect to U. The state s is considered not solved if there is a state in the greedy envelope of s whose utility residual is greater than threshold δ. If no such state is found, then s is marked as solved—as well as all states in the greedy envelope of s because they must have converged as well. If a state with a sufficiently large utility residual is found, then the utilities of all states traversed during the search of the greedy enveloped are updated.

Figure 9.6 shows several different greedy envelopes. Figure 9.7 shows the states traversed in a single iteration of labeled heuristic search. Figure 9.8 shows the progression of heuristic search on the hex world problem.

9.9 Open-Loop Planning

The online methods discussed in this chapter, as well as the offline methods discussed in the previous chapters, are examples of *closed-loop planning*, which involves accounting for future state information in the planning process.[10] Often, *open-loop planning* can provide a satisfactory approximation of an optimal closed-loop plan while greatly enhancing computational efficiency by avoiding having to reason about the acquisition of future information. Sometimes this open-loop planning approach is referred to as *model predictive control*.[11] As with receding horizon control, model predictive control solves the open-loop problem, executes the action from our current state, transitions to the next state, and then replans.

Open-loop plans can be represented as a sequence of actions up to a depth d. The planning process reduces to an optimization problem:

$$\underset{a_{1:d}}{\text{maximize}} \quad U(a_{1:d}) \tag{9.3}$$

where $U(a_{1:d})$ is the expected return when executing the sequence of actions $a_{1:d}$. Depending on the application, this optimization problem may be convex or lend itself to a convex approximation, meaning that it can be solved quickly using a variety of algorithms.[12] Later in this section, we will discuss a few different formulations that can be used to transform equation (9.3) into a convex problem.

[10] The loop in this context refers to the observe-act loop introduced in section 1.1.

[11] F. Borrelli, A. Bemporad, and M. Morari, *Predictive Control for Linear and Hybrid Systems*. Cambridge University Press, 2019.

[12] Appendix A.6 reviews convexity. An introduction to convex optimization is provided by S. Boyd and L. Vandenberghe, *Convex Optimization*. Cambridge University Press, 2004.

```
function expand(π::LabeledHeuristicSearch, U, solved, s)
    𝒫, δ = π.𝒫, π.δ
    S, 𝒜, T = 𝒫.S, 𝒫.𝒜, 𝒫.T
    found, toexpand, envelope = false, Set(s), []
    while !isempty(toexpand)
        s = pop!(toexpand)
        push!(envelope, s)
        a, u = greedy(𝒫, U, s)
        if abs(U[s] - u) > δ
            found = true
        else
            for s' in S
                if T(s,a,s') > 0 && s' ∉ (solved ∪ envelope)
                    push!(toexpand, s')
                end
            end
        end
    end
    return (found, envelope)
end

function label!(π::LabeledHeuristicSearch, U, solved, s)
    if s ∈ solved
        return false
    end
    found, envelope = expand(π, U, solved, s)
    if found
        for s ∈ reverse(envelope)
            U[s] = greedy(π.𝒫, U, s).u
        end
    else
        union!(solved, envelope)
    end
    return found
end
```

Algorithm 9.11. The `label!` function will attempt to find a state in the greedy envelope of s whose utility residual exceeds a threshold δ. The function `expand` computes the greedy envelope of s and determines whether any of those states have utility residuals above the threshold. If a state has a residual that exceeds the threshold, then we update the utilities of the states in the envelope. Otherwise, we add that envelope to the set of solved states.

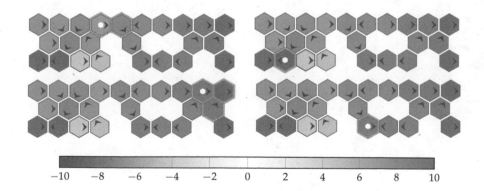

Figure 9.6. The greedy envelope for $\delta = 1$ for several states visualized for a value function on the hex world problem. The value function was obtained by running basic heuristic search for 10 iterations from an initial state, shown with a white hex center, to a maximum depth of 8. We find that the size of the greedy envelope, outlined in gray, can vary widely depending on the state.

Figure 9.7. A single iteration of labeled heuristic search conducts an exploratory run (arrows), followed by labeling (hexagonal border). Only two states are labeled in this iteration: the hidden terminal state and the state with a hexagonal border. Both the exploratory run and the labeling step update the value function.

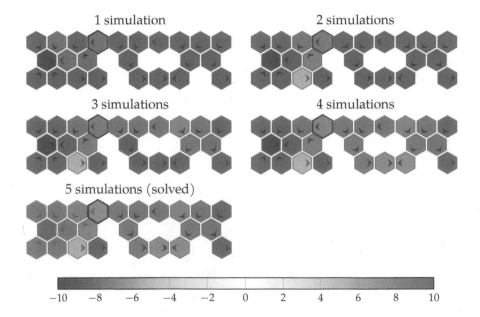

1 simulation

2 simulations

3 simulations

4 simulations

5 simulations (solved)

Figure 9.8. A progression of heuristic search on the hex world problem using $\delta = 1$ and a heuristic $\overline{U}(s) = 10$. The solved states in each iteration are covered in a gray wash. The set of solved states grows from the terminal reward state back toward the initial state with the dark border.

-10	-8	-6	-4	-2	0	2	4	6	8	10

Open-loop planning can often allow us to devise effective decision strategies in high-dimensional spaces where closed-loop planning is computationally infeasible. This type of planning gains this efficiency by not accounting for future information. Example 9.9 provides a simple instance of where open-loop planning can result in poor decisions, even when we account for stochasticity.

Consider a problem with nine states, as shown in the margin, with two decision steps starting from the initial state s_1. In our decisions, we must decide between going up (blue arrows) and going down (green arrows). The effects of these actions are deterministic, except that if we go up from s_1, then we end up in state s_2 half the time and in state s_3 half the time. We receive a reward of 30 in states s_5 and s_7 and a reward of 20 in states s_8 and s_9, as indicated in the illustration.

There are exactly four open-loop plans: (up, up), (up, down), (down, up), and (down, down). In this simple example, it is easy to compute their expected utilities:

- $U(\text{up}, \text{up}) = 0.5 \times 30 + 0.5 \times 0 = 15$

- $U(\text{up}, \text{down}) = 0.5 \times 0 + 0.5 \times 30 = 15$

- $U(\text{down}, \text{up}) = 20$

- $U(\text{down}, \text{down}) = 20$

According to the set of open-loop plans, it is best to choose down from s_1 because our expected reward is 20 instead of 15.

Closed-loop planning, in contrast, takes into account the fact that we can base our next decision on the observed outcome of our first action. If we choose to go up from s_1, then we can choose to go down or up depending on whether we end up in s_2 or s_3, thereby guaranteeing a reward of 30.

Example 9.9. Suboptimality of open-loop planning.

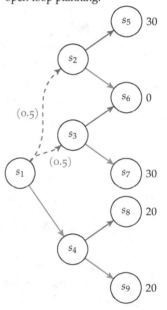

9.9.1   *Deterministic Model Predictive Control*

A common approximation to make $U(a_{1:d})$ amenable to optimization is to assume deterministic dynamics:

$$\begin{aligned}
\underset{a_{1:d},s_{2:d}}{\text{maximize}} \quad & \sum_{t=1}^{d} \gamma^t R(s_t, a_t) \\
\text{subject to} \quad & s_{t+1} = T(s_t, a_t), \quad t \in 1:d-1
\end{aligned} \tag{9.4}$$

where s_1 is the current state and $T(s,a)$ is a deterministic transition function that returns the state that results from taking action a from state s. A common strategy for producing a suitable deterministic transition function from a stochastic transition function is to use the most likely transition. If the dynamics in equation (9.4) are linear and the reward function is convex, then the problem is convex.

Example 9.10 provides an instance involving navigating to a goal state while avoiding an obstacle and minimizing acceleration effort. Both the state space and action space are continuous, and we can find a solution in well under a second. Replanning after every step can help compensate for stochasticity or unexpected events. For example, if the obstacle moves, we can readjust our plan, as illustrated in figure 9.9.

9.9.2   *Robust Model Predictive Control*

We can change the problem formulation to provide robustness to outcome uncertainty. There are many *robust model predictive control* formulations,[13] but one involves choosing the best open-loop plan given the worst-case state transitions. This formulation defines $T(s,a)$ to be an *uncertainty set* consisting of all possible states that can result from taking action a in state s. In other words, the uncertainty set is the support of the distribution $T(\cdot \mid s,a)$. Optimizing with respect to worst-case state transitions requires transforming the optimization problem in equation (9.4) into a *minimax* problem:

$$\begin{aligned}
\underset{a_{1:d}}{\text{maximize}} \; \underset{s_{2:d}}{\text{minimize}} \; & \sum_{t=1}^{d} \gamma^t R(s_t, a_t) \\
\text{subject to} \quad & s_{t+1} \in T(s_t, a_t), \quad t \in 1:d-1
\end{aligned} \tag{9.5}$$

[13] A. Bemporad and M. Morari, "Robust Model Predictive Control: A Survey," in *Robustness in Identification and Control*, A. Garulli, A. Tesi, and A. Vicino, eds., Springer, 1999, pp. 207–226.

In this problem, our state **s** represents our agent's two-dimensional position concatenated with its two-dimensional velocity vector, with **s** initially set to $[0,0,0,0]$. Our action **a** is an acceleration vector, where each component must be between ± 1. At each step, we use our action to update our velocity, and we use our velocity to update our position. Our objective is to reach a goal state of $\mathbf{s}_{\text{goal}} = [10,10,0,0]$. We plan up to $d = 10$ steps with no discounting. With each step, we accumulate a cost of $\|\mathbf{a}_t\|_2^2$ to minimize acceleration effort. At the last step, we want to be as close to the goal state as possible, with a penalty of $100\|\mathbf{s}_d - \mathbf{s}_{\text{goal}}\|_2^2$. We also have to ensure that we avoid a circular obstacle with radius 2 centered at $[3,4]$. We can formulate this problem as follows and extract the first action from the plan:

```
model = Model(Ipopt.Optimizer)
d = 10
current_state = zeros(4)
goal = [10,10,0,0]
obstacle = [3,4]
@variables model begin
    s[1:4, 1:d]
    -1 ≤ a[1:2,1:d] ≤ 1
end
# velocity update
@constraint(model, [i=2:d,j=1:2], s[2+j,i] == s[2+j,i-1] + a[j,i-1])
# position update
@constraint(model, [i=2:d,j=1:2], s[j,i] == s[j,i-1] + s[2+j,i-1])
# initial condition
@constraint(model, s[:,1] .== current_state)
# obstacle
@constraint(model, [i=1:d], sum((s[1:2,i] - obstacle).^2) ≥ 4)
@objective(model, Min, 100*sum((s[:,d] - goal).^2) + sum(a.^2))
optimize!(model)
action = value.(a[:,1])
```

Example 9.10. Open-loop planning in a deterministic environment. We attempt to find a path around a circular obstacle. This implementation uses the JuMP.jl interface to the Ipopt solver. A. Wächter and L. T. Biegler, "On the Implementation of an Interior-Point Filter Line-Search Algorithm for Large-Scale Nonlinear Programming," *Mathematical Programming*, vol. 106, no. 1, pp. 25–57, 2005.

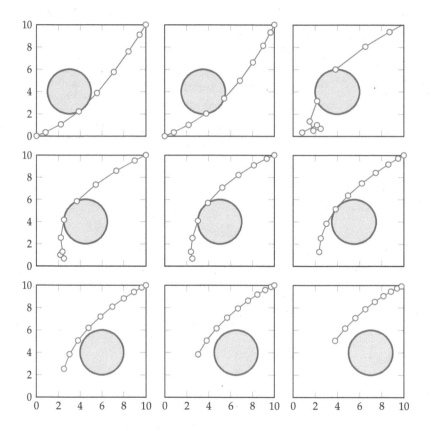

Figure 9.9. Model predictive control applied to the problem in example 9.10, with the addition of a moving obstacle. The sequence progresses left-to-right, and top-to-bottom. Initially, we have a plan that passes to the right of the obstacle, but in the third cell, we see that we must change our mind and pass to the left. We have to maneuver around a little to adjust our velocity vector appropriately with minimal effort. Of course, we could have created a better path (in terms of our utility function) if our planning process had known that the obstacle was moving in a particular direction.

Unfortunately, this formulation can result in extremely conservative behavior. If we adapt example 9.10 to model the uncertainty in the motion of the obstacle, the accumulation of uncertainty may become quite large, even when planning with a relatively short horizon. One way to reduce the accumulation of uncertainty is to restrict the uncertainty set output by $T(s, a)$ to contain only, say, 95 % of the probability mass. Another issue with this approach is that the minimax optimization problem is often not convex and difficult to solve.

9.9.3 *Multiforecast Model Predictive Control*

One way to address the computational challenge within the minimax problem in equation (9.5) is to use m forecast scenarios, each of which follows its own deterministic transition function.[14] There are various formulations of this kind of *multiforecast model predictive control*, which is a type of *hindsight optimization*.[15] One common approach is to have the deterministic transition functions depend on the step k, $T_i(s, a, k)$, which is the same as augmenting the state space to include depth. Example 9.11 demonstrates how this might be done for a linear Gaussian model.

[14] S. Garatti and M. C. Campi, "Modulating Robustness in Control Design: Principles and Algorithms," *IEEE Control Systems Magazine*, vol. 33, no. 2, pp. 36–51, 2013.

[15] It is called hindsight optimization because it represents a solution that is optimizing using knowledge about action outcomes that can only be known in hindsight. E. K. P. Chong, R. L. Givan, and H. S. Chang, "A Framework for Simulation-Based Network Control via Hindsight Optimization," in *IEEE Conference on Decision and Control (CDC)*, 2000.

Suppose we have a problem with linear Gaussian dynamics:

$$T(\mathbf{s}' \mid \mathbf{s}, \mathbf{a}) = \mathcal{N}(\mathbf{T}_s\mathbf{s} + \mathbf{T}_a\mathbf{a}, \mathbf{\Sigma})$$

The problem in figure 9.9 is linear, with no uncertainty, but if we allow the obstacle to move according to a Gaussian distribution at each step, then the dynamics become linear Gaussian. We can approximate the dynamics using a set of m forecast scenarios, each consisting of d steps. We can pull $m \times d$ samples $\epsilon_{ik} \sim \mathcal{N}(\mathbf{0}, \mathbf{\Sigma})$ and define the deterministic transition functions:

$$T_i(\mathbf{s}, \mathbf{a}, k) = \mathbf{T}_s\mathbf{s} + \mathbf{T}_a\mathbf{a} + \epsilon_{ik}$$

Example 9.11. Modeling linear Gaussian transition dynamics in multiforecast model predictive control.

We try to find the best sequence of actions for the worst sampled scenario:

$$\begin{aligned} \underset{a_{1:d}}{\text{maximize}} \quad & \underset{i,\, s_{2:d}}{\text{minimize}} \sum_{k=1}^{d} \gamma^k R(s_k, a_k) \\ \text{subject to} \quad & s_{k+1} = T_i(s_k, a_k, k), \quad k \in 1:d-1 \end{aligned} \tag{9.6}$$

This problem can be much easier to solve than the original robust problem.

We can also use a multiforecast approach to optimize the average case.[16] The formulation is similar to equation (9.6), except that we replace the minimization with an expectation and allow different action sequences to be taken for different scenarios, with the constraint that the first action must agree:

$$
\begin{aligned}
\underset{a_{1:d}^{(1:m)},\, s_{2:d}^{(i)}}{\text{maximize}} \quad & \frac{1}{m} \sum_{i=1}^{m} \sum_{k=1}^{d} \gamma^k R(s_k^{(i)}, a_k^{(i)}) \\
\text{subject to} \quad & s_{k+1}^{(i)} = T_i(s_k^{(i)}, a_k^{(i)}, k), \quad k \in 1:d-1, i \in 1:m \\
& a_1^{(i)} = a_1^{(j)}, \qquad\qquad\quad i \in 1:m, j \in 1:m
\end{aligned}
\tag{9.7}
$$

This formulation can result in robust behavior without being overly conservative, while still maintaining computational tractability. Both formulations in equations (9.6) and (9.7) can be made more robust by increasing the number of forecast scenarios m at the expense of additional computation.

9.10   Summary

- Online methods plan from the current state, focusing computation on states that are reachable.

- Receding horizon planning involves planning to a certain horizon and then replanning with each step.

- Lookahead with rollouts involves acting greedily with respect to values estimated using simulations of a rollout policy; it is computationally efficient compared to other algorithms, but there are no guarantees on performance.

- Forward search considers all state-action transitions up to a certain depth, resulting in computational complexity that grows exponentially in both the number of states and the number of actions.

- Branch and bound uses upper and lower bound functions to prune portions of the search tree that will not lead to a better outcome in expectation.

- Sparse sampling avoids the exponential complexity in the number of states by limiting the number of sampled transitions from every search node.

[16] This approach was applied to optimizing power flow policies by N. Moehle, E. Busseti, S. Boyd, and M. Wytock, "Dynamic Energy Management," in *Large Scale Optimization in Supply Chains and Smart Manufacturing*, Springer, 2019, pp. 69–126.

- Monte Carlo tree search guides search to promising areas of the search space by taking actions that balance exploration with exploitation.

- Heuristic search runs simulations of a policy that is greedy with respect to a value function that is updated along the way using lookahead.

- Labeled heuristic search reduces computation by not reevaluating states whose values have converged.

- Open-loop planning aims to find the best possible sequence of actions and can be computationally efficient if the optimization problem is convex.

9.11   Exercises

Exercise 9.1. Why does branch and bound have the same worst-case computational complexity as forward search?

Solution: In the worst case, branch and bound will never prune, resulting in a traversal of the same search tree as forward search with the same complexity.

Exercise 9.2. Given two admissible heuristics h_1 and h_2, how can we use both of them in heuristic search?

Solution: Create a new heuristic $h(s) = \min\{h_1(s), h_2(s)\}$ and use it instead. This new heuristic is guaranteed to be admissible and cannot be a worse bound than either h_1 or h_2. Both $h_1(s) \geq U^*(s)$ and $h_2(s) \geq U^*(s)$ imply that $h(s) \geq U^*(s)$.

Exercise 9.3. Given two inadmissible heuristics h_1 and h_2, describe a way we can use both of them in heuristic search.

Solution: We could define a new heuristic $h_3(s) = \max(h_1(s), h_2(s))$ to get a potentially admissible, or "less-inadmissible," heuristic. It may be slower to converge, but it may be more likely to not miss out on a better solution.

Exercise 9.4. Suppose we have a discrete MDP with state space $\mathcal{S}$ and action space $\mathcal{A}$ and we want to perform forward search to depth d. Due to computational constraints and the requirement that we must simulate to depth d, we decide to generate new, smaller state and action spaces by re-discretizing the original state and action spaces on a coarser scale with $|\mathcal{S}'| < |\mathcal{S}|$ and $|\mathcal{A}'| < |\mathcal{A}|$. In terms of the original state and action spaces, what would the size of the new state and action spaces need to be in order to make the computational complexity of forward search approximately depth-invariant with respect to the size of our original state and action spaces, that is, $O\left(|\mathcal{S}||\mathcal{A}|\right)$?

Solution: We need

$$|\mathcal{S}'| = |\mathcal{S}|^{\frac{1}{d}} \qquad \text{and} \qquad |\mathcal{A}'| = |\mathcal{A}|^{\frac{1}{d}}$$

This results in the following complexity:

$$O\left(|\mathcal{S}'|^d|\mathcal{A}'|^d\right) = O\left(\left(|\mathcal{S}|^{\frac{1}{d}}\right)^d\left(|\mathcal{A}|^{\frac{1}{d}}\right)^d\right) = O(|\mathcal{S}||\mathcal{A}|)$$

Exercise 9.5. Building on the previous exercise, suppose now that we want to keep all the original actions in our action space and only re-discretize the state space. What would the size of the new state space need to be to make the computational complexity of forward search approximately depth-invariant with respect to the size of our original state and action spaces?

Solution: The computational complexity of forward search is given by $O\left((|\mathcal{S}||\mathcal{A}|)^d\right)$, which can also be written as $O\left(|\mathcal{S}|^d|\mathcal{A}|^d\right)$. Thus, in order for our coarser state space to lead to forward search that is approximately depth-invariant with respect to the size of our original state and action spaces, we need

$$|\mathcal{S}'| = \left(\frac{|\mathcal{S}|}{|\mathcal{A}|^{d-1}}\right)^{\frac{1}{d}}$$

This gives us:

$$O\left(|\mathcal{S}'|^d|\mathcal{A}'|^d\right) = O\left(\left[\left(\frac{|\mathcal{S}|}{|\mathcal{A}|^{d-1}}\right)^{\frac{1}{d}}\right]^d|\mathcal{A}|^d\right) = O\left(|\mathcal{S}|\frac{|\mathcal{A}|^d}{|\mathcal{A}|^{d-1}}\right) = O(|\mathcal{S}||\mathcal{A}|)$$

Exercise 9.6. Will changing the ordering of the action space cause forward search to take different actions? Will changing the ordering of the action space cause branch and bound to take different actions? Can the ordering of the action space affect how many states are visited by branch and bound?

Solution: Forward search enumerates over all possible future actions. It may return different actions if there are ties in their expected utilities. Branch and bound maintains the same optimality guarantee over the horizon as forward search by sorting by upper bound. The ordering of the action space can affect branch and bound's visitation rate when the upper bound produces the same expected value for two or more actions. Below we show this effect on the modified mountain car problem from example 9.2. The plot compares the number of states visited in forward search to that of branch and bound for different action orderings to depth 6. Branch and bound consistently visits far fewer states than forward search, but action ordering can still affect state visitation.

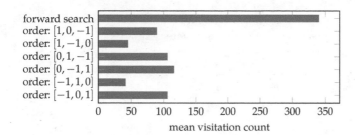

Exercise 9.7. Is sparse sampling with $m = |\mathcal{S}|$ equivalent to forward search?

Solution: No. While the computational complexities are identical at $O\left(|\mathcal{S}|^d|\mathcal{A}|^d\right)$, forward search will branch on all states in the state space, while sparse sampling will branch on $|\mathcal{S}|$ randomly sampled states.

Exercise 9.8. Given an MDP with $|\mathcal{S}| = 10$, $|\mathcal{A}| = 3$, and a uniform transition distribution $T(s' \mid s,a) = 1/|\mathcal{S}|$ for all s and a, what is the probability that sparse sampling with $m = |\mathcal{S}|$ samples and depth $d = 1$ yields the exact same search tree produced by forward search with depth $d = 1$?

Solution: For both forward search and sparse sampling, we branch on all actions from the current state node. For forward search, at each of these action nodes, we branch on all states, while for sparse sampling, we will branch on $m = |\mathcal{S}|$ sampled states. If these sampled states are exactly equal to the state space, that action branch is equivalent to the branch produced in forward search. Thus, for a single action branch we have:

the probability the first state is unique $\qquad\qquad\qquad\qquad \dfrac{10}{10}$

the probability the second state is unique (not equal to the first state) $\quad \dfrac{9}{10}$

the probability the third state is unique (not equal to the first or second state) $\quad \dfrac{8}{10}$

$\qquad\vdots\qquad\qquad\qquad\qquad\qquad\qquad\qquad\qquad\qquad\qquad\qquad\qquad\vdots$

Since each of these sampled states is independent, this leads to the probability of all unique states in the state space being selected with probability

$$\frac{10 \times 9 \times 8 \times \cdots}{10 \times 10 \times 10 \times \cdots} = \frac{10!}{10^{10}} \approx 0.000363$$

Since each of the sampled states across different action branches is independent, the probability that all three action branches sample the unique states in the state space is

$$\left(\frac{10!}{10^{10}}\right)^3 \approx (0.000363)^3 \approx 4.78 \times 10^{-11}$$

Exercise 9.9. Given the following tables of $Q(s,a)$ and $N(s,a)$, use the upper confidence bound in equation (9.1) to compute the MCTS traversal action for each state with an exploration parameter of $c_1 = 10$ and again for $c_2 = 20$.

	$Q(s,a_1)$	$Q(s,a_2)$
s_1	10	-5
s_2	12	10

	$N(s,a_1)$	$N(s,a_2)$
s_1	27	4
s_2	32	18

Solution: For the first exploration parameter $c_1 = 10$, we tabulate the upper confidence bound of each state-action pair and select the action maximizing the bound for each state:

	$UCB(s,a_1)$	$UCB(s,a_2)$	$\arg\max_a UCB(s,a)$
s_1	$10 + 10\sqrt{\frac{\log 31}{27}} \approx 13.566$	$-5 + 10\sqrt{\frac{\log 31}{4}} \approx 4.266$	a_1
s_2	$12 + 10\sqrt{\frac{\log 50}{32}} \approx 15.496$	$10 + 10\sqrt{\frac{\log 50}{18}} \approx 14.662$	a_1

And for $c_2 = 20$, we have:

	$UCB(s,a_1)$	$UCB(s,a_2)$	$\arg\max_a UCB(s,a)$
s_1	$10 + 20\sqrt{\frac{\log 31}{27}} \approx 17.133$	$-5 + 20\sqrt{\frac{\log 31}{4}} \approx 13.531$	a_1
s_2	$12 + 20\sqrt{\frac{\log 50}{32}} \approx 18.993$	$10 + 20\sqrt{\frac{\log 50}{18}} \approx 19.324$	a_2

10 Policy Search

Policy search involves searching the space of policies without directly computing a value function. The policy space is often lower-dimensional than the state space and can often be searched more efficiently. Policy optimization optimizes the parameters in a *parameterized policy* in order to maximize utility. This parameterized policy can take many forms, such as neural networks, decision trees, and computer programs. This chapter begins by discussing a way to estimate the value of a policy given an initial state distribution. We will then discuss search methods that do not use estimates of the gradient of the policy, saving gradient methods for the next chapter. Although local search can be quite effective in practice, we will also discuss a few alternative optimization approaches that can avoid local optima.[1]

[1] There are many other optimization approaches, as discussed by M. J. Kochenderfer and T. A. Wheeler, *Algorithms for Optimization*. MIT Press, 2019.

10.1 Approximate Policy Evaluation

As introduced in section 7.2, we can compute the expected discounted return when following a policy π from a state s. This expected discounted return $U^\pi(s)$ can be computed iteratively (algorithm 7.3) or through matrix operations (algorithm 7.4) when the state space is discrete and relatively small. We can use these results to compute the expected discounted return of π:

$$U(\pi) = \sum_s b(s) U^\pi(s) \tag{10.1}$$

assuming an *initial state distribution* $b(s)$.

We will use this definition of $U(\pi)$ throughout this chapter. However, we often cannot compute $U(\pi)$ exactly when the state space is large or continuous. Instead, we can approximate $U(\pi)$ by sampling *trajectories*, consisting of states, actions, and rewards when following π. The definition of $U(\pi)$ can be rewritten as

$$U(\pi) = \mathbb{E}_\tau[R(\tau)] = \int p_\pi(\tau)R(\tau)\,d\tau \qquad (10.2)$$

where $p_\pi(\tau)$ is the probability density associated with trajectory τ when following policy π, starting from initial state distribution b. The *trajectory reward* $R(\tau)$ is the discounted return associated with τ. Figure 10.1 illustrates the computation of $U(\pi)$ in terms of trajectories sampled from an initial state distribution.

Monte Carlo policy evaluation (algorithm 10.1) involves approximating equation (10.2) with m trajectory rollouts of π:

$$U(\pi) \approx \frac{1}{m}\sum_{i=1}^{m} R(\tau^{(i)}) \qquad (10.3)$$

where $\tau^{(i)}$ is the ith trajectory sample.

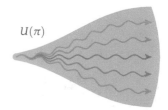

$U(\pi)$

Figure 10.1. The utility associated with a policy from an initial state distribution is computed from the return associated with all possible trajectories under the given policy, weighted according to their likelihood.

```
struct MonteCarloPolicyEvaluation
    𝒫 # problem
    b # initial state distribution
    d # depth
    m # number of samples
end

function (U::MonteCarloPolicyEvaluation)(π)
    R(π) = rollout(U.𝒫, rand(U.b), π, U.d)
    return mean(R(π) for i = 1:U.m)
end

(U::MonteCarloPolicyEvaluation)(π, θ) = U(s→π(θ, s))
```

Algorithm 10.1. Monte Carlo policy evaluation of a policy π. The method runs m rollouts to depth d according to the dynamics specified by the problem $\mathcal{P}$. Each rollout is run from an initial state sampled from state distribution b. The final line in this algorithm block evaluates a policy π parameterized by θ, which will be useful in the algorithms in this chapter that attempt to find a value of θ that maximizes U.

Monte Carlo policy evaluation is stochastic. Multiple evaluations of equation (10.1) with the same policy can give different estimates. Increasing the number of rollouts decreases the variance of the evaluation, as demonstrated in figure 10.2.

We will use π_θ to denote a policy parameterized by θ. For convenience, we will use $U(\theta)$ as shorthand for $U(\pi_\theta)$ in cases where it is not ambiguous. The parameter θ may be a vector or some other more complex representation. For example, we may want to represent our policy using a neural network with a particular structure. We would use θ to represent the weights in the network. Many optimization algorithms assume that θ is a vector with a fixed number of

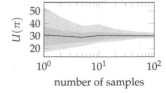

Figure 10.2. The effect of the depth and sample count for Monte Carlo policy evaluation of a uniform random policy on the cart-pole problem (appendix F.3). The variance decreases as the number of samples increases. The blue regions indicate the 5 % to 95 % and 25 % to 75 % empirical quantiles of $U(\pi)$.

components. Other optimization algorithms allow more flexible representations, including representations like decision trees or computational expressions.[2]

[2] We will not be discussing those representations here, but some are implemented in ExprOptimization.jl.

10.2 Local Search

A common approach to optimization is *local search*, where we begin with an initial parameterization and incrementally move from neighbor to neighbor in the search space until convergence occurs. We discussed this type of approach in chapter 5, in the context of optimizing Bayesian network structures with respect to the Bayesian score. Here, we are optimizing policies parameterized by θ. We are trying to find a value of θ that maximizes $U(\theta)$.

There are many local search algorithms, but this section will focus on the *Hooke-Jeeves method* (algorithm 10.2).[3] This algorithm assumes that our policy is parameterized by an n-dimensional vector θ. The algorithm takes a step of size $\pm\alpha$ in each of the coordinate directions from the current θ. These $2n$ points correspond to the neighborhood of θ. If no improvements to the policy are found, then the step size α is decreased by some factor. If an improvement is found, it moves to the best point. The process continues until α drops below some threshold $\epsilon > 0$. An example involving policy optimization is provided in example 10.1, and figure 10.3 illustrates this process.

[3] R. Hooke and T. A. Jeeves, "Direct Search Solution of Numerical and Statistical Problems," *Journal of the ACM (JACM)*, vol. 8, no. 2, pp. 212–229, 1961.

10.3 Genetic Algorithms

A potential issue with local search algorithms like the Hooke-Jeeves method is that the optimization can get stuck in a local optimum. There are a wide variety of approaches that involve maintaining a *population* consisting of samples of points in the parameter space, evaluating them in parallel with respect to our objective, and then recombining them in some way to drive the population toward a global optimum. A *genetic algorithm*[4] is one such approach, which derives inspiration from biological evolution. It is a general optimization method, but it has been successful in the context of optimizing policies. For example, this approach has been used to optimize policies for Atari video games, where the policy parameters correspond to weights in a neural network.[5]

A simple version of this approach (algorithm 10.3) begins with a population of m random parameterizations, $\theta^{(1)}, \ldots, \theta^{(m)}$. We compute $U(\theta^{(i)})$ for each sample

[4] D. E. Goldberg, *Genetic Algorithms in Search, Optimization, and Machine Learning*. Addison-Wesley, 1989.

[5] F. P. Such, V. Madhavan, E. Conti, J. Lehman, K. O. Stanley, and J. Clune, "Deep Neuroevolution: Genetic Algorithms Are a Competitive Alternative for Training Deep Neural Networks for Reinforcement Learning," 2017. arXiv: 1712.06567v3. The implementation in this section follows their relatively simple formulation. Their formulation does not include crossover, which is typically used to mix parameterizations across a population.

```
struct HookeJeevesPolicySearch
    θ # initial parameterization
    α # step size
    c # step size reduction factor
    ε # termination step size
end

function optimize(M::HookeJeevesPolicySearch, π, U)
    θ, θ′, α, c, ε = copy(M.θ), similar(M.θ), M.α, M.c, M.ε
    u, n = U(π, θ), length(θ)
    while α > ε
        copyto!(θ′, θ)
        best = (i=0, sgn=0, u=u)
        for i in 1:n
            for sgn in (-1,1)
                θ′[i] = θ[i] + sgn*α
                u′ = U(π, θ′)
                if u′ > best.u
                    best = (i=i, sgn=sgn, u=u′)
                end
            end
            θ′[i] = θ[i]
        end
        if best.i != 0
            θ[best.i] += best.sgn*α
            u = best.u
        else
            α *= c
        end
    end
    return θ
end
```

Algorithm 10.2. Policy search using the Hooke-Jeeves method, which returns a θ that has been optimized with respect to U. The policy π takes as input a parameter θ and state s. This implementation starts with an initial value of θ. The step size α is reduced by a factor of c if no neighbor improves the objective. Iterations are run until the step size is less than ε.

Suppose we want to optimize a policy for the simple regulator problem described in appendix F.5. We define a stochastic policy π parameterized by θ such that the action is generated according to

$$a \sim \mathcal{N}(\theta_1 s, (|\theta_2| + 10^{-5})^2) \qquad (10.4)$$

The following code defines the parameterized stochastic policy π, evaluation function U, and method M. It then calls optimize(M, π, U), which returns an optimized value for θ. In this case, we use the Hooke-Jeeves method, but the other methods discussed in this chapter can be passed in as M instead:

```
function π(θ, s)
    return rand(Normal(θ[1]*s, abs(θ[2]) + 0.00001))
end
b, d, n_rollouts = Normal(0.3,0.1), 10, 3
U = MonteCarloPolicyEvaluation(𝒫, b, d, n_rollouts)
θ, α, c, ε = [0.0,1.0], 0.75, 0.75, 0.01
M = HookeJeevesPolicySearch(θ, α, c, ε)
θ = optimize(M, π, U)
```

Example 10.1. Using a policy optimization algorithm to optimize the parameters of a stochastic policy.

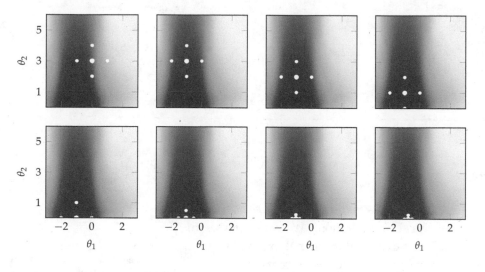

Figure 10.3. The Hooke-Jeeves method applied to optimizing a policy in the simple regulator problem discussed in example 10.1. The evaluations at each iteration are shown as white points. Iterations proceed left to right and top to bottom, and the background is colored according to the expected utility, with yellow indicating lower utility and dark blue indicating higher utility.

i in the population. Since these evaluations potentially involve many rollout simulations and are therefore computationally expensive, they are often run in parallel. These evaluations help us identify the *elite samples*, which are the top m_{elite} samples according to U.

The population at the next iteration is generated by producing $m - 1$ new parameterizations by repeatedly selecting a random elite sample θ and perturbing it with isotropic Gaussian noise, $\theta + \sigma \epsilon$, where $\epsilon \sim \mathcal{N}(\mathbf{0}, \mathbf{I})$. The best parameterization, unperturbed, is included as the mth sample. Because the evaluations involve stochastic rollouts, a variation of this algorithm could involve running additional rollouts to help identify which of the elite samples is truly the best. Figure 10.4 shows several iterations, or *generations*, of this approach in a sample problem.

```
struct GeneticPolicySearch
    θs      # initial population
    σ       # initial standard deviation
    m_elite # number of elite samples
    k_max   # number of iterations
end

function optimize(M::GeneticPolicySearch, π, U)
    θs, σ = M.θs, M.σ
    n, m = length(first(θs)), length(θs)
    for k in 1:M.k_max
        us = [U(π, θ) for θ in θs]
        sp = sortperm(us, rev=true)
        θ_best = θs[sp[1]]
        rand_elite() = θs[sp[rand(1:M.m_elite)]]
        θs = [rand_elite() + σ.*randn(n) for i in 1:(m-1)]
        push!(θs, θ_best)
    end
    return last(θs)
end
```

Algorithm 10.3. A genetic policy search method for iteratively updating a population of policy parameterizations θs, which takes a policy evaluation function U, a policy π(θ, s), a perturbation standard deviation σ, an elite sample count m_elite, and an iteration count k_max. The best m_elite samples from each iteration are used to generate the samples for the subsequent iteration.

10.4   Cross Entropy Method

The *cross entropy method* (algorithm 10.4) involves updating a *search distribution* over the parameterized space of policies at each iteration.[6] We parameterize this search distribution $p(\theta \mid \psi)$ with ψ.[7] This distribution can belong to any family, but a Gaussian distribution is a common choice, where ψ represents the mean and

[6] S. Mannor, R. Y. Rubinstein, and Y. Gat, "The Cross Entropy Method for Fast Policy Search," in *International Conference on Machine Learning (ICML)*, 2003.

[7] Often, θ and ψ are vectors, but because this assumption is not required for this method, we will not bold them in this section.

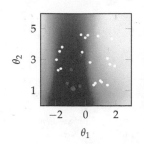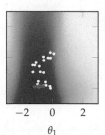

Figure 10.4. Genetic policy search with $\sigma = 0.25$ applied to the simple regulator problem using 25 samples per iteration. The five elite samples in each generation are shown in red, with the best sample indicated by a larger dot.

covariance of the distribution. The objective is to find a value of ψ^* that maximizes the expectation of $U(\theta)$ when θ is drawn from the search distribution:

$$\psi^* = \arg\max_{\psi} \mathbb{E}_{\theta \sim p(\cdot|\psi)}[U(\theta)] = \arg\max_{\psi} \int U(\theta) p(\theta \mid \psi)\, d\theta \qquad (10.5)$$

Directly maximizing equation (10.5) is typically computationally infeasible. The approach taken in the cross entropy method is to start with an initial value of ψ, typically chosen so that the distribution is spread over the relevant parameter space. At each iteration, we draw m samples from the associated distribution and then update ψ to fit the elite samples. For the fit, we typically use the maximum likelihood estimate (section 4.1).[8] We stop after a fixed number of iterations, or until the search distribution becomes highly focused on an optimum. Figure 10.5 demonstrates the algorithm on a simple problem.

[8] The maximum likelihood estimate corresponds to the choice of ψ that minimizes the *cross entropy* (see appendix A.9) between the search distribution and the elite samples.

10.5 Evolution Strategies

Evolution strategies[9] update a search distribution parameterized by a vector $\boldsymbol{\psi}$ at each iteration. However, instead of fitting the distribution to a set of elite samples, they update the distribution by taking a step in the direction of the gradient.[10] The gradient of the objective in equation (10.5) can be computed as follows:[11]

[9] D. Wierstra, T. Schaul, T. Glasmachers, Y. Sun, J. Peters, and J. Schmidhuber, "Natural Evolution Strategies," *Journal of Machine Learning Research*, vol. 15, pp. 949–980, 2014.

[10] We are effectively doing gradient ascent, which is reviewed in appendix A.11.

[11] The policy parameter θ is not bolded here because it is not required to be a vector. However, $\boldsymbol{\psi}$ is in bold because we require it to be a vector when we work with the gradient of the objective.

```julia
struct CrossEntropyPolicySearch
    p       # initial distribution
    m       # number of samples
    m_elite # number of elite samples
    k_max   # number of iterations
end

function optimize_dist(M::CrossEntropyPolicySearch, π, U)
    p, m, m_elite, k_max = M.p, M.m, M.m_elite, M.k_max
    for k in 1:k_max
        θs = rand(p, m)
        us = [U(π, θs[:,i]) for i in 1:m]
        θ_elite = θs[:,sortperm(us)[(m-m_elite+1):m]]
        p = Distributions.fit(typeof(p), θ_elite)
    end
    return p
end

function optimize(M, π, U)
    return Distributions.mode(optimize_dist(M, π, U))
end
```

Algorithm 10.4. Cross entropy policy search, which iteratively improves a search distribution initially set to p. This algorithm takes as input a parameterized policy $\pi(\theta, s)$ and a policy evaluation function U. In each iteration, m samples are drawn and the top m_elite are used to refit the distribution. The algorithm terminates after k_max iterations. The distribution p can be defined using the Distributions.jl package. For example, we might define
```julia
μ = [0.0,1.0]
Σ = [1.0 0.0; 0.0 1.0]
p = MvNormal(μ,Σ)
```

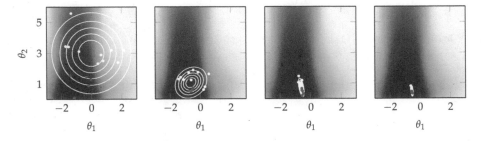

Figure 10.5. The cross entropy method applied to the simple regulator problem using a multivariate Gaussian search distribution. The five elite samples in each iteration are shown in red. The initial distribution is set to $\mathcal{N}([0,3], 2\mathbf{I})$.

$$\nabla_{\psi} \mathop{\mathbb{E}}_{\theta \sim p(\cdot|\psi)}[U(\theta)] = \nabla_{\psi} \int U(\theta) p(\theta \mid \psi)\, d\theta \tag{10.6}$$

$$= \int U(\theta) \nabla_{\psi} p(\theta \mid \psi)\, d\theta \tag{10.7}$$

$$= \int U(\theta) \nabla_{\psi} p(\theta \mid \psi) \frac{p(\theta \mid \psi)}{p(\theta \mid \psi)}\, d\theta \tag{10.8}$$

$$= \int \big(U(\theta) \nabla_{\psi} \log p(\theta \mid \psi) \big) p(\theta \mid \psi)\, d\theta \tag{10.9}$$

$$= \mathop{\mathbb{E}}_{\theta \sim p(\cdot|\psi)}\big[U(\theta) \nabla_{\psi} \log p(\theta \mid \psi) \big] \tag{10.10}$$

The introduction of the logarithm above comes from what is called the *log derivative trick*, which observes that $\nabla_{\psi} \log p(\theta \mid \psi) = \nabla_{\psi} p(\theta \mid \psi) / p(\theta \mid \psi)$. This computation requires knowing $\nabla_{\psi} \log p(\theta \mid \psi)$, but we can often compute this analytically, as discussed in example 10.2.

The search gradient can be estimated from m samples: $\theta^{(1)}, \ldots, \theta^{(m)} \sim p(\cdot \mid \psi)$:

$$\nabla_{\psi} \mathop{\mathbb{E}}_{\theta \sim p(\cdot|\psi)}[U(\theta)] \approx \frac{1}{m} \sum_{i=1}^{m} U(\theta^{(i)}) \nabla_{\psi} \log p(\theta^{(i)} \mid \psi) \tag{10.11}$$

This estimate depends on the evaluated expected utility, which itself can vary widely. We can make our gradient estimate more resilient with *rank shaping*, which replaces the utility values with weights based on the relative performance of each sample to the other samples in its iteration. The m samples are sorted in descending order of expected utility. Weight $w^{(i)}$ is assigned to sample i according to a weighting scheme with $w^{(1)} \geq \cdots \geq w^{(m)}$. The search gradient becomes

$$\nabla_{\psi} \mathop{\mathbb{E}}_{\theta \sim p(\cdot|\psi)}[U(\theta)] \approx \sum_{i=1}^{m} w^{(i)} \nabla_{\psi} \log p(\theta^{(i)} \mid \psi) \tag{10.12}$$

A common weighting scheme is[12]

$$w^{(i)} = \frac{\max\big(0, \log\big(\frac{m}{2} + 1\big) - \log(i)\big)}{\sum_{j=1}^{m} \max\big(0, \log\big(\frac{m}{2} + 1\big) - \log(j)\big)} - \frac{1}{m} \tag{10.13}$$

These weights, shown in figure 10.6, favor better samples and give most samples a small negative weight. Rank-shaping reduces the influence of outliers.

Algorithm 10.5 provides an implementation of the evolution strategies method. Figure 10.7 shows an example of a search progression.

[12] N. Hansen and A. Ostermeier, "Adapting Arbitrary Normal Mutation Distributions in Evolution Strategies: The Covariance Matrix Adaptation," in *IEEE International Conference on Evolutionary Computation*, 1996.

The multivariate normal distribution $\mathcal{N}(\boldsymbol{\mu}, \boldsymbol{\Sigma})$, with mean $\boldsymbol{\mu}$ and covariance $\boldsymbol{\Sigma}$, is a common distribution family. The likelihood in d dimensions takes the form

$$p(\mathbf{x} \mid \boldsymbol{\mu}, \boldsymbol{\Sigma}) = (2\pi)^{-\frac{d}{2}} |\boldsymbol{\Sigma}|^{-\frac{1}{2}} \exp\left(-\frac{1}{2}(\mathbf{x} - \boldsymbol{\mu})^{\top} \boldsymbol{\Sigma}^{-1}(\mathbf{x} - \boldsymbol{\mu})\right)$$

where $|\boldsymbol{\Sigma}|$ is the determinant of $\boldsymbol{\Sigma}$. The log likelihood is

$$\log p(\mathbf{x} \mid \boldsymbol{\mu}, \boldsymbol{\Sigma}) = -\frac{d}{2}\log(2\pi) - \frac{1}{2}\log|\boldsymbol{\Sigma}| - \frac{1}{2}(\mathbf{x} - \boldsymbol{\mu})^{\top} \boldsymbol{\Sigma}^{-1}(\mathbf{x} - \boldsymbol{\mu})$$

The parameters can be updated using their log likelihood gradients:

$$\nabla_{\boldsymbol{\mu}} \log p(\mathbf{x} \mid \boldsymbol{\mu}, \boldsymbol{\Sigma}) = \boldsymbol{\Sigma}^{-1}(\mathbf{x} - \boldsymbol{\mu})$$

$$\nabla_{\boldsymbol{\Sigma}} \log p(\mathbf{x} \mid \boldsymbol{\mu}, \boldsymbol{\Sigma}) = \frac{1}{2}\boldsymbol{\Sigma}^{-1}(\mathbf{x} - \boldsymbol{\mu})(\mathbf{x} - \boldsymbol{\mu})^{\top}\boldsymbol{\Sigma}^{-1} - \frac{1}{2}\boldsymbol{\Sigma}^{-1}$$

The term $\nabla_{\boldsymbol{\Sigma}}$ contains the partial derivative of each entry of $\boldsymbol{\Sigma}$ with respect to the log likelihood.

Directly updating $\boldsymbol{\Sigma}$ may not result in a positive definite matrix, as is required for covariance matrices. One solution is to represent $\boldsymbol{\Sigma}$ as a product $\mathbf{A}^{\top}\mathbf{A}$, which guarantees that $\boldsymbol{\Sigma}$ remains positive semidefinite, and then to update $\mathbf{A}$ instead. Replacing $\boldsymbol{\Sigma}$ by $\mathbf{A}^{\top}\mathbf{A}$ and taking the gradient with respect to $\mathbf{A}$ yields

$$\nabla_{(\mathbf{A})} \log p(\mathbf{x} \mid \boldsymbol{\mu}, \mathbf{A}) = \mathbf{A}\left[\nabla_{\boldsymbol{\Sigma}} \log p(\mathbf{x} \mid \boldsymbol{\mu}, \boldsymbol{\Sigma}) + \nabla_{\boldsymbol{\Sigma}} \log p(\mathbf{x} \mid \boldsymbol{\mu}, \boldsymbol{\Sigma})^{\top}\right]$$

Example 10.2. A derivation of the log likelihood gradient equations for the multivariate Gaussian distribution. For the original derivation and several more sophisticated solutions for handling the positive definite covariance matrix, see D. Wierstra, T. Schaul, T. Glasmachers, Y. Sun, J. Peters, and J. Schmidhuber, "Natural Evolution Strategies," *Journal of Machine Learning Research*, vol. 15, pp. 949–980, 2014.

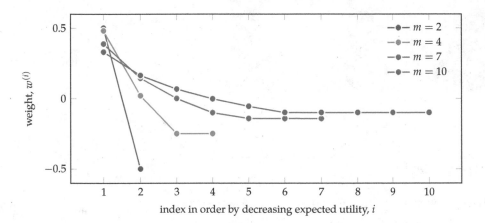

Figure 10.6. Several weightings constructed using equation (10.13).

```
struct EvolutionStrategies
    D         # distribution constructor
    ψ         # initial distribution parameterization
    ∇logp     # log search likelihood gradient
    m         # number of samples
    α         # step factor
    k_max     # number of iterations
end

function evolution_strategy_weights(m)
    ws = [max(0, log(m/2+1) - log(i)) for i in 1:m]
    ws ./= sum(ws)
    ws .-= 1/m
    return ws
end

function optimize_dist(M::EvolutionStrategies, π, U)
    D, ψ, m, ∇logp, α = M.D, M.ψ, M.m, M.∇logp, M.α
    ws = evolution_strategy_weights(m)
    for k in 1:M.k_max
        θs = rand(D(ψ), m)
        us = [U(π, θs[:,i]) for i in 1:m]
        sp = sortperm(us, rev=true)
        ∇ = sum(w.*∇logp(ψ, θs[:,i]) for (w,i) in zip(ws,sp))
        ψ += α.*∇
    end
    return D(ψ)
end
```

Algorithm 10.5. An evolution strategies method for updating a search distribution $D(\psi)$ over policy parameterizations for policy $\pi(\theta, s)$. This implementation also takes an initial search distribution parameterization ψ, the log search likelihood gradient $\nabla\text{logp}(\psi, \theta)$, a policy evaluation function U, and an iteration count k_max. In each iteration, m parameterization samples are drawn and are used to estimate the search gradient. This gradient is then applied with a step factor α. We can use Distributions.jl to define $D(\psi)$. For example, if we want to define D to construct a Gaussian with a given mean ψ and fixed covariance Σ, we can use
$D(\psi) = \text{MvNormal}(\psi, \Sigma)$.

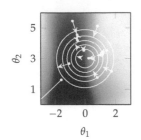 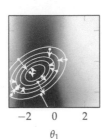 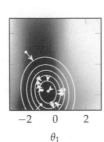 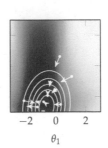

Figure 10.7. Evolution strategies (algorithm 10.5) applied to the simple regulator problem using a multivariate Gaussian search distribution. Samples are shown in white, along with their search gradient contributions, $w\nabla \log p$.

10.6   Isotropic Evolutionary Strategies

The previous section introduced evolutionary strategies that can work with general search distributions. This section will make the assumption that the search distribution is a *spherical* or *isotropic* Gaussian, where the covariance matrix takes the form $\sigma^2\mathbf{I}$.[13] Under this assumption, the expected utility of the distribution introduced in equation (10.5) simplifies to[14]

$$\underset{\theta\sim\mathcal{N}(\psi,\sigma^2\mathbf{I})}{\mathbb{E}}[U(\theta)] = \underset{\epsilon\sim\mathcal{N}(0,\mathbf{I})}{\mathbb{E}}[U(\psi+\sigma\epsilon)] \tag{10.14}$$

The search gradient reduces to

$$\nabla_\psi \underset{\theta\sim\mathcal{N}(\psi,\sigma^2\mathbf{I})}{\mathbb{E}}[U(\theta)] = \underset{\theta\sim\mathcal{N}(\psi,\sigma^2\mathbf{I})}{\mathbb{E}}\left[U(\theta)\nabla_\psi \log p(\theta \mid \psi,\sigma^2\mathbf{I})\right] \tag{10.15}$$

$$= \underset{\theta\sim\mathcal{N}(\psi,\sigma^2\mathbf{I})}{\mathbb{E}}\left[U(\theta)\frac{1}{\sigma^2}(\theta-\psi)\right] \tag{10.16}$$

$$= \underset{\epsilon\sim\mathcal{N}(0,\mathbf{I})}{\mathbb{E}}\left[U(\psi+\sigma\epsilon)\frac{1}{\sigma^2}(\sigma\epsilon)\right] \tag{10.17}$$

$$= \frac{1}{\sigma}\underset{\epsilon\sim\mathcal{N}(0,\mathbf{I})}{\mathbb{E}}[U(\psi+\sigma\epsilon)\epsilon] \tag{10.18}$$

Algorithm 10.6 provides an implementation of this strategy. This implementation incorporates *mirrored sampling*.[15] We sample $m/2$ values from the search distribution and then generate the other $m/2$ samples by mirroring them about the mean. Mirrored samples reduce the variance of the gradient estimate.[16] The benefit of using this technique is shown in figure 10.8.

[13] An example of this approach applied to policy search is explored by T. Salimans, J. Ho, X. Chen, S. Sidor, and I. Sutskever, "Evolution Strategies as a Scalable Alternative to Reinforcement Learning," 2017. arXiv: 1703.03864v2.

[14] In general, if $\mathbf{A}^\top\mathbf{A} = \mathbf{\Sigma}$, then $\theta = \mu + \mathbf{A}^\top\epsilon$ transforms $\epsilon \sim \mathcal{N}(0,\mathbf{I})$ into a sample $\theta \sim \mathcal{N}(\mu,\mathbf{\Sigma})$.

[15] D. Brockhoff, A. Auger, N. Hansen, D. Arnold, and T. Hohm, "Mirrored Sampling and Sequential Selection for Evolution Strategies," in *International Conference on Parallel Problem Solving from Nature*, 2010.

[16] This technique was implemented by T. Salimans, J. Ho, X. Chen, S. Sidor, and I. Sutskever, "Evolution Strategies as a Scalable Alternative to Reinforcement Learning," 2017. arXiv: 1703.03864v2. They included other techniques as well, including weight decay.

```
struct IsotropicEvolutionStrategies
    ψ        # initial mean
    σ        # initial standard deviation
    m        # number of samples
    α        # step factor
    k_max    # number of iterations
end

function optimize_dist(M::IsotropicEvolutionStrategies, π, U)
    ψ, σ, m, α, k_max = M.ψ, M.σ, M.m, M.α, M.k_max
    n = length(ψ)
    ws = evolution_strategy_weights(2*div(m,2))
    for k in 1:k_max
        εs = [randn(n) for i in 1:div(m,2)]
        append!(εs, -εs) # weight mirroring
        us = [U(π, ψ + σ.*ε) for ε in εs]
        sp = sortperm(us, rev=true)
        ∇ = sum(w.*εs[i] for (w,i) in zip(ws,sp)) / σ
        ψ += α.*∇
    end
    return MvNormal(ψ, σ)
end
```

Algorithm 10.6. An evolution strategies method for updating an isotropic multivariate Gaussian search distribution with mean ψ and covariance $\sigma^2 I$ over policy parameterizations for a policy $\pi(\theta, s)$. This implementation also takes a policy evaluation function U, a step factor α, and an iteration count k_max. In each iteration, m/2 parameterization samples are drawn and mirrored and are then used to estimate the search gradient.

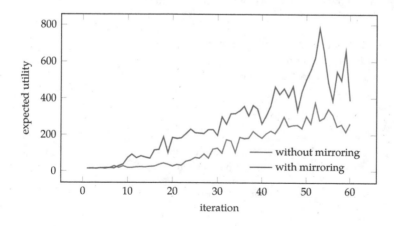

Figure 10.8. A demonstration of the effect that mirrored sampling has on isotropic evolution strategies. Two-layer neural network policies were trained on the cart-pole problem (appendix F.3) using m = 10, and σ = 0.25, with six rollouts per evaluation. Mirrored sampling significantly speeds and stabilizes learning.

10.7   Summary

- Monte Carlo policy evaluation involves computing the expected utility associated with a policy using a large number of rollouts from states sampled from an initial state distribution.

- Local search methods, such as the Hooke-Jeeves method, improve a policy based on small, local changes.

- Genetic algorithms maintain a population of points in the parameter space, recombining them in different ways in attempt to drive the population toward a global optimum.

- The cross entropy method iteratively improves a search distribution over policy parameters by refitting the distribution to elite samples at each iteration.

- Evolutionary strategies attempt to improve the search distribution using gradient information from samples from that distribution.

- Isotropic evolutionary strategies make the assumption that the search distribution is an isotropic Gaussian.

10.8   Exercises

Exercise 10.1. In Monte Carlo policy evaluation, how is the variance of the utility estimate affected by the number of samples?

Solution: The variance of Monte Carlo policy evaluation is the variance of the mean of m samples. These samples are assumed to be independent, and so the variance of the mean is the variance of a single rollout evaluation divided by the sample size:

$$\text{Var}[\hat{U}(\pi)] = \text{Var}\left[\sum_{i=1}^{m} R(\tau^{(i)})\right] = \frac{1}{m}\,\text{Var}_\tau[R(\tau)]$$

where $\hat{U}(\pi)$ is the utility from Monte Carlo policy evaluation and $R(\tau)$ is the trajectory reward for a sampled trajectory τ. The sample variance, therefore, decreases with $1/m$.

Exercise 10.2. What effect does varying the number of samples m and the number of elite samples m_{elite} have on cross entropy policy search?

Solution: The computational cost per iteration scales linearly with the number of samples. More samples will better cover the search space, resulting in a better chance of identifying better elite samples to improve the policy. The number of elite samples also has an effect. Making all samples elite provides no feedback to the improvement process. Having too few elite samples can lead to premature convergence to a suboptimal solution.

Exercise 10.3. Consider using evolution strategies with a univariate Gaussian distribution, $\theta \sim \mathcal{N}(\mu, \nu)$. What is the search gradient with respect to the variance ν? What issue arises as the variance becomes small?

Solution: The search gradient is the gradient of the log-likelihood:

$$\frac{\partial}{\partial \nu} \log p(x \mid \mu, \nu) = \frac{\partial}{\partial \nu} \log \frac{1}{\sqrt{2\pi\nu}} \exp\left(-\frac{(x-\mu)^2}{2\nu}\right)$$

$$= \frac{\partial}{\partial \nu}\left(-\frac{1}{2}\log(2\pi) - \frac{1}{2}\log(\nu) - \frac{(x-\mu)^2}{2\nu}\right)$$

$$= -\frac{1}{2\nu} + \frac{(x-\mu)^2}{2\nu^2}$$

We find that the gradient goes to infinity as the variance approaches zero. This is a problem because the variance should be small when the search distribution converges. Very large gradients can cause simple ascent methods to overshoot optima.

Exercise 10.4. Equation (10.14) defines the objective in terms of a search distribution $\theta \sim \mathcal{N}(\psi, \Sigma)$. What advantage does this objective have over directly optimizing θ using the expected utility objective in equation (10.1)?

Solution: The added Gaussian noise around the policy parameters can smooth discontinuities in the original objective, which can make optimization more reliable.

Exercise 10.5. Which of the methods in this chapter are best suited to the fact that multiple types of policies could perform well in a given problem?

Solution: The Hooke-Jeeves method improves a single policy parameterization, so it cannot retain multiple policies. Both the cross entropy method and evolution strategies use search distributions. In order to successfully represent multiple types of policies, a multimodal distribution would have to be used. One common multimodal distribution is a mixture of Gaussians. A mixture of Gaussians cannot be fit analytically, but they can be reliably fit using expectation maximization (EM), as demonstrated in example 4.4. Genetic algorithms can retain multiple policies if the population size is sufficiently large.

Exercise 10.6. Suppose we have a parameterized policy π_θ that we would like to optimize using the Hooke-Jeeves method. If we initialize our parameter $\theta = 0$ and the utility function is $U(\theta) = -3\theta^2 + 4\theta + 1$, what is the largest step size α that would still guarantee policy improvement in the first iteration of the Hooke-Jeeves method?

Solution: The Hooke-Jeeves method evaluates the objective function at the center point $\pm\alpha$ along each coordinate direction. In order to guarantee improvement in the first iteration of Hooke-Jeeves search, at least one of the objective function values at the new points must improve the objective function value. For our policy optimization problem, this means that we are searching for the largest step size α such that either $U(\theta + \alpha)$ or $U(\theta - \alpha)$ is greater than $U(\theta)$.

Since the underlying utility function is parabolic and concave, the largest step size that would still lead to improvement is slightly less than the width of the parabola at the current point. Thus, we compute the point on the parabola opposite the current point, θ' at which $U(\theta') = U(\theta)$:

$$U(\theta) = -3\theta^2 + 4\theta + 1 = -3(0)^2 + 4(0) + 1 = 1$$
$$U(\theta) = U(\theta')$$
$$1 = -3\theta'^2 + 4\theta' + 1$$
$$0 = -3\theta'^2 + 4\theta' + 0$$
$$\theta' = \frac{-4 \pm \sqrt{4^2 - 4(-3)(0)}}{2(-3)} = \frac{-4 \pm 4}{-6} = \frac{2 \pm 2}{3} = \left\{0, \tfrac{4}{3}\right\}$$

The point on the parabola opposite the current point is thus $\theta' = \frac{4}{3}$. The distance between θ and θ' is $\frac{4}{3} - 0 = \frac{4}{3}$. Thus, the maximal step size we can take and still guarantee improvement in the first iteration is just under $\frac{4}{3}$.

Exercise 10.7. Suppose we have a policy parameterized by a single parameter θ. We take an evolution strategies approach with a search distribution that follows a Bernoulli distribution $p(\theta \mid \psi) = \psi^\theta (1 - \psi)^{1-\theta}$. Compute the log-likelihood gradient $\nabla_\psi \log p(\theta \mid \psi)$.

Solution: The log-likelihood gradient can be computed as follows:

$$p(\theta \mid \psi) = \psi^\theta (1 - \psi)^{1-\theta}$$
$$\log p(\theta \mid \psi) = \log \left(\psi^\theta (1 - \psi)^{1-\theta} \right)$$
$$\log p(\theta \mid \psi) = \theta \log \psi + (1 - \theta) \log(1 - \psi)$$
$$\nabla_\psi \log p(\theta \mid \psi) = \frac{d}{d\psi} \left[\theta \log \psi + (1 - \theta) \log(1 - \psi) \right]$$
$$\nabla_\psi \log p(\theta \mid \psi) = \frac{\theta}{\psi} - \frac{1 - \theta}{1 - \psi}$$

Exercise 10.8. Compute the sample weights for search gradient estimation with rank shaping given $m = 3$ samples.

Solution: We first compute the numerator of the first term from equation (10.13), for all i:

$$i = 1 \quad \max\left(0, \log\left(\tfrac{3}{2} + 1\right) - \log 1\right) = \log \tfrac{5}{2}$$
$$i = 2 \quad \max\left(0, \log\left(\tfrac{3}{2} + 1\right) - \log 2\right) = \log \tfrac{5}{4}$$
$$i = 3 \quad \max\left(0, \log\left(\tfrac{3}{2} + 1\right) - \log 3\right) = 0$$

Now, we compute the weights:

$$w^{(1)} = \frac{\log \tfrac{5}{2}}{\log \tfrac{5}{2} + \log \tfrac{5}{4} + 0} - \frac{1}{3} = 0.47$$

$$w^{(2)} = \frac{\log \tfrac{5}{4}}{\log \tfrac{5}{2} + \log \tfrac{5}{4} + 0} - \frac{1}{3} = -0.14$$

$$w^{(3)} = \frac{0}{\log \tfrac{5}{2} + \log \tfrac{5}{4} + 0} - \frac{1}{3} = -0.33$$

11 Policy Gradient Estimation

The previous chapter discussed several ways to go about directly optimizing the parameters of a policy to maximize expected utility. In many applications, it is often useful to use the gradient of the utility with respect to the policy parameters to guide the optimization process. This chapter discusses several approaches to estimating this gradient from trajectory rollouts.[1] A major challenge with this approach is the variance of the estimate due to the stochastic nature of the trajectories arising from both the environment and our exploration of it. The next chapter will discuss how to use these algorithms to estimate gradients for the purpose of policy optimization.

[1] An additional resource on this topic is M. C. Fu, "Gradient Estimation," in *Simulation*, S. G. Henderson and B. L. Nelson, eds., Elsevier, 2006, pp. 575–616.

11.1 Finite Difference

Finite difference methods estimate the gradient of a function from small changes in its evaluation. Recall that the derivative of a univariate function f is

$$\frac{\mathrm{d}f}{\mathrm{d}x}(x) = \lim_{\delta \to 0} \frac{f(x+\delta) - f(x)}{\delta} \tag{11.1}$$

The derivative at x can be approximated by a sufficiently small step $\delta > 0$:

$$\frac{\mathrm{d}f}{\mathrm{d}x}(x) \approx \frac{f(x+\delta) - f(x)}{\delta} \tag{11.2}$$

This approximation is illustrated in figure 11.1.

The gradient of a multivariate function f with an input of length n is

$$\nabla f(\mathbf{x}) = \left[\frac{\partial f}{\partial x_1}(\mathbf{x}), \ldots, \frac{\partial f}{\partial x_n}(\mathbf{x}) \right] \tag{11.3}$$

Finite differences can be applied to each dimension to estimate the gradient.

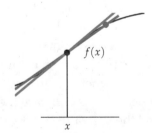

Figure 11.1. The finite difference method approximates the derivative of $f(x)$ using an evaluation of a point near x. The finite-difference approximation, in red, is not a perfect match for the true derivative, in blue.

In the context of policy optimization, we want to estimate the gradient of the utility expected from following a policy parameterized by θ:

$$\nabla U(\theta) = \left[\frac{\partial U}{\partial \theta_1}(\theta), \ldots, \frac{\partial U}{\partial \theta_n}(\theta) \right] \tag{11.4}$$

$$\approx \left[\frac{U(\theta + \delta \mathbf{e}^{(1)}) - U(\theta)}{\delta}, \ldots, \frac{U(\theta + \delta \mathbf{e}^{(n)}) - U(\theta)}{\delta} \right] \tag{11.5}$$

where $\mathbf{e}^{(i)}$ is the ith *standard basis* vector, consisting of zeros except for the ith component, which is set to 1.

As discussed in section 10.1, we need to simulate policy rollouts to estimate $U(\theta)$. We can use algorithm 11.1 to generate trajectories. From these trajectories, we can compute their return and estimate the utility associated with the policy. Algorithm 11.2 implements the gradient estimate in equation (11.5) by simulating m rollouts for each component and averaging the returns.

```
function simulate(𝒫::MDP, s, π, d)
    τ = []
    for i = 1:d
        a = π(s)
        s′, r = 𝒫.TR(s,a)
        push!(τ, (s,a,r))
        s = s′
    end
    return τ
end
```

Algorithm 11.1. A method for generating a trajectory associated with problem 𝒫 starting in state s and executing policy π to depth d. It creates a vector τ containing state-action-reward tuples.

A major challenge in arriving at accurate estimates of the policy gradient is the fact that the variance of the trajectory rewards can be quite high. One approach to reduce the resulting variance in the gradient estimate is to have each rollout share the same random generator seeds.[2] This approach can be helpful, for example, in cases where one rollout happens to hit a low-probability transition early on. Other rollouts will have the same tendency due to the shared random generator, and their rewards will tend to be biased in the same way.

Policy representations have a significant effect on the policy gradient. Example 11.1 demonstrates the sensitivity of the policy gradient to the policy parameterization. Finite differences for policy optimization can perform poorly when the parameters differ in scale.

[2] This random seed sharing is used in the PEGASUS algorithm. A. Y. Ng and M. Jordan, "A Policy Search Method for Large MDPs and POMDPs," in *Conference on Uncertainty in Artificial Intelligence* (*UAI*), 2000.

```
struct FiniteDifferenceGradient
    𝒫 # problem
    b # initial state distribution
    d # depth
    m # number of samples
    δ # step size
end

function gradient(M::FiniteDifferenceGradient, π, θ)
    𝒫, b, d, m, δ, γ, n = M.𝒫, M.b, M.d, M.m, M.δ, M.𝒫.γ, length(θ)
    Δθ(i) = [i == k ? δ : 0.0 for k in 1:n]
    R(τ) = sum(r*γ^(k-1) for (k, (s,a,r)) in enumerate(τ))
    U(θ) = mean(R(simulate(𝒫, rand(b), s→π(θ, s), d)) for i in 1:m)
    ΔU = [U(θ + Δθ(i)) - U(θ) for i in 1:n]
    return ΔU ./ δ
end
```

Algorithm 11.2. A method for estimating a policy gradient using finite differences for a problem $\mathcal{P}$, a parameterized policy $\pi(\theta, s)$, and a policy parameterization vector θ. Utility estimates are made from m rollouts to depth d. The step size is given by δ.

Consider a single-state, single-step MDP with a one-dimensional continuous action space and a reward function $R(s, a) = a$. In this case, larger actions produce higher rewards.

Suppose we have a stochastic policy π_θ that samples its action according to a uniform distribution between θ_1 and θ_2 for $\theta_2 > \theta_1$. The expected value is

$$U(\theta) = \mathbb{E}[a] = \int_{\theta_1}^{\theta_2} a \frac{1}{\theta_2 - \theta_1}\, \mathrm{d}a = \frac{\theta_1 + \theta_2}{2}$$

The policy gradient is

$$\nabla U(\theta) = [1/2, 1/2]$$

The policy could be reparameterized to draw actions from a uniform distribution between θ_1' and $100\theta_2'$, for $100\theta_2' > \theta_1'$. Now the expected reward is $(\theta_1' + 100\theta_2')/2$ and the policy gradient is $[1/2, 50]$.

The two parameterizations can represent the same policies, but they have very different gradients. Finding a suitable perturbation scalar for the second policy is much more difficult because the parameters vary widely in scale.

Example 11.1. An example of how policy parameterization has a significant impact on the policy gradient.

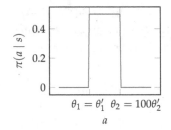

11.2   Regression Gradient

Instead of estimating the gradient at θ by taking a fixed step along each coordinate axis, as done in the previous section, we can use *linear regression*[3] to estimate the gradient from the results of random perturbations from θ. These perturbations are stored in a matrix as follows:[4]

$$\Delta\Theta = \begin{bmatrix} (\Delta\theta^{(1)})^\top \\ \vdots \\ (\Delta\theta^{(m)})^\top \end{bmatrix} \qquad (11.6)$$

More policy parameter perturbations will tend to produce better gradient estimates.[5]

For each of these perturbations, we perform a rollout and estimate the change in utility:[6]

$$\Delta\mathbf{U} = \left[U(\theta + \Delta\theta^{(1)}) - U(\theta), \ldots, U(\theta + \Delta\theta^{(m)}) - U(\theta) \right] \qquad (11.7)$$

The policy gradient estimate using linear regression is then[7]

$$\nabla U(\theta) \approx \Delta\Theta^+ \Delta\mathbf{U} \qquad (11.8)$$

Algorithm 11.3 provides an implementation of this approach in which the perturbations are drawn uniformly from a hypersphere with radius δ. Example 11.2 demonstrates this approach with a simple function.

11.3   Likelihood Ratio

The *likelihood ratio* approach[8] to gradient estimation uses an analytical form of $\nabla\pi_\theta$ to improve our estimate of $\nabla U(\theta)$. Recall from equation (10.2) that

$$U(\theta) = \int p_\theta(\tau) R(\tau) \, d\tau \qquad (11.9)$$

[3] Linear regression is covered in section 8.6.

[4] This general approach is sometimes referred to as *simultaneous perturbation stochastic approximation* by J. C. Spall, *Introduction to Stochastic Search and Optimization*. Wiley, 2003. The general connection to linear regression is provided by J. Peters and S. Schaal, "Reinforcement Learning of Motor Skills with Policy Gradients," *Neural Networks*, vol. 21, no. 4, pp. 682–697, 2008.

[5] A recommended rule of thumb is to use about twice as many perturbations as the number of parameters.

[6] This equation shows the *forward difference*. Other finite-difference formulations, such as the central difference, can also be used.

[7] As discussed in section 8.6, $\mathbf{X}^+$ denotes the pseudoinverse of $\mathbf{X}$.

[8] P. W. Glynn, "Likelihood Ratio Gradient Estimation for Stochastic Systems," *Communications of the ACM*, vol. 33, no. 10, pp. 75–84, 1990.

```
struct RegressionGradient
    𝒫 # problem
    b # initial state distribution
    d # depth
    m # number of samples
    δ # step size
end

function gradient(M::RegressionGradient, π, θ)
    𝒫, b, d, m, δ, γ = M.𝒫, M.b, M.d, M.m, M.δ, M.𝒫.γ
    ΔΘ = [δ.*normalize(randn(length(θ)), 2) for i = 1:m]
    R(τ) = sum(r*γ^(k-1) for (k, (s,a,r)) in enumerate(τ))
    U(θ) = R(simulate(𝒫, rand(b), s→π(θ,s), d))
    ΔU = [U(θ + Δθ) - U(θ) for Δθ in ΔΘ]
    return pinv(reduce(hcat, ΔΘ)') * ΔU
end
```

Algorithm 11.3. A method for estimating a policy gradient using finite differences for an MDP $\mathcal{P}$, a stochastic parameterized policy $\pi(\theta, s)$, and a policy parameterization vector θ. Policy variation vectors are generated by normalizing normally distributed samples and scaling by a perturbation scalar δ. A total of m parameter perturbations are generated, and each is evaluated in a rollout from an initial state drawn from b to depth d and compared to the original policy parameterization.

Hence,

$$\nabla U(\theta) = \nabla_\theta \int p_\theta(\tau) R(\tau) \, d\tau \tag{11.10}$$

$$= \int \nabla_\theta p_\theta(\tau) R(\tau) \, d\tau \tag{11.11}$$

$$= \int p_\theta(\tau) \frac{\nabla_\theta p_\theta(\tau)}{p_\theta(\tau)} R(\tau) \, d\tau \tag{11.12}$$

$$= \mathbb{E}_\tau \left[\frac{\nabla_\theta p_\theta(\tau)}{p_\theta(\tau)} R(\tau) \right] \tag{11.13}$$

The name for this method comes from this trajectory likelihood ratio. This likelihood ratio can be seen as a weight in likelihood weighted sampling (section 3.7) over trajectory rewards.

Applying the log derivative trick,[9] we have

$$\nabla U(\theta) = \mathbb{E}_\tau [\nabla_\theta \log p_\theta(\tau) R(\tau)] \tag{11.14}$$

[9] The log derivative trick was introduced in section 10.5. It uses the following equality:

$$\nabla_\theta \log p_\theta(\tau) = \nabla_\theta p_\theta(\tau) / p_\theta(\tau)$$

We can estimate this expectation using trajectory rollouts. For each trajectory τ, we need to compute the product $\nabla_\theta \log p_\theta(\tau) R(\tau)$. Recall that $R(\tau)$ is the return associated with trajectory τ. If we have a stochastic policy,[10] the gradient $\nabla_\theta \log p_\theta(\tau)$ is

[10] We use $\pi_\theta(a \mid s)$ to represent the probability (either density or mass) the policy π_θ assigns to taking action a from state s.

$$\nabla_\theta \log p_\theta(\tau) = \sum_{k=1}^{d} \nabla_\theta \log \pi_\theta(a^{(k)} \mid s^{(k)}) \tag{11.15}$$

We would like to apply the regression gradient to estimate the gradient of a simple, one-dimensional function $f(x) = x^2$, evaluated at $x_0 = 2$ from $m = 20$ samples. To imitate the stochasticity inherent in policy evaluation, we add noise to the function evaluations. We generate a set of disturbances ΔX, sampled from $\mathcal{N}(0, \delta^2)$, and evaluate $f(x_0 + \Delta x) - f(x_0)$ for each disturbance Δx in ΔX. We can then estimate the one-dimensional gradient (or derivative) $\Delta X^+ \Delta F$ with this code:

```
f(x) = x^2 + 1e-2*randn()
m = 20
δ = 1e-2
ΔX = [δ.*randn() for i = 1:m]
x0 = 2.0
ΔF = [f(x0 + Δx) - f(x0) for Δx in ΔX]
pinv(ΔX) * ΔF
```

The samples and linear regression are shown here. The slope of the regression line is close to the exact solution of 4:

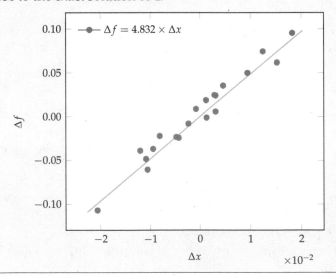

Example 11.2. Using the regression gradient method on a one-dimensional function.

because $p_\theta(\tau)$ takes the form

$$p_\theta(\tau) = p(s^{(1)}) \prod_{k=1}^{d} T(s^{(k+1)} \mid s^{(k)}, a^{(k)}) \pi_\theta(a^{(k)} \mid s^{(k)}) \tag{11.16}$$

where $s^{(k)}$ and $a^{(k)}$ are the kth state and action, respectively, in trajectory τ. Algorithm 11.4 provides an implementation in which m trajectories are sampled to arrive at a gradient estimate. Example 11.3 illustrates the process.

If we have a deterministic policy, the gradient requires computing:[11]

$$\nabla_\theta \log p_\theta(\tau) = \nabla_\theta \log \left[p(s^{(1)}) \prod_{k=1}^{d} T(s^{(k+1)} \mid s^{(k)}, \pi_\theta(s^{(k)})) \right] \tag{11.17}$$

$$= \sum_{k=1}^{d} \nabla_\theta \pi_\theta(s^{(k)}) \frac{\partial}{\partial a^{(k)}} \log T(s^{(k+1)} \mid s^{(k)}, a^{(k)}) \tag{11.18}$$

Equations (11.17) and (11.18) require knowing the transition likelihood, which is in contrast with equation (11.15) for stochastic policies.

[11] Many problems have vector-valued actions $\mathbf{a} \in \mathbb{R}^n$. In this case, $\nabla_\theta \pi_\theta(s^{(k)})$ is replaced with a Jacobian matrix whose jth column is the gradient with respect to the jth action component, and the $\frac{\partial}{\partial a^{(k)}} \log T(s^{(k+1)} \mid s^{(k)}, a^{(k)})$ is replaced with an action gradient.

```
struct LikelihoodRatioGradient
    𝒫 # problem
    b # initial state distribution
    d # depth
    m # number of samples
    ∇logπ # gradient of log likelihood
end

function gradient(M::LikelihoodRatioGradient, π, θ)
    𝒫, b, d, m, ∇logπ, γ = M.𝒫, M.b, M.d, M.m, M.∇logπ, M.𝒫.γ
    πθ(s) = π(θ, s)
    R(τ) = sum(r*γ^(k-1) for (k, (s,a,r)) in enumerate(τ))
    ∇U(τ) = sum(∇logπ(θ, a, s) for (s,a) in τ)*R(τ)
    return mean(∇U(simulate(𝒫, rand(b), πθ, d)) for i in 1:m)
end
```

Algorithm 11.4. A method for estimating a policy gradient of a policy $\pi(s)$ for an MDP $\mathcal{P}$ with initial state distribution b using the likelihood ratio trick. The gradient with respect to the parameterization vector θ is estimated from m rollouts to depth d using the log policy gradients $\nabla log\pi$.

11.4 Reward-to-Go

The likelihood ratio policy gradient method is unbiased but has high variance. Example 11.4 reviews bias and variance. The variance generally increases significantly with rollout depth due to the correlation between actions, states, and

Consider the single-step, single-state problem from example 11.1. Suppose we have a stochastic policy π_θ that samples its action according to a Gaussian distribution $\mathcal{N}(\theta_1, \theta_2^2)$, where θ_2^2 is the variance.

$$\log \pi_\theta(a \mid s) = \log\left(\frac{1}{\sqrt{2\pi\theta_2^2}} \exp\left(-\frac{(a-\theta_1)^2}{2\theta_2^2}\right)\right)$$

$$= -\frac{(a-\theta_1)^2}{2\theta_2^2} - \frac{1}{2}\log\left(2\pi\theta_2^2\right)$$

The gradient of the log policy likelihood is

$$\frac{\partial}{\partial\theta_1} \log \pi_\theta(a \mid s) = \frac{a-\theta_1}{\theta_2^2}$$

$$\frac{\partial}{\partial\theta_2} \log \pi_\theta(a \mid s) = \frac{(a-\theta_1)^2 - \theta_2^2}{\theta_2^3}$$

Suppose we run three rollouts with $\theta = [0, 1]$, taking actions $\{0.5, -1, 0.7\}$ and receiving the same rewards $(R(s,a) = a)$. The estimated policy gradient is

$$\nabla U(\theta) \approx \frac{1}{m}\sum_{i=1}^{m} \nabla_\theta \log p_\theta(\tau^{(i)}) R(\tau^{(i)})$$

$$= \frac{1}{3}\left(\begin{bmatrix} 0.5 \\ -0.75 \end{bmatrix} 0.5 + \begin{bmatrix} -1.0 \\ 0.0 \end{bmatrix}(-1) + \begin{bmatrix} 0.7 \\ -0.51 \end{bmatrix} 0.7\right)$$

$$= [0.58, -0.244]$$

Example 11.3. Applying the likelihood ratio trick to estimate a policy gradient in a simple problem.

When estimating a quantity of interest from a collection of simulations, we generally want to use a scheme that has both low *bias* and low *variance*. In this chapter, we want to estimate $\nabla U(\theta)$. Generally, with more simulation samples, we can arrive at a better estimate. Some methods can lead to bias, where—even with infinitely many samples—it does not lead to an accurate estimate. Sometimes methods with nonzero bias may still be attractive if they also have low variance, meaning that they require fewer samples to converge.

Here are plots of the estimates from four notional methods for estimating $\nabla U(\theta)$. The true value is 17.5, as indicated by the red lines. We ran 100 simulations 100 times for each method. The variance decreases as the number of samples increases. The blue regions indicate the 5 % to 95 % and 25 % to 75 % empirical quantiles of the estimates.

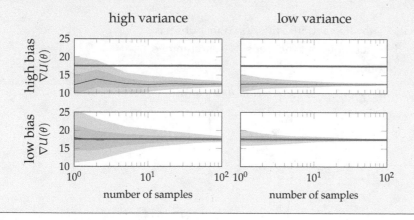

Example 11.4. An empirical demonstration of bias and variance when estimating $\nabla U(\theta)$.

rewards across time steps. The *reward-to-go* approach attempts to reduce the variance in the estimate.

To derive this approach, we begin by expanding equation (11.14):

$$\nabla U(\theta) = \mathbb{E}_\tau \left[\left(\sum_{k=1}^d \nabla_\theta \log \pi_\theta(a^{(k)} \mid s^{(k)}) \right) \left(\sum_{k=1}^d r^{(k)} \gamma^{k-1} \right) \right] \qquad (11.19)$$

Let $f^{(k)}$ replace $\nabla_\theta \log \pi_\theta(a^{(k)} \mid s^{(k)})$ for convenience. We then expand as follows:

$$\nabla U(\theta) = \mathbb{E}_\tau \left[\left(\sum_{k=1}^d f^{(k)} \right) \left(\sum_{k=1}^d r^{(k)} \gamma^{k-1} \right) \right] \qquad (11.20)$$

$$= \mathbb{E}_\tau \left[\left(f^{(1)} + f^{(2)} + f^{(3)} + \cdots + f^{(d)} \right) \left(r^{(1)} + r^{(2)} \gamma + r^{(3)} \gamma^2 + \cdots + r^{(d)} \gamma^{d-1} \right) \right] \qquad (11.21)$$

$$= \mathbb{E}_\tau \begin{bmatrix} f^{(1)}r^{(1)} + f^{(1)}r^{(2)}\gamma + f^{(1)}r^{(3)}\gamma^2 + \cdots + f^{(1)}r^{(d)}\gamma^{d-1} \\ +f^{(2)}r^{(1)} + f^{(2)}r^{(2)}\gamma + f^{(2)}r^{(3)}\gamma^2 + \cdots + f^{(2)}r^{(d)}\gamma^{d-1} \\ +f^{(3)}r^{(1)} + f^{(3)}r^{(2)}\gamma + f^{(3)}r^{(3)}\gamma^2 + \cdots + f^{(3)}r^{(d)}\gamma^{d-1} \\ \vdots \\ +f^{(d)}r^{(1)} + f^{(d)}r^{(2)}\gamma + f^{(d)}r^{(3)}\gamma^2 + \cdots + f^{(d)}r^{(d)}\gamma^{d-1} \end{bmatrix} \qquad (11.22)$$

The first reward, $r^{(1)}$, is affected only by the first action. Thus, its contribution to the policy gradient should not depend on subsequent time steps. We can remove other such causality-violating terms as follows:[12]

$$\nabla U(\theta) = \mathbb{E}_\tau \begin{bmatrix} f^{(1)}r^{(1)} + f^{(1)}r^{(2)}\gamma + f^{(1)}r^{(3)}\gamma^2 + \cdots + f^{(1)}r^{(d)}\gamma^{d-1} \\ + f^{(2)}r^{(2)}\gamma + f^{(2)}r^{(3)}\gamma^2 + \cdots + f^{(2)}r^{(d)}\gamma^{d-1} \\ + f^{(3)}r^{(3)}\gamma^2 + \cdots + f^{(3)}r^{(d)}\gamma^{d-1} \\ \vdots \\ + f^{(d)}r^{(d)}\gamma^{d-1} \end{bmatrix} \qquad (11.23)$$

$$= \mathbb{E}_\tau \left[\sum_{k=1}^d \nabla_\theta \log \pi_\theta(a^{(k)} \mid s^{(k)}) \left(\sum_{\ell=k}^d r^{(\ell)} \gamma^{\ell-1} \right) \right] \qquad (11.24)$$

$$= \mathbb{E}_\tau \left[\sum_{k=1}^d \nabla_\theta \log \pi_\theta(a^{(k)} \mid s^{(k)}) \left(\gamma^{k-1} \sum_{\ell=k}^d r^{(\ell)} \gamma^{\ell-k} \right) \right] \qquad (11.25)$$

$$= \mathbb{E}_\tau \left[\sum_{k=1}^d \nabla_\theta \log \pi_\theta(a^{(k)} \mid s^{(k)}) \gamma^{k-1} r_{\text{to-go}}^{(k)} \right] \qquad (11.26)$$

[12] The term $\sum_{\ell=k}^d r^{(\ell)} \gamma^{\ell-k}$ is often called the *reward-to-go* from step k.

Algorithm 11.5 provides an implementation of this.

Notice that the reward-to-go for a state-action pair (s, a) under a policy parameterized by θ is really an approximation of the state-action value from that state, $Q_\theta(s, a)$. The action value function, if known, can be used to obtain the policy gradient:

$$\nabla U(\theta) = \mathbb{E}_\tau \left[\sum_{k=1}^d \nabla_\theta \log \pi_\theta(a^{(k)} \mid s^{(k)}) \gamma^{k-1} Q_\theta\left(s^{(k)}, a^{(k)}\right) \right] \qquad (11.27)$$

```
struct RewardToGoGradient
    𝒫 # problem
    b # initial state distribution
    d # depth
    m # number of samples
    ∇logπ # gradient of log likelihood
end

function gradient(M::RewardToGoGradient, π, θ)
    𝒫, b, d, m, ∇logπ, γ = M.𝒫, M.b, M.d, M.m, M.∇logπ, M.𝒫.γ
    πθ(s) = π(θ, s)
    R(τ, j) = sum(r*γ^(k-1) for (k,(s,a,r)) in zip(j:d, τ[j:end]))
    ∇U(τ) = sum(∇logπ(θ, a, s)*R(τ,j) for (j, (s,a,r)) in enumerate(τ))
    return mean(∇U(simulate(𝒫, rand(b), πθ, d)) for i in 1:m)
end
```

Algorithm 11.5. A method that uses reward-to-go for estimating a policy gradient of a policy $\pi(s)$ for an MDP $\mathcal{P}$ with initial state distribution b. The gradient with respect to the parameterization vector θ is estimated from m rollouts to depth d using the log policy gradient ∇logπ.

11.5 Baseline Subtraction

We can further build on the approach presented in the previous section by subtracting a *baseline* value from the reward-to-go[13] to reduce the variance of the gradient estimate. This subtraction does not bias the gradient.

We now subtract a baseline $r_{\text{base}}(s^{(k)})$:

[13] We could also subtract a baseline from a state-action value.

$$\nabla U(\theta) = \mathbb{E}_\tau \left[\sum_{k=1}^d \nabla_\theta \log \pi_\theta(a^{(k)} \mid s^{(k)}) \gamma^{k-1} \left(r_{\text{to-go}}^{(k)} - r_{\text{base}}(s^{(k)}) \right) \right] \qquad (11.28)$$

To show that baseline subtraction does not bias the gradient, we first expand:

$$\nabla U(\theta) = \mathbb{E}_\tau \left[\sum_{k=1}^d \nabla_\theta \log \pi_\theta(a^{(k)} \mid s^{(k)}) \gamma^{k-1} r_{\text{to-go}}^{(k)} - \sum_{k=1}^d \nabla_\theta \log \pi_\theta(a^{(k)} \mid s^{(k)}) \gamma^{k-1} r_{\text{base}}(s^{(k)}) \right] \qquad (11.29)$$

The *linearity of expectation* states that $\mathbb{E}[a + b] = \mathbb{E}[a] + \mathbb{E}[b]$, so it is sufficient to prove that equation (11.29) is equivalent to equation (11.26), if for each step k, the expected associated baseline term is **0**:

$$\mathbb{E}_{\tau}\left[\nabla_{\theta} \log \pi_{\theta}(a^{(k)} \mid s^{(k)})\gamma^{k-1}r_{\text{base}}(s^{(k)})\right] = \mathbf{0} \tag{11.30}$$

We begin by converting the expectation into nested expectations, as illustrated in figure 11.2:

$$\mathbb{E}_{\tau}\left[\nabla_{\theta} \log \pi_{\theta}(a^{(k)} \mid s^{(k)})\gamma^{k-1}r_{\text{base}}(s^{(k)})\right] = \mathbb{E}_{\tau_{1:k}}\left[\mathbb{E}_{\tau_{k+1:d}}\left[\nabla_{\theta} \log \pi_{\theta}(a^{(k)} \mid s^{(k)})\gamma^{k-1}r_{\text{base}}(s^{(k)})\right]\right] \tag{11.31}$$

$$\mathbb{E}_{\tau}[f(\tau)] \qquad\qquad \mathbb{E}_{\tau_{1:k}}\left[\mathbb{E}_{\tau_{k+1:d}}[f(\tau)]\right]$$

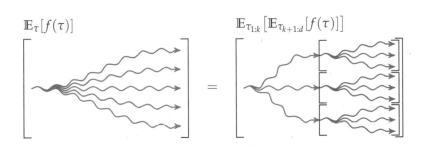

Figure 11.2. The expectation of a function of trajectories sampled from a policy can be viewed as an expectation over a nested expectation of subtrajectories. For a mathematical derivation, see exercise 11.4.

We continue with our derivation, using the same log derivative trick from section 11.3:

$$\mathbb{E}_{\tau_{1:k}}\left[\mathbb{E}_{\tau_{k+1:d}}\left[\nabla_{\theta} \log \pi_{\theta}(a^{(k)} \mid s^{(k)})\gamma^{k-1}r_{\text{base}}(s^{(k)})\right]\right]$$

$$= \mathbb{E}_{\tau_{1:k}}\left[\gamma^{k-1}r_{\text{base}}(s^{(k)})\;\mathbb{E}_{\tau_{k+1:d}}\left[\nabla_{\theta} \log \pi_{\theta}(a^{(k)} \mid s^{(k)})\right]\right] \tag{11.32}$$

$$= \mathbb{E}_{\tau_{1:k}}\left[\gamma^{k-1}r_{\text{base}}(s^{(k)})\;\mathbb{E}_{a^{(k)}}\left[\nabla_{\theta} \log \pi_{\theta}(a^{(k)} \mid s^{(k)})\right]\right] \tag{11.33}$$

$$= \mathbb{E}_{\tau_{1:k}}\left[\gamma^{k-1}r_{\text{base}}(s^{(k)})\int \nabla_{\theta} \log \pi_{\theta}(a^{(k)} \mid s^{(k)})\pi_{\theta}(a^{(k)} \mid s^{(k)})\,\mathrm{d}a^{(k)}\right] \tag{11.34}$$

$$= \mathbb{E}_{\tau_{1:k}}\left[\gamma^{k-1}r_{\text{base}}(s^{(k)})\int \frac{\nabla_{\theta} \pi_{\theta}(a^{(k)} \mid s^{(k)})}{\pi_{\theta}(a^{(k)} \mid s^{(k)})}\pi_{\theta}(a^{(k)} \mid s^{(k)})\,\mathrm{d}a^{(k)}\right] \tag{11.35}$$

$$= \mathbb{E}_{\tau_{1:k}}\left[\gamma^{k-1}r_{\text{base}}(s^{(k)})\,\nabla_{\theta}\int \pi_{\theta}(a^{(k)} \mid s^{(k)})\,\mathrm{d}a^{(k)}\right] \tag{11.36}$$

$$= \mathbb{E}_{\tau_{1:k}}\left[\gamma^{k-1}r_{\text{base}}(s^{(k)})\,\nabla_{\theta}1\right] \tag{11.37}$$

$$= \mathbb{E}_{\tau_{1:k}}\left[\gamma^{k-1}r_{\text{base}}(s^{(k)})\,\mathbf{0}\right] \tag{11.38}$$

Therefore, subtracting a term $r_{\text{base}}(s^{(k)})$ does not bias the estimate. This derivation assumed continuous state and action spaces. The same result applies to discrete spaces.

We can choose a different $r_{\text{base}}(s)$ for every component of the gradient, and we will select them to minimize the variance. For simplicity, we will drop the dependence on s and treat each baseline component as constant.[14] For compactness in writing the equations in our derivation, we define

[14] Some methods approximate a state-dependent baseline using $r_{\text{base}}(s^{(k)}) = \phi(s^{(k)})^\top \mathbf{w}$. Selecting appropriate baseline functions tends to be difficult. J. Peters and S. Schaal, "Reinforcement Learning of Motor Skills with Policy Gradients," *Neural Networks*, vol. 21, no. 4, pp. 682–697, 2008.

$$\ell_i(a,s,k) = \gamma^{k-1} \frac{\partial}{\partial \theta_i} \log \pi_\theta(a \mid s) \tag{11.39}$$

The variance of the ith component of our gradient estimate in equation (11.28) is

$$\mathop{\mathbb{E}}_{a,s,r_{\text{to-go}},k}\left[\left(\ell_i(a,s,k)\left(r_{\text{to-go}} - r_{\text{base},i}\right)\right)^2\right] - \mathop{\mathbb{E}}_{a,s,r_{\text{to-go}},k}\left[\ell_i(a,s,k)\left(r_{\text{to-go}} - r_{\text{base},i}\right)\right]^2 \tag{11.40}$$

where the expectation is over the $(a, s, r_{\text{to-go}})$ tuples in our trajectory samples, and k is each tuple's depth.

We have just shown that the second term is zero. Hence, we can focus on choosing $r_{\text{base},i}$ to minimize the first term by taking the derivative with respect to the baseline and setting it to zero:

$$\frac{\partial}{\partial r_{\text{base},i}} \mathop{\mathbb{E}}_{a,s,r_{\text{to-go}},k}\left[\left(\ell_i(a,s,k)\left(r_{\text{to-go}} - r_{\text{base},i}\right)\right)^2\right]$$

$$= \frac{\partial}{\partial r_{\text{base},i}}\left(\mathop{\mathbb{E}}_{a,s,r_{\text{to-go}},k}\left[\ell_i(a,s,k)^2 r_{\text{to-go}}^2\right] - 2\mathop{\mathbb{E}}_{a,s,r_{\text{to-go}},k}\left[\ell_i(a,s,k)^2 r_{\text{to-go}} r_{\text{base},i}\right] + r_{\text{base},i}^2 \mathop{\mathbb{E}}_{a,s,k}\left[\ell_i(a,s,k)^2\right]\right) \tag{11.41}$$

$$= -2 \mathop{\mathbb{E}}_{a,s,r_{\text{to-go}},k}\left[\ell_i(a,s,k)^2 r_{\text{to-go}}\right] + 2 r_{\text{base},i} \mathop{\mathbb{E}}_{a,s,k}\left[\ell_i(a,s,k)^2\right] = 0 \tag{11.42}$$

Solving for $r_{\text{base},i}$ yields the baseline component that minimizes the variance:

$$r_{\text{base},i} = \frac{\mathbb{E}_{a,s,r_{\text{to-go}},k}\left[\ell_i(a,s,k)^2 r_{\text{to-go}}\right]}{\mathbb{E}_{a,s,k}\left[\ell_i(a,s,k)^2\right]} \tag{11.43}$$

```
struct BaselineSubtractionGradient
    𝒫 # problem
    b # initial state distribution
    d # depth
    m # number of samples
    ∇logπ # gradient of log likelihood
end

function gradient(M::BaselineSubtractionGradient, π, θ)
    𝒫, b, d, m, ∇logπ, γ = M.𝒫, M.b, M.d, M.m, M.∇logπ, M.𝒫.γ
    πθ(s) = π(θ, s)
    ℓ(a, s, k) = ∇logπ(θ, a, s)*γ^(k-1)
    R(τ, k) = sum(r*γ^(j-1) for (j,(s,a,r)) in enumerate(τ[k:end]))
    numer(τ) = sum(ℓ(a,s,k).^2*R(τ,k) for (k,(s,a,r)) in enumerate(τ))
    denom(τ) = sum(ℓ(a,s,k).^2 for (k,(s,a)) in enumerate(τ))
    base(τ) = numer(τ) ./ denom(τ)
    trajs = [simulate(𝒫, rand(b), πθ, d) for i in 1:m]
    rbase = mean(base(τ) for τ in trajs)
    ∇U(τ) = sum(ℓ(a,s,k).*(R(τ,k).-rbase) for (k,(s,a,r)) in enumerate(τ))
    return mean(∇U(τ) for τ in trajs)
end
```

Algorithm 11.6. Likelihood ratio gradient estimation with reward-to-go and baseline subtraction for an MDP 𝒫, policy π, and initial state distribution b. The gradient with respect to the parameterization vector θ is estimated from m rollouts to depth d using the log policy gradients ∇logπ.

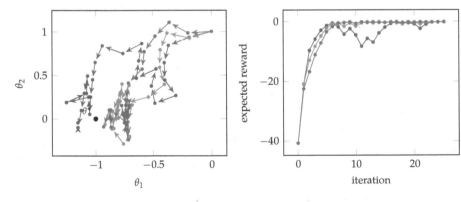

— • — likelihood ratio
— • — reward-to-go
— • — baseline subtraction

Figure 11.3. Several policy gradient methods used to optimize policies for the simple regulator problem from the same initial parameterization. Each gradient evaluation ran six rollouts to depth 10. The magnitude of the gradient was limited to 1, and step updates were applied with step size 0.2. The optimal policy parameterization is shown in black.

It is common to use likelihood ratio policy gradient estimation with this baseline subtraction (algorithm 11.6).[15]. Figure 11.3 compares the methods discussed here.

Qualitatively, when considering the gradient contribution of state-action pairs, what we really care about is the relative value of one action over another. If all actions in a particular state produce the same high value, there is no real signal in the gradient, and baseline subtraction can zero that out. We want to identify the actions that produce a higher value than others, regardless of the mean value across actions.

An alternative to the action value is the *advantage*, $A(s,a) = Q(s,a) - U(s)$. Using the state value function in baseline subtraction produces the advantage. The policy gradient using the advantage is unbiased and typically has much lower variance. The gradient computation takes the following form:

$$\nabla U(\theta) = \mathbb{E}_\tau \left[\sum_{k=1}^{d} \nabla_\theta \log \pi_\theta \left(a^{(k)} \mid s^{(k)}\right) \gamma^{k-1} A_\theta \left(s^{(k)}, a^{(k)}\right) \right] \qquad (11.44)$$

As with the state and action value functions, the advantage function is typically unknown. Other methods, covered in chapter 13, are needed to approximate it.

11.6 Summary

- A gradient can be estimated using finite differences.

- Linear regression can also be used to provide more robust estimates of the policy gradient.

- The likelihood ratio can be used to derive a form of the policy gradient that does not depend on the transition model for stochastic policies.

- The variance of the policy gradient can be significantly reduced using the reward-to-go and baseline subtraction.

[15] This combination is used in the class of algorithms called *REINFORCE* as introduced by R. J. Williams, "Simple Statistical Gradient-Following Algorithms for Connectionist Reinforcement Learning," *Machine Learning*, vol. 8, pp. 229–256, 1992.

11.7   Exercises

Exercise 11.1. If we estimate the expected discounted return of a given parameterized policy π_θ defined by an n-dimensional vector of parameters θ using m rollouts, how many total rollouts do we need to perform to compute the policy gradient using a finite difference approach?

Solution: In order to estimate the policy gradient using a finite difference approach, we need to estimate the utility of the policy given the current parameter vector $U(\theta)$, as well as all n variations of the current parameter vector $U(\theta + \delta \mathbf{e}^{(i)})$ for $i = 1:n$. Since we estimate each of these using m rollouts, we need to perform a total of $m(n+1)$ rollouts.

Exercise 11.2. Suppose we have a robotic arm with which we are able to run experiments manipulating a wide variety of objects. We would like to use the likelihood ratio policy gradient or one of its extensions to train a policy that is efficient at picking up and moving these objects. Would it be more straightforward to use a deterministic or a stochastic policy, and why?

Solution: The likelihood ratio policy gradient requires an explicit representation of the transition likelihood when used with deterministic policies. Specifying an accurate explicit transition model for a real-world robotic arm manipulation task would be challenging. Computing the policy gradient for a stochastic policy does not require having an explicit representation of the transition likelihood, making theh use of a stochastic policy more straightforward.

Exercise 11.3. Consider policy gradients of the form

$$\nabla_\theta U(\theta) = \mathbb{E}_\tau \left[\sum_{k=1}^{d} \gamma^{k-1} y \, \nabla_\theta \log \pi_\theta \left(a^{(k)} \mid s^{(k)} \right) \right]$$

Which of the following values of y result in a valid policy gradient? Explain why.

(a) $\gamma^{1-k} \sum_{\ell=1}^{\infty} r^{(\ell)} \gamma^{\ell-1}$

(b) $\sum_{\ell=k}^{\infty} r^{(\ell)} \gamma^{\ell-k}$

(c) $\left(\sum_{\ell=k}^{\infty} r^{(\ell)} \gamma^{\ell-k} \right) - r_{\text{base}}\left(s^{(k)}\right)$

(d) $U\left(s^{(k)}\right)$

(e) $Q\left(s^{(k)}, a^{(k)}\right)$

(f) $A\left(s^{(k)}, a^{(k)}\right)$

(g) $r^{(k)} + \gamma U\left(s^{(k+1)}\right) - U\left(s^{(k)}\right)$

Solution:

(a) $\sum_{\ell=1}^{\infty} r^{(\ell)}$ results in the total discounted reward, as

$$\gamma^{k-1}\gamma^{1-k}\sum_{\ell=1}^{\infty} r^{(\ell)}\gamma^{\ell-1} = \sum_{\ell=1}^{\infty} r^{(\ell)}\gamma^{\ell-1}$$

and produces a valid policy gradient, as given in equation (11.19).

(b) $\sum_{\ell=k}^{\infty} r^{(\ell)}\gamma^{\ell-k}$ is the reward-to-go and produces a valid policy gradient, as given in equation (11.26).

(c) $\left(\sum_{\ell=k}^{\infty} r^{(\ell)}\right) - r_{\text{base}}(s^{(k)})$ is the baseline subtracted reward-to-go and produces a valid policy gradient, as given in equation (11.28).

(d) $U(s^{(k)})$ is the state value function and does not produce a valid policy gradient.

(e) $Q(s^{(k)}, a^{(k)})$ is the state-action value function and produces a valid policy gradient, as given in equation (11.27).

(f) $A(s^{(k)}, a^{(k)})$ is the advantage function and produces a valid policy gradient, as given in equation (11.44).

(g) $r^{(k)} + \gamma U(s^{(k+1)}) - U(s^{(k)})$ is the temporal difference residual (to be discussed further in chapter 13) and produces a valid policy gradient because it is an unbiased approximation of the advantage function.

Exercise 11.4. Show that $\mathbb{E}_{\tau \sim \pi}[f(\tau)] = \mathbb{E}_{\tau_{1:k} \sim \pi}[\mathbb{E}_{\tau_{k:d} \sim \pi}[f(\tau)]]$ for step k.

Solution: The nested expectations can be proven by writing the expectation in integral form and then converting back:

$$\mathbb{E}_{\tau \sim \pi}[f(\tau)] =$$

$$= \int p(\tau)f(\tau)\, d\tau$$

$$= \int \left(p(s^{(1)}) \prod_{k=1}^{d} p(s^{(k+1)} \mid s^{(k)}, a^{(k)})\pi(a^{(k)} \mid s^{(k)})\right) f(\tau)\, d\tau$$

$$= \int\int\int\int \cdots \int \left(p(s^{(1)}) \prod_{k=1}^{d} p(s^{(k+1)} \mid s^{(k)}, a^{(k)})\pi(a^{(k)} \mid s^{(k)})\right) f(\tau)\, ds^{(d)} \cdots da^{(2)}\, ds^{(2)}\, da^{(1)}\, ds^{(1)}$$

$$= \underset{\tau_{1:k} \sim \pi}{\mathbb{E}} \left[\int\int\int\int \cdots \int \left(\prod_{q=k}^{d} p(s^{(q+1)} \mid s^{(q)}, a^{(q)})\pi(a^{(q)} \mid s^{(q)})\right) f(\tau)\, ds^{(d)} \cdots da^{(k+1)}\, ds^{(k+1)}\, da^{(k)}\, ds^{(k)} \right]$$

$$= \mathbb{E}_{\tau_{1:k} \sim \pi}[\mathbb{E}_{\tau_{k:d} \sim \pi}[f(\tau)]]$$

Exercise 11.5. Our implementation of the regression gradient (algorithm 11.3) fits a linear mapping from perturbations to the difference in returns, $U(\theta + \Delta\theta^{(i)}) - U(\theta)$. We evaluate $U(\theta + \Delta\theta^{(i)})$ and $U(\theta)$ for each of the m perturbations, thus reevaluating $U(\theta)$ a total of m times. How might we reallocate the samples in a more effective manner?

Solution: One approach is to evaluate $U(\theta)$ once and use the same value for each perturbation, thereby conducting only $m + 1$ evaluations. Having an accurate estimate of $U(\theta)$ is particularly important for an accurate regression gradient estimate. An alternative is to still compute $U(\theta)$ once, but use m rollouts, thus preserving the total number of rollouts per iteration. This approach uses the same amount of computation as algorithm 11.3, but it can produce a more reliable gradient estimate.

12 *Policy Gradient Optimization*

We can use estimates of the policy gradient to drive the search of the parameter space toward an optimal policy. The previous chapter outlined methods for estimating this gradient. This chapter explains how to use these estimates to guide the optimization. We begin with gradient ascent, which simply takes steps in the direction of the gradient at each iteration. Determining the step size is a major challenge. Large steps can lead to faster progress to the optimum, but they can overshoot. The natural policy gradient modifies the direction of the gradient to better handle variable levels of sensitivity across parameter components. We conclude with the trust region method, which starts in exactly the same way as the natural gradient method to obtain a candidate policy. It then searches along the line segment in policy space connecting the original policy to this candidate to find a better policy.

12.1 *Gradient Ascent Update*

We can use *gradient ascent* (reviewed in appendix A.11) to find a policy parameterized by θ that maximizes the expected utility $U(\theta)$. Gradient ascent is a type of *iterated ascent* method, which involves taking steps in the parameter space at each iteration in an attempt to improve the quality of the associated policy. All the methods discussed in this chapter are iterated ascent methods, but they differ in how they take steps. The gradient ascent method discussed in this section takes steps in the direction of $\nabla U(\theta)$, which may be estimated using one of the methods discussed in the previous chapter. The update of θ is

$$\theta \leftarrow \theta + \alpha \nabla U(\theta) \qquad (12.1)$$

where the step length is equal to a step factor $\alpha > 0$ times the magnitude of the gradient.

Algorithm 12.1 implements a method that takes such a step. This method can be called for either a fixed number of iterations or until θ or $U(\theta)$ converges. Gradient ascent, as well as the other algorithms discussed in this chapter, is not guaranteed to converge to the optimal policy. However, there are techniques to encourage convergence to a *locally optimal* policy, in which taking an infinitesimally small step in parameter space cannot result in a better policy. One approach is to decay the step factor with each step.[1]

[1] This approach, as well as many others, are covered in detail by M. J. Kochenderfer and T. A. Wheeler, *Algorithms for Optimization*. MIT Press, 2019.

```
struct PolicyGradientUpdate
    ∇U # policy gradient estimate
    α  # step factor
end

function update(M::PolicyGradientUpdate, θ)
    return θ + M.α * M.∇U(θ)
end
```

Algorithm 12.1. The gradient ascent method for policy optimization. It takes a step from a point θ in the direction of the gradient ∇U with step factor α. We can use one of the methods in the previous chapter to compute ∇U.

Very large gradients tend to overshoot the optimum and may occur due to a variety of reasons. Rewards for some problems, such as for the 2048 problem (appendix F.2), can vary by orders of magnitude. One approach for keeping the gradients manageable is to use *gradient scaling*, which limits the magnitude of a gradient estimate before using it to update the policy parameterization. Gradients are commonly limited to having an L_2-norm of 1. Another approach is *gradient clipping*, which conducts elementwise clamping of the gradient before using it to update the policy. Clipping commonly limits the entries to lie between ± 1. Both techniques are implemented in algorithm 12.2.

```
scale_gradient(∇, L2_max) = min(L2_max/norm(∇), 1)*∇
clip_gradient(∇, a, b) = clamp.(∇, a, b)
```

Algorithm 12.2. Methods for gradient scaling and clipping. Gradient scaling limits the magnitude of the provided gradient vector ∇ to L2_max. Gradient clipping provides elementwise clamping of the provided gradient vector ∇ to between a and b.

Scaling and clipping differ in how they affect the final gradient direction, as demonstrated in figure 12.1. Scaling will leave the direction unaffected, whereas clipping affects each component individually. Whether this difference is advantageous depends on the problem. For example, if a single component dominates the gradient vector, scaling will zero out the other components.

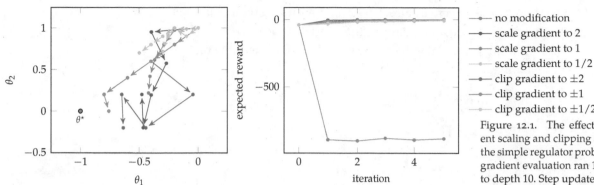

- no modification
- scale gradient to 2
- scale gradient to 1
- scale gradient to 1/2
- clip gradient to ± 2
- clip gradient to ± 1
- clip gradient to $\pm 1/2$

Figure 12.1. The effect of gradient scaling and clipping applied to the simple regulator problem. Each gradient evaluation ran 10 rollouts to depth 10. Step updates were applied with a step size of 0.2. The optimal policy parameterization is shown in black.

12.2   Restricted Gradient Update

The remaining algorithms in this chapter attempt to optimize an approximation of the objective function $U(\theta)$, subject to a constraint that the policy parameters at the next step θ' are not too far from θ at the current step. The constraint takes the form $g(\theta, \theta') \leq \epsilon$, where $\epsilon > 0$ is a free parameter in the algorithm. The methods differ in their approximation of $U(\theta)$ and the form of g. This section describes a simple *restricted step* method.

We use the first-order Taylor approximation (appendix A.12) obtained from our gradient estimate at θ to approximate U:

$$U(\theta') \approx U(\theta) + \nabla U(\theta)^\top (\theta' - \theta) \qquad (12.2)$$

For the constraint, we use

$$g(\theta, \theta') = \frac{1}{2}(\theta' - \theta)^\top \mathbf{I}(\theta' - \theta) = \frac{1}{2}\|\theta' - \theta\|_2^2 \qquad (12.3)$$

We can view this constraint as limiting the step length to no more than $\sqrt{2\epsilon}$. In other words, the feasible region in our optimization is a ball of radius $\sqrt{2\epsilon}$ centered at θ.

The optimization problem is, then,

$$\begin{aligned}
\underset{\theta'}{\text{maximize}} \quad & U(\theta) + \nabla U(\theta)^\top (\theta' - \theta) \\
\text{subject to} \quad & \frac{1}{2}(\theta' - \theta)^\top \mathbf{I}(\theta' - \theta) \leq \epsilon
\end{aligned} \qquad (12.4)$$

We can drop $U(\theta)$ from the objective since it does not depend on θ'. In addition, we can change the inequality to an equality in the constraint because the linear objective forces the optimal solution to be on the boundary of the feasible region. These changes result in an equivalent optimization problem:

$$\underset{\theta'}{\text{maximize}} \quad \nabla U(\theta)^\top (\theta' - \theta)$$

$$\text{subject to} \quad \frac{1}{2}(\theta' - \theta)^\top \mathbf{I}(\theta' - \theta) = \epsilon \tag{12.5}$$

This optimization problem can be solved analytically:

$$\theta' = \theta + \mathbf{u}\sqrt{\frac{2\epsilon}{\mathbf{u}^\top \mathbf{u}}} = \theta + \sqrt{2\epsilon}\frac{\mathbf{u}}{\|\mathbf{u}\|} \tag{12.6}$$

where the unnormalized search direction $\mathbf{u}$ is simply $\nabla U(\theta)$. Of course, we do not know $\nabla U(\theta)$ exactly, but we can use any of the methods described in the previous chapter to estimate it. Algorithm 12.3 provides an implementation.

```
struct RestrictedPolicyUpdate
    𝒫      # problem
    b      # initial state distribution
    d      # depth
    m      # number of samples
    ∇logπ  # gradient of log likelihood
    π      # policy
    ϵ      # divergence bound
end

function update(M::RestrictedPolicyUpdate, θ)
    𝒫, b, d, m, ∇logπ, π, γ = M.𝒫, M.b, M.d, M.m, M.∇logπ, M.π, M.𝒫.γ
    πθ(s) = π(θ, s)
    R(τ) = sum(r*γ^(k-1) for (k, (s,a,r)) in enumerate(τ))
    τs = [simulate(𝒫, rand(b), πθ, d) for i in 1:m]
    ∇log(τ) = sum(∇logπ(θ, a, s) for (s,a) in τ)
    ∇U(τ) = ∇log(τ)*R(τ)
    u = mean(∇U(τ) for τ in τs)
    return θ + u*sqrt(2*M.ϵ/dot(u,u))
end
```

Algorithm 12.3. The update function for the restricted policy gradient method at θ for a problem $\mathcal{P}$ with initial state distribution b. The gradient is estimated from an initial state distribution b to depth d with m simulations of parameterized policy $\pi(\theta, s)$ with log policy gradient $\nabla\log\pi$.

12.3   Natural Gradient Update

The *natural gradient* method[2] is a variation of the restricted step method discussed in the previous section to better handle situations when some components of the parameter space are more sensitive than others. *Sensitivity* in this context refers to how much the utility of a policy varies with respect to small changes in one of the parameters. The sensitivity in gradient methods is largely determined by the choice of scaling of the policy parameters. The natural policy gradient method makes the search direction **u** invariant to parameter scaling. Figure 12.2 illustrates the differences between the true gradient and the natural gradient.

[2] S. Amari, "Natural Gradient Works Efficiently in Learning," *Neural Computation*, vol. 10, no. 2, pp. 251–276, 1998.

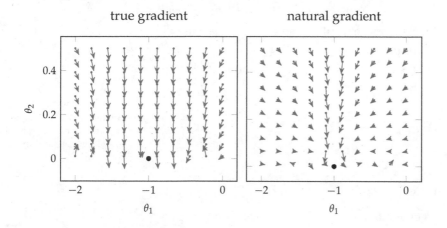

true gradient   natural gradient

Figure 12.2. A comparison of the true gradient and the natural gradient on the simple regulator problem (see appendix F.5). The true gradient generally points strongly in the negative θ_2 direction, whereas the natural gradient generally points toward the optimum (black dot) at $[-1, 0]$. A similar figure is presented in J. Peters and S. Schaal, "Reinforcement Learning of Motor Skills with Policy Gradients," *Neural Networks*, vol. 21, no. 4, pp. 682–697, 2008.

The natural policy gradient method uses the same first-order approximation of the objective as in the previous section. The constraint, however, is different. The intuition is that we want to restrict changes in θ that result in large changes in the distribution over trajectories. A way to measure how much a distribution changes is to use the *Kullback-Leibler divergence*, or KL divergence (appendix A.10). We could impose the constraint

$$g(\theta, \theta') = D_{KL}\left(p(\cdot \mid \theta) \,\|\, p(\cdot \mid \theta')\right) \leq \epsilon \qquad (12.7)$$

but instead we will use a second-order Taylor approximation:

$$g(\theta, \theta') = \frac{1}{2}(\theta' - \theta)^{\top} \mathbf{F}_{\theta} (\theta' - \theta) \leq \epsilon \qquad (12.8)$$

where the *Fisher information matrix* has the following form:

$$\mathbf{F}_\theta = \int p(\tau \mid \theta) \nabla \log p(\tau \mid \theta) \nabla \log p(\tau \mid \theta)^\top \, d\tau \qquad (12.9)$$

$$= \mathbb{E}_\tau \left[\nabla \log p(\tau \mid \theta) \nabla \log p(\tau \mid \theta)^\top \right] \qquad (12.10)$$

The resulting optimization problem is

$$\underset{\theta'}{\text{maximize}} \quad \nabla U(\theta)^\top (\theta' - \theta)$$

$$\text{subject to} \quad \frac{1}{2}(\theta' - \theta)^\top \mathbf{F}_\theta (\theta' - \theta) = \epsilon \qquad (12.11)$$

which looks identical to equation (12.5) except that instead of the identity matrix $\mathbf{I}$, we have the Fisher matrix $\mathbf{F}_\theta$. This difference results in an ellipsoid feasible set. Figure 12.3 shows an example in two dimensions.

This optimization problem can be solved analytically and has the same form as the update in the previous section:

$$\theta' = \theta + \mathbf{u}\sqrt{\frac{2c}{\nabla U(\theta)^\top \mathbf{u}}} \qquad (12.12)$$

except that we now have[3]

$$\mathbf{u} = \mathbf{F}_\theta^{-1} \nabla U(\theta) \qquad (12.13)$$

We can use sampled trajectories to estimate $\mathbf{F}_\theta$ and $\nabla U(\theta)$. Algorithm 12.4 provides an implementation.

12.4   Trust Region Update

This section discusses a method for searching within the *trust region*, defined by the elliptical feasible region from the previous section. This category of approach is referred to as *trust region policy optimization (TRPO)*.[4] It works by computing the next evaluation point θ' that would be taken by the natural policy gradient and then conducting a *line search* along the line segment connecting θ to θ'. A key property of this line search phase is that evaluations of the approximate objective and constraint do not require any additional rollout simulations.

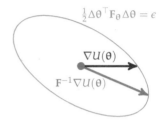

Figure 12.3. The natural policy gradient places a constraint on the approximated Kullback-Leibler divergence. This constraint takes the form of an ellipse. The ellipse may be elongated in certain directions, allowing larger steps if the gradient is rotated.

[3] This computation can be done using conjugate gradient descent, which reduces computation when the dimension of θ is large. S. M. Kakade, "A Natural Policy Gradient," in *Advances in Neural Information Processing Systems (NIPS)*, 2001.

[4] J. Schulman, S. Levine, P. Moritz, M. Jordan, and P. Abbeel, "Trust Region Policy Optimization," in *International Conference on Machine Learning (ICML)*, 2015.

```
struct NaturalPolicyUpdate
    𝒫        # problem
    b        # initial state distribution
    d        # depth
    m        # number of samples
    ∇logπ    # gradient of log likelihood
    π        # policy
    ϵ        # divergence bound
end

function natural_update(θ, ∇f, F, ϵ, τs)
    ∇fθ = mean(∇f(τ) for τ in τs)
    u = mean(F(τ) for τ in τs) \ ∇fθ
    return θ + u*sqrt(2ϵ/dot(∇fθ,u))
end

function update(M::NaturalPolicyUpdate, θ)
    𝒫, b, d, m, ∇logπ, π, γ = M.𝒫, M.b, M.d, M.m, M.∇logπ, M.π, M.𝒫.γ
    πθ(s) = π(θ, s)
    R(τ) = sum(r*γ^(k-1) for (k, (s,a,r)) in enumerate(τ))
    ∇log(τ) = sum(∇logπ(θ, a, s) for (s,a) in τ)
    ∇U(τ) = ∇log(τ)*R(τ)
    F(τ) = ∇log(τ)*∇log(τ)'
    τs = [simulate(𝒫, rand(b), πθ, d) for i in 1:m]
    return natural_update(θ, ∇U, F, M.ϵ, τs)
end
```

Algorithm 12.4. The update function for the natural policy gradient, given policy $\pi(\theta, s)$, for an MDP $\mathcal{P}$ with initial state distribution b. The natural gradient with respect to the parameter vector θ is estimated from m rollouts to depth d using the log policy gradients $\nabla\log\pi$. The natural_update helper method conducts an update according to equation (12.12), given an objective gradient $\nabla f(\tau)$ and a Fisher matrix $F(\tau)$ for a list of trajectories.

During the line search phase, we no longer use a first-order approximation. Instead, we use an approximation derived from an equality involving the advantage function[5]

$$U(\theta') = U(\theta) + \mathop{\mathbb{E}}_{\tau \sim \pi_{\theta'}} \left[\sum_{k=1}^{d} A_\theta\left(s^{(k)}, a^{(k)}\right) \right] \quad (12.14)$$

Another way to write this is to use $b_{\gamma,\theta}$, which is the *discounted visitation distribution* of state s under policy π_θ, where

$$b_{\gamma,\theta}(s) \propto P(s^{(1)} = s) + \gamma P(s^{(2)} = s) + \gamma^2 P(s^{(3)} = s) + \cdots \quad (12.15)$$

Using the discounted visitation distribution, the objective becomes

$$U(\theta') = U(\theta) + \mathop{\mathbb{E}}_{s \sim b_{\gamma,\theta'}} \left[\mathop{\mathbb{E}}_{a \sim \pi_{\theta'}(\cdot|s)} [A_\theta(s,a)] \right] \quad (12.16)$$

We would like to pull our samples from our policy parameterized by θ instead of θ' so that we do not have to run more simulations during the line search. The samples associated with the inner expectation can be replaced with samples from our original policy so long as we appropriately weight the advantage:[6]

$$U(\theta') = U(\theta) + \mathop{\mathbb{E}}_{s \sim b_{\gamma,\theta'}} \left[\mathop{\mathbb{E}}_{a \sim \pi_\theta(\cdot|s)} \left[\frac{\pi_{\theta'}(a \mid s)}{\pi_\theta(a \mid s)} A_\theta(s,a) \right] \right] \quad (12.17)$$

The next step involves replacing the state distribution with $b_{\gamma,\theta}$. The quality of the approximation degrades as θ' gets further from θ, but it is hypothesized that it is acceptable within the trust region. Since $U(\theta)$ does not depend on θ', we can drop it from the objective. We can also drop the state value function from the advantage function, leaving us with the action value function. What remains is referred to as the *surrogate objective*:

$$f(\theta, \theta') = \mathop{\mathbb{E}}_{s \sim b_{\gamma,\theta}} \left[\mathop{\mathbb{E}}_{a \sim \pi_\theta(\cdot|s)} \left[\frac{\pi_{\theta'}(a \mid s)}{\pi_\theta(a \mid s)} Q_\theta(s,a) \right] \right] \quad (12.18)$$

This equation can be estimated from the same set of trajectories that was used to estimate the natural gradient update. We can estimate $Q_\theta(s,a)$ using the reward-to-go in the sampled trajectories.[7]

The *surrogate constraint* in the line search is given by

$$g(\theta, \theta') = \mathop{\mathbb{E}}_{s \sim b_{\gamma,\theta}} [D_{\text{KL}}(\pi_\theta(\cdot \mid s) \| \pi_{\theta'}(\cdot \mid s))] \leq \epsilon \quad (12.19)$$

[5] A variation of this equality is proven in lemma 6.1 of S. M. Kakade and J. Langford, "Approximately Optimal Approximate Reinforcement Learning," in *International Conference on Machine Learning (ICML)*, 2002.

[6] This weighting comes from *importance sampling*, which is reviewed in appendix A.14.

[7] Algorithm 12.5 instead uses $\sum_{\ell=k} r^{(\ell)} \gamma^{\ell-1}$, which effectively discounts the reward-to-go by γ^{k-1}. This discount is needed to weight each sample's contribution to match the discounted visitation distribution. The surrogate constraint is similarly discounted.

Line search involves iteratively evaluating our surrogate objective f and surrogate constraint g for different points in the policy space. We begin with the θ' obtained from the same process as the natural gradient update. We then iteratively apply

$$\theta' \leftarrow \theta + \alpha(\theta' - \theta) \tag{12.20}$$

until we have an improvement in our objective with $f(\theta, \theta') > f(\theta, \theta)$ and our constraint is met with $g(\theta, \theta') \leq \epsilon$. The step factor $0 < \alpha < 1$ shrinks the distance between θ and θ' at each iteration, with α typically set to 0.5.

Algorithm 12.5 provides an implementation of this approach. Figure 12.4 illustrates the relationship between the feasible regions associated with the natural gradient and the line search. Figure 12.5 demonstrates the approach on a regulator problem, and example 12.1 shows an update for a simple problem.

12.5   Clamped Surrogate Objective

We can avoid detrimental policy updates from overly optimistic estimates of the trust region surrogate objective by *clamping*.[8] The surrogate objective from equation (12.18), after exchanging the action value advantage, is

$$\underset{s \sim b_{\gamma,\theta}}{\mathbb{E}} \left[\underset{a \sim \pi_\theta(\cdot|s)}{\mathbb{E}} \left[\frac{\pi_{\theta'}(a \mid s)}{\pi_\theta(a \mid s)} A_\theta(s, a) \right] \right] \tag{12.21}$$

The probability ratio $\pi_{\theta'}(a \mid s)/\pi_\theta(a \mid s)$ can be overly optimistic. A pessimistic lower bound on the objective can significantly improve performance:

$$\underset{s \sim b_{\gamma,\theta}}{\mathbb{E}} \left[\underset{a \sim \pi_\theta(\cdot|s)}{\mathbb{E}} \left[\min\left(\frac{\pi_{\theta'}(a \mid s)}{\pi_\theta(a \mid s)} A_\theta(s, a), \mathrm{clamp}\left(\frac{\pi_{\theta'}(a \mid s)}{\pi_\theta(a \mid s)}, 1 - \epsilon, 1 + \epsilon \right) A_\theta(s, a) \right) \right] \right] \tag{12.22}$$

where ϵ is a small positive value[9] and $\mathrm{clamp}(x, a, b)$ forces x to be between a and b. By definition, $\mathrm{clamp}(x, a, b) = \min\{\max\{x, a\}, b\}$.

Clamping the probability ratio alone does not produce a lower bound; we must also take the minimum of the clamped and original objectives. The lower bound is shown in figure 12.6, together with the original and clamped objectives. The end result of the lower bound is that the change in probability ratio is ignored when it would cause the objective to improve significantly. Using the lower bound thus prevents large, often detrimental, updates in these situations and removes the need for the trust region surrogate constraint equation (12.19). Without the

[8] Clamping is a key idea in what is known as *proximal policy optimization (PPO)* as discussed by J. Schulman, F. Wolski, P. Dhariwal, A. Radford, and O. Klimov, "Proximal Policy Optimization Algorithms," 2017. arXiv: 1707.06347v2.

[9] While this ϵ does not directly act as a threshold on divergence, as it did in previous algorithms, its role is similar. A typical value is 0.2.

```
struct TrustRegionUpdate
    𝒫      # problem
    b      # initial state distribution
    d      # depth
    m      # number of samples
    π      # policy π(s)
    p      # policy likelihood p(θ, a, s)
    ∇logπ  # log likelihood gradient
    KL     # KL divergence KL(θ, θ', s)
    ε      # divergence bound
    α      # line search reduction factor (e.g., 0.5)
end

function surrogate_objective(M::TrustRegionUpdate, θ, θ', τs)
    d, p, γ = M.d, M.p, M.𝒫.γ
    R(τ, j) = sum(r*γ^(k-1) for (k,(s,a,r)) in zip(j:d, τ[j:end]))
    w(a,s) = p(θ',a,s) / p(θ,a,s)
    f(τ) = mean(w(a,s)*R(τ,k) for (k,(s,a,r)) in enumerate(τ))
    return mean(f(τ) for τ in τs)
end

function surrogate_constraint(M::TrustRegionUpdate, θ, θ', τs)
    γ = M.𝒫.γ
    KL(τ) = mean(M.KL(θ, θ', s)*γ^(k-1) for (k,(s,a,r)) in enumerate(τ))
    return mean(KL(τ) for τ in τs)
end

function linesearch(M::TrustRegionUpdate, f, g, θ, θ')
    fθ = f(θ)
    while g(θ') > M.ε || f(θ') ≤ fθ
        θ' = θ + M.α*(θ' - θ)
    end
    return θ'
end

function update(M::TrustRegionUpdate, θ)
    𝒫, b, d, m, ∇logπ, π, γ = M.𝒫, M.b, M.d, M.m, M.∇logπ, M.π, M.𝒫.γ
    πθ(s) = π(θ, s)
    R(τ) = sum(r*γ^(k-1) for (k, (s,a,r)) in enumerate(τ))
    ∇log(τ) = sum(∇logπ(θ, a, s) for (s,a) in τ)
    ∇U(τ) = ∇log(τ)*R(τ)
    F(τ) = ∇log(τ)*∇log(τ)'
    τs = [simulate(𝒫, rand(b), πθ, d) for i in 1:m]
    θ' = natural_update(θ, ∇U, F, M.ε, τs)
    f(θ') = surrogate_objective(M, θ, θ', τs)
    g(θ') = surrogate_constraint(M, θ, θ', τs)
    return linesearch(M, f, g, θ, θ')
end
```

Algorithm 12.5. The update procedure for trust region policy optimization, which augments the natural gradient with a line search. It generates m trajectories using policy π in problem $\mathcal{P}$ with initial state distribution b and depth d. To obtain the starting point of the line search, we need the gradient of the log-probability of the policy generating a particular action from the current state, which we denote as ∇logπ. For the surrogate objective, we need the probability function p, which gives the probability that our policy generates a particular action from the current state. For the surrogate constraint, we need the divergence between the action distributions generated by π_θ and $\pi_{\theta'}$. At each step of the line search, we shrink the distance between the considered point θ' and θ while maintaining the search direction.

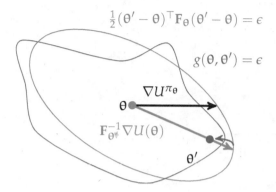

$$\frac{1}{2}(\theta' - \theta)^\top \mathbf{F}_\theta (\theta' - \theta) = \epsilon$$

$$g(\theta, \theta') = \epsilon$$

$$\nabla U^{\pi_\theta}$$

$$\theta$$

$$\mathbf{F}_{\theta^*}^{-1} \nabla U(\theta)$$

$$\theta'$$

Figure 12.4. Trust region policy optimization searches within the elliptical constraint generated by a second-order approximation of the Kullback-Leibler divergence. After computing the natural policy gradient ascent direction, a line search is conducted to ensure that the updated policy improves the policy reward and adheres to the divergence constraint. The line search starts from the estimated maximum step size and reduces the step size along the ascent direction until a satisfactory point is found.

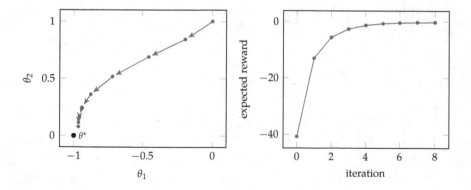

Figure 12.5. Trust region policy optimization applied to the simple regulator problem with rollouts to depth 10 with $\epsilon = 1$ and $c = 2$. The optimal policy parameterization is shown in black.

Consider applying TRPO to the Gaussian policy $\mathcal{N}(\theta_1, \theta_2^2)$ from example 11.3 to the single-state MDP from example 11.1 with $\gamma = 1$. Recall that the gradient of the log policy likelihood is

$$\frac{\partial}{\partial \theta_1} \log \pi_\theta(a \mid s) = \frac{a - \theta_1}{\theta_2^2}$$

$$\frac{\partial}{\partial \theta_2} \log \pi_\theta(a \mid s) = \frac{(a - \theta_1)^2 - \theta_2^2}{\theta_2^3}$$

Suppose that we run two rollouts with $\theta = [0, 1]$ (this problem only has one state):

$$\tau_1 = \{(a = r = -0.532), (a = r = 0.597), (a = r = 1.947)\}$$
$$\tau_2 = \{(a = r = -0.263), (a = r = -2.212), (a - r = 2.364)\}$$

The estimated Fisher information matrix is

$$\mathbf{F}_\theta = \frac{1}{2}\left(\nabla \log p(\tau^{(1)}) \nabla \log p(\tau^{(1)})^\top + \nabla \log p(\tau^{(2)}) \nabla \log p(\tau^{(2)})^\top\right)$$

$$= \frac{1}{2}\left(\begin{bmatrix} 4.048 & 2.878 \\ 2.878 & 2.046 \end{bmatrix} + \begin{bmatrix} 0.012 & -0.838 \\ -0.838 & 57.012 \end{bmatrix}\right) = \begin{bmatrix} 2.030 & 1.020 \\ 1.019 & 29.529 \end{bmatrix}$$

The objective function gradient is $[2.030, 1.020]$. The resulting descent direction $\mathbf{u}$ is $[1, 0]$. Setting $\epsilon = 0.1$, we compute our updated parameterization vector and obtain $\theta' = [0.314, 1]$.

The surrogate objective function value at θ is 1.485. Line search begins at θ', where the surrogate objective function value is 2.110 and the constraint yields 0.049. This satisfies our constraint (as $0.049 < \epsilon$), so we return the new parameterization.

constraint, we can also eliminate line search and use standard gradient ascent methods.

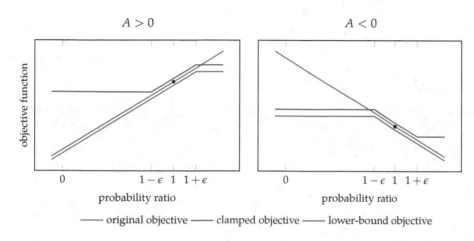

Figure 12.6. A visualization of the lower-bound objective for positive and negative advantages compared to the original objective and the clamped objective. The black point shows the baseline around which the optimization is performed, $\pi_{\theta'}(a \mid s)/\pi_\theta(a \mid s) = 1$. The three line plots in each axis are vertically separated for clarity.

The gradient of the unclamped objective equation (12.21) with action values is

$$\nabla_{\theta'} f(\theta, \theta') = \mathop{\mathbb{E}}_{s \sim b_{\gamma,\theta}} \left[\mathop{\mathbb{E}}_{a \sim \pi_\theta(\cdot|s)} \left[\frac{\nabla_{\theta'} \pi_{\theta'}(a \mid s)}{\pi_\theta(a \mid s)} Q_\theta(s,a) \right] \right] \qquad (12.23)$$

where $Q_\theta(s,a)$ can be estimated from reward-to-go. The gradient of the lower-bound objective equation (12.22) (with clamping), is the same, except there is no contribution from experience tuples for which the objective is actively clamped. That is, if either the reward-to-go is positive and the probability ratio is greater than $1 + \epsilon$, or if the reward-to-go is negative and the probability ratio is less than $1 - \epsilon$, the gradient contribution is zero.

Like TRPO, the gradient can be computed for a parameterization θ' from experience generated from θ. Hence, several gradient updates can be run in a row using the same set of sampled trajectories. Algorithm 12.6 provides an implementation of this.

The clamped surrogate objective is compared to several other surrogate objectives in figure 12.7, which includes a line plot for the effective objective for TRPO:

$$\mathop{\mathbb{E}}_{\substack{s \sim b_{\gamma,\theta} \\ a \sim \pi_\theta(\cdot|s)}} \left[\frac{\pi_{\theta'}(a \mid s)}{\pi_\theta(a \mid s)} A_\theta(s,a) - \beta D_{\mathrm{KL}}(\pi_\theta(\cdot \mid s) \mid\mid \pi_{\theta'}(\cdot \mid s)) \right] \qquad (12.24)$$

```
struct ClampedSurrogateUpdate
    𝒫      # problem
    b      # initial state distribution
    d      # depth
    m      # number of trajectories
    π      # policy
    p      # policy likelihood
    ∇π     # policy likelihood gradient
    ϵ      # divergence bound
    α      # step size
    k_max  # number of iterations per update
end

function clamped_gradient(M::ClampedSurrogateUpdate, θ, θ′, τs)
    d, p, ∇π, ϵ, γ = M.d, M.p, M.∇π, M.ϵ, M.𝒫.γ
    R(τ, j) = sum(r*γ^(k-1) for (k,(s,a,r)) in zip(j:d, τ[j:end]))
    ∇f(a,s,r_togo) = begin
        P = p(θ, a,s)
        w = p(θ′,a,s) / P
        if (r_togo > 0 && w > 1+ϵ) || (r_togo < 0 && w < 1-ϵ)
            return zeros(length(θ))
        end
        return ∇π(θ′, a, s) * r_togo / P
    end
    ∇f(τ) = mean(∇f(a,s,R(τ,k)) for (k,(s,a,r)) in enumerate(τ))
    return mean(∇f(τ) for τ in τs)
end

function update(M::ClampedSurrogateUpdate, θ)
    𝒫, b, d, m, π, α, k_max= M.𝒫, M.b, M.d, M.m, M.π, M.α, M.k_max
    πθ(s) = π(θ, s)
    τs = [simulate(𝒫, rand(b), πθ, d) for i in 1:m]
    θ′ = copy(θ)
    for k in 1:k_max
        θ′ += α*clamped_gradient(M, θ, θ′, τs)
    end
    return θ′
end
```

Algorithm 12.6. An implementation of clamped surrogate policy optimization, which returns a new policy parameterization for policy $\pi(s)$ of an MDP $\mathcal{P}$ with initial state distribution b. This implementation samples m trajectories to depth d, and then uses them to estimate the policy gradient in k_max subsequent updates. The policy gradient using the clamped objective is constructed using the policy gradients ∇p with clamping parameter ϵ.

which is the trust region policy objective where the constraint is implemented as a penalty for some coefficient β. TRPO typically uses a hard constraint rather than a penalty because it is difficult to choose a value of β that performs well within a single problem, let alone across multiple problems.

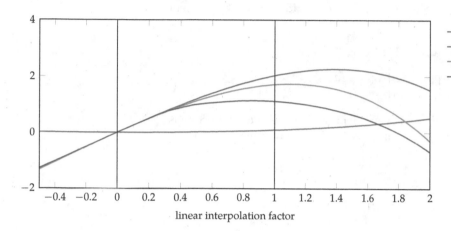

———— surrogate objective
———— surrogate constraint
———— TRPO effective objective
———— clamped surrogate objective

Figure 12.7. A comparison of surrogate objectives related to clamped surrogate policy optimization using the linear quadratic regulator problem. The x-axis shows surrogate objectives as we travel from θ at 0 toward θ', given a natural policy update at 1. The surrogate objectives were centered at 0 by subtracting the surrogate objective function value for θ. We see that the clamped surrogate objective behaves very similarly to the effective TRPO objective without needing a constraint. Note that ϵ and β can be adjusted for both algorithms, which would affect where the maximum is in each case.

12.6 Summary

- The gradient ascent algorithm can use the gradient estimates obtained from the methods discussed in the previous chapter to iteratively improve our policy.

- Gradient ascent can be made more robust by scaling, clipping, or forcing the size of the improvement steps to be uniform.

- The natural gradient approach uses a first-order approximation of the objective function with a constraint on the divergence between the trajectory distribution at each step, approximated using an estimate of the Fisher information matrix.

- Trust region policy optimization involves augmenting the natural gradient method with a line search to further improve the policy without additional trajectory simulations.

- We can use a pessimistic lower bound of the TRPO objective to obtain a clamped surrogate objective that performs similarly without the need for line search.

12.7   Exercises

Exercise 12.1. TRPO starts its line search from a new parameterization given by a natural policy gradient update. However, TRPO conducts the line search using a different objective than the natural policy gradient. Show that the gradient of the surrogate objective equation (12.18) used in TRPO is actually the same as the reward-to-go policy gradient equation (11.26).

Solution: The gradient of TRPO's surrogate objective is

$$\nabla_{\theta'} U_{\text{TRPO}} = \mathop{\mathbb{E}}_{s \sim b_{\gamma,\theta}} \left[\mathop{\mathbb{E}}_{a \sim \pi_\theta(\cdot|s)} \left[\frac{\nabla_{\theta'} \pi_{\theta'}(a \mid s)}{\pi_\theta(a \mid s)} Q_\theta(s,a) \right] \right]$$

When conducting the initial natural policy gradient update, the search direction is evaluated at $\theta' = \theta$. Furthermore, the action value is approximated with the reward-to-go:

$$\nabla_{\theta'} U_{\text{TRPO}} = \mathop{\mathbb{E}}_{s \sim b_{\gamma,\theta}} \left[\mathop{\mathbb{E}}_{a \sim \pi_\theta(\cdot|s)} \left[\frac{\nabla_\theta \pi_\theta(a \mid s)}{\pi_\theta(a \mid s)} r_{\text{to-go}} \right] \right]$$

Recall that the derivative of $\log f(x)$ is $f'(x)/f(x)$. It thus follows that

$$\nabla_{\theta'} U_{\text{TRPO}} = \mathop{\mathbb{E}}_{s \sim b_{\gamma,\theta}} \left[\mathop{\mathbb{E}}_{a \sim \pi_\theta(\cdot|s)} \left[\nabla_\theta \log \pi_\theta(a \mid s) r_{\text{to-go}} \right] \right]$$

which takes the same form as the reward-to-go policy gradient equation (11.26).

Exercise 12.2. Perform the calculations of example 12.1. First, compute the inverse of the Fisher information matrix $\mathbf{F}_\theta^{-1}$, compute $\mathbf{u}$, and compute the updated parameters θ'.

Solution: We start by computing the inverse of the Fisher information matrix:

$$\mathbf{F}_\theta^{-1} \approx \frac{1}{0.341(29.529) - 0.332(0.332)} \begin{bmatrix} 29.529 & -0.332 \\ -0.332 & 0.341 \end{bmatrix} \approx \begin{bmatrix} 0.501 & -0.017 \\ 0.017 & 0.034 \end{bmatrix}$$

Now, we update $\mathbf{u}$ as follows:

$$\mathbf{u} = \mathbf{F}_\theta^{-1} \nabla U(\theta) \approx \begin{bmatrix} 0.501 & -0.017 \\ -0.017 & 0.034 \end{bmatrix} \begin{bmatrix} 2.030 \\ 1.020 \end{bmatrix} \approx \begin{bmatrix} 1 \\ 0 \end{bmatrix}$$

Finally, we estimate the updated parameters θ:

$$\theta' = \theta + \mathbf{u}\sqrt{\frac{2\epsilon}{\nabla U(\theta)^\top \mathbf{u}}}$$

$$\approx \begin{bmatrix} 0 \\ 1 \end{bmatrix} + \begin{bmatrix} 1 \\ 0 \end{bmatrix} \sqrt{\frac{2(0.1)}{\begin{bmatrix} 2.030 & 1.020 \end{bmatrix}\begin{bmatrix} 1 \\ 0 \end{bmatrix}}}$$

$$\approx \begin{bmatrix} 0 \\ 1 \end{bmatrix} + \begin{bmatrix} 1 \\ 0 \end{bmatrix} \sqrt{\frac{0.2}{2.030}}$$

$$\approx \begin{bmatrix} 0.314 \\ 1 \end{bmatrix}$$

Exercise 12.3. Suppose we have the parameterized policies π_θ and $\pi_{\theta'}$ given in the following table:

	a_1	a_2	a_3	a_4
$\pi_\theta(a \mid s_1)$	0.1	0.2	0.3	0.4
$\pi_{\theta'}(a \mid s_1)$	0.4	0.3	0.2	0.1
$\pi_\theta(a \mid s_2)$	0.1	0.1	0.6	0.2
$\pi_{\theta'}(a \mid s_2)$	0.1	0.1	0.5	0.3

Given that we sample the following five states, s_1, s_2, s_1, s_1, s_2, approximate $\mathbb{E}_s\left[D_{\mathrm{KL}}(\pi_\theta(\cdot \mid s) \| \pi_{\theta'}(\cdot \mid s))\right]$ using the definition

$$D_{\mathrm{KL}}(P \| Q) = \sum_x P(x) \log \frac{P(x)}{Q(x)}$$

Solution: First, we compute the KL divergence for a state sample s_1:

$$D_{\mathrm{KL}}(\pi_\theta(\cdot \mid s_1) \| \pi_{\theta'}(\cdot \mid s_1)) = 0.1 \log\left(\tfrac{0.1}{0.4}\right) + 0.2 \log\left(\tfrac{0.2}{0.3}\right) + 0.3 \log\left(\tfrac{0.3}{0.3}\right) + 0.4 \log\left(\tfrac{0.4}{0.1}\right) \approx 0.456$$

Now, we compute the KL divergence for a state sample s_2:

$$D_{\mathrm{KL}}(\pi_\theta(\cdot \mid s_2) \| \pi_{\theta'}(\cdot \mid s_2)) = 0.1 \log\left(\tfrac{0.1}{0.1}\right) + 0.1 \log\left(\tfrac{0.1}{0.1}\right) + 0.6 \log\left(\tfrac{0.6}{0.5}\right) + 0.2 \log\left(\tfrac{0.2}{0.3}\right) \approx 0.0283$$

Finally, we compute the approximation of the expectation, which is the average KL divergence of the parameterized policies over the n state samples:

$$\mathbb{E}_s[D_{\mathrm{KL}}(\pi_\theta(\cdot \mid s) \| \pi_{\theta'}(\cdot \mid s))] \approx \frac{1}{n} \sum_{i=1}^{n} D_{\mathrm{KL}}\left(\pi_\theta(\cdot \mid s^{(i)}) \| \pi_{\theta'}(\cdot \mid s^{(i)})\right)$$

$$\approx \frac{1}{5}(0.456 + 0.0283 + 0.456 + 0.456 + 0.0283)$$

$$\approx 0.285$$

13 Actor-Critic Methods

The previous chapter discussed ways to improve a parameterized policy through gradient information estimated from rollouts. This chapter introduces *actor-critic methods*, which use an estimate of a value function to help direct the optimization. The actor, in this context, is the policy, and the critic is the value function. Both are trained in parallel. We will discuss several methods that differ in whether they approximate the value function, advantage function, or action value function. Most focus on stochastic policies, but we will also discuss one method that supports deterministic policies that output continuous actions. Finally, we will discuss a way to incorporate an online method for generating more informative trajectories for training the actor and critic.

13.1 Actor-Critic

In actor-critic methods, we have an actor represented by a policy π_θ, parameterized by θ with the help of a critic that provides an estimate of the value function $U_\phi(s)$, $Q_\phi(s,a)$, or $A_\phi(s,a)$ parameterized by ϕ. We will start this chapter with a simple actor-critic approach in which the optimization of π_θ is done through gradient ascent, with the gradient of our objective being the same as in equation (11.44):

$$\nabla U(\theta) = \mathbb{E}_\tau \left[\sum_{k=1}^{d} \nabla_\theta \log \pi_\theta(a^{(k)} \mid s^{(k)}) \gamma^{k-1} A_\theta\left(s^{(k)}, a^{(k)}\right) \right] \qquad (13.1)$$

The advantage when following a policy parameterized by θ can be estimated using a set of observed transitions from s to s' with reward r:

$$A_\theta(s,a) = \mathbb{E}_{r,s'} \left[r + \gamma U^{\pi_\theta}(s') - U^{\pi_\theta}(s) \right] \qquad (13.2)$$

The $r + \gamma U^{\pi_\theta}(s') - U^{\pi_\theta}(s)$ inside the expectation is referred to as the *temporal difference residual*.

The critic allows us to estimate the true value function U^{π_θ} when following π_θ, resulting in the following gradient for the actor:

$$\nabla U(\theta) \approx \mathbb{E}_\tau \left[\sum_{k=1}^{d} \nabla_\theta \log \pi_\theta (a^{(k)} \mid s^{(k)}) \gamma^{k-1} \left(r^{(k)} + \gamma U_\phi (s^{(k+1)}) - U_\phi (s^{(k)}) \right) \right] \tag{13.3}$$

This expectation can be estimated through rollout trajectories, as done in chapter 11.

The critic is also updated through gradient optimization. We want to find a ϕ that minimizes our loss function:

$$\ell(\phi) = \frac{1}{2} \mathbb{E}_s \left[(U_\phi (s) - U^{\pi_\theta}(s))^2 \right] \tag{13.4}$$

To minimize this objective, we can take steps in the opposite direction of the gradient:

$$\nabla \ell(\phi) = \mathbb{E}_s \left[(U_\phi (s) - U^{\pi_\theta}(s)) \nabla_\phi U_\phi (s) \right] \tag{13.5}$$

Of course, we do not know U^{π_θ} exactly, but it can be estimated using the reward-to-go along rollout trajectories, resulting in

$$\nabla \ell(\phi) = \mathbb{E}_\tau \left[\sum_{k=1}^{d} \left(U_\phi (s^{(k)}) - r^{(k)}_{\text{to-go}} \right) \nabla_\phi U_\phi (s^{(k)}) \right] \tag{13.6}$$

where $r^{(k)}_{\text{to-go}}$ is the reward-to-go at step k in a particular trajectory τ.

Algorithm 13.1 shows how to estimate $\nabla U(\theta)$ and $\nabla \ell(\phi)$ from rollouts. With each iteration, we step θ in the direction of $\nabla U(\theta)$ to maximize utility, and we step ϕ in the opposite direction of $\nabla \ell(\phi)$ to minimize our loss. This approach can become unstable due to the dependency between the estimation of θ and ϕ, but this approach has worked well for a variety of problems. It is a common practice to update the policy more frequently than the value function to improve stability. The implementations in this chapter can easily be adapted to update the value function only for a subset of the iterations that the policy is updated.

```
struct ActorCritic
    𝒫       # problem
    b       # initial state distribution
    d       # depth
    m       # number of samples
    ∇logπ   # gradient of log likelihood ∇logπ(θ,a,s)
    U       # parameterized value function U(ɸ, s)
    ∇U      # gradient of value function ∇U(ɸ,s)
end

function gradient(M::ActorCritic, π, θ, ɸ)
    𝒫, b, d, m, ∇logπ = M.𝒫, M.b, M.d, M.m, M.∇logπ
    U, ∇U, γ = M.U, M.∇U, M.𝒫.γ
    πθ(s) = π(θ, s)
    R(τ,j) = sum(r*γ^(k-1) for (k,(s,a,r)) in enumerate(τ[j:end]))
    A(τ,j) = τ[j][3] + γ*U(ɸ,τ[j+1][1]) - U(ɸ,τ[j][1])
    ∇Uθ(τ) = sum(∇logπ(θ,a,s)*A(τ,j)*γ^(j-1) for (j, (s,a,r))
                    in enumerate(τ[1:end-1]))
    ∇ℓɸ(τ) = sum((U(ɸ,s) - R(τ,j))*∇U(ɸ,s) for (j, (s,a,r))
                    in enumerate(τ))
    trajs = [simulate(𝒫, rand(b), πθ, d) for i in 1:m]
    return mean(∇Uθ(τ) for τ in trajs), mean(∇ℓɸ(τ) for τ in trajs)
end
```

Algorithm 13.1. A basic actor-critic method for computing both a policy gradient and a value function gradient for an MDP 𝒫 with initial state distribution b. The policy π is parameterized by θ and has a log-gradient ∇logπ. The value function U is parameterized by ɸ and the gradient of its objective function is ∇U. This method runs m rollouts to depth d. The results are used to update θ and ɸ. The policy parameterization is updated in the direction of ∇θ to maximize the expected value, whereas the value function parameterization is updated in the negative direction of ∇ɸ to minimize the value loss.

13.2 Generalized Advantage Estimation

Generalized advantage estimation (algorithm 13.2) is an actor-critic method that uses a more general version of the advantage estimate shown in equation (13.2) that allows us to balance between bias and variance.[1] Approximation with the temporal difference residual has low variance, but it introduces bias due to a potentially inaccurate U_ϕ used to approximate U^{π_θ}. An alternative is to replace $r + \gamma U^{\pi_\theta}(s')$ with the sequence of rollout rewards $r_1, \ldots, r_d$:

[1] J. Schulman, P. Moritz, S. Levine, M. Jordan, and P. Abbeel, "High-Dimensional Continuous Control Using Generalized Advantage Estimation," in *International Conference on Learning Representations (ICLR)*, 2016. arXiv: 1506.02438v6.

$$A_\theta(s,a) = \mathbb{E}_{r_1,\ldots,r_d}\left[r_1 + \gamma r_2 + \gamma^2 r_3 + \cdots + \gamma^{d-1}r_d - U^{\pi_\theta}(s)\right] \quad (13.7)$$

$$= \mathbb{E}_{r_1,\ldots,r_d}\left[-U^{\pi_\theta}(s) + \sum_{\ell=1}^{d}\gamma^{\ell-1}r_\ell\right] \quad (13.8)$$

We can obtain an unbiased estimate of this expectation through rollout trajectories, as done in the policy gradient estimation methods (chapter 11). However, the estimate is high variance, meaning that we need many samples to arrive at an accurate estimate.

The approach taken by generalized advantage estimation is to balance between these two extremes of using temporal difference residuals and full rollouts. We define $\hat{A}^{(k)}$ to be the advantage estimate obtained from k steps of a rollout and the utility associated with the resulting state s':

$$\hat{A}^{(k)}(s,a) = \mathbb{E}_{r_1,\ldots,r_k,s'}\left[r_1 + \gamma r_2 + \cdots + \gamma^{k-1} r_k + \gamma^k U^{\pi_\theta}(s') - U^{\pi_\theta}(s) \right] \quad (13.9)$$

$$= \mathbb{E}_{r_1,\ldots,r_k,s'}\left[-U^{\pi_\theta}(s) + \gamma^k U^{\pi_\theta}(s') + \sum_{\ell=1}^{k} \gamma^{\ell-1} r_\ell \right] \quad (13.10)$$

An alternative way to write $\hat{A}^{(k)}$ is in terms of an expectation over temporal difference residuals. We can define

$$\delta_t = r_t + \gamma U(s_{t+1}) - U(s_t) \quad (13.11)$$

where s_t, r_t, and s_{t+1} are the state, reward, and subsequent state along a sampled trajectory and U is our value function estimate. Then,

$$\hat{A}^{(k)}(s,a) = \mathbb{E}\left[\sum_{\ell=1}^{k} \gamma^{\ell-1} \delta_\ell \right] \quad (13.12)$$

Instead of committing to a particular value for k, generalized advantage estimation introduces a parameter $\lambda \in [0,1]$ that provides an *exponentially weighted average* of $\hat{A}^{(k)}$ for k ranging from 1 to d:[2]

[2] The exponentially weighted average of a series $x_1, x_2, \ldots$ is $(1-\lambda)(x_1 + \lambda x_2 + \lambda^2 x_3 + \cdots)$.

$$\hat{A}^{\text{GAE}}(s,a)\,|_{d=1} = \hat{A}^{(1)} \quad (13.13)$$

$$\hat{A}^{\text{GAE}}(s,a)\,|_{d=2} = (1-\lambda)\hat{A}^{(1)} + \lambda\hat{A}^{(2)} \quad (13.14)$$

$$\hat{A}^{\text{GAE}}(s,a)\,|_{d=3} = (1-\lambda)\hat{A}^{(1)} + \lambda\left((1-\lambda)\hat{A}^{(2)} + \lambda\hat{A}^{(3)}\right) \quad (13.15)$$

$$= (1-\lambda)\hat{A}^{(1)} + \lambda(1-\lambda)\hat{A}^{(2)} + \lambda^2\hat{A}^{(3)} \quad (13.16)$$

$$\vdots$$

$$\hat{A}^{\text{GAE}}(s,a) = (1-\lambda)\left(\hat{A}^{(1)} + \lambda\hat{A}^{(2)} + \lambda^2\hat{A}^{(3)} + \cdots + \lambda^{d-2}\hat{A}^{(d-1)}\right) + \lambda^{d-1}\hat{A}^{(d)} \quad (13.17)$$

For an infinite horizon, the generalized advantage estimate simplifies to

$$\hat{A}^{\text{GAE}}(s,a) = (1-\lambda)\left(\hat{A}^{(1)} + \lambda\hat{A}^{(2)} + \lambda^2\hat{A}^{(3)} + \cdots\right) \tag{13.18}$$

$$= (1-\lambda)\left(\delta_1\left(1 + \lambda + \lambda^2 + \cdots\right) + \gamma\delta_2\left(\lambda + \lambda^2 + \cdots\right) + \gamma^2\delta_3\left(\lambda^2 + \cdots\right) + \cdots\right) \tag{13.19}$$

$$= (1-\lambda)\left(\delta_1\frac{1}{1-\lambda} + \gamma\delta_2\frac{\lambda}{1-\lambda} + \gamma^2\delta_3\frac{\lambda^2}{1-\lambda} + \cdots\right) \tag{13.20}$$

$$= \mathbb{E}\left[\sum_{k=1}^{\infty}(\gamma\lambda)^{k-1}\delta_k\right] \tag{13.21}$$

We can tune parameter λ to balance between bias and variance. If $\lambda = 0$, then we have the high-bias, low-variance estimate for the temporal difference residual from the previous section. If $\lambda = 1$, we have the unbiased full rollout with increased variance. Figure 13.1 demonstrates the algorithm with different values for λ.

```
struct GeneralizedAdvantageEstimation
    𝒫        # problem
    b        # initial state distribution
    d        # depth
    m        # number of samples
    ∇logπ    # gradient of log likelihood ∇logπ(θ,a,s)
    U        # parameterized value function U(φ, s)
    ∇U       # gradient of value function ∇U(φ,s)
    λ        # weight ∈ [0,1]
end

function gradient(M::GeneralizedAdvantageEstimation, π, θ, φ)
    𝒫, b, d, m, ∇logπ = M.𝒫, M.b, M.d, M.m, M.∇logπ
    U, ∇U, γ, λ = M.U, M.∇U, M.𝒫.γ, M.λ
    πθ(s) = π(θ, s)
    R(τ,j) = sum(r*γ^(k-1) for (k,(s,a,r)) in enumerate(τ[j:end]))
    δ(τ,j) = τ[j][3] + γ*U(φ,τ[j+1][1]) - U(φ,τ[j][1])
    A(τ,j) = sum((γ*λ)^(ℓ-1)*δ(τ, j+ℓ-1) for ℓ in 1:d-j)
    ∇Uθ(τ) = sum(∇logπ(θ,a,s)*A(τ,j)*γ^(j-1)
                    for (j, (s,a,r)) in enumerate(τ[1:end-1]))
    ∇ℓφ(τ) = sum((U(φ,s) - R(τ,j))*∇U(φ,s)
                    for (j, (s,a,r)) in enumerate(τ))
    trajs = [simulate(𝒫, rand(b), πθ, d) for i in 1:m]
    return mean(∇Uθ(τ) for τ in trajs), mean(∇ℓφ(τ) for τ in trajs)
end
```

Algorithm 13.2. Generalized advantage estimation for computing both a policy gradient and a value function gradient for an MDP $\mathcal{P}$ with initial state distribution b. The policy is parameterized by θ and has a log-gradient ∇logπ. The value function U is parameterized by φ and has gradient ∇U. This method runs m rollouts to depth d. The generalized advantage is computed with exponential weighting λ using equation (13.21) with a finite horizon. The implementation here is a simplified version of what was presented in the original paper, which included aspects of trust regions when taking steps.

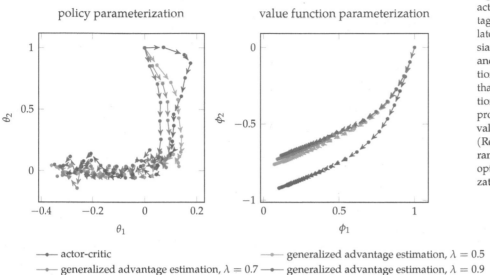

Figure 13.1. A comparison of basic actor-critic to generalized advantage estimation on the simple regulator problem with $\gamma = 0.9$, a Gaussian policy $\pi_\theta(s) = \mathcal{N}(\theta_1 s, \theta_2^2)$, and an approximate value function $U_\phi(s) = \phi_1 s + \phi_2 s^2$. We find that generalized advantage estimation is more efficiently able to approach well-performing policy and value function parameterizations. (Recall that the optimal policy parameterization is $[-1, 0]$ and the optimal value function parameterization is near $[0, -0.7]$.)

13.3   *Deterministic Policy Gradient*

The *deterministic policy gradient* approach[3] involves optimizing a deterministic policy $\pi_\theta(s)$ that produces continuous actions with the help of a critic in the form of a parameterized action value function $Q_\phi(s, a)$. As with the actor-critic methods discussed so far, we define a loss function with respect to the parameterization ϕ:

$$\ell(\phi) = \frac{1}{2} \mathop{\mathbb{E}}_{s,a,r,s'} \left[\left(r + \gamma Q_\phi(s', \pi_\theta(s')) - Q_\phi(s, a) \right)^2 \right] \tag{13.22}$$

[3] D. Silver, G. Lever, N. Heess, T. Degris, D. Wierstra, and M. Riedmiller, "Deterministic Policy Gradient Algorithms," in *International Conference on Machine Learning (ICML)*, 2014.

where the expectation is over the experience tuples generated by rollouts of π_θ. This loss function attempts to minimize the residual of Q_ϕ, similar to how the actor-critic method in the first section tried to minimize the residual of U_ϕ.

Similar to the other methods, we update ϕ by taking a step in the opposite direction of the gradient:

$$\nabla \ell(\phi) = \mathop{\mathbb{E}}_{s,a,r,s'} \left[\left(r + \gamma Q_\phi(s', \pi_\theta(s')) - Q_\phi(s, a) \right) \left(\gamma \nabla_\phi Q_\phi(s', \pi_\theta(s')) - \nabla_\phi Q_\phi(s, a) \right) \right] \tag{13.23}$$

We thus need a differentiable parameterized action value function from which we can compute $\nabla_\phi Q_\phi(s, a)$, such as a neural network.

For the actor, we want to find a value of θ that maximizes

$$U(\theta) = \mathop{\mathbb{E}}_{s \sim b_{\gamma,\theta}} \left[Q_\phi(s, \pi_\theta(s)) \right] \tag{13.24}$$

where the expectation is over the states from the discounted visitation frequency when following π_θ. Again, we can use gradient ascent to optimize θ with the gradient given by

$$\nabla U(\theta) = \mathbb{E}_s \left[\nabla_\theta Q_\phi(s, \pi_\theta(s)) \right] \tag{13.25}$$

$$= \mathbb{E}_s \left[\nabla_\theta \pi_\theta(s) \nabla_a Q_\phi(s, a)|_{a=\pi_\theta(s)} \right] \tag{13.26}$$

Here, $\nabla_\theta \pi_\theta(s)$ is a Jacobian matrix whose ith column is the gradient with respect to the ith action dimension of the policy under parameterization θ. An example for this term is given in example 13.1. The gradient $\nabla_a Q_\phi(s, a)|_{a=\pi_\theta(s)}$ is a vector that indicates how much our estimated action value changes as we perturb the action given by our policy at state s. In addition to the Jacobian, we need to supply this gradient to use this method.

Consider the following deterministic policy for a two-dimensional action space and a one-dimensional state space:

$$\pi_\theta(s) = \begin{bmatrix} \theta_1 + \theta_2 s + \theta_3 s^2 \\ \theta_1 + \sin(\theta_4 s) + \cos(\theta_5 s) \end{bmatrix}$$

The matrix $\nabla_\theta \pi_\theta(s)$ then takes the following form:

$$\nabla_\theta \pi_\theta(s) = \begin{bmatrix} \nabla_\theta \pi_\theta(s)\,|_{a_1} & \nabla_\theta \pi_\theta(s)\,|_{a_2} \end{bmatrix} = \begin{bmatrix} 1 & 1 \\ s & 0 \\ s^2 & 0 \\ 0 & \cos(\theta_4 s)s \\ 0 & -\sin(\theta_5 s)s \end{bmatrix}$$

Example 13.1. An example of the Jacobian in the deterministic policy gradient.

As with the other actor-critic methods, we perform gradient descent on $\ell(\phi)$ and gradient ascent on $U(\theta)$. For this approach to work in practice, a few additional techniques are needed. One is to generate experiences from a stochastic policy to allow better exploration. It is often adequate to simply add zero-mean

Gaussian noise to actions generated by our deterministic policy π_θ, as done in algorithm 13.3. To encourage stability when learning θ and ϕ, we can use experience replay.[4]

An example of this method and the effect of σ on performance is given in example 13.2.

```
struct DeterministicPolicyGradient
    𝒫      # problem
    b      # initial state distribution
    d      # depth
    m      # number of samples
    ∇π     # gradient of deterministic policy π(θ, s)
    Q      # parameterized value function Q(ϕ,s,a)
    ∇Qϕ    # gradient of value function with respect to ϕ
    ∇Qa    # gradient of value function with respect to a
    σ      # policy noise
end

function gradient(M::DeterministicPolicyGradient, π, θ, ϕ)
    𝒫, b, d, m, ∇π = M.𝒫, M.b, M.d, M.m, M.∇π
    Q, ∇Qϕ, ∇Qa, σ, γ = M.Q, M.∇Qϕ, M.∇Qa, M.σ, M.𝒫.γ
    π_rand(s) = π(θ, s) + σ*randn()*I
    ∇Uθ(τ) = sum(∇π(θ,s)*∇Qa(ϕ,s,π(θ,s))*γ^(j-1) for (j,(s,a,r))
                in enumerate(τ))
    ∇ℓϕ(τ,j) = begin
        s, a, r = τ[j]
        s′ = τ[j+1][1]
        a′ = π(θ,s′)
        δ = r + γ*Q(ϕ,s′,a′) - Q(ϕ,s,a)
        return δ*(γ*∇Qϕ(ϕ,s′,a′) - ∇Qϕ(ϕ,s,a))
    end
    ∇ℓϕ(τ) = sum(∇ℓϕ(τ,j) for j in 1:length(τ)-1)
    trajs = [simulate(𝒫, rand(b), π_rand, d) for i in 1:m]
    return mean(∇Uθ(τ) for τ in trajs), mean(∇ℓϕ(τ) for τ in trajs)
end
```

[4] We will discuss experience replay in section 17.7 in the context of reinforcement learning. Other techniques for stabilizing learning include using *target parameterizations*, described in the context of neural representations by T. P. Lillicrap, J. J. Hunt, A. Pritzel, N. Heess, T. Erez, Y. Tassa, D. Silver, and D. Wierstra, "Continuous Control with Deep Reinforcement Learning," in *International Conference on Learning Representations (ICLR)*, 2016. arXiv: 1509.02971v6.

Algorithm 13.3. The deterministic policy gradient method for computing a policy gradient $\nabla\theta$ for a deterministic policy π and a value function gradient $\nabla\phi$ for a continuous action MDP $\mathcal{P}$ with initial state distribution b. The policy is parameterized by θ and has a gradient $\nabla\pi$ that produces a matrix where each column is the gradient with respect to that continuous action component. The value function Q is parameterized by ϕ and has a gradient $\nabla Q\phi$ with respect to the parameterization and gradient ∇Qa with respect to the action. This method runs m rollouts to depth d, and performs exploration using 0-mean Gaussian noise with standard deviation σ.

13.4   Actor-Critic with Monte Carlo Tree Search

We can extend concepts from online planning (chapter 9) to the actor-critic setting in which we improve a parameterized policy $\pi_\theta(a \mid s)$ and a parameterized value function $U_\phi(s)$.[5] This section discusses the application of Monte Carlo tree search (section 9.6) to learning a stochastic policy with a discrete action space. We use our parameterized policy and value function to guide Monte Carlo tree search,

[5] Deterministic policy gradient used Q_ϕ, but this approach uses U_ϕ like the other actor-critic methods discussed in this chapter.

Consider applying the deterministic policy gradient algorithm to the simple regulator problem. Suppose we use a simple parameterized deterministic policy $\pi_\theta(s) = \theta_1$ and the parameterized state-action value function:

$$Q_\phi(s,a) = \phi_1 + \phi_2 s + \phi_3 s^2 + \phi_4(s+a)^2$$

Here, we plot a progression of the deterministic policy gradient algorithm starting with $\theta = [0]$ and $\phi = [0,1,0,-1]$ for different values of σ. Each iteration was run with five rollouts to depth 10 with $\gamma = 0.9$.

Example 13.2. An application of the deterministic policy gradient method to the simple regulator problem and an exploration of the impact of the policy stochasticity parameter σ.

For this simple problem, the policy quickly converges to optimality almost regardless of σ. However, if σ is either too small or too large, the value function takes longer to improve. In the case of very small values of σ, our policy conducts insufficient exploration from which to effectively learn the value function. For larger values of σ, we explore more, but we also tend to make poor move choices more frequently.

and we use the results from Monte Carlo tree search to refine our parameterized policy and value function. As with the other actor critic methods, we apply gradient-based optimization of θ and ϕ.[6]

As we perform Monte Carlo tree search, we want to direct our exploration to some extent by our parameterized policy $\pi_\theta(a \mid s)$. One approach is to use an action that maximizes the *probabilistic upper confidence bound*:

$$a = \arg\max_a Q(s,a) + c\pi_\theta(a \mid s)\frac{\sqrt{N(s)}}{1 + N(s,a)} \tag{13.27}$$

where $Q(s,a)$ is the action value estimated through the tree search, $N(s,a)$ is the visit count as discussed in section 9.6, and $N(s) = \sum_a N(s,a)$.[7]

After running tree search, we can use the statistics that we collect to obtain $\pi_{\text{MCTS}}(a \mid s)$. One way to define this is in terms of the counts:[8]

$$\pi_{\text{MCTS}}(a \mid s) \propto N(s,a)^\eta \tag{13.28}$$

where $\eta \geq 0$ is a hyperparameter that controls the greediness of the policy. If $\eta = 0$, then π_{MCTS} will generate actions at random. As $\eta \to \infty$, it will select the action that was selected the most from that state.

In our optimization of θ, we want our model π_θ to match what we obtain through Monte Carlo tree search. One loss function that we can define is the expected cross entropy of $\pi_\theta(\cdot \mid s)$ relative to $\pi_{\text{MCTS}}(\cdot \mid s)$:

$$\ell(\theta) = -\mathbb{E}_s\left[\sum_a \pi_{\text{MCTS}}(a \mid s) \log \pi_\theta(a \mid s)\right] \tag{13.29}$$

where the expectation is over states experienced during the tree exploration. The gradient is

$$\nabla\ell(\theta) = -\mathbb{E}_s\left[\sum_a \frac{\pi_{\text{MCTS}}(a \mid s)}{\pi_\theta(a \mid s)} \nabla_\theta \pi_\theta(a \mid s)\right] \tag{13.30}$$

To learn ϕ, we define a loss function in terms of a value function generated during the tree search:

$$U_{\text{MCTS}}(s) = \max_a Q(s,a) \tag{13.31}$$

which is defined at least at the states that we explore during tree search. The loss function aims to make U_ϕ agree with the estimates from the tree search:

$$\ell(\phi) = \frac{1}{2}\mathbb{E}_s\left[(U_\phi(s) - U_{\text{MCTS}}(s))^2\right] \tag{13.32}$$

[6] This general approach was introduced by D. Silver, J. Schrittwieser, K. Simonyan, I. Antonoglou, A. Huang, A. Guez, T. Hubert, L. Baker, M. Lai, A. Bolton, et al., "Mastering the Game of Go Without Human Knowledge," *Nature*, vol. 550, pp. 354–359, 2017. The discussion here loosely follows their *AlphaGo Zero* algorithm, but instead of trying to solve the game of Go, we are trying to solve a general MDP. Both the fact that Alpha Zero plays as both Go players and that games tend to have a winner and a loser allow the original method to reinforce the winning behavior and punish the losing behavior. The generalized MDP formulation will tend to suffer from sparse rewards when applied to similar problems.

[7] There are some notable differences from the upper confidence bound presented in equation (9.1); for example, there is no logarithm in equation (13.27) and we add 1 to the denominator to follow the form used by AlphaGo Zero.

[8] In algorithm 9.5, we select the greedy action with respect to Q. Other strategies are surveyed by C. B. Browne, E. Powley, D. Whitehouse, S. M. Lucas, P. I. Cowling, P. Rohlfshagen, S. Tavener, D. Perez, S. Samothrakis, and S. Colton, "A Survey of Monte Carlo Tree Search Methods," *IEEE Transactions on Computational Intelligence and AI in Games*, vol. 4, no. 1, pp. 1–43, 2012. The approach suggested here follows AlphaGo Zero.

The gradient is

$$\nabla \ell(\phi) = \mathbb{E}_s \big[(U_\phi(s) - U_{\mathrm{MCTS}}(s)) \nabla_\phi U_\phi(s) \big] \qquad (13.33)$$

Like the actor-critic method in the first section, we need to be able to compute the gradient of our parameterized value function.

After performing some number of Monte Carlo tree search simulations, we update θ by stepping in the direction opposite to $\nabla \ell(\theta)$ and ϕ by stepping in the direction opposite to $\nabla \ell(\phi)$.[9]

[9] The AlphaGo Zero implementation uses a single neural network to represent both the value function and the policy instead of independent parameterizations as discussed in this section. The gradient used to update the network parameters is a mixture of equations (13.30) and (13.33). This enhancement significantly reduces evaluation time and feature learning time.

13.5 Summary

- In actor-critic methods, an actor attempts to optimize a parameterized policy with the help of a critic that provides a parameterized estimate of the value function.

- Generally, actor-critic methods use gradient-based optimization to learn the parameters of both the policy and value function approximation.

- The basic actor-critic method uses a policy gradient for the actor and minimizes the squared temporal difference residual for the critic.

- The generalized advantage estimate attempts to reduce the variance of its policy gradient at the expense of some bias by accumulating temporal difference residuals across multiple time steps.

- The deterministic policy gradient can be applied to problems with continuous action spaces and uses a deterministic policy actor and an action value critic.

- Online methods, such as Monte Carlo tree search, can be used to direct the optimization of the policy and value function estimate.

13.6 Exercises

Exercise 13.1. Would the actor-critic method with Monte Carlo tree search, as presented in section 13.4, be a good method for solving the cart-pole problem (appendix F.3)?

Solution: The Monte Carlo tree search expands a tree based on visited states. The cart-pole problem has a continuous state space, leading to a search tree with an infinite branching factor. Use of this algorithm would require adjusting the problem, such as discretizing the state space.

Exercise 13.2. In the following expressions of advantage functions, determine which ones are correct and explain what they are referring to:

(a) $\mathbb{E}_{r,s'}\left[r + \gamma U^{\pi_\theta}(s) - U^{\pi_\theta}(s')\right]$

(b) $\mathbb{E}_{r,s'}\left[r + \gamma U^{\pi_\theta}(s') - U^{\pi_\theta}(s)\right]$

(c) $\mathbb{E}_{r_{1:d},s'}\left[-U^{\pi_\theta}(s) + \gamma^k U^{\pi_\theta}(s') + \sum_{\ell=1}^{k} \gamma^{l-1} r_l\right]$

(d) $\mathbb{E}_{r_{1:d},s'}\left[-U^{\pi_\theta}(s) + \gamma U^{\pi_\theta}(s') + \sum_{\ell=1}^{k} \gamma^{l-1} r_l\right]$

(e) $\mathbb{E}\left[-U^{\pi_\theta}(s) + \sum_{\ell=1}^{d} \gamma^{l-1} r_l\right]$

(f) $\mathbb{E}\left[-\gamma U^{\pi_\theta}(s') + \sum_{\ell=1}^{d+1} \gamma^{l-1} r_l\right]$

(g) $\mathbb{E}\left[\sum_{\ell=1}^{k} \gamma^{l-1} \delta_{l-1}\right]$

(h) $\mathbb{E}\left[\sum_{\ell=1}^{k} \gamma^{l-1} \delta_l\right]$

(i) $\mathbb{E}\left[\sum_{k=1}^{\infty} (\gamma\lambda)^{k-1} \delta_k\right]$

(j) $\mathbb{E}\left[\sum_{k=1}^{\infty} (\lambda)^{k-1} \delta_k\right]$

Solution: The following table lists the correct expressions:

(b)	Advantage with temporal difference residual
(c)	Advantage estimate after k-step rollouts
(e)	Advantage with the sequence of rollout rewards
(h)	Advantage estimate with temporal difference residuals
(i)	Generalized advantage estimate

Exercise 13.3. What are the benefits of using a temporal difference residual over a sequence of rollout rewards and vice versa?

Solution: Approximation using a temporal difference residual is more computationally efficient than using a sequence of rollouts. Temporal difference residual approximation has low variance but high bias due to using the critic value function U_ϕ as an approximator of the true value function U^{π_θ}. On the other hand, rollout approximation has high variance but is unbiased. Obtaining an accurate estimate using a temporal difference residual approximation typically requires far fewer samples than when using a rollout approximation, at the cost of introducing bias into our estimate.

Exercise 13.4. Consider the action value function given in example 13.2, $Q_\phi(s,a) = \phi_1 + \phi_2 s + \phi_3 s^2 + \phi_4 (s+a)^2$. Calculate the gradients required for the deterministic policy gradient approach.

Solution: We need to calculate two gradients. For the actor, we need to compute $\nabla_\phi Q_\phi(s,a)$, while for the critic, we need to compute $\nabla_a Q_\phi(s,a)$.

$$\nabla_\phi Q(s,a) \doteq \left[1, s, s^2, (s+a)^2\right]$$
$$\nabla_a Q(s,a) = 2\phi_4(s+a)$$

14 Policy Validation

The methods presented in the earlier chapters show how to construct an optimal or approximately optimal solution with respect to a model of the dynamics and reward. However, before deploying a decision-making system in the real world, it is generally desirable to validate in simulation that the behavior of the resulting policy is consistent with what is actually desired. This chapter discusses various analytical tools for validating decision strategies.[1] We will start by discussing how to go about evaluating performance metrics. Accurately computing such metrics can be computationally challenging, especially when they pertain to rare events such as failures. We will discuss methods that can help address computational efficiency. It is important that our systems be robust to differences between the models that we use for analysis and the real world. This chapter suggests methods for analyzing robustness. Fundamental to the design of many decision-making systems is the trade-off between multiple objectives, and we will outline ways of analyzing these trade-offs. The chapter concludes with a discussion of adversarial analysis, which can be used for finding the most likely failure trajectory.

[1] A more extensive discussion is provided by A. Corso, R. J. Moss, M. Koren, R. Lee, and M. J. Kochenderfer, "A Survey of Algorithms for Black-Box Safety Validation," *Journal of Artificial Intelligence Research*, vol. 72, pp. 377–428, 2021.

14.1 Performance Metric Evaluation

Once we have a policy, we are often interested in evaluating it with respect to various *performance metrics*. For example, suppose that we constructed a collision avoidance system—either through some form of optimization of a scalar reward function or just heuristically, as discussed in example 14.1—and we want to assess its safety by computing the probability of collision when following our policy.[2] Or, if we created a policy for constructing investment portfolios, we might be interested in understanding the probability that our policy will result in an extreme loss or what the expected return may be.

[2] Other safety risk metrics are discussed by I. L. Johansen and M. Rausand, "Foundations and Choice of Risk Metrics," *Safety Science*, vol. 62, pp. 386–399, 2014.

For the moment, we will consider a single metric f, evaluated on a policy π. Often, this metric is defined as the expectation of a trajectory metric f_{traj}, evaluated on trajectories $\tau = (s_1, a_1, \ldots)$ produced by following the policy:

$$f(\pi) = \mathbb{E}_\tau[f_{\text{traj}}(\tau)] \tag{14.1}$$

This expectation is over the trajectory distribution. To define a trajectory distribution associated with an MDP, we need to specify an *initial state distribution b*. The probability of generating a trajectory τ is

$$P(\tau) = P(s_1, a_1, \ldots) = b(s_1) \prod_t T(s_{t+1} \mid s_t, a_t) \tag{14.2}$$

In the collision avoidance context, f_{traj} may be 1 if the trajectory led to a collision, and 0 otherwise. The expectation would correspond to the collision probability.

In some cases, we are interested in studying the distribution over the output of f_{traj}. Figure 14.1 shows an example of such a distribution. The expectation in equation (14.1) is just one of many ways to convert a distribution over trajectory metrics to a single value. We will focus primarily on this expectation in our discussion, but examples of other transformations of the distribution to a value include variance, fifth percentile, and mean of the values below the fifth percentile.[3]

The trajectory metric can sometimes be written in this form:

$$f_{\text{traj}}(\tau) = f_{\text{traj}}(s_1, a_1, \ldots) = \sum_t f_{\text{step}}(s_t, a_t) \tag{14.3}$$

where f_{step} is a function that depends on the current state and action, much like the reward function in MDPs. If $f(\pi)$ is defined as the expectation of f_{traj}, the objective is the same as when solving an MDP, where f_{step} is simply the reward function. We can thus use the policy evaluation algorithms introduced in section 7.2 to evaluate our policy with respect to any performance metric of the form in equation (14.3).

Policy evaluation will output a value function that is a function of the state,[4] corresponding to the expected value of the performance metric when starting from that state. Example 14.2 shows slices of this value function for the collision avoidance problem. The overall performance is given by

$$f(\pi) = \sum_s f_{\text{state}}(s) b(s) \tag{14.4}$$

where f_{state} is the value function obtained through policy evaluation.

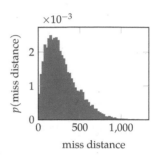

Figure 14.1. Distribution over the miss distance estimated from 10^4 simulations when following a simple collision avoidance policy from initial states with
$h \sim \mathcal{U}(-10,10)$ (m)
$\dot{h} \sim \mathcal{U}(-200,200)$ (m/s)
$a_{\text{prev}} = 0\,\text{m/s}$
$t_{\text{col}} = 40\,\text{s}$

[3] Various risk measures have been discussed in the literature. An overview of some of these that have been used in the context of MDPs is provided by A. Ruszczyński, "Risk-Averse Dynamic Programming for Markov Decision Processes," *Mathematical Programming*, vol. 125, no. 2, pp. 235–261, 2010.

[4] We used U^π to represent the value function associated with policy π in previous chapters.

In the aircraft collision avoidance problem, we need to decide when to issue a climb or descend advisory to our aircraft to avoid an intruder aircraft. The intruder is approaching us head on, with a constant horizontal closing speed. The state is specified by the altitude h of our aircraft measured relative to the intruder aircraft, our vertical rate $\dot{h}$, the previous action a_{prev}, and the time to potential collision t_{col}. There is a penalty of 1 when there is a collision, defined as when the intruder comes within 50 m when $t_{\text{col}} = 0$. In addition, there is a penalty of 0.01 when $a \neq a_{\text{prev}}$ to discourage advisory changes.

We can use dynamic programming with linear interpolation (section 8.4) to derive an optimal policy. Alternatively, we can define a simple heuristic policy parameterized by thresholds on t_{col} and h that works as follows. If $|h| < h_{\text{thresh}}$ and $t_{\text{col}} < t_{\text{thresh}}$, then an advisory is generated. This advisory is to climb if $h > 0$ and to descend otherwise. By default, we use $h_{\text{thresh}} = 50\,\text{m}$ and $t_{\text{thresh}} = 30\,\text{s}$. The following are plots of both the optimal and simple policies for two slices through the state space:

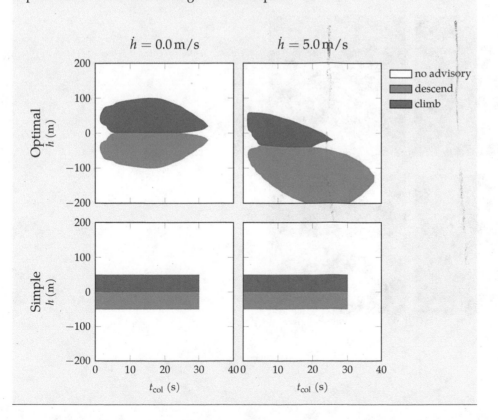

Example 14.1. Optimal and simple collision avoidance policies. Additional details of the problem are given in appendix F.6.

Here is the result of applying policy evaluation to both an optimal policy and the simple policy introduced in example 14.1. Each point in the plot corresponds to the value of the metric, conditioned on starting from the associated state. We define $f_{\text{state}}(s, a) = 1$ if s is a collision, and 0 otherwise. This plot shows where in the state space there is significant collision risk, indicated by "hotter" colors, when following the policy. We can see that the optimal policy is quite safe, especially if $t_{\text{col}} > 20\,\text{s}$. When t_{col} is low, even the optimal policy cannot avoid collision due to the physical acceleration constraints of the vehicle. The simple policy has a much higher level of risk compared to the optimal policy, especially when $t_{\text{col}} > 20\,\text{s}$, $\dot{h} = 5\,\text{m/s}$, and the intruder is below us—in part because the choice to produce an advisory in the simple strategy does not take $\dot{h}$ into account.

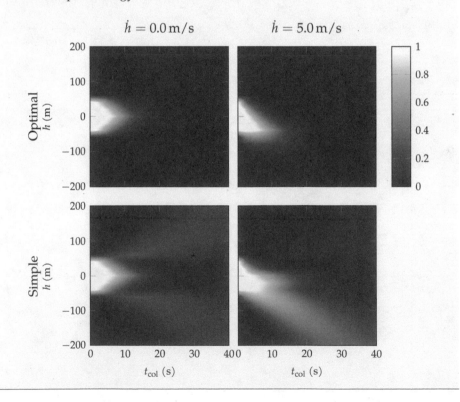

Example 14.2. Probability of a collision when following the optimal and simple collision avoidance policies.

If the state space is discrete, then equation (14.4) can be computed analytically. However, if the state space is large or continuous, we may want to estimate $f(\pi)$ through sampling. We can pull a sample from the initial state distribution and then roll out the policy and compute the trajectory metric. We can then estimate the value of the overall metric from the mean of the trajectory metrics. The quality of the estimate generally improves with more samples. Example 14.3 illustrates this process for estimating various metrics associated with collision avoidance policies.

We often use the *standard error* to measure the quality of our estimate:

$$\mathrm{SE} = \hat{\sigma}/\sqrt{n} \qquad (14.5)$$

where $\hat{\sigma}$ is the standard deviation of our samples and n is the number of samples. In example 14.3, the standard deviation of our collision metric is 0.0173, making the standard error of our collision probability metric 0.000173.

We can convert the standard error to a *confidence interval*. For example, a 95 % confidence interval would be $\hat{\mu} \pm 1.96\,\mathrm{SE}$, where $\hat{\mu}$ is the mean of our samples. For our collision avoidance example, this interval is $(-3.94 \times 10^{-5}, 6.39 \times 10^{-4})$. Alternatively, we can take a Bayesian approach and represent our posterior as a beta distribution, as discussed in section 4.2.

For small probabilities, such as failure probabilities in a relatively safe system, we are often interested in the *relative standard error*, which is given by

$$\frac{\hat{\sigma}}{\hat{\mu}\sqrt{n}} \qquad (14.6)$$

This is equivalent to dividing the standard error by the mean. In our collision avoidance problem, our relative error is 0.578. Although the absolute error might be small, the relative error is quite high since we are trying to estimate a small probability.

14.2 Rare Event Simulation

As we see in example 14.3, we may need many samples to accurately estimate metrics where rare events are very influential, such as estimating collision probability. In the collision avoidance example, our 10^4 samples contained only three collisions, as indicated by the three spikes in the plot. When we are designing algorithms for high-stakes systems, such as systems that trade money or drive cars,

We want to estimate the probability of collision and the probability of generating an advisory. Here, we will consider the optimal and simple policies introduced in example 14.1. To evaluate these metrics, we use 10^4 samples from the initial state distribution used in figure 14.1 and then perform rollouts. The plots here show the convergence curves:

Example 14.3. Probability of a collision and an advisory when following the optimal and simple collision avoidance policies.

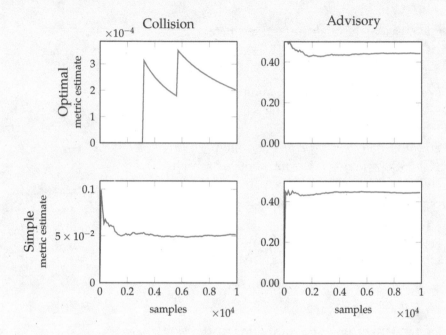

What we can see is that the optimal policy is much safer than the simple policy, while producing advisories at approximately the same frequency. The advisory metric estimate converges much more quickly than the collision estimates. The reason for the faster convergence for the advisory metric is that advisories are more common than collisions. Collisions involving the optimal policy are so rare that even 10^4 samples appear inadequate for an accurate estimate. The curve is very jagged, with large spikes at samples involving collisions, followed by a decay in the collision probability estimate as collision-free samples are simulated.

accurately estimating failure probabilities through direct sampling and simulation can be computationally challenging.

A common approach to improve efficiency is called *importance sampling*, which involves sampling from an alternative distribution and weighting the results appropriately to arrive at an unbiased estimate.[5] We used this same kind of approach in the context of inference in Bayesian networks by the name of likelihood weighted sampling (section 3.7). The alternative sampling distribution is often called a *proposal distribution*, and we will use $P'(\tau)$ to represent the probability our proposal distribution assigns to trajectory τ.

[5] A more elaborate introduction to importance sampling and other techniques for rare event simulation is provided by J. A. Bucklew, *Introduction to Rare Event Simulation*. Springer, 2004.

We will derive the appropriate way to weight samples from P'. If we have $\tau^{(1)}, \ldots, \tau^{(n)}$ drawn from the true distribution P, then we have

$$f(\pi) = \mathbb{E}_\tau[f_{\text{traj}}(\tau)] \tag{14.7}$$

$$= \sum_\tau f_{\text{traj}}(\tau) P(\tau) \tag{14.8}$$

$$\approx \frac{1}{n} \sum_i f_{\text{traj}}(\tau^{(i)}) \text{ with } \tau^{(i)} \sim P \tag{14.9}$$

We can multiply equation (14.8) by $P'(\tau)/P'(\tau)$ and obtain the following:

$$f(\pi) = \sum_\tau f_{\text{traj}}(\tau) P(\tau) \frac{P'(\tau)}{P'(\tau)} \tag{14.10}$$

$$= \sum_\tau f_{\text{traj}}(\tau) P'(\tau) \frac{P(\tau)}{P'(\tau)} \tag{14.11}$$

$$\approx \frac{1}{n} \sum_i f_{\text{traj}}(\tau^{(i)}) \frac{P(\tau^{(i)})}{P'(\tau^{(i)})} \text{ with } \tau^{(i)} \sim P' \tag{14.12}$$

In other words, we need to weight the outcomes of the samples from the proposal distribution, where the weight[6] given to sample i is $P(\tau^{(i)})/P'(\tau^{(i)})$.

We want to choose the proposal distribution P' to focus the generation of samples on those that are "important," in the sense that they are more likely to contribute to the overall performance estimate. In the case of collision avoidance, we will want this proposal distribution to encourage collisions so that we have more than just a few collision situations to estimate collision risk. However, we do not want all of our samples to result in collision. In general, assuming that the space of histories is discrete, the optimal proposal distribution is

[6] Importantly, P' must not assign zero likelihood to any trajectory to which P assigns positive likelihood.

$$P^*(\tau) = \frac{|f_{\text{traj}}(\tau)| P(\tau)}{\sum_{\tau'} |f_{\text{traj}}(\tau')| P(\tau')} \tag{14.13}$$

If f_{traj} is nonnegative, then the denominator is exactly the same as the metric that we are trying to estimate in equation (14.1).

Although equation (14.13) is generally not practical to compute exactly (this is why we are using importance sampling in the first place), it can provide some intuition as to how to use our domain expertise to construct a proposal distribution. It is common to bias the initial state distribution or the transition model slightly toward more important trajectories, such as toward collision.

To illustrate the construction of an importance distribution, we will use the optimal policy for the collision avoidance problem in example 14.1. Instead of starting at $t_{\text{col}} = 40\,\text{s}$, we will start the aircraft closer, with $t_{\text{col}} = 20\,\text{s}$, to make the collision avoidance problem more challenging. The true distribution has $h \sim \mathcal{U}(-10, 10)$ (m) and $\dot{h} \sim \mathcal{U}(-200, 200)$ (m/s). However, certain combinations of h and $\dot{h}$ are more challenging for the optimal policy to resolve. We used dynamic programming on a discrete version of the problem to determine the probability of collision for different values of h and $\dot{h}$. We can take these results and normalize them to turn them into the proposal distribution shown in figure 14.2.

Using the proposal distribution shown in figure 14.2 results in better estimates of the collision probability than direct sampling with the same number of samples. Figure 14.3 shows the convergence curves. By 5×10^4 samples, both sampling methods converge to the same estimate. However, importance sampling converges closely to the true value within 10^4 samples. Using our proposal distribution, importance sampling generated 939 collisions, while direct sampling generated only 246. Even more collisions could be generated if we also biased the transition distribution, rather than solely the initial state distribution.

14.3 Robustness Analysis

Before deploying a system in the real world, it is important to study its robustness to modeling errors. We can use the tools mentioned in the previous sections, such as policy evaluation and importance sampling, but evaluate our policies on environments that deviate from the model assumed when optimizing the policy. Figure 14.4 shows how performance varies as the true model deviates from the one used for optimization. We can also study the sensitivity of our metrics to modeling assumptions over the state space (example 14.4). If performance on the relevant metrics appears to be preserved under plausible perturbations of the

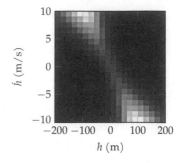

Figure 14.2. Proposal distribution generated from the probability of collision when following the optimal collision avoidance policies from different initial states with $t_{\text{col}} = 20\,\text{s}$ and $a_{\text{prev}} = 0\,\text{m/s}$. Yellow indicates higher probability density.

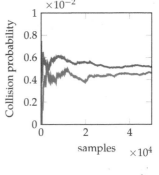

—— importance sampling
—— direct sampling

Figure 14.3. Collision probability when following the optimal policy as estimated by importance sampling and direct sampling.

environment model, then we can have greater confidence that our system will behave as planned when deployed.

We typically want our *planning model*, the model we use for optimizing our policies, to be relatively simple to prevent overfitting to potentially erroneous modeling assumptions that are not representative of the real world. A side benefit of simpler planning models is that they can make planning more computationally efficient. However, our *evaluation model* can be as complex as we can justify. For example, we may use a simple, low-dimensional, discrete model of aircraft dynamics when generating a collision avoidance policy, but then evaluate that policy in a continuous, high-fidelity simulation. A simpler planning model is often more robust to perturbations in the evaluation model.

The process of evaluating our policies on a variety of evaluation models is sometimes referred to as *stress testing*, especially if the spectrum of evaluation models includes fairly extreme scenarios. In collision avoidance, extreme scenarios might include those where the aircraft are converging on each other with extreme climb rates that may not be physically achievable. Understanding what categories of scenarios can lead to system failure can be useful during the design phase, even if we choose not to optimize the behavior of the system for these scenarios because they are deemed unrealistic.

If we find that our policies are overly sensitive to our modeling assumptions, we may consider using a method known as *robust dynamic programming*.[7] Instead of committing to a particular transition model, we have a suite of transition models $T_{1:n}$ and reward models $R_{1:n}$. We can revise the Bellman update equation from equation (7.16) to provide robustness to different models as follows:

$$U_{k+1}(s) = \max_a \min_i \left(R_i(s,a) + \gamma \sum_{s'} T_i(s' \mid s,a) U_k(s') \right) \quad (14.14)$$

The update uses the action that maximizes expected utility when using the model that minimizes our utility.

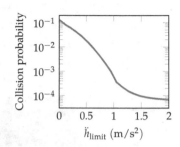

Figure 14.4. Analysis of robustness of a policy optimized for $\ddot{h}_{\text{limit}} = 1\,\text{m/s}^2$ but evaluated in environments with different values for $\ddot{h}_{\text{limit}}$.

[7] G. N. Iyengar, "Robust Dynamic Programming," *Mathematics of Operations Research*, vol. 30, no. 2, pp. 257–280, 2005. This approach can improve robustness in the context of collision avoidance. M. J. Kochenderfer, J. P. Chryssanthacopoulos, and P. Radecki, "Robustness of Optimized Collision Avoidance Logic to Modeling Errors," in *Digital Avionics Systems Conference (DASC)*, 2010.

14.4 Trade Analysis

Many interesting tasks involve multiple, often competing, objectives. For autonomous systems, there is often a trade-off between safety and efficiency. In designing a collision avoidance system, we want to be very safe without making

We can plot collision probability when starting from different initial states, similar to example 14.2. Here, we use a policy optimized for the parameters in appendix F.6, but we vary the limit $\ddot{h}_{\text{limit}}$ in the evaluation model.

Example 14.4. Probability of a collision when following the optimal collision avoidance policies when there is a mismatch between the model used for planning and the model used for evaluation.

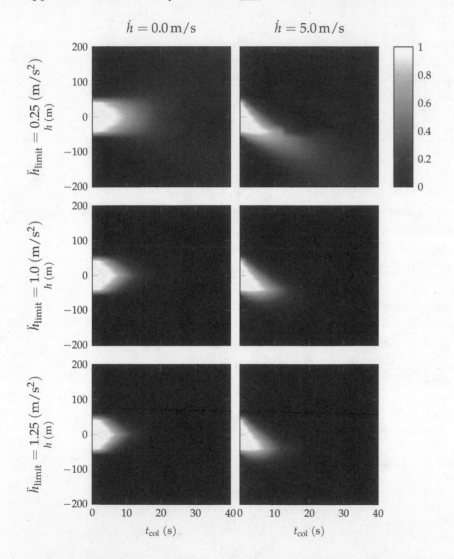

We optimized the policy with $\ddot{h}_{\text{limit}} = 1\,\text{m}/\text{s}^2$. If it was actually $0.25\,\text{m}/\text{s}^2$, then the policy performs poorly in some states since it takes longer to achieve a target vertical rate. If the limit was $1.25\,\text{m}/\text{s}^2$, we are a bit safer.

too many unnecessary avoidance maneuvers. A *trade analysis* studies how the various performance metrics are traded as the design parameters are changed.

If we consider only two performance metrics, we can plot a *trade-off curve* like the one discussed in example 14.5. By varying parameters in the policy, we obtain different values for the two metrics. These curves are useful when comparing different methodologies for generating policies. For example, the curves in example 14.5 suggest that a dynamic programming approach to generating policies can bring significant benefit over simple threshold-based policies—at least in the way we defined them.

For each of the curves in example 14.5, we vary only one parameter at a time, but to arrive at a satisfactory system, we may need to study the effects of varying multiple parameters. As we vary multiple parameters, we obtain a space of possible policies. Some of those policies may perform worse on all performance metrics relative to at least one other policy in that space. We can often eliminate from consideration those policies that are *dominated* by others. A policy is called *Pareto optimal*[8] or *Pareto efficient* if it is not dominated by any other policy in that space. The set of Pareto optimal policies is called the *Pareto frontier* or (in two dimensions) the *Pareto curve*. Figure 14.5 shows an example of a Pareto curve.

14.5   Adversarial Analysis

It can be useful to study the robustness of a policy from the perspective of an *adversarial analysis*. At each time step, an *adversary* selects the state that results from applying the action specified by the policy from the current state. The adversary has two objectives to balance: minimizing our return and maximizing the likelihood of the resulting trajectory according to our transition model. We can transform our original problem into an adversarial problem. The adversarial state space is the same as in the original problem, but the adversarial action space is the state space of the original problem. The adversarial reward is

$$R'(s,a) = -R(s,\pi(s)) + \lambda \log(T(a \mid s, \pi(s))) \tag{14.15}$$

where π is our policy, R is our original reward function, T is our original transition model, and $\lambda \geq 0$ is a parameter that controls the importance of maximizing the resulting likelihood of the trajectory. Since an adversary attempts to maximize the sum of adversarial reward, it is maximizing our expected negative return plus λ times the log probability of the resulting trajectory.[9] The adversarial transition

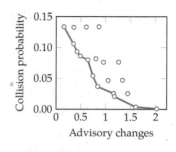

Figure 14.5. Performance of policies generated by varying the parameters of the simple policy from example 14.1. The approximate Pareto curve is highlighted in blue.

[8] Named after the Italian economist Vilfredo Federico Damaso Pareto (1848–1923).

[9] The log probability of a trajectory is equal to the sum of the log of the individual state transition probabilities.

In our aircraft collision avoidance problem, we must balance safety in terms of collision probability with other metrics, such as the expected number of advisory changes. Both of these can be implemented using trajectory metrics that are additively decomposed by steps as done in equation (14.3), allowing us to compute them using exact policy evaluation.

The plot here shows three curves associated with different parameterized versions of the simple and optimal policies. The first curve shows the performance of the simple policy on the two metrics as the h_{thresh} parameter (defined in example 14.1) is varied. The second curve shows the performance of the simple policy as t_{thresh} is varied. The third curve shows the optimal policy as the parameter θ is varied, where the cost of collision is $-\theta$ and the cost of changing advisories is $-(1 - \theta)$.

Example 14.5. An analysis of the trade-off between safety and operational efficiency when varying parameters of different collision avoidance systems.

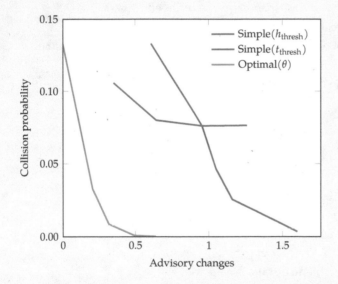

We can see that the optimal policy dominates the curves generated by the parameterized simple policies. When θ is close to 1, then we are very safe, but we have to tolerate more advisory changes. As θ goes to 0, we are less safe but do not produce advisories. Given a particular threshold level of safety, we are able to create an optimized policy that has fewer advisory changes in expectation than either of the simple parametric policies.

model is deterministic; the state transitions to exactly what the adversary specifies as its action.

Algorithm 14.1 implements this conversion to an adversarial problem. It assumes a discrete state and action space, which can then be solved using one of the dynamic programming algorithms in chapter 7. The solution is an adversarial policy that maps states to states. Given an initial state, we can generate a trajectory that minimizes our reward given some level of probability. Since the problem is deterministic, it is actually a search problem, and any of the algorithms in appendix E can be used. If our problem is high-dimensional or continuous, we may use one of the approximate solution techniques discussed in chapters 8 and 9.

```
function adversarial(𝒫::MDP, π, λ)
    S, 𝒜, T, R, γ = 𝒫.S, 𝒫.𝒜, 𝒫.T, 𝒫.R, 𝒫.γ
    S′ = 𝒜′ = S
    R′ = zeros(length(S′), length(𝒜′))
    T′ = zeros(length(S′), length(𝒜′), length(S′))
    for s in S′
        for a in 𝒜′
            R′[s,a] = -R(s, π(s)) + λ*log(T(s, π(s), a))
            T′[s,a,a] = 1
        end
    end
    return MDP(T′, R′, γ)
end
```

Algorithm 14.1. Conversion to an adversarial problem, given a policy π. An adversarial agent tries to change the outcomes of our policy actions so as to balance minimizing our original utility and maximizing the likelihood of the trajectory. The parameter λ controls how important it is to maximize the likelihood of the resulting trajectory. It returns an MDP whose transition and reward models are represented as matrices.

Sometimes we are interested in finding the *most likely failure* associated with a policy for a particular definition of failure. In some problems, failure can be defined as entering a particular state. For example, a collision may be considered a failure in our collision avoidance problem. Other problems may require a more complicated definition of failure that goes beyond just entering a subset of the state space. For example, we may want to specify failure using a *temporal logic*, which is a way to represent and reason about propositions qualified in terms of time. In many cases, however, we can use these failure specifications to create an augmented state space that we can then solve.[10]

[10] M. Bouton, J. Tumova, and M. J. Kochenderfer, "Point-Based Methods for Model Checking in Partially Observable Markov Decision Processes," in *AAAI Conference on Artificial Intelligence* (*AAAI*), 2020.

With the failure states defined, we can solve for the most likely failure trajectory by changing the reward function in equation (14.15) to

$$R'(s,a) = \begin{cases} -\infty & \text{if } s \text{ is terminal and not a failure} \\ 0 & \text{if } s \text{ is terminal and a failure} \\ \log(T(a \mid s, \pi(s))) & \text{otherwise} \end{cases} \quad (14.16)$$

We can find these most likely failures using a variety of approximation methods. Depending on the approximation method, it may be important to relax the infinite penalty for not reaching a failure at termination so that the search can be guided to failures. If applying Monte Carlo tree search to collision avoidance, the penalty could be related to the miss distance.[11]

We can play back the most likely failure trajectory and gauge whether that trajectory merits concern. If the trajectory is deemed extremely implausible, then we can feel more confident that our policy is safe. If the failure trajectory does merit concern, however, then we might have a few options:

1. *Change the action space.* We may add more extreme maneuvers to our action set for our collision avoidance problem.

2. *Change the reward function.* We may decrease the cost for changing advisories with the aim of lowering collision risk, as illustrated in the trade-off curve in example 14.5.

3. *Change the transition function.* We may increase the acceleration limit so that the aircraft can achieve the target vertical rates more quickly when directed by our policy.

4. *Improve the solver.* We may have used a discretization of the state space that is too coarse to capture important features of the optimal policy. In exchange for additional computation time, we may be able to refine the discretization to obtain a better policy. Alternatively, we may adopt a different approximation technique.

5. *Do not deploy the system.* If the policy is unsafe, it may be better not to deploy it in the real world.

[11] This strategy was used by R. Lee, M. J. Kochenderfer, O. J. Mengshoel, G. P. Brat, and M. P. Owen, "Adaptive Stress Testing of Airborne Collision Avoidance Systems," in *Digital Avionics Systems Conference (DASC)*, 2015.

14.6   Summary

- Performance metrics for policies may be evaluated using the dynamic programming techniques discussed in earlier chapters or through sampling rollouts.

- We can assess our confidence in our performance metric evaluations using standard error, confidence intervals, or one of the Bayesian approaches discussed earlier.

- Estimating the probability of rare events can be done more efficiently using a method called importance sampling.

- Importance sampling involves sampling from an alternative distribution and weighting the results appropriately.

- Because the model used for optimization may be an inaccurate representation of the real world, it is important to study the sensitivity of our policy to modeling assumptions.

- Robust dynamic programming can help improve robustness to model uncertainty by optimizing with respect to a set of different transition and reward models.

- Trade analysis can help us determine how to balance multiple performance objectives when optimizing a policy.

- Adversarial analyses involve an adversary that chooses the state to which we transition at each step so as to minimize our objective while maximizing the likelihood of the trajectory.

14.7   Exercises

Exercise 14.1. We have a trajectory τ with

s_1	a_1	s_2	a_2	s_3
6.0	2.2	1.4	0.7	6.0

Our dynamics are linear Gaussian, with $T(s' \mid s, a) = \mathcal{N}(s' \mid 2s + a, 5^2)$, and our initial state distribution is given by $\mathcal{N}(5, 6^2)$. What is the log-likelihood of the trajectory τ?

Solution: The log-likelihood of the trajectory is

$$\log \mathcal{N}(6.0 \mid 5, 6^2) + \log \mathcal{N}(1.4 \mid 2 \cdot 6.0 + 2.2, 5^2) + \log \mathcal{N}(6.0 \mid 2 \cdot 1.4 + 0.7, 5^2) \approx -11.183$$

Exercise 14.2. We ran a million simulations and found that our collision avoidance system resulted in 10 collisions. What is our collision probability estimate and the relative standard error?

Solution: The collision probability estimate is

$$\hat{\mu} = 10/10^6 = 10^{-5}$$

The ith sample x_i is 1 if there is a collision, and 0 otherwise. The standard deviation is

$$\hat{\sigma} = \sqrt{\frac{1}{10^6 - 1} \sum_{i=1}^{n} (x_i - \hat{\mu})^2} = \sqrt{\frac{1}{10^6 - 1} \left(10(1 - \hat{\mu})^2 + (10^6 - 10)\hat{\mu}^2 \right)} \approx 0.00316$$

The relative error is

$$\frac{\hat{\sigma}}{\hat{\mu}\sqrt{n}} \approx \frac{0.00316}{10^{-5}\sqrt{10^6}} = 0.316$$

Exercise 14.3. We want to compute the expectation $\mathbb{E}_{x \sim \mathcal{U}(0,5)}[f(x)]$, where $f(x)$ is -1 if $|x| \leq 1$, and 0 otherwise. What is the optimal proposal distribution?

Solution: The optimal proposal distribution is

$$p^*(x) = \frac{|f(x)|p(x)}{\int |f(x)|p(x)\,dx}$$

which is equivalent to $\mathcal{U}(0,1)$ because $f(x)$ is only nonzero for $x \in [-1,1]$, $\mathcal{U}(0,5)$ only has support for $x \in [0,5]$, and both $f(x)$ and $p(x)$ produce constant values when nonzero.

Exercise 14.4. Suppose we draw the sample 0.3 from the proposal distribution in the previous exercise. What is its weight? What is the estimate of $\mathbb{E}_{x \sim \mathcal{U}(0,5)}[f(x)]$?

Solution: The weight is $p(x)/p^*(x) = 0.2/1$. Since $f(0.3) = -1$, the estimate is -0.2, which is the exact answer.

Exercise 14.5. Suppose we have the following four policies, which have been evaluated on three metrics that we want to maximize:

System	f_1	f_2	f_3
π_1	2.7	1.1	2.8
π_2	1.8	2.8	4.5
π_3	9.0	4.5	2.3
π_4	5.3	6.0	2.8

Which policies are on the Pareto frontier?

Solution: Only π_1 is dominated by other policies. Hence, π_2, π_3, and π_4 are on the Pareto frontier.

PART III

MODEL UNCERTAINTY

In our discussion of sequential decision problems thus far, we have assumed that the transition and reward models are known. In many problems, however, these models are not known exactly, and the agent must learn to act through experience. By observing the outcomes of its actions in the form of state transitions and rewards, the agent is to choose actions that maximize its long-term accumulation of rewards. Solving such problems in which there is model uncertainty is the subject of the field of *reinforcement learning*, which is the focus of this part of the book. We will discuss several challenges in addressing model uncertainty. First, the agent must carefully balance exploration of the environment with the exploitation of that knowledge gained through experience. Second, rewards may be received long after the important decisions have been made, so credit for later rewards must be assigned to earlier decisions. Third, the agent must generalize from limited experience. We will review the theory and some of the key algorithms for addressing these challenges.

15 Exploration and Exploitation

Reinforcement learning agents[1] must balance *exploration* of the environment with *exploitation* of knowledge obtained through its interactions.[2] Pure exploration will allow the agent to build a comprehensive model, but the agent will likely have to sacrifice the gathering of reward. Pure exploitation has the agent continually choosing the action it thinks best to accumulate reward, but there may be other, better actions that could be taken. This chapter introduces the challenges associated with the exploration-exploitation trade-off by focusing on a problem with a single state. We conclude by introducing exploration in MDPs with multiple states.

15.1 Bandit Problems

Early analyses of the exploration-exploitation trade-off were focused on slot machines, also called *one-armed bandits*.[3] The name comes from older slot machines having a single pull lever, as well as the fact that the machine tends to take the gambler's money. Many real-world problems can be framed as *multiarmed bandit problems*,[4] such as the allocation of clinical trials and adaptive network routing. Many bandit problem formulations exist in the literature, but this chapter will focus on what is called a *binary bandit*, *Bernoulli bandit*, or *binomial bandit*. In these problems, arm a pays off 1 with probability θ_a, and 0 otherwise. Pulling an arm costs nothing, but we have only h pulls.

A bandit problem can be framed as an h-step MDP with a single state, n actions, and an unknown, stochastic reward function $R(s, a)$, as shown in figure 15.1. Recall that $R(s, a)$ is the expected reward when taking action a in s, but individual rewards realized in the environment may come from a probability distribution.

[1] A review of the field of reinforcement learning is provided in M. Wiering and M. van Otterlo, eds., *Reinforcement Learning: State of the Art*. Springer, 2012.

[2] In some applications, we want to optimize a policy given a fixed set of trajectories. This context is known as *batch reinforcement learning*. This chapter assumes that we have to collect our own data through interaction, which makes choosing an appropriate exploration strategy important.

[3] These bandit problems were explored during World War II and proved exceptionally challenging to solve. According to Peter Whittle, "efforts to solve [bandit problems] so sapped the energies and minds of Allied analysts that the suggestion was made that the problem be dropped over Germany as the ultimate instrument of intellectual sabotage." J. C. Gittins, "Bandit Processes and Dynamic Allocation Indices," *Journal of the Royal Statistical Society. Series B (Methodological)*, vol. 41, no. 2, pp. 148–177, 1979.

[4] C. Szepesvári and T. Lattimore, *Bandit Algorithms*. Cambridge University Press, 2020.

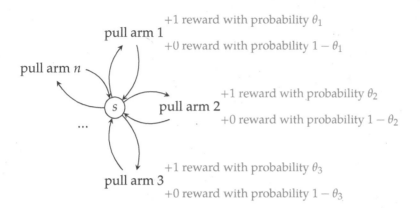

Figure 15.1. The multiarmed bandit problem is a single-state MDP where actions can differ only in the likelihood that they produce reward.

Algorithm 15.1 defines the simulation loop for a bandit problem. At each step, we evaluate our exploration policy π on our current model of the payoff probabilities to generate an action a. The next section will discuss a way to model payoff probabilities, and the remainder of the chapter will outline several exploration strategies. After obtaining a, we simulate a pull of that arm, returning binary reward r. The model is then updated using the observed a and r. The simulation loop is repeated to horizon h.

```
struct BanditProblem
    θ # vector of payoff probabilities
    R # reward sampler
end

function BanditProblem(θ)
    R(a) = rand() < θ[a] ? 1 : 0
    return BanditProblem(θ, R)
end

function simulate(𝒫::BanditProblem, model, π, h)
    for i in 1:h
        a = π(model)
        r = 𝒫.R(a)
        update!(model, a, r)
    end
end
```

Algorithm 15.1. Simulation of a bandit problem. A bandit problem is defined by a vector θ of payoff probabilities, one per action. We also define a function R that simulates the generation of a stochastic binary reward in response to the selection of an action. Each step of a simulation involves generating an action a from the exploration policy π. The exploration policy generally consults the model in the selection of the action. The selection of that action results in a randomly generated reward, which is then used to update the model. Simulations are run to horizon h.

15.2 Bayesian Model Estimation

We would like to track our belief over the win probability θ_a for arm a. The beta distribution (section 4.2) is often used for representing such a belief. Assuming a uniform prior of $\text{Beta}(1,1)$, the posterior for θ_a after w_a wins and ℓ_a losses is $\text{Beta}(w_a + 1, \ell_a + 1)$. The posterior probability of winning is

$$\rho_a = P(\text{win}_a \mid w_a, \ell_a) = \int_0^1 \theta \times \text{Beta}(\theta \mid w_a + 1, \ell_a + 1)\, d\theta = \frac{w_a + 1}{w_a + \ell_a + 2} \quad (15.1)$$

Algorithm 15.2 provides an implementation of this. Example 15.1 illustrates how to compute these posterior distributions from counts of wins and losses.

```
struct BanditModel
    B # vector of beta distributions
end

function update!(model::BanditModel, a, r)
    α, β = StatsBase.params(model.B[a])
    model.B[a] = Beta(α + r, β + (1-r))
    return model
end
```

Algorithm 15.2. The Bayesian update function for bandit models. After observing reward r after taking action a, we update the beta distribution associated with that action by incrementing the appropriate parameter.

A *greedy action* is one that maximizes our expected immediate reward—or, in other words, the posterior probability of winning in the context of our binary bandit problem. There may be multiple greedy actions. We do not always want to select a greedy action because we may miss out on discovering another action that may actually provide higher reward in expectation. We can use the information from the beta distributions associated with the different actions to drive our exploration of nongreedy actions.

15.3 Undirected Exploration Strategies

There are several *ad hoc exploration* strategies that are commonly used to balance exploration with exploitation. This section discusses a type of ad hoc exploration called *undirected exploration*, where we do not use information from previous outcomes to guide exploration of nongreedy actions.

Suppose we have a two-armed bandit that we have played six times. The first arm has 1 win and 0 losses, and the other arm has 4 wins and 1 loss. Assuming a uniform prior, the posterior distribution for θ_1 is Beta$(2,1)$, and the posterior distribution for θ_2 is Beta$(5,2)$.

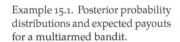

Example 15.1. Posterior probability distributions and expected payouts for a multiarmed bandit.

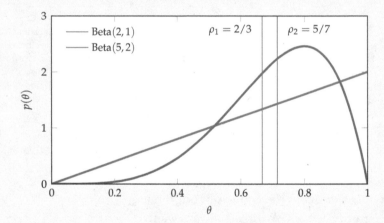

These posteriors assign nonzero likelihood to the win probabilities between 0 and 1. The density at 0 is 0 for both arms because they both received at least one win. Similarly, the density at 1 for arm 2 is 0 because it received at least one loss. The payoff probabilities $\rho_1 = 2/3$ and $\rho_2 = 5/7$ are shown with vertical lines. We believe that the second arm has the best chance of producing a payout.

One of the most common undirected exploration strategies is *ε-greedy exploration* (algorithm 15.3). This strategy chooses a random arm with probability ϵ. Otherwise, we choose a greedy arm, $\arg\max_a \rho_a$. This ρ_a is the posterior probability of a win with action a using the Bayesian model given in the previous section. Alternatively, we can use the maximum likelihood estimate, but with enough pulls, the difference between the two approaches is small. Larger values of ϵ lead to more exploration, thereby resulting in faster identification of the best arm, but more pulls are wasted on suboptimal arms. Example 15.2 demonstrates this exploration strategy and the evolution of our beliefs.

The ϵ-greedy method maintains a constant amount of exploration, despite there being far more uncertainty earlier in the interaction with the bandit than later. One common adjustment is to decay ϵ over time, such as with an exponential decay schedule with the following update:

$$\epsilon \leftarrow \alpha\epsilon \tag{15.2}$$

for an $\alpha \in (0, 1)$ typically close to 1.

```
mutable struct EpsilonGreedyExploration
    ϵ # probability of random arm
end

function (π::EpsilonGreedyExploration)(model::BanditModel)
    if rand() < π.ϵ
        return rand(eachindex(model.B))
    else
        return argmax(mean.(model.B))
    end
end
```

Algorithm 15.3. The ϵ-greedy exploration strategy. With probability ϵ, it will return a random action. Otherwise, it will return a greedy action.

Another strategy is *explore-then-commit exploration* (algorithm 15.4), where we select actions uniformly at random for the first k time steps. From that point on, we choose a greedy action.[5] Large values for k reduce the risk of committing to a suboptimal action, but we waste more time exploring potentially suboptimal actions.

[5] A. Garivier, T. Lattimore, and E. Kaufmann, "On Explore-Then-Commit Strategies," in *Advances in Neural Information Processing Systems (NIPS)*, 2016.

15.4 Directed Exploration Strategies

Directed exploration uses information gathered from previous pulls to guide exploration of the nongreedy actions. For example, the *softmax strategy* (algorithm 15.5)

Example 15.2. Application of the
ϵ-greedy exploration strategy to a
two-armed bandit problem.

We would like to apply the ϵ-greedy exploration strategy to a two-armed bandit. We can construct the model with a uniform prior and the exploration policy with $\epsilon = 0.3$:

```
model(fill(Beta(),2))
π = EpsilonGreedyExploration(0.3)
```

To obtain our first action, we call $\pi(\text{model})$, which returns 1 based on the current state of the random number generator. We observe a loss, with $r = 0$, and then call

```
update!(model, 1, 0)
```

which updates the beta distributions within the model to reflect that we took action 1 and received a reward of 0.

The plots here show the evolution of the payoff beliefs after each of six steps of execution using our exploration strategy. Blue corresponds to the first arm, and red corresponds to the second arm:

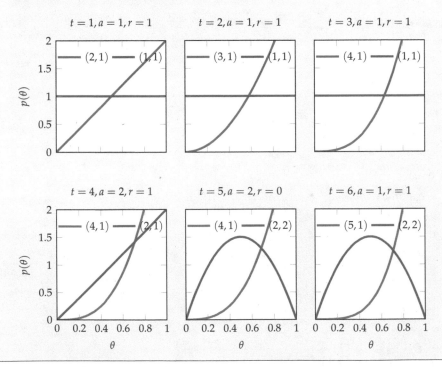

```
mutable struct ExploreThenCommitExploration
    k # pulls remaining until commitment
end

function (π::ExploreThenCommitExploration)(model::BanditModel)
    if π.k > 0
        π.k -= 1
        return rand(eachindex(model.B))
    end
    return argmax(mean.(model.B))
end
```

Algorithm 15.4. The explore-then-commit exploration strategy. If k is strictly positive, it will return a random action after decrementing k. Otherwise, it will return a greedy action.

pulls arm a with probability proportional to $\exp(\lambda\rho_a)$, where the *precision parameter* $\lambda \geq 0$ controls the amount of exploration. We have uniform random selection as $\lambda \to 0$ and greedy selection as $\lambda \to \infty$. As more data is accumulated, we may want to increase λ by a multiplicative factor to reduce exploration.

```
mutable struct SoftmaxExploration
    λ # precision parameter
    α # precision factor
end

function (π::SoftmaxExploration)(model::BanditModel)
    weights = exp.(π.λ * mean.(model.B))
    π.λ *= π.α
    return rand(Categorical(normalize(weights, 1)))
end
```

Algorithm 15.5. The softmax exploration strategy. It selects action a with probability proportional to $\exp(\lambda\rho_a)$. The precision parameter λ is scaled by a factor α at each step.

A variety of exploration strategies are grounded in the idea of *optimism under uncertainty*. If we are optimistic about the outcomes of our actions to the extent that our data statistically allows, we will be implicitly driven to balance exploration and exploitation. One such approach is *quantile exploration* (algorithm 15.6),[6] where we choose the arm with the highest α-quantile (section 2.2.2) for the payoff probability. Values for $\alpha > 0.5$ result in optimism under uncertainty, incentivizing the exploration of actions that have not been tried as often. Larger values of α result in more exploration. Example 15.3 shows quantile estimation and compares it with the other exploration strategies.

An alternative to computing the upper confidence bound for our posterior distribution exactly is to use *UCB1 exploration* (algorithm 15.7), originally introduced in section 9.6 for exploration in Monte Carlo tree search. In this strategy,

[6] This general strategy is related to *upper confidence bound exploration*, *interval exploration*, and *interval estimation*, referring to the upper bound of a confidence interval. L. P. Kaelbling, *Learning in Embedded Systems*. MIT Press, 1993. See also E. Kaufmann, "On Bayesian Index Policies for Sequential Resource Allocation," *Annals of Statistics*, vol. 46, no. 2, pp. 842–865, 2018.

```
mutable struct QuantileExploration
    α # quantile (e.g., 0.95)
end

function (π::QuantileExploration)(model::BanditModel)
    return argmax([quantile(B, π.α) for B in model.B])
end
```

Algorithm 15.6. Quantile exploration, which returns the action with the highest α quantile.

we select the action a that maximizes

$$\rho_a + c\sqrt{\frac{\log N}{N(a)}} \qquad (15.3)$$

where $N(a)$ is the number of times that we have taken action a, and $N = \sum_a N(a)$. The parameter $c \geq 0$ controls the amount of exploration that is encouraged through the second term. Larger values of c lead to more exploration. This strategy is often used with maximum likelihood estimates of the payoff probabilities, but we can adapt it to the Bayesian context by having $N(a)$ be the sum of the beta distribution parameters associated with a.

Another general approach to exploration is to use *posterior sampling* (algorithm 15.8), also referred to as *randomized probability matching* or *Thompson sampling*.[7] It is simple to implement and does not require careful parameter tuning. The idea is to sample from the posterior distribution over the rewards associated with the various actions. The action with the largest sampled value is selected.

15.5 Optimal Exploration Strategies

The beta distribution associated with arm a is parameterized by counts (w_a, ℓ_a). Together, these counts $w_1, \ell_1, \ldots, w_n, \ell_n$ represent our belief about payoffs, and thus represent a *belief state*. These $2n$ numbers can describe n continuous probability distributions over possible payoff probabilities.

We can construct an MDP whose states are vectors of length $2n$ that represent the agent's belief over the n-armed bandit problem. Dynamic programming can be used to solve this MDP to obtain an optimal policy π^* that specifies which arm to pull given the counts.

[7] W. R. Thompson, "On the Likelihood That One Unknown Probability Exceeds Another in View of the Evidence of Two Samples," *Biometrika*, vol. 25, no. 3/4, pp. 285–294, 1933. For a recent tutorial, see D. Russo, B. V. Roy, A. Kazerouni, I. Osband, and Z. Wen, "A Tutorial on Thompson Sampling," *Foundations and Trends in Machine Learning*, vol. 11, no. 1, pp. 1–96, 2018.

Consider using exploration strategies given the information obtained in the two-armed bandit problem of example 15.1, where the posterior distribution for θ_1 is Beta$(2,1)$, and the posterior distribution for θ_2 is Beta$(5,2)$. The second arm has the higher payoff probability.

An ϵ-greedy strategy with $\epsilon = 0.2$ has a 20 % chance of choosing randomly between the arms and an 80 % chance of choosing the second arm. Hence, the overall probability of choosing the first arm is 0.1, and the probability of choosing the second arm is 0.9.

A softmax strategy with $\lambda = 1$ assigns a weight of $\exp(\rho_1) = \exp(2/3) \approx 1.948$ to the first arm and a weight of $\exp(\rho_2) = \exp(5/7) \approx 2.043$ to the second. The probability of choosing the first arm is $1.948/(1.948 + 2.043) \approx 0.488$, and the probability of choosing the second arm is 0.512. The plot here shows how the probability of choosing the first arm varies with λ:

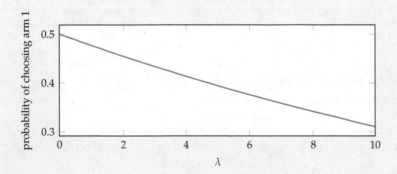

Quantile exploration with $\alpha = 0.9$ computes the payoff probability that is greater than 90 % of the probability mass associated with each posterior distribution. The 0.9 quantile for θ_1 is 0.949 and for θ_2 is 0.907, as shown here. The first arm (blue) has the higher quantile and would be pulled next.

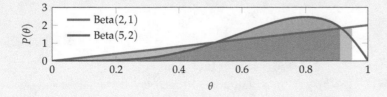

Example 15.3. Exploration strategies used with the two-armed bandit problem from example 15.1.

```
mutable struct UCB1Exploration
    c # exploration constant
end

function bonus(π::UCB1Exploration, B, a)
    N = sum(b.α + b.β for b in B)
    Na = B[a].α + B[a].β
    return π.c * sqrt(log(N)/Na)
end

function (π::UCB1Exploration)(model::BanditModel)
    B = model.B
    ρ = mean.(B)
    u = ρ .+ [bonus(π, B, a) for a in eachindex(B)]
    return argmax(u)
end
```

Algorithm 15.7. The UCB1 exploration strategy with exploration constant c. We compute equation (15.3) for each action from the pseudocount parameters in B. We then return the action that maximizes that quantity.

```
struct PosteriorSamplingExploration end

(π::PosteriorSamplingExploration)(model::BanditModel) =
    argmax(rand.(model.B))
```

Algorithm 15.8. The posterior sampling exploration strategy. It has no free parameters. It simply samples from the beta distributions associated with each action and then returns the action associated with the largest sample.

Let $Q^*(w_1, \ell_1, \ldots, w_n, \ell_n, a)$ represent the expected payoff after pulling arm a and thereafter acting optimally. The optimal utility function and optimal policy can be written in terms of Q^*:

$$U^*(w_1, \ell_1, \ldots, w_n, \ell_n) = \max_a Q^*(w_1, \ell_1, \ldots, w_n, \ell_n, a) \qquad (15.4)$$

$$\pi^*(w_1, \ell_1, \ldots, w_n, \ell_n) = \arg\max_a Q^*(w_1, \ell_1, \ldots, w_n, \ell_n, a) \qquad (15.5)$$

We can decompose Q^* into two terms:

$$Q^*(w_1, \ell_1, \ldots, w_n, \ell_n, a) = \frac{w_a + 1}{w_a + \ell_a + 2}(1 + U^*(\ldots, w_a + 1, \ell_a, \ldots))$$
$$+ \left(1 - \frac{w_a + 1}{w_a + \ell_a + 2}\right) U^*(\ldots, w_a, \ell_a + 1, \ldots) \qquad (15.6)$$

The first term is associated with a win for arm a, and the second term is associated with a loss. The value $(w_a + 1)/(w_a + \ell_a + 2)$ is the posterior probability of a win, which comes from equation (15.1).[8] The first U^* in equation (15.6) records a win, whereas the second U^* records a loss.

[8] This probability can be adjusted if we have a nonuniform prior.

We can compute Q^* for the entire belief space, as we have assumed a finite horizon h. We start with all terminal belief states with $\sum_a (w_a + \ell_a) = h$, where $U^* = 0$. We can then work backward to states with $\sum_a (w_a + \ell_a) = h - 1$ and apply equation (15.6). This process is repeated until we reach our initial state. Such an optimal policy is computed in example 15.4.

Although this dynamic programming solution is optimal, the number of belief states is $O(h^{2n})$. We can formulate an infinite horizon, discounted version of the problem that can be solved efficiently using the *Gittins allocation index*,[9] which can be stored as a lookup table that specifies a scalar allocation index value, given the number of pulls and the number of wins associated with an arm.[10] The arm that has the highest allocation index is the one that should be pulled next.

15.6   Exploration with Multiple States

In the general reinforcement learning context with multiple states, we must use observations about state transitions to inform our decisions. We can modify the simulation process in algorithm 15.1 to account for state transitions and update our model appropriately. Algorithm 15.9 provides an implementation of this. There are many ways to model the problem and perform exploration, as we will discuss over the next few chapters, but the simulation structure is exactly the same.

15.7   Summary

- The exploration-exploitation trade-off is a balance between exploring the state-action space for higher rewards and exploiting the already-known favorable state actions.

- Multiarmed bandit problems involve a single state where the agent receives stochastic rewards for taking different actions.

- A beta distribution can be used to maintain a belief over multiarmed bandit rewards.

- Undirected exploration strategies, including ϵ-greedy and explore-then-commit, are simple to implement but do not use information from previous outcomes to guide the exploration of nongreedy actions.

[9] J.C. Gittins, "Bandit Processes and Dynamic Allocation Indices," *Journal of the Royal Statistical Society. Series B (Methodological)*, vol. 41, no. 2, pp. 148–177, 1979. J. Gittins, K. Glazebrook, and R. Weber, *Multi-Armed Bandit Allocation Indices*, 2nd ed. Wiley, 2011.

[10] A survey of algorithms for computing this lookup table are provided in J. Chakravorty and A. Mahajan, "Multi-Armed Bandits, Gittins Index, and Its Calculation," in *Methods and Applications of Statistics in Clinical Trials*, N. Balakrishnan, ed., vol. 2, Wiley, 2014, pp. 416–435.

Next, we have constructed the state-action tree for a two-armed bandit problem with a two-step horizon. State vectors are shown as $[w_1, \ell_1, w_2, \ell_2]$; blue arrows indicate wins and red arrows indicate losses.

Example 15.4. Computing the optimal policy for a two-armed, two-step horizon bandit problem.

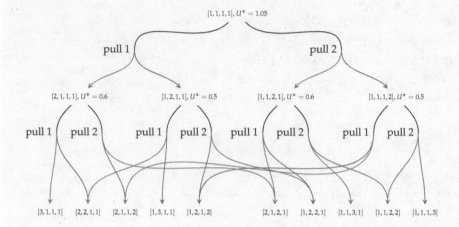

Unsurprisingly, the policy is symmetric with respect to arms 1 and 2. We find that the first arm does not matter, and it is best to pull a winning arm twice and not to pull a losing arm twice.

The optimal value functions were computed using

$$Q^*([2,1,1,1],1) = \frac{3}{5}(1+0) + \frac{2}{5}(0) = 0.6$$

$$Q^*([2,1,1,1],2) = \frac{2}{4}(1+0) + \frac{2}{4}(0) = 0.5$$

$$Q^*([1,2,1,1],1) = \frac{2}{5}(1+0) + \frac{3}{5}(0) = 0.4$$

$$Q^*([1,2,1,1],2) = \frac{2}{4}(1+0) + \frac{2}{4}(0) = 0.5$$

$$Q^*([1,1,1,1],1) = \frac{2}{4}(1+0.6) + \frac{2}{4}(0.5) = 1.05$$

```
function simulate(𝒫::MDP, model, π, h, s)
    for i in 1:h
        a = π(model, s)
        s′, r = 𝒫.TR(s, a)
        update!(model, s, a, r, s′)
        s = s′
    end
end
```

Algorithm 15.9. The simulation loop for reinforcement learning problems. The exploration policy π generates the next action based on information in the model and the current state s. The MDP problem 𝒫 is treated as the ground truth and is used to sample the next state and reward. The state transition and reward are used to update the model. The simulation is run to horizon h.

- Directed exploration strategies, including softmax, quantile, UCB1, and posterior sampling exploration, use information from past actions to better explore promising actions.

- Dynamic programming can be used to derive optimal exploration strategies for finite horizons, but these strategies can be expensive to compute.

15.8   Exercises

Exercise 15.1. Consider again the three-armed bandit problems in which each arm has a win probability drawn uniformly between 0 and 1. Compare the softmax, quantile, and UCB1 exploration strategies. Qualitatively, what values for λ, α, and c produce the highest expected reward on randomly generated bandit problems?

Solution: Here we plot the expected reward per step for each of the three strategies. Again, the effectiveness of the parameterization depends on the problem horizon, so several different depths are shown as well.

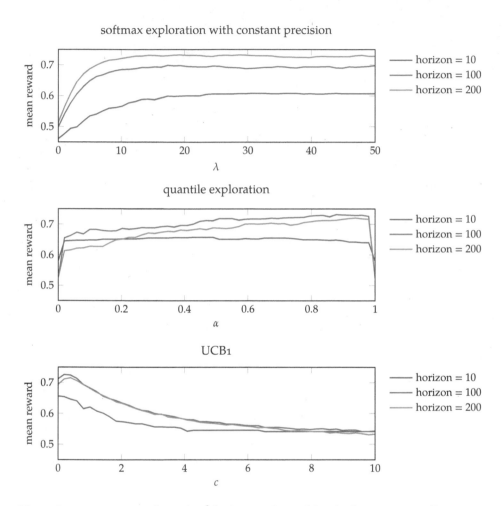

The softmax strategy performs best for large values of λ, which prioritize pulling arms with higher expected reward according to the current belief. Upper confidence bound exploration performs better with longer horizons, independent of its parameterization. The size of the confidence bound α does not significantly affect performance except for values very close to 0 or 1. The UCB1 strategy performs best with small positive values of the exploration scalar c. The expected reward decays as c increases. All three policies can be tuned to produce similar maximal expected rewards.

Exercise 15.2. Give an example of a practical application of a multiarmed bandit problem.

Solution: There are many multiarmed bandit problems. Consider, for example, a news company that would like to maximize interaction (clicks) on articles on its website. The company may have several articles to display, but it must select one article to display at any given time. This problem is a multiarmed bandit problem because a user will either click article i with probability θ_i or not click with probability $1 - \theta_i$. Exploration would consist of displaying articles on the website and observing the number of clicks, and exploitation would consist of displaying the article likely to lead to the highest number of clicks. This problem is related to *A/B testing*, where companies test different versions of a website to determine which version yields the most interactions.

Exercise 15.3. Given a one-armed bandit with a prior of $\theta \sim \text{Beta}(7,2)$, provide bounds on the posterior probability of winning after 10 additional pulls.

Solution: A lower bound on our posterior probability of winning ρ can be computed assuming that all pulls result in a loss, (e.g., $\underline{\ell} = 10$ and $\underline{w} = 0$). We can similarly compute an upper bound $\bar{\rho}$, assuming that all pulls result in a win (e.g., $\bar{w} = 10$ and $\bar{\ell} = 0$). The bounds are thus

$$\underline{\rho} = \frac{\underline{w} + 7}{\underline{w} + \underline{\ell} + 9} = \frac{0 + 7}{0 + 10 + 9} = \frac{7}{19}$$

$$\bar{\rho} = \frac{\bar{w} + 7}{\bar{w} + \bar{\ell} + 9} = \frac{10 + 7}{10 + 0 + 9} = \frac{17}{19}$$

Exercise 15.4. Suppose that we have a bandit with arms a and b, and we use an ϵ-greedy exploration strategy with $\epsilon = 0.3$ and an exploration decay factor of $\alpha = 0.9$. We generate a random number x between 0 and 1 to determine if we explore ($x < \epsilon$) or exploit ($x > \epsilon$). Given we have $\rho_a > \rho_b$, which arm is selected if $x = 0.2914$ in the first iteration? Which arm is selected if $x = 0.1773$ in the ninth iteration?

Solution: Since $x < \epsilon_1$ in the first iteration, we explore and choose a with probability 0.5 and b with probability 0.5. At the ninth iteration, $\epsilon_9 = \alpha^8 \epsilon_1 \approx 0.129$. Since $x > \epsilon_9$, we exploit and select a.

Exercise 15.5. We have a four-armed bandit, and we want to use a softmax exploration strategy with precision parameter $\lambda = 2$ and a prior belief $\theta_a \sim \text{Beta}(2,2)$ for each arm a. Suppose that we pull each arm four times, with the result that arms 1, 2, 3, and 4 pay off 1, 2, 3, and 4 times, respectively. List the posterior distributions over θ_a and calculate the probability that we select arm 2.

Solution: The posterior distributions for each arm are: Beta$(3,5)$, Beta$(4,4)$, Beta$(5,3)$, and Beta$(6,2)$, respectively. The probability of selecting arm 2 can be computed in the following steps:

$$P(a = i) \propto \exp\left(\lambda \rho_i\right)$$

$$P(a = i) = \frac{\exp\left(\lambda \rho_i\right)}{\sum_a \exp\left(\lambda \rho_a\right)}$$

$$P(a = 2) = \frac{\exp\left(2 \times \frac{4}{8}\right)}{\exp\left(2 \times \frac{3}{8}\right) + \exp\left(2 \times \frac{4}{8}\right) + \exp\left(2 \times \frac{5}{8}\right) + \exp\left(2 \times \frac{6}{8}\right)}$$

$$P(a = 2) \approx 0.2122$$

Exercise 15.6. Rewrite equation (15.6) for an arbitrary Beta(α, β) prior.

Solution: We can rewrite the equation more generally as follows:

$$Q^*(w_1, \ell_1, \ldots, w_n, \ell_n, a) = \frac{w_a + \alpha}{w_a + \ell_a + \alpha + \beta}(1 + U^*(\ldots, w_a + 1, \ell_a, \ldots))$$
$$+ \left(1 - \frac{w_a + \alpha}{w_a + \ell_a + \alpha + \beta}\right)U^*(\ldots, w_a, \ell_a + 1, \ldots)$$

Exercise 15.7. Recall example 15.4. Instead of having a payoff of 1 for each arm, let us assume that arm 1 gives a payoff of 1, while arm 2 gives a payoff of 2. Calculate the new action value functions for both arms.

Solution: For arm 1, we have

$$Q^*([2,1,1,1],1) = \frac{3}{5}(1+0) + \frac{2}{5}(0) = 0.6$$
$$Q^*([2,1,1,1],2) = \frac{2}{4}(2+0) + \frac{2}{4}(0) = 1$$
$$Q^*([1,2,1,1],1) = \frac{2}{5}(1+0) + \frac{3}{5}(0) = 0.4$$
$$Q^*([1,2,1,1],2) = \frac{2}{4}(2+0) + \frac{2}{4}(0) = 1$$
$$Q^*([1,1,1,1],1) = \frac{2}{4}(1+0.6) + \frac{2}{4}(1) = 1.3$$

And for arm 2, we have

$$Q^*([1,1,2,1],1) = \frac{2}{4}(1+0) + \frac{2}{4}(0) = 0.5$$

$$Q^*([1,1,2,1],2) = \frac{3}{5}(2+0) + \frac{2}{5}(0) = 1.2$$

$$Q^*([1,1,1,2],1) = \frac{2}{4}(1+0) + \frac{2}{4}(0) = 0.5$$

$$Q^*([1,1,1,2],2) = \frac{2}{5}(2+0) + \frac{3}{5}(0) = 0.8$$

$$Q^*([1,1,1,1],2) = \frac{2}{4}(2+1.2) + \frac{2}{4}(0.8) = 2$$

Exercise 15.8. Prove that the number of belief states in an n-armed bandit problem with a horizon of h is $O(h^{2n})$.

Solution: We begin by counting the number of solutions to $w_1 + \ell_1 + \cdots + w_n + \ell_n = k$, where $0 \le k \le h$. If $n = 2$ and $k = 6$, one solution is $2 + 0 + 3 + 1 = 6$. For our counting argument, we will use tally marks to represent integers. For example, we can write a solution like $2 + 0 + 3 + 1 = ||+$ $+|||+| = 6$. For general values for n and k, we would have k tally marks and $2n - 1$ plus signs. Given that many tally marks and plus signs, we can arrange them in any order we want. We can represent a solution as a string of $k + 2n - 1$ characters, where a character is either $|$ or $+$, with k of those characters being $|$. To obtain the number of solutions, we count the number of ways we can choose k positions for $|$ from the set of $k + 2n - 1$ positions, resulting in

$$\frac{(k+2n-1)!}{(2n-1)!k!} = O(h^{2n-1})$$

solutions. The number of belief states is this expression summed for k from 0 to h, which is $O(h \times h^{2n-1}) = O(h^{2n})$.

16   Model-Based Methods

This chapter discusses both maximum likelihood and Bayesian approaches for learning the underlying dynamics and reward through interaction with the environment. Maximum likelihood methods involve counting state transitions and recording the amount of reward received to estimate the model parameters. We will discuss a few approaches for planning using models that are continuously updated. Even if we solve the estimated problem exactly, we generally have to rely on heuristic exploration strategies to arrive at a suitable solution. Bayesian methods involve computing a posterior distribution over model parameters. Solving for the optimal exploration strategy is generally intractable, but we can often obtain a sensible approximation through posterior sampling.

16.1   Maximum Likelihood Models

As introduced in section 15.6 and implemented in algorithm 15.9, reinforcement learning involves using information about past state transitions and rewards to inform decisions. This section describes how to obtain a *maximum likelihood estimate* of the underlying problem. This maximum likelihood estimate can be used to generate a value function estimate that can be used with an exploration strategy to generate actions.

We record the transition counts $N(s, a, s')$, indicating the number of times a transition from s to s' was observed when taking action a. The maximum likelihood estimate of the transition function given these transition counts is

$$T(s' \mid s, a) \approx N(s, a, s')/N(s, a) \qquad (16.1)$$

where $N(s, a) = \sum_{s'} N(s, a, s')$. If $N(s, a) = 0$, then the estimate of the transition probability is 0.

The reward function can also be estimated. As we receive rewards, we update $\rho(s,a)$, the sum of all rewards obtained when taking action a in state s. The maximum likelihood estimate of the reward function is the mean reward:

$$R(s,a) \approx \rho(s,a)/N(s,a) \qquad (16.2)$$

If $N(s,a) = 0$, then our estimate of $R(s,a)$ is 0. If we have prior knowledge about the transition probabilities or rewards, then we can initialize $N(s,a,s')$ and $\rho(s,a)$ to values other than 0.

Algorithm 16.1 updates N and ρ after observing the transition from s to s' after taking action a and receiving reward r. Algorithm 16.2 converts the maximum likelihood model into an MDP representation. Example 16.1 illustrates this process. We can use this maximum likelihood model to select actions while interacting with the environment and improving the model.

16.2   Update Schemes

As we update our maximum likelihood estimate of the model, we also need to update our plan. This section discusses several update schemes in response to our continuously changing model. A major consideration is computational efficiency because we will want to perform these updates fairly frequently while interacting with the environment.

16.2.1   Full Updates

Algorithm 16.3 solves the maximum likelihood model using the linear programming formulation from section 7.7, though we could have used value iteration or some other algorithm. After each step, we obtain a new model estimate and re-solve.

16.2.2   Randomized Updates

Recomputing an optimal policy with each state transition is typically computationally expensive. An alternative is to perform a Bellman update on the estimated model at the previously visited state, as well as a few randomly chosen states.[1] Algorithm 16.4 implements this approach.

[1] This approach is related to the *Dyna* approach suggested by R. S. Sutton, "Dyna, an Integrated Architecture for Learning, Planning, and Reacting," *SIGART Bulletin,* vol. 2, no. 4, pp. 160–163, 1991.

```
mutable struct MaximumLikelihoodMDP
    𝒮 # state space (assumes 1:nstates)
    𝒜 # action space (assumes 1:nactions)
    N # transition count N(s,a,s')
    ρ # reward sum ρ(s, a)
    γ # discount
    U # value function
    planner
end

function lookahead(model::MaximumLikelihoodMDP, s, a)
    𝒮, U, γ = model.𝒮, model.U, model.γ
    n = sum(model.N[s,a,:])
    if n == 0
        return 0.0
    end
    r = model.ρ[s, a] / n
    T(s,a,s') = model.N[s,a,s'] / n
    return r + γ * sum(T(s,a,s')*U[s'] for s' in 𝒮)
end

function backup(model::MaximumLikelihoodMDP, U, s)
    return maximum(lookahead(model, s, a) for a in model.𝒜)
end

function update!(model::MaximumLikelihoodMDP, s, a, r, s')
    model.N[s,a,s'] += 1
    model.ρ[s,a] += r
    update!(model.planner, model, s, a, r, s')
    return model
end
```

Algorithm 16.1. A method for updating the transition and reward model for maximum likelihood reinforcement learning with discrete state and action spaces. We increment N[s,a,s'] after observing a transition from s to s' after taking action a, and we add r to ρ[s,a]. The model also contains an estimate of the value function U and a planner. This algorithm block also includes methods for performing backup and lookahead with respect to this model.

```
function MDP(model::MaximumLikelihoodMDP)
    N, ρ, 𝒮, 𝒜, γ = model.N, model.ρ, model.𝒮, model.𝒜, model.γ
    T, R = similar(N), similar(ρ)
    for s in 𝒮
        for a in 𝒜
            n = sum(N[s,a,:])
            if n == 0
                T[s,a,:] .= 0.0
                R[s,a] = 0.0
            else
                T[s,a,:] = N[s,a,:] / n
                R[s,a] = ρ[s,a] / n
            end
        end
    end
    return MDP(T, R, γ)
end
```

Algorithm 16.2. A method for converting a maximum likelihood model to an MDP problem.

We would like to apply maximum likelihood model estimation to the hex world problem. The true transition matrices look like this:

There are six transition matrices, one for each action. The rows correspond to the current state, and the columns correspond to the next state. There are 26 states. The intensity in the images relate to the probability of making the corresponding transition. In a reinforcement learning context, we do not know these transition probabilities ahead of time. However, we can interact with the environment and record the transitions we observe. After 10 simulations of 10 steps each from random initial states, maximum likelihood estimation results in the following matrices:

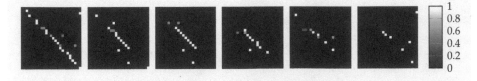

After 1000 simulations, our estimate becomes

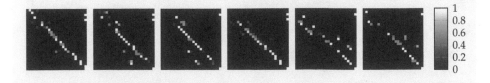

Example 16.1. Applying maximum likelihood estimation to the hex world problem.

```
struct FullUpdate end

function update!(planner::FullUpdate, model, s, a, r, s′)
    𝒫 = MDP(model)
    U = solve(𝒫).U
    copy!(model.U, U)
    return planner
end
```

Algorithm 16.3. A method that performs a full update of the value function of U using the linear programming formulation from section 7.7.

```
struct RandomizedUpdate
    m # number of updates
end

function update!(planner::RandomizedUpdate, model, s, a, r, s′)
    U = model.U
    U[s] = backup(model, U, s)
    for i in 1:planner.m
        s = rand(model.𝒮)
        U[s] = backup(model, U, s)
    end
    return planner
end
```

Algorithm 16.4. Maximum likelihood model-based reinforcement learning with updates at randomized states. This approach performs a Bellman update at the previously visited state, as well as at m additional states chosen randomly.

16.2.3   Prioritized Updates

An approach called *prioritized sweeping*[2] (algorithm 16.5) uses a priority queue to help identify which states are most in need of updating. A transition from s to s′ is followed by an update of $U(s)$ based on our updated transition and reward models. We then iterate over all state-action pairs (s^-, a^-) that can immediately transition into s. The priority of any such s^- is increased to $T(s \mid s^-, a^-) \times |U(s) - u|$, where u was the value of $U(s)$ before the update. Hence, the larger the change in $U(s)$ and the more likely the transition to s, the higher the priority of states leading to s. The process of updating the highest-priority state in the queue continues for a fixed number of iterations or until the queue becomes empty.

[2] A. W. Moore and C. G. Atkeson, "Prioritized Sweeping: Reinforcement Learning with Less Data and Less Time," *Machine Learning*, vol. 13, no. 1, pp. 103–130, 1993.

16.3   Exploration

Regardless of the update scheme, some form of exploration strategy generally must be followed to avoid the pitfalls of pure exploitation mentioned in the previous chapter. We can adapt the exploration algorithms presented in that chapter

```
struct PrioritizedUpdate
    m  # number of updates
    pq # priority queue
end

function update!(planner::PrioritizedUpdate, model, s)
    N, U, pq = model.N, model.U, planner.pq
    S, 𝒜 = model.S, model.𝒜
    u = U[s]
    U[s] = backup(model, U, s)
    for s⁻ in S
        for a⁻ in 𝒜
            n_sa = sum(N[s⁻,a⁻,s'] for s' in S)
            if n_sa > 0
                T = N[s⁻,a⁻,s] / n_sa
                priority = T * abs(U[s] - u)
                if priority > 0
                    pq[s⁻] = max(get(pq, s⁻, 0.0), priority)
                end
            end
        end
    end
    return planner
end

function update!(planner::PrioritizedUpdate, model, s, a, r, s')
    planner.pq[s] = Inf
    for i in 1:planner.m
        if isempty(planner.pq)
            break
        end
        update!(planner, model, dequeue!(planner.pq))
    end
    return planner
end
```

Algorithm 16.5.   The prioritized sweeping algorithm maintains a priority queue pq of states that determines which are to be updated. With each update, we set the previous state to have infinite priority. We then perform m Bellman updates of the value function U at the highest-priority states.

for use in multistate problems. Algorithm 16.6 provides an implementation of the ϵ-greedy exploration strategy.

```
function (π::EpsilonGreedyExploration)(model, s)
    𝒜, ϵ = model.𝒜, π.ϵ
    if rand() < ϵ
        return rand(𝒜)
    end
    Q(s,a) = lookahead(model, s, a)
    return argmax(a→Q(s,a), 𝒜)
end
```

Algorithm 16.6.   The ϵ-greedy exploration strategy for maximum likelihood model estimates. It chooses a random action with probability ϵ; otherwise, it uses the model to extract the greedy action.

A limitation of the exploration strategies discussed in the previous chapter is that they do not reason about exploring actions from states besides the current one. For instance, we might want to take actions that bring ourselves into an area of the state space that has not been explored. Several algorithms have been suggested for addressing this issue, which also provide probabilistic bounds on the quality of the resulting policy after a finite number of interactions.[3]

One such algorithm is known as *R-MAX* (algorithm 16.7).[4] Its name comes from assigning maximal reward to underexplored state-action pairs. State-action pairs with fewer than m visitations are considered underexplored. Instead of using the maximum likelihood estimate for the reward (equation (16.2)), we use

$$R(s,a) = \begin{cases} r_{\max} & \text{if } N(s,a) < m \\ \rho(s,a)/N(s,a) & \text{otherwise} \end{cases} \quad (16.3)$$

where $r_{\max}$ is the maximum achievable reward.

The transition model in R-MAX is also modified so that underexplored state-action pairs result in staying in the same state:

$$T(s' \mid s,a) = \begin{cases} (s' = s) & \text{if } N(s,a) < m \\ N(s,a,s')/N(s,a) & \text{otherwise} \end{cases} \quad (16.4)$$

Hence, underexplored states have value $r_{\max}/(1-\gamma)$, providing an incentive to explore them. This exploration incentive relieves us of needing a separate exploration mechanism. We simply choose our actions greedily with respect to the value function derived from our transition and reward estimates. Example 16.2 demonstrates ϵ-greedy and R-MAX exploration.

[3] M. Kearns and S. Singh, "Near-Optimal Reinforcement Learning in Polynomial Time," *Machine Learning*, vol. 49, no. 2/3, pp. 209–232, 2002.

[4] R. I. Brafman and M. Tennenholtz, "R-MAX—A General Polynomial Time Algorithm for Near-Optimal Reinforcement Learning," *Journal of Machine Learning Research*, vol. 3, pp. 213–231, 2002.

```
mutable struct RmaxMDP
    S # state space (assumes 1:nstates)
    𝒜 # action space (assumes 1:nactions)
    N # transition count N(s,a,s')
    ρ # reward sum ρ(s, a)
    γ # discount
    U # value function
    planner
    m     # count threshold
    rmax # maximum reward
end

function lookahead(model::RmaxMDP, s, a)
    S, U, γ = model.S, model.U, model.γ
    n = sum(model.N[s,a,:])
    if n < model.m
        return model.rmax / (1-γ)
    end
    r = model.ρ[s, a] / n
    T(s,a,s') = model.N[s,a,s'] / n
    return r + γ * sum(T(s,a,s')*U[s'] for s' in S)
end

function backup(model::RmaxMDP, U, s)
    return maximum(lookahead(model, s, a) for a in model.𝒜)
end

function update!(model::RmaxMDP, s, a, r, s')
    model.N[s,a,s'] += 1
    model.ρ[s,a] += r
    update!(model.planner, model, s, a, r, s')
    return model
end

function MDP(model::RmaxMDP)
    N, ρ, S, 𝒜, γ = model.N, model.ρ, model.S, model.𝒜, model.γ
    T, R, m, rmax = similar(N), similar(ρ), model.m, model.rmax
    for s in S
        for a in 𝒜
            n = sum(N[s,a,:])
            if n < m
                T[s,a,:] .= 0.0
                T[s,a,s] = 1.0
                R[s,a] = rmax
            else
                T[s,a,:] = N[s,a,:] / n
                R[s,a] = ρ[s,a] / n
            end
        end
    end
    return MDP(T, R, γ)
end
```

Algorithm 16.7. The R-MAX exploration strategy modifies the transition and reward model from maximum likelihood estimation. It assigns the maximum reward `rmax` to any underexplored state-action pair, defined as being those that have been tried fewer than `m` times. In addition, all underexplored state-action pairs are modeled as transitioning to the same state. This `RmaxMDP` can be used as a replacement for the `MaximumLikelihoodMDP` introduced in algorithm 16.1.

We can apply ϵ-greedy exploration to maximum likelihood model estimates constructed while interacting with the environment. The code that follows initializes the counts, rewards, and utilities to zero. It uses full updates to the value function with each step. For exploration, we choose a random action with probability 0.1. The last line runs a simulation (algorithm 15.9) of problem $\mathcal{P}$ for 100 steps starting in a random initial state:

```
N = zeros(length(S), length(A), length(S))
ρ = zeros(length(S), length(A))
U = zeros(length(S))
planner = FullUpdate()
model = MaximumLikelihoodMDP(S, A, N, ρ, γ, U, planner)
π = EpsilonGreedyExploration(0.1)
simulate(P, model, π, 100, rand(S))
```

Alternatively, we can use R-MAX with an exploration threshold of $m = 3$. We can act greedily with respect to the R-MAX model:

```
rmax = maximum(P.R(s,a) for s in S, a in A)
m = 3
model = RmaxMDP(S, A, N, ρ, γ, U, planner, m, rmax)
π = EpsilonGreedyExploration(0)
simulate(P, model, π, 100, rand(S))
```

Example 16.2. Demonstration of ϵ-greedy and R-MAX exploration.

16.4   Bayesian Methods

In contrast with the maximum likelihood methods discussed so far, Bayesian methods balance exploration and exploitation without having to rely on heuristic exploration policies. This section describes a generalization of the Bayesian methods covered in section 15.5. In *Bayesian reinforcement learning*, we specify a prior distribution over all model parameters θ.[5] These model parameters may include the parameters governing the distribution over immediate rewards, but this section focuses on the parameters governing the state transition probabilities.

The structure of the problem can be represented using the dynamic decision network shown in figure 16.1, wherein the model parameters are made explicit. The shaded nodes indicate that the states are observed but the model parameters are not. We generally assume that the model parameters are time invariant with $\theta_{t+1} = \theta_t$. However, our belief about θ evolves with time as we transition to new states.

The belief over transition probabilities can be represented using a collection of Dirichlet distributions, one for each source state and action. Each Dirichlet distribution represents the distribution over s' for a given s and a. If $\theta_{(s,a)}$ is an $|\mathcal{S}|$-element vector representing the distribution over the next state, then the prior distribution is given by

$$\text{Dir}(\theta_{(s,a)} \mid \mathbf{N}(s,a)) \tag{16.5}$$

where $\mathbf{N}(s,a)$ is the vector of counts associated with transitions starting in state s taking action a. It is common to use a uniform prior with all components set to 1, but prior knowledge of the transition dynamics can be used to initialize the counts differently. Example 16.3 illustrates how these counts are used by the Dirichlet distribution to represent the distribution over possible transition probabilities.

The distribution over θ is the result of the product of the Dirichlet distributions:

$$b(\theta) = \prod_s \prod_a \text{Dir}\left(\theta_{(s,a)} \mid \mathbf{N}(s,a)\right) \tag{16.6}$$

Algorithm 16.8 provides an implementation of the Bayesian update for this type of posterior model. For problems with larger or continuous spaces, we can use other posterior representations.

[5] A survey of this topic is provided by M. Ghavamzadeh, S. Mannor, J. Pineau, and A. Tamar, "Bayesian Reinforcement Learning: A Survey," *Foundations and Trends in Machine Learning*, vol. 8, no. 5–6, pp. 359–483, 2015. It covers methods for incorporating priors over reward functions, which are not discussed here.

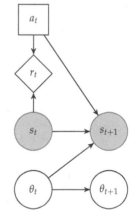

Figure 16.1. A dynamic decision network for an MDP with model uncertainty.

Suppose our agent randomly explores an environment with three states. The agent takes action a_1 from state s_1 five times. It transitions to s_3 four times and remains in s_1 once. The counts associated with s_1 and a_1 are $\mathbf{N}(s_1, a_1) = [1, 0, 4]$. If we want to assume a uniform prior over resulting states, we would increment the counts by 1 to get $\mathbf{N}(s_1, a_1) = [2, 1, 5]$. The transition function from s_1 taking action a_1 is a three-valued categorical distribution because there are three possible successor states. Each successor state has an unknown transition probability. The space of possible transition probabilities is the set of three-element vectors that sum to 1. The Dirichlet distribution represents a probability distribution over these possible transition probabilities. Here is a plot of the density function:

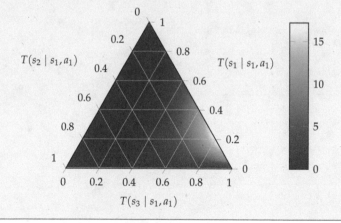

Example 16.3. A posterior Dirichlet distribution over transition probabilities from a particular state when taking a particular action. An agent learning the transition function in an unknown MDP may choose to maintain such a distribution over each state-action pair.

```
mutable struct BayesianMDP
    𝒮 # state space (assumes 1:nstates)
    𝒜 # action space (assumes 1:nactions)
    D # Dirichlet distributions D[s,a]
    R # reward function as matrix (not estimated)
    γ # discount
    U # value function
    planner
end

function lookahead(model::BayesianMDP, s, a)
    𝒮, U, γ = model.𝒮, model.U, model.γ
    n = sum(model.D[s,a].alpha)
    if n == 0
        return 0.0
    end
    r = model.R(s,a)
    T(s,a,s′) = model.D[s,a].alpha[s′] / n
    return r + γ * sum(T(s,a,s′)*U[s′] for s′ in 𝒮)
end

function update!(model::BayesianMDP, s, a, r, s′)
    α = model.D[s,a].alpha
    α[s′] += 1
    model.D[s,a] = Dirichlet(α)
    update!(model.planner, model, s, a, r, s′)
    return model
end
```

Algorithm 16.8. A Bayesian update method when the posterior distribution over transition models is represented as a product of Dirichlet distributions. We assume in this implementation that the reward model R is known, though we can use Bayesian methods to estimate expected reward from experience. The matrix D associates Dirichlet distributions with every state-action pair to model uncertainty in the transition to their successor states.

16.5 Bayes-Adaptive Markov Decision Processes

We can formulate the problem of acting optimally in an MDP with an unknown model as a higher-dimensional MDP with a known model. This MDP is known as a *Bayes-adaptive Markov decision process*, which is related to the partially observable Markov decision process discussed in part IV.

The state space in the Bayes-adaptive MDP is the Cartesian product $\mathcal{S} \times \mathcal{B}$, where $\mathcal{B}$ is the space of possible beliefs over the model parameters θ. Although $\mathcal{S}$ is discrete, $\mathcal{B}$ is often a high-dimensional continuous state space.[6] A state in a Bayes-adaptive MDP is a pair (s, b) consisting of the current state s in the base MDP and a belief state b. The action space and reward function are the same as in the base MDP.

The transition function in a Bayes-adaptive MDP is $T(s', b' \mid s, b, a)$, which is the probability of transitioning to a state s' with a belief state b', given that the agent starts in s with belief b and takes action a. The new belief state b' can be deterministically computed according to Bayes' rule. If we let this deterministic function be denoted as τ so that $b' = \tau(s, b, a, s')$, then we can decompose the Bayes-adaptive MDP transition function as

$$T(s', b' \mid s, b, a) = \delta_{\tau(s,b,a,s')}(b')\, P(s' \mid s, b, a) \tag{16.7}$$

where $\delta_x(y)$ is the *Kronecker delta function*[7] such that $\delta_x(y) = 1$ if $x = y$, and 0 otherwise.

The second term can be computed using integration:

$$P(s' \mid s, b, a) = \int_\theta b(\theta) P(s' \mid s, b, a)\, \mathrm{d}\theta = \int_\theta b(\theta)\theta_{(s,a,s')}\, \mathrm{d}\theta \tag{16.8}$$

This equation can be evaluated analytically in a manner similar to equation (15.1). In the case where our belief b is represented by the factored Dirichlet in equation (16.6), we have

$$P(s' \mid s, b, a) = N(s, a, s') \Big/ \sum_{s''} N(s, a, s'') \tag{16.9}$$

We can generalize the Bellman optimality equation (equation (7.16)) for MDPs with a known model to the case in which the model is unknown:

$$U^*(s, b) = \max_a \left(R(s, a) + \gamma \sum_{s'} P(s' \mid s, b, a) U^*(s', \tau(s, b, a, s')) \right) \tag{16.10}$$

[6] It is continuous in the case of Dirichlet distributions over transition probabilities, as shown in example 16.3.

[7] This function is named after the German mathematician Leopold Kronecker (1823–1891).

330   CHAPTER 16. MODEL-BASED METHODS

Unfortunately, we cannot simply directly apply policy iteration or value iteration because b is continuous. We can, however use the approximation methods of chapter 8 or the online methods of chapter 9. Chapter 16 presents methods that better use the structure of the Bayes-adaptive MDP.

16.6 Posterior Sampling

An alternative to solving for the optimal value function over the belief space is to use *posterior sampling*,[8] which was originally introduced in the context of exploration in bandit problems in section 15.4.[9] Here, we draw a sample θ from the current belief b and then solve for the best action, assuming that θ is the true model. We then update our belief, draw a new sample, and solve the corresponding MDP. Example 16.4 provides an example instance of this.

An advantage of posterior sampling is that we do not have to decide on heuristic exploration parameters. However, solving the MDP at every step can be expensive. A method for sampling a discrete MDP from the posterior is implemented in algorithm 16.9.

[8] M. J. A. Strens, "A Bayesian Framework for Reinforcement Learning," in *International Conference on Machine Learning (ICML)*, 2000.
[9] In that section, we sampled from a posterior distribution over the probability of payoffs and then assumed that the sampled probabilities were correct when selecting an action.

```
struct PosteriorSamplingUpdate end

function Base.rand(model::BayesianMDP)
    S, A = model.S, model.A
    T = zeros(length(S), length(A), length(S))
    for s in S
        for a in A
            T[s,a,:] = rand(model.D[s,a])
        end
    end
    return MDP(T, model.R, model.γ)
end

function update!(planner::PosteriorSamplingUpdate, model, s, a, r, s′)
    P = rand(model)
    U = solve(P).U
    copy!(model.U, U)
end
```

Algorithm 16.9. The update method for posterior sampling. After updating the parameters of the Bayesian posterior, we sample an MDP problem from that posterior. This implementation assumes a discrete state and action space with a Dirichlet modeling our uncertainty in the transition probabilities from each state-action pair. To generate the transition model, we iterate over every state and action and sample from the associated Dirichlet distribution. Once we have a sampled problem P, we solve it using the linear programming formulation and store the resulting value function U.

We want to apply Bayesian model estimation to hex world. We start with associating uniform Dirichlet priors with every state-action pair. After 100 simulations of length 10 and adding our transition counts to our pseudo-counts in our prior, the parameters of our posterior distributions over our successor states appear as follows:

We can sample from this distribution to produce the model shown here. Notice that it has many more nonzero transition probabilities than the maximum likelihood models shown in example 16.1.

Example 16.4. Application of Bayesian model estimation and posterior sampling to the hex world problem.

16.7   Summary

- Model-based methods learn the transition and reward models through interaction with the environment.

- Maximum likelihood models use transition counts to maintain an estimate of the transition probabilities to successor states and to track the mean reward associated with state-action pairs.

- Maximum likelihood models must be paired with an exploration strategy, such as those introduced in the previous chapter in the context of bandits.

- Although we can replan with each step of experience, doing so exactly can be costly.

- Prioritized sweeping can focus replanning by updating the values of states that appear to need it the most in our evolving model of the environment.

- Bayesian model-based methods maintain a probability distribution over possible problems, allowing principled reasoning about exploration.

- In Bayes-adaptive MDPs, their states augment the original MDP with the probability distribution over the possible MDP models.

- Posterior sampling reduces the high computational complexity of solving a Bayes-adaptive MDP by solving an MDP sampled from the belief state rather than reasoning about all possible MDPs.

16.8   Exercises

Table 16.1. Transition data.

s	a	r	s'
s_2	a_1	2	s_1
s_1	a_2	1	s_2
s_2	a_2	1	s_1
s_1	a_2	1	s_2
s_2	a_2	1	s_3
s_3	a_2	2	s_2
s_2	a_2	1	s_3
s_3	a_2	2	s_3
s_3	a_1	2	s_2
s_2	a_1	2	s_3

Exercise 16.1. Suppose we have an agent interacting in an environment with three states and two actions with unknown transition and reward models. We perform one sequence of direct interaction with the environment. Table 16.1 tabulates the state, action, reward, and resulting state. Use maximum likelihood estimation to estimate the transition and reward functions from this data.

Solution: We first tabulate the number of transitions from each state and action $N(s,a)$, the rewards received $\rho(s,a)$, and the maximum likelihood estimate of the reward function $\hat{R}(s,a) = \rho(s,a)/N(s,a)$ as follows:

s	a	$N(s,a)$	$\rho(s,a)$	$\hat{R}(s,a) = \frac{\rho(s,a)}{N(s,a)}$
s_1	a_1	0	0	0
s_1	a_2	2	2	1
s_2	a_1	2	4	2
s_2	a_2	3	3	1
s_3	a_1	1	2	2
s_3	a_2	2	4	2

In the next set of tables, we compute the number of observed transitions $N(s,a,s')$ and the maximum likelihood estimate of the transition model $\hat{T}(s' \mid s,a) = N(s,a,s')/N(s,a)$. When $N(s,a) = 0$, we use a uniform distribution over the resulting states.

s	a	s'	$N(s,a,s')$	$\hat{T}(s' \mid s,a) = \frac{N(s,a,s')}{N(s,a)}$
s_1	a_1	s_1	0	1/3
s_1	a_1	s_2	0	1/3
s_1	a_1	s_3	0	1/3
s_1	a_2	s_1	0	0
s_1	a_2	s_2	2	1
s_1	a_2	s_3	0	0
s_2	a_1	s_1	1	1/2
s_2	a_1	s_2	0	0
s_2	a_1	s_3	1	1/2
s_2	a_2	s_1	1	1/3
s_2	a_2	s_2	0	0
s_2	a_2	s_3	2	2/3
s_3	a_1	s_1	0	0
s_3	a_1	s_2	1	1
s_3	a_1	s_3	0	0
s_3	a_2	s_1	0	0
s_3	a_2	s_2	1	1/2
s_3	a_2	s_3	1	1/2

Exercise 16.2. Provide a lower bound and an upper bound on the number of updates that could be performed during an iteration of prioritized sweeping.

Solution: A lower bound on the number of updates performed in an iteration of prioritized sweeping is 1. This could occur during our first iteration using a maximum likelihood model, where the only nonzero entry in our transition model is $T(s' \mid s,a)$. Since no state-action pairs (s^-, a^-) transition to s, our priority queue would be empty, and thus the only update performed would be for $U(s)$.

An upper bound on the number of updates performed in an iteration of prioritized sweeping is $|\mathcal{S}|$. Suppose that we just transitioned to s', and $\hat{T}(s' \mid s, a) > 0$ for all s and a. If we do not provide a maximum number of updates, we will perform $|\mathcal{S}|$ updates. If we provide a maximum number of updates $m < |\mathcal{S}|$, the upper bound is reduced to m.

Exercise 16.3. In performing Bayesian reinforcement learning of the transition model parameters for a discrete MDP with state space $\mathcal{S}$ and action space $\mathcal{A}$, how many independent parameters are there when using Dirichlet distributions to represent uncertainty over the transition model?

Solution: For each state and action, we specify a Dirichlet distribution over the transition probability parameters, so we will have $|\mathcal{S}||\mathcal{A}|$ Dirichlet distributions. Each Dirichlet is specified using $|\mathcal{S}|$ independent parameters. In total, we have $|\mathcal{S}|^2|\mathcal{A}|$ independent parameters.

Exercise 16.4. Consider the problem statement in exercise 16.1, but this time we want to use Bayesian reinforcement learning with a prior distribution represented by a Dirichlet distribution. Assuming a uniform prior, what is the posterior distribution over the next state, given that we are in state s_2 and take action a_1?

Solution: $\text{Dir}(\theta_{(s_2, a_1)} \mid [2, 1, 2])$

17   *Model-Free Methods*

In contrast with model-based methods, *model-free reinforcement learning* does not require building explicit representations of the transition and reward models.[1] The model-free methods discussed in this chapter model the action value function directly. Avoiding explicit representations is attractive, especially when the problem is high dimensional. This chapter begins by introducing incremental estimation of the mean of a distribution, which plays an important role in estimating the mean of returns. We then discuss some common model-free algorithms and methods for handling delayed reward more efficiently. Finally, we discuss how to use function approximation to generalize from our experience.[2]

17.1   *Incremental Estimation of the Mean*

Many model-free methods *incrementally estimate* the action value function $Q(s, a)$ from samples. For the moment, suppose that we are only concerned with the expectation of a single variable X from m samples:

$$\hat{x}_m = \frac{1}{m} \sum_{i=1}^{m} x^{(i)} \tag{17.1}$$

where $x^{(1)}, \ldots x^{(m)}$ are the samples. We can derive an incremental update:

$$\hat{x}_m = \frac{1}{m} \left(x^{(m)} + \sum_{i=1}^{m-1} x^{(i)} \right) \tag{17.2}$$

$$= \frac{1}{m} \left(x^{(m)} + (m-1)\hat{x}_{m-1} \right) \tag{17.3}$$

$$= \hat{x}_{m-1} + \frac{1}{m} \left(x^{(m)} - \hat{x}_{m-1} \right) \tag{17.4}$$

[1] Many of the topics in this chapter are covered in greater depth by R. S. Sutton and A. G. Barto, *Reinforcement Learning: An Introduction*, 2nd ed. MIT Press, 2018. See also D. P. Bertsekas, *Reinforcement Learning and Optimal Control*. Athena Scientific, 2019.

[2] Although this part of the book has been focusing on problems where the model of the environment is unknown, reinforcement learning is often used for problems with known models. The model-free methods discussed in this chapter can be especially useful in complex environments as a form of approximate dynamic programming. They can be used to produce policies offline, or as a means to generate the next action in an online context.

We can rewrite this equation with the introduction of a *learning rate* function $\alpha(m)$:

$$\hat{x}_m = \hat{x}_{m-1} + \alpha(m)\left(x^{(m)} - \hat{x}_{m-1}\right) \tag{17.5}$$

The learning rate can be a function other than $1/m$. To ensure convergence, we generally select $\alpha(m)$ such that we have $\sum_{m=1}^{\infty} \alpha(m) = \infty$ and $\sum_{m=1}^{\infty} \alpha^2(m) < \infty$. The first condition ensures that the steps are sufficiently large, and the second condition ensures that the steps are sufficiently small.[3]

If the learning rate is constant, which is common in reinforcement learning applications, then the weights of older samples decay exponentially at the rate $(1 - \alpha)$. With a constant learning rate, we can update our estimate after observing x using the following rule:

$$\hat{x} \leftarrow \hat{x} + \alpha(x - \hat{x}) \tag{17.6}$$

Algorithm 17.1 provides an implementation of this. An example of several learning rates is shown in example 17.1.

The update rule discussed here will appear again in later sections and is related to stochastic gradient descent. The magnitude of the update is proportional to the difference between the sample and the previous estimate. The difference between the sample and previous estimate is called the *temporal difference error*.

17.2   Q-Learning

Q-learning (algorithm 17.2) involves applying incremental estimation of the action value function $Q(s,a)$.[4] The update is derived from the action value form of the Bellman expectation equation:

$$Q(s,a) = R(s,a) + \gamma \sum_{s'} T(s' \mid s,a)U(s') \tag{17.7}$$

$$= R(s,a) + \gamma \sum_{s'} T(s' \mid s,a) \max_{a'} Q(s',a') \tag{17.8}$$

Instead of using T and R, we can rewrite the equation above in terms of an expectation over samples of reward r and the next state s':

$$Q(s,a) = \mathbb{E}_{r,s'}[r + \gamma \max_{a'} Q(s',a')] \tag{17.9}$$

[3] For a discussion of convergence and its application to some of the other algorithms discussed in this chapter, see T. Jaakkola, M. I. Jordan, and S. P. Singh, "On the Convergence of Stochastic Iterative Dynamic Programming Algorithms," *Neural Computation*, vol. 6, no. 6, pp. 1185–1201, 1994.

[4] C. J. C. H. Watkins, "Learning from Delayed Rewards," Ph.D. dissertation, University of Cambridge, 1989.

Consider estimating the expected value obtained when rolling a fair six-sided die. What follows are *learning curves* that show the incremental estimates over 100 trials associated with different learning rate functions. As we can see, convergence is not guaranteed if $\alpha(m)$ decays too quickly, and it is slow if $\alpha(m)$ does not decay quickly enough.

For constant values of $\alpha \in (0,1]$, the mean estimate will continue to fluctuate. Larger values of constant α fluctuate wildly, whereas lower values take longer to converge.

Example 17.1. The effect of decaying the learning rate with different functions for $\alpha(m)$.

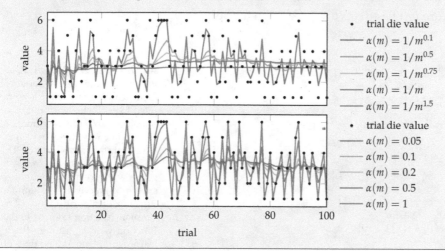

Algorithm 17.1. A type for maintaining an incremental estimate of the mean of a random variable. The associated type maintains a current mean value μ, a learning rate function α, and an iteration count m. Calling update! with a new value x updates the estimate.

```
mutable struct IncrementalEstimate
    μ # mean estimate
    α # learning rate function
    m # number of updates
end

function update!(model::IncrementalEstimate, x)
    model.m += 1
    model.μ += model.α(model.m) * (x - model.μ)
    return model
end
```

We can use equation (17.6) to produce an incremental update rule to estimate the action value function:[5]

$$Q(s,a) \leftarrow Q(s,a) + \alpha\left(r + \gamma \max_{a'} Q(s',a') - Q(s,a)\right) \qquad (17.10)$$

Our choice of actions affects which states we end up in, and therefore our ability to estimate $Q(s,a)$ accurately. To guarantee convergence of our action value function, we need to adopt some form of exploration policy, such as ϵ-greedy or softmax, just as we did for our model-based methods in the previous chapter. Example 17.2 shows how to run a simulation with the Q-learning update rule and an exploration policy. Figure 17.1 illustrates this process on the hex world problem.

[5] The maximization in this equation can introduce a bias. Algorithms like *double Q-learning* attempt to correct for this bias and can lead to better performance. H. van Hasselt, "Double Q-Learning," in *Advances in Neural Information Processing Systems (NIPS)*, 2010.

```
mutable struct QLearning
    S # state space (assumes 1:nstates)
    𝒜 # action space (assumes 1:nactions)
    γ # discount
    Q # action value function
    α # learning rate
end

lookahead(model::QLearning, s, a) = model.Q[s,a]

function update!(model::QLearning, s, a, r, s′)
    γ, Q, α = model.γ, model.Q, model.α
    Q[s,a] += α*(r + γ*maximum(Q[s′,:]) - Q[s,a])
    return model
end
```

Algorithm 17.2. The Q-learning update for model-free reinforcement learning, which can be applied to problems with unknown transition and reward functions. The update modifies Q, which is a matrix of state-action values. This update function can be used together with an exploration strategy, such as ϵ-greedy, in the simulate function of algorithm 15.9. That simulate function calls the update function with s′, though this Q-learning implementation does not use it.

17.3   Sarsa

Sarsa (algorithm 17.3) is an alternative to Q-learning.[6] It derives its name from the fact that it uses (s,a,r,s',a') to update the Q function at each step. It uses the actual next action a' to update Q instead of maximizing over all possible actions:

$$Q(s,a) \leftarrow Q(s,a) + \alpha\left(r + \gamma Q(s',a') - Q(s,a)\right) \qquad (17.11)$$

With a suitable exploration strategy, the a' will converge to $\arg\max_{a'} Q(s',a')$, which is what is used in the Q-learning update.

[6] This approach was suggested with a different name in G. A. Rummery and M. Niranjan, "On-Line Q-Learning Using Connectionist Systems," Cambridge University, Tech. Rep. CUED/F-INFENG/TR 166, 1994.

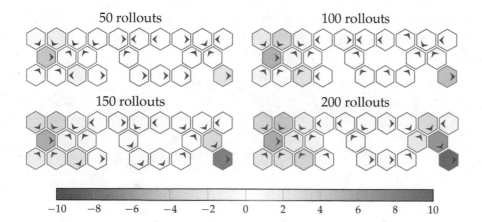

Figure 17.1. Q-learning used to iteratively learn an action value function for the hex world problem. Each state is colored according to the expected value of the best action in that state according to Q. Actions are similarly the best expected actions. Q-learning was run with $\alpha = 0.1$ and 10 steps per rollout.

Suppose we want to apply Q-learning to an MDP problem $\mathcal{P}$. We can construct an exploration policy, such as the ϵ-greedy policy implemented in algorithm 16.6 from the previous chapter. The Q-learning model comes from algorithm 17.2, and the simulate function is implemented in algorithm 15.9.

```
Q = zeros(length(𝒫.𝒮), length(𝒫.𝒜))
α = 0.2 # learning rate
model = QLearning(𝒫.𝒮, 𝒫.𝒜, 𝒫.γ, Q, α)
ε = 0.1 # probability of random action
π = EpsilonGreedyExploration(ε)
k = 20 # number of steps to simulate
s = 1  # initial state
simulate(𝒫, model, π, k, s)
```

Example 17.2. How to use an exploration strategy with Q-learning in simulation. The parameter settings are notional.

Sarsa is referred to as a type of *on-policy* reinforcement learning method because it attempts to directly estimate the value of the exploration policy as it follows it. In contrast, Q-learning is an *off-policy* method because it attempts to find the value of the optimal policy while following the exploration strategy. Although Q-learning and Sarsa both converge to an optimal strategy, the speed of convergence depends on the application. Sarsa is run on the hex world problem in figure 17.2.

```
mutable struct Sarsa
    𝒮 # state space (assumes 1:nstates)
    𝒜 # action space (assumes 1:nactions)
    γ # discount
    Q # action value function
    α # learning rate
    ℓ # most recent experience tuple (s,a,r)
end

lookahead(model::Sarsa, s, a) = model.Q[s,a]

function update!(model::Sarsa, s, a, r, s′)
    if model.ℓ != nothing
        γ, Q, α, ℓ = model.γ, model.Q, model.α,  model.ℓ
        model.Q[ℓ.s,ℓ.a] += α*(ℓ.r + γ*Q[s,a] - Q[ℓ.s,ℓ.a])
    end
    model.ℓ = (s=s, a=a, r=r)
    return model
end
```

Algorithm 17.3. The Sarsa update for model-free reinforcement learning. We update the matrix Q containing the state-action values, α is a constant learning rate, and ℓ is the most recent experience tuple. As with the Q-learning implementation, the update function can be used in the simulator in algorithm 15.9.

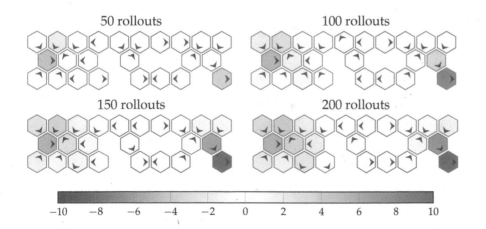

50 rollouts

100 rollouts

150 rollouts

200 rollouts

−10   −8   −6   −4   −2   0   2   4   6   8   10

Figure 17.2. Sarsa used to iteratively learn an action value function for the hex world problem in a manner otherwise identical to figure 17.1. We find that Sarsa is slower to converge to the true action value function.

17.4   Eligibility Traces

One of the disadvantages of Q-learning and Sarsa is that learning can be very slow, especially with *sparse rewards*. For example, suppose that the environment has a single goal state that provides a large reward, and the reward is zero at all other states. After an amount of random exploration in the environment, we reach the goal state. Regardless of whether we use Q-learning or Sarsa, we only update the action value of the state immediately preceding the goal state. The values at all other states leading up to the goal remain at zero. A large amount of exploration is required to slowly propagate nonzero values to the remainder of the state space.

Q-learning and Sarsa can be modified to propagate reward backward to the states and actions leading to the source of the reward using *eligibility traces*.[7] The credit is decayed exponentially so that states closer to the reward are assigned larger values. It is common to use $0 < \lambda < 1$ as the exponential decay parameter. Versions of Q-learning and Sarsa with eligibility traces are often called $Q(\lambda)$ and Sarsa(λ).[8]

A version of Sarsa(λ) is implemented in algorithm 17.4, which maintains an exponentially decaying visit count $N(s,a)$ for all state-action pairs. When action a is taken in state s, $N(s,a)$ is incremented by 1. The Sarsa temporal difference update is then partially applied to every state-action pair according to this decaying visit count.

Let δ denote the Sarsa temporal difference update:

$$\delta = r + \gamma Q(s',a') - Q(s,a) \tag{17.12}$$

Every entry in the action value function is then updated according to

$$Q(s,a) \leftarrow Q(s,a) + \alpha \delta N(s,a) \tag{17.13}$$

The visit counts are then decayed using both the discount factor and the exponential decay parameter:

$$N(s,a) \leftarrow \gamma \lambda N(s,a) \tag{17.14}$$

Although the impact of eligibility traces is especially pronounced in environments with sparse reward, the algorithm can speed learning in general environments where reward is more distributed.

[7] Eligibility traces were proposed in the context of temporal difference learning by R. Sutton, "Learning to Predict by the Methods of Temporal Differences," *Machine Learning*, vol. 3, no. 1, pp. 9–44, 1988.

[8] These algorithms were introduced by C. J. C. H. Watkins, "Learning from Delayed Rewards," Ph.D. dissertation, University of Cambridge, 1989. and J. Peng and R. J. Williams, "Incremental Multi-Step Q-Learning," *Machine Learning*, vol. 22, no. 1–3, pp. 283–290, 1996.

```
mutable struct SarsaLambda
    𝒮 # state space (assumes 1:nstates)
    𝒜 # action space (assumes 1:nactions)
    γ # discount
    Q # action value function
    N # trace
    α # learning rate
    λ # trace decay rate
    ℓ # most recent experience tuple (s,a,r)
end

lookahead(model::SarsaLambda, s, a) = model.Q[s,a]

function update!(model::SarsaLambda, s, a, r, s′)
    if model.ℓ != nothing
        γ, λ, Q, α, ℓ = model.γ, model.λ, model.Q, model.α, model.ℓ
        model.N[ℓ.s,ℓ.a] += 1
        δ = ℓ.r + γ*Q[s,a] - Q[ℓ.s,ℓ.a]
        for s in model.𝒮
            for a in model.𝒜
                model.Q[s,a] += α*δ*model.N[s,a]
                model.N[s,a] *= γ*λ
            end
        end
    else
        model.N[:,:] .= 0.0
    end
    model.ℓ = (s=s, a=a, r=r)
    return model
end
```

Algorithm 17.4. The Sarsa(λ) update, which uses eligibility traces to propagate reward back in time to speed learning of sparse rewards. The matrix Q contains the state-action values, the matrix N contains exponentially decaying state-action visit counts, α is a constant learning rate, λ is an exponential decay parameter, and ℓ is the most recent experience tuple.

Special care must be taken when applying eligibility traces to an off-policy algorithm like Q-learning that attempts to learn the value of the optimal policy.[9] Eligibility traces propagate back values obtained from an exploration policy. This mismatch can result in learning instabilities.

17.5 Reward Shaping

Reward function augmentation can also improve learning, especially in problems with sparse rewards. For example, if we are trying to reach a single goal state, we could supplement the reward function by an amount that is inversely proportional to the distance to the goal. Alternatively, we could add another penalty based on how far we are from the goal. If we are playing chess, for instance, we might add a penalty to our reward function when we lose a piece, even though we only care about winning or losing the game at the end, not about winning or losing individual pieces.

Modifying the reward function during training by incorporating domain knowledge to speed training is known as *reward shaping*. Suppose that rewards in our problem are generated according to $R(s, a, s')$, allowing rewards to depend on the resulting state. We will use $F(s, a, s')$ to represent our *shaping function*. During training, instead of using $R(s, a, s')$ as our reward, we use $R(s, a, s') + F(s, a, s')$.

Adding $F(s, a, s')$ to our reward can change the optimal policy, of course. We are often interested in shaping reward without changing what is optimal. It turns out that a policy that is optimal under the original reward remains optimal under the shaped reward if and only if

$$F(s, a, s') = \gamma \beta(s') - \beta(s) \qquad (17.15)$$

for some potential function $\beta(s)$.[10]

17.6 Action Value Function Approximation

The algorithms discussed so far in this chapter have assumed discrete state and action spaces where the action value function can be stored in a lookup table. We can adapt our algorithms to use value function approximation, allowing us to apply them to problems with large or continuous spaces and generalize from limited experience. Similar to the approach taken in chapter 8 in the context of a

[9] For an overview of this problem and a potential solution, see A. Harutyunyan, M. G. Bellemare, T. Stepleton, and R. Munos, "Q(λ) with Off-Policy Corrections," in *International Conference on Algorithmic Learning Theory (ALT)*, 2016.

[10] A. Y. Ng, D. Harada, and S. Russell, "Policy Invariance Under Reward Transformations: Theory and Application to Reward Shaping," in *International Conference on Machine Learning (ICML)*, 1999.

known model, we will use $Q_\theta(s,a)$ to represent a parametric approximation of our action value function when the model is unknown.[11]

To illustrate this concept, we will derive a version of Q-learning that uses our parametric approximation. We want to minimize the loss between our approximation and the optimal action value function $Q^*(s,a)$, which we define to be[12]

$$\ell(\theta) = \frac{1}{2} \mathop{\mathbb{E}}_{(s,a)\sim\pi^*} \left[(Q^*(s,a) - Q_\theta(s,a))^2 \right] \tag{17.16}$$

The expectation is over the state-action pairs that are experienced when following the optimal policy π^*.

A common approach to minimizing this loss is to use some form of gradient descent. The gradient of the loss is

$$\nabla\ell(\theta) = -\mathop{\mathbb{E}}_{(s,a)\sim\pi^*} \left[(Q^*(s,a) - Q_\theta(s,a))\nabla_\theta Q_\theta(s,a) \right] \tag{17.17}$$

We typically choose parametric representations of the action value function that are differentiable and where $\nabla_\theta Q_\theta(s,a)$ is easy to compute, such as linear or neural network representations. If we apply gradient descent,[13] our update rule is

$$\theta \leftarrow \theta + \alpha \mathop{\mathbb{E}}_{(s,a)\sim\pi^*} \left[(Q^*(s,a) - Q_\theta(s,a))\nabla_\theta Q_\theta(s,a) \right] \tag{17.18}$$

where α is our step factor or learning rate. We can approximate the update rule above using samples of our state-action pairs (s,a) as we experience them:

$$\theta \leftarrow \theta + \alpha(Q^*(s,a) - Q_\theta(s,a))\nabla_\theta Q_\theta(s,a) \tag{17.19}$$

Of course, we cannot compute equation (17.19) directly because that would require knowing the optimal policy, which is precisely what we are attempting to find. Instead, we attempt to estimate it from our observed transition and our action value approximation:

$$Q^*(s,a) \approx r + \gamma \max_{a'} Q_\theta(s',a') \tag{17.20}$$

which results in the following update rule:

$$\theta \leftarrow \theta + \alpha(r + \gamma \max_{a'} Q_\theta(s',a') - Q_\theta(s,a))\nabla_\theta Q_\theta(s,a) \tag{17.21}$$

[11] In recent years, a major focus has been on *deep reinforcement learning*, where deep neural networks are used for this parametric approximation. A discussion of practical implementations is provided by L. Graesser and W. L. Keng, *Foundations of Deep Reinforcement Learning*. Addison Wesley, 2020.

[12] The 1/2 in the front is for convenience because we will later be computing the derivative of this quadratic.

[13] We want to descend rather than ascend because we are trying to minimize our loss.

This update is implemented in algorithm 17.5 with the addition of a scaled gradient step (algorithm 12.2), which is often needed to ensure that the gradient steps do not become too large. Example 17.3 shows how to use this update with a linear action value approximation. Figure 17.3 demonstrates this algorithm with the mountain car problem.

```
struct GradientQLearning
    𝒜  # action space (assumes 1:nactions)
    γ  # discount
    Q  # parameterized action value function Q(θ,s,a)
    ∇Q # gradient of action value function
    θ  # action value function parameter
    α  # learning rate
end

function lookahead(model::GradientQLearning, s, a)
    return model.Q(model.θ, s,a)
end

function update!(model::GradientQLearning, s, a, r, s′)
    𝒜, γ, Q, θ, α = model.𝒜, model.γ, model.Q, model.θ, model.α
    u = maximum(Q(θ,s′,a′) for a′ in 𝒜)
    Δ = (r + γ*u - Q(θ,s,a))*model.∇Q(θ,s,a)
    θ[:] += α*scale_gradient(Δ, 1)
    return model
end
```

Algorithm 17.5. The Q-learning update with action value function approximation. With each new experience tuple s, a, r, s′, we update our vector θ with constant learning rate α. Our parameterized action value function is given by Q(θ,s,a) and its gradient is ∇Q(θ,s,a).

17.7   Experience Replay

A major challenge of using global function approximation with reinforcement learning is *catastrophic forgetting*. For example, we might initially discover that our particular policy brings us to a low-reward region of the state space. We then refine our policy to avoid that area. However, after some amount of time, we may forget why it was important to avoid that region of the state space, and we may risk reverting to a poorly performing policy.

Catastrophic forgetting can be mitigated with *experience replay*,[14] where a fixed number of the most recent experience tuples are stored across training iterations. A *batch* of tuples are sampled uniformly from this *replay memory* to remind us to avoid strategies that we have already discovered are poor.[15] The update equation from equation (17.21) is modified to become

[14] Experience replay played an important role in the work of V. Mnih, K. Kavukcuoglu, D. Silver, A. Graves, I. Antonoglou, D. Wierstra, and M. Riedmiller, "Playing Atari with Deep Reinforcement Learning," 2013. arXiv: 1312 . 5602v1 . This concept was explored earlier by L.-J. Lin, "Reinforcement Learning for Robots Using Neural Networks," Ph.D. dissertation, Carnegie Mellon University, 1993.

[15] Variations of this approach include prioritizing experiences. T. Schaul, J. Quan, I. Antonoglou, and D. Silver, "Prioritized Experience Replay," in *International Conference on Learning Representations (ICLR)*, 2016.

We are interested in applying Q-learning with a linear action value approximation to the simple regulator problem with $\gamma = 1$. Our action value approximation is $Q_\theta(s,a) = \theta^\top \beta(s,a)$, where our basis function is

$$\beta(s,a) = [s, s^2, a, a^2, 1]$$

With this linear model,

$$\nabla_\theta Q_\theta(s,a) = \beta(s,a)$$

We can implement this as follows for problem $\mathcal{P}$:

```
β(s,a) = [s,s^2,a,a^2,1]
Q(θ,s,a) = dot(θ,β(s,a))
∇Q(θ,s,a) = β(s,a)
θ = [0.1,0.2,0.3,0.4,0.5] # initial parameter vector
α = 0.5 # learning rate
model = GradientQLearning(𝒫.𝒜, 𝒫.γ, Q, ∇Q, θ, α)
ε = 0.1 # probability of random action
π = EpsilonGreedyExploration(ε)
k = 20  # number of steps to simulate
s = 0.0 # initial state
simulate(𝒫, model, π, k, s)
```

Example 17.3. How to use an exploration strategy with Q-learning with action value function approximation in simulation. The parameter settings are notional.

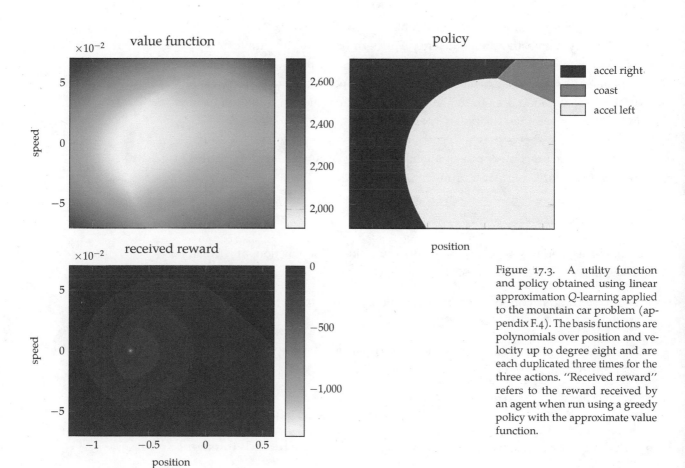

Figure 17.3. A utility function and policy obtained using linear approximation Q-learning applied to the mountain car problem (appendix F.4). The basis functions are polynomials over position and velocity up to degree eight and are each duplicated three times for the three actions. "Received reward" refers to the reward received by an agent when run using a greedy policy with the approximate value function.

$$\theta \leftarrow \theta + \alpha \frac{1}{m_{\text{grad}}} \sum_i (r^{(i)} + \gamma \max_{a'} Q_\theta(s'^{(i)}, a') - Q_\theta(s^{(i)}, a^{(i)})) \nabla_\theta Q_\theta(s^{(i)}, a^{(i)}) \qquad (17.22)$$

where $s^{(i)}$, $a^{(i)}$, $r^{(i)}$, and $s'^{(i)}$ is the ith experience tuple in a random batch of size m_{grad}.

Experience replay allows experience tuples to contribute to learning multiple times, thereby increasing data efficiency. Furthermore, sampling uniformly at random from the replay memory breaks apart otherwise correlated sequences that are obtained from rollouts, thereby reducing the variance of the gradient estimate. Experience replay stabilizes the learning process by retaining information from previous policy parameterizations.

Algorithm 17.6 shows how to incorporate experience replay into Q-learning with action value function approximation. Example 17.4 shows how to apply this approach to a simple regulator problem.

17.8   Summary

- Model-free methods seek to directly learn an action value function rather than transition and reward models.

- Simple techniques can be used to incrementally learn a mean from sequential updates.

- The Q-learning algorithm incrementally learns an action value function using an approximation of the Bellman equation.

- In contrast with Q-learning, Sarsa uses the action taken by the exploration policy rather than maximizing over all subsequent actions in its update.

- Eligibility traces can speed learning by propagating sparse rewards through the state-action space.

- Q-learning can be applied to approximate value functions using stochastic gradient descent.

- The catastrophic forgetting experienced by Q-learning and Sarsa can be mitigated using experience replay, which reuses past experience tuples.

```
struct ReplayGradientQLearning
    𝒜        # action space (assumes 1:nactions)
    γ        # discount
    Q        # parameterized action value function Q(θ,s,a)
    ∇Q       # gradient of action value function
    θ        # action value function parameter
    α        # learning rate
    buffer # circular memory buffer
    m        # number of steps between gradient updates
    m_grad # batch size
end

function lookahead(model::ReplayGradientQLearning, s, a)
    return model.Q(model.θ, s,a)
end

function update!(model::ReplayGradientQLearning, s, a, r, s′)
    𝒜, γ, Q, θ, α = model.𝒜, model.γ, model.Q, model.θ, model.α
    buffer, m, m_grad = model.buffer, model.m, model.m_grad
    if isfull(buffer)
        U(s) = maximum(Q(θ,s,a) for a in 𝒜)
        ∇Q(s,a,r,s′) = (r + γ*U(s′) - Q(θ,s,a))*model.∇Q(θ,s,a)
        Δ = mean(∇Q(s,a,r,s′) for (s,a,r,s′) in rand(buffer, m_grad))
        θ[:] += α*scale_gradient(Δ, 1)
        for i in 1:m # discard oldest experiences
            popfirst!(buffer)
        end
    else
        push!(buffer, (s,a,r,s′))
    end
    return model
end
```

Algorithm 17.6. *Q*-learning with function approximation and experience replay. The update depends on a parameterized policy $Q(\theta,s,a)$ and gradient $\nabla Q(\theta,s,a)$. It updates the parameter vector θ and the circular memory buffer provided by DataStructures.jl. It updates θ every m steps using a gradient estimated from m_grad samples from the buffer.

Suppose we want to add experience replay to example 17.3. When constructing the model, we need to provide a replay buffer with the desired capacity:

```
capacity = 100 # maximum size of the replay buffer
ExperienceTuple = Tuple{Float64,Float64,Float64,Float64}
M = CircularBuffer{ExperienceTuple}(capacity) # replay buffer
m_grad = 20 # batch size
model = ReplayGradientQLearning(𝒫.𝒜, 𝒫.γ, Q, ∇Q, θ, α, M, m, m_grad)
```

We can vary the number of steps between gradient updates m and the
depth of each simulation d. In the plot shown here, we limit all training runs
to $md = 30$ experience tuples with each iteration. It indicates that rollouts to
a sufficient depth are necessary for training to succeed. In addition, very few
rollouts to an excessive depth do not perform as well as a moderate number
of rollouts to a moderate depth.

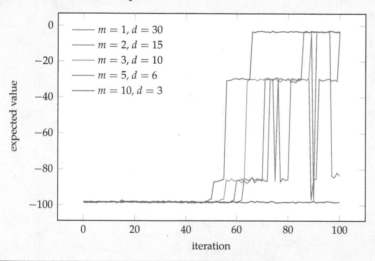

Example 17.4. An application of experience replay to the simple regulator problem with Q-learning and
action value approximation.

17.9   Exercises

Exercise 17.1. Given the following set of samples, perform incremental estimation of the mean twice: once using a learning rate of $\alpha = 0.1$ and once using a learning rate of $\alpha = 0.5$. In both, use an initial mean equal to the first sample:

$$x^{(1:5)} = \{1.0, 1.8, 2.0, 1.6, 2.2\}$$

Solution: We set the mean at the first iteration equal to the first sample and proceed to incrementally estimate the mean using equation (17.6):

$$\hat{x}_1 = 1.0 \qquad\qquad\qquad\qquad \hat{x}_1 = 1.0$$
$$\hat{x}_2 = 1.0 + 0.1(1.8 - 1.0) = 1.08 \qquad \hat{x}_2 = 1.0 + 0.5(1.8 - 1.0) = 1.4$$
$$\hat{x}_3 = 1.08 + 0.1(2.0 - 1.08) = 1.172 \qquad \hat{x}_3 = 1.4 + 0.5(2.0 - 1.4) = 1.7$$
$$\hat{x}_4 = 1.172 + 0.1(1.6 - 1.172) \approx 1.215 \qquad \hat{x}_4 = 1.7 + 0.5(1.6 - 1.7) = 1.65$$
$$\hat{x}_5 = 1.215 + 0.1(2.2 - 1.215) \approx 1.313 \qquad \hat{x}_5 = 1.65 + 0.5(2.2 - 1.65) = 1.925$$

Exercise 17.2. Following the previous exercise, suppose that once we have estimated the mean with five samples for both methods, we are provided with a single additional sample, $x^{(6)}$, that we will use as the final sample in estimating our mean. Which of the two incremental estimation methods (i.e., $\alpha = 0.1$ or $\alpha = 0.5$) would be preferable?

Solution: While we do not know what the sample would be or what the underlying mean of the process is, we would likely prefer the second incrementally estimated mean that uses $\alpha = 0.5$. Since we only have one sample left, the first learning rate is too small to considerably change the mean, while the second learning rate is large enough to be responsive, without neglecting the past samples. Consider two cases:

1. If we assume that the next sample is approximately equal to the *incremental* mean of all previous samples, then we have $x^{(6)} \approx \hat{x}_5$. Thus, performing an incremental update of the mean yields no change to our estimate. We have $\hat{x}_6 \approx 1.313$ for a learning rate of 0.1, and we have $\hat{x}_6 = 1.925$ for a learning rate of 0.5.

2. If we assume the next sample is approximately equal to the *exact* mean of all previous samples, then we have $x^{(6)} \approx 1.72$. The update using a learning rate of 0.1 yields $\hat{x}_6 \approx 1.354$, while the update using a learning rate of 0.5 yields $\hat{x}_6 \approx 1.823$.

In both of these cases, supposing that the next sample is equal to the mean of all previous samples, then the estimate using a learning rate of 0.5 is more accurate.

Exercise 17.3. Consider applying Q-learning with function approximation to a problem with a continuous action space by discretizing the action space. Suppose that the continuous action space is in $\mathbb{R}^n$, such as a robot with n actuators, and each dimension is discretized into m intervals. How many actions are in the resulting discrete action space? Is Q-learning with function approximation well suited for continuous problems with many dimensions?

Solution: An action space with n dimensions and m intervals per dimension results in m^n discrete actions. The number of discrete actions increases exponentially in n. Even if m is small, larger values of n can quickly result in very high action counts. Hence, Q-learning with function approximation is not well suited for use on continuous problems with many action dimensions.

Exercise 17.4. What is the complexity of Q-learning if we interact with the environment for d time steps? What is the complexity of Sarsa if we interact with the environment for d time steps?

Solution: For Q-learning, our update rule is

$$Q(s,a) \leftarrow Q(s,a) + \alpha \left(r + \gamma \max_{a'} Q(s',a') - Q(s,a) \right)$$

At each time step, we must perform a maximization over actions, so for d time steps, the complexity of Q-learning is $O(d|\mathcal{A}|)$. For Sarsa, our update rule is

$$Q(s,a) \leftarrow Q(s,a) + \alpha \left(r + \gamma Q(s',a') - Q(s,a) \right) \tag{17.23}$$

At each time step, unlike Q-learning, we do not have to perform a maximization over actions, so for d time steps, the complexity of Sarsa is simply $O(d)$.

Exercise 17.5. Is the computational complexity of Sarsa per experience tuple (s_t, a_t, r_t, s_{t+1}) more or less than that of Sarsa(λ)?

Solution: For Sarsa, our update rule is

$$Q(s,a) \leftarrow Q(s,a) + \alpha \left(r + \gamma Q(s',a') - Q(s,a) \right) \tag{17.24}$$

So, for each experience tuple, we have $O(1)$ complexity. For Sarsa(λ), our update rules are

$$\delta \leftarrow r_t + \gamma Q(s_{t+1}, a_{t+1}) - Q(s_t, a_t)$$
$$N(s_t, a_t) \leftarrow N(s_t, a_t) + 1$$
$$Q(s,a) \leftarrow Q(s,a) + \alpha \delta N(s,a) \quad \text{for all } s, a$$
$$N(s,a) \leftarrow \gamma \lambda N(s,a) \quad \text{for all } s, a$$

For each experience tuple, we need to compute δ and increment the visit count at (s_t, a_t), which are both $O(1)$. However, we need to update both the action value function and the visit counts for all states and actions, which are both $O(|\mathcal{S}||\mathcal{A}|)$. Thus, the computational complexity per experience tuple is greater for Sarsa(λ). However, Sarsa(λ) often converges using fewer experience tuples.

Exercise 17.6. What is the behavior of $Q(\lambda)$ in the limit as $\lambda \to 0$? What is the behavior of $Q(\lambda)$ in the limit as $\lambda \to 1$?

Solution: For $Q(\lambda)$, we perform the following update rules:

$$\delta \leftarrow r_t + \gamma \max_{a'} Q(s_{t+1}, a') - Q(s_t, a_t)$$

$$N(s_t, a_t) \leftarrow N(s_t, a_t) + 1$$

$$Q(s, a) \leftarrow Q(s, a) + \alpha \delta N(s, a) \qquad \text{for all } s, a$$

$$N(s, a) \leftarrow \gamma \lambda N(s, a) \qquad \text{for all } s, a$$

In the limit as $\lambda \to 0$, for our first iteration, we compute the temporal difference error δ and we increment the visit count $N(s_t, a_t)$. In the action value function update, the only nonzero $N(s, a)$ is at $N(s_t, a_t)$, so we perform $Q(s_t, a_t) \leftarrow Q(s_t, a_t) + \alpha \delta N(s_t, a_t)$. Finally, we reset all the visit counts to zero. From this, we can see that in the limit as $\lambda \to 0$, we have no eligibility traces and we are performing a straightforward Q-learning update.

In the limit as $\lambda \to 1$, our visit counts will accumulate and we have full eligibility traces, which will spread the reward over all previously visited state-action pairs.

Exercise 17.7. Compute $Q(s, a)$ using Sarsa(λ) after following the trajectory

$$(s_1, a_R, 0, s_2, a_R, 0, s_3, a_L, 10, s_2, a_R, 4, s_1, a_R)$$

Use $\alpha = 0.5$, $\lambda = 1$, $\gamma = 0.9$, and initial action value function and visit counts equal to zero everywhere. Assume that $\mathcal{S} = \{s_1, s_2, s_3, s_4\}$ and $\mathcal{A} = \{a_L, a_R\}$.

Solution: The Sarsa(λ) update rules are

$$\delta \leftarrow r_t + \gamma Q(s_{t+1}, a_{t+1}) - Q(s_t, a_t)$$

$$N(s_t, a_t) \leftarrow N(s_t, a_t) + 1$$

$$Q(s, a) \leftarrow Q(s, a) + \alpha \delta N(s, a) \qquad \text{for all } s, a$$

$$N(s, a) \leftarrow \gamma \lambda N(s, a) \qquad \text{for all } s, a$$

For the first experience tuple, we have $\delta = 0 + 0.9 \times 0 - 0 = 0$, we increment the visit count at $N(s_1, a_R)$, the action value function does not change since $\delta = 0$, and we update our counts. After this, we have

$Q(s,a)$	s_1	s_2	s_3	s_4		$N(s,a)$	s_1	s_2	s_3	s_4
a_L	0	0	0	0		a_L	0	0	0	0
a_R	0	0	0	0		a_R	0.9	0	0	0

For the second experience tuple, we have $\delta = 0$, we increment the visit count at $N(s_2, a_R)$, the action value function does not change since $\delta = 0$, and we update our counts. After this, we have

$Q(s,a)$	s_1	s_2	s_3	s_4
a_L	0	0	0	0
a_R	0	0	0	0

$N(s,a)$	s_1	s_2	s_3	s_4
a_L	0	0	0	0
a_R	0.81	0.9	0	0

For the third experience tuple, we have $\delta = 10$, we increment the visit count at $N(s_3, a_L)$, we update the action value function, and we update our counts. After this, we have

$Q(s,a)$	s_1	s_2	s_3	s_4
a_L	0	0	5	0
a_R	4.05	4.5	0	0

$N(s,a)$	s_1	s_2	s_3	s_4
a_L	0	0	0.9	0
a_R	0.729	0.81	0	0

For the fourth experience tuple, we have $\delta = 4 + 0.9 \times 4.05 - 4.5 = 3.145$, we increment the visit count at $N(s_2, a_R) = 0.81 + 1 = 1.81$, we update the action value function, and we update our counts. After this, we have

$Q(s,a)$	s_1	s_2	s_3	s_4
a_L	0	0	6.415	0
a_R	5.196	7.346	0	0

$N(s,a)$	s_1	s_2	s_3	s_4
a_L	0	0	0.81	0
a_R	0.656	1.629	0	0

18 Imitation Learning

Previous chapters have assumed either that a reward function is known or that rewards are received while interacting with the environment. For some applications, it may be easier for an expert to demonstrate the desired behavior rather than specify a reward function. This chapter discusses algorithms for *imitation learning*, where the desired behavior is learned from expert demonstration. We will cover a variety of methods ranging from very simple likelihood-maximization methods to more complicated iterative methods that involve reinforcement learning.[1]

18.1 Behavioral Cloning

A simple form of imitation learning is to treat it as a supervised learning problem. This method, called *behavioral cloning*,[2] trains a stochastic policy π_θ parameterized by θ to maximize the likelihood of actions from a data set $\mathcal{D}$ of expert state-action pairs:

$$\underset{\theta}{\text{maximize}} \prod_{(s,a) \in \mathcal{D}} \pi_\theta(a \mid s) \qquad (18.1)$$

As done in earlier chapters, we can transform the maximization over the product over $\pi_\theta(a \mid s)$ to a sum over $\log \pi_\theta(a \mid s)$.

Depending on how we want to represent the conditional distribution $\pi_\theta(a \mid s)$, we may compute the maximum likelihood estimate of θ analytically. For example, if we use a discrete conditional model (section 2.4), θ would consist of the counts $N(s,a)$ from $\mathcal{D}$ and $\pi_\theta(a \mid s) = N(s,a) / \sum_a N(s,a)$. Example 18.1 applies a discrete conditional model to data from the mountain car problem.

If we have a factored representation of our policy, we can use a Bayesian network to represent the joint distribution over our state and action variables. Figure 18.1 shows an example. We can learn both the structure (chapter 5) and

[1] Additional methods and applications are surveyed by A. Hussein, M. M. Gaber, E. Elyan, and C. Jayne, "Imitation Learning: A Survey of Learning Methods," *ACM Computing Surveys*, vol. 50, no. 2, pp. 1–35, 2017.

[2] D. A. Pomerleau, "Efficient Training of Artificial Neural Networks for Autonomous Navigation," *Neural Computation*, vol. 3, no. 1, pp. 88–97, 1991.

Consider using behavioral cloning on expert demonstrations for the mountain car problem (appendix F.4). We are given 10 rollouts from an expert policy. We fit a conditional distribution and plot the results. The continuous trajectories were discretized with 10 bins each for position and for speed.

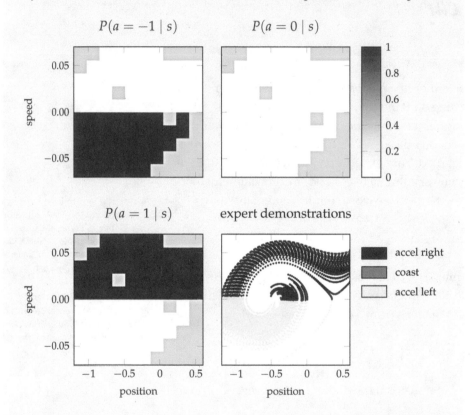

Example 18.1. A demonstration of behavioral cloning applied to the mountain car problem. The light blue regions are areas without training data, resulting in poor policy performance when the agent encounters those states.

The state space is not fully covered by expert demonstrations, which is typical of imitation learning problems. The resulting policy may perform well when used in regions with coverage, but it assigns a uniform distribution to actions in regions without coverage. Even if we start in a region with coverage, we may transition to regions without coverage due to stochasticity in the environment.

the parameters (chapter 4) from the data $\mathcal{D}$. Given the current state, we can then infer the distribution over actions using one of the inference algorithms discussed earlier (chapter 3).

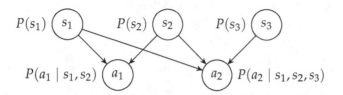

Figure 18.1. Bayesian networks can be used to represent a joint distribution over the state and action variables. We can apply an inference algorithm to generate a distribution over actions, given the current values of the state variables.

We can use many other representations for π_θ. For example, we might want to use a neural network, where the input corresponds to the values of the state variables and the output corresponds to parameters of a distribution over the action space. If our representation is differentiable, which is the case with neural networks, we can attempt to optimize equation (18.1) using gradient ascent. This approach is implemented in algorithm 18.1.

```
struct BehavioralCloning
    α      # step size
    k_max  # number of iterations
    ∇logπ  # log likelihood gradient
end

function optimize(M::BehavioralCloning, D, θ)
    α, k_max, ∇logπ = M.α, M.k_max, M.∇logπ
    for k in 1:k_max
        ∇ = mean(∇logπ(θ, a, s) for (s,a) in D)
        θ += α*∇
    end
    return θ
end
```

Algorithm 18.1. A method for learning a parameterized stochastic policy from expert demonstrations in the form of a set of state-action tuples D. The policy parameterization vector θ is iteratively improved by maximizing the log likelihood of the actions given the states. Behavioral cloning requires a step size α, an iteration count k_max, and a log likelihood gradient ∇logπ.

The closer the expert demonstrations are to optimal, the better the resulting behavioral cloning policy will perform.[3] However, behavioral cloning suffers from *cascading errors*. As discussed in example 18.2, small inaccuracies compound during a rollout and eventually lead to states that are poorly represented in the training data, thereby leading to worse decisions, and ultimately to invalid or unseen situations. Although behavioral cloning is attractive due to its simplicity, cascading errors cause the method to perform poorly on many problems, especially when policies must be used for long time horizons.

[3] U. Syed and R. E. Schapire, "A Reduction from Apprenticeship Learning to Classification," in *Advances in Neural Information Processing Systems (NIPS)*, 2010.

> Consider applying behavioral cloning to train a policy for driving an autonomous race car. A human race car driver provides expert demonstrations. Being an expert, the driver never drifts onto the grass or too close to a railing. A model trained with behavioral cloning would have no information to use when near a railing or when drifting onto the grass, and thus it would not know how to recover.

Example 18.2. A brief example of the generalization issue inherent to behavioral cloning approaches.

18.2   Data Set Aggregation

One way to address the problem of cascading errors is to correct a trained policy using additional expert input. *Sequential interactive demonstration* methods alternate between collecting data from an expert in situations generated by a trained policy and using this data to improve this policy.

One type of sequential interactive demonstration method is called *data set aggregation (DAgger)* (algorithm 18.2).[4] It starts by training a stochastic policy using behavioral cloning. The policy is then used to run several rollouts from an initial state distribution b, which are then given to an expert to provide the correct actions for each state. The new data is aggregated with the previous data set and a new policy is trained. Example 18.3 illustrates this process.

These interactive demonstrations iteratively build a data set covering the regions of the state space that the agent is likely to encounter, based on previous learning iterations. With each iteration, newly added examples compose a smaller fraction of the data set, thereby leading to smaller policy changes. While sequential interactive demonstration can work well in practice, it is not guaranteed to converge. It can be shown that mixing in influence from the expert policy can guarantee convergence, which is the subject of the next section.

[4] S. Ross, G. J. Gordon, and J. A. Bagnell, "A Reduction of Imitation Learning and Structured Prediction to No-Regret Online Learning," in *International Conference on Artificial Intelligence and Statistics (AISTATS)*, vol. 15, 2011.

18.3   Stochastic Mixing Iterative Learning

Sequential interactive methods can also iteratively build up a policy by stochastically mixing in newly trained policies. One such method is *stochastic mixing iterative learning (SMILe)* (algorithm 18.3).[5] It uses behavioral cloning in every iteration but mixes the newly trained policy with the previous ones.

We start with the expert policy, $\pi^{(1)} = \pi_E$.[6] In each iteration, we execute the

[5] S. Ross and J. A. Bagnell, "Efficient Reductions for Imitation Learning," in *International Conference on Artificial Intelligence and Statistics (AISTATS)*, 2010.

[6] We do not have an explicit representation of π_E. Evaluating π_E requires interactively querying the expert, as done in the previous section.

```
struct DataSetAggregation
    𝒫      # problem with unknown reward function
    bc     # behavioral cloning struct
    k_max  # number of iterations
    m      # number of rollouts per iteration
    d      # rollout depth
    b      # initial state distribution
    πE     # expert
    πθ     # parameterized policy
end

function optimize(M::DataSetAggregation, D, θ)
    𝒫, bc, k_max, m = M.𝒫, M.bc, M.k_max, M.m
    d, b, πE, πθ = M.d, M.b, M.πE, M.πθ
    θ = optimize(bc, D, θ)
    for k in 2:k_max
        for i in 1:m
            s = rand(b)
            for j in 1:d
                push!(D, (s, πE(s)))
                a = rand(πθ(θ, s))
                s = rand(𝒫.T(s, a))
            end
        end
        θ = optimize(bc, D, θ)
    end
    return θ
end
```

Algorithm 18.2. The DAgger method of data set aggregation for learning a stochastic parameterized policy from expert demonstrations. This method takes an initial data set of state-action tuples D, a stochastic parameterized policy πθ(θ, s), an MDP 𝒫 that defines a transition function, and an initial state distribution b. Behavioral cloning (algorithm 18.1) is used in each iteration to improve the policy.

An expert policy πE labels trajectories sampled from the latest learned policy to augment the data set. The original paper generated trajectories by stochastically mixing in the expert policy. This implementation is thus the original DAgger with an extreme mixing value of zero.

In practice, an expert policy would not exist, and calls to this policy would be replaced with queries to a human expert.

Consider using DAgger to train a policy on the mountain car problem where the reward is not observed. We use an expert policy that accelerates in the direction of travel. In this example, we train a policy using the following features:

$$\mathbf{f}(s) = [1[v > 0], 1[v < 0], x, x^2, v, v^2, xv]$$

where x and v are the position and speed of the car.

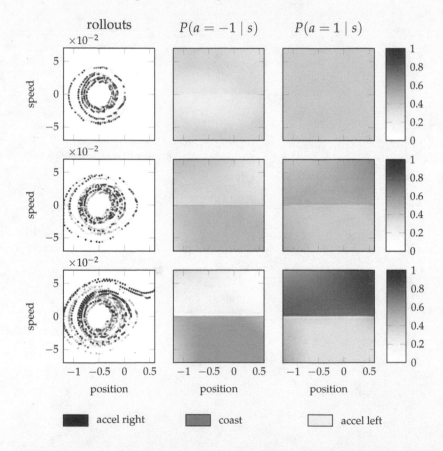

Example 18.3. DAgger applied to the mountain car problem, with iterations running from top to bottom. Trajectories accumulate in the data set over time. The behavior of the agent improves with each iteration.

Trajectories are colored according to the action. In the first iteration, the agent behaves randomly, unable to make progress toward the goal ($x \geq 0.6$). With additional iterations, the agent learns to mimic the expert policy of accelerating in the direction of travel. This behavior is apparent in the new trajectories, which spiral outward, and the policy, which assigns high likelihood to $a = 1$ when $v > 0$ and $a = -1$ when $v < 0$.

latest policy $\pi^{(k)}$ to generate a new data set, querying the expert to provide the correct actions. Behavioral cloning is applied only to this new data set to train a new *component policy* $\hat{\pi}^{(k)}$. This component policy is mixed with component policies from the previous iterations to produce a new policy $\pi^{(k+1)}$.

The mixing of component policies to generate $\pi^{(k+1)}$ is governed by a mixing scalar $\beta \in (0,1)$. The probability of acting according to the expert policy is $(1-\beta)^k$, and the probability of acting according to $\hat{\pi}^{(i)}$ is $\beta(1-\beta)^{i-1}$. This scheme assigns more weight to older policies under the hypothesis that older policy components were trained on the states most likely to be encountered.[7] With each iteration, the probability of acting according to the original expert policy decays to zero. The mixing scalar is typically small, such that the agent does not abandon the expert's policy too quickly. Example 18.4 demonstrates this approach with the mountain car problem.

[7] In SMILe, we are acting according to our latest learned policy. We expect that this learned policy will match the expert fairly well and primarily mispredict when we deviate from the expert policy. The learned component policies generally only need to make smaller and smaller contributions with each iteration to make up the difference in what has not already been learned.

18.4   Maximum Margin Inverse Reinforcement Learning

In many application settings, we have no expert that can be interactively queried; but instead we have a batch of expert demonstration trajectories. We will assume that the expert demonstration data $\mathcal{D}$ consists of m trajectories. Each trajectory τ in $\mathcal{D}$ involves a rollout to depth d. In *inverse reinforcement learning*, we assume that the expert is optimizing an unknown reward function. From $\mathcal{D}$, we attempt to derive that reward function. With that reward function, we can use the methods discussed in prior chapters to derive an optimal policy.

There are different approaches to inverse reinforcement learning. We generally need to define a parameterization of the reward function. A common assumption is that this parameterization is linear, with $R_{\phi}(s,a) = \phi^{\top}\beta(s,a)$, where $\beta(s,a)$ is a feature vector and ϕ is a vector of weightings. In this section, we will focus on an approach known as *maximum margin inverse reinforcement learning*,[8] where the features are assumed to be binary. Since optimal policies remain optimal with positive scaling of the reward function, this method additionally constrains the weight vector such that $\|\phi\|_2 \leq 1$. The expert data activates each binary feature with different frequencies, perhaps pursuing some and avoiding others. This approach attempts to learn this pattern of activation and trains an agent to mimic these activation frequencies.

[8] P. Abbeel and A. Y. Ng, "Apprenticeship Learning via Inverse Reinforcement Learning," in *International Conference on Machine Learning (ICML)*, 2004.

```
struct SMILe
    𝒫      # problem with unknown reward
    bc     # Behavioral cloning struct
    k_max  # number of iterations
    m      # number of rollouts per iteration
    d      # rollout depth
    b      # initial state distribution
    β      # mixing scalar (e.g., d^-3)
    πE     # expert policy
    πθ     # parameterized policy
end

function optimize(M::SMILe, θ)
    𝒫, bc, k_max, m = M.𝒫, M.bc, M.k_max, M.m
    d, b, β, πE, πθ = M.d, M.b, M.β, M.πE, M.πθ
    𝒜, T = 𝒫.𝒜, 𝒫.T
    θs = []
    π = s → πE(s)
    for k in 1:k_max
        # execute latest π to get new data set D
        D = []
        for i in 1:m
            s = rand(b)
            for j in 1:d
                push!(D, (s, πE(s)))
                a = π(s)
                s = rand(T(s, a))
            end
        end
        # train new policy classifier
        θ = optimize(bc, D, θ)
        push!(θs, θ)
        # compute a new policy mixture
        Pπ = Categorical(normalize([(1-β)^(i-1) for i in 1:k],1))
        π = s → begin
            if rand() < (1-β)^(k-1)
                return πE(s)
            else
                return rand(Categorical(πθ(θs[rand(Pπ)], s)))
            end
        end
    end
    Ps = normalize([(1-β)^(i-1) for i in 1:k_max],1)
    return Ps, θs
end
```

Algorithm 18.3. The SMILe algorithm for training a stochastic parameterized policy from expert demonstrations for an MDP 𝒫. It successively mixes in new component policies with smaller and smaller weights, while simultaneously reducing the probability of acting according to the expert policy. The method returns the probabilities Ps and parameterizations θs for the component policies.

Consider using SMILe to train a policy on the mountain car problem where the reward is not observed. We use the same features that were used for DAgger in example 18.3. Both DAgger and SMILe receive a new expert-labeled data set with each iteration. Instead of accumulating a larger data set of expert-labeled data, SMILe trains a new policy component using only the most recent data, mixing the new policy component with the previous policy components.

Example 18.4. Using SMILe to learn a policy for the mountain car problem. In contrast with DAgger in example 18.3, SMILe mixes the expert into the policy during rollouts. This expert component, whose influence wanes with each iteration, causes the initial rollouts to better progress toward the goal.

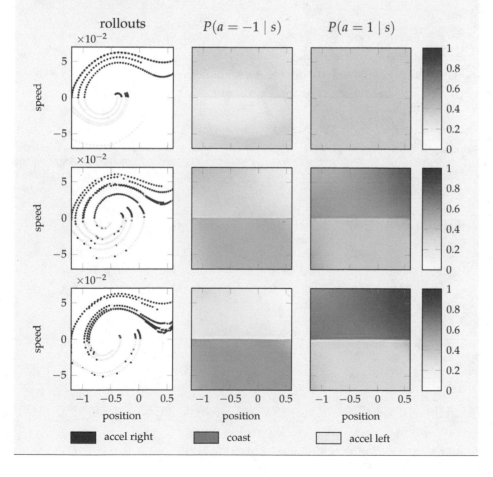

An important part of this algorithm involves reasoning about the expected return under a policy π for a weighting ϕ and initial state distribution b:

$$\mathbb{E}_{s \sim b}[U(s)] = \mathbb{E}_\tau \left[\sum_{k=1}^{d} \gamma^{k-1} R_\phi(s^{(k)}, a^{(k)}) \right] \tag{18.2}$$

$$= \mathbb{E}_\tau \left[\sum_{k=1}^{d} \gamma^{k-1} \phi^\top \beta(s^{(k)}, a^{(k)}) \right] \tag{18.3}$$

$$= \phi^\top \left(\mathbb{E}_\tau \left[\sum_{k=1}^{d} \gamma^{k-1} \beta(s^{(k)}, a^{(k)}) \right] \right) \tag{18.4}$$

$$= \phi^\top \mu_\pi \tag{18.5}$$

where τ corresponds to trajectories generated by π to depth d. Here, we introduce the *feature expectations* vector μ_π, which is the expected discounted accumulated feature values. These feature expectations can be estimated from m rollouts, as implemented in algorithm 18.4.

```
struct InverseReinforcementLearning
    𝒫  # problem
    b  # initial state distribution
    d  # depth
    m  # number of samples
    π  # parameterized policy
    β  # binary feature mapping
    μE # expert feature expectations
    RL # reinforcement learning method
    ϵ  # tolerance
end

function feature_expectations(M::InverseReinforcementLearning, π)
    𝒫, b, m, d, β, γ = M.𝒫, M.b, M.m, M.d, M.β, M.𝒫.γ
    μ(τ) = sum(γ^(k-1)*β(s, a) for (k,(s,a)) in enumerate(τ))
    τs = [simulate(𝒫, rand(b), π, d) for i in 1:m]
    return mean(μ(τ) for τ in τs)
end
```

Algorithm 18.4. A structure for inverse reinforcement learning and a method for estimating a feature expectations vector from rollouts.

We can use the expert demonstrations to estimate the expert feature expectations μ_E, and we want to find a policy that matches these feature expectations as closely as possible. At the first iteration, we begin with a randomized policy $\pi^{(1)}$ and estimate its feature expectations, denoted as $\mu^{(1)}$. At iteration k, we find a new $\phi^{(k)}$ corresponding to a reward function $R_{\phi^{(k)}}(s, a) = \phi^{(k)\top} \beta(s, a)$, such that the expert outperforms all previously found policies by the greatest *margin t*:

$$\underset{t,\boldsymbol{\phi}}{\text{maximize}} \quad t$$
$$\text{subject to} \quad \boldsymbol{\phi}^{\top}\boldsymbol{\mu}_E \geq \boldsymbol{\phi}^{\top}\boldsymbol{\mu}^{(i)} + t \ \text{ for } \ i = 1,\dots,k-1 \qquad (18.6)$$
$$\|\boldsymbol{\phi}\|_2 \leq 1$$

Equation (18.6) is a quadratic program that can be easily solved. We then solve for a new policy $\pi^{(k)}$ using the reward function $R(s,a) = \boldsymbol{\phi}^{(k)\top}\boldsymbol{\beta}(s,a)$, and produce a new vector of feature expectations. Figure 18.2 illustrates this margin maximization process.

We iterate until the margin is sufficiently small, with $t \leq \epsilon$. At convergence, we can solve for a mixed policy that attempts to have feature expectations as close as possible to that of the expert policy:

$$\underset{\lambda}{\text{minimize}} \quad \|\boldsymbol{\mu}_E - \boldsymbol{\mu}_\lambda\|_2$$
$$\text{subject to} \quad \lambda \geq 0 \qquad (18.7)$$
$$\|\lambda\|_1 = 1$$

where $\boldsymbol{\mu}_\lambda = \sum_i \lambda_i \boldsymbol{\mu}^{(i)}$. The mixture weights λ combine the policies found at each iteration. With probability λ_i, we follow policy $\pi^{(i)}$. Maximum margin inverse reinforcement learning is implemented in algorithm 18.5.

18.5 Maximum Entropy Inverse Reinforcement Learning

The inverse reinforcement learning approach from the previous section is under-specified, meaning that there are often multiple policies that can produce the same feature expectations as the expert demonstrations. This section introduces *maximum entropy inverse reinforcement learning*, which avoids this ambiguity by preferring the policy that results in the distribution over trajectories that has maximum *entropy* (appendix A.8).[9] The problem can be transformed into one of finding the best reward function parameters $\boldsymbol{\phi}$ in a maximum likelihood estimation problem, given the expert data $\mathcal{D}$.

[9] B. D. Ziebart, A. Maas, J. A. Bagnell, and A. K. Dey, "Maximum Entropy Inverse Reinforcement Learning," in *AAAI Conference on Artificial Intelligence (AAAI)*, 2008.

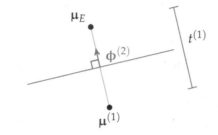

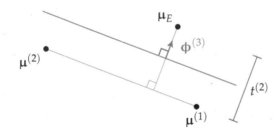

Figure 18.2. A geometric visualization of three example iterations of the maximum-margin inverse reinforcement learning algorithm, going top to bottom. In each iteration, the new weight vector points in the direction perpendicular to the hyperplane that separates the expert feature expectation vector from that of the previous policy with the largest possible margin. The margin decreases with each iteration.

```
function calc_weighting(M::InverseReinforcementLearning, μs)
    μE = M.μE
    k = length(μE)
    model = Model(Ipopt.Optimizer)
    @variable(model, t)
    @variable(model, ϕ[1:k] ≥ 0)
    @objective(model, Max, t)
    for μ in μs
        @constraint(model, ϕ⋅μE ≥ ϕ⋅μ + t)
    end
    @constraint(model, ϕ⋅ϕ ≤ 1)
    optimize!(model)
    return (value(t), value.(ϕ))
end

function calc_policy_mixture(M::InverseReinforcementLearning, μs)
    μE = M.μE
    k = length(μs)
    model = Model(Ipopt.Optimizer)
    @variable(model, λ[1:k] ≥ 0)
    @objective(model, Min, (μE - sum(λ[i]*μs[i] for i in 1:k))⋅
                           (μE - sum(λ[i]*μs[i] for i in 1:k)))
    @constraint(model, sum(λ) == 1)
    optimize!(model)
    return value.(λ)
end

function optimize(M::InverseReinforcementLearning, θ)
    π, ϵ, RL = M.π, M.ϵ, M.RL
    θs = [θ]
    μs = [feature_expectations(M, s→π(θ,s))]
    while true
        t, ϕ = calc_weighting(M, μs)
        if t ≤ ϵ
            break
        end
        copyto!(RL.ϕ, ϕ) # R(s,a) = ϕ⋅β(s,a)
        θ = optimize(RL, π, θ)
        push!(θs, θ)
        push!(μs, feature_expectations(M, s→π(θ,s)))
    end
    λ = calc_policy_mixture(M, μs)
    return λ, θs
end
```

Algorithm 18.5. Maximum margin inverse reinforcement learning, which computes a mixed policy whose feature expectations match those of given expert demonstrations. We use JuMP.jl to solve constrained optimization problems. This implementation requires that the provided reinforcement learning struct has a weight vector ϕ that can be updated with new values. The method returns the stochastic weightings λ and parameterizations θs for the component policies.

Any policy π induces a distribution over trajectories[10] $P_\pi(\tau)$. Different policies produce different trajectory distributions. We are free to choose any of these distributions over trajectories that match the expert feature expectations. The *principle of maximum entropy* chooses the least informative distribution, which corresponds to the one with maximum entropy.[11] It can be shown that the least informative trajectory distribution takes the following form:

$$P_\phi(\tau) = \frac{1}{Z(\phi)} \exp(R_\phi(\tau)) \qquad (18.8)$$

where $P_\phi(\tau)$ is the likelihood of a trajectory τ given reward parameter ϕ, and

$$R_\phi(\tau) = \sum_{k=1}^{d} \gamma^{k-1} R_\phi(s^{(k)}, a^{(k)}) \qquad (18.9)$$

is the discounted trajectory reward. We make no assumption on the parameterization of $R_\phi(s^{(k)}, a^{(k)})$ other than that it is differentiable, allowing representations such as neural networks. The normalization scalar $Z(\phi)$ ensures that the probabilities sum to 1:

$$Z(\phi) = \sum_\tau \exp(R_\phi(\tau)) \qquad (18.10)$$

The summation is over all possible trajectories.

We have chosen a particular class of trajectory distributions for our policy. We now fit that class to our trajectories using maximum likelihood to obtain the parameters that best describe our data:

$$\max_\phi f(\phi) = \max_\phi \sum_{\tau \in \mathcal{D}} \log P_\phi(\tau) \qquad (18.11)$$

We can rewrite the objective function $f(\phi)$ from equation (18.11):

$$f(\phi) = \sum_{\tau \in \mathcal{D}} \log \frac{1}{Z(\phi)} \exp(R_\phi(\tau)) \qquad (18.12)$$

$$= \left(\sum_{\tau \in \mathcal{D}} R_\phi(\tau) \right) - |\mathcal{D}| \log Z(\phi) \qquad (18.13)$$

$$= \left(\sum_{\tau \in \mathcal{D}} R_\phi(\tau) \right) - |\mathcal{D}| \log \sum_\tau \exp(R_\phi(\tau)) \qquad (18.14)$$

[10] For simplicity, this section assumes a finite horizon and that the state and action spaces are discrete, making $P_\phi(\tau)$ a probability mass. To extend maximum entropy inverse reinforcement learning both to problems with continuous state and action spaces where the dynamics may be unknown, consider guided cost learning. C. Finn, S. Levine, and P. Abbeel, "Guided Cost Learning: Deep Inverse Optimal Control via Policy Optimization," in *International Conference on Machine Learning (ICML)*, 2016.

[11] For an introduction to this principle, see E. T. Jaynes, "Information Theory and Statistical Mechanics," *Physical Review*, vol. 106, no. 4, pp. 620–630, 1957.

We can attempt to optimize this objective function through gradient ascent. The gradient of f is

$$\nabla_\phi f = \left(\sum_{\tau \in \mathcal{D}} \nabla_\phi R_\phi(\tau) \right) - \frac{|\mathcal{D}|}{\sum_\tau \exp(R_\phi(\tau))} \sum_\tau \exp(R_\phi(\tau)) \nabla_\phi R_\phi(\tau) \tag{18.15}$$

$$= \left(\sum_{\tau \in \mathcal{D}} \nabla_\phi R_\phi(\tau) \right) - |\mathcal{D}| \sum_\tau P_\phi(\tau) \nabla_\phi R_\phi(\tau) \tag{18.16}$$

$$= \left(\sum_{\tau \in \mathcal{D}} \nabla_\phi R_\phi(\tau) \right) - |\mathcal{D}| \sum_s b_{\gamma,\phi}(s) \sum_a \pi_\phi(a \mid s) \nabla_\phi R_\phi(s,a) \tag{18.17}$$

If the reward function is linear, with $R_\phi(s,a) = \phi^\top \beta(s,a)$, as in the previous section, then $\nabla_\phi R_\phi(s,a)$ is simply $\beta(s,a)$.

Updating the parameter vector ϕ thus requires both the discounted state visitation frequency $b_{\gamma,\phi}$ and the optimal policy under the current parameter vector, $\pi_\phi(a \mid s)$. We can obtain the optimal policy by running reinforcement learning. To compute the discounted state visitation frequencies, we can use rollouts or take a dynamic programming approach.

If we take a dynamic programming approach to compute the discounted state visitation frequencies, we can start with the initial state distribution $b_{\gamma\phi}^{(1)} = b(s)$ and iteratively work forward in time:

$$b_{\gamma,\phi}^{(k+1)}(s) = \gamma \sum_a \sum_{s'} b_{\gamma,\phi}^{(k)}(s) \pi(a \mid s) T(s' \mid s,a) \tag{18.18}$$

This version of maximum entropy inverse reinforcement learning is implemented in algorithm 18.6.

18.6   Generative Adversarial Imitation Learning

In *generative adversarial imitation learning (GAIL)*,[12] we optimize a differentiable parameterized policy π_θ, often represented by a neural network. Rather than provide a reward function, we use *adversarial learning* (appendix D.7). We also train a *discriminator* $C_\phi(s,a)$, typically also a neural network, to return the probability that it assigns to the state-action pair coming from the learned policy. The process involves alternating between training this discriminator to become better

[12] J. Ho and S. Ermon, "Generative Adversarial Imitation Learning," in *Advances in Neural Information Processing Systems (NIPS)*, 2016.

```
struct MaximumEntropyIRL
    𝒫      # problem
    b      # initial state distribution
    d      # depth
    π      # parameterized policy π(θ,s)
    Pπ     # parameterized policy likelihood π(θ, a, s)
    ∇R     # reward function gradient
    RL     # reinforcement learning method
    α      # step size
    k_max  # number of iterations
end

function discounted_state_visitations(M::MaximumEntropyIRL, θ)
    𝒫, b, d, Pπ = M.𝒫, M.b, M.d, M.Pπ
    S, 𝒜, T, γ = 𝒫.S, 𝒫.𝒜, 𝒫.T, 𝒫.γ
    b_sk = zeros(length(𝒫.S), d)
    b_sk[:,1] = [pdf(b, s) for s in S]
    for k in 2:d
        for (si′, s′) in enumerate(S)
            b_sk[si′,k] = γ*sum(sum(b_sk[si,k-1]*Pπ(θ, a, s)*T(s, a, s′)
                    for (si,s) in enumerate(S))
                for a in 𝒜)
        end
    end
    return normalize!(vec(mean(b_sk, dims=2)),1)
end

function optimize(M::MaximumEntropyIRL, D, ϕ, θ)
    𝒫, π, Pπ, ∇R, RL, α, k_max = M.𝒫, M.π, M.Pπ, M.∇R, M.RL, M.α, M.k_max
    S, 𝒜, γ, nD = 𝒫.S, 𝒫.𝒜, 𝒫.γ, length(D)
    for k in 1:k_max
        copyto!(RL.ϕ, ϕ) # update parameters
        θ = optimize(RL, π, θ)
        b = discounted_state_visitations(M, θ)
        ∇Rτ = τ → sum(γ^(i-1)*∇R(ϕ,s,a) for (i,(s,a)) in enumerate(τ))
        ∇f = sum(∇Rτ(τ) for τ in D) - nD*sum(b[si]*sum(Pπ(θ,a,s)*∇R(ϕ,s,a)
                    for (ai,a) in enumerate(𝒜))
                for (si, s) in enumerate(S))
        ϕ += α*∇f
    end
    return ϕ, θ
end
```

Algorithm 18.6.   Maximum entropy inverse reinforcement learning, which finds a stochastic policy that maximizes the likelihood of the expert demonstrations under a maximum-entropy trajectory distribution. This implementation computes the expected visitations using dynamic programming over all states, which requires that the problem be discrete.

at distinguishing between simulated and expert state-action pairs, and training the policy to look indistinguishable from the expert demonstrations. The process is sketched in figure 18.3.

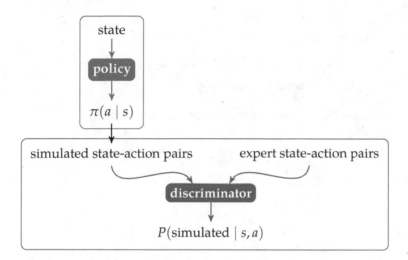

Figure 18.3. Instead of inferring a reward function, generative adversarial imitation learning optimizes a discriminator to distinguish between simulated and expert state-action pairs, and it optimizes a policy to appear indistinguishable to the discriminator. The aim is to eventually produce a policy that resembles the expert.

The discriminator and policy have opposing objectives. GAIL seeks to find a saddle point (θ, ϕ) of the negative log loss of the discriminator's binary classification problem:[13]

$$\max_{\phi} \min_{\theta} \mathbb{E}_{(s,a)\sim\pi_\theta}\left[\log(C_\phi(s,a))\right] + \mathbb{E}_{(s,a)\sim\mathcal{D}}\left[\log(1 - C_\phi(s,a))\right] \quad (18.19)$$

[13] The original paper also includes the following entropy term:

$$-\lambda\, \mathbb{E}_{(s,a)\sim\mathcal{D}}[-\log \pi_\theta(a \mid s)]$$

where we use $(s, a) \sim \mathcal{D}$ to represent samples from the distribution represented by the expert data set $\mathcal{D}$. We can alternate between gradient ascent on ϕ to increase the objective and trust region policy optimization (section 12.4) on θ to reduce the objective, generating the necessary trajectory samples from the policy to conduct each of these steps. The discriminator provides a learning signal to the policy similar to the way that a reward signal would if it were known.

18.7 Summary

- Imitation learning involves learning the desired behavior from expert demonstration without the use of a reward function.

- One type of imitation learning is behavioral cloning, which produces a stochastic policy that maximizes the conditional likelihood of the actions in the data set.

- When an expert can be queried multiple times, we can use iterative approaches like data set aggregation or stochastic mixing iterative learning.

- Inverse reinforcement learning involves inferring a reward function from expert data and then using traditional methods for finding an optimal policy.

- Maximum margin inverse reinforcement learning attempts to find a policy that matches the frequency of binary features found in the expert data set.

- Maximum entropy inverse reinforcement learning frames the problem of finding the best reward parameter as a maximum likelihood estimation problem, which it tries to solve using gradient ascent.

- Generative adversarial imitation learning iteratively optimizes a discriminator and a policy; the discriminator tries to discriminate between decisions made by the policy and decisions made by the expert, and the policy attempts to deceive the discriminator.

18.8   Exercises

Exercise 18.1.   Consider applying behavioral cloning to a discrete problem where we have been given expert demonstrations. We could define a feature function $\beta(s)$ and represent the policy with a softmax distribution:

$$\pi(a \mid s) \propto \exp(\theta_a^\top \beta(s))$$

We would then learn the parameters θ_a for each action from the expert data. Why might we want to use this approach over one where we directly estimate a discrete distribution for each state, with one parameter per state-action pair?

Solution: In imitation learning, we are generally limited to a relatively small set of expert demonstrations. The distribution $P(a \mid s)$ has $(|\mathcal{A}| - 1)|\mathcal{S}|$ independent parameters that must be learned, which is often prohibitively large. Expert demonstrations typically cover only a small portion of the state space. Even if $P(a \mid s)$ can be reliably trained for the states covered in the provided data set, the resulting policy would be untrained in other states. Using a feature function allows generalization to unseen states.

Exercise 18.2. Section 18.1 suggested using a maximum likelihood approach for training a policy from expert data. This approach attempts to find the parameters of the policy that maximizes the likelihood assigned to the training examples. In some problems, however, we know that assigning high probability to one incorrect action is not as bad as assigning high probability to another incorrect action. For example, predicting an acceleration of -1 in the mountain car problem when the expert dictates an acceleration of 1 is worse than predicting an acceleration of 0. How might behavioral cloning be modified to allow different penalties to be given to different misclassifications?

Solution: We can instead supply a cost function $C(s, a_{\text{true}}, a_{\text{pred}})$ that defines the cost of predicting action a_{pred} for state s when the expert's action is a_{true}. For example, with the mountain car problem, we might use

$$C(s, a_{\text{true}}, a_{\text{pred}}) = -|a_{\text{true}} - a_{\text{pred}}|$$

which penalizes greater deviations more than smaller deviations. The cost associated with the expert's action is typically zero.

If we have a stochastic policy $\pi(a \mid s)$, we then seek to minimize the cost over our data set:

$$\underset{\theta}{\text{minimize}} \quad \sum_{(s, a_{\text{true}}) \in \mathcal{D}} \sum_{a_{\text{pred}}} C\left(s, a_{\text{true}}, a_{\text{pred}}\right) \pi\left(a_{\text{pred}} \mid s\right)$$

This technique is called *cost-sensitive classification*.[14] One benefit of cost-sensitive classification is that we can use a wide variety of off-the-shelf classification models, such as k-nearest neighbors, support vector machines, or decision trees, to train a policy.

[14] C. Elkan, "The Foundations of Cost-Sensitive Learning," in *International Joint Conference on Artificial Intelligence (IJCAI)*, 2001.

Exercise 18.3. Provide an example of where maximum margin inverse reinforcement learning does not uniquely define an optimal policy.

Solution: Maximum margin inverse reinforcement learning extracts binary features from the expert data and seeks a reward function whose optimal policy produces trajectories with the same frequencies of these binary features. There is no guarantee that multiple policies do not produce the same feature expectations. For example, an autonomous car that makes only left lane changes could have the same lane change frequencies as an autonomous car that makes only right lane changes.

Exercise 18.4. Maximum margin inverse reinforcement learning measures how similar a policy is to expert demonstrations using feature expectations. How is this similarity measure affected if nonbinary features are used?

Solution: If we use nonbinary features, then it is possible that some features can get larger than others, incentivizing the agent to match those features rather than those that tend to be smaller. Scale is not the only issue. Even if all features are constrained to lie within $[0, 1]$, then a policy that consistently produces $\phi(s, a)_1 = 0.5$ will have the same feature expectations as one that produces $\phi(s, a)_1 = 0$ half the time and $\phi(s, a)_1 = 1$ half the time. Depending on what the feature encodes, this can result in very different policies. Any set of continuous features can be discretized, and thus approximated by a set of binary features.

Exercise 18.5. Suppose we are building a system in a high-rise that must choose which floor to send an elevator. We have trained several policies to match the feature expectations of expert demonstrations, such as how long customers must wait for an elevator or how long they have to wait to get to their destinations. We run multiple rollouts for each policy and plot the relative duration spent on each floor. Which policy should we prefer according to the principle of maximum entropy, assuming that each policy matches the feature expectations equally?

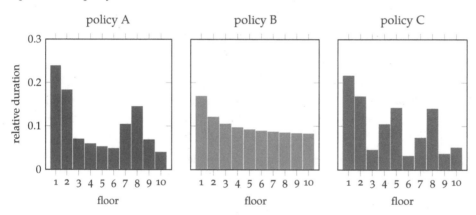

Solution: These distributions over relative duration are analogous to distributions over trajectories for this elevator problem. In applying the principle of maximum entropy, we prefer the distribution with most entropy. Hence, we would choose policy B, which, in being most uniform, has the greatest entropy.

Exercise 18.6. Consider the policy optimization step in generative adversarial imitation learning. Rewrite the objective in the form of a reward function so that traditional reinforcement learning techniques can be applied.

Solution: We rewrite equation (18.19), dropping the terms dependent on the expert data set, and flip the sign to change from minimization over θ to a maximization over θ of the reward, producing the surrogate reward function:

$$\tilde{R}_\phi(s, a) = -\log C_\phi(s, a)$$

Although $\tilde{R}_\phi(s,a)$ may be quite different from the unknown true reward function, it can be used to drive the learned policy into regions of the state-action space similar to those covered by the expert.

Exercise 18.7. Explain how generative adversarial imitation learning could be changed such that the discriminator takes in trajectories rather than state-action pairs. Why might this be useful?

Solution: Changing generative adversarial imitation learning such that the discriminator takes trajectories is straightforward, especially if the trajectories are of fixed length. The expert data set is split into trajectories, and the learned policy is used to produce trajectories, just as it was before. Rather than operating on state-action pairs, the discriminator takes in trajectories using a representation such as a recurrent neural network (appendix D.5) and produces a classification probability. The objective function remains largely unchanged:

$$\max_\phi \min_\theta \mathbb{E}_{\tau \sim \pi_\theta}\left[\log(C_\phi(\tau))\right] + \mathbb{E}_{\tau \sim \mathcal{D}}\left[\log(1 - C_\phi(\tau))\right]$$

The advantage of running the discriminator over entire trajectories is that it can help the discriminator capture features that are not apparent from individual state-action pairs, which can result in better policies. For example, when looking at individual accelerations and turn rates for an autonomous driving policy, there is very little for a discriminator to learn. A discriminator trained to look at longer trajectories can see more of the vehicle's behavior, such as lane change aggressiveness and smoothness, to better match expert driving demonstrations.[15]

[15] This approach was used in A. Kuefler, J. Morton, T. A. Wheeler, and M. J. Kochenderfer, "Imitating Driver Behavior with Generative Adversarial Networks," in *IEEE Intelligent Vehicles Symposium (IV)*, 2017.

PART IV

STATE UNCERTAINTY

Previous chapters have included uncertainty in the transition function, in terms of the uncertainty both in the resulting state and in the model. In this part, we extend uncertainty to include the state. Instead of observing the state exactly, we receive observations that have only a probabilistic relationship with the state. Such problems can be modeled as a *partially observable Markov decision process (POMDP)*. A common approach to solving POMDPs involves inferring a belief distribution over the underlying state at the current time step and then applying a policy that maps beliefs to actions. We will show how to update our belief distribution, given a past sequence of observations and actions. This enables us to devise exact solution methods for optimizing these belief-based policies. Unfortunately, POMDPs are intractable to optimally solve for all but the smallest of problems. We review a variety of offline approximation methods that tend to scale much better than exact methods to larger problems. We also show how to extend some of the online approximations discussed earlier in this book to accommodate partial observability. Finally, we introduce finite state controllers as an alternative policy representation and discuss methods that optimize them to solve POMDPs.

19   Beliefs

A POMDP is an MDP with state uncertainty. The agent receives a potentially imperfect *observation* of the current state rather than the true state. From the past sequence of observations and actions, the agent develops an understanding of the world. This chapter discusses how the *belief* of the agent can be represented by a probability distribution over the underlying state. Various algorithms are presented for updating our belief based on the observation and action taken by the agent.[1] We can perform exact belief updates if the state space is discrete or if certain linear Gaussian assumptions are met. In cases where these assumptions do not hold, we can use approximations based on linearization or sampling.

[1] Different methods for belief updating are discussed in the context of robotic applications by S. Thrun, W. Burgard, and D. Fox, *Probabilistic Robotics*. MIT Press, 2006.

19.1   Belief Initialization

There are different ways to represent our beliefs. In this chapter, we will discuss *parametric* representations, where the belief distribution is represented by a set of parameters of a fixed distribution family, such as the categorical or multivariate normal distribution. We will also discuss *nonparametric* representations, where the belief distribution is represented by particles, or points sampled from the state space. Associated with the different representations are different procedures for updating the belief based on the action taken by the agent and the observation.

Before the agent takes any actions or makes any observations, we start with an initial belief distribution. If we have some prior information about where the agent might be in the state space, we can encode this in the initial belief. We generally want to use diffuse initial beliefs in the absence of information to avoid being overly confident in the agent being in a region of the state space where it might not actually be. A strong initial belief focused on states that are far from the true state can lead to poor state estimates, even after many observations.

A diffuse initial belief can cause difficulties, especially for nonparametric representations of the belief, where the state space can be only very sparsely sampled. In some cases, it may be useful to wait to initialize our beliefs until an informative observation is made. For example, in robot navigation problems, we might want to wait until the sensors detect a known *landmark*, and then initialize the belief appropriately. The landmark can help narrow down the relevant region of the state space so that we can focus our sampling of the space in the area consistent with the landmark observation. Example 19.1 illustrates this concept.

Consider an autonomous car equipped with a localization system that uses camera, radar, and lidar data to track its position. The car is able to identify a unique landmark at a range r and bearing θ from its current pose:

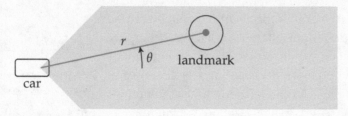

The range and bearing measurements have zero-mean Gaussian noise with variance v_r and v_θ, respectively, and the landmark is known to be at (x, y). Given a measurement r and θ, we can produce a distribution over the car's position $(\hat{x}, \hat{y})$ and orientation $\hat{\psi}$:

$$\hat{r} \sim \mathcal{N}(r, v_r) \qquad \hat{\theta} \sim \mathcal{N}(\theta, v_\theta) \qquad \hat{\phi} \sim \mathcal{U}(0, 2\pi)$$
$$\hat{x} \leftarrow x + \hat{r}\cos\hat{\phi} \qquad \hat{y} \leftarrow y + \hat{r}\sin\hat{\phi} \qquad \hat{\psi} \leftarrow \hat{\phi} - \hat{\theta} - \pi$$

where $\hat{\phi}$ is the angle of the car from the landmark in the global frame.

Example 19.1. Generating an initial nonparametric belief based on a landmark observation. In this case, the autonomous car could be anywhere in a ring around the landmark:

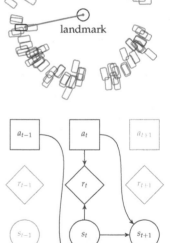

Figure 19.1. A dynamic decision network for the POMDP problem formulation. As with figure 7.1, informational edges into the action nodes are not shown.

19.2   Discrete State Filter

In a POMDP, the agent does not directly observe the underlying state of the environment. Instead, the agent receives an observation, which belongs to some *observation space* $\mathcal{O}$, at each time step. The probability of observing o, given that the agent took action a and transitioned to state s', is given by $O(o \mid a, s')$. If $\mathcal{O}$

is continuous, then $O(o \mid a, s')$ is a probability density. Figure 19.1 shows the dynamic decision network associated with POMDPs. Algorithm 19.1 provides an implementation of the POMDP data structure.

```
struct POMDP
    γ   # discount factor
    S   # state space
    A   # action space
    O   # observation space
    T   # transition function
    R   # reward function
    O   # observation function
    TRO # sample transition, reward, and observation
end
```

Algorithm 19.1.   A data structure for POMDPs. We will use the TRO field to sample the next state, reward, and observation given the current state and action: s', r, o = TRO(s, a). A comprehensive package for specifying and solving POMDPs is provided by M. Egorov, Z. N. Sunberg, E. Balaban, T. A. Wheeler, J. K. Gupta, and M. J. Kochenderfer, "POMDPs.jl: A Framework for Sequential Decision Making Under Uncertainty," *Journal of Machine Learning Research*, vol. 18, no. 26, pp. 1–5, 2017. In mathematical writing, POMDPs are sometimes defined in terms of a tuple consisting of the various components of the MDP, written as $(S, A, O, T, R, O, \gamma)$.

A kind of inference known as *recursive Bayesian estimation* can be used to update our belief distribution over the current state, given the most recent action and observation. We use $b(s)$ to represent the probability (or probability density for continuous state spaces) assigned to state s. A particular belief b belongs to a *belief space* $\mathcal{B}$, which contains all possible beliefs.

When the state and observation spaces are finite, we can use a *discrete state filter* to perform this inference exactly. Beliefs for problems with discrete state spaces can be represented using categorical distributions, where a probability mass is assigned to each state. This categorical distribution can be represented as a vector of length $|\mathcal{S}|$ and is often called a *belief vector*. In cases where b can be treated as a vector, we will use $\mathbf{b}$. In this case, $\mathcal{B} \subset \mathbb{R}^{|\mathcal{S}|}$. Sometimes $\mathcal{B}$ is referred to as a *probability simplex* or *belief simplex*.

Because a belief vector represents a probability distribution, the elements must be strictly nonnegative and must sum to 1:

$$b(s) \geq 0 \text{ for all } s \in \mathcal{S} \qquad \sum_s b(s) = 1 \qquad (19.1)$$

In vector form, we have

$$\mathbf{b} \geq \mathbf{0} \qquad \mathbf{1}^\top \mathbf{b} = 1 \qquad (19.2)$$

The belief space for a POMDP with three states is given in figure 19.2. A discrete POMDP problem is given in example 19.2.

If an agent with belief b takes an action a and receives an observation o, the new belief b' can be calculated as follows due to the independence assumptions

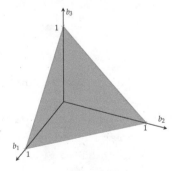

Figure 19.2. The set of valid belief vectors for problems with three states. Although the state space is discrete, the belief space is continuous.

The *crying baby problem* is a simple POMDP with two states, three actions, and two observations. Our goal is to care for a baby, and we do so by choosing at each time step whether to feed the baby, sing to it, or ignore it.

The baby becomes hungry over time. One does not directly observe whether the baby is hungry, but instead receives a noisy observation in the form of whether the baby is crying. A hungry baby cries 80 % of the time, whereas a sated baby cries 10 % of the time. Singing to the baby yields a perfect observation. The state, action, and observation spaces are:

$$\mathcal{S} = \{\text{sated}, \text{hungry}\}$$
$$\mathcal{A} = \{\text{feed}, \text{sing}, \text{ignore}\}$$
$$\mathcal{O} = \{\text{crying}, \text{quiet}\}$$

The transition dynamics are:

$$T(\text{sated} \mid \text{hungry}, \text{feed}) = 100\%$$
$$T(\text{hungry} \mid \text{hungry}, \text{sing}) = 100\%$$
$$T(\text{hungry} \mid \text{hungry}, \text{ignore}) = 100\%$$
$$T(\text{sated} \mid \text{sated}, \text{feed}) = 100\%$$
$$T(\text{hungry} \mid \text{sated}, \text{sing}) = 10\%$$
$$T(\text{hungry} \mid \text{sated}, \text{ignore}) = 10\%$$

The reward function assigns −10 reward if the baby is hungry and an additional −5 reward for feeding the baby because of the effort required. Thus, feeding a hungry baby results in −15 reward. Singing to a baby takes extra effort, and incurs a further −0.5 reward. As baby caretakers, we seek the optimal infinite horizon policy with discount factor $\gamma = 0.9$.

Example 19.2. The crying baby problem is a simple POMDP used to demonstrate decision making with state uncertainty.

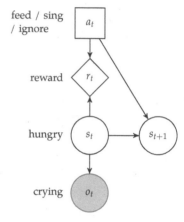

in figure 19.1:

$$b'(s') = P(s' \mid b, a, o) \tag{19.3}$$
$$\propto P(o \mid b, a, s')P(s' \mid b, a) \tag{19.4}$$
$$= O(o \mid a, s')P(s' \mid b, a) \tag{19.5}$$
$$= O(o \mid a, s')\sum_s P(s' \mid a, b, s)P(s \mid b, a) \tag{19.6}$$
$$= O(o \mid a, s')\sum_s T(s' \mid s, a)b(s) \tag{19.7}$$

An instance of updating discrete beliefs is given in example 19.3, and the belief update is implemented in algorithm 19.2. The success of the belief update depends on having accurate observation and transition models. In cases where these models are not well known, it is generally advisable to use simplified models with more diffuse distributions to help prevent overconfidence, which leads to brittleness in the state estimates.

19.3 Kalman Filter

We can adapt equation (19.7) to handle continuous state spaces as follows:

$$b'(s') \propto O(o \mid a, s') \int T(s' \mid s, a)b(s)\, ds \tag{19.8}$$

The integration above can be challenging unless we make some assumptions about the form of T, O, and b. A special type of filter, known as a *Kalman filter* (algorithm 19.3),[2] provides an exact update under the assumption that T and O are linear Gaussian and b is Gaussian:[3]

$$T(\mathbf{s}' \mid \mathbf{s}, \mathbf{a}) = \mathcal{N}(\mathbf{s}' \mid \mathbf{T}_s\mathbf{s} + \mathbf{T}_a\mathbf{a}, \mathbf{\Sigma}_s) \tag{19.9}$$
$$O(\mathbf{o} \mid \mathbf{s}') = \mathcal{N}(\mathbf{o} \mid \mathbf{O}_s\mathbf{s}', \mathbf{\Sigma}_o) \tag{19.10}$$
$$b(\mathbf{s}) = \mathcal{N}(\mathbf{s} \mid \mathbf{\mu}_b, \mathbf{\Sigma}_b) \tag{19.11}$$

The Kalman filter begins with a *predict step*, which uses the transition dynamics to get a predicted distribution with the following mean and covariance:

$$\mathbf{\mu}_p \leftarrow \mathbf{T}_s\mathbf{\mu}_b + \mathbf{T}_a\mathbf{a} \tag{19.12}$$
$$\mathbf{\Sigma}_p \leftarrow \mathbf{T}_s\mathbf{\Sigma}_b\mathbf{T}_s^\top + \mathbf{\Sigma}_s \tag{19.13}$$

[2] Named after the Hungarian-American electrical engineer Rudolf E. Kálmán (1930–2016) who was involved in the early development of this filter.

[3] R. E. Kálmán, "A New Approach to Linear Filtering and Prediction Problems," *ASME Journal of Basic Engineering*, vol. 82, pp. 35–45, 1960. A comprehensive overview of the Kalman filter and its variants is provided by Y. Bar-Shalom, X. R. Li, and T. Kirubarajan, *Estimation with Applications to Tracking and Navigation*. Wiley, 2001.

Example 19.3. Discrete belief updating in the crying baby problem.

The crying baby problem (example 19.2) assumes a uniform initial belief state: $[b(\text{sated}), b(\text{hungry})] = [0.5, 0.5]$.

Suppose we ignore the baby and the baby cries. We update our belief according to equation (19.7) as follows:

$$b'(\text{sated}) \propto O(\text{crying} \mid \text{ignore}, \text{sated}) \sum_s T(\text{sated} \mid s, \text{ignore}) b(s)$$

$$\propto 0.1(0.0 \cdot 0.5 + 0.9 \cdot 0.5)$$

$$\propto 0.045$$

$$b'(\text{hungry}) \propto O(\text{crying} \mid \text{ignore}, \text{hungry}) \sum_s T(\text{hungry} \mid s, \text{ignore}) b(s)$$

$$\propto 0.8(1.0 \cdot 0.5 + 0.1 \cdot 0.5)$$

$$\propto 0.440$$

After normalizing, our new belief is approximately $[0.0928, 0.9072]$. A crying baby is likely to be hungry.

Suppose we then feed the baby and the crying stops. Feeding deterministically caused the baby to be sated, so the new belief is $[1, 0]$.

Finally, we sing to the baby, and the baby is quiet. Equation (19.7) is used again to update the belief, resulting in $[0.9890, 0.0110]$. A sated baby only becomes hungry 10 % of the time, and this percentage is further reduced by not observing any crying.

```
function update(b::Vector{Float64}, 𝒫, a, o)
    𝒮, T, O = 𝒫.𝒮, 𝒫.T, 𝒫.O
    b' = similar(b)
    for (i', s') in enumerate(𝒮)
        po = O(a, s', o)
        b'[i'] = po * sum(T(s, a, s') * b[i] for (i, s) in enumerate(𝒮))
    end
    if sum(b') ≈ 0.0
        fill!(b', 1)
    end
    return normalize!(b', 1)
end
```

Algorithm 19.2. A method that updates a discrete belief based on equation (19.7), where b is a vector and 𝒫 is the POMDP model. If the given observation has a zero likelihood, a uniform distribution is returned.

In the *update step*, we use this predicted distribution with the current observation to update our belief:

$$K \leftarrow \Sigma_p O_s^\top \left(O_s \Sigma_p O_s^\top + \Sigma_o \right)^{-1} \tag{19.14}$$

$$\mu_b \leftarrow \mu_p + K \left(o - O_s \mu_p \right) \tag{19.15}$$

$$\Sigma_b \leftarrow (I - K O_s) \Sigma_p \tag{19.16}$$

where K is called the *Kalman gain*.

```
struct KalmanFilter
    μb # mean vector
    Σb # covariance matrix
end

function update(b::KalmanFilter, 𝒫, a, o)
    μb, Σb = b.μb, b.Σb
    Ts, Ta, Os = 𝒫.Ts, 𝒫.Ta, 𝒫.Os
    Σs, Σo = 𝒫.Σs, 𝒫.Σo
    # predict
    μp = Ts*μb + Ta*a
    Σp = Ts*Σb*Ts' + Σs
    # update
    Σpo = Σp*Os'
    K = Σpo/(Os*Σp*Os' + Σo)
    μb' = μp + K*(o - Os*μp)
    Σb' = (I - K*Os)*Σp
    return KalmanFilter(μb', Σb')
end
```

Algorithm 19.3. The Kalman filter, which updates beliefs in the form of Gaussian distributions. The current belief is represented by μb and Σb, and 𝒫 contains the matrices that define linear Gaussian dynamics and observation model. This 𝒫 can be defined using a composite type or a named tuple.

Kalman filters are often applied to systems that do not actually have linear Gaussian dynamics and observations. A variety of modifications to the basic Kalman filter have been proposed to better accommodate such systems.[4]

[4] S. Thrun, W. Burgard, and D. Fox, *Probabilistic Robotics*. MIT Press, 2006.

19.4 Extended Kalman Filter

The *extended Kalman filter* (EKF) is a simple extension of the Kalman filter to problems whose dynamics are nonlinear with Gaussian noise:

$$T(s' \mid s, a) = \mathcal{N}(s' \mid f_T(s, a), \Sigma_s) \tag{19.17}$$

$$O(o \mid s') = \mathcal{N}(o \mid f_O(s'), \Sigma_o) \tag{19.18}$$

where $\mathbf{f}_T(\mathbf{s}, \mathbf{a})$ and $\mathbf{f}_O(\mathbf{s}')$ are differentiable functions.

Exact belief updates through nonlinear dynamics are not guaranteed to produce new Gaussian beliefs, as shown in figure 19.3. The extended Kalman filter uses a local linear approximation to the nonlinear dynamics, thereby producing a new Gaussian belief that approximates the true updated belief. We can use similar update equations as the Kalman filter, but we must compute the matrices $\mathbf{T}_s$ and $\mathbf{O}_s$ at every iteration based on the current belief.

The local linear approximation to the dynamics, or *linearization*, is given by first-order Taylor expansions in the form of Jacobians.[5] For the state matrix, the Taylor expansion is conducted at $\mathbf{\mu}_b$ and the current action, whereas for the observation matrix, it is computed at the predicted mean, $\mathbf{\mu}_p = \mathbf{f}_T(\mathbf{\mu}_b)$.

The extended Kalman filter is implemented in algorithm 19.4. Although it is an approximation, it is fast and performs well on a variety of real-world problems. The EKF does not generally preserve the true mean and variance of the posterior, and it does not model multimodal posterior distributions.

[5] The Jacobian of a multivariate function $\mathbf{f}$ with n inputs and m outputs is an $m \times n$ matrix where the (i, j)th entry is $\partial f_i / \partial x_j$.

```
struct ExtendedKalmanFilter
    μb # mean vector
    Σb # covariance matrix
end

import ForwardDiff: jacobian
function update(b::ExtendedKalmanFilter, 𝒫, a, o)
    μb, Σb = b.μb, b.Σb
    fT, fO = 𝒫.fT, 𝒫.fO
    Σs, Σo = 𝒫.Σs, 𝒫.Σo
    # predict
    μp = fT(μb, a)
    Ts = jacobian(s→fT(s, a), μb)
    Os = jacobian(fO, μp)
    Σp = Ts*Σb*Ts' + Σs
    # update
    Σpo = Σp*Os'
    K = Σpo/(Os*Σp*Os' + Σo)
    μb' = μp + K*(o - fO(μp))
    Σb' = (I - K*Os)*Σp
    return ExtendedKalmanFilter(μb', Σb')
end
```

Algorithm 19.4. The extended Kalman filter, an extension of the Kalman filter to problems with nonlinear Gaussian dynamics. The current belief is represented by mean μb and covariance Σb. The problem 𝒫 specifies the nonlinear dynamics using the mean transition dynamics function fT and mean observation dynamics function fO. The Jacobians are obtained using the ForwardDiff.jl package.

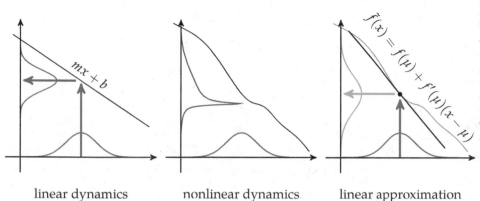

Figure 19.3. Updating a Gaussian belief with a linear transform (left) produces another Gaussian distribution. Updating a Gaussian belief with a nonlinear transform (center) does not in general produce a Gaussian distribution. The extended Kalman filter uses a linear approximation of the transform (right), thereby producing another Gaussian distribution that approximates the posterior.

linear dynamics   nonlinear dynamics   linear approximation

19.5   Unscented Kalman Filter

The *unscented Kalman filter (UKF)*[6] is another extension to the Kalman filter to problems that are nonlinear with Gaussian noise.[7] Unlike the extended Kalman filter, the unscented Kalman filter is derivative free, and relies on a deterministic sampling strategy to approximate the effect of a distribution undergoing a (typically nonlinear) transformation.

The unscented Kalman filter was developed to estimate the effect of transforming a distribution over $\mathbf{x}$ with a nonlinear function $\mathbf{f}(\mathbf{x})$, producing a distribution over $\mathbf{x}'$. We would like to estimate the mean $\boldsymbol{\mu}'$ and covariance $\boldsymbol{\Sigma}'$ of the distribution over $\mathbf{x}'$. The unscented transform allows for more information of $p(\mathbf{x})$ to be used than the mean $\boldsymbol{\mu}$ and covariance $\boldsymbol{\Sigma}$ of the distribution over $\mathbf{x}$.[8]

An *unscented transform* passes a set of *sigma points S* through $\mathbf{f}$ and uses the transformed points to approximate the transformed mean $\boldsymbol{\mu}'$ and covariance $\boldsymbol{\Sigma}'$. The original mean and covariance are constructed using the sigma points and a vector of weights $\mathbf{w}$:

$$\boldsymbol{\mu} = \sum_i w_i \mathbf{s}_i \tag{19.19}$$

$$\boldsymbol{\Sigma} = \sum_i w_i (\mathbf{s}_i - \boldsymbol{\mu})(\mathbf{s}_i - \boldsymbol{\mu})^\top \tag{19.20}$$

[6] S. J. Julier and J. K. Uhlmann, "Unscented Filtering and Nonlinear Estimation," *Proceedings of the IEEE*, vol. 92, no. 3, pp. 401–422, 2004.

[7] According to Jeffrey K. Uhlmann, the term "unscented" comes from a label on a deodorant container that he saw on someone's desk. He used that term to avoid calling it the "Uhlmann filter." IEEE History Center Staff, "Proceedings of the IEEE Through 100 Years: 2000–2009," *Proceedings of the IEEE*, vol. 100, no. 11, pp. 3131–3145, 2012.

[8] We need not necessarily assume that the prior distribution is Gaussian.

where the ith sigma point $\mathbf{s}_i$ has weight w_i. These weights must sum to 1 in order to provide an unbiased estimate, but they need not all be positive.

The updated mean and covariance matrix given by the unscented transform through $\mathbf{f}$ are thus:

$$\boldsymbol{\mu}' = \sum_i w_i \mathbf{f}(\mathbf{s}_i) \tag{19.21}$$

$$\boldsymbol{\Sigma}' = \sum_i w_i \big(\mathbf{f}(\mathbf{s}_i) - \boldsymbol{\mu}'\big)\big(\mathbf{f}(\mathbf{s}_i) - \boldsymbol{\mu}'\big)^\top \tag{19.22}$$

A common set of sigma points include the mean $\boldsymbol{\mu} \in \mathbb{R}^n$ and an additional $2n$ points formed from perturbations of $\boldsymbol{\mu}$ in directions determined by the covariance matrix $\boldsymbol{\Sigma}$:[9]

$$\mathbf{s}_1 = \boldsymbol{\mu} \tag{19.23}$$

$$\mathbf{s}_{2i} = \boldsymbol{\mu} + \left(\sqrt{(n+\lambda)\boldsymbol{\Sigma}}\right)_i \text{ for } i \text{ in } 1:n \tag{19.24}$$

$$\mathbf{s}_{2i+1} = \boldsymbol{\mu} - \left(\sqrt{(n+\lambda)\boldsymbol{\Sigma}}\right)_i \text{ for } i \text{ in } 1:n \tag{19.25}$$

These sigma points are associated with the weights:

$$w_i = \begin{cases} \frac{\lambda}{n+\lambda} & \text{for } i = 1 \\ \frac{1}{2(n+\lambda)} & \text{otherwise} \end{cases} \tag{19.26}$$

The scalar *spread parameter* λ determines how far the sigma points are spread from the mean.[10] Several sigma point sets for different values of λ are shown in figure 19.4.

[9] The square root of a matrix $\mathbf{A}$ is a matrix $\mathbf{B}$ such that $\mathbf{BB}^\top = \mathbf{A}$. In Julia, the sqrt method produces a matrix $\mathbf{C}$ such that $\mathbf{CC} = \mathbf{A}$, which is not the same. One common square root matrix can be obtained from the Cholesky decomposition.

[10] It is common to use $\lambda = 2$, which is optimal for matching the fourth moment of Gaussian distributions. Motivations for choosing sigma point sets of this form are provided in exercise 19.13 and exercise 19.14.

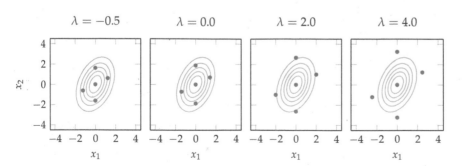

Figure 19.4. The effect of varying λ on the sigma points from equation (19.23) generated for a Gaussian distribution with zero mean and covariance:
$\Sigma = [1\ 1/2;\ 1/2\ 2]$.

The unscented Kalman filter performs two unscented transformations: one for the prediction step and one for the observation update. Algorithm 19.5 provides an implementation of this.

```
struct UnscentedKalmanFilter
    μb # mean vector
    Σb # covariance matrix
    λ  # spread parameter
end

function unscented_transform(μ, Σ, f, λ, ws)
    n = length(μ)
    Δ = cholesky((n + λ) * Σ).L
    S = [μ]
    for i in 1:n
        push!(S, μ + Δ[:,i])
        push!(S, μ - Δ[:,i])
    end
    S′ = f.(S)
    μ′ = sum(w*s for (w,s) in zip(ws, S′))
    Σ′ = sum(w*(s - μ′)*(s - μ′)' for (w,s) in zip(ws, S′))
    return (μ′, Σ′, S, S′)
end

function update(b::UnscentedKalmanFilter, 𝒫, a, o)
    μb, Σb, λ = b.μb, b.Σb, b.λ
    fT, fO = 𝒫.fT, 𝒫.fO
    n = length(μb)
    ws = [λ / (n + λ); fill(1/(2(n + λ)), 2n)]
    # predict
    μp, Σp, Sp, Sp′ = unscented_transform(μb, Σb, s→fT(s,a), λ, ws)
    Σp += 𝒫.Σs
    # update
    μo, Σo, So, So′ = unscented_transform(μp, Σp, fO, λ, ws)
    Σo += 𝒫.Σo
    Σpo = sum(w*(s - μp)*(s′ - μo)' for (w,s,s′) in zip(ws, So, So′))
    K = Σpo / Σo
    μb′ = μp + K*(o - μo)
    Σb′ = Σp - K*Σo*K'
    return UnscentedKalmanFilter(μb′, Σb′, λ)
end
```

Algorithm 19.5. The unscented Kalman filter, an extension of the Kalman filter to problems with nonlinear Gaussian dynamics. The current belief is represented by mean μb and covariance Σb. The problem 𝒫 specifies the nonlinear dynamics using the mean transition dynamics function fT and mean observation dynamics function fO. The sigma points used in the unscented transforms are controlled by the spread parameter λ.

19.6   Particle Filter

Discrete problems with large state spaces or continuous problems with dynamics that are not well approximated by the linear Gaussian assumption of the Kalman filter must often resort to approximation techniques to represent the belief and to perform the belief update. One common approach is to use a *particle filter*, which represents the belief state as a collection of states.[11] Each state in the approximate belief is called a *particle*.

A particle filter is initialized by selecting or randomly sampling a collection of particles that represent the initial belief. The belief update for a particle filter with m particles begins by propagating each state s_i by sampling from the transition distribution to obtain a new state s'_i with probability $T(s'_i \mid s_i, a)$. The new belief is constructed by drawing m particles from the propagated states weighted according to the observation function $w_i = O(o \mid a, s')$. This procedure is given in algorithm 19.6. Example 19.4 illustrates an application of a particle filter.

In problems with discrete observations, we can also perform particle belief updates with rejection. We repeat the following process m times to generate the set of next state samples. First, we randomly select some state s_i in the filter and then sample a next state s'_i according to our transition model. Second, we generate a random observation o_i according to our observation model. If o_i does not equal the true observation o, it is rejected, and we generate a new s'_i and o_i until the observations match. This *particle filter with rejection* is implemented in algorithm 19.7.

As the number of particles in a particle filter increases, the distribution represented by the particles approaches the true posterior distribution. Unfortunately, particle filters can fail in practice. Low particle coverage and the stochastic nature of the resampling procedure can cause there to be no particles near the true state. This problem of *particle deprivation* can be somewhat mitigated by several strategies. A motivational example is given in example 19.5.

[11] A tutorial on particle filters is provided by M. S. Arulampalam, S. Maskell, N. Gordon, and T. Clapp, "A Tutorial on Particle Filters for Online Nonlinear / Non-Gaussian Bayesian Tracking," *IEEE Transactions on Signal Processing*, vol. 50, no. 2, pp. 174–188, 2002.

Suppose that we want to determine our position based on imperfect distance measurements to radio beacons whose locations are known. We remain approximately still for a few steps to collect independent measurements. The particle filter states are our potential locations. We can compare the ranges that we would expect to measure for each particle to the observed ranges.

We assume that individual range observations from each beacon are observed with zero-mean Gaussian noise. Our particle transition function adds zero-mean Gaussian noise since we remain only approximately still.

The images here show the evolution of the particle filter. The rows correspond to different numbers of beacons. The red dots indicate our true location, and the blue dots are particles. The circles indicate the positions consistent with noiseless distance measurements from each sensor.

Example 19.4. A particle filter applied to different beacon configurations.

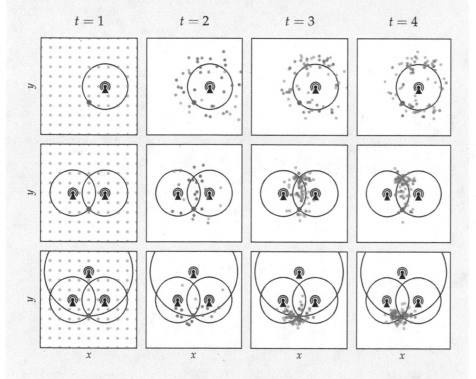

Three beacons are required to identify our location accurately. A strength of the particle filter is that it is able to represent the multimodal distributions that are especially apparent when there are only one or two beacons.

```
struct ParticleFilter
    states # vector of state samples
end

function update(b::ParticleFilter, 𝒫, a, o)
    T, O = 𝒫.T, 𝒫.O
    states = [rand(T(s, a)) for s in b.states]
    weights = [O(a, s′, o) for s′ in states]
    D = SetCategorical(states, weights)
    return ParticleFilter(rand(D, length(states)))
end
```

Algorithm 19.6. A belief updater for particle filters, which updates a vector of states representing the belief based on the agent's action a and its observation o. Appendix G.5 provides an implementation of SetCategorical for defining distributions over discrete sets.

```
struct RejectionParticleFilter
    states # vector of state samples
end

function update(b::RejectionParticleFilter, 𝒫, a, o)
    T, O = 𝒫.T, 𝒫.O
    states = similar(b.states)
    i = 1
    while i ≤ length(states)
        s = rand(b.states)
        s′ = rand(T(s,a))
        if rand(O(a,s′)) == o
            states[i] = s′
            i += 1
        end
    end
    return RejectionParticleFilter(states)
end
```

Algorithm 19.7. Updating a particle filter with rejection, which forces sampled states to match the input observation o.

Spelunker Joe is lost in a grid-based maze. He lost his lantern, so he can observe his surroundings only by touch. At any given moment, Joe can tell whether his location in the maze has walls in each cardinal direction. Joe is fairly confident in his ability to feel walls, so he assumes that his observations are perfect.

Joe uses a particle filter to track his belief over time. At some point, he stops to rest. He continues to run his particle filter to update his belief. The figures below show his belief over time, with dots indicating belief particles in his particle filter corresponding to those locations in the maze.

The initial belief has one particle in each grid location that matches his current observation of a wall to the north and south. Spelunker Joe does not move and does not gain new information, so his belief should not change over time. Due to the stochastic nature of resampling, subsequent beliefs may not contain all the initial states. Over time, his belief will continue to lose states until it only contains a single state. It is possible that this state is not where Spelunker Joe is located.

Example 19.5. A particle filter run for enough time can lose particles in relevant regions of the state space due to the stochastic nature of resampling. The problem is more pronounced when there are fewer particles or when the particles are spread over a large state space.

19.7   Particle Injection

Particle injection involves injecting random particles to protect against particle deprivation. Algorithm 19.8 injects a fixed number of particles from a broader distribution, such as a uniform distribution over the state space.[12] While particle injection can help prevent particle deprivation, it also reduces the accuracy of the posterior belief represented by the particle filter.

```
struct InjectionParticleFilter
    states # vector of state samples
    m_inject # number of samples to inject
    D_inject # injection distribution
end

function update(b::InjectionParticleFilter, 𝒫, a, o)
    T, O, m_inject, D_inject = 𝒫.T, 𝒫.O, b.m_inject, b.D_inject
    states = [rand(T(s, a)) for s in b.states]
    weights = [O(a, s′, o) for s′ in states]
    D = SetCategorical(states, weights)
    m = length(states)
    states = vcat(rand(D, m - m_inject), rand(D_inject, m_inject))
    return InjectionParticleFilter(states, m_inject, D_inject)
end
```

[12] For robotic localization problems, it is a common practice to inject particles from a uniform distribution over all possible robot poses, weighted by the current observation.

Algorithm 19.8.   Particle filter update with injection, in which m_inject particles are sampled from the injection distribution D_inject to reduce the risk of particle deprivation.

Instead of using a fixed number of injected particles at each update, we can take a more adaptive approach. When the particles are all being given very low weights, we generally want to inject more particles. It might be tempting to choose the number of injected particles based solely on the mean weight of the current set of particles. However, doing so can make the success of the filter sensitive to naturally low observation probabilities in the early periods when the filter is still converging or in moments of high sensor noise.[13]

Algorithm 19.9 presents an *adaptive injection* algorithm that keeps track of two exponential moving averages of the mean particle weight and bases the number of injections on their ratio.[14] If w_{mean} is the current mean particle weight, the two moving averages are updated according to

$$w_{\mathrm{fast}} \leftarrow w_{\mathrm{fast}} + \alpha_{\mathrm{fast}}(w_{\mathrm{mean}} - w_{\mathrm{fast}}) \tag{19.27}$$

$$w_{\mathrm{slow}} \leftarrow w_{\mathrm{slow}} + \alpha_{\mathrm{slow}}(w_{\mathrm{mean}} - w_{\mathrm{slow}}) \tag{19.28}$$

where $0 \leq \alpha_{\mathrm{slow}} < \alpha_{\mathrm{fast}} \leq 1$.

[13] S. Thrun, W. Burgard, and D. Fox, *Probabilistic Robotics*. MIT Press, 2006.

[14] D. E. Goldberg and J. Richardson, "An Experimental Comparison of Localization Methods," in *International Conference on Genetic Algorithms*, 1987.

The number of injected samples in a given iteration is obtained by comparing the fast and slow mean particle weights:[15]

$$m_{\text{inject}} = \left\lfloor m \max\left(0, 1 - \nu \frac{w_{\text{fast}}}{w_{\text{slow}}}\right) \right\rceil \qquad (19.29)$$

The scalar $\nu \geq 1$ allows us to tune the injection rate.

[15] Note that $\lfloor x \rceil$ denotes the integer nearest to x.

```
mutable struct AdaptiveInjectionParticleFilter
    states   # vector of state samples
    w_slow   # slow moving average
    w_fast   # fast moving average
    α_slow   # slow moving average parameter
    α_fast   # fast moving average parameter
    ν        # injection parameter
    D_inject # injection distribution
end

function update(b::AdaptiveInjectionParticleFilter, 𝒫, a, o)
    T, O = 𝒫.T, 𝒫.O
    w_slow, w_fast, α_slow, α_fast, ν, D_inject =
        b.w_slow, b.w_fast, b.α_slow, b.α_fast, b.ν, b.D_inject
    states = [rand(T(s, a)) for s in b.states]
    weights = [O(a, s', o) for s' in states]
    w_mean = mean(weights)
    w_slow += α_slow*(w_mean - w_slow)
    w_fast += α_fast*(w_mean - w_fast)
    m = length(states)
    m_inject = round(Int, m * max(0, 1.0 - ν*w_fast / w_slow))
    D = SetCategorical(states, weights)
    states = vcat(rand(D, m - m_inject), rand(D_inject, m_inject))
    b.w_slow, b.w_fast = w_slow, w_fast
    return AdaptiveInjectionParticleFilter(states,
        w_slow, w_fast, α_slow, α_fast, ν, D_inject)
end
```

Algorithm 19.9.   A particle filter with adaptive injection, which maintains fast and slow exponential moving averages w_fast and w_slow of the mean particle weight with smoothness factors α_fast and α_slow, respectively. Particles are injected only if the fast moving average of the mean particle weight is less than $1/\nu$ of the slow moving average. Recommended values from the original paper are α_fast = 0.1, α_slow = 0.001, and ν = 2.

19.8   Summary

- Partially observable Markov decision processes (POMDPs) extend MDPs to include state uncertainty.

- The uncertainty requires agents in a POMDP to maintain a belief over their state.

Spelunker Joe from example 19.6 now moves one tile to the east and moves all particles in his particle filter one tile east as well. He now senses walls only to the north and east, and unfortunately, this observation does not agree with any of the updated particles in his filter. He decides to use adaptive injection to fix his particle deprivation problem. Here, we see how his filter injects particles from a uniform random distribution, along with the values for the fast and slow filters:

Example 19.6. A particle filter with adaptive injection α_slow = 0.01, α_fast = 0.3, and ν = 2.0, starting from a deprived state with 16 identical particles. The moving averages are initialized to 1 to reflect a long period of observations that perfectly match every particle in the filter. Over the next iterations, these moving averages change at different rates based on the quantity of particles that match the observation. The iterations proceed left to right and top to bottom.

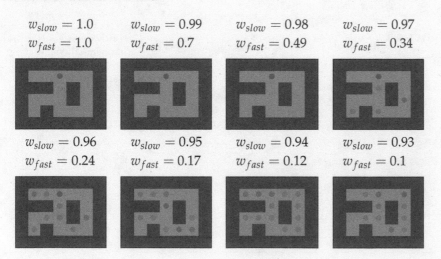

$w_{slow} = 1.0$ $w_{slow} = 0.99$ $w_{slow} = 0.98$ $w_{slow} = 0.97$
$w_{fast} = 1.0$ $w_{fast} = 0.7$ $w_{fast} = 0.49$ $w_{fast} = 0.34$

$w_{slow} = 0.96$ $w_{slow} = 0.95$ $w_{slow} = 0.94$ $w_{slow} = 0.93$
$w_{fast} = 0.24$ $w_{fast} = 0.17$ $w_{fast} = 0.12$ $w_{fast} = 0.1$

Iterations proceed left to right and top to bottom. Each blue dot represents a particle in the particle filter, corresponding to a partial belief in being in that location of the grid.

- Beliefs for POMDPs with discrete state spaces can be represented using categorical distributions and can be updated analytically.

- Beliefs for linear Gaussian POMDPs can be represented using Gaussian distributions and can also be updated analytically.

- Beliefs for nonlinear, continuous POMDPs can also be represented using Gaussian distributions, but they cannot typically be updated analytically. In this case, the extended Kalman filter and the unscented Kalman filter can be used.

- Continuous problems can sometimes be modeled under the assumption that they are linear Gaussian.

- Particle filters approximate the belief with a large collection of state particles.

19.9   Exercises

Exercise 19.1. Can every MDP be framed as a POMDP?

Solution: Yes. The POMDP formulation extends the MDP formulation by introducing state uncertainty in the form of the observation distribution. Any MDP can be framed as a POMDP with $\mathcal{O} = \mathcal{S}$ and $O(o \mid a, s') = (o = s')$.

Exercise 19.2. What is the belief update for a discrete POMDP with no observation? What is the belief update for a POMDP with linear Gaussian dynamics with no observation?

Solution: If an agent in a POMDP without an observation with belief b takes an action a, the new belief b' can be calculated as follows:

$$b'(s') = P(s' \mid b, a) = \sum_s P(s' \mid a, b, s)P(s \mid b, a) = \sum_s T(s' \mid s, a)b(s)$$

This belief update is equivalent to having a uniform observation distribution. A POMDP with linear Gaussian dynamics that has no observation will update its belief using only the Kalman filter predict step in equation (19.12).

Exercise 19.3. An autonomous vehicle represents its belief over its position using a multivariate normal distribution. It comes to a rest at a traffic light, and the belief updater continues to run while it sits. Over time, the belief concentrates and becomes extremely confident in a particular location. Why might this be a problem? How might this extreme confidence be avoided?

Solution: Overconfidence in a belief can be a problem when the models or belief updates do not perfectly represent reality. The overconfident belief may have converged on a state that does not match the true state. Once the vehicle moves again, new observations may be inconsistent with the belief and result in poor estimates. To help address this issue, we can require that the values of the diagonal elements of the covariance matrix be above threshold.

Exercise 19.4. Consider tracking our belief over the dud rate for widgets produced at a factory. We use a Poisson distribution to model the probability that k duds are produced in one day of factory operation given that the factory has a dud rate of λ:

$$P(k \mid \lambda) = \frac{1}{k!}\lambda^k e^{-\lambda}$$

Suppose that our initial belief over the dud rate follows a gamma distribution:

$$p(\lambda \mid \alpha, \beta) = \frac{\beta^\alpha}{\Gamma(\alpha)}\lambda^{\alpha-1}e^{-\beta\lambda}$$

where $\lambda \in (0, \infty)$, and the belief is parameterized by the shape $\alpha > 0$ and the rate $\beta > 0$. After a day of factory operation, we observe that $d \geq 0$ duds were produced. Show that our updated belief over the dud rate is also a gamma distribution.[16]

Solution: We seek the posterior distribution $p(\lambda \mid d, \alpha, \beta)$, which we can obtain through Bayes' rule:

$$p(\lambda \mid d, \alpha, \beta) \propto p(d \mid \lambda)p(\lambda \mid \alpha, \beta)$$
$$\propto \frac{1}{d!}\lambda^d e^{-\lambda}\frac{\beta^\alpha}{\Gamma(\alpha)}\lambda^{\alpha-1}e^{-\beta\lambda}$$
$$\propto \lambda^{\alpha+d-1}e^{-(\beta+1)\lambda}$$

This is a gamma distribution:

$$p(\lambda \mid \alpha+d, \beta+1) = \frac{(\beta+1)^{\alpha+d}}{\Gamma(\alpha+d)}\lambda^{\alpha+d-1}e^{-(\beta+1)\lambda}$$
$$\propto \lambda^{\alpha+d-1}e^{-(\beta+1)\lambda}$$

[16] The gamma distribution is a conjugate prior to the Poisson distribution. A *conjugate prior* is a family of probability distributions that remain within the same family when updated with an observation. Conjugate priors are useful for modeling beliefs because their form remains constant.

Exercise 19.5. Why are particle filters with rejection not used for updating beliefs in POMDPs with continuous observations?

Solution: Rejection sampling requires repeatedly sampling the transition and observation functions until the sampled observation matches the true observation. The probability of sampling any particular value in a continuous probability distribution is zero, making rejection sampling run forever. In practice, we would use a finite representation for continuous values, such as 64-bit floating point numbers, but rejection sampling can run for an extremely long time for each particle.

Exercise 19.6. Explain why Spelunker Joe would not benefit from switching to a particle filter with adaptive injection with $\nu \geq 1$ in example 19.5.

Solution: Adaptive injection injects new particles when $\nu w_{\text{fast}}/w_{\text{slow}} < 1$. Spelunker Joe assumes perfect observations and has a belief with particles that match his current observation. Thus, every particle has a weight of 1, and both w_{fast} and w_{slow} are 1. It follows that $w_{\text{fast}}/w_{\text{slow}}$ is always 1, leading to no new particles.

Exercise 19.7. Why is the injection rate scalar ν in a particle filter with adaptive injection typically not set to a value less than 1?

Solution: Particle injection was designed to inject particles when the current observations have lower likelihood than a historic trend over the observation likelihood. Thus, injection typically occurs only when the short-term estimate of the mean particle weight w_{fast} is less than the long-term estimate of the mean particle weight w_{slow}. If $\nu < 1$, then particles can still be generated even if $w_{\text{fast}} \geq w_{\text{slow}}$, despite indicating that current observations have a higher likelihood than the past average.

Exercise 19.8. Suppose we are dropped into a rectangular forest at an initial location chosen uniformly at random. We do not know which direction we are facing. Fortunately, we do know the dimensions of the forest (it has width w and length $\ell \gg w$).[17] We can move in a continuous path, continuously observing whether we are still in the forest. How can we apply belief updating to this problem? Here are three possible policies, each defining a different path. Which of these policies are guaranteed to escape the forest? Which policy is best?

[17] This problem was motivated by Richard Bellman's "Lost in a Forest Problem," in which we start at a random location and orientation in a forest with a known geometry and must find a policy that minimizes the average (or maximum) time to exit. R. Bellman, "Minimization Problem," *Bulletin of the American Mathematical Society*, vol. 62, no. 3, p. 270, 1956.

A straight path of length $2w$

Two perpendicular segments, each of length $\sqrt{2}w$

Two legs of an equilateral triangle, each of length $\frac{2\sqrt{3}}{3}w$

Solution: Our initial belief is a uniform distribution over all two-dimensional locations and orientations (states) in the forest. We can represent an updated belief using the path that we have traveled thus far. If we are still in the forest, our belief consists of all states that can be reached from a state within the forest by following our path while remaining entirely in the forest. As soon as we exit the forest, our belief consists of all states that reach the edge by following our path while remaining entirely in the forest.

Of the given policies, only the last two are guaranteed to escape the forest. The path formed by the two perpendicular segments and by the two sides of the equilateral triangle will always intersect with the forest's border. The straight segment, however, may not leave the forest. We prefer the shorter of the two escaping policies, which is the equilateral triangle.

Exercise 19.9. Algorithm 19.2 checks whether the updated belief is a zero vector. When can a belief update yield a zero vector? Why might this arise in real-world applications?

Solution: A zero belief vector can result from an observation o that is considered impossible. This situation can arise after taking action a from belief b when $O(o \mid a, s') = 0$ for all possible next states s' according to b and our transition model. Algorithm 19.2 handles this case by returning a uniform belief. In practical applications, there may be a mismatch between the model and the real world. We generally want to be careful to avoid assigning zero probability to observations, just in case our belief, transition, or observations models are incorrect.

Exercise 19.10. Suppose we are performing in-flight monitoring of an aircraft. The aircraft is either in a state of normal operation s^0 or a state of malfunction s^1. We receive observations through the absence of a warning w^0 or the presence of a warning w^1. We can choose to allow the plane to continue to fly m^0 or send the plane in for maintenance m^1. We have the following transition and observation dynamics, where we assume that the warnings are independent of the actions, given the status of the plane:

$$T(s^0 \mid s^0, m^0) = 0.95 \qquad\qquad O(w^0 \mid s^0) = 0.99$$
$$T(s^0 \mid s^0, m^1) = 1 \qquad\qquad\quad O(w^1 \mid s^1) = 0.7$$
$$T(s^1 \mid s^1, m^0) = 1$$
$$T(s^0 \mid s^1, m^1) = 0.98$$

Given the initial belief $\mathbf{b} = [0.95, 0.05]$, compute the updated belief $\mathbf{b}'$, given that we allow the plane to continue to fly and we observe a warning.

Solution: Using equation (19.7), we update the belief for s^0:

$$b'(s^0) \propto O(w^1 \mid s^0) \sum_s T(s^0 \mid s, m^0) b(s)$$
$$b'(s^0) \propto O(w^1 \mid s^0)(T(s^0 \mid s^0, m^0) b(s^0) + T(s^0 \mid s^1, m^0) b(s^1))$$
$$b'(s^0) \propto (1 - 0.99)(0.95 \times 0.95 + (1 - 1) \times 0.05) = 0.009025$$

We repeat the update for s^1:

$$b'(s^1) \propto O(w^1 \mid s^1) \sum_s T(s^1 \mid s, m^0)b(s)$$

$$b'(s^1) \propto O(w^1 \mid s^1)(T(s^1 \mid s^0, m^0)b(s^0) + T(s^1 \mid s^1, m^0)b(s^1))$$

$$b'(s^1) \propto 0.7((1 - 0.95) \times 0.95 + 1 \times 0.05) = 0.06825$$

After normalization, we obtain the following updated belief:

$$b'(s^0) = \frac{b'(s^0)}{b'(s^0) + b'(s^1)} \approx 0.117$$

$$b'(s^1) = \frac{b'(s^1)}{b'(s^0) + b'(s^1)} \approx 0.883$$

$$b' \approx [0.117, 0.883]$$

Exercise 19.11. Consider a robot moving along a line with position x, velocity v, and acceleration a. At each time step, we directly control the acceleration and observe the velocity. The equations of motion for the robot are

$$x' = x + v\Delta t + \tfrac{1}{2}a\Delta t^2$$
$$v' = v + a\Delta t$$

where Δt is the duration of each step. Suppose we would like to implement a Kalman filter to update our belief. The state vector is $\mathbf{s} = [x, v]$. Determine $\mathbf{T}_s$, $\mathbf{T}_a$, and $\mathbf{O}_s$.

Solution: The transition and observation dynamics can be written in linear form as follows:

$$\begin{bmatrix} x' \\ v' \end{bmatrix} = \begin{bmatrix} 1 & \Delta t \\ 0 & 1 \end{bmatrix} \begin{bmatrix} x \\ v \end{bmatrix} + \begin{bmatrix} \tfrac{1}{2}\Delta t^2 \\ \Delta t \end{bmatrix} a$$

$$o = \begin{bmatrix} 0 & 1 \end{bmatrix} \begin{bmatrix} x' \\ v' \end{bmatrix}$$

Through these equations, we can identify $\mathbf{T}_s$, $\mathbf{T}_a$, and $\mathbf{O}_s$:

$$\mathbf{T}_s = \begin{bmatrix} 1 & \Delta t \\ 0 & 1 \end{bmatrix} \qquad \mathbf{T}_a = \begin{bmatrix} \tfrac{1}{2}\Delta t^2 \\ \Delta t \end{bmatrix} \qquad \mathbf{O}_s = \begin{bmatrix} 0 & 1 \end{bmatrix}$$

Exercise 19.12. Consider a robot with a differential drive moving in two dimensions at a constant speed v. The robot's state is its position (x, y) and its heading θ. At each time step, we control the robot's turn rate ω. The equations of motion for the robot are

$$x' = x + v\cos(\theta)\Delta t$$
$$y' = y + v\sin(\theta)\Delta t$$
$$\theta' = \theta + \omega\Delta t$$

This transition function is nonlinear. What is its linearization, $\mathbf{T_s}$, as a function of the state $\mathbf{s} = [x, y, \theta]$?

Solution: The linearization is given by the Jacobian as follows:

$$\mathbf{T_s} = \begin{bmatrix} \frac{\partial x'}{\partial x} & \frac{\partial x'}{\partial y} & \frac{\partial x'}{\partial \theta} \\ \frac{\partial y'}{\partial x} & \frac{\partial y'}{\partial y} & \frac{\partial y'}{\partial \theta} \\ \frac{\partial \theta'}{\partial x} & \frac{\partial \theta'}{\partial y} & \frac{\partial \theta'}{\partial \theta} \end{bmatrix} = \begin{bmatrix} 1 & 0 & -v\sin(\theta)\Delta t \\ 0 & 1 & v\cos(\theta)\Delta t \\ 0 & 0 & 1 \end{bmatrix}$$

This linearization can be used in an extended Kalman filter to maintain a belief.

Exercise 19.13. Suppose we choose the following $2n$ sigma points for an n-dimensional distribution:

$$\mathbf{s}_{2i} = \boldsymbol{\mu} + \sqrt{n\boldsymbol{\Sigma}}_i \text{ for } i \text{ in } 1:n$$
$$\mathbf{s}_{2i-1} = \boldsymbol{\mu} - \sqrt{n\boldsymbol{\Sigma}}_i \text{ for } i \text{ in } 1:n$$

Show that we can reconstruct the mean and the covariance from these sigma points using the weights $w_i = 1/(2n)$.

Solution: If we use the weights $w_i = 1/(2n)$, the reconstructed mean is

$$\sum_i w_i \mathbf{s}_i = \sum_{i=1}^n \frac{1}{2n}\left(\boldsymbol{\mu} + \sqrt{n\boldsymbol{\Sigma}}_i\right) + \frac{1}{2n}\left(\boldsymbol{\mu} - \sqrt{n\boldsymbol{\Sigma}}_i\right) = \sum_{i=1}^n \frac{1}{n}\boldsymbol{\mu} = \boldsymbol{\mu}$$

and the reconstructed covariance is

$$\sum_i w_i (\mathbf{s}_i - \boldsymbol{\mu}')(\mathbf{s}_i - \boldsymbol{\mu}')^\top = 2\sum_{i=1}^n \frac{1}{2n}\left(\sqrt{n\boldsymbol{\Sigma}}_i\right)\left(\sqrt{n\boldsymbol{\Sigma}}_i\right)^\top$$
$$= \frac{1}{n}\sum_{i=1}^n \left(\sqrt{n\boldsymbol{\Sigma}}_i\right)\left(\sqrt{n\boldsymbol{\Sigma}}_i\right)^\top$$
$$= \sqrt{\boldsymbol{\Sigma}}\sqrt{\boldsymbol{\Sigma}}^\top$$
$$= \boldsymbol{\Sigma}$$

Exercise 19.14. Recall the $2n$ sigma points and weights from the previous problem that represent a mean $\boldsymbol{\mu}$ and covariance $\boldsymbol{\Sigma}$. We would like to parameterize the sigma points and weights in order to control the concentration of the points about the mean. Show that we can construct a new set of sigma points by uniformly down-weighting the original sigma points and then including the mean $\boldsymbol{\mu}$ as an additional sigma point. Show that this new set of $2n+1$ sigma points matches the form in equation (19.23).

Solution: We can include the mean $\boldsymbol{\mu}$ in the sigma points from exercise 19.13 to obtain a new set of $2n + 1$ sigma points:

$$\mathbf{s}_1 = \boldsymbol{\mu}$$

$$\mathbf{s}_{2i} = \boldsymbol{\mu} + \left(\sqrt{\frac{n}{1 - w_1} \boldsymbol{\Sigma}} \right)_i \text{ for } i \text{ in } 1 : n$$

$$\mathbf{s}_{2i+1} = \boldsymbol{\mu} - \left(\sqrt{\frac{n}{1 - w_1} \boldsymbol{\Sigma}} \right)_i \text{ for } i \text{ in } 1 : n$$

where w_1 is the weight of the first sigma point. The weights of the remaining sigma points are uniformly reduced from $1/(2n)$ to $(1 - w_1)/(2n)$. The reconstructed mean is still $\boldsymbol{\mu}$, and the reconstructed covariance is still $\boldsymbol{\Sigma}$.

We can vary w_1 to produce different sets of sigma points. Setting $w_1 > 0$ causes the sigma points to spread away from the mean; setting $w_1 < 0$ moves the sigma points closer to the mean. This results in a scaled set of sigma points with different higher-order moments, but it preserves the same mean and covariance.

We can match equation (19.23) by substituting $w_1 = \lambda/(n + \lambda)$. It follows that $(1 - w_1)/2n = 1/(2(n + \lambda))$ and $n/(1 - w_1) = n + \lambda$.

Exercise 19.15. Compute the set of sigma points and weights with $\lambda = 2$ for a multivariate Gaussian distribution with

$$\boldsymbol{\mu} = \begin{bmatrix} 1 \\ 2 \end{bmatrix} \qquad \boldsymbol{\Sigma} = \begin{bmatrix} 4 & 0 \\ 0 & 2.25 \end{bmatrix}$$

Solution: Since we have a two-dimensional Gaussian distribution and we are given $\lambda = 2$, we need to compute $2n + 1 = 5$ sigma points. We need to compute the square-root matrix $\mathbf{B} = \sqrt{(n + \lambda)\boldsymbol{\Sigma}}$, such that $\mathbf{B}\mathbf{B}^\top = (n + \lambda)\boldsymbol{\Sigma}$. Since the scaled covariance matrix is diagonal, the square-root matrix is simply the elementwise square root of $(n + \lambda)\boldsymbol{\Sigma}$:

$$\sqrt{(n + \lambda)\boldsymbol{\Sigma}} = \sqrt{(2 + 2) \begin{bmatrix} 4 & 0 \\ 0 & 2.25 \end{bmatrix}} = \begin{bmatrix} 4 & 0 \\ 0 & 3 \end{bmatrix}$$

Now, we can compute the sigma points and weights:

$$\mathbf{s}_1 = \begin{bmatrix} 1 \\ 2 \end{bmatrix} \qquad w_1 = \frac{2}{2+2} = \frac{1}{2}$$

$$\mathbf{s}_2 = \begin{bmatrix} 1 \\ 2 \end{bmatrix} + \begin{bmatrix} 4 \\ 0 \end{bmatrix} = \begin{bmatrix} 5 \\ 2 \end{bmatrix} \qquad w_2 = \frac{1}{2(2+2)} = \frac{1}{8}$$

$$\mathbf{s}_3 = \begin{bmatrix} 1 \\ 2 \end{bmatrix} - \begin{bmatrix} 4 \\ 0 \end{bmatrix} = \begin{bmatrix} -3 \\ 2 \end{bmatrix} \qquad w_3 = \frac{1}{2(2+2)} = \frac{1}{8}$$

$$\mathbf{s}_4 = \begin{bmatrix} 1 \\ 2 \end{bmatrix} + \begin{bmatrix} 0 \\ 3 \end{bmatrix} = \begin{bmatrix} 1 \\ 5 \end{bmatrix} \qquad w_4 = \frac{1}{2(2+2)} = \frac{1}{8}$$

$$\mathbf{s}_5 = \begin{bmatrix} 1 \\ 2 \end{bmatrix} - \begin{bmatrix} 0 \\ 3 \end{bmatrix} = \begin{bmatrix} 1 \\ -1 \end{bmatrix} \qquad w_5 = \frac{1}{2(2+2)} = \frac{1}{8}$$

Exercise 19.16. Using the sigma points and weights from the previous exercise, compute the updated mean and covariance given by the unscented transform through $\mathbf{f}(\mathbf{x}) = [2x_1, x_1 x_2]$.

Solution: The transformed sigma points are

$$\mathbf{f}(\mathbf{s}_1) = \begin{bmatrix} 2 \\ 2 \end{bmatrix} \quad \mathbf{f}(\mathbf{s}_2) = \begin{bmatrix} 10 \\ 10 \end{bmatrix} \quad \mathbf{f}(\mathbf{s}_3) = \begin{bmatrix} -6 \\ -6 \end{bmatrix} \quad \mathbf{f}(\mathbf{s}_4) = \begin{bmatrix} 2 \\ 5 \end{bmatrix} \quad \mathbf{f}(\mathbf{s}_5) = \begin{bmatrix} 2 \\ -1 \end{bmatrix}$$

We can reconstruct the mean as the weighted sum of transformed sigma points:

$$\boldsymbol{\mu}' = \sum_i w_i \mathbf{f}(\mathbf{s}_i)$$

$$\boldsymbol{\mu}' = \frac{1}{2}\begin{bmatrix} 2 \\ 2 \end{bmatrix} + \frac{1}{8}\begin{bmatrix} 10 \\ 10 \end{bmatrix} + \frac{1}{8}\begin{bmatrix} -6 \\ -6 \end{bmatrix} + \frac{1}{8}\begin{bmatrix} 2 \\ 5 \end{bmatrix} + \frac{1}{8}\begin{bmatrix} 2 \\ -1 \end{bmatrix} = \begin{bmatrix} 2 \\ 2 \end{bmatrix}$$

The covariance matrix can be reconstructed from the weighted sum of point-wise covariance matrices:

$$\Sigma' = \sum_i w_i \left(\mathbf{f}(\mathbf{s}_i) - \boldsymbol{\mu}'\right)\left(\mathbf{f}(\mathbf{s}_i) - \boldsymbol{\mu}'\right)^\top$$

$$\Sigma' = \frac{1}{2}\begin{bmatrix} 0 & 0 \\ 0 & 0 \end{bmatrix} + \frac{1}{8}\begin{bmatrix} 64 & 64 \\ 64 & 64 \end{bmatrix} + \frac{1}{8}\begin{bmatrix} 64 & 64 \\ 64 & 64 \end{bmatrix} + \frac{1}{8}\begin{bmatrix} 0 & 0 \\ 0 & 9 \end{bmatrix} + \frac{1}{8}\begin{bmatrix} 0 & 0 \\ 0 & 9 \end{bmatrix} = \begin{bmatrix} 16 & 16 \\ 16 & 18.25 \end{bmatrix}$$

Exercise 19.17. Both the Kalman filter and the extended Kalman filter compute the cross-covariance matrix Σ_{po} using the observation covariance $\mathbf{O}_s$. The unscented Kalman filter does not directly compute this observation matrix, but instead computes Σ_{po} directly. Show that the covariance update for the unscented Kalman filter, $\Sigma_{b'} \leftarrow \Sigma_p - \mathbf{K}\Sigma_o\mathbf{K}^\top$, matches the covariance update for the Kalman filter and extended Kalman filter, $\Sigma_{b'} \leftarrow (\mathbf{I} - \mathbf{K}\mathbf{O}_s)\Sigma_p$.

Solution: We can use the relations $\mathbf{K} = \Sigma_{po}\Sigma_o^{-1}$ and $\Sigma_{po} = \Sigma_p \mathbf{O}_s^\top$ to show that the two updates are equivalent. Note also that a symmetric matrix is its own transpose, and that covariance matrices are symmetric.

$$
\begin{aligned}
\Sigma_{b'} &= \Sigma_p - \mathbf{K}\Sigma_o\mathbf{K}^\top \\
&= \Sigma_p - \mathbf{K}\Sigma_o\left(\Sigma_{po}\Sigma_o^{-1}\right)^\top \\
&= \Sigma_p - \mathbf{K}\Sigma_o\left(\Sigma_o^{-1}\right)^\top \Sigma_{po}^\top \\
&= \Sigma_p - \mathbf{K}\Sigma_{po}^\top \\
&= \Sigma_p - \mathbf{K}\left(\Sigma_p\mathbf{O}_s^\top\right)^\top \\
&= \Sigma_p - \mathbf{K}\mathbf{O}_s\Sigma_p^\top \\
&= \Sigma_p - \mathbf{K}\mathbf{O}_s\Sigma_p \\
&= (\mathbf{I} - \mathbf{K}\mathbf{O}_s)\Sigma_p
\end{aligned}
$$

Exercise 19.18. What are some advantages and disadvantages of using a particle filter instead of a Kalman filter?

Solution: A Kalman filter can provide an exact belief update when the system is linear Gaussian. Particle filters can work better when the system is nonlinear and the uncertainty is multimodal. Particle filters are generally more computationally expensive and may suffer from particle deprivation.

Exercise 19.19. Consider using a particle filter to maintain a belief in a problem where observations are very reliable, with observations having either high or low likelihood. For example, in the Spelunker Joe problem, we can reliably determine which of the four walls are present, allowing us to immediately discount any states that do not match the observation. Why might a particle filter with rejection be a better match than a traditional particle filter for such problems?

Solution: A traditional particle filter produces a set of particles and assigns weights to them according to their observation likelihoods. In problems like the one with Spelunker Joe, many particles may end up with little to no weight. Having many particles with low weight makes the belief vulnerable to particle deprivation. A particle filter with rejection ensures that each particle's successor state is compatible with the observation, thus mitigating the issue of particle deprivation.

20 Exact Belief State Planning

The objective in a POMDP is to choose actions that maximize the accumulation of reward while interacting with the environment. In contrast with MDPs, states are not directly observable, requiring the agent to use its past history of actions and observations to inform a belief. As discussed in the previous chapter, beliefs can be represented as probability distributions over states. There are different approaches for computing an optimal policy that maps beliefs to actions given models of the transitions, observations, and rewards.[1] One approach is to convert a POMDP into an MDP and apply dynamic programming. Other approaches include representing policies as conditional plans or as piecewise linear value functions over the belief space. The chapter concludes with an algorithm for computing an optimal policy that is analogous to value iteration for MDPs.

[1] A discussion of exact solution methods is provided by L. P. Kaelbling, M. L. Littman, and A. R. Cassandra, "Planning and Acting in Partially Observable Stochastic Domains," *Artificial Intelligence*, vol. 101, no. 1–2, pp. 99–134, 1998.

20.1 Belief-State Markov Decision Processes

Any POMDP can be viewed as an MDP that uses beliefs as states, also called a *belief-state MDP*.[2] The state space of a belief-state MDP is the set of all beliefs $\mathcal{B}$. The action space is identical to that of the POMDP.

The reward function for a belief-state MDP depends on the belief and action taken. It is simply the expected value of the reward. For a discrete state-space, it is given by

$$R(b,a) = \sum_s R(s,a)b(s) \tag{20.1}$$

[2] K. J. Åström, "Optimal Control of Markov Processes with Incomplete State Information," *Journal of Mathematical Analysis and Applications*, vol. 10, no. 1, pp. 174–205, 1965.

If the state and observation spaces are discrete, the belief-state transition function for a belief-state MDP is given by

$$T(b' \mid b,a) = P(b' \mid b,a) \tag{20.2}$$

$$= \sum_o P(b' \mid b,a,o)P(o \mid b,a) \tag{20.3}$$

$$= \sum_o P(b' \mid b,a,o) \sum_s P(o \mid b,a,s)P(s \mid b,a) \tag{20.4}$$

$$= \sum_o P(b' \mid b,a,o) \sum_s P(o \mid b,a,s)b(s) \tag{20.5}$$

$$= \sum_o P(b' \mid b,a,o) \sum_{s'} \sum_s P(o \mid b,a,s,s')P(s' \mid b,s,a)b(s) \tag{20.6}$$

$$= \sum_o (b' = \text{Update}(b,a,o)) \sum_{s'} O(o \mid a,s') \sum_s T(s' \mid s,a)b(s) \tag{20.7}$$

In equation (20.7), $\text{Update}(b,a,o)$ returns the updated belief using the deterministic process discussed in the previous chapter.[3] For continuous problems, we replace the summations with integrals.

Solving belief-state MDPs is challenging because the state space is continuous. We can use the approximate dynamic programming techniques presented in earlier chapters, but we can often do better by taking advantage of the structure of the belief-state MDP, as will be discussed in the remainder of this chapter.

20.2 Conditional Plans

There are a number of ways to represent policies for POMDPs. One approach is to use a *conditional plan* represented as a tree. Figure 20.1 shows an example of a three-step conditional plan with binary action and observation spaces. The nodes correspond to belief states. The edges are annotated with observations, and the nodes are annotated with actions. If we have a plan π, the action associated with the root is denoted as $\pi()$ and the subplan associated with observation o is denoted as $\pi(o)$. Algorithm 20.1 provides an implementation of this.

A conditional plan tells us what to do in response to our observations up to the horizon represented by the tree. To execute a conditional plan, we start with the root node and execute the action associated with it. We proceed down the tree according to our observations, taking the actions associated with the nodes through which we pass.

[3] As a reminder, we use the convention where a logical statement in parentheses is treated numerically as 1 when true and 0 when false.

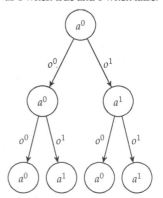

Figure 20.1.   A three-step conditional plan.

```
struct ConditionalPlan
    a          # action to take at root
    subplans # dictionary mapping observations to subplans
end

ConditionalPlan(a) = ConditionalPlan(a, Dict())

(π::ConditionalPlan)() = π.a
(π::ConditionalPlan)(o) = π.subplans[o]
```

Algorithm 20.1. The conditional plan data structure consisting of an action and a mapping from observations to subplans. The subplans field is a Dict from observations to conditional plans. For convenience, we have created a special constructor for plans that consist of a single node.

Suppose we have a conditional plan π, and we want to compute its expected utility when starting from state s. This computation can be done recursively:

$$U^\pi(s) = R(s, \pi()) + \gamma \left[\sum_{s'} T(s' \mid s, \pi()) \sum_o O(o \mid \pi(), s') U^{\pi(o)}(s') \right] \quad (20.8)$$

An implementation for this procedure is given in algorithm 20.2.

```
function lookahead(𝒫::POMDP, U, s, a)
    S, O, T, O, R, γ = 𝒫.S, 𝒫.O, 𝒫.T, 𝒫.O, 𝒫.R, 𝒫.γ
    u′ = sum(T(s,a,s′)*sum(O(a,s′,o)*U(o,s′) for o in O) for s′ in S)
    return R(s,a) + γ*u′
end

function evaluate_plan(𝒫::POMDP, π::ConditionalPlan, s)
    U(o,s′) = evaluate_plan(𝒫, π(o), s′)
    return isempty(π.subplans) ? 𝒫.R(s,π()) : lookahead(𝒫, U, s, π())
end
```

Algorithm 20.2. A method for evaluating a conditional plan π for MDP 𝒫 starting at state s. Plans are represented as tuples consisting of an action and a dictionary mapping observations to subplans.

We can compute the utility of our belief b as follows:

$$U^\pi(b) = \sum_s b(s) U^\pi(s) \quad (20.9)$$

Example 20.1 shows how to compute the utility associated with a three-step conditional plan.

Now that we have a way to evaluate conditional plans up to a horizon h, we can compute the optimal h-step value function:

$$U^*(b) = \max_\pi U^\pi(b) \quad (20.10)$$

An optimal action can be generated from the action associated with the root of a maximizing π.

Consider the following three-step conditional plan for the crying baby problem:

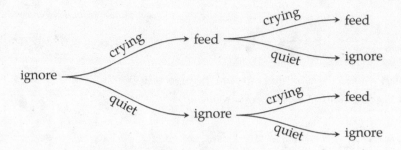

In this plan, we begin by ignoring the baby. If we observe any crying, we feed the baby. If we do not observe any crying, we ignore the baby. Our third action again feeds if there is crying.

The expected utility for this plan in belief space is plotted alongside a three-step plan that always feeds the baby and one that always ignores the baby.

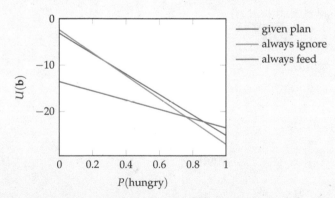

We find that the given plan is not universally better than either always ignoring or always feeding the baby.

Example 20.1. A conditional plan for the three-step crying baby problem (appendix F.7), evaluated and compared to two simpler conditional plans.

Solving an h-step POMDP by directly enumerating all h-step conditional plans is generally computationally intractable, as shown in figure 20.2. There are $(|\mathcal{O}|^h - 1)/(|\mathcal{O}| - 1)$ nodes in an h-step plan. In general, any action can be inserted into any node, resulting in $|\mathcal{A}|^{(|\mathcal{O}|^h-1)/(|\mathcal{O}|-1)}$ possible h-step plans. This exponential growth means that enumerating over all plans is intractable even for modest values of h. As will be discussed later in this chapter, there are alternatives to explicitly enumerating over all possible plans.

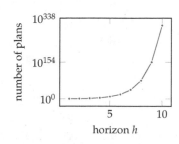

20.3   Alpha Vectors

We can rewrite equation (20.9) in vector form:

$$U^\pi(b) = \sum_s b(s)U^\pi(s) = \boldsymbol{\alpha}_\pi^\top \mathbf{b} \tag{20.11}$$

The vector $\boldsymbol{\alpha}_\pi$, called an *alpha vector*, contains the expected utility under plan π for each state. As with belief vectors, alpha vectors have dimension $|\mathcal{S}|$. Unlike beliefs, the components in alpha vectors represent utilities, not probability masses. Algorithm 20.3 shows how to compute an alpha vector.

Figure 20.2.   Even for small POMDPs with only two actions and two observations, the number of possible plans grows extremely quickly with the planning horizon. We can often significantly prune the set of alpha vectors at each iteration and only consider far fewer plans.

```
function alphavector(𝒫::POMDP, π::ConditionalPlan)
    return [evaluate_plan(𝒫, π, s) for s in 𝒫.S]
end
```

Algorithm 20.3.   We can generate an alpha vector from a conditional plan by calling evaluate_plan from all possible initial states.

Each alpha vector defines a hyperplane in belief space. The optimal value function given in equation (20.11) is the maximum over these hyperplanes:

$$U^*(\mathbf{b}) = \max_\pi \boldsymbol{\alpha}_\pi^\top \mathbf{b} \tag{20.12}$$

making the value function piecewise-linear and convex.[4]

An alternative to using a conditional plan to represent a policy is to use a set of alpha vectors Γ, each annotated with an action. Although it is not practical, one way to generate set Γ is to enumerate the set of h-step conditional plans and then compute their alpha vectors. The action associated with an alpha vector is the action at the root of the associated conditional plan. We execute a policy represented by Γ by updating our belief state and performing the action associated with the dominating alpha vector at the new belief $\mathbf{b}$. The dominating alpha vector $\boldsymbol{\alpha}$ at $\mathbf{b}$ is the one that maximizes $\boldsymbol{\alpha}^\top \mathbf{b}$. This strategy can be used to select actions

[4] The optimal value function for continuous-state POMDPs is also convex, as can be seen by approximating the POMDP through state space discretization and taking the limit as the number of discrete states approaches infinity.

beyond the horizon of the original conditional plans. Algorithm 20.4 provides an implementation.

```
struct AlphaVectorPolicy
    𝒫 # POMDP problem
    Γ # alpha vectors
    a # actions associated with alpha vectors
end

function utility(π::AlphaVectorPolicy, b)
    return maximum(α⋅b for α in π.Γ)
end

function (π::AlphaVectorPolicy)(b)
    i = argmax([α⋅b for α in π.Γ])
    return π.a[i]
end
```

Algorithm 20.4. An alpha vector policy is defined in terms of a set of alpha vectors Γ and an array of associated actions a. Given the current belief b, it will find the alpha vector that gives the highest value at that belief point. It will return the associated action.

If we use *one-step lookahead*, we do not have to keep track of the actions associated with the alpha vectors in Γ. The one-step lookahead action from belief b using the value function represented by Γ, denoted as U^Γ, is

$$\pi^\Gamma(b) = \arg\max_a \left[R(b,a) + \gamma \sum_o P(o \mid b,a) U^\Gamma(\text{Update}(b,a,o)) \right] \quad (20.13)$$

where

$$P(o \mid b,a) = \sum_s P(o \mid s,a) b(s) \quad (20.14)$$

$$P(o \mid s,a) = \sum_{s'} T(s' \mid s,a) O(o \mid s',a) \quad (20.15)$$

Algorithm 20.5 provides an implementation of this. Example 20.2 demonstrates using one-step lookahead on the crying baby problem.

20.4   Pruning

If we have a collection of alpha vectors Γ, we may want to *prune* alpha vectors that do not contribute to our representation of the value function or plans that are not optimal for any belief. Removing such alpha vectors or plans can improve computational efficiency. We can check whether an alpha vector α is *dominated* by

```
function lookahead(𝒫::POMDP, U, b::Vector, a)
    𝒮, 𝒪, T, O, R, γ = 𝒫.𝒮, 𝒫.𝒪, 𝒫.T, 𝒫.O, 𝒫.R, 𝒫.γ
    r = sum(R(s,a)*b[i] for (i,s) in enumerate(𝒮))
    Posa(o,s,a) = sum(O(a,s′,o)*T(s,a,s′) for s′ in 𝒮)
    Poba(o,b,a) = sum(b[i]*Posa(o,s,a) for (i,s) in enumerate(𝒮))
    return r + γ*sum(Poba(o,b,a)*U(update(b, 𝒫, a, o)) for o in 𝒪)
end

function greedy(𝒫::POMDP, U, b::Vector)
    u, a = findmax(a→lookahead(𝒫, U, b, a), 𝒫.𝒜)
    return (a=a, u=u)
end

struct LookaheadAlphaVectorPolicy
    𝒫 # POMDP problem
    Γ # alpha vectors
end

function utility(π::LookaheadAlphaVectorPolicy, b)
    return maximum(α·b for α in π.Γ)
end

function greedy(π, b)
    U(b) = utility(π, b)
    return greedy(π.𝒫, U, b)
end

(π::LookaheadAlphaVectorPolicy)(b) = greedy(π, b).a
```

Algorithm 20.5. A policy represented by a set of alpha vectors Γ. It uses one-step lookahead to produce an optimal action and associated utility. Equation (20.13) is used to compute the lookahead.

Consider using one-step lookahead on the crying baby problem with a value function given by the alpha vectors $[-3.7, -15]$ and $[-2, -21]$. Suppose that our current belief is $b = [0.5, 0.5]$, meaning that we believe it is equally likely the baby is hungry as not hungry. We apply equation (20.13)

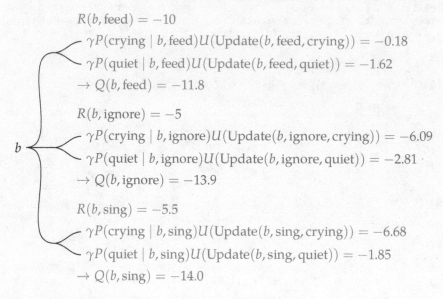

$$R(b, \text{feed}) = -10$$
$$\gamma P(\text{crying} \mid b, \text{feed}) U(\text{Update}(b, \text{feed}, \text{crying})) = -0.18$$
$$\gamma P(\text{quiet} \mid b, \text{feed}) U(\text{Update}(b, \text{feed}, \text{quiet})) = -1.62$$
$$\rightarrow Q(b, \text{feed}) = -11.8$$

$$R(b, \text{ignore}) = -5$$
$$\gamma P(\text{crying} \mid b, \text{ignore}) U(\text{Update}(b, \text{ignore}, \text{crying})) = -6.09$$
$$\gamma P(\text{quiet} \mid b, \text{ignore}) U(\text{Update}(b, \text{ignore}, \text{quiet})) = -2.81$$
$$\rightarrow Q(b, \text{ignore}) = -13.9$$

$$R(b, \text{sing}) = -5.5$$
$$\gamma P(\text{crying} \mid b, \text{sing}) U(\text{Update}(b, \text{sing}, \text{crying})) = -6.68$$
$$\gamma P(\text{quiet} \mid b, \text{sing}) U(\text{Update}(b, \text{sing}, \text{quiet})) = -1.85$$
$$\rightarrow Q(b, \text{sing}) = -14.0$$

We use $Q(b, a)$ to represent the action value function from a belief state. The policy predicts that feeding the baby will result in the highest expected utility, so it takes that action.

Example 20.2. Applying a lookahead policy to the crying baby problem.

the alpha vectors in a set Γ by solving a linear program to maximize the utility gap δ that vector achieves over all other vectors:[5]

$$\begin{aligned}
\underset{\delta, \mathbf{b}}{\text{maximize}} \quad & \delta \\
\text{subject to} \quad & \mathbf{b} \geq \mathbf{0} \\
& \mathbf{1}^\top \mathbf{b} = 1 \\
& \boldsymbol{\alpha}^\top \mathbf{b} \geq \boldsymbol{\alpha}'^\top \mathbf{b} + \delta, \qquad \boldsymbol{\alpha}' \in \Gamma
\end{aligned} \quad (20.16)$$

[5] Constraints of the form $\mathbf{a} \geq \mathbf{b}$ are elementwise. That is, we mean $a_i \geq b_i$ for all i.

The first two constraints ensure that $\mathbf{b}$ is a categorical distribution, and the final set of constraints ensures that we find a belief vector for which α has a higher expected reward than all alpha vectors in Γ. If, after solving the linear program, the utility gap δ is negative, then α is dominated. If δ is positive, then α is not dominated and $\mathbf{b}$ is a belief at which α is not dominated. Algorithm 20.6 provides an implementation for solving equation (20.16) to determine a belief, if one exists, where δ is most positive.

```
function find_maximal_belief(α, Γ)
    m = length(α)
    if isempty(Γ)
        return fill(1/m, m) # arbitrary belief
    end
    model = Model(GLPK.Optimizer)
    @variable(model, δ)
    @variable(model, b[i=1:m] ≥ 0)
    @constraint(model, sum(b) == 1.0)
    for a in Γ
        @constraint(model, (α-a)⋅b ≥ δ)
    end
    @objective(model, Max, δ)
    optimize!(model)
    return value(δ) > 0 ? value.(b) : nothing
end
```

Algorithm 20.6. A method for finding the belief vector b for which the alpha vector α improves the most compared to the set of alpha vectors Γ. Nothing is returned if no such belief exists. The packages JuMP.jl and GLPK.jl provide a mathematical optimization framework and a solver for linear programs, respectively.

Algorithm 20.7 shows a procedure that uses algorithm 20.6 to find the dominating alpha vectors in a set Γ. Initially, all the alpha vectors are candidates for being dominating. We then choose one of these candidates and determine the belief b where the candidate leads to the greatest improvement in value compared to all other alpha vectors in the dominating set. If the candidate does not bring improvement, we remove it from the set. If it does bring improvement, we move an alpha vector from the candidate set that brings the greatest improvement at b to the dominating set. The process continues until there are no longer any candidates. We can prune away any alpha vectors and associated conditional plans that are not dominating at any belief point. Example 20.3 demonstrates pruning on the crying baby problem.

```
function find_dominating(Γ)
    n = length(Γ)
    candidates, dominating = trues(n), falses(n)
    while any(candidates)
        i = findfirst(candidates)
        b = find_maximal_belief(Γ[i], Γ[dominating])
        if b === nothing
            candidates[i] = false
        else
            k = argmax([candidates[j] ? b·Γ[j] : -Inf for j in 1:n])
            candidates[k], dominating[k] = false, true
        end
    end
    return dominating
end

function prune(plans, Γ)
    d = find_dominating(Γ)
    return (plans[d], Γ[d])
end
```

Algorithm 20.7. A method for pruning dominated alpha vectors and associated plans. The find_dominating function identifies all the dominating alpha vectors in set Γ. It uses binary vectors candidates and dominating to track which alpha vectors are candidates for inclusion in the dominating set and which are currently in the dominating set, respectively.

20.5 Value Iteration

The value iteration algorithm for MDPs can be adapted for POMDPs.[6] POMDP *value iteration* (algorithm 20.8) begins by constructing all one-step plans. We prune any plans that are never optimal for any initial belief. Then, we expand all combinations of one-step plans to produce two-step plans. Again, we prune any suboptimal plans from consideration. This procedure of alternating between expansion and pruning is repeated until the desired horizon is reached. Figure 20.3 demonstrates value iteration on the crying baby problem.

[6] This section describes a version of value iteration in terms of conditional plans and alpha vectors. For a version that only uses alpha vectors, see A. R. Cassandra, M. L. Littman, and N. L. Zhang, "Incremental Pruning: A Simple, Fast, Exact Method for Partially Observable Markov Decision Processes," in *Conference on Uncertainty in Artificial Intelligence (UAI)*, 1997.

We can construct all two-step plans for the crying baby problem. There are $3^3 = 27$ such plans.

The expected utility for each plan in belief space is plotted below. We find that two plans dominate all others. These dominating plans are the only ones that need to be considered as subplans for optimal three-step plans.

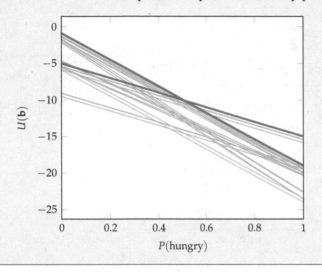

Example 20.3. The expected utility over the belief space for all two-step plans for the crying baby problem (appendix F.7). The thick lines are optimal for some beliefs, whereas the thin lines are dominated.

```
function value_iteration(𝒫::POMDP, k_max)
    S, 𝒜, R = 𝒫.S, 𝒫.𝒜, 𝒫.R
    plans = [ConditionalPlan(a) for a in 𝒜]
    Γ = [[R(s,a) for s in S] for a in 𝒜]
    plans, Γ = prune(plans, Γ)
    for k in 2:k_max
        plans, Γ = expand(plans, Γ, 𝒫)
        plans, Γ = prune(plans, Γ)
    end
    return (plans, Γ)
end

function solve(M::ValueIteration, 𝒫::POMDP)
    plans, Γ = value_iteration(𝒫, M.k_max)
    return LookaheadAlphaVectorPolicy(𝒫, Γ)
end
```

Algorithm 20.8. Value iteration for POMDPs, which finds the dominating h-step plans for a finite horizon POMDP of horizon k_max by iteratively constructing optimal subplans. The ValueIteration structure is the same as what was defined in algorithm 7.8 in the context of MDPs.

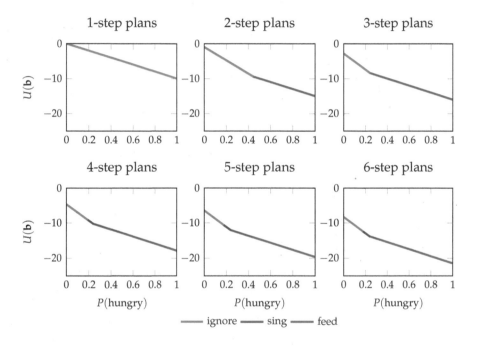

Figure 20.3. POMDP value iteration used to find the optimal value function for the crying baby problem to various horizons.

The expansion step (algorithm 20.9) in this process constructs all possible $(k + 1)$-step plans from a set of k-step plans. New plans can be constructed using a new first action and all possible combinations of the k-step plans as subplans, as shown in figure 20.4. While plans can also be extended by adding actions to the ends of subplans, top-level expansion allows alpha vectors constructed for the k-step plans to be used to efficiently construct alpha vectors for the $(k + 1)$-step plans.

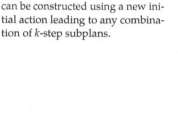

Figure 20.4. A $(k + 1)$-step plan can be constructed using a new initial action leading to any combination of k-step subplans.

Computing the alpha vector associated with a plan π from a set of alpha vectors associated with its subplans can be done as follows. We use α_o to represent the alpha vector associated with subplan $\pi(o)$. The alpha vector associated with π is then

$$\alpha(s) = R(s, \pi()) + \gamma \sum_{s'} T(s' \mid s, \pi()) \sum_o O(o \mid \pi(), s')\alpha_o(s') \qquad (20.17)$$

Even for relatively simple problems to shallow depths, computing alpha vectors from subplans in this way is much more efficient than computing them from scratch, as in algorithm 20.2.

20.6   Linear Policies

As discussed in section 19.3, the belief state in a problem with linear Gaussian dynamics can be represented by a Gaussian distribution, $\mathcal{N}(\mu_b, \Sigma_b)$. If the reward function is quadratic, then it can be shown that the optimal policy can be computed exactly offline using a process that is often called *linear quadratic Gaussian (LQG)* control. The optimal action is obtained in an identical manner as in section 7.8, but the μ_b computed using the linear Gaussian filter is treated as the true state.[7] With each observation, we simply use the filter to update our μ_b and obtain an optimal action by multiplying μ_b with the policy matrix from algorithm 7.11. Example 20.4 demonstrates this process.

[7] Our ability to simply use the mean of the distribution is another instance of the *certainty equivalence* principle, originally introduced in section 7.8.

20.7   Summary

- Exact solutions for POMDPs typically can be obtained only for finite horizon discrete POMDPs.

```
function ConditionalPlan(𝒫::POMDP, a, plans)
    subplans = Dict(o⇒π for (o, π) in zip(𝒫.𝒪, plans))
    return ConditionalPlan(a, subplans)
end

function combine_lookahead(𝒫::POMDP, s, a, Γo)
    S, 𝒪, T, O, R, γ = 𝒫.S, 𝒫.𝒪, 𝒫.T, 𝒫.O, 𝒫.R, 𝒫.γ
    U′(s′,i) = sum(O(a,s′,o)*α[i] for (o,α) in zip(𝒪,Γo))
    return R(s,a) + γ*sum(T(s,a,s′)*U′(s′,i) for (i,s′) in enumerate(S))
end

function combine_alphavector(𝒫::POMDP, a, Γo)
    return [combine_lookahead(𝒫, s, a, Γo) for s in 𝒫.S]
end

function expand(plans, Γ, 𝒫)
    S, 𝒜, 𝒪, T, O, R = 𝒫.S, 𝒫.𝒜, 𝒫.𝒪, 𝒫.T, 𝒫.O, 𝒫.R
    plans′, Γ′ = [], []
    for a in 𝒜
        # iterate over all possible mappings from observations to plans
        for inds in product([eachindex(plans) for o in 𝒪]...)
            πo = plans[[inds...]]
            Γo = Γ[[inds...]]
            π = ConditionalPlan(𝒫, a, πo)
            α = combine_alphavector(𝒫, a, Γo)
            push!(plans′, π)
            push!(Γ′, α)
        end
    end
    return (plans′, Γ′)
end
```

Algorithm 20.9. The expansion step in value iteration, which constructs all $(k+1)$–step conditional plans and associated alpha vectors from a set of k-step conditional plans and alpha vectors. The way that we combine alpha vectors of subplans follows equation (20.17).

Consider a satellite navigating in two dimensions, neglecting gravity, drag, and other external forces. The satellite can use its thrusters to accelerate in any direction with linear dynamics:

$$\begin{bmatrix} x \\ y \\ \dot{x} \\ \dot{y} \end{bmatrix} \leftarrow \begin{bmatrix} 1 & 0 & \Delta t & 0 \\ 0 & 1 & 0 & \Delta t \\ 0 & 0 & 1 & 0 \\ 0 & 0 & 0 & 1 \end{bmatrix} \begin{bmatrix} x \\ y \\ \dot{x} \\ \dot{y} \end{bmatrix} + \begin{bmatrix} \frac{1}{2}\Delta t^2 & 0 \\ 0 & \frac{1}{2}\Delta t^2 \\ \Delta t & 0 \\ 0 & \Delta t \end{bmatrix} \begin{bmatrix} \ddot{x} \\ \ddot{y} \end{bmatrix} + \boldsymbol{\epsilon}$$

where Δt is the duration of a time step and ϵ is zero-mean Gaussian noise with covariance $\Delta t / 20 \mathbf{I}$.

We seek to place the satellite in its orbital slot at the origin, while minimizing fuel use. Our quadratic reward function is

$$R(\mathbf{s}, \mathbf{a}) = -\mathbf{s}^\top \begin{bmatrix} \mathbf{I}_{2 \times 2} & \mathbf{0}_{2 \times 2} \\ \mathbf{0}_{2 \times 2} & \mathbf{0}_{2 \times 2} \end{bmatrix} \mathbf{s} - 2\mathbf{a}^\top \mathbf{a}$$

The satellite's sensors measure its position according to:

$$\mathbf{o} = \begin{bmatrix} \mathbf{I}_{2 \times 2} & \mathbf{0}_{2 \times 2} \end{bmatrix} \mathbf{s} + \boldsymbol{\varepsilon}$$

where ε is zero-mean Gaussian noise with covariance $\Delta t / 10 \mathbf{I}$.

Here are 50 trajectories from 10-step rollouts using the optimal policy for $\Delta t = 1$ and a Kalman filter to track the belief. In each case, the satellite was started at $\mathbf{s} = \boldsymbol{\mu}_b = [-5, 2, 0, 1]$ with $\boldsymbol{\Sigma}_b = [\mathbf{I}\ 0;\ 0\ 0.25\mathbf{I}]$.

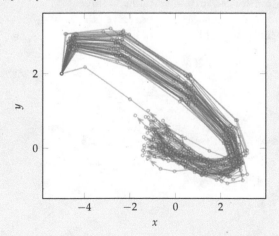

Example 20.4. An optimal policy used for a POMDP with linear Gaussian dynamics and quadratic reward.

- Policies for these problems can be represented as conditional plans, which are trees that describe the actions to take based on the observations.

- Alpha vectors contain the expected utility when starting from different states and following a particular conditional plan.

- Alpha vectors can also serve as an alternative representation of a POMDP policy.

- POMDP value iteration can avoid the computational burden of enumerating all conditional plans by iteratively computing subplans and pruning those that are suboptimal.

- Linear Gaussian problems with quadratic reward can be solved exactly using methods very similar to those derived for the fully observable case.

20.8   Exercises

Exercise 20.1. Can every POMDP be framed as an MDP?

Solution: Yes. Any POMDP can equivalently be viewed as a belief-state MDP whose state space is the space of beliefs in the POMDP, whose action space is the same as that of the POMDP and whose transition function is given by equation (20.2).

Exercise 20.2. What are the alpha vectors for the one-step crying baby problem (appendix F.7)? Are all the available actions dominant?

Solution: There are three one-step conditional plans, one for each action, resulting in three alpha vectors. The optimal one-step policy must choose between these actions, given the current belief. The one-step alpha vectors for a POMDP can be obtained from the optimal one-step belief value function:

$$U^*(b) = \max_a \sum_s b(s)R(s,a)$$

Feeding the baby yields an expected reward:

$$R(\text{hungry}, \text{feed})P(\text{hungry}) + R(\text{sated}, \text{feed})P(\text{sated})$$
$$= -15P(\text{hungry}) - 5(1 - P(\text{hungry}))$$
$$= -10P(\text{hungry}) - 5$$

Singing to the baby yields an expected reward:

$$R(\text{hungry}, \text{sing})P(\text{hungry}) + R(\text{sated}, \text{sing})P(\text{sated})$$
$$= -10.5P(\text{hungry}) - 0.5(1 - P(\text{hungry}))$$
$$= -10P(\text{hungry}) - 0.5$$

Ignoring the baby yields an expected reward:

$$R(\text{hungry}, \text{ignore})P(\text{hungry}) + R(\text{sated}, \text{ignore})P(\text{sated})$$
$$= -10P(\text{hungry})$$

The expected reward for each action is plotted as follows over the belief space:

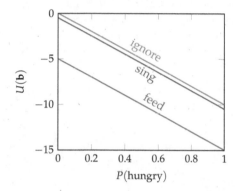

We find that under a one-step horizon, it is never optimal to feed or sing to the baby. The ignore action is dominant.

Exercise 20.3. Why does the implementation of value iteration in algorithm 20.8 call expand in algorithm 20.9 rather than evaluating the plan in algorithm 20.2 to obtain alpha vectors for each new conditional plan?

Solution: The plan evaluation method applies equation (20.8) recursively to evaluate the expected utility for a conditional plan. Conditional plans grow very large as the horizon increases. POMDP value iteration can save computation by using the alpha vectors for the subplans from the previous iteration:

$$U^{\pi}(s) = R(s, \pi()) + \gamma \left[\sum_{s'} T(s' \mid s, \pi()) \sum_{o} O(o \mid \pi(), s') \alpha_{s'}^{\pi(o)} \right]$$

Exercise 20.4. Does the number of conditional plans increase faster with the number of actions or with the number of observations?

Solution: Recall that there are $|\mathcal{A}|^{(|\mathcal{O}|^h - 1)/(|\mathcal{O}| - 1)}$ possible h-step plans. Exponential growth (n^x) is faster than polynomial growth (x^n), and we have better-than exponential growth in $|\mathcal{O}|$ and polynomial growth in $|\mathcal{A}|$. The number of plans thus increases faster with respect to the number of observations. To demonstrate, let us use $|\mathcal{A}| = 3$, $|\mathcal{O}| = 3$, and $h = 3$ as a baseline. The baseline has 1,594,323 plans. Incrementing the number of actions results in 67,108,864 plans, whereas incrementing the number of observations results in 10,460,353,203 plans.

Exercise 20.5. Suppose that we have a patient and we are unsure whether they have a particular disease. We do have three diagnostic tests, each with different probabilities that they will correctly indicate whether the disease is present. While the patient is in our office, we have the option to administer multiple diagnostic tests in sequence. We observe the outcome of each diagnostic test immediately. In addition, we can repeat any diagnostic test multiple times, with the outcomes of all tests being conditionally independent of each other, given the presence or absence of the disease. When we are done with the tests, we decide whether to treat the disease or send the patient home without treatment. Explain how you would define the various components of a POMDP formulation.

Solution: We have three states:

1. $s_{\text{no-disease}}$: the patient does not have the disease

2. s_{disease}: the patient has the disease

3. s_{terminal}: the interaction is over (terminal state)

We have five actions:

1. a_1: administer test 1

2. a_2: administer test 2

3. a_3: administer test 3

4. a_{treat}: administer treatment and send patient home

5. a_{stop}: send patient home without treatment

We have three observations:

1. $o_{\text{no-disease}}$: the outcome of the test (if administered) indicates the patient does not have the disease

2. o_{disease}: the outcome of the test (if administered) indicates the patient has the disease

3. o_{terminal}: a test was not administered

The transition model would be deterministic, with

$$T(s' \mid s, a) = \begin{cases} 1 & \text{if } a \in \{a_{\text{treat}}, a_{\text{stop}}\} \wedge s' = s_{\text{terminal}} \\ 1 & \text{if } s = s' \\ 0 & \text{otherwise} \end{cases}$$

The reward function would be a function of the cost of administering treatment and each test, as well as the cost of not treating the disease if it is indeed present. The reward available from $s_{terminal}$ is 0. The observation model assigns probabilities to correct and incorrect observations of the disease state as a result of a diagnostic test from one of the nonterminal states. The initial belief would assign our prior probability to whether the patient has the disease, with zero probability assigned to the terminal state.

Exercise 20.6. Why might we want to perform the same test multiple times in the previous exercise?

Solution: Depending on the probability of incorrect results, we may want to perform the same test multiple times to improve our confidence in whether the patient has the disease. The results of the tests are independent given the disease state.

Exercise 20.7. Suppose we have three alpha vectors, $[1,0]$, $[0,1]$, and $[\theta,\theta]$, for a constant θ. Under what conditions on θ can we prune alpha vectors?

Solution: We can prune alpha vectors if $\theta < 0.5$ or $\theta > 1$. If $\theta < 0.5$, then $[\theta,\theta]$ is dominated by the other two alpha vectors. If $\theta > 1$, then $[\theta,\theta]$ dominates the other two alpha vectors.

Exercise 20.8. We have $\Gamma = \{[1,0],[0,1]\}$ and $\alpha = [0.7,0.7]$. What belief **b** maximizes the utility gap δ, as defined by the linear program in equation (20.16)?

Solution: The alpha vectors in Γ are shown in blue and the alpha vector α is shown in red. We care only about the region where $0.3 \leq b_2 \leq 0.7$, where α dominates the alpha vectors in Γ; in other words, where the red line is above the blue lines. The point where the gap between the red line and the maximum of the blue lines occurs at $b_2 = 0.5$, with a gap of $\delta = 0.2$. Hence, the belief that maximizes this gap is **b** $= [0.5,0.5]$.

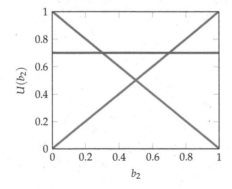

21 *Offline Belief State Planning*

In the worst case, an exact solution for a general finite-horizon POMDP is *PSPACE-complete*, which is a complexity class that includes NP-complete problems and is suspected to include problems that are even more difficult.[1] General infinite-horizon POMDPs have been shown to be uncomputable.[2] Hence, there has been a tremendous amount of research recently on approximation methods. This chapter discusses various offline POMDP solution methods, which involve performing all or most of the computation prior to execution. We focus on methods that represent the value function as alpha vectors and different forms of interpolation.

21.1 *Fully Observable Value Approximation*

One of the simplest offline approximation techniques is *QMDP*, which derives its name from the action value function associated with a fully observed MDP.[3] This approach, as well as several others discussed in this chapter, involve iteratively updating a set Γ of alpha vectors, as shown in algorithm 21.1. The resulting set Γ defines a value function and a policy that can be used directly or with one-step lookahead as discussed in the previous chapter, though the resulting policy will only be an approximation of the optimal solution.

```
function alphavector_iteration(𝒫::POMDP, M, Γ)
    for k in 1:M.k_max
        Γ = update(𝒫, M, Γ)
    end
    return Γ
end
```

[1] C. Papadimitriou and J. Tsitsiklis, "The Complexity of Markov Decision Processes," *Mathematics of Operation Research*, vol. 12, no. 3, pp. 441–450, 1987.

[2] O. Madani, S. Hanks, and A. Condon, "On the Undecidability of Probabilistic Planning and Related Stochastic Optimization Problems," *Artificial Intelligence*, vol. 147, no. 1–2, pp. 5–34, 2003.

[3] M. L. Littman, A. R. Cassandra, and L. P. Kaelbling, "Learning Policies for Partially Observable Environments: Scaling Up," in *International Conference on Machine Learning* (ICML), 1995. A proof that QMDP provides an upper bound on the optimal value function is given by M. Hauskrecht, "Value-Function Approximations for Partially Observable Markov Decision Processes," *Journal of Artificial Intelligence Research*, vol. 13, pp. 33–94, 2000.

Algorithm 21.1. Iteration structure for updating a set of alpha vectors Γ used by several of the methods in this chapter. The various methods, including QMDP, differ in their implementation of update. After k_max iterations, this function returns a policy represented by the alpha vectors in Γ.

QMDP (algorithm 21.2) constructs a single alpha vector α_a for each action a using value iteration. Each alpha vector is initialized to zero, and then we iterate:

$$\alpha_a^{(k+1)}(s) = R(s,a) + \gamma \sum_{s'} T(s' \mid s,a) \max_{a'} \alpha_{a'}^{(k)}(s') \qquad (21.1)$$

Each iteration requires $O(|\mathcal{A}|^2|\mathcal{S}|^2)$ operations. Figure 21.1 illustrates the process.

```
struct QMDP
    k_max # maximum number of iterations
end

function update(𝒫::POMDP, M::QMDP, Γ)
    S, 𝒜, R, T, γ = 𝒫.S, 𝒫.𝒜, 𝒫.R, 𝒫.T, 𝒫.γ
    Γ′ = [[R(s,a) + γ*sum(T(s,a,s′)*maximum(α′[j] for α′ in Γ)
        for (j,s′) in enumerate(S)) for s in S] for a in 𝒜]
    return Γ′
end

function solve(M::QMDP, 𝒫::POMDP)
    Γ = [zeros(length(𝒫.S)) for a in 𝒫.𝒜]
    Γ = alphavector_iteration(𝒫, M, Γ)
    return AlphaVectorPolicy(𝒫, Γ, 𝒫.𝒜)
end
```

Algorithm 21.2. The QMDP algorithm, which finds an approximately optimal policy for an infinite-horizon POMDP with a discrete state and action space, where k_max is the number of iterations. QMDP assumes perfect observability.

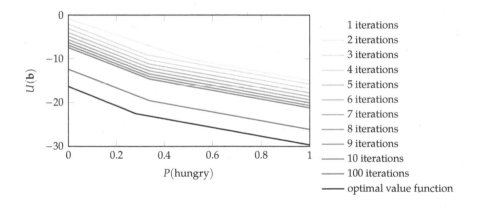

Figure 21.1. Value functions obtained for the crying baby problem (appendix F.7) using QMDP. In the first iteration, a single alpha vector dominates. In subsequent iterations, two alpha vectors dominate.

When QMDP is run to the horizon in finite horizon problems or to convergence for infinite-horizon problems, the resulting policy is equivalent to assuming that there will be full observability after taking the first step. Because we can do better only if we have full observability, QMDP will produce an upper bound on the true optimal value function $U^*(\mathbf{b})$. In other words, $\max_a \alpha_a^\top \mathbf{b} \geq U^*(\mathbf{b})$ for all $\mathbf{b}$.[4]

If QMDP is not run to convergence for infinite-horizon problems, it might not provide an upper bound. One way to guarantee that QMDP will provide an upper bound after a finite number of iterations is to initialize the value function to some upper bound. One rather loose upper bound is the *best-action best-state upper bound*, which is the utility obtained from taking the best action from the best state forever:

$$\overline{U}(b) = \max_{s,a} \frac{R(s,a)}{1-\gamma} \tag{21.2}$$

The assumption of full observability after the first step can cause QMDP to poorly approximate the value of *information-gathering* actions, which are actions that significantly reduce the uncertainty in the state. For example, looking over one's shoulder before changing lanes when driving is an information-gathering action. QMDP can perform well in problems where the optimal policy does not include costly information gathering.

We can generalize the QMDP approach to problems that may not have a small, discrete state space. In such problems, the iteration in equation (21.1) may not be feasible, but we may use one of the many methods discussed in earlier chapters for obtaining an approximate action value function $Q(s,a)$. This value function might be defined over a high-dimensional, continuous state space using, for example, a neural network representation. The value function evaluated at a belief point is, then,

$$U(b) = \max_a \int Q(s,a)b(s)\,\mathrm{d}s \tag{21.3}$$

The integral above may be approximated through sampling.

21.2   Fast Informed Bound

As with QMDP, the *fast informed bound* computes one alpha vector for each action. However, the fast informed bound takes into account, to some extent, the observation model.[5] The iteration is

$$\alpha_a^{(k+1)}(s) = R(s,a) + \gamma \sum_o \max_{a'} \sum_{s'} O(o \mid a,s')T(s' \mid s,a)\alpha_{a'}^{(k)}(s') \tag{21.4}$$

which requires $O(|\mathcal{A}|^2|\mathcal{S}|^2|\mathcal{O}|)$ operations per iteration.

[4] Although the value function represented by the QMDP alpha vectors upper-bounds the optimal value function, the utility realized by a QMDP policy will not exceed that of an optimal policy in expectation, of course.

[5] The relationship between QMDP and the fast informed bound, together with empirical results, are discussed by M. Hauskrecht, "Value-Function Approximations for Partially Observable Markov Decision Processes," *Journal of Artificial Intelligence Research*, vol. 13, pp. 33–94, 2000.

The fast informed bound provides an upper bound on the optimal value function. That upper bound is guaranteed to be no looser than that provided by QMDP, and it also tends to be tighter. The fast informed bound is implemented in algorithm 21.3 and is used in figure 21.2 to compute optimal value functions.

```
struct FastInformedBound
    k_max # maximum number of iterations
end

function update(𝒫::POMDP, M::FastInformedBound, Γ)
    S, 𝒜, O, R, T, O, γ = 𝒫.S, 𝒫.𝒜, 𝒫.O, 𝒫.R, 𝒫.T, 𝒫.O, 𝒫.γ
    Γ′ = [[R(s, a) + γ*sum(maximum(sum(O(a,s′,o)*T(s,a,s′)*α′[j]
        for (j,s′) in enumerate(S)) for α′ in Γ) for o in O)
        for s in S] for a in 𝒜]
    return Γ′
end

function solve(M::FastInformedBound, 𝒫::POMDP)
    Γ = [zeros(length(𝒫.S)) for a in 𝒫.𝒜]
    Γ = alphavector_iteration(𝒫, M, Γ)
    return AlphaVectorPolicy(𝒫, Γ, 𝒫.𝒜)
end
```

Algorithm 21.3. The fast informed bound algorithm, which finds an approximately optimal policy for an infinite-horizon POMDP with discrete state, action, and observation spaces, where k_max is the number of iterations.

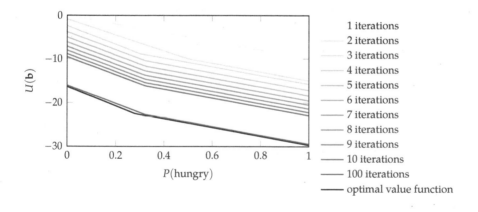

1 iterations
2 iterations
3 iterations
4 iterations
5 iterations
6 iterations
7 iterations
8 iterations
9 iterations
10 iterations
100 iterations
optimal value function

Figure 21.2. Value functions obtained for the crying baby problem using the fast informed bound. The value function after 10 iterations is noticeably lower than that of the QMDP algorithm.

21.3   Fast Lower Bounds

The previous two sections introduced methods that can be used to produce upper bounds on the value function represented as alpha vectors. This section introduces a couple of methods for quickly producing lower bounds represented as alpha vectors without any planning in the belief space. Although the upper-bound methods can often be used directly to produce sensible policies, the lower bounds discussed in this section are generally only used to seed other planning algorithms. Figure 21.3 plots the two lower-bound methods discussed in this section.

A common lower bound is the *best-action worst-state (BAWS) lower bound* (algorithm 21.4). It is the discounted reward obtained by taking the best action in the worst state forever:

$$r_{\text{baws}} = \max_a \sum_{k=1}^{\infty} \gamma^{k-1} \min_s R(s,a) = \frac{1}{1-\gamma} \max_a \min_s R(s,a) \qquad (21.5)$$

This lower bound is represented by a single alpha vector. This bound is typically very loose, but it can be used to seed other algorithms that can tighten the bound, as we will discuss shortly.

```
function baws_lowerbound(𝒫::POMDP)
    𝒮, 𝒜, R, γ = 𝒫.𝒮, 𝒫.𝒜, 𝒫.R, 𝒫.γ
    r = maximum(minimum(R(s, a) for s in 𝒮) for a in 𝒜) / (1-γ)
    α = fill(r, length(𝒮))
    return α
end
```

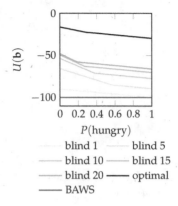

Figure 21.3. Blind lower bounds with different numbers of iterations and the BAWS lower bound applied to the crying baby problem.

Algorithm 21.4. Implementation of the best-action worst-state lower bound from equation (21.5) represented as an alpha vector.

The *blind lower bound* (algorithm 21.5) represents a lower bound with one alpha vector per action. It makes the assumption that we are forced to commit to a single action forever, blind to what we observe in the future. To compute these alpha vectors, we start with another lower bound (typically the best-action worst-state lower bound) and then perform a number of iterations:

$$\alpha_a^{(k+1)}(s) = R(s,a) + \gamma \sum_{s'} T(s' \mid s,a)\alpha_a^{(k)}(s') \qquad (21.6)$$

This iteration is similar to the QMDP update in equation (21.1), except that it does not have a maximization over the alpha vectors on the right-hand side.

21.4 *Point-Based Value Iteration*

QMDP and the fast informed bound generate one alpha vector for each action, but the optimal value function is often better approximated by many more

```
function blind_lowerbound(𝒫, k_max)
    S, 𝒜, T, R, γ = 𝒫.S, 𝒫.𝒜, 𝒫.T, 𝒫.R, 𝒫.γ
    Q(s,a,α) = R(s,a) + γ*sum(T(s,a,s')*α[j] for (j,s') in enumerate(S))
    Γ = [baws_lowerbound(𝒫) for a in 𝒜]
    for k in 1:k_max
        Γ = [[Q(s,a,α) for s in S] for (α,a) in zip(Γ, 𝒜)]
    end
    return Γ
end
```

Algorithm 21.5. Implementation of the blind lower bound represented as a set of alpha vectors.

alpha vectors. *Point-based value iteration*[6] computes m different alpha vectors $\Gamma = \{\alpha_1, \dots, \alpha_m\}$, each associated with different belief points $B = \{\mathbf{b}_1, \dots, \mathbf{b}_m\}$. Methods for selecting these beliefs will be discussed in section 21.7. As before, these alpha vectors define an approximately optimal value function:

$$U^\Gamma(\mathbf{b}) = \max_{\alpha \in \Gamma} \alpha^\top \mathbf{b} \qquad (21.7)$$

The algorithm maintains a lower bound on the optimal value function, $U^\Gamma(\mathbf{b}) \le U^*(\mathbf{b})$ for all $\mathbf{b}$. We initialize our alpha vectors to start with a lower bound and then perform a *backup* to update the alpha vectors at each point in B. The backup operation (algorithm 21.6) takes a belief $\mathbf{b}$ and a set of alpha vectors Γ and constructs a new alpha vector. The algorithm iterates through every possible action a and observation o and extracts the alpha vector from Γ that is maximal at the resulting belief state:

$$\alpha_{a,o} = \arg\max_{\alpha \in \Gamma} \alpha^\top \text{Update}(\mathbf{b}, a, o) \qquad (21.8)$$

Then, for each available action a, we construct a new alpha vector based on these $\alpha_{a,o}$ vectors:

$$\alpha_a(s) = R(s,a) + \gamma \sum_{s',o} O(o \mid a, s') T(s' \mid s, a) \alpha_{a,o}(s') \qquad (21.9)$$

The alpha vector that is ultimately produced by the backup operation is

$$\alpha = \arg\max_{\alpha_a} \alpha_a^\top \mathbf{b} \qquad (21.10)$$

If Γ is a lower bound, the backup operation will produce only alpha vectors that are also a lower bound.

[6] A survey of point-based value iteration methods are provided by G. Shani, J. Pineau, and R. Kaplow, "A Survey of Point-Based POMDP Solvers," *Autonomous Agents and Multi-Agent Systems*, vol. 27, pp. 1–51, 2012. That reference provides a slightly different way to compute a belief backup, though the result is the same.

Repeated application of the backup operation over the beliefs in B gradually increases the lower bound on the value function represented by the alpha vectors until convergence. The converged value function will not necessarily be optimal because B typically does not include all beliefs reachable from the initial belief. However, so long as the beliefs in B are well distributed across the reachable belief space, the approximation may be acceptable. In any case, the resulting value function is guaranteed to provide a lower bound that can be used with other algorithms, potentially online, to further improve the policy.

Point-based value iteration is implemented in algorithm 21.7. Figure 21.4 shows several iterations on an example problem.

```
function backup(𝒫::POMDP, Γ, b)
    𝒮, 𝒜, 𝒪, γ = 𝒫.𝒮, 𝒫.𝒜, 𝒫.𝒪, 𝒫.γ
    R, T, O = 𝒫.R, 𝒫.T, 𝒫.O
    Γa = []
    for a in 𝒜
        Γao = []
        for o in 𝒪
            b′ = update(b, 𝒫, a, o)
            push!(Γao, argmax(α→α⋅b′, Γ))
        end
        α = [R(s, a) + γ*sum(sum(T(s, a, s′)*O(a, s′, o)*Γao[i][j]
            for (j,s′) in enumerate(𝒮)) for (i,o) in enumerate(𝒪))
            for s in 𝒮]
        push!(Γa, α)
    end
    return argmax(α→α⋅b, Γa)
end
```

Algorithm 21.6. A method for backing up a belief for a POMDP with discrete state and action spaces, where Γ is a vector of alpha vectors and b is a belief vector at which to apply the backup. The `update` method for vector beliefs is defined in algorithm 19.2.

21.5 Randomized Point-Based Value Iteration

Randomized point-based value iteration (algorithm 21.8) is a variation of the point-based value iteration approach from the previous section.[7] The primary difference is the fact that we are not forced to maintain an alpha vector at every belief in B. We initialize the algorithm with a single alpha vector in Γ, and then update Γ at every iteration, potentially increasing or decreasing the number of alpha vectors in Γ as appropriate. This modification of the update step can improve efficiency.

[7] M. T. J. Spaan and N. A. Vlassis, "Perseus: Randomized Point-Based Value Iteration for POMDPs," *Journal of Artificial Intelligence Research*, vol. 24, pp. 195–220, 2005.

434   CHAPTER 21. OFFLINE BELIEF STATE PLANNING

```
struct PointBasedValueIteration
    B      # set of belief points
    k_max  # maximum number of iterations
end

function update(𝒫::POMDP, M::PointBasedValueIteration, Γ)
    return [backup(𝒫, Γ, b) for b in M.B]
end

function solve(M::PointBasedValueIteration, 𝒫)
    Γ = fill(baws_lowerbound(𝒫), length(𝒫.𝒜))
    Γ = alphavector_iteration(𝒫, M, Γ)
    return LookaheadAlphaVectorPolicy(𝒫, Γ)
end
```

Algorithm 21.7. Point-based value iteration, which finds an approximately optimal policy for an infinite-horizon POMDP with discrete state, action, and observation spaces, where B is a vector of beliefs and k_max is the number of iterations.

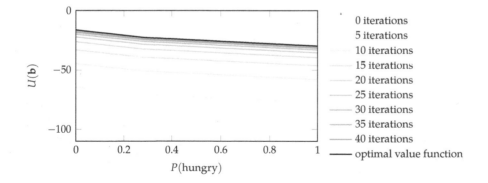

Figure 21.4. Approximate value functions obtained using point-based value iteration on the crying baby problem with belief vectors $[1/4, 3/4]$ and $[3/4, 1/4]$. Unlike QMDP and the fast informed bound, the value function of point-based value iteration is always a lower bound of the true value function.

Each update takes a set of alpha vectors Γ as input and outputs a set of alpha vectors Γ' that improve on the value function represented by Γ at the beliefs in B. In other words, it outputs Γ' such that $U^{\Gamma'}(\mathbf{b}) \geq U^{\Gamma}(\mathbf{b})$ for all $\mathbf{b} \in B$. We begin by initializing Γ' to the empty set and initializing B' to B. We then remove a point $\mathbf{b}$ randomly from B' and perform a belief backup (algorithm 21.6) on $\mathbf{b}$, using Γ to get a new alpha vector, $\boldsymbol{\alpha}$. We then find the alpha vector in $\Gamma \cup \{\boldsymbol{\alpha}\}$ that dominates at $\mathbf{b}$ and add it to Γ'. All belief points in B' whose value is improved with this alpha vector is then removed from B'. As the algorithm progresses, B' becomes smaller and contains the set of points that have not been improved by Γ'. The update finishes when B' is empty. Figure 21.5 illustrates this process with the crying baby problem.

```
struct RandomizedPointBasedValueIteration
    B      # set of belief points
    k_max  # maximum number of iterations
end

function update(𝒫::POMDP, M::RandomizedPointBasedValueIteration, Γ)
    Γ', B' = [], copy(M.B)
    while !isempty(B')
        b = rand(B')
        α = argmax(α→α⋅b, Γ)
        α' = backup(𝒫, Γ, b)
        if α'⋅b ≥ α⋅b
            push!(Γ', α')
        else
            push!(Γ', α)
        end
        filter!(b→maximum(α⋅b for α in Γ') <
            maximum(α⋅b for α in Γ), B')
    end
    return Γ'
end

function solve(M::RandomizedPointBasedValueIteration, 𝒫)
    Γ = [baws_lowerbound(𝒫)]
    Γ = alphavector_iteration(𝒫, M, Γ)
    return LookaheadAlphaVectorPolicy(𝒫, Γ)
end
```

Algorithm 21.8. Randomized point-based value iteration, which finds an approximately optimal policy for an infinite-horizon POMDP with discrete state, action, and observation spaces, where B is a vector of beliefs and k_max is the number of iterations.

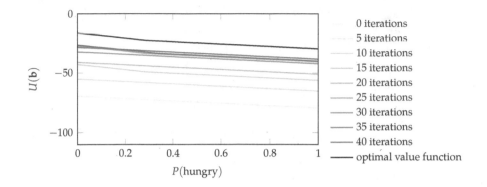

Figure 21.5. Approximate value functions obtained using randomized point-based value iteration on the crying baby problem with belief points at $[1/4, 3/4]$ and $[3/4, 1/4]$.

21.6 Sawtooth Upper Bound

The *sawtooth upper bound* is an alternative way to represent the value function. Instead of storing a set of alpha vectors Γ, we store a set of belief-utility pairs:

$$V = \{(b_1, U(b_1)), \ldots, (b_m, U(b_m))\} \qquad (21.11)$$

with the requirement that V contains all the standard basis beliefs:

$$E = \{e_1 = [1, 0, \ldots, 0], \ldots, e_n = [0, 0, \ldots, 1]\} \qquad (21.12)$$

such that

$$\{(e_1, U(e_1)), \ldots, (e_n, U(e_n))\} \subseteq V \qquad (21.13)$$

If these utilities are upper bounds (e.g., as obtained from the fast informed bound), then the way that we use V to estimate $U(b)$ at arbitrary beliefs b will result in an upper bound.[8]

The "sawtooth" name comes from the way that we estimate $U(b)$ by interpolating points in V. For each belief-utility pair $(b, U(b))$ in V, we form a single, pointed "tooth." If the belief space is n-dimensional, each tooth is an inverted, n-dimensional pyramid. When multiple pairs are considered, it forms a "sawtooth" shape. The bases of the pyramids are formed by the standard basis beliefs $(e_i, U(e_i))$. The apex point of each tooth corresponds to each belief-utility pair $(b, U(b)) \in V$. Since these are pyramids in general, each tooth has walls equivalently defined by n-hyperplanes with bounded regions. These hyperplanes can also be interpreted as alpha vectors that act over a bounded region of the belief

[8] The relationship between sawtooth and other bounds are discussed by M. Hauskrecht, "Value-Function Approximations for Partially Observable Markov Decision Processes," *Journal of Artificial Intelligence Research*, vol. 13, pp. 33–94, 2000.

space, not the entire belief space as with normal alpha vectors. The combination of multiple pyramids forms the n-dimensional sawtooth. The sawtooth upper bound at any belief is similarly the minimum value among these pyramids at that belief.

Consider the sawtooth representation in a two-state POMDP, such as in the crying baby problem as shown in figure 21.6. The corners of each tooth are the values $U(e_1)$ and $U(e_2)$ for each standard basis belief e_i. The sharp lower point of each tooth is the value $U(b)$, since each tooth is a point-set pair $(b, U(b))$. The linear interpolation from $U(e_1)$ to $U(b)$, and again from $U(b)$ to $U(e_2)$, form the tooth. To combine multiple teeth and form the upper bound, we take the minimum interpolated value at any belief, creating the distinctive sawtooth shape.

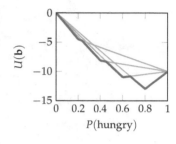

Figure 21.6. The sawtooth upper bound representation applied to the crying baby problem.

To compute the sawtooth at any belief b, we iterate over each belief-utility pair $(b', U(b'))$ in V. The key idea is to compute the utility $U'(b)$ for this hyperpyramid, first by finding the farthest basis point, then using this to determine the matching hyperplane from the hyperpyramid, and finally computing a utility using a rescaled version of the hyperplane. The farthest basis belief e_i is computed using L_1 distances from b and b':

$$i \leftarrow \arg\max_{j} \|b - e_j\|_1 - \|b' - e_j\|_1 \qquad (21.14)$$

This e_i uniquely identifies the particular hyperplane among those forming the hyperpyramid for $U(b')$. Specifically, this hyperplane is defined by all corners $e_j \neq e_i$ and using b' as a replacement for e_i. At this point, we know that this is the hyperplane for the region of the utility that b is contained within. The hyperplane's utilities are $U(e_j)$ for $e_j \neq e_i$ and $U(b')$ as a replacement for $U(e_i)$. However, we cannot directly compute the desired utility $U'(b)$ using a dot product because this is not the standard simplex. We instead compute the weight w of b in terms of the weighted distance from the hyperplane's corners, $e_j \neq e_i$ and b'. This allows us to be able to compute $U'(b)$, essentially creating a simplex amenable to a dot product with $U(e_j)$ and $U(b')$:

$$U'(b) = w_i U(b') + \sum_{j \neq i} w_j U(e_j) \qquad (21.15)$$

This entire process is done among all $(b', U(b'))$, resulting in

$$U(b) = \min_{(b', U(b')) \in V} U'(b) \qquad (21.16)$$

Algorithm 21.9 provides an implementation. We can also derive a policy using greedy one-step lookahead.

```
struct SawtoothPolicy
    𝒫 # POMDP problem
    V # dictionary mapping beliefs to utilities
end

function basis(𝒫)
    n = length(𝒫.S)
    e(i) = [j == i ? 1.0 : 0.0 for j in 1:n]
    return [e(i) for i in 1:n]
end

function utility(π::SawtoothPolicy, b)
    𝒫, V = π.𝒫, π.V
    if haskey(V, b)
        return V[b]
    end
    n = length(𝒫.S)
    E = basis(𝒫)
    u = sum(V[E[i]] * b[i] for i in 1:n)
    for (b', u') in V
        if b' ∉ E
            i = argmax([norm(b-e, 1) - norm(b'-e, 1) for e in E])
            w = [norm(b - e, 1) for e in E]
            w[i] = norm(b - b', 1)
            w /= sum(w)
            w = [1 - wi for wi in w]
            α = [V[e] for e in E]
            α[i] = u'
            u = min(u, w⋅α)
        end
    end
    return u
end

(π::SawtoothPolicy)(b) = greedy(π, b).a
```

Algorithm 21.9. The sawtooth upper bound representation for value functions and policies. It is defined using a dictionary V that maps belief vectors to upper bounds on their utility obtained, such as, from the fast informed bound. A requirement of this representation is that V contain belief-utility pairs at the standard basis beliefs, which can be obtained from the basis function. We can use one-step lookahead to obtain greedy action-utility pairs from arbitrary beliefs b.

We can iteratively apply greedy one-step lookahead at a set of beliefs B to tighten our estimates of the upper bound. The beliefs in B can be a superset of the beliefs in V. Algorithm 21.10 provides an implementation of this. Example 21.1 shows the effect of multiple iterations of the sawtooth approximation on the crying baby problem.

```
struct SawtoothIteration
    V      # initial mapping from beliefs to utilities
    B      # beliefs to compute values including those in V map
    k_max  # maximum number of iterations
end

function solve(M::SawtoothIteration, 𝒫::POMDP)
    E = basis(𝒫)
    π = SawtoothPolicy(𝒫, M.V)
    for k in 1:M.k_max
        V = Dict(b ⇒ (b ∈ E ? M.V[b] : greedy(π, b).u) for b in M.B)
        π = SawtoothPolicy(𝒫, V)
    end
    return π
end
```

Algorithm 21.10. Sawtooth iteration iteratively applies one-step lookahead at points in B to improve the utility estimates at the points in V. The beliefs in B are a superset of those contained in V. To preserve the upper bound at each iteration, updates are not made at the standard basis beliefs stored in E. We run k_max iterations.

Suppose that we want to maintain an upper bound of the value for the crying baby problem with regularly spaced belief points with a step size of 0.2. To obtain an initial upper bound, we use the fast informed bound. We can then run sawtooth iteration for three steps as follows:

Example 21.1. An illustration of sawtooth's ability to maintain an upper bound at regularly spaced beliefs for the crying baby problem.

```
n = length(𝒫.𝒮)
πfib = solve(FastInformedBound(1), 𝒫)
V = Dict(e ⇒ utility(πfib, e) for e in basis(𝒫))
B = [[p, 1 - p] for p in 0.0:0.2:1.0]
π = solve(SawtoothIteration(V, B, 2), 𝒫)
```

The sawtooth upper bound improves as follows:

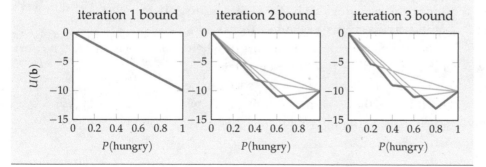

21.7   Point Selection

Algorithms like point-based value iteration and sawtooth iteration require a set of beliefs B. We want to choose B so that there are more points in the relevant areas of the belief space; we do not want to waste computation on beliefs that we are not likely to reach under our (hopefully approximately optimal) policy. One way to explore the potentially reachable space is to take steps in the belief space (algorithm 21.11). The outcome of the step will be random because the observation is generated according to our probability model.

```
function randstep(𝒫::POMDP, b, a)
    s = rand(SetCategorical(𝒫.S, b))
    s′, r, o = 𝒫.TRO(s, a)
    b′ = update(b, 𝒫, a, o)
    return b′, r
end
```

Algorithm 21.11. A function for randomly sampling the next belief b' and reward r, given the current belief b and action a in problem $\mathcal{P}$.

We can create B from the belief states reachable from some initial belief under a random policy. This *random belief expansion* procedure (algorithm 21.12) may explore much more of the belief space than might be necessary; the belief space reachable by a random policy can be much larger than the space reachable by an optimal policy. Of course, computing the belief space that is reachable by an optimal policy generally requires knowing the optimal policy, which is what we want to compute in the first place. One approach that can be taken is to use successive approximations of the optimal policy to iteratively generate B.[9]

In addition to wanting our belief points to be focused on the reachable belief space, we want those points to be spread out to allow better value function approximation. The quality of the approximation provided by the alpha vectors associated with the points in B degrades as we evaluate points farther from B. We can take an *exploratory belief expansion* approach (algorithm 21.13), where we try every action for every belief in B and add the resulting belief states that are farthest from the beliefs already in the set. Distance in belief space can be measured in different ways. This algorithm uses the L_1-norm.[10] Figure 21.7 shows an example of the belief points added to B using this approach.

[9] This is the intuition behind the algorithm known as *Successive Approximations of the Reachable Space under Optimal Policies* (SARSOP). H. Kurniawati, D. Hsu, and W. S. Lee, "SARSOP: Efficient Point-Based POMDP Planning by Approximating Optimally Reachable Belief Spaces," in *Robotics: Science and Systems*, 2008.

[10] The L_1 distance between $\mathbf{b}$ and $\mathbf{b}'$ is $\sum_s |b(s) - b'(s)|$ and is denoted as $\|\mathbf{b} - \mathbf{b}'\|_1$. See appendix A.4.

```
function random_belief_expansion(𝒫, B)
    B′ = copy(B)
    for b in B
        a = rand(𝒫.𝒜)
        b′, r = randstep(𝒫, b, a)
        push!(B′, b′)
    end
    return unique!(B′)
end
```

Algorithm 21.12. Randomly expanding a finite set of beliefs B used in point-based value iteration based on reachable beliefs.

```
function exploratory_belief_expansion(𝒫, B)
    B′ = copy(B)
    for b in B
        best = (b=copy(b), d=0.0)
        for a in 𝒫.𝒜
            b′, r = randstep(𝒫, b, a)
            d = minimum(norm(b - b′, 1) for b in B′)
            if d > best.d
                best = (b=b′, d=d)
            end
        end
        push!(B′, best.b)
    end
    return unique!(B′)
end
```

Algorithm 21.13. Expanding a finite set of beliefs B used in point-based value iteration by exploring the reachable beliefs and adding those that are farthest from the current beliefs.

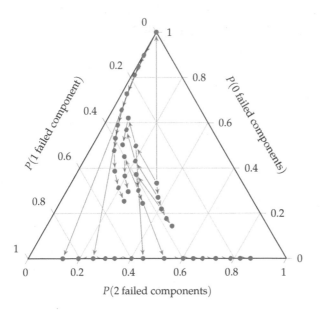

Figure 21.7. Exploratory belief expansion run on the three-state machine replacement problem, starting with an initial uniform belief $\mathbf{b} = [1/3, 1/3, 1/3]$. New beliefs were added if the distance to any previous belief was at least 0.05.

21.8   Sawtooth Heuristic Search

Chapter 9 introduced the concept of heuristic search as an online method in the fully observable context. This section discusses *sawtooth heuristic search* (algorithm 21.14) as an offline method that produces a set of alpha vectors that can be used to represent an offline policy. However, like the online POMDP methods discussed in the next chapter, the computational effort is focused on beliefs that are reachable from some specified initial belief. The heuristic that drives the exploration of the reachable belief space is the gap between the upper and lower bounds of the value function.[11]

The algorithm is initialized with an upper bound on the value function represented by a set of sawtooth belief-utility pairs V, together with a lower bound on the value function represented by a set of alpha vectors Γ. The belief-utility pairs defining the sawtooth upper bound can be obtained from the fast informed bound. The lower bound can be obtained from the best-action worst-state bound, as shown in algorithm 21.14, or some other method, such as point-based value iteration.

[11] The *heuristic search value iteration* (*HSVI*) algorithm introduced the concept of using the sawtooth-based action heuristic and gap-based observation heuristic. T. Smith and R. G. Simmons, "Heuristic Search Value Iteration for POMDPs," in *Conference on Uncertainty in Artificial Intelligence (UAI)*, 2004. The SARSOP algorithm built on this work. H. Kurniawati, D. Hsu, and W. S. Lee, "SARSOP: Efficient Point-Based POMDP Planning by Approximating Optimally Reachable Belief Spaces," in *Robotics: Science and Systems*, 2008.

```
struct SawtoothHeuristicSearch
    b     # initial belief
    δ     # gap threshold
    d     # depth
    k_max # maximum number of iterations
    k_fib # number of iterations for fast informed bound
end

function explore!(M::SawtoothHeuristicSearch, 𝒫, πhi, πlo, b, d=0)
    𝒮, 𝒜, 𝒪, γ = 𝒫.𝒮, 𝒫.𝒜, 𝒫.𝒪, 𝒫.γ
    ϵ(b') = utility(πhi, b') - utility(πlo, b')
    if d ≥ M.d || ϵ(b) ≤ M.δ / γ^d
        return
    end
    a = πhi(b)
    o = argmax(o → ϵ(update(b, 𝒫, a, o)), 𝒪)
    b' = update(b, 𝒫, a, o)
    explore!(M, 𝒫, πhi, πlo, b', d+1)
    if b' ∉ basis(𝒫)
        πhi.V[b'] = greedy(πhi, b').u
    end
    push!(πlo.Γ, backup(𝒫, πlo.Γ, b'))
end

function solve(M::SawtoothHeuristicSearch, 𝒫::POMDP)
    πfib = solve(FastInformedBound(M.k_fib), 𝒫)
    Vhi = Dict(e ⇒ utility(πfib, e) for e in basis(𝒫))
    πhi = SawtoothPolicy(𝒫, Vhi)
    πlo = LookaheadAlphaVectorPolicy(𝒫, [baws_lowerbound(𝒫)])
    for i in 1:M.k_max
        explore!(M, 𝒫, πhi, πlo, M.b)
        if utility(πhi, M.b) - utility(πlo, M.b) < M.δ
            break
        end
    end
    return πlo
end
```

Algorithm 21.14. The sawtooth heuristic search policy. The solver starts from belief b and explores to a depth d for no more than k_max iterations. It uses an upper bound obtained through the fast informed bound computed with k_fib iterations. The lower bound is obtained from the best-action worst-state bound. The gap threshold is δ.

At each iteration, we explore beliefs that are reachable from our initial belief to a maximum depth. As we explore, we update the set of belief-action pairs forming our sawtooth upper bound and the set of alpha vectors forming our lower bound. We stop exploring after a certain number of iterations or until the gap at our initial state is below a threshold $\delta > 0$.

When we encounter a belief b along our path from the initial node during our exploration, we check whether the gap at b is below a threshold δ / γ^d, where d is our current depth. If we are below that threshold, then we can stop exploring along that branch. We want the threshold to increase as d increases because the gap at b after an update is at most γ times the weighted average of the gap at the beliefs that are immediately reachable.

If the gap at b is above the threshold and we have not reached our maximum depth, then we can explore the next belief, b'. First, we determine the action a recommended by our sawtooth policy. Then, we choose the observation o that maximizes the gap at the resulting belief.[12] We recursively explore down the tree. After exploring the descendants of b', we add (b', u) to V, where u is the one-step lookahead value of b'. We add to Γ the alpha vector that results from a backup at b'. Figure 21.8 shows the tightening of the bounds.

[12] Some variants simply sample the next observations. Others select the observation that maximizes the gap weighted by its likelihood.

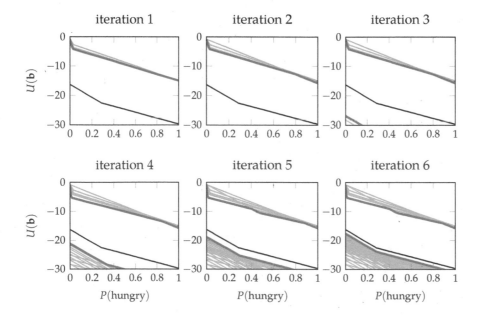

Figure 21.8. The evolution of the upper bound, represented by sawtooth pairs, and the lower bound, represented by alpha vectors for the crying baby problem. The optimal value function is shown in black.

21.9 Triangulated Value Functions

As discussed in section 20.1, a POMDP can be converted to a belief-state MDP. The state space in that belief-state MDP is continuous, corresponding to the space of possible beliefs in the original POMDP. We can approximate the value function in a way similar to what was described in chapter 8 and then apply a dynamic programming algorithm such as value iteration to the approximation. This section discusses a particular kind of local value function approximation that involves *Freudenthal triangulation*[13] over a discrete set of belief points B. This triangulation allows us to interpolate the value function at arbitrary points in the belief space. As with the sawtooth representation, we use a set of belief-utility pairs $V = \{(b, U(b)) \mid b \in B\}$ to represent our value function. This approach can be used to obtain an upper bound on the value function.

Freudenthal interpolation in belief space involves spreading the belief points in B evenly over the space, as shown in figure 21.9. The number of beliefs in B depends on the dimensionality n and granularity m of the Freudenthal triangulation:[14]

$$|B| = \frac{(m+n-1)!}{m!(n-1)!} \tag{21.17}$$

We can estimate $U(\mathbf{b})$ at an arbitrary point b by interpolating values at the discrete points in B. Similar to the simplex interpolation introduced in section 8.5, we find the set of belief points in B that form a simplex that encloses b and weight their values together. In n-dimensional belief spaces, there are up to $n+1$ vertices whose values need to be weighted together. If $b^{(1)}, \ldots, b^{(n+1)}$ are the enclosing points and $\lambda_1, \ldots, \lambda_{n+1}$ are their weights, then the estimate of the value at b is

$$U(b) = \sum_i \lambda_i U(b^{(i)}) \tag{21.18}$$

Algorithm 21.15 extracts this utility function and policy from the pairs in V.

Algorithm 21.16 applies a variation of approximate value iteration (introduced in algorithm 8.1) to our triangulated policy representation. We simply iteratively apply backups over our beliefs in B using one-step lookahead with our value function interpolation. If U is initialized with an upper bound, value iteration will result in an upper bound even after a finite number of iterations. This property holds because value functions are convex and the linear interpolation between vertices on the value function must lie on or above the underlying convex function.[15] Figure 21.10 shows an example of a policy and utility function.

[13] H. Freudenthal, "Simplizialzerlegungen von Beschränkter Flachheit," *Annals of Mathematics*, vol. 43, pp. 580–582, 1942. This triangulation method was applied to POMDPs in W. S. Lovejoy, "Computationally Feasible Bounds for Partially Observed Markov Decision Processes," *Operations Research*, vol. 39, no. 1, pp. 162–175, 1991.

[14] `FreudenthalTriangulations.jl` provides an implementation for generating these beliefs.

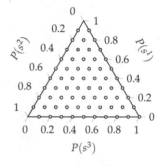

Figure 21.9. A belief state discretization using Freudenthal triangulation in $n = 3$-dimensional belief space with granularity $m = 10$.

[15] See lemma 4 of W. S. Lovejoy, "Computationally Feasible Bounds for Partially Observed Markov Decision Processes," *Operations Research*, vol. 39, no. 1, pp. 162–175, 1991.

```
struct TriangulatedPolicy
    𝒫 # POMDP problem
    V # dictionary mapping beliefs to utilities
    B # beliefs
    T # Freudenthal triangulation
end

function TriangulatedPolicy(𝒫::POMDP, m)
    T = FreudenthalTriangulation(length(𝒫.S), m)
    B = belief_vertices(T)
    V = Dict(b ⟹ 0.0 for b in B)
    return TriangulatedPolicy(𝒫, V, B, T)
end

function utility(π::TriangulatedPolicy, b)
    B, λ = belief_simplex(π.T, b)
    return sum(λi*π.V[b] for (λi, b) in zip(λ, B))
end

(π::TriangulatedPolicy)(b) = greedy(π, b).a
```

Algorithm 21.15. A policy representation using Freudenthal triangulation with granularity m. As with the sawtooth method, we maintain a dictionary that maps belief vectors to utilities. This implementation initializes the utilities to 0, but if we want to represent an upper bound, then we would need to initialize those utilities appropriately. We define a function to estimate the utility of a given belief using interpolation. We can extract a policy using greedy lookahead. The Freudenthal triangulation structure is passed the dimensionality and granularity at construction. The FreudenthalTriangulations.jl package provides the function belief_vertices, which returns B, given a particular triangulation. It also provides belief_simplex, which returns the set of enclosing points and weights for a belief.

```
struct TriangulatedIteration
    m     # granularity
    k_max # maximum number of iterations
end

function solve(M::TriangulatedIteration, 𝒫)
    π = TriangulatedPolicy(𝒫, M.m)
    U(b) = utility(π, b)
    for k in 1:M.k_max
        U′ = [greedy(𝒫, U, b).u for b in π.B]
        for (b, u′) in zip(π.B, U′)
            π.V[b] = u′
        end
    end
    return π
end
```

Algorithm 21.16. Approximate value iteration with k_max iterations using a triangulated policy with granularity m. At each iteration, we update the utilities associated with the beliefs in B using greedy one-step lookahead with triangulated utilities.

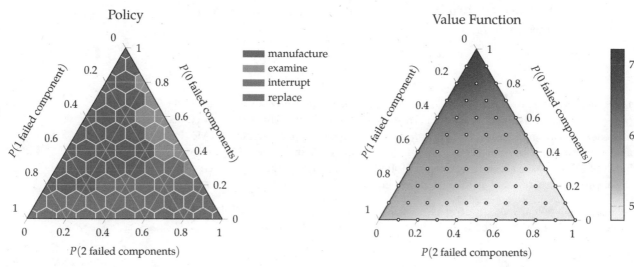

Figure 21.10. The policy and value function for the maintenance problem with granularity $m = 10$ after 11 iterations. The value function plot shows the discrete belief points as white dots. This policy approximates the exact policy given in appendix F.8.

21.10 Summary

- The QMDP algorithm assumes perfect observability after the first step, resulting in an upper bound on the true value function.

- The fast informed bound provides a tighter upper bound on the value function than QMDP by accounting for the observation model.

- Point-based value iteration provides a lower bound on the value function using alpha vectors at a finite set of beliefs.

- Randomized point-based value iteration performs updates at randomly selected points in the belief set until the values at all points in the set are improved.

- The sawtooth upper bound allows iterative improvement of the fast informed bound using an efficient point-set representation.

- Carefully selecting which belief points to use in point-based value iteration can improve the quality of the resulting policies.

- Sawtooth heuristic search attempts to tighten the upper and lower bounds of the value function represented by sawtooth pairs and alpha vectors, respectively.

- One approach to approximately solving POMDPs is to discretize the belief space, and then to apply dynamic programming to extract an upper bound on the value function and a policy.

21.11   Exercises

Exercise 21.1. Suppose that we are in a variation of the straight-line hex world problem (appendix F.1) consisting of four cells corresponding to states $s_{1:4}$. There are two actions: move left (ℓ) and move right (r). The effects of those actions are deterministic. Moving left in s_1 or moving right in s_4 gives a reward of 100 and ends the game. With a discount factor of 0.9, compute alpha vectors using QMDP. Then, using the alpha vectors, compute the approximately optimal action, given the belief $\mathbf{b} = [0.3, 0.1, 0.5, 0.1]$.

Solution: We denote the alpha vector associated with moving left as α_ℓ and the alpha vector associated with moving right as α_r. We initialize the alpha vectors to zero:

$$\alpha_\ell^{(1)} = [R(s_1, \ell), R(s_2, \ell), R(s_3, \ell), R(s_4, \ell)] = [0, 0, 0, 0]$$
$$\alpha_r^{(1)} = [R(s_1, r), R(s_2, r), R(s_3, r), R(s_4, r)] = [0, 0, 0, 0]$$

In the first iteration, since all the entries in the alpha vectors are zero, only the reward term contributes to the QMDP update (equation (21.1)):

$$\alpha_\ell^{(2)} = [100, 0, 0, 0]$$
$$\alpha_r^{(2)} = [0, 0, 0, 100]$$

In the next iteration, we apply the update, which leads to new values for s_2 for the left alpha vector and for s_3 for the right alpha vector. The updates for the left alpha vector are as follows (with the right alpha vector updates being symmetric):

$$\alpha_\ell^{(3)}(s_1) = 100 \quad \text{(terminal state)}$$
$$\alpha_\ell^{(3)}(s_2) = 0 + 0.9 \times \max(\alpha_\ell^{(2)}(s_1), \alpha_r^{(2)}(s_1)) = 90$$
$$\alpha_\ell^{(3)}(s_3) = 0 + 0.9 \times \max(\alpha_\ell^{(2)}(s_2), \alpha_r^{(2)}(s_2)) = 0$$
$$\alpha_\ell^{(3)}(s_4) = 0 + 0.9 \times \max(\alpha_\ell^{(2)}(s_3), \alpha_r^{(2)}(s_3)) = 0$$

This leads to the following:

$$\alpha_\ell^{(3)} = [100, 90, 0, 0]$$
$$\alpha_r^{(3)} = [0, 0, 90, 100]$$

In the third iteration, the updates for the left alpha vector are

$$\alpha_\ell^{(4)}(s_1) = 100 \quad \text{(terminal state)}$$
$$\alpha_\ell^{(4)}(s_2) = 0 + 0.9 \times \max(\alpha_\ell^{(3)}(s_1), \alpha_r^{(3)}(s_1)) = 90$$
$$\alpha_\ell^{(4)}(s_3) = 0 + 0.9 \times \max(\alpha_\ell^{(3)}(s_2), \alpha_r^{(3)}(s_2)) = 81$$
$$\alpha_\ell^{(4)}(s_4) = 0 + 0.9 \times \max(\alpha_\ell^{(3)}(s_3), \alpha_r^{(3)}(s_3)) = 81$$

Our alpha vectors are, then,

$$\alpha_\ell^{(4)} = [100, 90, 81, 81]$$
$$\alpha_r^{(4)} = [81, 81, 90, 100]$$

At this point, our alpha vector estimates have converged. We now determine the optimal action by maximizing the utility associated with our belief over all actions:

$$\alpha_\ell^\top b = 100 \times 0.3 + 90 \times 0.1 + 81 \times 0.5 + 81 \times 0.1 = 87.6$$
$$\alpha_r^\top b = 81 \times 0.3 + 81 \times 0.1 + 90 \times 0.5 + 100 \times 0.1 = 87.4$$

Thus, we find that moving left is the optimal action for this belief state, despite a higher probability of being on the right half of the grid world. This is due to the relatively high likelihood that we assign to being in state s_1, where we would receive a large, immediate reward by moving left.

Exercise 21.2. Recall the simplified hex world problem from exercise 21.1. Compute alpha vectors for each action using the blind lower bound. Then, using the alpha vectors, compute the value at the belief $\mathbf{b} = [0.3, 0.1, 0.5, 0.1]$.

Solution: The blind lower bound, shown in equation (21.6), is like the QMDP update, but it lacks the maximization. We initialize the components of the alpha vectors to zero and run to convergence as follows:

$$\alpha_\ell^{(2)} = [100, 0, 0, 0]$$
$$\alpha_r^{(2)} = [0, 0, 0, 100]$$

$$\alpha_\ell^{(3)} = [100, 90, 0, 0]$$
$$\alpha_r^{(3)} = [0, 0, 90, 100]$$

$$\alpha_\ell^{(4)} = [100, 90, 81, 0]$$
$$\alpha_r^{(4)} = [0, 81, 90, 100]$$

$$\alpha_\ell^{(5)} = [100, 90, 81, 72.9]$$
$$\alpha_r^{(5)} = [72.9, 81, 90, 100]$$

At this point, our alpha vector estimates have converged. We now determine the value by maximizing the utility associated with our belief over all actions:

$$\alpha_\ell^\top \mathbf{b} = 100 \times 0.3 + 90 \times 0.1 + 81 \times 0.5 + 72.9 \times 0.1 = 86.79$$
$$\alpha_r^\top \mathbf{b} = 72.9 \times 0.3 + 81 \times 0.1 + 90 \times 0.5 + 100 \times 0.1 = 84.97$$

Thus, the lower bound at $\mathbf{b}$ is 86.79.

Exercise 21.3. What is the complexity of a backup at a single belief point in point-based value iteration assuming that $|\Gamma| > |S|$?

Solution: In the process of doing a backup, we compute an $\alpha_{a,o}$ for every action a and observation o. Computing $\alpha_{a,o}$ in equation (21.8) requires finding the alpha vector α in Γ that maximizes $\alpha^\top \text{Update}(\mathbf{b}, a, o)$. A belief update, as shown in equation (19.7), is $O(|S|^2)$ because it iterates over all initial and successor states. Hence, computing $\alpha_{a,o}$ requires $O(|\Gamma||S| + |S|^2) = O(|\Gamma||S|)$ operations for a specific a and o, resulting in a total of $O(|\Gamma||S||A||O|)$ operations. We then compute α_a in equation (21.9) for every action a using these values for $\alpha_{a,o}$, requiring in a total of $O(|S|^2|A||O|)$. Finding the alpha vector α_a that maximizes $\alpha_a^\top \mathbf{b}$ requires $O(|S||A|)$ operations once we have the α_a values. Together, we have $O(|\Gamma||S||A||O|)$ operations for a backup at belief $\mathbf{b}$.

Exercise 21.4. Consider the set of belief-utility pairs given by

$$V = \{([1,0], 0), ([0,1], -10), ([0.8, 0.2], -4), ([0.4, 0.6], -6)\}$$

Using weights $w_i = 0.5$ for all i, determine the utility for belief $\mathbf{b} = [0.5, 0.5]$ using the sawtooth upper bound.

Solution: We interpolate with the belief-utility pairs. For each nonbasis belief, we start by finding the farthest basis belief, $\mathbf{e}_i$. Starting with $\mathbf{b}_3$, we compute as follows:

$$i_3 = \arg\max_j \left\| \mathbf{b} - \mathbf{e}_j \right\|_1 - \left\| \mathbf{b}_3 - \mathbf{e}_j \right\|_1$$

$$\left\| \mathbf{b} - \mathbf{e}_1 \right\|_1 - \left\| \mathbf{b}_3 - \mathbf{e}_1 \right\|_1 = \left\| \begin{bmatrix} 0.5 \\ 0.5 \end{bmatrix} - \begin{bmatrix} 1 \\ 0 \end{bmatrix} \right\|_1 - \left\| \begin{bmatrix} 0.8 \\ 0.2 \end{bmatrix} - \begin{bmatrix} 1 \\ 0 \end{bmatrix} \right\|_1$$

$$= \left\| \begin{bmatrix} -0.5 \\ 0.5 \end{bmatrix} \right\|_1 - \left\| \begin{bmatrix} -0.2 \\ 0.2 \end{bmatrix} \right\|_1$$

$$= 0.6$$

$$\left\| \mathbf{b} - \mathbf{e}_2 \right\|_1 - \left\| \mathbf{b}_3 - \mathbf{e}_2 \right\|_1 = \left\| \begin{bmatrix} 0.5 \\ 0.5 \end{bmatrix} - \begin{bmatrix} 0 \\ 1 \end{bmatrix} \right\|_1 - \left\| \begin{bmatrix} 0.8 \\ 0.2 \end{bmatrix} - \begin{bmatrix} 0 \\ 1 \end{bmatrix} \right\|_1$$

$$= \left\| \begin{bmatrix} 0.5 \\ -0.5 \end{bmatrix} \right\|_1 - \left\| \begin{bmatrix} 0.8 \\ -0.8 \end{bmatrix} \right\|_1$$

$$= -0.6$$

$$i_3 = 1$$

Thus, $\mathbf{e}_1$ is the farthest basis belief from $\mathbf{b}_3$.

For $\mathbf{b}_4$, we compute the following:

$$i_4 = \arg\max_j \left\| \mathbf{b} - \mathbf{e}_j \right\|_1 - \left\| \mathbf{b}_4 - \mathbf{e}_j \right\|_1$$

$$\left\| \mathbf{b} - \mathbf{e}_1 \right\|_1 - \left\| \mathbf{b}_3 - \mathbf{e}_1 \right\|_1 = \left\| \begin{bmatrix} 0.5 \\ 0.5 \end{bmatrix} - \begin{bmatrix} 1 \\ 0 \end{bmatrix} \right\|_1 - \left\| \begin{bmatrix} 0.4 \\ 0.6 \end{bmatrix} - \begin{bmatrix} 1 \\ 0 \end{bmatrix} \right\|_1$$

$$= \left\| \begin{bmatrix} -0.5 \\ 0.5 \end{bmatrix} \right\|_1 - \left\| \begin{bmatrix} -0.6 \\ 0.6 \end{bmatrix} \right\|_1$$

$$= -0.2$$

$$\left\| \mathbf{b} - \mathbf{e}_2 \right\|_1 - \left\| \mathbf{b}_3 - \mathbf{e}_2 \right\|_1 = \left\| \begin{bmatrix} 0.5 \\ 0.5 \end{bmatrix} - \begin{bmatrix} 0 \\ 1 \end{bmatrix} \right\|_1 - \left\| \begin{bmatrix} 0.4 \\ 0.6 \end{bmatrix} - \begin{bmatrix} 0 \\ 1 \end{bmatrix} \right\|_1$$

$$= \left\| \begin{bmatrix} 0.5 \\ -0.5 \end{bmatrix} \right\|_1 - \left\| \begin{bmatrix} 0.4 \\ -0.4 \end{bmatrix} \right\|_1$$

$$= 0.2$$

$$i_4 = 2$$

Thus, $\mathbf{e}_2$ is the farthest basis belief from $\mathbf{b}_4$.

We can compute $U(\mathbf{b})$ using our weights, along with the appropriate corners and utility pairs $(\mathbf{e}_2, \mathbf{b}_3)$ and $(\mathbf{e}_1, \mathbf{b}_4)$:

$$U_3(\mathbf{b}) = 0.5 \times -4 + 0.5 \times (-10) = -7$$
$$U_4(\mathbf{b}) = 0.5 \times -6 + 0.5 \times 0 = -3$$

Finally, we compute $U(\mathbf{b})$ by taking the minimum of $U_3(\mathbf{b})$ and $U_4(\mathbf{b})$. Thus, $U(\mathbf{b}) = -7$.

Exercise 21.5. Suppose that we have a valid lower bound represented as a set of alpha vectors Γ. Is it possible for a backup at a belief state b to result in an alpha vector $\boldsymbol{\alpha}'$, such that $\boldsymbol{\alpha}'^\top \mathbf{b}$ is lower than the utility function represented by Γ? In other words, can a backup at a belief b result in an alpha vector that assigns a lower utility to b than the value function represented by Γ?

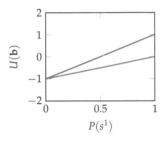

Figure 21.11. An example of how a backup at a belief can result in an alpha vector that, on its own, lowers the value at that belief compared to the original value function. The belief $\mathbf{b}$ where we do the update corresponds to $P(s^1) = 0.5$. The original value function, represented by Γ, is shown in red. The alpha vector resulting from a backup at $\mathbf{b}$ is shown in blue.

Solution: It is possible. Suppose we have only one action, observations are perfect, there is no discounting, and the state space is $\{s^0, s^1\}$. The reward is $R(s^i) = i$ for all i, and states transition deterministically to s^0. We start with a valid lower bound, $\Gamma = \{[-1, +1]\}$, as shown in red in figure 21.11. We choose $\mathbf{b} = [0.5, 0.5]$ for the belief where we do the backup. Using equation (21.9), we obtain

$$\alpha(s^0) = R(s^0) + U^\Gamma(s^0) = 0 + (-1) = -1$$
$$\alpha(s^1) = R(s^1) + U^\Gamma(s^0) = 1 + (-1) = 0$$

Hence, the alpha vector that we get after a backup is $[-1, 0]$, shown in blue in figure 21.11. The utility at $\mathbf{b}$ with that alpha vector is -0.5. However, $U^\Gamma(\mathbf{b}) = 0$, showing that backing up a belief can result in an alpha vector that represents a lower utility at that belief. This fact motivates the use of the if statement in randomized point-based value iteration (algorithm 21.8). That if statement will use either the alpha vector from the backup or the dominating alpha vector in Γ at belief $\mathbf{b}$, whichever gives the greatest utility estimate.

22 *Online Belief State Planning*

Online methods determine the optimal policy by planning from the current belief state. The belief space reachable from the current state is typically small compared with the full belief space. As introduced in the fully observable context, many online methods use variations of tree-based search up to some horizon.[1] Various strategies can be used to try to avoid the exponential computational growth with the tree depth. Although online methods require more computation per decision step during execution than offline approaches, online methods are sometimes easier to apply to high-dimensional problems.

[1] A survey is provided by S. Ross, J. Pineau, S. Paquet, and B. Chaib-draa, "Online Planning Algorithms for POMDPs," *Journal of Artificial Intelligence Research*, vol. 32, pp. 663–704, 2008.

22.1 *Lookahead with Rollouts*

Algorithm 9.1 introduced lookahead with rollouts as an online method in fully observed problems. The algorithm can be used directly for partially observed problems. It uses a function for randomly sampling the next state, which corresponds to a belief state in the context of partial observability. This function was already introduced in algorithm 21.11. Because we can use a generative model rather than an explicit model for transitions, rewards, and observations, we can accommodate problems with high-dimensional state and observation spaces.

22.2 *Forward Search*

We can apply the forward search strategy from algorithm 9.2 to partially observed problems without modification. The difference between MDPs and POMDPs is encapsulated by one-step lookahead, which branches on actions and observations, as shown in figure 22.1. The value of taking action a from belief b can be defined

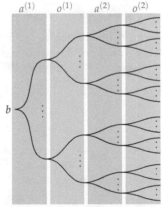

Figure 22.1. Forward search searches the action-observation-belief graph to an arbitrary finite depth in order to select the action that produces the highest expected reward. This illustration shows a search to depth 2.

recursively to a depth d:

$$Q_d(b,a) = \begin{cases} R(b,a) + \gamma \sum_o P(o \mid b,a) U_{d-1}(\text{Update}(b,a,o)) & \text{if } d > 0 \\ U(b) & \text{otherwise} \end{cases} \quad (22.1)$$

where $U_d(b) = \max_a Q_d(b,a)$. When $d = 0$, we have reached maximum depth and return the utility using the approximate value function $U(b)$, which may be obtained from one of the methods discussed in the previous chapter, heuristically chosen, or estimated from one or more rollouts. When $d > 0$, we continue to search deeper, recursing down another level. Example 22.1 shows how to combine QMDP with forward search for the machine replacement problem. Example 22.2 demonstrates forward search on the crying baby problem.

Consider applying forward search to the machine replacement problem. We can first obtain an approximate value function through QMDP (algorithm 21.2). We can then construct a `ForwardSearch` object, which was originally defined in algorithm 9.2. The call to `lookahead` within that function will use the one defined for POMDPs in algorithm 20.5. The following code applies forward search to the problem $\mathcal{P}$ from belief state $[0.5, 0.2, 0.3]$ to depth 5 using our estimate of the utility obtained from QMDP at the leaf nodes:

```
k_max = 10 # maximum number of iterations of QMDP
πQMDP = solve(QMDP(k_max), 𝒫)
d = 5 # depth
U(b) = utility(πQMDP, b)
π = ForwardSearch(𝒫, d, U)
π([0.5,0.2,0.3])
```

Example 22.1. Applying forward search to the machine replacement problem (appendix F.8).

The computation associated with the recursion in equation (22.1) grows exponentially with depth, $O(|\mathcal{A}|^d |\mathcal{O}|^d)$. Hence, forward search is generally limited to a relatively shallow depth. To go deeper, we can limit the action or observation branching. For example, if we have some domain knowledge, we may restrict the action set either at the root or farther down the tree. For the observation branching, we may restrict our consideration to a small set of likely observations—or even just the most likely observation.[2] Branching can be avoided entirely by adopting the open loop or hindsight optimization methods described in section 9.9.3 with states sampled from the current belief.

[2] R. Platt Jr., R. Tedrake, L. P. Kaelbling, and T. Lozano-Pérez, "Belief Space Planning Assuming Maximum Likelihood Observations," in *Robotics: Science and Systems*, 2010.

Consider forward search with the crying baby problem with an approximate value function given by the alpha vectors $[-3.7, -15]$ and $[-2, -21]$. Running forward search to depth 2 from the initial belief $b = [0.5, 0.5]$ proceeds as follows:

$$\begin{aligned}
Q_2(b, a_{\text{feed}}) &= R(b, a_{\text{feed}}) + \gamma(P(\text{crying} \mid b, \text{feed})U_1([1.0, 0.0]) \\
&\qquad + P(\text{quiet} \mid b, \text{feed})U_1([1.0, 0.0])) \\
&= -10 + 0.9(0.1 \times -3.2157 + 0.9 \times -3.2157) \\
&= -12.894 \\
Q_2(b, a_{\text{ignore}}) &= R(b, a_{\text{ignore}}) + \gamma(P(\text{crying} \mid b, \text{ignore})U_1([0.093, 0.907]) \\
&\qquad + P(\text{quiet} \mid b, \text{ignore})U_1([0.786, 0.214])) \\
&= -5 + 0.9(0.485 \times -15.872 + 0.515 \times -7.779) \\
&= -15.534 \\
Q_2(b, a_{\text{sing}}) &= R(b, a_{\text{sing}}) + \gamma(P(\text{crying} \mid b, \text{sing})U_1([0.0, 1.0]) \\
&\qquad + P(\text{quiet} \mid b, \text{sing})U_1([0.891, 0.109])) \\
&= -5.5 + 0.9(0.495 \times -16.8 + 0.505 \times -5.543) \\
&= -15.503
\end{aligned}$$

Recall that feeding the baby always results in a sated baby ($b = [1, 0]$), and singing to the baby ensures that it cries only if it is hungry ($b = [0, 1]$). Each U_1 value is evaluated by recursing one level deeper in equation (22.1) using $U_d(b) = \max_a Q_d(b, a)$. At maximum depth, we use the approximate value function given by the alpha vectors, $Q_0(b, a) = \max(b^\top[-3.7, -15], b^\top[-2, -21])$.

The policy predicts that feeding the baby will result in the highest expected utility, so it recommends that action.

22.3   Branch and Bound

The *branch and bound* technique originally introduced in the context of MDPs can be extended to POMDPs as well. The same algorithm in section 9.4 can be used without modification (see example 22.3), relying on the appropriate lookahead implementation to update beliefs and account for the observations. The efficiency of the algorithm still depends on the quality of the upper and lower bounds for pruning.

Although we can use domain-specific heuristics for the upper and lower bounds, as we did in the fully observed case, we can alternatively use one of the methods introduced in the previous chapter for discrete state spaces. For example, we can use the fast informed bound for the upper bound and point-based value iteration for the lower bound. So long as the lower bound $\underline{U}$ and upper bound $\overline{Q}$ are true lower and upper bounds, the result of the branch and bound algorithm will be the same as the forward search algorithm with $\underline{U}$ as the approximate value function.

In this example, we apply branch and bound to the crying baby problem with a depth of 5. The upper bound comes from the fast informed bound, and the lower bound comes from point-based value iteration. We compute the action from belief $[0.4, 0.6]$ as follows:

```
k_max = 10 # maximum number of iterations for bounds
πFIB = solve(FastInformedBound(k_max), 𝒫)
d = 5 # depth
Uhi(b) = utility(πFIB, b)
Qhi(b,a) = lookahead(𝒫, Uhi, b, a)
B = [[p, 1 - p] for p in 0.0:0.2:1.0]
πPBVI = solve(PointBasedValueIteration(B, k_max), 𝒫)
Ulo(b) = utility(πPBVI, b)
π = BranchAndBound(𝒫, d, Ulo, Qhi)
π([0.4,0.6])
```

Example 22.3. An application of branch and bound to the crying baby problem.

22.4   Sparse Sampling

Forward search sums over all possible observations, resulting in a runtime exponential in $|\mathcal{O}|$. As introduced in section 9.5, we can use sampling to avoid exhaustive summation. We can generate m observations for each action and then compute

$$Q_d(b,a) = \begin{cases} \frac{1}{m}\sum_{i=1}^{m}\left(r_a^{(i)} + \gamma U_{d-1}\left(\text{Update}(b,a,o_a^{(i)})\right)\right) & \text{if } d > 0 \\ U(b) & \text{otherwise} \end{cases} \qquad (22.2)$$

where $r_a^{(i)}$ and $o_a^{(i)}$ are the ith-sampled observation and reward associated with action a from belief b, and $U(b)$ is the value function estimate at maximum depth. We may use algorithm 9.4 without modification. The resulting complexity is $O(|\mathcal{A}|^d m^d)$.

22.5   Monte Carlo Tree Search

The *Monte Carlo tree search* approach for MDPs can be extended to POMDPs, though we cannot use the same exact implementation.[3] The input to the algorithm is a belief state b, depth d, exploration factor c, and rollout policy π.[4] The main difference between the POMDP algorithm (algorithm 22.1) and the MDP algorithm is that the counts and values are associated with *histories* instead of states. A history is a sequence of past actions and observations. For example, if we have two actions a_1 and a_2 and two observations o_1 and o_2, then a possible history could be the sequence $h = a_1 o_2 a_2 o_2 a_1 o_1$. During the execution of the algorithm, we update the value estimates $Q(h,a)$ and counts $N(h,a)$ for a set of history-action pairs.[5]

The histories associated with Q and N may be organized in a tree similar to the one in figure 22.2. The root node represents the empty history starting from the initial belief state b. During the execution of the algorithm, the tree structure expands. The layers of the tree alternate between action nodes and observation nodes. Associated with each action node are values $Q(h,a)$ and $N(h,a)$, where the history is determined by the path from the root node. As with the MDP version, when searching down the tree, the algorithm takes the action that maximizes

$$Q(h,a) + c\sqrt{\frac{\log N(h)}{N(h,a)}} \qquad (22.3)$$

where $N(h) = \sum_a N(h,a)$ is the total visit count for history h and c is an exploration parameter. Importantly, c augments the value of actions that are unexplored and underexplored, thus representing the relative trade-off between exploration and exploitation.

[3] Silver and Veness present a Monte Carlo tree search algorithm for POMDPs called *Partially Observable Monte Carlo Planning* (POMCP) and show its convergence. D. Silver and J. Veness, "Monte-Carlo Planning in Large POMDPs," in *Advances in Neural Information Processing Systems* (NIPS), 2010.

[4] Monte Carlo tree search can be implemented with a POMDP rollout policy that operates on beliefs, or on an MDP rollout policy that operates on states. Random policies are commonly used.

[5] There are many variations of the basic algorithm introduced here, including some that incorporate aspects of double progressive widening, discussed in section 9.6. Z. N. Sunberg and M. J. Kochenderfer, "Online Algorithms for POMDPs with Continuous State, Action, and Observation Spaces," in *International Conference on Automated Planning and Scheduling* (ICAPS), 2018.

```
struct HistoryMonteCarloTreeSearch
    𝒫 # problem
    N # visit counts
    Q # action value estimates
    d # depth
    m # number of simulations
    c # exploration constant
    U # value function estimate
end

function explore(π::HistoryMonteCarloTreeSearch, h)
    𝒜, N, Q, c = π.𝒫.𝒜, π.N, π.Q, π.c
    Nh = sum(get(N, (h,a), 0) for a in 𝒜)
    return argmax(a→Q[(h,a)] + c*bonus(N[(h,a)], Nh), 𝒜)
end

function simulate(π::HistoryMonteCarloTreeSearch, s, h, d)
    if d ≤ 0
        return π.U(s)
    end
    𝒫, N, Q, c = π.𝒫, π.N, π.Q, π.c
    S, 𝒜, TRO, γ = 𝒫.S, 𝒫.𝒜, 𝒫.TRO, 𝒫.γ
    if !haskey(N, (h, first(𝒜)))
        for a in 𝒜
            N[(h,a)] = 0
            Q[(h,a)] = 0.0
        end
        return π.U(s)
    end
    a = explore(π, h)
    s', r, o = TRO(s,a)
    q = r + γ*simulate(π, s', vcat(h, (a,o)), d-1)
    N[(h,a)] += 1
    Q[(h,a)] += (q-Q[(h,a)])/N[(h,a)]
    return q
end

function (π::HistoryMonteCarloTreeSearch)(b, h=[])
    for i in 1:π.m
        s = rand(SetCategorical(π.𝒫.S, b))
        simulate(π, s, h, π.d)
    end
    return argmax(a→π.Q[(h,a)], π.𝒫.𝒜)
end
```

Algorithm 22.1. Monte Carlo tree search for POMDPs from belief b. The initial history h is optional. This implementation is similar to the one in algorithm 9.5.

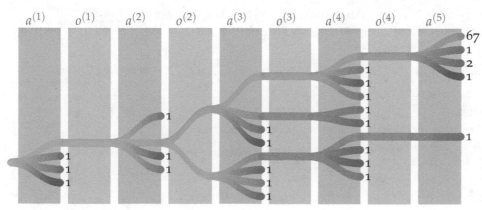

$$a^{(1)} \quad o^{(1)} \quad a^{(2)} \quad o^{(2)} \quad a^{(3)} \quad o^{(3)} \quad a^{(4)} \quad o^{(4)} \quad a^{(5)}$$

Figure 22.2. A search tree containing all the histories covered when running a Monte Carlo tree search with 100 samples on the machine replacement problem. Visitations are given beneath each action node, and color indicates node values with high values in blue and low values in red. Expanded nodes with zero visitations are not shown. This search used an exploration constant $c = 0.5$, a maximum depth $d = 5$, and a uniform random rollout policy. The initial belief is certainty in a fully working system. Monte Carlo tree search is able to avoid certain actions and instead focus samples on more promising paths.

As with the MDP version, the Monte Carlo tree search algorithm is an anytime algorithm. The loop in algorithm 22.1 can be terminated at any time, and the best solution found up to that point will be returned. With a sufficient number of iterations, the algorithm converges to the optimal action.

Prior knowledge can be incorporated into Monte Carlo tree search in how we initialize N and Q. Our implementation uses zero, but other choices are possible, including having the initialization of the action values be a function of history. The value estimates can again be obtained from simulations of a rollout policy.

The algorithm does not need to be reinitialized with each decision. The *history tree* and associated counts and value estimates can be maintained between calls. The observation node associated with the selected action and actual observation becomes the root node at the next time step.

22.6   Determinized Sparse Tree Search

Determinized sparse tree search strives to reduce the overall amount of sampling in both sparse sampling and Monte Carlo tree search by making the observation resulting from performing an action deterministic.[6] It does so by building a *determinized belief tree* from a special particle belief representation to form a sparse approximation of the true belief tree. Each particle refers to one of *m scenarios*, each of depth *d*. A scenario represents a fixed history that the particle will follow for any given sequence of actions $a^{(1)}, a^{(2)}, \ldots, a^{(d)}$. Every distinct action sequence

[6] Ye, Somani, Hsu, and Lee present a determinized sparse tree search algorithm for POMDPs called *Determinized Sparse Partially Observable Tree* (DESPOT) N. Ye, A. Somani, D. Hsu, and W. S. Lee, "DESPOT: Online POMDP Planning with Regularization," *Journal of Artificial Intelligence Research*, vol. 58, pp. 231–266, 2017. In addition, the algorithm includes branch and bound, heuristic search, and regularization techniques.

produces a distinct history under a particular scenario.[7] This determinization reduces the size of the search tree to $O(|\mathcal{A}|^d m)$. An example of a history is given in example 22.4. A determinized tree is shown in figure 22.3.

[7] A similar idea was discussed in section 9.9.3 and is related to the PEGASUS algorithm mentioned in section 11.1.

Suppose we have two states s_1 and s_2, two actions a_1 and a_2, and two observations o_1 and o_2. A possible history of depth $d = 2$ for the particle with initial state s_2 is the sequence $h = s_2 a_1 o_2 s_1 a_2 o_1$. If this history is used as a scenario, then this history is returned every time the belief tree is traversed from the initial state with the action sequence $a^{(1)} = a_1$ and $a^{(2)} = a_2$.

Example 22.4. A history and a scenario in the context of determinized sparse tree search.

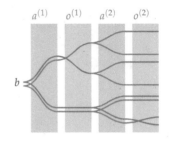

Figure 22.3. A determinized sparse search tree with two scenarios, shown in blue and purple. The line traces show the possible paths for each scenario under different action sequences.

A search tree with m scenarios up to depth d can be fully specified by a compact $m \times d$ *determinizing matrix* $\boldsymbol{\Phi}$ containing probability masses. The element Φ_{ij} contains the information needed for a particle following the ith scenario at depth j to identify its successor state and observation. Specifically, Φ_{ij} is a uniformly distributed random number that can generate the successor pair (s', o) from a state-action pair (s, a), following the distribution $P(s', o \mid s, a) = T(s' \mid s, a)O(o \mid a, s')$. We can generate a determinizing matrix by filling it with values sampled uniformly between 0 and 1.

Beliefs are represented as vectors of belief particles. Each belief particle ϕ contains a state s and indices i and j into the determinizing matrix $\boldsymbol{\Phi}$ corresponding to a scenario i and current depth j. Given a particular action a, Φ_{ij} is used to deterministically transition to successor state s' and observation o. The successor particle $\phi' = (s', i, j + 1)$ receives s' as its state and increments j by 1. Example 22.5 demonstrates this tree traversal process. The particle belief representation is implemented in algorithm 22.2 and is used in forward search in algorithm 22.3.

22.7 Gap Heuristic Search

Similar to the offline heuristic search presented in section 21.8, *gap heuristic search* uses the gap between the upper and lower bounds to guide our search toward beliefs that have uncertainty in their associated value and as an indication of when we can stop exploring. The gap at a belief b is the difference between the upper-bound and lower-bound values: $\overline{U}(b) - \underline{U}(b)$. Search algorithms with the gap heuristic select the observation that maximizes the gap because they are more likely to benefit from a belief backup. Actions are often selected according to a

Suppose that we generate a determinizing matrix Φ for a problem with four histories up to depth 3:

$$\Phi = \begin{bmatrix} 0.393 & 0.056 & 0.369 \\ 0.313 & 0.749 & 0.273 \\ 0.078 & 0.262 & 0.009 \\ 0.969 & 0.598 & 0.095 \end{bmatrix}$$

Suppose that we take action a_3 in state s_2 when at depth 2 while following history 3. The corresponding belief particle is $\phi = (2, 3, 2)$, and the determinizing value in Φ is $\Phi_{3,2} = 0.262$.

The deterministic successor action and observation are given by iterating over all successor state-observation pairs and accumulating their transition probabilities. We begin with $p = 0$ and evaluate $s' = s_1$, $o = o_1$. Suppose we get $T(s_1 \mid s_2, a_3)O(o_1 \mid a_3, s_1) = 0.1$. We increase p to 0.1, which is less than $\Phi_{3,2}$, so we continue.

Next, we evaluate $s' = s_1$, $o = o_2$. Suppose we get $T(s_1 \mid s_2, a_3)O(o_2 \mid a_3, s_2) = 0.17$. We increase p to 0.27, which is greater than $\Phi_{3,2}$. We thus deterministically proceed to $s' = s_1$, $o = o_2$ as our successor state, resulting in a new particle $\phi' = (1, 3, 3)$.

Example 22.5.   Determinized sparse tree search uses a matrix to make tree traversal deterministic for a given particle.

```
struct DeterminizedParticle
    s # state
    i # scenario index
    j # depth index
end

function successor(𝒫, Φ, ϕ, a)
    S, 𝒪, T, O = 𝒫.S, 𝒫.𝒪, 𝒫.T, 𝒫.O
    p = 0.0
    for (s′, o) in product(S, 𝒪)
        p += T(ϕ.s, a, s′) * O(a, s′, o)
        if p ≥ Φ[ϕ.i, ϕ.j]
            return (s′, o)
        end
    end
    return last(S), last(𝒪)
end

function possible_observations(𝒫, Φ, b, a)
    𝒪 = []
    for ϕ in b
        s′, o = successor(𝒫, Φ, ϕ, a)
        push!(𝒪, o)
    end
    return unique(𝒪)
end

function update(b, Φ, 𝒫, a, o)
    b′ = []
    for ϕ in b
        s′, o′ = successor(𝒫, Φ, ϕ, a)
        if o == o′
            push!(b′, DeterminizedParticle(s′, ϕ.i, ϕ.j + 1))
        end
    end
    return b′
end
```

Algorithm 22.2. The determinized particle belief update used in determinized sparse tree search for a POMDP 𝒫. Each belief b consists of particles ϕ that each encode a particular scenario and depth along the scenario. Their scenario's trajectory is determinized through a matrix Φ containing random values in $[0,1]$. Each particle ϕ represents a particular scenario i at a particular depth j, referring to the ith row and jth column of Φ.

```
struct DeterminizedSparseTreeSearch
    𝒫 # problem
    d # depth
    Φ # m×d determinizing matrix
    U # value function to use at leaf nodes
end

function determinized_sparse_tree_search(𝒫, b, d, Φ, U)
    S, 𝒜, 𝒪, T, R, O, γ = 𝒫.S, 𝒫.𝒜, 𝒫.𝒪, 𝒫.T, 𝒫.R, 𝒫.O, 𝒫.γ
    if d == 0
        return (a=nothing, u=U(b))
    end
    best = (a=nothing, u=-Inf)
    for a in 𝒜
        u = sum(R(φ.s, a) for φ in b) / length(b)
        for o in possible_observations(𝒫, Φ, b, a)
            Poba = sum(sum(O(a,s′,o)*T(φ.s,a,s′) for s′ in S)
                        for φ in b) / length(b)
            b′ = update(b, Φ, 𝒫, a, o)
            u′ = determinized_sparse_tree_search(𝒫,b′,d-1,Φ,U).u
            u += γ*Poba*u′
        end
        if u > best.u
            best = (a=a, u=u)
        end
    end
    return best
end

function determinized_belief(b, 𝒫, m)
    particles = []
    for i in 1:m
        s = rand(SetCategorical(𝒫.S, b))
        push!(particles, DeterminizedParticle(s, i, 1))
    end
    return particles
end

function (π::DeterminizedSparseTreeSearch)(b)
    particles = determinized_belief(b, π.𝒫, size(π.Φ,1))
    return determinized_sparse_tree_search(π.𝒫,particles,π.d,π.Φ,π.U).a
end
```

Algorithm 22.3. An implementation of determinized sparse tree search, a modification of forward search, for POMDPs. The policy takes a belief b in the form of a vector of probabilities, which is approximated by a vector of determinized particles by determinized_belief.

lookahead using an approximate value function. Algorithm 22.4 provides an implementation.[8]

The initial lower- and upper-bound values used in heuristic search play an important role in the algorithm's performance. Example 22.6 uses a random rollout policy for the lower bound $\underline{U}(b)$. A rollout is not guaranteed to produce a lower bound, of course, because it is based on a single trial up to a fixed depth. As the number of samples increases, it will converge to a true lower bound. That example uses the best-action best-state upper bound from equation (21.2). Many other forms of upper and lower bounds exist that can provide faster convergence, but at the cost of run time and implementation complexity. For example, using the fast informed bound (algorithm 21.3) for the upper bound can improve exploration and help reduce the gap. For the lower bound, we can use a problem-specific rollout policy to better guide the search.

[8] There are a variety of different heuristic search algorithms for POMDPs that attempt to minimize the gap. For example, see S. Ross and B. Chaib-draa, "AEMS: An Anytime Online Search Algorithm for Approximate Policy Refinement in Large POMDPs," in *International Joint Conference on Artificial Intelligence (IJCAI)*, 2007. This implementation is similar to the one used by DESPOT, referenced in the previous section.

22.8   Summary

- A simple online strategy is to perform a one-step lookahead, which considers each action taken from the current belief and estimates its expected value using an approximate value function.

- Forward search is a generalization of lookahead to arbitrary horizons, which can lead to better policies, but its computational complexity grows exponentially with the horizon.

- Branch and bound is a more efficient version of forward search that can avoid searching certain paths by placing upper and lower bounds on the value function.

- Sparse sampling is an approximation method that can reduce the computational burden of iterating over the space of all possible observations.

- Monte Carlo tree search can be adapted to POMDPs by operating over histories rather than states.

- Determinized sparse tree search uses a special form of particle belief that ensures that observations are determinized, greatly reducing the search tree.

```
struct GapHeuristicSearch
    𝒫       # problem
    Ulo     # lower bound on value function
    Uhi     # upper bound on value function
    δ       # gap threshold
    k_max   # maximum number of simulations
    d_max   # maximum depth
end

function heuristic_search(π::GapHeuristicSearch, Ulo, Uhi, b, d)
    𝒫, δ = π.𝒫, π.δ
    S, 𝒜, 𝒪, R, γ = 𝒫.S, 𝒫.𝒜, 𝒫.𝒪, 𝒫.R, 𝒫.γ
    B = Dict((a,o)⇒update(b,𝒫,a,o) for (a,o) in product(𝒜,𝒪))
    B = merge(B, Dict(()⇒copy(b)))
    for (ao, b′) in B
        if !haskey(Uhi, b′)
            Ulo[b′], Uhi[b′] = π.Ulo(b′), π.Uhi(b′)
        end
    end
    if d == 0 || Uhi[b] - Ulo[b] ≤ δ
        return
    end
    a = argmax(a → lookahead(𝒫,b′→Uhi[b′],b,a), 𝒜)
    o = argmax(o → Uhi[B[(a, o)]] - Ulo[B[(a, o)]], 𝒪)
    b′ = update(b,𝒫,a,o)
    heuristic_search(π,Ulo,Uhi,b′,d-1)
    Ulo[b] = maximum(lookahead(𝒫,b′→Ulo[b′],b,a) for a in 𝒜)
    Uhi[b] = maximum(lookahead(𝒫,b′→Uhi[b′],b,a) for a in 𝒜)
end

function (π::GapHeuristicSearch)(b)
    𝒫, k_max, d_max, δ = π.𝒫, π.k_max, π.d_max, π.δ
    Ulo = Dict{Vector{Float64}, Float64}()
    Uhi = Dict{Vector{Float64}, Float64}()
    for i in 1:k_max
        heuristic_search(π, Ulo, Uhi, b, d_max)
        if Uhi[b] - Ulo[b] < δ
            break
        end
    end
    return argmax(a → lookahead(𝒫,b′→Ulo[b′],b,a), 𝒫.𝒜)
end
```

Algorithm 22.4. An implementation of heuristic search that uses bounds, a gap criterion, and initial lower and upper bounds on the value function. We update a dictionary Ulo and Uhi to maintain the lower and upper bounds on the value function as specific beliefs. At belief b, the gap is Uhi[b] - Ulo[b]. Exploration stops when the gap is smaller than the threshold δ or the maximum depth d_max is reached. A maximum number of iterations k_max is allotted to search.

The following code demonstrates how to apply gap heuristic search to the crying baby problem.

Example 22.6. The use of gap heuristic search lower and upper bounds for the crying baby problem over iterations of heuristic search.

```
δ = 0.001  # gap threshold
k_max = 5  # maximum number of iterations
d_max = 10 # maximum depth
πrollout(b) = rand(𝒜) # random rollout policy
Ulo(b) = rollout(𝒫, b, πrollout, d_max) # initial lower bound
Rmax = maximum(R(s,a) for (s,a) in product(𝒮,𝒜)) # max reward
Uhi(b) = Rmax / (1.0 - 𝒫.γ) # best action best state upper bound
π = GapHeuristicSearch(𝒫, Ulo, Uhi, δ, k_max, d_max)
π([0.5, 0.5]) # evaluate at initial belief point
```

Here, we show six iterations of heuristic search with an initial belief b of $[0.5, 0.5]$. In each iteration, the upper bound is shown in green and the lower bound is shown in blue.

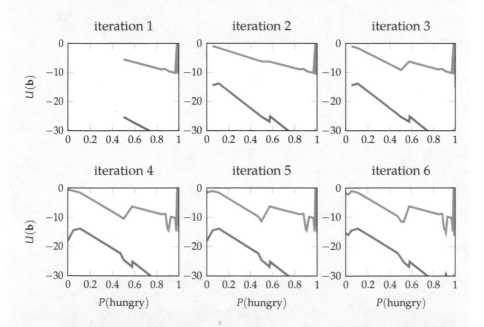

The jagged bounds are due to some beliefs not being reexplored based on the action and observation selection. In the bottom row, we see that it has explored many of the beliefs once, but the bounds are still loose. Heuristic search seeks to reduce the maximum gap.

- Heuristic search intelligently selects action-observation pairs to explore regions with a high gap between the upper and lower bounds on the value function that it maintains.

22.9   Exercises

Exercise 22.1. Suppose we have $\mathcal{A} = \{a^1, a^2\}$ and a belief $\mathbf{b} = [0.5, 0.5]$. The reward is always 1. The observation function is given by $P(o^1 \mid a^1) = 0.8$ and $P(o^1 \mid a^2) = 0.4$. We have an approximate value function represented by an alpha vector $\boldsymbol{\alpha} = [-3, 4]$. With $\gamma = 0.9$, use forward search to a depth of 1 to compute $U(\mathbf{b})$. Use the following updated beliefs in the calculation:

a	o	Update$(\mathbf{b}, a, o)$
a^1	o^1	$[0.3, 0.7]$
a^2	o^1	$[0.2, 0.8]$
a^1	o^2	$[0.5, 0.5]$
a^2	o^2	$[0.8, 0.2]$

Solution: We need to calculate the action value function at depth 1 according to equation (22.1):

$$Q_d(\mathbf{b}, a) = R(\mathbf{b}, a) + \gamma \sum_o P(o \mid b, a) U_{d-1}(\text{Update}(\mathbf{b}, a, o))$$

First, we calculate the utility for the updated beliefs:

$$U_0(\text{Update}(\mathbf{b}, a^1, o^1)) = \boldsymbol{\alpha}^\top \mathbf{b}' = 0.3 \times -3 + 0.7 \times 4 = 1.9$$
$$U_0(\text{Update}(\mathbf{b}, a^2, o^1)) = 0.2 \times -3 + 0.8 \times 4 = 2.6$$
$$U_0(\text{Update}(\mathbf{b}, a^1, o^2)) = 0.5 \times -3 + 0.5 \times 4 = 0.5$$
$$U_0(\text{Update}(\mathbf{b}, a^2, o^2)) = 0.8 \times -3 + 0.2 \times 4 = -1.6$$

Second, we compute the action value function for both actions:

$$Q_1(\mathbf{b}, a^1) = 1 + 0.9((P(o^1 \mid \mathbf{b}, a^1) U_0(\text{Update}(\mathbf{b}, a^1, o^1)) + (P(o^2 \mid \mathbf{b}, a^1) U_0(\text{Update}(\mathbf{b}, a^1, o^2))))$$
$$= 1 + 0.9(0.8 \times 1.9 + 0.2 \times 0.5) = 2.458$$
$$Q_1(\mathbf{b}, a^2) = 1 + 0.9((P(o^1 \mid \mathbf{b}, a^2) U_0(\text{Update}(\mathbf{b}, a^2, o^1)) + (P(o^2 \mid \mathbf{b}, a^2) U_0(\text{Update}(\mathbf{b}, a^2, o^2))))$$
$$= 1 + 0.9(0.4 \times 2.6 + 0.6 \times -1.6) = 1.072$$

Finally, we have $U_1(\mathbf{b}) = \max_a Q_1(\mathbf{b}, a) = 2.458$.

Exercise 22.2. Using the following trajectory samples, compute the action value function for belief $\mathbf{b}$ and actions a^1 and a^2 based on sparse sampling to depth 1. Use the following updated beliefs, discount factor $\gamma = 0.9$, and approximate value function represented by an alpha vector $\boldsymbol{\alpha} = [10, 1]$.

a	o	r	Update($\mathbf{b}, a, o$)
1	1	0	$[0.47, 0.53]$
2	1	1	$[0.22, 0.78]$
1	2	1	$[0.49, 0.51]$
2	1	1	$[0.22, 0.78]$
2	2	1	$[0.32, 0.68]$
1	2	1	$[0.49, 0.51]$

Solution: We first calculate the utility for the updated beliefs:

a	o	r	Update($\mathbf{b}, a, o_a$)	U_0(Update($\mathbf{b}, a, o$))
1	1	0	$[0.47, 0.53]$	5.23
2	1	1	$[0.22, 0.78]$	2.98
1	2	1	$[0.49, 0.51]$	5.41
2	1	1	$[0.22, 0.78]$	2.98
2	2	1	$[0.32, 0.68]$	3.88
1	2	1	$[0.49, 0.51]$	5.41

Then, we can compute the action value function over all actions using equation (22.2):

$$Q_1(\mathbf{b}, a^1) = \frac{1}{3}(0 + 1 + 1 + 0.9(5.23 + 5.41 + 5.41)) = 5.48$$

$$Q_1(\mathbf{b}, a^2) = \frac{1}{3}(1 + 1 + 1 + 0.9(2.98 + 2.98 + 3.88)) = 3.95$$

Exercise 22.3. Consider example 22.5. Suppose we have the following transition functions:

$$T(s_2 \mid s_1, a_3) = 0.4 \qquad O(o_1 \mid s_1, a_3) = 0.6$$
$$T(s_3 \mid s_1, a_3) = 0.45 \qquad O(o_2 \mid s_1, a_3) = 0.5$$

What is the path taken by a particle associated with $\phi = (1, 4, 2)$ if we take action a_3?

Solution: From the determinizing matrix, our determinizing value is $\Phi_{4,2} = 0.598$ and we are in state s_1. Then, we calculate p as follows:

$$p \leftarrow T(s_2 \mid s_1, a_3)O(o_1 \mid s_1, a_3) = 0.4 \times 0.6 = 0.24$$
$$p \leftarrow p + T(s_2 \mid s_1, a_3)O(o_2 \mid s_1, a_3) = 0.24 + 0.4 \times 0.5 = 0.44$$
$$p \leftarrow p + T(s_3 \mid s_1, a_3)O(o_1 \mid s_1, a_3) = 0.44 + 0.45 \times 0.6 = 0.71$$

We stop our iteration because $p > 0.598$. Thus, from our final iteration, we proceed to (s_3, o_1).

Exercise 22.4. Summarize the techniques covered in this chapter to reduce branching over actions.

Solution: Branch and bound can reduce action branching by using an upper bound on the value function. It skips actions that cannot improve on the value obtained from actions that it explored earlier. Gap heuristic search and Monte Carlo tree search use approximations of action values to guide the selection of actions during exploration.

Exercise 22.5. Summarize the techniques covered in this chapter to reduce branching over observations.

Solution: Sparse sampling reduces observation branching by sampling only a small number of observations. Observations are sampled from $P(o \mid b, a)$, which means that observations that have greater probability are more likely to be sampled. Determinized sparse tree search uses a similar approach, but the sampling occurs once and is then fixed. Branching over observations can also be reduced based on the lookahead value $U(b')$. Gap heuristic search evaluates the gap and avoids branching on observations for which we have high confidence in the value function.

23 Controller Abstractions

This chapter introduces controller representations for POMDP policies, which allow policies to maintain their own internal state. These representations can improve scalability over previous methods that enumerate over belief points. This chapter presents algorithms that construct controllers using policy iteration, nonlinear programming, and gradient ascent.

23.1 Controllers

A *controller* is a policy representation that maintains its own internal state. It is represented as a graph consisting of a finite set of nodes X.[1] The active *node* changes as actions are taken and new observations are made. Having a finite set of nodes makes these controllers more computationally tractable than belief-point methods that must consider the reachable belief space.

Actions are selected according to an *action distribution* $\psi(a \mid x)$ that depends on the current node. When selecting an action, in addition to transitioning to an unobserved s' and receiving an observation o, the control state also advances according to a *successor distribution* $\eta(x' \mid x, a, o)$. Figure 23.1 shows how these distributions are used as a controller policy is followed. Algorithm 23.1 provides an implementation, and example 23.1 shows a controller for the crying baby problem.

Controllers generalize conditional plans, which were introduced in section 20.2. Conditional plans represent policies as trees, with each node deterministically assigning an action and each edge specifying a unique successor node. Controllers represent policies as directed graphs, and actions may have stochastic transitions to multiple successor nodes. Example 23.2 compares these two representations.

[1] Such a policy representation is also called a *finite state controller*. We will refer to the controller states as "nodes" rather than "states" to reduce ambiguity with the environment state.

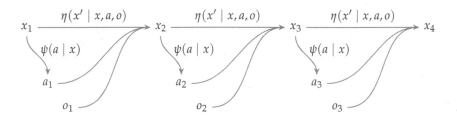

Figure 23.1. In a controller representation, the action is sampled from the action selection distribution. This action, as well as the subsequent observation it produces, are used alongside the previous node x to produce the successor node x'.

We can construct a simple controller for the crying baby problem (appendix F.7). This example is shown here as a graph with two nodes, x^1 and x^2. When in x^1, the controller always ignores the baby. When in x^2, the controller always feeds the baby. If the baby cries, we always transition to x^2, and if the baby is quiet, we always transition to x^1.

Example 23.1. A two-node controller for the crying baby problem. This compact representation captures a straightforward solution to the crying baby problem (namely, to react immediately to the most recent observation).

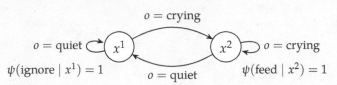

```
mutable struct ControllerPolicy
    𝒫 # problem
    X # set of controller nodes
    ψ # action selection distribution
    η # successor selection distribution
end

function (π::ControllerPolicy)(x)
    𝒜, ψ = π.𝒫.𝒜, π.ψ
    dist = [ψ[x, a] for a in 𝒜]
    return rand(SetCategorical(𝒜, dist))
end

function update(π::ControllerPolicy, x, a, o)
    X, η = π.X, π.η
    dist = [η[x, a, o, x'] for x' in X]
    return rand(SetCategorical(X, dist))
end
```

Algorithm 23.1. A finite state controller policy representation for a POMDP $\mathcal{P}$. The nodes in X are an abstract representation of reachable beliefs. Actions and controller successor nodes are selected stochastically. Given a node x, actions are selected following the distribution ψ. The function π(x) implements this mechanism to stochastically select actions. After performing action a in node x and observing observation o, the successor is selected following the distribution η. The function update implements this mechanism to stochastically select successor nodes.

Consider a three-step conditional plan (left) compared with the more general, two-node finite state controller (right) from example 23.1. In this case, actions and successors are selected deterministically. The deterministic action is marked in the center of a node, and the outgoing edges represent the deterministic successor nodes. This problem has two actions (a^1 and a^2) and two observations (o^1 and o^2).

Example 23.2. A comparison of a simple conditional plan with a simple deterministic controller.

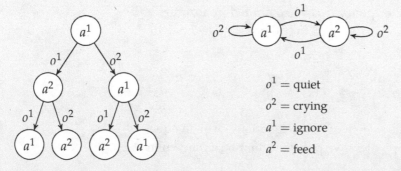

$o^1 = $ quiet
$o^2 = $ crying
$a^1 = $ ignore
$a^2 = $ feed

The conditional plan performs action a^1 first, toggles the previously chosen action if it observes o^1, and preserves the previously chosen action if it observes o^2. The controller performs the same logic, with five fewer controller nodes. Moreover, the controller represents the described infinite horizon policy perfectly with only two nodes (compared to seven). The conditional plan cannot capture this infinite horizon policy because it would require a tree of infinite depth.

Controllers have several advantages over conditional plans. First, controllers can provide a more compact representation. The number of nodes in a conditional plan grows exponentially with depth, but this need not be the case with finite state controllers. The approximation methods from previous chapters might also not be as efficient because they must maintain a large set of beliefs and corresponding alpha vectors. Controllers can be much more compact, considering infinitely many possible reachable beliefs with a small, finite number of nodes. Another advantage of controllers is that they do not require that a belief be maintained. Each controller node corresponds to a subset of the belief space. These subsets are not necessarily mutually exclusive. A controller transitions between these subsets that together cover the reachable belief space. The controller itself selects a new node based on each observation rather than relying on a belief update, which can be expensive for some domains.

The utility of following a controller policy can be computed by forming a product MDP whose state space is $X \times \mathcal{S}$. The value of being in state s with node x active is

$$U(x,s) = \sum_a \psi(a \mid x) \left(R(s,a) + \gamma \sum_{s'} T(s' \mid s,a) \sum_o O(o \mid a,s') \sum_{x'} \eta(x' \mid x,a,o) U(x',s') \right) \qquad (23.1)$$

Policy evaluation involves solving the system of linear equations given in equation (23.1). Alternatively, we can apply iterative policy evaluation as shown in algorithm 23.2.

If a belief is known, then the current value is

$$U(x,b) = \sum_s b(s) U(x,s) \qquad (23.2)$$

We can think of $U(x,s)$ as defining a set of alpha vectors, one for each node x in X. Each alpha vector α_x is defined by $\alpha_x(s) = U(x,s)$. The current value for a given alpha vector is $U(x,b) = \mathbf{b}^\top \alpha_x$.

Given a controller and an initial belief, we can select an initial node by maximizing as follows:

$$x^* = \arg\max_x U(x,b) = \arg\max_x \mathbf{b}^\top \alpha_x \qquad (23.3)$$

```
function utility(π::ControllerPolicy, U, x, s)
    𝒮, 𝒜, 𝒪 = π.𝒫.𝒮, π.𝒫.𝒜, π.𝒫.𝒪
    T, O, R, γ = π.𝒫.T, π.𝒫.O, π.𝒫.R, π.𝒫.γ
    X, ψ, η = π.X, π.ψ, π.η
    U′(a,s′,o) = sum(η[x,a,o,x′]*U[x′,s′] for x′ in X)
    U′(a,s′) = T(s,a,s′)*sum(O(a,s′,o)*U′(a,s′,o) for o in 𝒪)
    U′(a) = R(s,a) + γ*sum(U′(a,s′) for s′ in 𝒮)
    return sum(ψ[x,a]*U′(a) for a in 𝒜)
end

function iterative_policy_evaluation(π::ControllerPolicy, k_max)
    𝒮, X = π.𝒫.𝒮, π.X
    U = Dict((x, s) ⇒ 0.0 for x in X, s in 𝒮)
    for k in 1:k_max
        U = Dict((x, s) ⇒ utility(π, U, x, s) for x in X, s in 𝒮)
    end
    return U
end
```

Algorithm 23.2. An algorithm for performing iterative policy evaluation to compute the utility of a finite state controller π with k_max iterations. The utility function performs a single-step evaluation for the current controller node x and state s following equation (23.1). This algorithm was adapted from algorithm 7.3, which applies iterative policy evaluation to MDPs.

23.2   Policy Iteration

Section 20.5 showed how to incrementally add nodes in a conditional plan to arrive at optimal finite horizon policy (algorithm 20.8). This section shows how to incrementally add nodes to a controller to optimize for infinite horizon problems. Although the policy representation is different, the version of policy iteration for partially observable problems introduced in this section[2] has some similarities with the policy iteration algorithm for fully observed problems (section 7.4).

Policy iteration (algorithm 23.3) begins with any initial controller and then iterates between policy evaluation and policy improvement. In policy evaluation, we evaluate the utilities $U(x,s)$ by solving equation (23.1). In policy improvement, we introduce new nodes to our controller. Specifically, we introduce a new node x' for every combination of deterministic action assignments $\psi(a_i \mid x') = 1$ and deterministic successor selection distributions $\eta(x \mid x', a, o)$. This process adds $|\mathcal{A}||X^{(k)}|^{|\mathcal{O}|}$ new controller nodes to the set of nodes $X^{(k)}$ at iteration k.[3] An improvement step is demonstrated in example 23.3.

Policy improvement cannot worsen the expected value of the controller policy. The value of any nodes in $X^{(k)}$ remain unchanged, as they and their reachable successor nodes remain unchanged. It is guaranteed that if $X^{(k)}$ is not an optimal controller, then at least one of the new nodes introduced in policy improvement

[2] The policy iteration method given here was given by E. A. Hansen, "Solving POMDPs by Searching in Policy Space," in *Conference on Uncertainty in Artificial Intelligence* (*UAI*), 1998.

[3] Adding all possible combinations is often not feasible. An alternative algorithm called *bounded policy iteration* adds only one node. P. Poupart and C. Boutilier, "Bounded Finite State Controllers," in *Advances in Neural Information Processing Systems* (*NIPS*), 2003. Algorithms can also add a number in between. *Monte Carlo value iteration*, for example, adds $O(n|\mathcal{A}||X^{(k)}|)$ new nodes at each iteration k, where n is a parameter. H. Bai, D. Hsu, W. S. Lee, and V. A. Ngo, "Monte Carlo Value Iteration for Continuous-State POMDPs," in *International Workshop on the Algorithmic Foundations of Robotics* (*WAFR*), 2011.

```
struct ControllerPolicyIteration
    k_max    # number of iterations
    eval_max # number of evaluation iterations
end

function solve(M::ControllerPolicyIteration, 𝒫::POMDP)
    𝒜, 𝒪, k_max, eval_max = 𝒫.𝒜, 𝒫.𝒪, M.k_max, M.eval_max
    X = [1]
    ψ = Dict((x, a) ⇒ 1.0 / length(𝒜) for x in X, a in 𝒜)
    η = Dict((x, a, o, x′) ⇒ 1.0 for x in X, a in 𝒜, o in 𝒪, x′ in X)
    π = ControllerPolicy(𝒫, X, ψ, η)
    for i in 1:k_max
        prevX = copy(π.X)
        U = iterative_policy_evaluation(π, eval_max)
        policy_improvement!(π, U, prevX)
        prune!(π, U, prevX)
    end
    return π
end

function policy_improvement!(π::ControllerPolicy, U, prevX)
    S, 𝒜, 𝒪 = π.𝒫.S, π.𝒫.𝒜, π.𝒫.𝒪
    X, ψ, η = π.X, π.ψ, π.η
    repeatX𝒪 = fill(X, length(𝒪))
    assign𝒜X′ = vec(collect(product(𝒜, repeatX𝒪...)))
    for ax′ in assign𝒜X′
        x, a = maximum(X) + 1, ax′[1]
        push!(X, x)
        successor(o) = ax′[findfirst(isequal(o), 𝒪) + 1]
        U′(o,s′) = U[successor(o), s′]
        for s in S
            U[x, s] = lookahead(π.𝒫, U′, s, a)
        end
        for a′ in 𝒜
            ψ[x, a′] = a′ == a ? 1.0 : 0.0
            for (o, x′) in product(𝒪, prevX)
                η[x, a′, o, x′] = x′ == successor(o) ? 1.0 : 0.0
            end
        end
    end
    for (x, a, o, x′) in product(X, 𝒜, 𝒪, X)
        if !haskey(η, (x, a, o, x′))
            η[x, a, o, x′] = 0.0
        end
    end
end
```

Algorithm 23.3. Policy iteration for a POMDP 𝒫 given a fixed number of iterations k_max and number of policy evaluation iterations eval_max. The algorithm iteratively applies policy evaluation (algorithm 23.2) and policy improvement. Pruning is implemented in algorithm 23.4.

We can apply policy improvement to the crying baby controller from example 23.1. The actions are $\mathcal{A} = \{\text{feed}, \text{sing}, \text{ignore}\}$ and observations are $\mathcal{O} = \{\text{crying}, \text{quiet}\}$. The policy improvement backup step results in $|\mathcal{A}||X^{(1)}|^{|\mathcal{O}|} = 3 \times 2^2 = 12$ new nodes. The new controller policy has nodes $\{x^1, \ldots, x^{14}\}$ and distributions as follows:

Node	Action	Successors (for all a below)
x^3	$\psi(\text{feed} \mid x^3) = 1$	$\eta(x^1 \mid x^3, a, \text{crying}) = \eta(x^1 \mid x^3, a, \text{quiet}) = 1$
x^4	$\psi(\text{feed} \mid x^4) = 1$	$\eta(x^1 \mid x^4, a, \text{crying}) = \eta(x^2 \mid x^4, a, \text{quiet}) = 1$
x^5	$\psi(\text{feed} \mid x^5) = 1$	$\eta(x^2 \mid x^5, a, \text{crying}) = \eta(x^1 \mid x^5, a, \text{quiet}) = 1$
x^6	$\psi(\text{feed} \mid x^6) = 1$	$\eta(x^2 \mid x^6, a, \text{crying}) = \eta(x^2 \mid x^6, a, \text{quiet}) = 1$
x^7	$\psi(\text{sing} \mid x^7) = 1$	$\eta(x^1 \mid x^7, a, \text{crying}) = \eta(x^1 \mid x^7, a, \text{quiet}) = 1$
x^8	$\psi(\text{sing} \mid x^8) = 1$	$\eta(x^1 \mid x^8, a, \text{crying}) = \eta(x^2 \mid x^8, a, \text{quiet}) = 1$
$\vdots$	$\vdots$	$\vdots$

We have the following controller, with the new nodes in blue and the original two nodes in black:

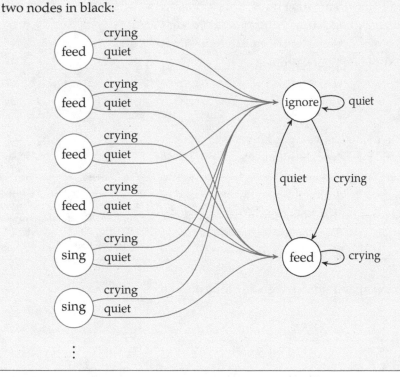

Example 23.3. An illustration of an improvement step as part of policy iteration on the crying baby problem with a controller policy representation.

will have better expected values for some states, and thus the overall controller must be improved.

Many of the nodes added during policy improvement tend not to improve the policy. Pruning is conducted after policy evaluation to eliminate unnecessary nodes. Doing so does not degrade the optimal value function of the controller. Pruning methods can help reduce the exponential growth in nodes that comes with the improvement step. In some cases, pruning can enable loops to form, resulting in compact controllers.

We prune any new nodes that are identical to existing nodes. We also prune any new nodes that are *dominated* by other nodes. A node x is dominated by another node x' when

$$U(x,s) \leq U(x',s) \quad \text{for all } s \tag{23.4}$$

Existing nodes can be pruned as well. Whenever a new node dominates an existing node, we prune the existing node from the controller. Any transitions to the deleted node are instead rerouted to the dominating node. This process is identical to pruning the new node instead and updating the dominated node's action and successor links to those of the new node. Example 23.4 demonstrates evaluation, expansion, and pruning on the crying baby problem.

23.3   *Nonlinear Programming*

The policy improvement problem can be framed as a single, large, *nonlinear programming* formulation (algorithm 23.5) that involves simultaneously optimizing ψ and η across all nodes.[4] This formulation allows general-purpose solvers to be applied. The nonlinear programming method directly searches the space of controllers to maximize the utility of a given initial belief while satisfying the Bellman expectation equation, equation (23.1). There is no alternating between policy evaluation and policy improvement steps, and the controller node count remains fixed.

We use x^1 to denote the initial node corresponding to the given initial belief b. The optimization problem is then

[4] C. Amato, D.S. Bernstein, and S. Zilberstein, "Optimizing Fixed-Size Stochastic Controllers for POMDPs and Decentralized POMDPs," *Autonomous Agents and Multi-Agent Systems*, vol. 21, no. 3, pp. 293–320, 2010.

```
function prune!(π::ControllerPolicy, U, prevX)
    S, 𝒜, 𝒪, X, ψ, η = π.𝒫.S, π.𝒫.𝒜, π.𝒫.𝒪, π.X, π.ψ, π.η
    newX, removeX = setdiff(X, prevX), []
    # prune dominated from previous nodes
    dominated(x,x′) = all(U[x,s] ≤ U[x′,s] for s in S)
    for (x,x′) in product(prevX, newX)
        if x′ ∉ removeX && dominated(x, x′)
            for s in S
                U[x,s] = U[x′,s]
            end
            for a in 𝒜
                ψ[x,a] = ψ[x′,a]
                for (o,x′′) in product(𝒪, X)
                    η[x,a,o,x′′] = η[x′,a,o,x′′]
                end
            end
            push!(removeX, x′)
        end
    end
    # prune identical from previous nodes
    identical_action(x,x′) = all(ψ[x,a] ≈ ψ[x′,a] for a in 𝒜)
    identical_successor(x,x′) = all(η[x,a,o,x′′] ≈ η[x′,a,o,x′′]
        for a in 𝒜, o in 𝒪, x′′ in X)
    identical(x,x′) = identical_action(x,x′) && identical_successor(x,x′)
    for (x,x′) in product(prevX, newX)
        if x′ ∉ removeX && identical(x,x′)
            push!(removeX, x′)
        end
    end
    # prune dominated from new nodes
    for (x,x′) in product(X, newX)
        if x′ ∉ removeX && dominated(x′,x) && x ≠ x′
            push!(removeX, x′)
        end
    end
    # update controller
    π.X = setdiff(X, removeX)
    π.ψ = Dict(k ⇒ v for (k,v) in ψ if k[1] ∉ removeX)
    π.η = Dict(k ⇒ v for (k,v) in η if k[1] ∉ removeX)
end
```

Algorithm 23.4. The pruning step of policy iteration. It reduces the number of nodes in the current policy π, using the utilities U computed by policy evaluation and the previous node list, prevX. Its first step replaces any point-wise dominated previous nodes by their improved nodes, marking the redundant node as now dominated. The second step marks any newly added nodes that are identical to previous nodes. The third step marks any point-wise dominated new nodes. Finally, all marked nodes are pruned.

Recall example 23.3. Here, we show the first iteration of policy iteration using the same initial controller. It consists of the two main steps: policy evaluation (left) and policy improvement (center), as well as the optional pruning step (right).

Example 23.4. Policy iteration, illustrating the evaluation, improvement, and pruning steps on the crying baby domain with a controller policy representation.

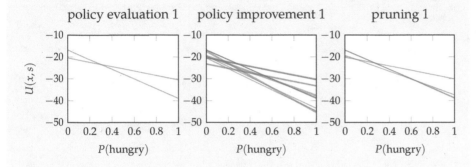

The second iteration of policy iteration follows the same pattern:

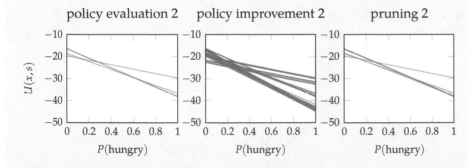

The utility has greatly improved after the second iteration, to near-optimal values. We see that the prune step removes dominated and duplicate nodes from previous iterations, as well as the current iteration's new nodes.

$$\underset{U,\psi,\eta}{\text{maximize}} \quad \sum_s b(s)U(x^1,s)$$

$$\text{subject to} \quad U(x,s) = \sum_a \psi(a \mid x)\left(R(s,a) + \gamma \sum_{s'} T(s' \mid s,a) \sum_o O(o \mid a,s') \sum_{x'} \eta(x' \mid x,a,o)U(x',s') \right)$$

$$\text{for all } x,s$$

$$\psi(a \mid x) \geq 0 \quad \text{for all } x,a$$

$$\sum_a \psi(a \mid x) = 1 \quad \text{for all } x$$

$$\eta(x' \mid x,a,o) \geq 0 \quad \text{for all } x,a,o,x'$$

$$\sum_{x'} \eta(x' \mid x,a,o) = 1 \quad \text{for all } x,a,o$$

(23.5)

This problem can be written as a *quadratically constrained linear program (QCLP)*, which can be solved effectively using a dedicated solver.[5] Example 23.5 demonstrates this approach.

[5] Solving a general QCLP is NP-hard, but dedicated solvers offer efficient approximations.

23.4 Gradient Ascent

A fixed-size controller policy can be iteratively improved using gradient ascent (covered in appendix A.11).[6] Although the gradient is challenging to compute, this opens up controller optimization to a wide variety of gradient-based optimization techniques. Algorithm 23.6 implements controller gradient ascent using algorithm 23.7.

[6] N. Meuleau, K.-E. Kim, L. P. Kaelbling, and A. R. Cassandra, "Solving POMDPs by Searching the Space of Finite Policies," in *Conference on Uncertainty in Artificial Intelligence (UAI)*, 1999.

Consider an explicit description of the nonlinear problem from section 23.3. For initial belief b and an arbitrary initial controller node x^1, we seek to maximize as follows:

$$\sum_s b(s)U(x^1,s) \tag{23.6}$$

with the utility $U(x,s)$ defined by the Bellman optimality equation for all x and s:

$$U(x,s) = \sum_a \psi(a \mid x)\left(R(s,a) + \gamma \sum_{s'} T(s' \mid s,a) \sum_o O(o \mid a,s') \sum_{x'} \eta(x' \mid x,a,o)U(x',s') \right) \tag{23.7}$$

In addition, ψ and η must be proper probability distributions. To apply gradient ascent, it is more convenient to rewrite this problem using linear algebra.

```
struct NonlinearProgramming
    b # initial belief
    ℓ # number of nodes
end

function tensorform(𝒫::POMDP)
    S, 𝒜, 𝒪, R, T, O = 𝒫.S, 𝒫.𝒜, 𝒫.𝒪, 𝒫.R, 𝒫.T, 𝒫.O
    S′ = eachindex(S)
    𝒜′ = eachindex(𝒜)
    𝒪′ = eachindex(𝒪)
    R′ = [R(s,a) for s in S, a in 𝒜]
    T′ = [T(s,a,s′) for s in S, a in 𝒜, s′ in S]
    O′ = [O(a,s′,o) for a in 𝒜, s′ in S, o in 𝒪]
    return S′, 𝒜′, 𝒪′, R′, T′, O′
end

function solve(M::NonlinearProgramming, 𝒫::POMDP)
    x1, X = 1, collect(1:M.ℓ)
    𝒫, γ, b = 𝒫, 𝒫.γ, M.b
    S, 𝒜, 𝒪, R, T, O = tensorform(𝒫)
    model = Model(Ipopt.Optimizer)
    @variable(model, U[X,S])
    @variable(model, ψ[X,𝒜] ≥ 0)
    @variable(model, η[X,𝒜,𝒪,X] ≥ 0)
    @objective(model, Max, b·U[x1,:])
    @NLconstraint(model, [x=X,s=S],
        U[x,s] == (sum(ψ[x,a]*(R[s,a] + γ*sum(T[s,a,s′]*sum(O[a,s′,o]
        *sum(η[x,a,o,x′]*U[x′,s′] for x′ in X)
        for o in 𝒪) for s′ in S)) for a in 𝒜)))
    @constraint(model, [x=X], sum(ψ[x,:]) == 1)
    @constraint(model, [x=X,a=𝒜,o=𝒪], sum(η[x,a,o,:]) == 1)
    optimize!(model)
    ψ′, η′ = value.(ψ), value.(η)
    return ControllerPolicy(𝒫, X,
        Dict((x, 𝒫.𝒜[a]) ⟹ ψ′[x, a] for x in X, a in 𝒜),
        Dict((x, 𝒫.𝒜[a], 𝒫.𝒪[o], x′) ⟹ η′[x, a, o, x′]
            for x in X, a in 𝒜, o in 𝒪, x′ in X))
end
```

Algorithm 23.5. A nonlinear programming approach to compute the optimal fixed-size controller policy for POMDP 𝒫 starting at initial belief b. The size of the finite state controller is specified by the number of nodes ℓ.

Here are optimal fixed-size controllers computed using nonlinear programming for the crying baby problem with $b_0 = [0.5, 0.5]$. The top node is x_1.

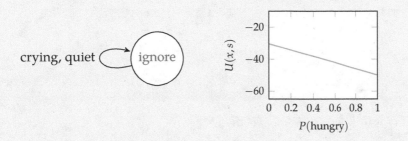

controller utility ($k = 1$)

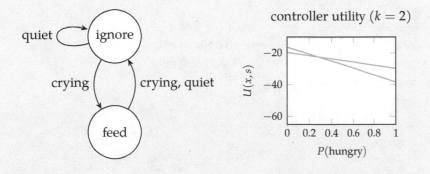

controller utility ($k = 2$)

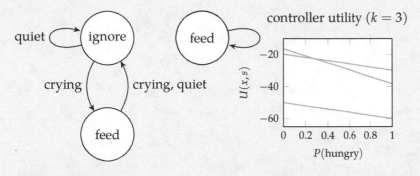

controller utility ($k = 3$)

Example 23.5. The nonlinear programming algorithm for controllers with a fixed size of k set to 1, 2, and 3. Each row shows the policy and its corresponding utilities (alpha vectors) on the left and right, respectively. The stochastic controllers are shown as circles, with the most likely action in the middle. The outgoing edges show successor node selections given an observation. The stochasticity in node actions and successors are shown as opacity (more opaque is higher probability, more transparent is lower probability).

With $k = 1$, the optimal policy is to simply ignore forever. With $k = 2$, the optimal policy is to ignore until crying is observed, at which point the best action is to feed the baby, and then return to ignoring. This policy is close to optimal for the infinite horizon crying baby POMDP. With $k = 3$, the optimal policy essentially remains unchanged from when $k = 2$.

We define the transition function with a controller, which has a state space $X \times S$. For any fixed-size controller policy parameterized by $\theta = (\psi, \eta)$, the transition matrix $\mathbf{T}_\theta \in \mathbb{R}^{|X \times S| \times |X \times S|}$ is

$$\mathbf{T}_\theta((x,s),(x',s')) = \sum_a \psi(x,a)T(s,a,s') \sum_o O(a,s',o)\eta(x,a,o,x') \qquad (23.8)$$

The reward for a parameterized policy is represented as vector $\mathbf{r}_\theta \in \mathbb{R}^{|X \times S|}$:

$$\mathbf{r}_\theta((x,s)) = \sum_a \psi(x,a)R(s,a) \qquad (23.9)$$

The Bellman expectation equation for utility $\mathbf{u}_\theta \in \mathbb{R}^{|X \times S|}$ is then

$$\mathbf{u}_\theta = \mathbf{r}_\theta + \gamma \mathbf{T}_\theta \mathbf{u}_\theta \qquad (23.10)$$

We can consider an initial node-belief vector $\beta \in \mathbb{R}^{|X \times S|}$ with $\beta_{xs} = b(s)$ if $x = x^1$, and $\beta_{xs} = 0$ otherwise. A utility vector $\mathbf{u}_\theta \in \mathbb{R}^{|X \times S|}$ is also defined over the nodes X and states S for any of these fixed-size parameterized controller policies $\theta = (\psi, \eta)$. We now seek to maximize as follows:

$$\beta^\top \mathbf{u}_\theta \qquad (23.11)$$

We begin by rewriting equation (23.10):

$$\mathbf{u}_\theta = \mathbf{r}_\theta + \gamma \mathbf{T}_\theta \mathbf{u}_\theta \qquad (23.12)$$

$$(\mathbf{I} - \gamma \mathbf{T}_\theta)\mathbf{u}_\theta = \mathbf{r}_\theta \qquad (23.13)$$

$$\mathbf{u}_\theta = (\mathbf{I} - \gamma \mathbf{T}_\theta)^{-1}\mathbf{r}_\theta \qquad (23.14)$$

$$\mathbf{u}_\theta = \mathbf{Z}^{-1}\mathbf{r}_\theta \qquad (23.15)$$

with $\mathbf{Z} = \mathbf{I} - \gamma \mathbf{T}_\theta$ for convenience. To perform gradient ascent, we need to know the partial derivatives of equation (23.15) with respect to the policy parameters:

$$\frac{\partial \mathbf{u}_\theta}{\partial \theta} = \frac{\partial \mathbf{Z}^{-1}}{\partial \theta}\mathbf{r}_\theta + \mathbf{Z}^{-1}\frac{\partial \mathbf{r}_\theta}{\partial \theta} \qquad (23.16)$$

$$= -\mathbf{Z}^{-1}\frac{\partial \mathbf{Z}}{\partial \theta}\mathbf{Z}^{-1}\mathbf{r}_\theta + \mathbf{Z}^{-1}\frac{\partial \mathbf{r}_\theta}{\partial \theta} \qquad (23.17)$$

$$= \mathbf{Z}^{-1}\left(\frac{\partial \mathbf{r}_\theta}{\partial \theta} - \frac{\partial \mathbf{Z}}{\partial \theta}\mathbf{Z}^{-1}\mathbf{r}_\theta\right) \qquad (23.18)$$

with $\partial \theta$ referring to both $\partial \psi(\hat{x}, \hat{a})$ and $\partial \eta(\hat{x}, \hat{a}, \hat{o}, \hat{x}')$ for convenience.

Computing the partial derivatives of $\mathbf{Z}$ and $\mathbf{r}_\theta$ results in four equations:

$$\frac{\partial \mathbf{r}_\theta((x,s))}{\partial \psi(\hat{x},\hat{a})} = \begin{cases} R(s,a) & \text{if } x = \hat{x} \\ 0 & \text{otherwise} \end{cases} \tag{23.19}$$

$$\frac{\partial \mathbf{r}_\theta((x,s))}{\partial \eta(\hat{x},\hat{a},\hat{o},\hat{x}')} = 0 \tag{23.20}$$

$$\frac{\partial \mathbf{Z}((x,s),(x',s'))}{\partial \psi(\hat{x},\hat{a})} = \begin{cases} -\gamma T(s,\hat{a},s') \sum_o O(\hat{a},s',o)\eta(\hat{x},\hat{a},o,x') & \text{if } x = \hat{x} \\ 0 & \text{otherwise} \end{cases} \tag{23.21}$$

$$\frac{\partial \mathbf{Z}((x,s),(x',s'))}{\partial \eta(\hat{x},\hat{a},\hat{o},\hat{x}')} = \begin{cases} -\gamma \psi(\hat{x},\hat{a})T(s,\hat{a},s')O(\hat{a},s',\hat{o})\eta(\hat{x},\hat{a},\hat{o},x') & \text{if } x = \hat{x} \text{ and } x' = \hat{x}' \\ 0 & \text{otherwise} \end{cases} \tag{23.22}$$

Finally, these four gradients are substituted into equation (23.18) as follows:

$$\frac{\partial \mathbf{u}_\theta}{\partial \psi(\hat{x},\hat{a})} = \mathbf{Z}^{-1}\left(\frac{\partial \mathbf{r}_\theta}{\partial \psi(\hat{x},\hat{a})} - \frac{\partial \mathbf{Z}}{\partial \psi(\hat{x},\hat{a})}\mathbf{Z}^{-1}\mathbf{r}_\theta \right) \tag{23.23}$$

$$\frac{\partial \mathbf{u}_\theta}{\partial \eta(\hat{x},\hat{a},\hat{o},\hat{x}')} = \mathbf{Z}^{-1}\left(\frac{\partial \mathbf{r}_\theta}{\partial \eta(\hat{x},\hat{a},\hat{o},\hat{x}')} - \frac{\partial \mathbf{Z}}{\partial \eta(\hat{x},\hat{a},\hat{o},\hat{x}')}\mathbf{Z}^{-1}\mathbf{r}_\theta \right) \tag{23.24}$$

We finally can return to the original objective in equation (23.11). Controller gradient ascent starts with a fixed number of nodes in X and an arbitrary policy ψ and η. At iteration k, it updates these parameters as follows:

$$\psi^{k+1}(x,a) = \psi^k(x,a) + \alpha \boldsymbol{\beta}^\top \frac{\partial \mathbf{u}_{\theta^k}}{\partial \psi^k(\hat{x},\hat{a})} \tag{23.25}$$

$$\eta^{k+1}(x,a,o,x') = \eta^k(x,a,o,x') + \alpha \boldsymbol{\beta}^\top \frac{\partial \mathbf{u}_{\theta^k}}{\partial \eta^k(\hat{x},\hat{a},\hat{o},\hat{x}')} \tag{23.26}$$

with gradient step size $\alpha > 0$. After this update, ψ^{k+1} and η^{k+1} may no longer be valid distributions. To make them valid, we project them onto the probability simplex. One approach to projecting a vector $\mathbf{y}$ onto the probability simplex is to find the closest distribution according to the L_2-norm:

$$\begin{aligned} \underset{\mathbf{b}}{\text{minimize}} \quad & \frac{1}{2}\|\mathbf{y} - \mathbf{b}\|_2^2 \\ \text{subject to} \quad & \mathbf{b} \geq 0 \\ & \mathbf{1}^\top \mathbf{b} = 1 \end{aligned} \tag{23.27}$$

This optimization can be solved exactly through a simple algorithm included in algorithm 23.6.[7] Example 23.6 demonstrates the process of updating the controller.

[7] J. Duchi, S. Shalev-Shwartz, Y. Singer, and T. Chandra, "Efficient Projections onto the ℓ_1-Ball for Learning in High Dimensions," in *International Conference on Machine Learning* (ICML), 2008.

The optimization objective in equation (23.6) is not necessarily convex.[8] Hence, normal gradient ascent can converge to a local optimum depending on the initial controller. Adaptive gradient algorithms can be applied to help smooth and speed convergence.

[8] This objective is distinct from the utility $U(x, b) = \sum_s b(s)U(x, s)$, which is guaranteed to be piece-wise linear and convex with respect to the belief state b, as discussed in section 20.3.

23.5   Summary

- Controllers are policy representations that do not rely on exploring or maintaining beliefs.

- Controllers consist of nodes, an action selection function, and a successor selection function.

- Nodes and the controller graph are abstract; however, they can be interpreted as sets of the countably infinite reachable beliefs.

- The value function for a controller node can be interpreted as an alpha vector.

- Policy iteration alternates between policy evaluation, which computes the utilities for each node, and policy improvement, which adds new nodes.

- Pruning during policy iteration can help reduce the exponential growth in nodes with each improvement step.

- Nonlinear programming reformulates finding the optimal fixed-sized controller as a general optimization problem, allowing off-the-shelf solvers and techniques to be used.

- Controller gradient ascent climbs in the space of policies to improve the value function directly, benefiting from an explicit, POMDP-based gradient step.

23.6   Exercises

Exercise 23.1. List any advantages that a controller policy representation has over tree-based conditional plan and belief-based representations.

Solution: Unlike tree-based conditional plans, controllers can represent policies that can be executed indefinitely. They do not have to grow exponentially in size with the horizon.

Compared to belief-based representations, the number of parameters in a controller representation tends to be far less than the number of alpha vectors for larger problems. We can also optimize controllers more easily for a fixed amount of memory.

```
struct ControllerGradient
    b        # initial belief
    ℓ        # number of nodes
    α        # gradient step
    k_max    # maximum iterations
end

function solve(M::ControllerGradient, 𝒫::POMDP)
    𝒜, 𝒪, ℓ, k_max = 𝒫.𝒜, 𝒫.𝒪, M.ℓ, M.k_max
    X = collect(1:ℓ)
    ψ = Dict((x, a) ⇒ rand() for x in X, a in 𝒜)
    η = Dict((x, a, o, x′) ⇒ rand() for x in X, a in 𝒜, o in 𝒪, x′ in X)
    π = ControllerPolicy(𝒫, X, ψ, η)
    for i in 1:k_max
        improve!(π, M, 𝒫)
    end
    return π
end

function improve!(π::ControllerPolicy, M::ControllerGradient, 𝒫::POMDP)
    S, 𝒜, 𝒪, X, x1, ψ, η = 𝒫.S, 𝒫.𝒜, 𝒫.𝒪, π.X, 1, π.ψ, π.η
    n, m, z, b, ℓ, α = length(S), length(𝒜), length(𝒪), M.b, M.ℓ, M.α
    ∂U′∂ψ, ∂U′∂η = gradient(π, M, 𝒫)
    UIndex(x, s) = (s - 1) * ℓ + (x - 1) + 1
    E(U, x1, b) = sum(b[s]*U[UIndex(x1,s)] for s in 1:n)
    ψ′ = Dict((x, a) ⇒ 0.0 for x in X, a in 𝒜)
    η′ = Dict((x, a, o, x′) ⇒ 0.0 for x in X, a in 𝒜, o in 𝒪, x′ in X)
    for x in X
        ψ′x = [ψ[x, a] + α * E(∂U′∂ψ(x, a), x1, b) for a in 𝒜]
        ψ′x = project_to_simplex(ψ′x)
        for (aIndex, a) in enumerate(𝒜)
            ψ′[x, a] = ψ′x[aIndex]
        end
        for (a, o) in product(𝒜, 𝒪)
            η′x = [(η[x, a, o, x′] +
                    α * E(∂U′∂η(x, a, o, x′), x1, b)) for x′ in X]
            η′x = project_to_simplex(η′x)
            for (x′Index, x′) in enumerate(X)
                η′[x, a, o, x′] = η′x[x′Index]
            end
        end
    end
    π.ψ, π.η = ψ′, η′
end

function project_to_simplex(y)
    u = sort(copy(y), rev=true)
    i = maximum([j for j in eachindex(u)
                    if u[j] + (1 - sum(u[1:j])) / j > 0.0])
    δ = (1 - sum(u[j] for j = 1:i)) / i
    return [max(y[j] + δ, 0.0) for j in eachindex(u)]
end
```

Algorithm 23.6. An implementation of a controller gradient ascent algorithm for POMDP 𝒫 at initial belief b. The controller itself has a fixed size of ℓ nodes. It is improved over k_max iterations by following the gradient of the controller, with a step size of α, to maximally improve the value of the initial belief.

```
function gradient(π::ControllerPolicy, M::ControllerGradient, 𝒫::POMDP)
    S, 𝒜, 𝒪, T, O, R, γ = 𝒫.S, 𝒫.𝒜, 𝒫.𝒪, 𝒫.T, 𝒫.O, 𝒫.R, 𝒫.γ
    X, x1, ψ, η = π.X, 1, π.ψ, π.η
    n, m, z = length(S), length(𝒜), length(𝒪)
    XS = vec(collect(product(X, S)))
    T' = [sum(ψ[x, a] * T(s, a, s') * sum(O(a, s', o) * η[x, a, o, x']
            for o in 𝒪) for a in 𝒜) for (x, s) in XS, (x', s') in XS]
    R' = [sum(ψ[x, a] * R(s, a) for a in 𝒜) for (x, s) in XS]
    Z = 1.0I(length(XS)) - γ * T'
    invZ = inv(Z)
    ∂Z∂ψ(hx, ha) = [x == hx ? (-γ * T(s, ha, s')
                    * sum(O(ha, s', o) * η[hx, ha, o, x']
                        for o in 𝒪)) : 0.0
                    for (x, s) in XS, (x', s') in XS]
    ∂Z∂η(hx, ha, ho, hx') = [x == hx && x' == hx' ? (-γ * ψ[hx, ha]
                    * T(s, ha, s') * O(ha, s', ho)) : 0.0
                    for (x, s) in XS, (x', s') in XS]
    ∂R'∂ψ(hx, ha) = [x == hx ? R(s, ha) : 0.0 for (x, s) in XS]
    ∂R'∂η(hx, ha, ho, hx') = [0.0 for (x, s) in XS]
    ∂U'∂ψ(hx, ha) = invZ * (∂R'∂ψ(hx, ha) - ∂Z∂ψ(hx, ha) * invZ * R')
    ∂U'∂η(hx, ha, ho, hx') = invZ * (∂R'∂η(hx, ha, ho, hx')
                            - ∂Z∂η(hx, ha, ho, hx') * invZ * R')
    return ∂U'∂ψ, ∂U'∂η
end
```

Algorithm 23.7. The gradient step of the controller gradient ascent method. It constructs the gradients of the utility U with respect to the policy gradients $\partial U'\partial\psi$ and $\partial U'\partial\eta$.

During execution, controllers will never divide by zero in the way that belief-based policies can. Belief-based methods require maintaining a belief. The discrete state filter from equation (19.7) will divide by zero if an impossible observation is made. This can happen when a noisy observation from a sensor returns an observation that the models of $T(s, a, s')$ and $O(o \mid a, s')$ does not accurately capture.

Exercise 23.2. Controller policy iteration only adds nodes with deterministic action selection functions and successor distributions. Does this mean that the resulting controller is necessarily suboptimal?

Solution: Controller policy iteration is guaranteed to converge on an optimal policy in the limit. However, the method cannot find more compact representations of optimal controller policies that may require stochastic nodes.

Exercise 23.3. Prove that node pruning in policy iteration does not affect the utility.

Solution: Let x' be the new node from some iteration i, and x be a previous node from iteration $i - 1$.

By construction, $\eta(x', a, o, x)$ defines all new nodes x' to only have a successor x from the previous iteration. Thus, for each state s, $U^{(i)}(x', s)$ only sums over the successors $U^{(i-1)}(x, s')$ in equation (23.1). This means that the other utilities in iteration i, including

Consider the catch problem (appendix F.9) with a uniform initial belief b_1. The diagrams here show the utility of the policy over gradient ascent iteration applied to the catch problem with $k = 3$ nodes. The left node is x_1.

At iteration 1, the policy is essentially random, both in action selection and successor selection:

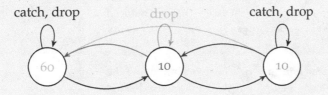

At iteration 50, the agent has determined a reasonable distance to throw the ball (50) but still has not used its three nodes to remember anything useful:

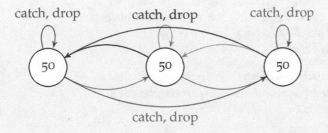

At iteration 500, the policy has constructed a reasonable plan, given its fixed three nodes of memory:

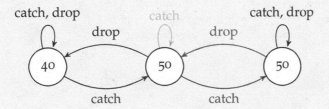

It first tries throwing the ball at a distance of 40. If the child catches the ball, then it increases the range to 50. It uses the final node to remember how many times the child caught the ball (up to twice) to choose the distance.

Example 23.6. A demonstration of the controller gradient algorithm for controllers with a fixed size of $\ell = 3$. The policy is shown to refine itself over the algorithm's iterations. The agent incrementally determines how to best use its fixed number of nodes, resulting in a reasonable and interpretable policy on convergence. The stochastic controllers are shown as circles, with the most likely action in the middle. The outgoing edges show successor node selections given an observation. The stochasticity in node actions and successors are shown as opacity (more opaque is higher probability, more transparent is lower probability).

a self-loop to x itself, do not affect the utility $U^{(i)}(x', s)$. Since the initial node is chosen by equation (23.3), we must ensure that the utility with and without the pruned node at all beliefs is the same. A node is pruned in one of two ways.

First, x' obtains a higher utility over all states than its pruned successor x. Formally, $U^{(i)}(x, s) \leq U^{(i-1)}(x', s)$ for all s. The pruning step replaces x with x', including U, ψ, and η. By construction, U has not decreased at any state s.

Second, x is identical to an existing previous node x'. Note that this means the transition $\eta(x, a, o, x') = \eta(x', a, o, x')$. This means that the utility is identical except that x is reduced by γ; in other words, $\gamma U^{(i)}(x, s) = U^{(i-1)}(x, s)$ by equation (23.1). Pruning x does not affect the final utility.

Exercise 23.4. Devise an algorithm that uses the nonlinear program algorithm to find the minimum fixed-sized controller required to obtain the optimality of a large fixed-sized controller of size ℓ. You can assume that the nonlinear optimizer returns the optimal policy in this case.

Solution: The idea is to create an outer loop that increments the fixed size of the controller, after knowing the utility of the large fixed-sized controller. First, we must compute the large fixed-sized controller's utility $U^* = \sum_s b_1(s)U(x_1, s)$ at initial node x_1 and initial belief b_1. Next, we create a loop that increments the size ℓ of the controller. At each step, we evaluate the policy and compute the utility U^ℓ. By our assumption, the returned controller produces a globally optimal utility for the fixed size ℓ. Once we arrive at a utility U^ℓ, if we see that $U^\ell = U^*$, then we stop and return the policy.

Exercise 23.5. Analyze the controller gradient ascent algorithm's gradient step. Assume that $|\mathcal{S}|$ is larger than $|\mathcal{A}|$ and $|\mathcal{O}|$. What is the most computationally expensive part of the gradient step? How might this be improved?

Solution: Computing the inverse $\mathbf{Z}^{-1} = (\mathbf{I} - \gamma \mathbf{T_\theta})$ is the most computationally expensive part of the gradient step, as well as the entire gradient algorithm. The matrix $\mathbf{Z}$ is of size $|X \times \mathcal{S}|$. Gauss–Jordan elimination requires $O(|X \times \mathcal{S}|^3)$ operations, though the 3 in the exponent can be reduced to 2.3728639 using a state-of-the-art matrix inversion algorithm.[9] The creation of the temporary matrix T_θ also requires $O(|X \times \mathcal{S}|^2 |\mathcal{A} \times \mathcal{O}|)$ operations to support computing the inverse. All other loops and other temporary array creations require far fewer operations. This can be improved using an approximate inverse technique.

[9] F. L. Gall, "Powers of Tensors and Fast Matrix Multiplication," in *International Symposium on Symbolic and Algebraic Computation (ISSAC)*, 2014.

PART V

MULTIAGENT SYSTEMS

Up to this point, we have focused on decision making from the perspective of a single agent. We now extend the core concepts that we have discussed so far to problems involving multiple agents. In multiagent systems, we can model other agents as potential allies or adversaries and adapt accordingly over time. These problems are inherently challenging due to complexities surrounding agent interactions and agents reasoning about other agents who reason about the agent, and so on. We begin by introducing multiagent reasoning in games and outline how to compute equilibria from simple interactions. We then discuss how to design algorithms for multiple agents interacting over time, describing learning algorithms that favor rational adaptation over convergence to equilibria. Introducing state uncertainty significantly increases problem complexity, and this part emphasizes the resulting challenges. The final chapter focuses on the various models and algorithms for collaborative agents that strive to work together with a common objective.

24 Multiagent Reasoning

So far, we have focused on making rational decisions for a single agent. These models have natural extensions to multiple agents. New challenges emerge as agents interact; agents can aid each other or act in their own best interests. Multiagent reasoning is a subject of *game theory*.[1] This chapter builds on the concepts introduced earlier, extending them to multiagent contexts. We will discuss the foundational game theoretic approaches to compute decision strategies and multiagent equilibria.

24.1 Simple Games

A *simple game* (algorithm 24.1) is a fundamental model for multiagent reasoning.[2] Each agent $i \in \mathcal{I}$ selects an action a^i to maximize their own accumulation of reward r^i. The *joint action space* $\mathcal{A} = \mathcal{A}^1 \times \cdots \times \mathcal{A}^k$ consists of all possible combinations of the actions $\mathcal{A}^i$ available to each agent. The actions selected simultaneously across agents can be combined to form a *joint action* $\mathbf{a} = (a^1, \dots, a^k)$ from this joint action space.[3] The *joint reward function* $\mathbf{R}(\mathbf{a}) = (R^1(\mathbf{a}), \dots, R^k(\mathbf{a}))$ represents the reward produced by the joint action $\mathbf{a}$. The *joint reward* is written $\mathbf{r} = (r^1, \dots, r^k)$. Simple games do not include states or transition functions. Example 24.1 introduces a simple game.

```
struct SimpleGame
    γ  # discount factor
    ℐ  # agents
    𝒜  # joint action space
    R  # joint reward function
end
```

[1] Game theory is a broad field. Several standard introductory books include D. Fudenberg and J. Tirole, *Game Theory*. MIT Press, 1991. R. B. Myerson, *Game Theory: Analysis of Conflict*. Harvard University Press, 1997. Y. Shoham and K. Leyton-Brown, *Multiagent Systems: Algorithmic, Game Theoretic, and Logical Foundations*. Cambridge University Press, 2009.

[2] Simple games encompass *normal form games* (also called *standard form games* or *matrix games*), finite-horizon *repeated games*, and infinite-horizon discounted repeated games. Y. Shoham and K. Leyton-Brown, *Multiagent Systems: Algorithmic, Game Theoretic, and Logical Foundations*. Cambridge University Press, 2009.

[3] A joint action is also called an *action profile*.

Algorithm 24.1. Data structure for a simple game.

Example 24.1.   A simple game known as the prisoner's dilemma. Additional detail is provided in appendix F.10.

The *prisoner's dilemma* is a two-agent, two-action game involving two prisoners that are on trial. They can choose to *cooperate* and remain silent about their shared crime, or *defect* and blame the other for their crime. If they both cooperate, they both serve a sentence of one year. If agent i cooperates and the other agent defects, then i serves four years and the other serves no time. If both defect, then they both serve three years.

Two-agent simple games can be represented by a table. Rows represent actions for agent 1. Columns represent actions for agent 2. The rewards for agent 1 and 2 are shown in each cell.

	agent 2 cooperate	agent 2 defect
agent 1 cooperate	$-1, -1$	$-4, 0$
agent 1 defect	$0, -4$	$-3, -3$

A *joint policy* π specifies a probability distribution over joint actions taken by the agents. Joint policies can be decomposed into individual agent policies. The probability that agent i selects action a is given by $\pi^i(a)$. In game theory, a deterministic policy is called a *pure strategy* and a stochastic policy is called a *mixed strategy*. The utility of a joint policy π from the perspective of agent i is

$$U^i(\pi) = \sum_{\mathbf{a}\in\mathcal{A}} R^i(\mathbf{a}) \prod_{j\in\mathcal{I}} \pi^j(a^j) \tag{24.1}$$

Algorithm 24.2 implements routines for representing policies and computing their utility.

A *zero-sum game* is a type of simple game where the sum of rewards across agents is zero. Here, any gain of an agent results as a loss to the other agents. A zero-sum game with two agents $\mathcal{I} = \{1,2\}$ has opposing reward functions $R^1(\mathbf{a}) = -R^2(\mathbf{a})$. They are typically solved with algorithms specialized for this reward structure. Example 24.2 describes such a game.

24.2   Response Models

Before exploring different concepts for solving for a joint policy, we will begin by discussing how to model the *response* of a single agent i, given fixed policies for the other agents. We will use the notation $-i$ as shorthand for $(1,\ldots,i-1,i+1,\ldots,k)$. Using this notation, a joint action is written as $\mathbf{a} = (a^i, \mathbf{a}^{-i})$, a joint reward is written as $\mathbf{R}(a^i, \mathbf{a}^{-i})$, and a joint policy is written as $\pi = (\pi^i, \pi^{-i})$. This section discusses various approaches for computing a response to a known π^{-i}.

Rock-paper-scissors is a zero-sum game for two agents. Each agent selects *rock*, *paper*, or *scissors*. Rock wins against scissors, paper wins against rock, and scissors wins against paper, with a reward of 1 for the winner and −1 for the loser. If the agents select the same action, both receive 0 reward. Generally, two-agent repeated games can be represented as a sequence of payoff matrices, as shown here:

Example 24.2. The well-known game of rock-paper-scissors is an example of a zero-sum game. Appendix F.11 provides additional details.

$t = 1$

agent 2

	rock	paper	scissors
rock	0,0	−1,1	1,−1
paper	1,−1	0,0	−1,1
scissors	−1,1	1,−1	0,0

$t = 2$

agent 2

	rock	paper	scissors
rock	0,0	−1,1	1,−1
paper	1,−1	0,0	−1,1
scissors	−1,1	1,−1	0,0

agent 1 (rows for both)

24.2.1 Best Response

A *best response* of agent i to the policies of the other agents π^{-i} is a policy π^i that satisfies

$$U^i(\pi^i, \pi^{-i}) \geq U^i(\pi^{i\prime}, \pi^{-i}) \tag{24.2}$$

for all other policies $\pi^{i\prime} \neq \pi^i$. In other words, a best response for an agent is a policy where there is no incentive for them to change their policy, given a fixed set of policies for the other agents. There may be multiple best responses.

If we restrict ourselves to deterministic policies, a *deterministic best response* to opponent policies π^{-i} is straightforward to compute. We simply iterate over all of agent i's actions and return the one that maximizes the utility as follows:

$$\arg\max_{a^i \in \mathcal{A}^i} U^i(a^i, \pi^{-i}) \tag{24.3}$$

Algorithm 24.3 provides an implementation of this.

```
struct SimpleGamePolicy
    p # dictionary mapping actions to probabilities

    function SimpleGamePolicy(p::Base.Generator)
        return SimpleGamePolicy(Dict(p))
    end

    function SimpleGamePolicy(p::Dict)
        vs = collect(values(p))
        vs ./= sum(vs)
        return new(Dict(k ⇒ v for (k,v) in zip(keys(p), vs)))
    end

    SimpleGamePolicy(ai) = new(Dict(ai ⇒ 1.0))
end

(πi::SimpleGamePolicy)(ai) = get(πi.p, ai, 0.0)

function (πi::SimpleGamePolicy)()
    D = SetCategorical(collect(keys(πi.p)), collect(values(πi.p)))
    return rand(D)
end

joint(X) = vec(collect(product(X...)))

joint(π, πi, i) = [i == j ? πi : πj for (j, πj) in enumerate(π)]

function utility(𝒫::SimpleGame, π, i)
    𝒜, R = 𝒫.𝒜, 𝒫.R
    p(a) = prod(πj(aj) for (πj, aj) in zip(π, a))
    return sum(R(a)[i]*p(a) for a in joint(𝒜))
end
```

Algorithm 24.2. A policy associated with an agent is represented by a dictionary that maps actions to probabilities. There are different ways to construct a policy. One way is to pass in a dictionary directory, in which case the probabilities are normalized. Another way is to pass in a generator that creates this dictionary. We can also construct a policy by passing in an action, in which case it assigns probability 1 to that action. If we have an individual policy πi, we can call $\pi i(ai)$ to compute the probability the policy associates with action ai. If we call $\pi i()$, then it will return a random action according to that policy. We can use $joint(\mathcal{A})$ to construct the joint action space from $\mathcal{A}$. We can use $utility(\mathcal{P}, \pi, i)$ to compute the utility associated with executing joint policy π in the game $\mathcal{P}$ from the perspective of agent i.

```
function best_response(𝒫::SimpleGame, π, i)
    U(ai) = utility(𝒫, joint(π, SimpleGamePolicy(ai), i), i)
    ai = argmax(U, 𝒫.𝒜[i])
    return SimpleGamePolicy(ai)
end
```

Algorithm 24.3. For a simple game $\mathcal{P}$, we can compute a deterministic best response for agent i, given that the other agents are playing the policies in π.

24.2.2 Softmax Response

We can use a *softmax response* to model how agent i will select their action.[4] As discussed in section 6.7, humans are often not perfectly rational optimizers of expected utility. The principle underlying the softmax response model is that (typically human) agents are more likely to make errors in their optimization when those errors are less costly. Given a *precision parameter* $\lambda \geq 0$, this model selects action a^i according to

$$\pi^i(a^i) \propto \exp(\lambda U^i(a^i, \boldsymbol{\pi}^{-i})) \tag{24.4}$$

As $\lambda \to 0$, the agent is insensitive to differences in utility, and selects actions uniformly at random. As $\lambda \to \infty$, the policy converges to a deterministic best response. We can treat λ as a parameter that can be learned from data using, for example, maximum likelihood estimation (section 4.1). This learning-based approach aims to be predictive of behavior rather than prescriptive of behavior, though having a predictive model of other human agents can be useful in building a system that prescribes optimal behavior. Algorithm 24.4 provides an implementation of a softmax response.

```
function softmax_response(𝒫::SimpleGame, π, i, λ)
    𝒜i = 𝒫.𝒜[i]
    U(ai) = utility(𝒫, joint(π, SimpleGamePolicy(ai), i), i)
    return SimpleGamePolicy(ai ⇒ exp(λ*U(ai)) for ai in 𝒜i)
end
```

[4] This kind of model is sometimes referred to as a *logit response* or *quantal response*. We introduced similar softmax models earlier in this book, in the context of directed exploration strategies for reinforcement learning (section 15.4).

Algorithm 24.4. For a simple game 𝒫 and a particular agent i, we can compute the softmax response policy πi, given that the other agents are playing the policies in π. This computation requires specifying the precision parameter λ.

24.3 Dominant Strategy Equilibrium

In some games, an agent has a *dominant strategy*, which is a policy that is a best response against all other possible agent policies. For example, in the prisoner's dilemma (example 24.1), the best response of agent 1 is to defect regardless of the policy of agent 2, making defect a dominant strategy for agent 1. A joint policy where all the agents use dominant strategies is called a *dominant strategy equilibrium*. In the prisoner's dilemma, a joint policy where both agents defect is a dominant strategy equilibrium.[5] Many games do not have a dominant strategy equilibrium. For example, in rock-paper-scissors (example 24.2), the best response of agent 1 depends on the strategy of agent 2.

[5] Interestingly, having both agents act greedily with respect to their own utility function results in a worse outcome for both of them. If they had both cooperated, then they would both get a sentence of one year instead of three years.

24.4   Nash Equilibrium

In contrast with the dominant strategy equilibrium concept, a Nash equilibrium[6] always exists for games with a finite action space.[7] A *Nash equilibrium* is a joint policy π in which all agents are following a best response. In other words, a Nash equilibrium is a joint policy in which no agents have an incentive to unilaterally switch their policy.

Multiple Nash equilibria can exist in a single game (exercise 24.2). Sometimes Nash equilibria may involve deterministic policies, but this is not always the case (see example 24.3). Computing a Nash equilibrium is *PPAD-complete*, a class that is distinct from NP-complete (appendix C.2) but also has no known polynomial time algorithm.[8]

The problem of finding a Nash equilibrium can be framed as an optimization problem:

$$
\begin{aligned}
\underset{\pi, U}{\text{minimize}} \quad & \sum_i \left(U^i - U^i(\pi) \right) \\
\text{subject to} \quad & U^i \geq U^i(a^i, \pi^{-i}) \text{ for all } i, a^i \\
& \sum_{a^i} \pi^i(a^i) = 1 \text{ for all } i \\
& \pi^i(a^i) \geq 0 \text{ for all } i, a^i
\end{aligned}
\tag{24.5}
$$

The optimization variables correspond to the parameters of π and U. At convergence, the objective will be 0, with U^i matching the utilities associated with policy π as computed in equation (24.1) for each agent i. The first constraint ensures that no agent will do better by unilaterally changing their action. Like the objective, this first constraint is nonlinear because it involves a product of the parameters in the optimization variable π. The last two constraints are linear, ensuring that π represents a valid set of probability distributions over actions. Algorithm 24.5 implements this optimization procedure.

24.5   Correlated Equilibrium

The *correlated equilibrium* generalizes the Nash equilibrium concept by relaxing the assumption that the agents act independently. The joint action in this case comes from a full joint distribution. A *correlated joint policy* $\pi(\mathbf{a})$ is a single distribution over the joint actions of all agents. Consequently, the actions of the various agents

[6] Named for the American mathematician John Forbes Nash, Jr. (1928–2015) who formalized the concept. J. Nash, "Non-Cooperative Games," *Annals of Mathematics*, pp. 286–295, 1951.

[7] Exercise 24.1 explores the case where the action space is infinite.

[8] C. Daskalakis, P. W. Goldberg, and C. H. Papadimitriou, "The Complexity of Computing a Nash Equilibrium," *Communications of the ACM*, vol. 52, no. 2, pp. 89–97, 2009.

Suppose that we wish to find a Nash equilibrium for the prisoner's dilemma from example 24.1. If both agents always defect, both receive -3 reward. Any deviation by any agent will result in a -4 reward for that agent; hence, there is no incentive to deviate. Having both agents defect is thus a Nash equilibrium for the prisoner's dilemma.

Suppose that we now wish to find a Nash equilibrium for the rock-paper-scissors scenario from example 24.2. Any deterministic strategy by one agent can be easily countered by the other agent. For example, if agent 1 plays rock, then agent 2's best response is paper. Because there is no deterministic Nash equilibrium for rock-paper-scissors, we know that there must be one involving stochastic policies. Suppose that each agent selects from the actions uniformly at random. This solution produces an expected utility of 0 for both agents:

$$
\begin{aligned}
U^i(\pi) = {} & 0\frac{1}{3}\frac{1}{3} - 1\frac{1}{3}\frac{1}{3} + 1\frac{1}{3}\frac{1}{3} \\
& + 1\frac{1}{3}\frac{1}{3} + 0\frac{1}{3}\frac{1}{3} - 1\frac{1}{3}\frac{1}{3} \\
& - 1\frac{1}{3}\frac{1}{3} + 1\frac{1}{3}\frac{1}{3} + 0\frac{1}{3}\frac{1}{3} \\
= {} & 0
\end{aligned}
$$

Any deviation by an agent would decrease their expected payoff, meaning that we have found a Nash equilibrium.

Example 24.3. Deterministic and stochastic Nash equilibria.

```
struct NashEquilibrium end

function tensorform(𝒫::SimpleGame)
    ℐ, 𝒜, R = 𝒫.ℐ, 𝒫.𝒜, 𝒫.R
    ℐ′ = eachindex(ℐ)
    𝒜′ = [eachindex(𝒜[i]) for i in ℐ]
    R′ = [R(a) for a in joint(𝒜)]
    return ℐ′, 𝒜′, R′
end

function solve(M::NashEquilibrium, 𝒫::SimpleGame)
    ℐ, 𝒜, R = tensorform(𝒫)
    model = Model(Ipopt.Optimizer)
    @variable(model, U[ℐ])
    @variable(model, π[i=ℐ, 𝒜[i]] ≥ 0)
    @NLobjective(model, Min,
        sum(U[i] - sum(prod(π[j,a[j]] for j in ℐ) * R[y][i]
            for (y,a) in enumerate(joint(𝒜))) for i in ℐ))
    @NLconstraint(model, [i=ℐ, ai=𝒜[i]],
        U[i] ≥ sum(
            prod(j==i ? (a[j]==ai ? 1.0 : 0.0) : π[j,a[j]] for j in ℐ)
                * R[y][i] for (y,a) in enumerate(joint(𝒜))))
    @constraint(model, [i=ℐ], sum(π[i,ai] for ai in 𝒜[i]) == 1)
    optimize!(model)
    πi′(i) = SimpleGamePolicy(𝒫.𝒜[i][ai] ⇒ value(π[i,ai]) for ai in 𝒜[i])
    return [πi′(i) for i in ℐ]
end
```

Algorithm 24.5. This nonlinear program computes a Nash equilibrium for a simple game $\mathcal{P}$.

may be correlated, preventing the policies from being decoupled into individual policies $\pi^i(a^i)$. Algorithm 24.6 shows how to represent such a policy.

```
mutable struct JointCorrelatedPolicy
    p # dictionary mapping from joint actions to probabilities
    JointCorrelatedPolicy(p::Base.Generator) = new(Dict(p))
end

(π::JointCorrelatedPolicy)(a) = get(π.p, a, 0.0)

function (π::JointCorrelatedPolicy)()
    D = SetCategorical(collect(keys(π.p)), collect(values(π.p)))
    return rand(D)
end
```

Algorithm 24.6. A joint correlated policy is represented by a dictionary that maps joint actions to probabilities. If π is a joint correlated policy, evaluating π(a) will return the probability associated with the joint action a.

A *correlated equilibrium* is a correlated joint policy where no agent i can increase their expected utility by deviating from their current action a^i to another action $a^{i\prime}$:

$$\sum_{\mathbf{a}^{-i}} R^i(a^i, \mathbf{a}^{-i}) \pi(a^i, \mathbf{a}^{-i}) \geq \sum_{\mathbf{a}^{-i}} R^i(a^{i\prime}, \mathbf{a}^{-i}) \pi(a^i, \mathbf{a}^{-i}) \qquad (24.6)$$

Example 24.4 demonstrates this concept.

Every Nash equilibrium is a correlated equilibrium because we can always form a joint policy from independent policies:

$$\pi(\mathbf{a}) = \prod_{i=1}^{k} \pi^i(a^i) \qquad (24.7)$$

If the individual policies satisfy equation (24.2), then the joint policy will satisfy equation (24.6). Not all correlated equilibria, however, are Nash equilibria.

A correlated equilibrium can be computed using linear programming (algorithm 24.7):

$$\begin{aligned} \underset{\pi}{\text{maximize}} \quad & \sum_i \sum_{\mathbf{a}} R^i(\mathbf{a}) \pi(\mathbf{a}) \\ \text{subject to} \quad & \sum_{\mathbf{a}^{-i}} R^i(a^i, \mathbf{a}^{-i}) \pi(a^i, \mathbf{a}^{-i}) \geq \sum_{\mathbf{a}^{-i}} R^i(a^{i\prime}, \mathbf{a}^{-i}) \pi(a^i, \mathbf{a}^{-i}) \quad \text{for all } i, a^i, a^{i\prime} \\ & \sum_{\mathbf{a}} \pi(\mathbf{a}) = 1 \\ & \pi(\mathbf{a}) \geq 0 \quad \text{for all } \mathbf{a} \end{aligned} \qquad (24.8)$$

Consider again the rock-paper-scissors scenario from example 24.2. In example 24.3, we found that a Nash equilibrium involves both agents selecting their actions uniformly at random. In correlated equilibria, we use a correlated joint policy $\pi(\mathbf{a})$, meaning that we need to find a distribution over (rock, rock), (rock, paper), (rock, scissors), (paper, rock), and so on. There are nine possible joint actions.

First, consider the joint policy in which agent 1 selects rock and agent 2 selects scissors. The utilities are

$$U^1(\pi) = 0\frac{0}{9} - 1\frac{0}{9} + 1\frac{9}{9} + 1\frac{0}{9} + \cdots = 1$$
$$U^2(\pi) = 0\frac{0}{9} + 1\frac{0}{9} - 1\frac{9}{9} - 1\frac{0}{9} + \cdots = -1$$

If agent 2 switched to paper, it would receive a utility of 1. Hence, this is not a correlated equilibrium.

Consider instead a correlated joint policy in which the joint action was chosen uniformly at random, with $\pi(\mathbf{a}) = 1/9$:

$$U^1(\pi) = 0\frac{1}{9} - 1\frac{1}{9} + 1\frac{1}{9} + 1\frac{1}{9} + \cdots = 0$$
$$U^2(\pi) = 0\frac{1}{9} + 1\frac{1}{9} - 1\frac{1}{9} - 1\frac{1}{9} + \cdots = 0$$

Any deviation from this results in one agent gaining utility and the other losing utility. This is a correlated equilibrium for rock-paper-scissors.

Example 24.4. Computing correlated equilibria in rock-paper-scissors.

Although linear programs can be solved in polynomial time, the size of the joint action space grows exponentially with the number of agents. The constraints enforce a correlated equilibrium. The objective, however, can be used to select among different valid correlated equilibria. Table 24.1 provides several common choices for the objective function.

```
struct CorrelatedEquilibrium end

function solve(M::CorrelatedEquilibrium, 𝒫::SimpleGame)
    ℐ, 𝒜, R = 𝒫.ℐ, 𝒫.𝒜, 𝒫.R
    model = Model(Ipopt.Optimizer)
    @variable(model, π[joint(𝒜)] ≥ 0)
    @objective(model, Max, sum(sum(π[a]*R(a) for a in joint(𝒜))))
    @constraint(model, [i=ℐ, ai=𝒜[i], ai'=𝒜[i]],
        sum(R(a)[i]*π[a] for a in joint(𝒜) if a[i]==ai)
        ≥ sum(R(joint(a,ai',i))[i]*π[a] for a in joint(𝒜) if a[i]==ai))
    @constraint(model, sum(π) == 1)
    optimize!(model)
    return JointCorrelatedPolicy(a ⇒ value(π[a]) for a in joint(𝒜))
end
```

Algorithm 24.7. Correlated equilibria are a more general notion of optimality for a simple game 𝒫 than a Nash equilibrium. They can be computed using a linear program. The resulting policies are correlated, meaning that the agents stochastically select their joint actions.

Name	Description	Objective Function
Utilitarian	Maximize the net utility.	$\text{maximize}_\pi \sum_i \sum_{\mathbf{a}} R^i(\mathbf{a})\pi(\mathbf{a})$
Egalitarian	Maximize the minimum of all agents' utilities.	$\text{maximize}_\pi \text{minimize}_i \sum_{\mathbf{a}} R^i(\mathbf{a})\pi(\mathbf{a})$
Plutocratic	Maximize the maximum of all agents' utilities.	$\text{maximize}_\pi \text{maximize}_i \sum_{\mathbf{a}} R^i(\mathbf{a})\pi(\mathbf{a})$
Dictatorial	Maximize agent i's utility.	$\text{maximize}_\pi \sum_{\mathbf{a}} R^i(\mathbf{a})\pi(\mathbf{a})$

Table 24.1. Alternative objective functions for equation (24.8), which select for various correlated equilibria. These descriptions were adapted from A. Greenwald and K. Hall, "Correlated Q-Learning," in *International Conference on Machine Learning* (ICML), 2003.

24.6 Iterated Best Response

Because computing a Nash equilibrium can be computationally expensive, an alternative approach is to iteratively apply best responses in a series of repeated games. In *iterated best response* (algorithm 24.8), we randomly cycle between agents, solving for each agent's best response policy in turn. This process may converge to a Nash equilibrium, but there are guarantees only for certain classes of games.[9] In many problems, it is common to observe cycles.

[9] Iterated best response will converge, for example, for a class known as *potential games*, as discussed in Theorem 19.12 of the textbook by N. Nisan, T. Roughgarden, É. Tardos, and V. V. Vazirani, eds., *Algorithmic Game Theory*. Cambridge University Press, 2007.

```
struct IteratedBestResponse
    k_max # number of iterations
    π     # initial policy
end

function IteratedBestResponse(𝒫::SimpleGame, k_max)
    π = [SimpleGamePolicy(ai ⇒ 1.0 for ai in 𝒜i) for 𝒜i in 𝒫.𝒜]
    return IteratedBestResponse(k_max, π)
end

function solve(M::IteratedBestResponse, 𝒫)
    π = M.π
    for k in 1:M.k_max
        π = [best_response(𝒫, π, i) for i in 𝒫.ℐ]
    end
    return π
end
```

Algorithm 24.8. Iterated best response involves cycling through the agents and applying their best response to the other agents. The algorithm starts with some initial policy and stops after k_max iterations. For convenience, we have a constructor that takes as input a simple game and creates an initial policy that has each agent select actions uniformly at random. The same solve function will be reused in the next chapter in the context of more complicated forms of games.

24.7   Hierarchical Softmax

An area known as *behavioral game theory* aims to model human agents. When building decision-making systems that must interact with humans, computing the Nash equilibrium is not always helpful. Humans often do not play a Nash equilibrium strategy. First, it may be unclear which equilibrium to adopt if there are many different equilibria in the game. For games with only one equilibrium, it may be difficult for a human to compute the Nash equilibrium because of cognitive limitations. Even if human agents can compute the Nash equilibrium, they may doubt that their opponents can perform that computation.

There are many behavioral models in the literature,[10] but one approach is to combine the iterated approach from the previous section with a softmax model. This *hierarchical softmax* approach (algorithm 24.9)[11] models the *depth of rationality* of an agent by a level of $k \geq 0$. A level 0 agent plays its actions uniformly at random. A level 1 agent assumes the other players adopt level 0 strategies and selects actions according to a softmax response with precision λ. A level k agent selects actions according to a softmax model of the other players playing level $k - 1$. Figure 24.1 illustrates this approach for a simple game.

We can learn the k and λ parameters of this behavioral model from data. If we have a collection of joint actions played by different agents, we can compute the associated likelihood for a given k and λ. We can then use an optimization algorithm to attempt to find values of k and λ that maximize likelihood. This

[10] C. F. Camerer, *Behavioral Game Theory: Experiments in Strategic Interaction*. Princeton University Press, 2003.

[11] This approach is sometimes called *quantal-level-k* or *logit-level-k*. D. O. Stahl and P. W. Wilson, "Experimental Evidence on Players' Models of Other Players," *Journal of Economic Behavior & Organization*, vol. 25, no. 3, pp. 309–327, 1994.

```
struct HierarchicalSoftmax
    λ # precision parameter
    k # level
    π # initial policy
end

function HierarchicalSoftmax(𝒫::SimpleGame, λ, k)
    π = [SimpleGamePolicy(ai ⇒ 1.0 for ai in 𝒜i) for 𝒜i in 𝒫.𝒜]
    return HierarchicalSoftmax(λ, k, π)
end

function solve(M::HierarchicalSoftmax, 𝒫)
    π = M.π
    for k in 1:M.k
        π = [softmax_response(𝒫, π, i, M.λ) for i in 𝒫.ℐ]
    end
    return π
end
```

Algorithm 24.9. The hierarchical softmax model with precision parameter λ and level k. By default, it starts with an initial joint policy that assigns uniform probability to all individual actions.

optimization typically cannot be done analytically, but we can use numerical methods to perform this optimization.[12] Alternatively, we can use a Bayesian approach to parameter learning.[13]

24.8 Fictitious Play

An alternative approach for computing policies for different agents is to have them play each other in simulation and learn how to best respond. Algorithm 24.10 provides an implementation of the simulation loop. At each iteration, we evaluate the various policies to obtain a joint action, and then this joint action is used by the agents to update their policies. We can use a number of ways to update the policies in response to observed joint actions. This section focuses on *fictitious play*, where the agents use maximum likelihood estimates (as described in section 16.1) of the policies followed by the other agents. Each agent follows its own best response, assuming that the other agents act according to those estimates.[14]

To compute a maximum likelihood estimate, agent i tracks the number of times that agent j takes action a^j, storing it in table $N^i(j, a^j)$. These counts can be initialized to any value, but they are often initialized to 1 to create initial uniform uncertainty. Agent i computes its best response, assuming that each agent j follows the stochastic policy:

$$\pi^j(a^j) \propto N^i(j, a^j) \qquad (24.9)$$

[12] J. R. Wright and K. Leyton-Brown, "Beyond Equilibrium: Predicting Human Behavior in Normal Form Games," in *AAAI Conference on Artificial Intelligence (AAAI)*, 2010.

[13] J. R. Wright and K. Leyton-Brown, "Behavioral Game Theoretic Models: A Bayesian Framework for Parameter Analysis," in *International Conference on Autonomous Agents and Multiagent Systems (AAMAS)*, 2012.

[14] G. W. Brown, "Iterative Solution of Games by Fictitious Play," *Activity Analysis of Production and Allocation*, vol. 13, no. 1, pp. 374–376, 1951. J. Robinson, "An Iterative Method of Solving a Game," *Annals of Mathematics*, pp. 296–301, 1951.

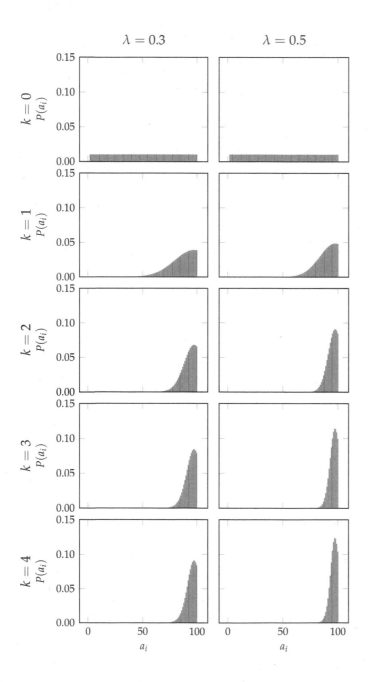

Figure 24.1. The hierarchical soft-max model applied to the traveler's dilemma (described in appendix F.12) for various depths of rationality k and precision parameters λ. People tend to select actions between \$97 and \$100, even though the Nash equilibrium is only \$2.

```
function simulate(𝒫::SimpleGame, π, k_max)
    for k = 1:k_max
        a = [πi() for πi in π]
        for πi in π
            update!(πi, a)
        end
    end
    return π
end
```

Algorithm 24.10. A simulation of a joint policy in simple game 𝒫 for k_max iterations. The joint policy π is a vector of policies that can be individually updated through calls to update!(πi, a).

At each iteration, we have each agent act according to a best response, assuming these stochastic count-based policies for the other agents. We then update the action counts for the actions taken. Algorithm 24.11 implements this simple adaptive procedure. Figures 24.2 and 24.3 show how the policies evolve over time using fictitious play. Fictitious play is not guaranteed to converge to a Nash equilibrium.[15]

[15] A concise background is provided by U. Berger, "Brown's Original Fictitious Play," *Journal of Economic Theory*, vol. 135, no. 1, pp. 572–578, 2007.

```
mutable struct FictitiousPlay
    𝒫  # simple game
    i  # agent index
    N  # array of action count dictionaries
    πi # current policy
end

function FictitiousPlay(𝒫::SimpleGame, i)
    N = [Dict(aj ⇒ 1 for aj in 𝒫.𝒜[j]) for j in 𝒫.ℐ]
    πi = SimpleGamePolicy(ai ⇒ 1.0 for ai in 𝒫.𝒜[i])
    return FictitiousPlay(𝒫, i, N, πi)
end

(πi::FictitiousPlay)() = πi.πi()

(πi::FictitiousPlay)(ai) = πi.πi(ai)

function update!(πi::FictitiousPlay, a)
    N, 𝒫, ℐ, i = πi.N, πi.𝒫, πi.𝒫.ℐ, πi.i
    for (j, aj) in enumerate(a)
        N[j][aj] += 1
    end
    p(j) = SimpleGamePolicy(aj ⇒ u/sum(values(N[j])) for (aj, u) in N[j])
    π = [p(j) for j in ℐ]
    πi.πi = best_response(𝒫, π, i)
end
```

Algorithm 24.11. Fictitious play is a simple learning algorithm for an agent i of a simple game 𝒫 that maintains counts of other agent action selections over time and averages them, assuming that this is their stochastic policy. It then computes a best response to this policy and performs the corresponding utility-maximizing action.

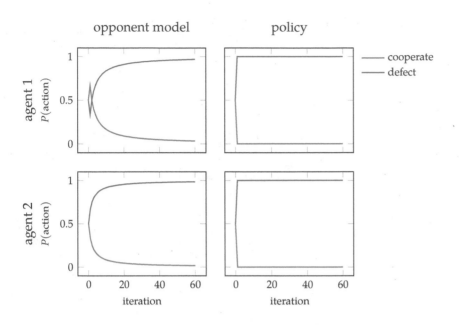

Figure 24.2. Two fictitious play agents learning and adapting to one another in a prisoner's dilemma game. The first row illustrates agent 1's learned model of 2 (left) and agent 1's policy (right) over iteration. The second row follows the same pattern, but for agent 2. To illustrate variation in learning behavior, the initial counts for each agent's model over the other agent's action were assigned to a random number between 1 and 10.

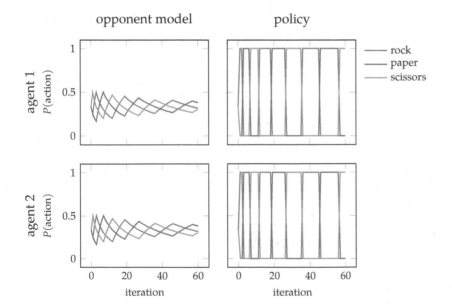

Figure 24.3. A visualization of two fictitious play agents learning and adapting to one another in a rock-paper-scissors game. The first row illustrates agent 1's learned model of 2 (left) and agent 1's policy (right) over time. The second row follows the same pattern, but for agent 2. To illustrate variation in learning behavior, the initial counts for each agent's model over the other agent's action were assigned to a random number between 1 and 10. In this zero-sum game, fictitious play agents approach convergence to their stochastic policy Nash equilibrium.

There are many variants of fictitious play. One variant, called *smooth fictitious play*,[16] selects a best response using expected utility plus a smoothing function, such as the entropy of the policy. Another variant is called *rational learning* or *Bayesian learning*. Rational learning expands the model of fictitious play to be any belief over other agents' actions, formulated as a Bayesian prior. Bayes' rule is then used to update the beliefs, given the history of joint actions. Traditional fictitious play can be seen as rational learning with a Dirichlet prior (section 4.2.2).

24.9 Gradient Ascent

Gradient ascent (algorithm 24.12) incrementally adjusts the agent's policy in the gradient with respect to its utility. At time t, the gradient for agent i is

$$\frac{\partial U^i(\boldsymbol{\pi}_t)}{\partial \pi_t^i(a^i)} = \frac{\partial}{\partial \pi_t^i}\left(\sum_{\mathbf{a}} R^i(\mathbf{a}) \prod_j \pi_t^j(a^j)\right) = \sum_{\mathbf{a}^{-i}} R^i(a^i, \mathbf{a}^{-i}) \prod_{j \neq i} \pi_t^j(a^j) \qquad (24.10)$$

We can then use standard gradient ascent with

$$\pi_{t+1}^i(a^i) = \pi_t^i(a^i) + \alpha_t^i \frac{\partial U^i(\boldsymbol{\pi}_t)}{\partial \pi_t^i(a^i)} \qquad (24.11)$$

with learning rate α_t^i.[17] This π_{t+1}^i may need to be projected back to a valid probability distribution, just as in section 23.4 for POMDP policies.

In practice, however, an agent i knows only its own policy π_t^i, not the policies of the others, making the computation of the gradient difficult. But agents do observe the joint actions $\mathbf{a}_t$ that are performed. Although we could try to estimate their policies as done in fictitious play, one simple approach is to assume the policy of the other agents is to replay their most recent action.[18] The gradient then simplifies to

$$\frac{\partial U^i(\boldsymbol{\pi}_t)}{\partial \pi_t^i(a^i)} = R^i(a^i, \mathbf{a}^{-i}) \qquad (24.12)$$

Figure 24.4 demonstrates this approach for a simple rock-paper-scissors game.

24.10 Summary

- In simple games, multiple agents compete to maximize expected reward.

[16] D. Fudenberg and D. Levine, "Consistency and Cautious Fictitious Play," *Journal of Economic Dynamics and Control*, vol. 19, no. 5–7, pp. 1065–1089, 1995.

[17] The *infinitesimal gradient ascent* method uses an inverse square root learning rate of $\alpha_t^i = 1/\sqrt{t}$. It is referred to as infinitesimal because $\alpha_t^i \to 0$ as $t \to \infty$. We use this learning rate in our implementation. S. Singh, M. Kearns, and Y. Mansour, "Nash Convergence of Gradient Dynamics in General-Sum Games," in *Conference on Uncertainty in Artificial Intelligence (UAI)*, 2000.

[18] This approach is used in *generalized infinitesimal gradient ascent* (GIGA). M. Zinkevich, "Online Convex Programming and Generalized Infinitesimal Gradient Ascent," in *International Conference on Machine Learning (ICML)*, 2003. A variation of the gradient update rule to encourage convergence is proposed by M. Bowling, "Convergence and No-Regret in Multiagent Learning," in *Advances in Neural Information Processing Systems (NIPS)*, 2005.

```
mutable struct GradientAscent
    𝒫  # simple game
    i  # agent index
    t  # time step
    πi # current policy
end

function GradientAscent(𝒫::SimpleGame, i)
    uniform() = SimpleGamePolicy(ai ⇒ 1.0 for ai in 𝒫.𝒜[i])
    return GradientAscent(𝒫, i, 1, uniform())
end

(πi::GradientAscent)() = πi.πi()

(πi::GradientAscent)(ai) = πi.πi(ai)

function update!(πi::GradientAscent, a)
    𝒫, 𝒯, 𝒜i, i, t = πi.𝒫, πi.𝒫.𝒯, πi.𝒫.𝒜[πi.i], πi.i, πi.t
    jointπ(ai) = [SimpleGamePolicy(j == i ? ai : a[j]) for j in 𝒯]
    r = [utility(𝒫, jointπ(ai), i) for ai in 𝒜i]
    π′ = [πi.πi(ai) for ai in 𝒜i]
    π = project_to_simplex(π′ + r / sqrt(t))
    πi.t = t + 1
    πi.πi = SimpleGamePolicy(ai ⇒ p for (ai, p) in zip(𝒜i, π))
end
```

Algorithm 24.12. An implementation of gradient ascent for an agent i of a simple game $\mathcal{P}$. The algorithm updates its distribution over actions incrementally following gradient ascent to improve the expected utility. The projection function from algorithm 23.6 is used to ensure that the resulting policy remains a valid probability distribution.

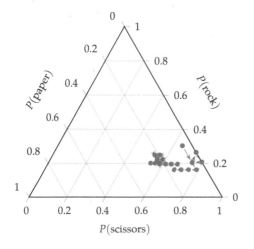 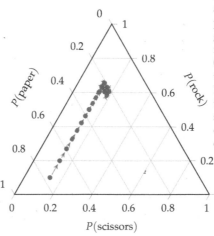

Figure 24.4. Two gradient ascent agents with randomly initialized policies in a rock-paper-scissors game. We use a variation of algorithm 24.12 with a learning rate of $0.1/\sqrt{t}$. Shown here are 20 policy updates. Although different simulation traces will converge because the step size goes to 0, different samples from the stochastic policies may result in convergence to different policies.

- Optimality is not as straightforward in the multiagent setting, with multiple possible solution concepts for extracting policies from a reward specification.

- A best response of an agent to a fixed set of policies of the other agents is one where there is no incentive to deviate.

- A Nash equilibrium is a joint policy where all agents follow a best response.

- A correlated equilibrium is the same as a Nash equilibrium, except that all the agents follow a single joint action distribution that allows correlation between agents.

- Iterated best response can quickly optimize a joint policy by iteratively applying best responses, but there are no general guarantees of convergence.

- Hierarchical softmax attempts to model agents in terms of their depth of rationality and precision, which can be learned from past joint actions.

- Fictitious play is a learning algorithm that uses maximum-likelihood action models for other agents to find best response policies, with the potential to converge to a Nash equilibrium.

- Gradient ascent, followed by projection onto the probability simplex, can be used to learn policies.

24.11   Exercises

Exercise 24.1. Give an example of a game with two agents and an infinite number of actions such that a Nash equilibrium does not exist.

Solution: Suppose that the action space of each agent consists of the negative real numbers and their reward is equal to their action. Since no greatest negative number exists, a Nash equilibrium cannot exist.

Exercise 24.2. Give an example of a game with two agents, two actions, and two Nash equilibria involving deterministic policies.

Solution: Here is one example.[19] Suppose that we have two aircraft on a collision course, and the pilots of each aircraft must choose between climb or descend to avoid collision. If the pilots both choose the same maneuver, then there is a crash, with utility -4 to both pilots. Because climbing requires more fuel than descending, there is an additional penalty of -1 to any pilot who decides to climb.

[19] This example comes from M. J. Kochenderfer, *Decision Making Under Uncertainty: Theory and Application*. MIT Press, 2015.

agent 2

	climb	descend
agent 1 — climb	$-5, -5$	$-1, 0$
agent 1 — descend	$0, -1$	$-4, -4$

Exercise 24.3. Given a stationary joint policy π that is a Nash equilibrium for a simple game with a horizon of 1, prove that it is also a Nash equilibrium for the same simple game repeated to any finite or infinite horizon.

Solution: By definition of a Nash equilibrium, all agents i are performing a best response π^i to all other policies $\pi^{i\prime} \neq \pi^i$ following equation (24.2):

$$U^i(\pi^i, \pi^{-i}) \geq U^i(\pi^{i\prime}, \pi^{-i})$$

By definition of U^i, we have

$$U^i(\pi) = \sum_{\mathbf{a} \in \mathbf{A}} R^i(\mathbf{a}) \prod_{j=1}^{k} \pi^j(a^j)$$

The joint policy remains constant over time for all agents. Apply any horizon n, with any discount factor ($\gamma = 1$ for $n < \infty$; $\gamma < 1$ for $n \to \infty$). The utility of agent i after n steps is

$$U^{i,n}(\pi) = \sum_{t=1}^{n} \gamma^{t-1} \sum_{\mathbf{a} \in \mathbf{A}} R^i(\mathbf{a}) \prod_{j=1}^{k} \pi^j(a^j)$$

$$= \sum_{\mathbf{a} \in \mathbf{A}} R^i(\mathbf{a}) \prod_{j=1}^{k} \pi^j(a^j) \sum_{t=1}^{n} \gamma^{t-1}$$

$$= U^i(\pi) \sum_{t=1}^{n} \gamma^{t-1}$$

$$= U^i(\pi) c$$

The discount factor becomes a constant multiplier $c > 0$. Therefore, any constant multiplication of equation (24.2) on both sides results in the same inequality, completing the proof:

$$U^i(\pi^i, \pi^{-i}) \geq U^i(\pi^{i'}, \pi^{-i})$$

$$U^i(\pi^i, \pi^{-i})c \geq U^i(\pi^{i'}, \pi^{-i})c$$

$$U^i(\pi^i, \pi^{-i}) \sum_{t=1}^{n} \gamma^{t-1} \geq U^i(\pi^{i'}, \pi^{-i}) \sum_{t=1}^{n} \gamma^{t-1}$$

$$\sum_{t=1}^{n} \gamma^{t-1} U^i(\pi^i, \pi^{-i}) \geq \sum_{t=1}^{n} \gamma^{t-1} U^i(\pi^{i'}, \pi^{-i})$$

$$U^{i,n}(\pi^i, \pi^{-i}) \geq U^{i,n}(\pi^{i'}, \pi^{-i})$$

Exercise 24.4. Prove that a Nash equilibrium is a correlated equilibrium.

Solution: Consider any uncorrelated joint policy $\pi(\mathbf{a})$. For any agent i:

$$\pi(\mathbf{a}) = \prod_{j=1}^{k} \pi^j(a^j) = \pi^i(a^i) \prod_{j \neq i} \pi^j(a^j) \tag{24.13}$$

It is sufficient to show that a correlated equilibrium under this constraint forms the exact definition of Nash equilibrium. Begin by applying equation (24.13) to the definition of a correlated equilibrium. For all i, any a^i with nonzero probability[20] in π, and all $a^{i'}$:

$$\sum_{\mathbf{a}^{-i}} R^i(a^i, \mathbf{a}^{-i}) \pi(a^i, \mathbf{a}^{-i}) \geq \sum_{\mathbf{a}^{-i}} R^i(a^{i'}, \mathbf{a}^{-i}) \pi(a^i, \mathbf{a}^{-i})$$

$$\sum_{\mathbf{a}^{-i}} R^i(a^i, \mathbf{a}^{-i}) \pi^i(a^i) \prod_{j \neq i} \pi^j(a^j) \geq \sum_{\mathbf{a}^{-i}} R^i(a^{i'}, \mathbf{a}^{-i}) \pi^i(a^i) \prod_{j \neq i} \pi^j(a^j)$$

$$\sum_{\mathbf{a}^{-i}} R^i(a^i, \mathbf{a}^{-i}) \prod_{j \neq i} \pi^j(a^j) \geq \sum_{\mathbf{a}^{-i}} R^i(a^{i'}, \mathbf{a}^{-i}) \prod_{j \neq i} \pi^j(a^j) \tag{24.14}$$

Now consider the definition of utility:

$$U^i(\pi^i, \pi^{-i}) = \sum_{\mathbf{a}} R^i(a^i, \mathbf{a}^{-i}) \prod_{j=1}^{k} \pi^j(a^j) = \sum_{a^i} \pi^i(a^i) \left(\sum_{\mathbf{a}^{-i}} R^i(a^i, \mathbf{a}^{-i}) \prod_{j \neq i} \pi^j(a^j) \right)$$

Next apply equation (24.14) to the terms inside the parentheses:

$$U^i(\pi^i, \pi^{-i}) \geq \sum_{a^i} \pi^i(a^i) \left(\sum_{\mathbf{a}^{-i}} R^i(a^{i'}, \mathbf{a}^{-i}) \prod_{j \neq i} \pi^j(a^j) \right) = \left(\sum_{\mathbf{a}^{-i}} R^i(a^{i'}, \mathbf{a}^{-i}) \prod_{j \neq i} \pi^j(a^j) \right) \sum_{a^i} \pi^i(a^i) = \sum_{\mathbf{a}^{-i}} R^i(a^{i'}, \mathbf{a}^{-i}) \prod_{j \neq i} \pi^j(a^j)$$

[20] That is, $\sum_{\mathbf{a}^{-i}} \pi(a^i, \mathbf{a}^{-i}) > 0$. If it is zero, then the inequality trivially becomes true with $0 \geq 0$.

This equation holds for any action $a^{i'}$. Consequently, applying any probability weighting preserves the right side of this inequality. Consider any other policy $\pi^{i'}$ as a weighting:

$$U^i(\pi^i, \pi^{-i}) \geq \sum_{a^i} \pi^{i'}(a^i) \sum_{\mathbf{a}^{-i}} R^i(a^i, \mathbf{a}^{-i}) \prod_{j \neq i} \pi^j(a^j) = U^i(\pi^{i'}, \pi^{-i})$$

This inequality is the definition of a best response. It must hold for all agents i and thus forms the definition of a Nash equilibrium. In summary, a Nash equilibrium is a special kind of correlated equilibrium that is constrained to an uncorrelated joint policy.

Exercise 24.5. Give an example of a two-agent game, each with two actions, for which the correlated equilibria cannot be represented as a Nash equilibrium.

Solution: Consider the following game, in which two people want to go on a date but have a conflicting preference on what kind of date (in this case, a dinner or a movie):

<table>
<tr><td></td><td></td><td colspan="2" align="center">agent 2</td></tr>
<tr><td></td><td></td><td align="center">dinner</td><td align="center">movie</td></tr>
<tr><td rowspan="2">agent 1</td><td>dinner</td><td align="center">2, 1</td><td align="center">0, 0</td></tr>
<tr><td>movie</td><td align="center">0, 0</td><td align="center">1, 2</td></tr>
</table>

There is a stochastic Nash equilibrium. Agent 1 follows $\pi^1(\text{dinner}) = 2/3$ and $\pi^1(\text{movie}) = 1/3$. Agent 2 follows $\pi^2(\text{dinner}) = 1/3$ and $\pi^2(\text{movie}) = 2/3$. The utilities are:

$$U^1(\pi) = \frac{2}{3} \cdot \frac{1}{3} \cdot 2 + \frac{2}{3} \cdot \frac{2}{3} \cdot 0 + \frac{1}{3} \cdot \frac{1}{3} \cdot 0 + \frac{1}{3} \cdot \frac{2}{3} \cdot 1 = \frac{2}{9} \cdot 2 + \frac{2}{9} \cdot 1 = \frac{2}{3}$$

$$U^2(\pi) = \frac{2}{3} \cdot \frac{1}{3} \cdot 1 + \frac{2}{3} \cdot \frac{2}{3} \cdot 0 + \frac{1}{3} \cdot \frac{1}{3} \cdot 0 + \frac{1}{3} \cdot \frac{2}{3} \cdot 2 = \frac{2}{9} \cdot 1 + \frac{2}{9} \cdot 2 = \frac{2}{3}$$

However, if the two agents correlated their actions on a fair coin flip $\pi(\text{movie}, \text{movie}) = \pi(\text{dinner}, \text{dinner}) = 0.5$, then they could coordinate either both going to dinner or both going to the movie. The utilities are:

$$U^1(\pi) = 0.5 \cdot 2 + 0.0 \cdot 0 + 0.0 \cdot 0 + 0.5 \cdot 1 = 0.5 \cdot 2 + 0.5 \cdot 1 = \frac{3}{2}$$

$$U^2(\pi) = 0.5 \cdot 1 + 0.0 \cdot 0 + 0.0 \cdot 0 + 0.5 \cdot 2 = 0.5 \cdot 1 + 0.5 \cdot 2 = \frac{3}{2}$$

This is not possible with a Nash equilibrium. Intuitively, in this example, this is because the probabilistic weight is spread out over each row independently for each player. Conversely, a correlated equilibrium can be targeted toward a specific cell (in this case, with a higher payoff).

Exercise 24.6. Algorithms such as iterated best response and fictitious play do not converge in every game. Construct a game that demonstrates this nonconvergence.

Solution: Iterated best response diverges in rock-paper-scissors. Here is an example of the first 10 iterations with random initialization:

Iteration	Agent 1's Action	Agent 2's Action	Rewards
1	paper	rock	1.0, −1.0
2	paper	scissors	−1.0, 1.0
3	rock	scissors	1.0, −1.0
4	rock	paper	−1.0, 1.0
5	scissors	paper	1.0, −1.0
6	scissors	rock	−1.0, 1.0
7	paper	rock	1.0, −1.0
8	paper	scissors	−1.0, 1.0
9	rock	scissors	1.0, −1.0
10	rock	paper	−1.0, 1.0

Fictitious play also will not converge in *almost-rock-paper-scissors*:[21]

		agent 2		
		rock	paper	scissors
agent 1	rock	0,0	0,1	1,0
	paper	1,0	0,0	0,1
	scissors	0,1	1,0	0,0

[21] This game and many others are discussed in greater detail by Y. Shoham and K. Leyton-Brown, *Multiagent Systems: Algorithmic, Game Theoretic, and Logical Foundations.* Cambridge University Press, 2009.

Here is an example of fictitious play agents playing this game for 60 iterations:

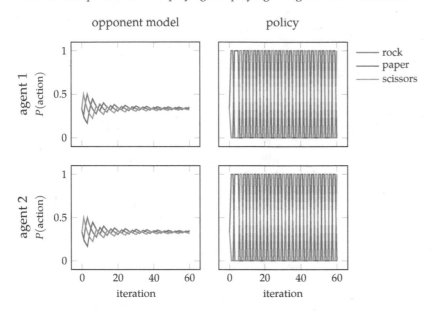

Exercise 24.7. What does iterated best response converge to in the traveler's dilemma (appendix F.12)?

Solution: It converges to the Nash equilibrium of $2.

25 Sequential Problems

This chapter extends simple games to a sequential context with multiple states. A *Markov game* (MG) can be viewed as a Markov decision process involving multiple agents with their own reward functions.[1] In this formulation, transitions depend on the joint action and all agents seek to maximize their own reward. We generalize the response models and the Nash equilibrium solution concept from simple games to take into account the state transition model. The last part of this chapter discusses learning-based models, where the agents adapt their policies based on information from observed interactions and knowledge of the reward and transition functions.

[1] MGs, also called *stochastic games*, were originally studied in the 1950s around the same time as MDPs. L. S. Shapley, "Stochastic Games," *Proceedings of the National Academy of Sciences*, vol. 39, no. 10, pp. 1095–1100, 1953. They were introduced into the multiagent artificial intelligence community decades later. M. L. Littman, "Markov Games as a Framework for Multi-Agent Reinforcement Learning," in *International Conference on Machine Learning* (ICML), 1994.

25.1 Markov Games

An MG (algorithm 25.1) extends a simple game to include a shared state $s \in \mathcal{S}$. The likelihood of transitioning from a state s to a state s' under a joint action $\mathbf{a}$ is given by the transition distribution $T(s' \mid s, \mathbf{a})$. Each agent i receives a reward according to its own reward function $R^i(s, \mathbf{a})$, which now also depends on the state. Example 25.1 sketches out how traffic routing can be framed as an MG.

```
struct MG
    γ  # discount factor
    ℐ  # agents
    𝒮  # state space
    𝒜  # joint action space
    T  # transition function
    R  # joint reward function
end
```

Algorithm 25.1. Data structure for an MG.

Consider commuters headed to work by car. Each car has a starting position and a destination. Each car can take any of several available roads to get to their destination, but these roads vary in the time it takes to drive them. The more cars that drive on a given road, the slower they all move.

This problem is an MG. The agents are the commuters in their cars, the states are the locations of all the cars on the roads, and the actions correspond to decisions of which road to take next. The state transition moves all car agents forward following their joint action. The negative reward is proportional to the time spent driving on a road.

Example 25.1. Traffic routing as an MG. The problem cannot be modeled using a single agent model like an MDP because we do not know the behavior of other agents, only their rewards. We can try to find equilibria or learn policies through interaction, similar to what we did for simple games.

The joint policy $\boldsymbol{\pi}$ in an MG specifies a probability distribution over joint actions, given the current state. As with MDPs, we will focus on policies that depend on the current state rather than the past history because future states and rewards are conditionally independent of the history, given the current state. In addition, we will focus on stationary policies, which do not depend on time. The probability that agent i selects action a at state s is given by $\pi^i(a \mid s)$. We will often use $\boldsymbol{\pi}(s)$ to represent a distribution over joint actions.

The utility of a joint policy $\boldsymbol{\pi}$ from the perspective of agent i can be computed using a variation of policy evaluation introduced in section 7.2 for MDPs. The reward to agent i from state s when following joint policy $\boldsymbol{\pi}$ is

$$R^i(s, \boldsymbol{\pi}(s)) = \sum_{\mathbf{a}} R^i(s, \mathbf{a}) \prod_{j \in \mathcal{I}} \pi^j(a^j \mid s) \tag{25.1}$$

The probability of transitioning from state s to s' when following $\boldsymbol{\pi}$ is

$$T(s' \mid s, \boldsymbol{\pi}(s)) = \sum_{\mathbf{a}} T(s' \mid s, \mathbf{a}) \prod_{j \in \mathcal{I}} \pi^j(a^j \mid s) \tag{25.2}$$

In an infinite-horizon discounted game, the utility for agent i from state s is

$$U^{\boldsymbol{\pi}, i}(s) = R^i(s, \boldsymbol{\pi}(s)) + \gamma \sum_{s'} T(s' \mid s, \boldsymbol{\pi}(s)) U^{\boldsymbol{\pi}, i}(s') \tag{25.3}$$

which can be solved exactly (algorithm 25.2).

```
struct MGPolicy
    p # dictionary mapping states to simple game policies
    MGPolicy(p::Base.Generator) = new(Dict(p))
end

(πi::MGPolicy)(s, ai) = πi.p[s](ai)
(πi::SimpleGamePolicy)(s, ai) = πi(ai)

probability(𝒫::MG, s, π, a) = prod(πj(s, aj) for (πj, aj) in zip(π, a))
reward(𝒫::MG, s, π, i) =
    sum(𝒫.R(s,a)[i]*probability(𝒫,s,π,a) for a in joint(𝒫.𝒜))
transition(𝒫::MG, s, π, s′) =
    sum(𝒫.T(s,a,s′)*probability(𝒫,s,π,a) for a in joint(𝒫.𝒜))

function policy_evaluation(𝒫::MG, π, i)
    S, 𝒜, R, T, γ = 𝒫.S, 𝒫.𝒜, 𝒫.R, 𝒫.T, 𝒫.γ
    p(s,a) = prod(πj(s, aj) for (πj, aj) in zip(π, a))
    R′ = [sum(R(s,a)[i]*p(s,a) for a in joint(𝒜)) for s in S]
    T′ = [sum(T(s,a,s′)*p(s,a) for a in joint(𝒜)) for s in S, s′ in S]
    return (I - γ*T′)\R′
end
```

Algorithm 25.2. An MG policy is a mapping from states to simple game policies, introduced in the previous chapter. We can construct it by passing in a generator to construct the dictionary. The probability that a policy (either for an MG or a simple game) assigns to taking action ai from state s is πi(s, ai). Functions are also provided for computing $R^i(s, \pi(s))$ and $T(s' \mid s, \pi(s))$. The policy evaluation function will compute a vector representing $U^{\pi, i}$.

25.2 Response Models

We can generalize the response models introduced in the previous chapter to MGs. Doing so requires taking into account the state transition model.

25.2.1 Best Response

A *response policy* for agent i is a policy π^i that maximizes expected utility, given the fixed policies of other agents $\boldsymbol{\pi}^{-i}$. If the policies of the other agents are fixed, then the problem reduces to an MDP. This MDP has state space $\mathcal{S}$ and action space $\mathcal{A}^i$. We can define the transition and reward functions as follows:

$$T'(s' \mid s, a^i) = T(s' \mid s, a^i, \boldsymbol{\pi}^{-i}(s)) \qquad (25.4)$$

$$R'(s, a^i) = R^i(s, a^i, \boldsymbol{\pi}^{-i}(s)) \qquad (25.5)$$

Because this is a best response for agent i, the MDP only uses reward R^i. Solving this MDP results in a best response policy for agent i. Algorithm 25.3 provides an implementation of this.

```
function best_response(𝒫::MG, π, i)
    S, 𝒜, R, T, γ = 𝒫.S, 𝒫.𝒜, 𝒫.R, 𝒫.T, 𝒫.γ
    T′(s,ai,s′) = transition(𝒫, s, joint(π, SimpleGamePolicy(ai), i), s′)
    R′(s,ai) = reward(𝒫, s, joint(π, SimpleGamePolicy(ai), i), i)
    πi = solve(MDP(γ, S, 𝒜[i], T′, R′))
    return MGPolicy(s ⇒ SimpleGamePolicy(πi(s)) for s in S)
end
```

Algorithm 25.3. For an MG 𝒫, we can compute a deterministic best response policy for agent i, given that the other agents are playing policies in π. We can solve the MDP exactly using one of the methods from chapter 7.

25.2.2   Softmax Response

Similar to what was done in the previous chapter, we can define a *softmax response policy*, which assigns a stochastic response to the policies of the other agents at each state. As we did in the construction of a deterministic best response policy, we solve an MDP where the agents with the fixed policies π^{-i} are folded into the environment. We then extract the action value function $Q(s,a)$ using one-step lookahead. The softmax response is

$$\pi^i(a^i \mid s) \propto \exp(\lambda Q(s,a^i)) \tag{25.6}$$

with precision parameter $\lambda \geq 0$. Algorithm 25.4 provides an implementation. This approach can be used to generate hierarchical softmax solutions (section 24.7). In fact, we can use algorithm 24.9 directly.

```
function softmax_response(𝒫::MG, π, i, λ)
    S, 𝒜, R, T, γ = 𝒫.S, 𝒫.𝒜, 𝒫.R, 𝒫.T, 𝒫.γ
    T′(s,ai,s′) = transition(𝒫, s, joint(π, SimpleGamePolicy(ai), i), s′)
    R′(s,ai) = reward(𝒫, s, joint(π, SimpleGamePolicy(ai), i), i)
    mdp = MDP(γ, S, joint(𝒜), T′, R′)
    πi = solve(mdp)
    Q(s,a) = lookahead(mdp, πi.U, s, a)
    p(s) = SimpleGamePolicy(a ⇒ exp(λ*Q(s,a)) for a in 𝒜[i])
    return MGPolicy(s ⇒ p(s) for s in S)
end
```

Algorithm 25.4. The softmax response of agent i to joint policy π with precision parameter λ.

25.3   Nash Equilibrium

The Nash equilibrium concept can be generalized to MGs.[2] As with simple games, all agents perform a best response to one another and have no incentive to deviate. All finite MGs with a discounted infinite horizon have a Nash equilibrium.[3]

[2] Because we assume that policies are *stationary*, in that they do not vary over time, the Nash equilibria covered here are *stationary Markov perfect equilibria*.

[3] A. M. Fink, "Equilibrium in a Stochastic n-Person Game," *Journal of Science of the Hiroshima University, Series A-I*, vol. 28, no. 1, pp. 89–93, 1964.

We can find a Nash equilibrium by solving a nonlinear optimization problem similar to the one that we solved in the context of simple games. This problem minimizes the sum of the lookahead utility deviations and constrains the policies to be valid distributions:

$$\underset{\pi,U}{\text{minimize}} \quad \sum_{i\in\mathcal{I}} \sum_s \left(U^i(s) - Q^i(s,\pi(s)) \right)$$

$$\text{subject to} \quad U^i(s) \geq Q^i(s,a^i,\pi^{-i}(s)) \text{ for all } i,s,a^i$$

$$\sum_{a^i} \pi^i(a^i \mid s) = 1 \text{ for all } i,s \tag{25.7}$$

$$\pi^i(a^i \mid s) \geq 0 \text{ for all } i,s,a^i$$

where

$$Q^i(s,\pi(s)) = R^i(s,\pi(s)) + \gamma \sum_{s'} T(s' \mid s,\pi(s))U^i(s') \tag{25.8}$$

This nonlinear optimization problem is implemented and solved in algorithm 25.5.[4]

[4] J. A. Filar, T. A. Schultz, F. Thuijsman, and O. Vrieze, "Nonlinear Programming and Stationary Equilibria in Stochastic Games," *Mathematical Programming*, vol. 50, no. 1–3, pp. 227–237, 1991.

25.4 Fictitious Play

As we did in the context of simple games, we can take a learning-based approach to arrive at joint policies by running agents in simulation. Algorithm 25.6 generalizes the simulation loop introduced in the previous chapter to handle state transitions. The various policies run in simulation update themselves based on the state transitions and the actions taken by the various agents.

One approach for updating policies is to use a generalization of *fictitious play* (algorithm 25.7) from the previous chapter,[5] which involves maintaining a maximum-likelihood model over the policies of the other agents. The maximum likelihood model tracks the state in addition to the action being taken by each agent. We track the number of times that agent j takes action a^j in state s, storing it in table $N(j,a^j,s)$, typically initialized to 1. Then, we can compute the best response, assuming that each agent j follows the state-dependent stochastic policy:

$$\pi^j(a^j \mid s) \propto N(j,a^j,s) \tag{25.9}$$

[5] W. Uther and M. Veloso, "Adversarial Reinforcement Learning," Carnegie Mellon University, Tech. Rep. CMU-CS-03-107, 1997. M. Bowling and M. Veloso, "An Analysis of Stochastic Game Theory for Multiagent Reinforcement Learning," Carnegie Mellon University, Tech. Rep. CMU-CS-00-165, 2000.

```
function tensorform(𝒫::MG)
    𝒯, 𝒮, 𝒜, R, T = 𝒫.𝒯, 𝒫.𝒮, 𝒫.𝒜, 𝒫.R, 𝒫.T
    𝒯′ = eachindex(𝒯)
    𝒮′ = eachindex(𝒮)
    𝒜′ = [eachindex(𝒜[i]) for i in 𝒯]
    R′ = [R(s,a) for s in 𝒮, a in joint(𝒜)]
    T′ = [T(s,a,s′) for s in 𝒮, a in joint(𝒜), s′ in 𝒮]
    return 𝒯′, 𝒮′, 𝒜′, R′, T′
end

function solve(M::NashEquilibrium, 𝒫::MG)
    𝒯, 𝒮, 𝒜, R, T = tensorform(𝒫)
    𝒮′, 𝒜′, γ = 𝒫.𝒮, 𝒫.𝒜, 𝒫.γ
    model = Model(Ipopt.Optimizer)
    @variable(model, U[𝒯, 𝒮])
    @variable(model, π[i=𝒯, 𝒮, ai=𝒜[i]] ≥ 0)
    @NLobjective(model, Min,
        sum(U[i,s] - sum(prod(π[j,s,a[j]] for j in 𝒯)
            * (R[s,y][i] + γ*sum(T[s,y,s′]*U[i,s′] for s′ in 𝒮))
            for (y,a) in enumerate(joint(𝒜))) for i in 𝒯, s in 𝒮))
    @NLconstraint(model, [i=𝒯, s=𝒮, ai=𝒜[i]],
        U[i,s] ≥ sum(
            prod(j==i ? (a[j]==ai ? 1.0 : 0.0) : π[j,s,a[j]] for j in 𝒯)
            * (R[s,y][i] + γ*sum(T[s,y,s′]*U[i,s′] for s′ in 𝒮))
            for (y,a) in enumerate(joint(𝒜))))
    @constraint(model, [i=𝒯, s=𝒮], sum(π[i,s,ai] for ai in 𝒜[i]) == 1)
    optimize!(model)
    π′ = value.(π)
    πi′(i,s) = SimpleGamePolicy(𝒜′[i][ai] ⇒ π′[i,s,ai] for ai in 𝒜[i])
    πi′(i) = MGPolicy(𝒮′[s] ⇒ πi′(i,s) for s in 𝒮)
    return [πi′(i) for i in 𝒯]
end
```

Algorithm 25.5. This nonlinear program computes a Nash equilibrium for an MG 𝒫.

```
function randstep(𝒫::MG, s, a)
    s′ = rand(SetCategorical(𝒫.𝒮, [𝒫.T(s, a, s′) for s′ in 𝒫.𝒮]))
    r = 𝒫.R(s,a)
    return s′, r
end

function simulate(𝒫::MG, π, k_max, b)
    s = rand(b)
    for k = 1:k_max
        a = Tuple(πi(s)() for πi in π)
        s′, r = randstep(𝒫, s, a)
        for πi in π
            update!(πi, s, a, s′)
        end
        s = s′
    end
    return π
end
```

Algorithm 25.6. Functions for taking a random step and running full simulations in MGs. The simulate function will simulate the joint policy π for k_max steps starting from a state randomly sampled from b.

After observing joint action **a** in states s, we update

$$N(j, a^j, s) \leftarrow N(j, a^j, s) + 1 \qquad (25.10)$$

for each agent j.

As the distributions of the other agents' actions change, we must update the utilities. The utilities in MGs are significantly more difficult to compute than simple games because of the state dependency. As described in section 25.2.1, any assignment of fixed policies of others π^{-i} induces an MDP. In fictitious play, π^{-i} is determined by equation (25.9). Instead of solving an MDP at each update, it is common to apply the update periodically, a strategy adopted from asynchronous value iteration. An example of fictitious play is given in example 25.2.

Our policy $\pi^i(s)$ for a state s is derived from a given opponent model π^{-i} and computed utility U^i. We then select a best response:

$$\arg\max_a Q^i(s, a, \pi^{-i}) \qquad (25.11)$$

In the implementation here, we use the property that each state of an MG policy is a simple game policy whose reward is the corresponding Q^i.

```
mutable struct MGFictitiousPlay
    𝒫  # Markov game
    i  # agent index
    Qi # state-action value estimates
    Ni # state-action counts
end

function MGFictitiousPlay(𝒫::MG, i)
    𝒯, 𝒮, 𝒜, R = 𝒫.𝒯, 𝒫.𝒮, 𝒫.𝒜, 𝒫.R
    Qi = Dict((s, a) ⇒ R(s, a)[i] for s in 𝒮 for a in joint(𝒜))
    Ni = Dict((j, s, aj) ⇒ 1.0 for j in 𝒯 for s in 𝒮 for aj in 𝒜[j])
    return MGFictitiousPlay(𝒫, i, Qi, Ni)
end


function (πi::MGFictitiousPlay)(s)
    𝒫, i, Qi = πi.𝒫, πi.i, πi.Qi
    𝒯, 𝒮, 𝒜, T, R, γ = 𝒫.𝒯, 𝒫.𝒮, 𝒫.𝒜, 𝒫.T, 𝒫.R, 𝒫.γ
    πi'(i,s) = SimpleGamePolicy(ai ⇒ πi.Ni[i,s,ai] for ai in 𝒜[i])
    πi'(i) = MGPolicy(s ⇒ πi'(i,s) for s in 𝒮)
    π = [πi'(i) for i in 𝒯]
    U(s,π) = sum(πi.Qi[s,a]*probability(𝒫,s,π,a) for a in joint(𝒜))
    Q(s,π) = reward(𝒫,s,π,i) + γ*sum(transition(𝒫,s,π,s')*U(s',π)
                                for s' in 𝒮)
    Q(ai) = Q(s, joint(π, SimpleGamePolicy(ai), i))
    ai = argmax(Q, 𝒫.𝒜[πi.i])
    return SimpleGamePolicy(ai)
end

function update!(πi::MGFictitiousPlay, s, a, s')
    𝒫, i, Qi = πi.𝒫, πi.i, πi.Qi
    𝒯, 𝒮, 𝒜, T, R, γ = 𝒫.𝒯, 𝒫.𝒮, 𝒫.𝒜, 𝒫.T, 𝒫.R, 𝒫.γ
    for (j,aj) in enumerate(a)
        πi.Ni[j,s,aj] += 1
    end
    πi'(i,s) = SimpleGamePolicy(ai ⇒ πi.Ni[i,s,ai] for ai in 𝒜[i])
    πi'(i) = MGPolicy(s ⇒ πi'(i,s) for s in 𝒮)
    π = [πi'(i) for i in 𝒯]
    U(π,s) = sum(πi.Qi[s,a]*probability(𝒫,s,π,a) for a in joint(𝒜))
    Q(s,a) = R(s,a)[i] + γ*sum(T(s,a,s')*U(π,s') for s' in 𝒮)
    for a in joint(𝒜)
        πi.Qi[s,a] = Q(s,a)
    end
end
```

Algorithm 25.7. Fictitious play for agent i in an MG 𝒫 that maintains counts Ni of other agent action selections over time for each state and averages them, assuming that this is their stochastic policy. It then computes a best response to this policy and performs the corresponding utility-maximizing action.

The predator-prey hex world MG (appendix F.13) has one predator (red) and one prey (blue). If the predator catches the prey, it receives a reward of 10 and the prey receives a reward of −100. Otherwise, both agents receive a −1 reward. The agents move simultaneously. We apply fictitious play with resets to the initial state every 10 steps.

We observe that the predator learns to chase the prey and the prey learns to flee. Interestingly, the predator also learns that the prey runs to the east corner and waits. The prey learns that if it waits at this corner, it can flee from the predator immediately as it jumps toward the prey. Here, the prey evades the predator by moving west when the predator moves north east.

Example 25.2. Fictitious play on the predator-prey hex world problem. Stochasticity was introduced when initializing the policies to better show learning trends.

Here is a plot of the learned opponent model of the highlighted state (both predator and prey hex locations) for both the predator and the prey:

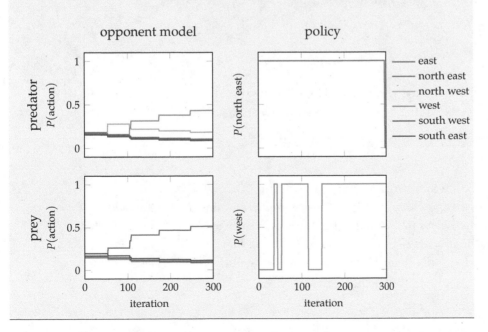

25.5   Gradient Ascent

We can use *gradient ascent* (algorithm 25.8) to learn policies in a way similar to what was done in the previous chapter for simple games. The state must now be considered and requires learning the action value function. At each time step t, all agents perform joint actions $\mathbf{a}_t$ in a state s_t. As in gradient ascent for simple games, an agent i assumes that the agents' policies π_t^{-i} are the observed actions $\mathbf{a}_t^{-i}$. The gradient is

$$\frac{\partial U^{\pi_{t,i}}(s_t)}{\partial \pi_t^i(a^i \mid s_t)} = \frac{\partial}{\partial \pi^i(a^i \mid s_t)} \left(\sum_{\mathbf{a}} \prod_j \pi^j(a^j \mid s_t) Q^{\pi_{t,i}}(s_t, \mathbf{a}_t) \right) \qquad (25.12)$$

$$= Q^{\pi_{t,i}}(s_t, a^i, \mathbf{a}_t^{-i}) \qquad (25.13)$$

The gradient step follows a similar pattern as in the previous chapter, except the state s is included and the expected utility estimate Q_t^i is used:

$$\pi_{t+1}^i(a^i \mid s_t) = \pi_t^i(a^i \mid s_t) + \alpha_t^i Q^i(s_t, a^i, \mathbf{a}^{-i}) \qquad (25.14)$$

Again, this update may require projection to ensure that the policy π_{t+1}^i at s_t is a valid probability distribution.

As with fictitious play in the previous section, we must estimate Q_t^i. We can use Q-learning:

$$Q_{t+1}^i(s_t, \mathbf{a}_t) = Q_t^i(s_t, \mathbf{a}_t) + \alpha_t \left(R^i(s_t, \mathbf{a}_t) + \gamma \max_{a^{i\prime}} Q_t^i(s_{t+1}, a^{i\prime}, \mathbf{a}_t^{-i}) - Q_t^i(s_t, \mathbf{a}_t) \right) \qquad (25.15)$$

We can use the inverse square root learning rate $\alpha_t = 1/\sqrt{t}$. Exploration is also necessary. We can use an ϵ-greedy strategy, perhaps also with $\epsilon_t = 1/\sqrt{t}$.

25.6   Nash Q-Learning

Another learning-based approach is *Nash Q-learning* (algorithm 25.9), which borrows inspiration from Q-learning (section 17.2).[6] The method maintains an estimate of the action value function, which is adapted as the agents react to each other's changing policies. In the process of updating the action value function, it computes a Nash equilibrium to model the behavior of the other agents.

[6] J. Hu and M. P. Wellman, "Nash Q-Learning for General-Sum Stochastic Games," *Journal of Machine Learning Research*, vol. 4, pp. 1039–1069, 2003.

```
mutable struct MGGradientAscent
    𝒫  # Markov game
    i  # agent index
    t  # time step
    Qi # state-action value estimates
    πi # current policy
end

function MGGradientAscent(𝒫::MG, i)
    𝒯, 𝒮, 𝒜 = 𝒫.𝒯, 𝒫.𝒮, 𝒫.𝒜
    Qi = Dict((s, a) ⇒ 0.0 for s in 𝒮, a in joint(𝒜))
    uniform() = Dict(s ⇒ SimpleGamePolicy(ai ⇒ 1.0 for ai in 𝒫.𝒜[i])
                     for s in 𝒮)
    return MGGradientAscent(𝒫, i, 1, Qi, uniform())
end

function (πi::MGGradientAscent)(s)
    𝒜i, t = πi.𝒫.𝒜[πi.i], πi.t
    ϵ = 1 / sqrt(t)
    π'(ai) = ϵ/length(𝒜i) + (1-ϵ)*πi.πi[s](ai)
    return SimpleGamePolicy(ai ⇒ π'(ai) for ai in 𝒜i)
end

function update!(πi::MGGradientAscent, s, a, s')
    𝒫, i, t, Qi = πi.𝒫, πi.i, πi.t, πi.Qi
    𝒯, 𝒮, 𝒜i, R, γ = 𝒫.𝒯, 𝒫.𝒮, 𝒫.𝒜[πi.i], 𝒫.R, 𝒫.γ
    jointπ(ai) = Tuple(j == i ? ai : a[j] for j in 𝒯)
    α = 1 / sqrt(t)
    Qmax = maximum(Qi[s', jointπ(ai)] for ai in 𝒜i)
    πi.Qi[s, a] += α * (R(s, a)[i] + γ * Qmax - Qi[s, a])
    u = [Qi[s, jointπ(ai)] for ai in 𝒜i]
    π' = [πi.πi[s](ai) for ai in 𝒜i]
    π = project_to_simplex(π' + u / sqrt(t))
    πi.t = t + 1
    πi.πi[s] = SimpleGamePolicy(ai ⇒ p for (ai, p) in zip(𝒜i, π))
end
```

Algorithm 25.8. Gradient ascent for an agent i of an MG 𝒫. The algorithm incrementally updates its distributions of actions at visited states following gradient ascent to improve the expected utility. The projection function from algorithm 23.6 is used to ensure that the resulting policy remains a valid probability distribution.

An agent following Nash Q-learning maintains an estimate of a joint action value function $\mathbf{Q}(s, \mathbf{a})$. This action value function is updated after every state transition using a Nash equilibrium computed from a simple game constructed from this value function. After a transition from s to s' following the joint action $\mathbf{a}$, we construct a simple game with the same number of agents and the same joint action space, but the reward function is equal to the estimated value of s' such that $\mathbf{R}(\mathbf{a}') = \mathbf{Q}(s', \mathbf{a}')$. The agent computes a Nash equilibrium policy π' over the next action $\mathbf{a}'$. Under the derived policy, the expected utility of the successor state is

$$\mathbf{U}(s') = \sum_{\mathbf{a}'} \mathbf{Q}(s', \mathbf{a}') \prod_{j \in \mathcal{I}} \pi^{j'}(a^{j'}) \tag{25.16}$$

The agent then updates its value function:

$$\mathbf{Q}(s, \mathbf{a}) \leftarrow \mathbf{Q}(s, \mathbf{a}) + \alpha \left(\mathbf{R}(s, \mathbf{a}) + \gamma \mathbf{U}(s') - \mathbf{Q}(s, \mathbf{a}) \right) \tag{25.17}$$

where the learning rate α is typically a function of the state-action count $\alpha = 1/\sqrt{N(s, \mathbf{a})}$.

As with regular Q-learning, we need to adopt an exploration strategy to ensure that all states and actions are tried often enough. In algorithm 25.9, the agent follows an ϵ-greedy policy. With probability $\epsilon = 1/\sum_{\mathbf{a}}(N(s, \mathbf{a}))$, it selects an action uniformly at random. Otherwise, it will use the result from the Nash equilibrium.

25.7 *Summary*

- MGs are an extension of MDPs to multiple agents or an extension of simple games to sequential problems. In these problems, multiple agents compete and individually receive rewards over time.

- The Nash equilibrium can be formulated for MGs, but it must now consider all actions for all agents in all states.

- The problem of finding a Nash equilibrium can be formulated as a nonlinear optimization problem.

- We can generalize fictitious play to MGs by using a known transition function and incorporating estimates of action values.

```
mutable struct NashQLearning
    𝒫 # Markov game
    i # agent index
    Q # state-action value estimates
    N # history of actions performed
end

function NashQLearning(𝒫::MG, i)
    𝒯, 𝒮, 𝒜 = 𝒫.𝒯, 𝒫.𝒮, 𝒫.𝒜
    Q = Dict((j, s, a) ⇒ 0.0 for j in 𝒯, s in 𝒮, a in joint(𝒜))
    N = Dict((s, a) ⇒ 1.0 for s in 𝒮, a in joint(𝒜))
    return NashQLearning(𝒫, i, Q, N)
end

function (π::NashQLearning)(s)
    𝒫, i, Q, N = π.𝒫, π.i, π.Q, π.N
    𝒯, 𝒮, 𝒜, 𝒜i, γ = 𝒫.𝒯, 𝒫.𝒮, 𝒫.𝒜, 𝒫.𝒜[π.i], 𝒫.γ
    M = NashEquilibrium()
    𝒢 = SimpleGame(γ, 𝒯, 𝒜, a → [Q[j, s, a] for j in 𝒯])
    π = solve(M, 𝒢)
    ϵ = 1 / sum(N[s, a] for a in joint(𝒜))
    πi'(ai) = ϵ/length(𝒜i) + (1-ϵ)*π[i](ai)
    return SimpleGamePolicy(ai ⇒ πi'(ai) for ai in 𝒜i)
end

function update!(π::NashQLearning, s, a, s')
    𝒫, 𝒯, 𝒮, 𝒜, R, γ = π.𝒫, π.𝒫.𝒯, π.𝒫.𝒮, π.𝒫.𝒜, π.𝒫.R, π.𝒫.γ
    i, Q, N = π.i, π.Q, π.N
    M = NashEquilibrium()
    𝒢 = SimpleGame(γ, 𝒯, 𝒜, a' → [Q[j, s', a'] for j in 𝒯])
    π = solve(M, 𝒢)
    π.N[s, a] += 1
    α = 1 / sqrt(N[s, a])
    for j in 𝒯
        π.Q[j,s,a] += α*(R(s,a)[j] + γ*utility(𝒢,π,j) - Q[j,s,a])
    end
end
```

Algorithm 25.9. Nash Q-learning for an agent i in an MG $𝒫$. The algorithm performs joint-action Q-learning to learn a state-action value function for all agents. A simple game is built with Q, and we compute a Nash equilibrium using algorithm 24.5. The equilibrium is then used to update the value function. This implementation also uses a variable learning rate proportional to the number of times state-joint-action pairs are visited, which is stored in N. In addition, it uses ϵ-greedy exploration to ensure that all states and actions are explored.

530 CHAPTER 25. SEQUENTIAL PROBLEMS

- Gradient ascent approaches iteratively improve a stochastic policy, and they do not need to assume a model.

- Nash Q-learning adapts traditional Q-learning to multiagent problems and involves solving for a Nash equilibrium of a simple game constructed from models of the other players.

25.8 Exercises

Exercise 25.1. Show that MGs are extensions of both MDPs and simple games. Show this by formulating an MDP as an MG and by formulating a simple game as an MG.

Solution: MGs generalize simple games. For any simple game with $\mathcal{I}$, $\mathcal{A}$, and $\mathbf{R}$, we can construct an MG by just having a single state that self-loops. In other words, this MG has $\mathcal{S} = \{s^1\}$, $T(s^1 \mid s^1, \mathbf{a}) = 1$, and $\mathbf{R}(s^1, \mathbf{a}) = \mathbf{R}(\mathbf{a})$.

MGs generalize MDPs. For any MDP with $\mathcal{S}$, $\mathcal{A}$, T, and R, we can construct an MG by just assigning the agents to be this single agent. In other words, this MG has $\mathcal{I} = \{1\}$, $\mathcal{A}^1 = \mathcal{A}$, $T(s' \mid s, \mathbf{a}) = T(s' \mid s', a)$, and $\mathbf{R}(s, a) = R(s, a)$.

Exercise 25.2. For an agent i, given the fixed policies of other agents $\boldsymbol{\pi}^{-i}$, can there be a stochastic best response that yields a greater utility than a deterministic best response? Why do we consider stochastic policies in a Nash equilibrium?

Solution: No, if given fixed policies of other agents $\boldsymbol{\pi}^{-i}$, a deterministic best response is sufficient to obtain the highest utility. The best response can be formulated as solving an MDP, as described in section 25.2. It has been shown that deterministic policies are sufficient to provide optimal utility maximization. Hence, the same is true for a best response in an MG.

In a Nash equilibrium, a best response has to hold for all agents. Although a deterministic best response might be equal in utility to a stochastic one, an equilibrium may require stochastic responses in order to prevent other agents from wanting to deviate.

Exercise 25.3. This chapter discussed only stationary Markov policies. What other categories of policies are there?

Solution: A so-called *behavioral policy* $\pi^i(\mathbf{h}_t)$ is one that has a dependence on the complete history $\mathbf{h}_t = (s_{1:t}, \mathbf{a}_{1:t-1})$. Such policies depend on the history of play of other agents. A *nonstationary Markov policy* $\pi^i(s, t)$ is one that depends on the time step t, but not on the complete history. For example, in the predator-prey hex world domain, for the first 10 time steps, the action at a hex might be to go east, and after 10 time steps, to go west.

There can be Nash equilibria that are in the space of nonstationary, non-Markov joint policies; stationary, non-Markov joint policies; and so forth. However, it has been proven that every stationary MG has a stationary Markov Nash equilibrium.

Exercise 25.4. In MGs, fictitious play requires the utilities to be estimated. List different approaches to compute utilities, with their benefits and drawbacks.

Solution: Algorithm 25.7 performs a single backup for the visited state s and all joint actions **a**. This approach has the benefit of being relatively efficient because it is a single backup. Updating all joint actions at that state results in exploring actions that were not observed. The drawback of this approach is that we may need to do this update at all states many times to obtain a suitable policy.

An alternative is only to update the visited state and the joint action that was actually taken, which results in a faster update step. The drawback is that it requires many more steps to explore the full range of joint actions.

Another alternative is to perform value iteration at all states s until convergence at every update step. Recall that the model of the opponent changes on each update. This induces a new MDP, as described for deterministic best response in section 25.2.1. Consequently, we would need to rerun value iteration after each update. The benefit of this approach is that it can result in the most informed decision at each step because the utilities Q^i consider all states over time. The drawback is that the update step is very computationally expensive.

26 State Uncertainty

The multiagent models discussed so far in this part of the book have assumed that all agents can observe the true state. Just as an MDP can be extended to include partial observability, so can an MG be extended to produce a *partially observable Markov game (POMG)*.[1] In fact, a POMG generalizes all the other problems presented in this book. These complex problems can be used to represent domains in which multiple agents receive partial or noisy observations of the environment. This generality makes modeling and solving POMGs computationally challenging. This chapter defines the POMG, outlines policy representations, and presents solution methods.

26.1 Partially Observable Markov Games

A POMG (algorithm 26.1) can be seen as either an extension of MGs to partial observability or as an extension of POMDPs to multiple agents. Each agent $i \in \mathcal{I}$ selects an action $a^i \in \mathcal{A}^i$ based only on local observations o^i made of a shared state s. The true state of the system $s \in \mathcal{S}$ is shared by all agents, but it is not necessarily fully observed. The initial state is drawn from a known initial state distribution b. The likelihood of transitioning from state s to state s' under their joint action $\mathbf{a}$ follows $T(s' \mid s, \mathbf{a})$. A joint reward $\mathbf{r}$ is generated following $R^i(s, \mathbf{a})$, as in MGs. Each agent strives to maximize its own accumulated reward. After all agents perform their joint action $\mathbf{a}$, a *joint observation* is emitted by the environment $\mathbf{o} = (o^1, \ldots, o^k)$ from a *joint observation space* $\mathcal{O} = \mathcal{O}^1 \times \cdots \times \mathcal{O}^k$. Each agent then receives an individual observation o^i from this joint observation. The crying baby problem is extended to multiple agents in example 26.1.

In POMDPs, we were able to maintain a belief state, as discussed in chapter 19, but this approach is not possible in POMGs. Individual agents cannot perform

[1] A POMG is also called a *partially observable stochastic game (POSG)*. POMGs are closely related to the extensive form game with imperfect information. H. Kuhn, "Extensive Games and the Problem of Information," in *Contributions to the Theory of Games II*, H. Kuhn and A. Tucker, eds., Princeton University Press, 1953, pp. 193–216. The model was later introduced to the artificial intelligence community. E. A. Hansen, D. S. Bernstein, and S. Zilberstein, "Dynamic Programming for Partially Observable Stochastic Games," in *AAAI Conference on Artificial Intelligence (AAAI)*, 2004.

the same kind of belief updates as in POMDPs because the joint actions and joint observations are not observed. Inferring a probability distribution over joint actions requires that each agent reason about the other agents reasoning about each other, who are in turn reasoning about each other, and so on. Inferring a distribution over the other observations is just as complicated because the observations depend on the actions of the other agents.[2]

Because of the difficulty of explicitly modeling beliefs in POMGs, we will focus on policy representations that do not require a belief to determine an action. We can use the tree-based conditional plan representation and the graph-based controller representation introduced in the earlier chapters on POMDPs. As in MGs, each agent in a POMG acts according to a policy π^i, or equivalently, the agents act together according to a joint policy $\pi = (\pi^1, \ldots, \pi^k)$.

```
struct POMG
    γ  # discount factor
    ℐ  # agents
    𝒮  # state space
    𝒜  # joint action space
    𝒪  # joint observation space
    T  # transition function
    O  # joint observation function
    R  # joint reward function
end
```

[2] The *Interactive POMDP (I-POMDP)* model attempts to capture this infinite regression. P. J. Gmytrasiewicz and P. Doshi, "A Framework for Sequential Planning in Multi-Agent Settings," *Journal of Artificial Intelligence Research*, vol. 24, no. 1, pp. 49–79, 2005. While this is a computationally complex framework because it reasons in both time and depth, algorithms for such models have advanced tremendously toward the goal of pragmatic use cases. E. Sonu, Y. Chen, and P. Doshi, "Decision-Theoretic Planning Under Anonymity in Agent Populations," *Journal of Artificial Intelligence Research*, vol. 59, pp. 725–770, 2017.

Algorithm 26.1. Data structure for a POMG.

Consider a multiagent POMG generalization of the crying baby problem. We have two caregivers taking care of a baby. As in the POMDP version, the states are the baby being hungry or sated. Each caregiver's actions are to feed, sing, or ignore the baby. If both caregivers choose to perform the same action, the cost is halved. For example, if both caregivers feed the baby, then the reward is only −2.5 instead of −5. However, the caregivers do not perfectly observe the state of the baby. Instead, they rely on the noisy observations of the baby crying, both with the same observation. As a consequence of the reward structure, there is a trade-off between helping each other and greedily choosing a less costly action.

Example 26.1. The multicaregiver crying baby problem as a POMG. Appendix F.14 provides additional details.

26.2   Policy Evaluation

This section discusses how to evaluate joint policies represented as either tree-based conditional plans or graph-based controllers. As in the context of POMDPs, we use conditional plans to represent deterministic policies and controllers to represent stochastic policies.

26.2.1   Evaluating Conditional Plans

Recall that a conditional plan (section 20.2) is a tree where actions are associated with nodes and observations are associated with edges. Each agent has its own tree and initially selects the action associated with its root. After making an observation, each agent proceeds down the tree, taking the edge associated with their observation. The process of taking actions and selecting edges based on observations continues until reaching the end of the tree. Example 26.2 shows a joint policy consisting of a conditional plan for each agent.

Here is a joint policy $\pi = (\pi^1, \pi^2)$ represented as two-step conditional plans for the multicaregiver crying baby problem:

agent 1's policy π^1 \qquad agent 2's policy π^2

$o_1^1 = $ quiet \quad $a_1^1 = $ ignore

$o_2^1 = $ crying \quad $a_2^1 = $ feed

$o_1^2 = $ quiet \quad $a_1^2 = $ ignore

$o_2^2 = $ crying \quad $a_2^2 = $ feed

Example 26.2. A two-agent, two-step joint policy using conditional plans for the multicaregiver crying baby problem.

We can compute the joint utility function $\mathbf{U}^\pi$ recursively, similar to what was done in equation (20.8) for POMDPs when starting in state s:

$$\mathbf{U}^\pi(s) = \mathbf{R}(s, \boldsymbol{\pi}()) + \gamma \left[\sum_{s'} T(s' \mid s, \boldsymbol{\pi}()) \sum_{\mathbf{o}} O(\mathbf{o} \mid \boldsymbol{\pi}(), s') \mathbf{U}^{\boldsymbol{\pi}(\mathbf{o})}(s') \right] \quad (26.1)$$

where $\boldsymbol{\pi}()$ is the vector of actions at the root of the tree associated with π and $\boldsymbol{\pi}(\mathbf{o})$ is the vector of subplans associated with the various agents observing their components of the joint observation $\mathbf{o}$.

The utility associated with policy π from initial state distribution b is given by

$$\mathbf{U}^\pi(b) = \sum_s b(s) \mathbf{U}^\pi(s) \quad (26.2)$$

Algorithm 26.2 provides an implementation of this.

```
function lookahead(𝒫::POMG, U, s, a)
    S, 𝒪, T, O, R, γ = 𝒫.S, joint(𝒫.𝒪), 𝒫.T, 𝒫.O, 𝒫.R, 𝒫.γ
    u' = sum(T(s,a,s')*sum(O(a,s',o)*U(o,s') for o in 𝒪) for s' in S)
    return R(s,a) + γ*u'
end

function evaluate_plan(𝒫::POMG, π, s)
    a = Tuple(πi() for πi in π)
    U(o,s') = evaluate_plan(𝒫, [πi(oi) for (πi, oi) in zip(π,o)], s')
    return isempty(first(π).subplans) ? 𝒫.R(s,a) : lookahead(𝒫, U, s, a)
end

function utility(𝒫::POMG, b, π)
    u = [evaluate_plan(𝒫, π, s) for s in 𝒫.S]
    return sum(bs * us for (bs, us) in zip(b, u))
end
```

Algorithm 26.2. Conditional plans represent policies in a finite-horizon POMG. They are defined for a single agent in algorithm 20.1. We can compute the utility associated with executing a joint policy π represented by conditional plans when starting from a state s. Computing the utility from an initial state distribution b involves taking a weighted average of utilities when starting from different states.

26.2.2 Evaluating Stochastic Controllers

A controller (section 23.1) is represented as a stochastic graph. The controller associated with agent i is defined by the action distribution $\psi^i(a^i \mid x^i)$ and successor distribution $\eta^i(x^{i\prime} \mid x^i, a^i, o^i)$. The utility of being in state s with joint node $\mathbf{x}$ active and following joint policy π is

$$\mathbf{U}^\pi(\mathbf{x},s) = \sum_{\mathbf{a}} \prod_i \psi^i(a^i \mid x^i) \left(\mathbf{R}(s,\mathbf{a}) + \gamma \sum_{s'} T(s' \mid s,\mathbf{a}) \sum_{\mathbf{o}} O(\mathbf{o} \mid \mathbf{a},s') \sum_{\mathbf{x'}} \prod_i \eta^i(x^{i\prime} \mid x^i,a^i,o^i) \mathbf{U}^\pi(\mathbf{x'},s') \right) \quad (26.3)$$

Policy evaluation in this context involves solving this system of linear equations. Alternatively, we can use iterative policy evaluation similar to algorithm 23.2 for POMDPs. The utility when starting from an initial state distribution b and joint controller state $\mathbf{x}$ is

$$\mathbf{U}^{\pi}(\mathbf{x}, b) = \sum_s b(s)\mathbf{U}(\mathbf{x}, s) \qquad (26.4)$$

Example 26.3 shows a joint stochastic controller.

Here is a joint controller policy $\boldsymbol{\pi} = (\pi^1, \pi^2)$ for the two caregivers in the crying baby problem. Each controller has two nodes, $X^i = \{x_1^i, x_2^i\}$:

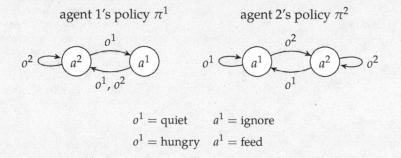

$$o^1 = \text{quiet} \qquad a^1 = \text{ignore}$$
$$o^1 = \text{hungry} \qquad a^1 = \text{feed}$$

Example 26.3. A two-agent joint policy using controllers for the multicaregiver crying baby problem.

26.3   Nash Equilibrium

As with simple games and MGs, a *Nash equilibrium* for a POMG is when all agents act according to a best response policy to each other, such that no agents have an incentive to deviate from their policy. Nash equilibria for POMGs tend to be incredibly computationally difficult to solve. Algorithm 26.3 computes a *d*-step Nash equilibrium for a POMG. It enumerates all of its possible *d*-step joint conditional plans to construct a simple game, as shown in example 26.4. A Nash equilibrium for this simple game is also a Nash equilibrium for the POMG.

The simple game has the same agents as the POMG. There is a joint action in the simple game for every joint conditional plan in the POMG. The reward received for each action is equal to the utilities under the joint conditional plan in the POMG. A Nash equilibrium of this constructed simple game can directly be applied as a Nash equilibrium of the POMG.

```
struct POMGNashEquilibrium
    b # initial belief
    d # depth of conditional plans
end

function create_conditional_plans(𝒫, d)
    𝒯, 𝒜, 𝒪 = 𝒫.𝒯, 𝒫.𝒜, 𝒫.𝒪
    Π = [[ConditionalPlan(ai) for ai in 𝒜[i]] for i in 𝒯]
    for t in 1:d
        Π = expand_conditional_plans(𝒫, Π)
    end
    return Π
end

function expand_conditional_plans(𝒫, Π)
    𝒯, 𝒜, 𝒪 = 𝒫.𝒯, 𝒫.𝒜, 𝒫.𝒪
    return [[ConditionalPlan(ai, Dict(oi ⇒ πi for oi in 𝒪[i]))
        for πi in Π[i] for ai in 𝒜[i]] for i in 𝒯]
end

function solve(M::POMGNashEquilibrium, 𝒫::POMG)
    𝒯, γ, b, d = 𝒫.𝒯, 𝒫.γ, M.b, M.d
    Π = create_conditional_plans(𝒫, d)
    U = Dict(π ⇒ utility(𝒫, b, π) for π in joint(Π))
    𝒢 = SimpleGame(γ, 𝒯, Π, π → U[π])
    π = solve(NashEquilibrium(), 𝒢)
    return Tuple(argmax(πi.p) for πi in π)
end
```

Algorithm 26.3. A Nash equilibrium is computed for a POMG $\mathcal{P}$ with initial state distribution b by creating a simple game of all conditional plans to some depth d. We solve for a Nash equilibrium in this simple game using algorithm 24.5. For simplicity, we select the most probable joint policy. Alternatively, we can randomly select the joint policy at the start of execution.

Consider the multicaregiver crying baby problem with a two-step horizon. Recall that for each agent i, there are three actions

$$\mathcal{A}^i = \{a_1^i, a_2^i, a_3^i\} = \{\text{feed}, \text{sing}, \text{ignore}\}$$

and two observations

$$\mathcal{O}^i = \{o_1^i, o_2^i\} = \{\text{cry}, \text{silent}\}$$

Converting this POMG to a simple game results in the following game table. Each caregiver selects simple game actions that correspond to a complete conditional plan. The simple game reward for each agent is the utility associated with the joint policy.

Example 26.4. Computing a Nash equilibrium for the multicaregiver crying baby problem by converting it into a simple game where the actions correspond to conditional plans.

26.4   Dynamic Programming

The approach taken in the previous section for computing a Nash equilibrium is typically extremely computationally expensive because the actions correspond to all possible conditional plans to some depth. We can adapt the value iteration approach for POMDPs (section 20.5), where we iterated between expanding the depth of the set of considered conditional plans and pruning suboptimal plans. While the worst-case computational complexity is the same as that of the full expansion of all policy trees, this incremental approach can lead to significant savings.

Algorithm 26.4 implements this dynamic programming approach. It begins by constructing all one-step plans. We prune any plans that are dominated by another plan, and we then expand all combinations of one-step plans to produce two-step plans. This procedure of alternating between expansion and pruning is repeated until the desired horizon is reached.

The pruning step eliminates all dominated policies. A policy π^i belonging to an agent i can be pruned if there exists another policy $\pi^{i\prime}$ that always performs at least as well as π^i. Although computationally expensive, this condition can be checked by solving a linear program. This process is related to controller node pruning in POMDPs (algorithm 23.4).

It would be computationally intractable to solve a separate linear program for every possible combination of the other agent's policies π^{-i}. Instead, we can take a much more efficient approach that will never prune an optimal policy but may not be able to prune all suboptimal policies. A policy π^i is dominated by $\pi^{i\prime}$ if there is no $b(\pi^{-i}, s)$ between other joint policies π^{-i} and states s such that

$$\sum_{\pi^{-i}} \sum_s b(\pi^{-i}, s) U^{\pi^{i\prime}, \pi^{-i}, i}(s) \geq \sum_{\pi^{-i}} \sum_s b(\pi^{-i}, s) U^{\pi^i, \pi^{-i}, i}(s) \qquad (26.5)$$

Here, b is a joint distribution over the policies of other agents and the state. As mentioned at the start of this chapter, it is generally infeasible to compute a belief state, but equation (26.5) checks the space of beliefs for individual policy domination.

We can construct a single linear program to check equation (26.5).[3] If the linear

[3] A similar linear program was created to prune alpha vectors in POMDPs in equation (20.16).

```
struct POMGDynamicProgramming
    b    # initial belief
    d    # depth of conditional plans
end

function solve(M::POMGDynamicProgramming, 𝒫::POMG)
    𝓘, 𝒮, 𝒜, R, γ, b, d = 𝒫.𝓘, 𝒫.𝒮, 𝒫.𝒜, 𝒫.R, 𝒫.γ, M.b, M.d
    Π = [[ConditionalPlan(ai) for ai in 𝒜[i]] for i in 𝓘]
    for t in 1:d
        Π = expand_conditional_plans(𝒫, Π)
        prune_dominated!(Π, 𝒫)
    end
    𝒢 = SimpleGame(γ, 𝓘, Π, π → utility(𝒫, b, π))
    π = solve(NashEquilibrium(), 𝒢)
    return Tuple(argmax(πi.p) for πi in π)
end

function prune_dominated!(Π, 𝒫::POMG)
    done = false
    while !done
        done = true
        for i in shuffle(𝒫.𝓘)
            for πi in shuffle(Π[i])
                if length(Π[i]) > 1 && is_dominated(𝒫, Π, i, πi)
                    filter!(πi′ → πi′ ≠ πi, Π[i])
                    done = false
                    break
                end
            end
        end
    end
end

function is_dominated(𝒫::POMG, Π, i, πi)
    𝓘, 𝒮 = 𝒫.𝓘, 𝒫.𝒮
    jointΠnoti = joint([Π[j] for j in 𝓘 if j ≠ i])
    π(πi′, πnoti) = [j==i ? πi′ : πnoti[j>i ? j-1 : j] for j in 𝓘]
    Ui = Dict((πi′, πnoti, s) ⇒ evaluate_plan(𝒫, π(πi′, πnoti), s)[i]
            for πi′ in Π[i], πnoti in jointΠnoti, s in 𝒮)
    model = Model(Ipopt.Optimizer)
    @variable(model, δ)
    @variable(model, b[jointΠnoti, 𝒮] ≥ 0)
    @objective(model, Max, δ)
    @constraint(model, [πi′=Π[i]],
        sum(b[πnoti, s] * (Ui[πi′, πnoti, s] - Ui[πi, πnoti, s])
        for πnoti in jointΠnoti for s in 𝒮) ≥ δ)
    @constraint(model, sum(b) == 1)
    optimize!(model)
    return value(δ) ≥ 0
end
```

Algorithm 26.4. Dynamic programming computes a Nash equilibrium π for a POMG 𝒫, given an initial belief b and horizon depth d. It iteratively computes the policy trees and their expected utilities at each step. The pruning phase at each iteration removes dominated policies, which are policy trees that result in lower expected utility than at least one other available policy tree.

program is feasible, then that means π^i is not dominated by any other $\pi^{i\prime}$:

$$
\begin{aligned}
&\underset{\delta,b}{\text{maximize}} \quad \delta \\
&\text{subject to} \quad b(\pi^{-i}, s) \geq 0 \text{ for all } \pi^{-i}, s \\
&\qquad\qquad \sum_{\pi^{-i}} \sum_{s} b(\pi^{-i}, s) = 1 \\
&\qquad\qquad \sum_{\pi^{-i}} \sum_{s} b(\pi^{-i}, s) \left(U^{\pi^{i\prime},\pi^{-i},i}(s) - U^{\pi^i,\pi^{-i},i}(s) \right) \geq \delta \text{ for all } \pi^{i\prime}
\end{aligned}
\tag{26.6}
$$

The pruning step removes dominated policies by randomly selecting an agent i and checking for domination of each of its policies. This process repeats until a pass over all agents fails to find any dominated policies. Example 26.5 shows this process on the multicaregiver crying baby problem.

26.5   Summary

- POMGs generalize POMDPs to multiple agents and MGs to partial observability.

- Because agents generally cannot maintain beliefs in POMGs, policies typically take the form of conditional plans or finite state controllers.

- Nash equilibria, in the form of d-step conditional plans for POMGs, can be obtained by finding Nash equilibria for simple games whose joint actions consist of all possible POMG joint policies.

- Dynamic programming approaches can be used to compute Nash equilibria more efficiently by iteratively constructing sets of deeper conditional plans while pruning dominated plans to restrict the search space.

26.6   Exercises

Exercise 26.1. Show that a POMG generalizes both a POMDP and an MG.

Consider the multicaregiver crying baby problem solved by dynamic programming. Initially, the policies at depth $d = 2$ are

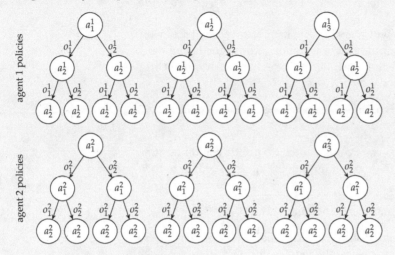

Example 26.5. Dynamic programming and a single pruning step for the multicaregiver crying baby problem.

After the pruning step, the agent policies are

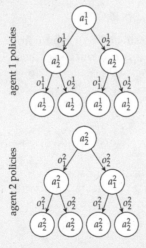

In this case, the pruning step finds the best joint policy. This approach significantly reduces the number of possible joint policies that the next iteration of the algorithm needs to consider.

Solution: For any POMDP, we can define a POMG with one agent $\mathcal{I} = \{1\}$. States $\mathcal{S}$ are identical, as are actions $\mathbf{A} = (\mathcal{A}^1)$ and observations $\mathbf{O} = (\mathcal{O}^1)$. Thus, the state transition, observation function, and rewards of the POMG directly follow. The Nash equilibrium optimization has only one agent, so it results in a simple maximization of expected value, which is identical to a POMDP.

For any MG, we can define a POMG with the same agents $\mathcal{I}$, states $\mathcal{S}$, joint actions $\mathbf{A}$, transitions T, and joint rewards $\mathbf{R}$. The individual observations are assigned to be states $\mathcal{O}^i = \mathcal{S}$. The observation function then deterministically provides each agent with the true state $O(\mathbf{o} \mid \mathbf{a}, s') = 1$ if $\mathbf{o} = (s', \ldots, s')$, and 0 otherwise.

Exercise 26.2. How can we incorporate communication between agents into the POMG framework?

Solution: The action space for the agents can be augmented to include communication actions. The other agents can observe these communication actions according to their observation model.

Exercise 26.3. Do agents always have an incentive to communicate?

Solution: Agents in POMGs are often competitive, in which case there would be no incentive to communicate with others. If their rewards are aligned to some degree, they may be inclined to communicate.

Exercise 26.4. How many possible joint conditional plans are there of depth d?

Solution: Recall that there are $|\mathcal{A}|^{(|\mathcal{O}|^d-1)/(|\mathcal{O}|-1)}$ possible d-step single-agent conditional plans. We can construct a joint policy of conditional plans using every combination of these single-agent conditional plans across agents. The number of d-step multiagent conditional plans is

$$\prod_{i \in \mathcal{I}} |\mathcal{A}^i|^{(|\mathcal{O}^i|^d-1)/(|\mathcal{O}^i|-1)}$$

Exercise 26.5. Define the best response for a POMG in terms of an agent i's utilities $U^{\pi,i}$. Propose the iterated best response for POMGs.

Solution: The best response π^i of agent i to other agents' policies $\boldsymbol{\pi}^{-i}$ is defined following equation (24.2) for an initial belief b:

$$U^{\pi^i, \boldsymbol{\pi}^{-i}, i}(b) \geq U^{\pi^{i\prime}, \boldsymbol{\pi}^{-i}, i}(b)$$

with any other policy $\pi^{i\prime}$. For conditional plans, $U^{\pi,i}$ is defined by equations (26.1) and (26.2).

The implementation of iterated best response follows from section 24.2.1. First, the conditional plans and simple game can be created, as in algorithm 26.3. Then, we can iterate best response using algorithm 24.8.

27 *Collaborative Agents*

Many multiagent domains are collaborative, where all agents act independently in an environment while working toward a common shared objective. Applications range from robotic search and rescue to interplanetary exploration rovers. The *decentralized partially observable Markov decision process (Dec-POMDP)* captures the generality of POMGs while focusing on such collaborative agent settings.[1] The model is more amenable to scalable approximate algorithms because of its single shared objective, as opposed to finding an equilibrium among multiple individual agent objectives. This chapter presents the Dec-POMDP model, highlights its subclasses, and describes algorithms that solve them optimally and approximately.

[1] D. S. Bernstein, R. Givan, N. Immerman, and S. Zilberstein, "The Complexity of Decentralized Control of Markov Decision Processes," *Mathematics of Operation Research*, vol. 27, no. 4, pp. 819–840, 2002. A more comprehensive introduction is provided by F. A. Oliehoek and C. Amato, *A Concise Introduction to Decentralized POMDPs*. Springer, 2016.

27.1 *Decentralized Partially Observable Markov Decision Processes*

A Dec-POMDP (algorithm 27.1) is a POMG where all agents share the same objective. Each agent $i \in \mathcal{I}$ selects a local action $a^i \in \mathcal{A}^i$ based on a history of local observations $o^i \in \mathcal{O}^i$. The true state of the system $s \in \mathcal{S}$ is shared by all agents. A single reward is generated by $R(s, \mathbf{a})$ based on state s and joint action $\mathbf{a}$. The goal of all agents is to maximize the shared expected reward over time under local partial observability. Example 27.1 describes a Dec-POMDP version of the predator-prey problem.

Consider a predator-prey hex world problem in which a team of predators $\mathcal{I}$ strives to capture a single fleeing prey. The predators move independently. The prey moves randomly to a neighboring cell not occupied by a predator. The predators must work together to capture the prey.

Example 27.1. The collaborative predator-prey problem as a Dec-POMDP. Additional detail is provided in appendix F.15.

Many of the same challenges of POMGs persist in Dec-POMDPs, such as the general inability of agents to maintain a belief state. We focus on policies represented as conditional plans or controllers. The same algorithms introduced in the previous chapter can be used to evaluate policies. All that is required is to create a POMG with $R^i(s, \mathbf{a})$ for each agent i equal to the $R(s, \mathbf{a})$ from the Dec-POMDP.

```
struct DecPOMDP
    γ  # discount factor
    ℐ  # agents
    𝒮  # state space
    𝒜  # joint action space
    𝒪  # joint observation space
    T  # transition function
    O  # joint observation function
    R  # reward function
end
```

Algorithm 27.1. Data structure for a Dec-POMDP. The joint function from algorithm 24.2 allows the creation of all combinations of a set provided, such as 𝒜 or 𝒪. The tensorform function converts the Dec-POMDP 𝒫 to a tensor representation.

27.2 Subclasses

There are many notable subclasses of Dec-POMDPs. Categorizing these subclasses is useful when designing algorithms that take advantage of their specific structure.

One attribute of interest is *joint full observability*, which is when each agent observes an aspect of the state, such that if they were to combine their observations, it would uniquely reveal the true state. The agents, however, do not share their observations. This property ensures that if $O(\mathbf{o} \mid \mathbf{a}, s') > 0$ then $P(s' \mid \mathbf{o}) = 1$. A Dec-POMDP with joint full observability is called a *decentralized Markov decision process (Dec-MDP)*. Both Dec-POMDP and Dec-MDP problems are *NEXP-complete* when the number of steps in the horizon is fewer than the number of states.[2]

In many settings, the state space of a Dec-POMDP is factored, one for each agent and one for the environment. This is called a *factored Dec-POMDP*. We have $\mathcal{S} = \mathcal{S}^0 \times \mathcal{S}^1 \times \mathcal{S}^k$, where $\mathcal{S}^i$ is the factored state component associated with agent i and $\mathcal{S}^0$ is the factored state component associated with the general environment. For example, in the collaborative predator-prey problem, each agent has its own state factor for their location, and the position of the prey is associated with the environment component of the state space.

[2] In contrast with the complexity classes NP and PSPACE, it is known that NEXP is not in P. Hence, we can prove that Dec-MDPs and Dec-POMDPs do not allow for polynomial time algorithms. D. S. Bernstein, R. Givan, N. Immerman, and S. Zilberstein, "The Complexity of Decentralized Control of Markov Decision Processes," *Mathematics of Operation Research*, vol. 27, no. 4, pp. 819–840, 2002.

In some problems, a factored Dec-POMDP may have one or more of the following properties:

- *Transition independence*, where agents may not affect each other's state:

$$T(\mathbf{s}' \mid \mathbf{s}, \mathbf{a}) = T^0(s^{0\prime} \mid s^0) \prod_i T^i(s^{i\prime} \mid s^i, a^i) \qquad (27.1)$$

- *Observation independence*, where the observations of agents depend only on their local state and actions:

$$O(\mathbf{o} \mid \mathbf{a}, \mathbf{s}') = \prod_i O^i(o^i \mid a^i, s^{i\prime}) \qquad (27.2)$$

- *Reward independence*, where the reward can be decomposed into multiple independent pieces:[3]

$$R(\mathbf{s}, \mathbf{a}) = R^0(s^0) + \sum_i R^i(s^i, a^i) \qquad (27.3)$$

[3] Here, we show the combination of the reward components as a summation, but any monotonically nondecreasing function can be used instead and preserve reward independence.

The computational complexity can vary significantly depending on which of these independence properties are satisfied, as summarized in table 27.1. It is important to take these independences into account when modeling a problem to improve scalability.

Independence	Complexity
Transitions, observations, and rewards	P-complete
Transitions and observations	NP-complete
Any other subset	NEXP-complete

Table 27.1. The complexity of factored Dec-POMDPs with different independence assumptions.

A *network distributed partially observable Markov decision process* (ND-POMDP) is a Dec-POMDP with transition and observation independence and a special reward structure. The reward structure is represented by a coordination graph. In contrast with the graphs used earlier in this book, a *coordination graph* is a type of hypergraph, which allows edges to connect any number of nodes. The nodes in the ND-POMDP hypergraph correspond to the various agents. The edges relate to interactions between the agents in the reward function. An ND-POMDP associates with each edge j in the hypergraph a reward component R_j that depends on the state and action components to which the edge connects. The reward function in an ND-POMDP is simply the sum of the reward components associated with the edges. Figure 27.1 shows a coordination graph resulting in a reward function that can be decomposed as follows:

$$R_{123}(s_1, s_2, s_3, a_1, a_2, a_3) + R_{34}(s_3, s_4, a_3, a_4) + R_5(s_5, a_5) \qquad (27.4)$$

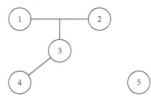

Figure 27.1. An ND-POMDP structure with five agents. There are three hyperedges: one involving agents 1, 2, and 3; another involving agents 3 and 4; and another involving agent 5 on its own.

Sensor network and target tracking problems are often framed as ND-POMDPs.

The ND-POMDP model is similar to the transition and observation independent Dec-MDP model, but it does not make the joint full observability assumption. Even if all observations are shared, the true state of the world may not be known. Furthermore, even with factored transitions and observations, a policy in an ND-POMDP is a mapping from observation histories to actions, unlike the transition and observation Dec-MDP case, in which policies are mappings from local states to actions. The worst-case complexity remains the same as for a Dec-POMDP, but algorithms for ND-POMDPs are typically much more scalable in the number of agents. Scalability can increase as the coordination graph becomes less connected.

If the agents are able to communicate their actions and observations perfectly without penalty, then they are able to maintain a collective belief state. This model is called a *multiagent MDP (MMDP)* or a *multiagent POMDP (MPOMDP)*. MMDPs and MPOMDPs can also result when there is transition, observation, and reward independence. Any MDP or POMDP algorithm discussed in earlier chapters can be applied to solve these problems.

Table 27.2 summarizes some of these subclasses. Figure 27.2 illustrates the relationships among the models discussed in this book.

Agents	Observability	Communication	Model
Single	Full	—	MDP
Single	Partial	—	POMDP
Multiple	Full	Free	MMDP
Multiple	Full	General	MMDP
Multiple	Joint full	Free	MMDP
Multiple	Joint full	General	Dec-MDP
Multiple	Partial	Free	MPOMDP
Multiple	Partial	General	Dec-POMDP

Table 27.2. Dec-POMDP subclasses categorized by type and computational complexity. "Observability" refers to the degree to which the shared state is observable. "Communication" refers to whether the cooperative agents can freely share all observations with each other. Free communication happens outside the model (e.g., a high-speed wireless connection in robots). General communication is when agents do not have this available and must communicate (typically imperfectly) via their actions.

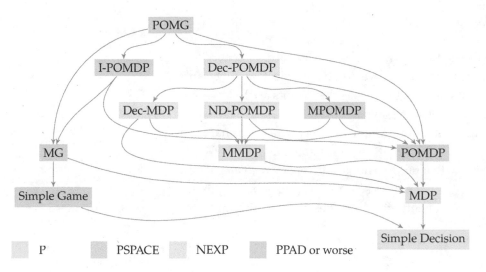

P   PSPACE   NEXP   PPAD or worse

Figure 27.2. A taxonomy for the models discussed in this book. Parents generalize their children in this diagram. For example, Dec-POMDPs generalize POMDPs by supporting multiple agents. The color of the nodes indicate computational complexity, as indicated in the key at the bottom left of the figure. The complexities listed here are for the common model, policy, and objective formulations presented in this book. For a more detailed treatment, see C. Papadimitriou and J. Tsitsiklis, "The Complexity of Markov Decision Processes," *Mathematics of Operation Research*, vol. 12, no. 3, pp. 441–450, 1987. Also, see S. Seuken and S. Zilberstein, "Formal Models and Algorithms for Decentralized Decision Making Under Uncertainty," *Autonomous Agents and Multi-Agent Systems*, vol. 17, no. 2, pp. 190–250, 2008.

27.3 Dynamic Programming

The *dynamic programming* algorithm for Dec-POMDPs applies the Bellman backup at each step and prunes dominated policies. This process is identical to dynamic programming for POMGs except that each agent shares the same reward. Algorithm 27.2 implements this procedure.

```
struct DecPOMDPDynamicProgramming
    b    # initial belief
    d    # depth of conditional plans
end

function solve(M::DecPOMDPDynamicProgramming, 𝒫::DecPOMDP)
    ℐ, 𝒮, 𝒜, 𝒪, T, O, R, γ = 𝒫.ℐ, 𝒫.𝒮, 𝒫.𝒜, 𝒫.𝒪, 𝒫.T, 𝒫.O, 𝒫.R, 𝒫.γ
    R′(s, a) = [R(s, a) for i in ℐ]
    𝒫′ = POMG(γ, ℐ, 𝒮, 𝒜, 𝒪, T, O, R′)
    M′ = POMGDynamicProgramming(M.b, M.d)
    return solve(M′, 𝒫′)
end
```

Algorithm 27.2. Dynamic programming computes the optimal joint policy π for a Dec-POMDP 𝒫, given an initial belief b and horizon depth d. We can directly use the POMG algorithm, as Dec-POMDPs are a special collaborative class of POMGs.

27.4   Iterated Best Response

Instead of exploring joint policies directly, we can perform a form of *iterated best response* (algorithm 27.3). In this approach, we iteratively select an agent and compute a best response policy, assuming that the other agents are following a fixed policy.[4] This approximate algorithm is typically fast because it is choosing the best policy for only one agent at a time. Moreover, since all agents share the same reward, it tends to terminate after relatively few iterations.

Iterated best response begins with a random initial joint policy π_1. The process randomly iterates over the agents. If agent i is selected, its policy π^i is updated with a best response to the other agents' fixed policies π^{-i} with initial belief distribution b:

$$\pi^i \leftarrow \arg\max_{\pi^{i\prime}} U^{\pi^{i\prime}, \pi^{-i}}(b) \qquad (27.5)$$

with ties favoring the current policy. This process can terminate when agents stop changing their policies.

While this algorithm is fast and guaranteed to converge, it does not always find the best joint policy. It relies on iterated best response to find a Nash equilibrium, but there may be many Nash equilibria, with different utilities associated with them. This approach will find only one of them.

27.5   Heuristic Search

Instead of expanding all joint policies, *heuristic search* (algorithm 27.4) explores a fixed number of policies,[5] which, stored over iterations, prevents exponential growth. The heuristic exploration guides the search by attempting to expand the best joint policies only until depth d is reached.

Each iteration k of the algorithm keeps a set of joint policies Π_k. This set initially consists of all one-step conditional plans. Subsequent iterations begin by fully expanding the conditional plans. The goal is to add a fixed number of these for the next iteration.

We prioritize the policies that are more likely to maximize the utility when deciding among the conditional plans to add to the set. However, since we expand the conditional plans from the bottom up, we cannot simply evaluate the policies from the initial belief state b. Instead, we need an estimate of the belief $d - k$ steps into the future, which we compute by taking random actions and simulating state

[4] This type of algorithm is also called *joint equilibrium-based search for policies (JESP)*. R. Nair, M. Tambe, M. Yokoo, D. Pynadath, and S. Marsella, "Taming Decentralized POMDPs: Towards Efficient Policy Computation for Multiagent Settings," in *International Joint Conference on Artificial Intelligence (IJCAI)*, 2003. It can be improved further by performing dynamic programming.

[5] This approach is also known as *memory-bounded dynamic programming (MBDP)*. S. Seuken and S. Zilberstein, "Memory-Bounded Dynamic Programming for Dec-POMDPs," in *International Joint Conference on Artificial Intelligence (IJCAI)*, 2007. There are other heuristic search algorithms as well, such as *multiagent A* (MMA*)*. D. Szer, F. Charpillet, and S. Zilberstein, "MAA*: A Heuristic Search Algorithm for Solving Decentralized POMDPs," in *Conference on Uncertainty in Artificial Intelligence (UAI)*, 2005.

```
struct DecPOMDPIteratedBestResponse
    b      # initial belief
    d      # depth of conditional plans
    k_max  # number of iterations
end

function solve(M::DecPOMDPIteratedBestResponse, 𝒫::DecPOMDP)
    ℐ, 𝒮, 𝒜, 𝒪, T, O, R, γ = 𝒫.ℐ, 𝒫.𝒮, 𝒫.𝒜, 𝒫.𝒪, 𝒫.T, 𝒫.O, 𝒫.R, 𝒫.γ
    b, d, k_max = M.b, M.d, M.k_max
    R'(s, a) = [R(s, a) for i in ℐ]
    𝒫' = POMG(γ, ℐ, 𝒮, 𝒜, 𝒪, T, O, R')
    Π = create_conditional_plans(𝒫, d)
    π = [rand(Π[i]) for i in ℐ]
    for k in 1:k_max
        for i in shuffle(ℐ)
            π'(πi) = Tuple(j == i ? πi : π[j] for j in ℐ)
            Ui(πi) = utility(𝒫', b, π'(πi))[i]
            π[i] = argmax(Ui, Π[i])
        end
    end
    return Tuple(π)
end
```

Algorithm 27.3. Iterated best response for a collaborative Dec-POMDP 𝒫 performs a deterministic best response for each agent to rapidly search the space of conditional plan policies. The `solve` function executes this procedure for up to k_max steps, maximizing the value at an initial belief b for conditional plans of depth d.

transitions and observations, updating the belief along the way. This belief at iteration k is denoted as b_k. For each available joint policy $\pi \in \Pi_k$, the utility $U^\pi(b_k)$ is examined to find a utility-maximizing joint policy to add. Example 27.2 demonstrates the process.

27.6 Nonlinear Programming

We can use *nonlinear programming* (NLP) (algorithm 27.5) to find an optimal joint controller policy representation of a fixed size.[6] This method generalizes the NLP approach for POMDPs from section 23.3.

[6] C. Amato, D.S. Bernstein, and S. Zilberstein, "Optimizing Fixed-Size Stochastic Controllers for POMDPs and Decentralized POMDPs," *Autonomous Agents and Multi-Agent Systems*, vol. 21, no. 3, pp. 293–320, 2010.

```
struct DecPOMDPHeuristicSearch
    b        # initial belief
    d        # depth of conditional plans
    π_max # number of policies
end

function solve(M::DecPOMDPHeuristicSearch, 𝒫::DecPOMDP)
    𝒾, 𝒮, 𝒜, 𝒪, T, O, R, γ = 𝒫.𝒾, 𝒫.𝒮, 𝒫.𝒜, 𝒫.𝒪, 𝒫.T, 𝒫.O, 𝒫.R, 𝒫.γ
    b, d, π_max = M.b, M.d, M.π_max
    R′(s, a) = [R(s, a) for i in 𝒾]
    𝒫′ = POMG(γ, 𝒾, 𝒮, 𝒜, 𝒪, T, O, R′)
    Π = [[ConditionalPlan(ai) for ai in 𝒜[i]] for i in 𝒾]
    for t in 1:d
        allΠ = expand_conditional_plans(𝒫, Π)
        Π = [[] for i in 𝒾]
        for z in 1:π_max
            b′ = explore(M, 𝒫, t)
            π = argmax(π → first(utility(𝒫′, b′, π)), joint(allΠ))
            for i in 𝒾
                push!(Π[i], π[i])
                filter!(πi → πi != π[i], allΠ[i])
            end
        end
    end
    return argmax(π → first(utility(𝒫′, b, π)), joint(Π))
end

function explore(M::DecPOMDPHeuristicSearch, 𝒫::DecPOMDP, t)
    𝒾, 𝒮, 𝒜, 𝒪, T, O, R, γ = 𝒫.𝒾, 𝒫.𝒮, 𝒫.𝒜, 𝒫.𝒪, 𝒫.T, 𝒫.O, 𝒫.R, 𝒫.γ
    b = copy(M.b)
    b′ = similar(b)
    s = rand(SetCategorical(𝒮, b))
    for τ in 1:t
        a = Tuple(rand(𝒜i) for 𝒜i in 𝒜)
        s′ = rand(SetCategorical(𝒮, [T(s,a,s′) for s′ in 𝒮]))
        o = rand(SetCategorical(joint(𝒪), [O(a,s′,o) for o in joint(𝒪)]))
        for (i′, s′) in enumerate(𝒮)
            po = O(a, s′, o)
            b′[i′] = po*sum(T(s,a,s′)*b[i] for (i,s) in enumerate(𝒮))
        end
        normalize!(b′, 1)
        b, s = b′, s′
    end
    return b′
end
```

Algorithm 27.4. Memory-bounded heuristic search uses a heuristic function to search the space of conditional plans for a Dec-POMDP $\mathcal{P}$. The solve function tries to maximize the value at an initial belief b for joint conditional plans of depth d. The explore function generates a belief t steps into the future by taking random actions and simulating actions and observations. The algorithm is memory-bounded, keeping only π_max conditional plans per agent.

Consider the collaborative predator-prey problem shown at right. We apply heuristic search to a depth of $d = 3$, with three policies retained at each iteration. After iteration $k = 1$, the policies are

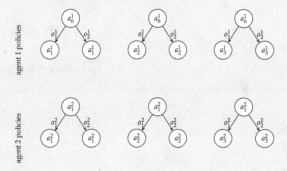

Example 27.2.   Heuristic search exploration and conditional plan expansion for the collaborative predator-prey hex world problem shown here. The predators are red and green. The prey is blue.

At the next iteration $k = 2$, heuristic search again starts at the initial belief and takes $d - k = 3 - 2 = 1$ steps following the heuristic exploration. The explored beliefs used to select the next three conditional plans are

$b_1 = [0.0, 0.0, 0.0, 0.0, 0.0, 0.0, 0.0, 0.17$
        $0.0, 0.03, 0.01, 0.0, 0.0, 0.05, 0.0$
        $0.01, 0.23, 0.0, 0.08, 0.01, 0.0, 0.0$
        $0.14, 0.0, 0.03, 0.22, 0.0, 0.01]$

$b_2 = [0.0, 0.21, 0.03, 0.0, 0.04, 0.01, 0.0$
        $0.05, 0.01, 0.0, 0.08, 0.03, 0.0, 0.0$
        $0.01, 0.0, 0.0, 0.01, 0.08, 0.34, 0.03$
        $0.02, 0.05, 0.01, 0.0, 0.01, 0.0]$

$b_3 = [0.0, 0.03, 0.01, 0.0, 0.03, 0.01, 0.0$
        $0.15, 0.05, 0.0, 0.01, 0.0, 0.0, 0.0$
        $0.0, 0.0, 0.0, 0.03, 0.06, 0.11, 0.32$
        $0.06, 0.03, 0.01, 0.01, 0.04, 0.06]$

The policies after iteration $k = 2$ are

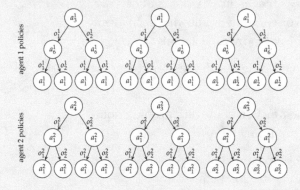

The beliefs were used to determine the root node's action and the two subtrees below it. These subtrees are built from the prior iteration's trees.

Given a fixed set of nodes X^i for each agent i, initial belief b, and initial joint nodes $\mathbf{x}_1$, the optimization problem is

$$
\underset{U, \psi, \eta}{\text{maximize}} \quad \sum_s b(s) U(\mathbf{x}_1, s)
$$

$$
\text{subject to} \quad U(\mathbf{x}, s) = \sum_{\mathbf{a}} \prod_i \psi^i(a^i \mid x^i) \left(R(s, \mathbf{a}) + \gamma \sum_{s'} T(s' \mid s, \mathbf{a}) \sum_{\mathbf{o}} O(\mathbf{o} \mid \mathbf{a}, s') \sum_{\mathbf{x}'} \prod_i \eta^i(x^{i\prime} \mid x^i, a^i, o^i) U(\mathbf{x}', s') \right)
$$

$$
\text{for all } \mathbf{x}, s
$$

$$
\psi^i(a^i \mid x^i) \geq 0 \quad \text{for all } i, x^i, a^i
$$

$$
\sum_a \psi^i(a^i \mid x^i) = 1 \quad \text{for all } i, x^i
$$

$$
\eta^i(x^{i\prime} \mid x^i, a^i, o^i) \geq 0 \quad \text{for all } i, x^i, a^i, o^i, x^{i\prime}
$$

$$
\sum_{x^{i\prime}} \eta^i(x^{i\prime} \mid x^i, a^i, o^i) = 1 \quad \text{for all } i, x^i, a^i, o^i
$$

$$
\text{(27.6)}
$$

27.7 Summary

- Dec-POMDPs are fully cooperative POMGs that model a team of agents working together toward a shared goal, each acting individually using only local information.

- Because determining a belief state is infeasible, as in POMGs, policies are generally represented as conditional plans or controllers, allowing each agent to map individual sequences of observations to individual actions.

- Many subclasses of Dec-POMDPs exist, with different degrees of computational complexity.

- Dynamic programming computes the value function iteratively, pruning dominated policies as it iterates using a linear program.

- Iterated best response computes a best utility-maximizing response policy for a single agent at a time, iteratively converging to a joint equilibrium.

- Heuristic search searches a fixed subset of policies at each iteration, guided by a heuristic.

- Nonlinear programming can be used to generate controllers of a fixed size.

```
struct DecPOMDPNonlinearProgramming
    b # initial belief
    ℓ # number of nodes for each agent
end

function tensorform(𝒫::DecPOMDP)
    𝒯, 𝒮, 𝒜, 𝒪, R, T, O = 𝒫.𝒯, 𝒫.𝒮, 𝒫.𝒜, 𝒫.𝒪, 𝒫.R, 𝒫.T, 𝒫.O
    𝒯′ = eachindex(𝒯)
    𝒮′ = eachindex(𝒮)
    𝒜′ = [eachindex(𝒜i) for 𝒜i in 𝒜]
    𝒪′ = [eachindex(𝒪i) for 𝒪i in 𝒪]
    R′ = [R(s,a) for s in 𝒮, a in joint(𝒜)]
    T′ = [T(s,a,s′) for s in 𝒮, a in joint(𝒜), s′ in 𝒮]
    O′ = [O(a,s′,o) for a in joint(𝒜), s′ in 𝒮, o in joint(𝒪)]
    return 𝒯′, 𝒮′, 𝒜′, 𝒪′, R′, T′, O′
end

function solve(M::DecPOMDPNonlinearProgramming, 𝒫::DecPOMDP)
    𝒫, γ, b = 𝒫, 𝒫.γ, M.b
    𝒯, 𝒮, 𝒜, 𝒪, R, T, O = tensorform(𝒫)
    X = [collect(1:M.ℓ) for i in 𝒯]
    jointX, joint𝒜, joint𝒪 = joint(X), joint(𝒜), joint(𝒪)
    x1 = jointX[1]
    model = Model(Ipopt.Optimizer)
    @variable(model, U[jointX,𝒮])
    @variable(model, ψ[i=𝒯,X[i],𝒜[i]] ≥ 0)
    @variable(model, η[i=𝒯,X[i],𝒜[i],𝒪[i],X[i]] ≥ 0)
    @objective(model, Max, b·U[x1,:])
    @NLconstraint(model, [x=jointX,s=𝒮],
        U[x,s] == (sum(prod(ψ[i,x[i],a[i]] for i in 𝒯)
                *(R[s,y] + γ*sum(T[s,y,s′]*sum(O[y,s′,z]
                    *sum(prod(η[i,x[i],a[i],o[i],x′[i]] for i in 𝒯)
                        *U[x′,s′] for x′ in jointX)
                    for (z, o) in enumerate(joint𝒪)) for s′ in 𝒮))
                for (y, a) in enumerate(joint𝒜))))
    @constraint(model, [i=𝒯,xi=X[i]],
            sum(ψ[i,xi,ai] for ai in 𝒜[i]) == 1)
    @constraint(model, [i=𝒯,xi=X[i],ai=𝒜[i],oi=𝒪[i]],
            sum(η[i,xi,ai,oi,xi′] for xi′ in X[i]) == 1)
    optimize!(model)
    ψ′, η′ = value.(ψ), value.(η)
    return [ControllerPolicy(𝒫, X[i],
            Dict((xi,𝒫.𝒜[i][ai]) ⇒ ψ′[i,xi,ai]
                for xi in X[i], ai in 𝒜[i]),
            Dict((xi,𝒫.𝒜[i][ai],𝒫.𝒪[i][oi]),xi′) ⇒ η′[i,xi,ai,oi,xi′]
                for xi in X[i], ai in 𝒜[i], oi in 𝒪[i], xi′ in X[i]))
        for i in 𝒯]
end
```

Algorithm 27.5. NLP computes the optimal joint controller policy π for a Dec-POMDP 𝒫, given an initial belief b and number of controller nodes ℓ for each agent. This generalizes the NLP solution in algorithm 23.5.

27.8   Exercises

Exercise 27.1. Why is a Dec-MDP with joint full observability different from agents knowing the state?

Solution: Full joint observability means if agents were to share their individual observations, then the team would know the true state. This can be done offline during planning. Thus in Dec-MDPs, the true state is essentially known during planning. The issue is that it requires agents to share their individual observations, which cannot be done online during execution. Therefore, planning still needs to reason about the uncertain observations made by the other agents.

Exercise 27.2. Propose a fast algorithm for a Dec-MDP with transition, observation, and reward independence. Prove that it is correct.

Solution: If a factored Dec-MDP satisfies all three independence assumptions, then we can solve it as $|\mathcal{I}|$ separate MDPs. The resulting policy π^i for each agent i's MDP can then be combined to form the optimal joint policy. To prove this fact, consider the utility of each agent's individual MDP:

$$U^{\pi^i}(s^i) = R\left(s^i, \pi^i()\right) + \gamma\left[\sum_{s^{i\prime}} T^i\left(s^{i\prime} \mid s^i, \pi^i()\right) \sum_{o^i} O^i\left(o^i \mid \pi^i(), s^{i\prime}\right) U^{\pi^i(o^i)}(s^{i\prime})\right]$$

As in equation (26.1), $\pi^i()$ refers to the root action of i's conditional plan, and $\pi^i(o^i)$ refers to i's subplans after making observation o^i. We sum up each of their individual contributions as follows:

$$\sum_i U^{\pi^i}(s) = \sum_i\left[R\left(s^i, \pi^i()\right) + \gamma\left[\sum_{s^{i\prime}} T^i\left(s^{i\prime} \mid s^i, \pi^i()\right) \sum_{o^i} O^i\left(o^i \mid \pi^i(), s^{i\prime}\right) U^{\pi^i(o^i)}(s^{i\prime})\right]\right]$$

We can combine T^i and O^i into a single probability distribution P, move the summation, and apply the definition of reward independence:

$$\sum_i U^{\pi^i}(s) = \sum_i\left[R\left(s^i, \pi^i()\right) + \gamma\left[\sum_{s^{i\prime}} P\left(s^{i\prime} \mid s^i, \pi^i()\right) \sum_{o^i} P\left(o^i \mid \pi^i(), s^{i\prime}\right) U^{\pi^i(o^i)}(s^{i\prime})\right]\right]$$

$$= \sum_i R\left(s^i, \pi^i()\right) + \sum_i\left[\gamma\left[\sum_{s^{i\prime}} P\left(s^{i\prime} \mid s^i, \pi^i()\right) \sum_{o^i} P\left(o^i \mid \pi^i(), s^{i\prime}\right) U^{\pi^i(o^i)}(s^{i\prime})\right]\right]$$

$$= R(s, \pi()) + \sum_i\left[\gamma\left[\sum_{s^{i\prime}} P\left(s^{i\prime} \mid s^i, \pi^i()\right) \sum_{o^i} P\left(o^i \mid \pi^i(), s^{i\prime}\right) U^{\pi^i(o^i)}(s^{i\prime})\right]\right]$$

Now, we marginalize over all successors s and observations o. Because of the transition and observation independence, we can freely condition the distributions on these other non-i state and observation factors, which is the same as conditioning on s and o. We can then apply the definition of transition and observation independence. Finally, we can move the summation in and recognize $U^\pi(s)$ results:

$$
\begin{aligned}
\sum_i U^{\pi^i}(s) &= R(s, \boldsymbol{\pi}()) + \sum_i \left[\gamma \left[\sum_{s'} P\left(s' \mid s^i, \pi^i()\right) \sum_o P\left(o \mid \pi^i(), s^{i\prime}\right) U^{\pi^{i}(o^i)}(s^{i\prime}) \right] \right] \\
&= R(s, \boldsymbol{\pi}()) + \sum_i \left[\gamma \left[\sum_{s'} P\left(s^{0\prime} \mid s^0\right) \prod_j P\left(s^{j\prime} \mid s^i, \pi^i()\right) \sum_o \prod_j P\left(o^j \mid \pi^i(), s^{i\prime}\right) U^{\pi^i(o^i)}(s^{i\prime}) \right] \right] \\
&= R(s, \boldsymbol{\pi}()) + \sum_i \left[\gamma \left[\sum_{s'} P\left(s^{0\prime} \mid s^0\right) \prod_j P\left(s^{j\prime} \mid s, \pi()\right) \sum_o \prod_j P\left(o^j \mid \pi(), s'\right) U^{\pi^i(o^i)}(s^{i\prime}) \right] \right] \\
&= R(s, \boldsymbol{\pi}()) + \sum_i \left[\gamma \left[\sum_{s'} T(s' \mid s, \boldsymbol{\pi}()) \sum_o O(o \mid \pi(), s') U^{\pi^i(o^i)}(s^{i\prime}) \right] \right] \\
&= R(s, \boldsymbol{\pi}()) + \gamma \left[\sum_{s'} T(s' \mid s, \boldsymbol{\pi}()) \sum_o O(o \mid \pi(), s') \left[\sum_i U^{\pi^i(o^i)}(s^{i\prime}) \right] \right] \\
&= R(s, \boldsymbol{\pi}()) + \gamma \left[\sum_{s'} T(s' \mid s, \boldsymbol{\pi}()) \sum_o O(o \mid \pi(), s') U^{\pi(o)}(s') \right] \\
&= U^\pi(s)
\end{aligned}
$$

This is the Dec-MDP utility function derived from equation (26.1), completing the proof.

Exercise 27.3. How can we use an MMDP or MPOMDP as a heuristic in Dec-POMDP heuristic search?

Solution: We can assume free communication for planning. At each time step t, all agents know $\mathbf{a}_t$ and $\mathbf{o}_t$, allowing us to maintain a multiagent belief b_t, resulting in an MPOMDP. This MPOMDP solution can be used as a heuristic to guide the search of policy trees. Alternatively, we create a heuristic where we assume that the true state and joint actions are known. This results in an MMDP, and it can also be used as a heuristic. These assumptions are used only for planning. Execution is still a Dec-POMDP wherein agents receive individual observations without free communication. Either heuristic results in a joint policy $\hat{\boldsymbol{\pi}}$ for heuristic exploration.

Exercise 27.4. How can we compute a best response controller? Describe how this could be used in an iterated best response.

Solution: For an agent i, the best response controller X^i, ψ^i, and η^i can be computed by solving a nonlinear program. The program is similar to what is given in section 27.6, except that $\mathbf{X}^{-i}$, ψ^{-i}, and η^{-i} are now given and are no longer variables:

$$\underset{U,\psi^i,\eta^i}{\text{maximize}} \quad \sum_s b(s)U(\mathbf{x}_1,s)$$

$$\text{subject to} \quad U(\mathbf{x},s) = \sum_{\mathbf{a}} \prod_i \psi^i(a^i \mid x^i)\left(R(s,\mathbf{a}) + \gamma \sum_{s'} T(s' \mid s,\mathbf{a}) \sum_{\mathbf{o}} O(\mathbf{o} \mid \mathbf{a},s') \sum_{\mathbf{x}'} \prod_i \eta^i(x^{i\prime} \mid x^i,a^i,o^i)U(\mathbf{x}',s') \right)$$

$$\text{for all } \mathbf{x}, s$$

$$\psi^i(a^i \mid x^i) \geq 0 \quad \text{for all } x^i, a^i$$

$$\sum_a \psi^i(a^i \mid x^i) = 1 \quad \text{for all } x^i$$

$$\eta^i(x^{i\prime} \mid x^i,a^i,o^i) \geq 0 \quad \text{for all } x^i, a^i, o^i, x^{i\prime}$$

$$\sum_{x^{i\prime}} \eta^i(x^{i\prime} \mid x^i,a^i,o^i) = 1 \quad \text{for all } x^i, a^i, o^i$$

Adapting algorithm 27.3 for controller policies, this program replaces the inner best response operation.

APPENDICES

A Mathematical Concepts

This appendix provides a brief overview of some of the mathematical concepts used in this book.

A.1 Measure Spaces

Before introducing the definition of a measure space, we will first discuss the notion of a sigma-algebra over a set Ω. A sigma-algebra is a collection Σ of subsets of Ω such that

1. $\Omega \in \Sigma$.

2. If $E \in \Sigma$, then $\Omega \setminus E \in \Sigma$ (*closed under complementation*).

3. If $E_1, E_2, E_3, \ldots \in \Sigma$, then $E_1 \cup E_2 \cup E_3 \ldots \in \Sigma$ (*closed under countable unions*).

An element $E \in \Sigma$ is called a *measurable set*.

A *measure space* is defined by a set Ω, a sigma-algebra Σ, and a *measure* $\mu : \Omega \to \mathbb{R} \cup \{\infty\}$. For μ to be a measure, the following properties must hold:

1. If $E \in \Sigma$, then $\mu(E) \geq 0$ (*nonnegativity*).

2. $\mu(\emptyset) = 0$.

3. If $E_1, E_2, E_3, \ldots \in \Sigma$ are pairwise disjoint, then $\mu(E_1 \cup E_2 \cup E_3 \ldots) = \mu(E_1) + \mu(E_2) + \mu(E_3) + \cdots$ (*countable additivity*).

A.2   Probability Spaces

A *probability space* is a measure space (Ω, Σ, μ) with the requirement that $\mu(\Omega) = 1$. In the context of probability spaces, Ω is called the *sample space*, Σ is called the *event space*, and μ (or, more commonly, P) is the *probability measure*. The *probability axioms*[1] refer to the nonnegativity and countable additivity properties of measure spaces, together with the requirement that $\mu(\Omega) = 1$.

[1] These axioms are sometimes called the *Kolmorogov axioms*. A. Kolmogorov, *Foundations of the Theory of Probability*, 2nd ed. Chelsea, 1956.

A.3   Metric Spaces

A set with a *metric* is called a *metric space*. A metric d, sometimes called a *distance metric*, is a function that maps pairs of elements in X to nonnegative real numbers such that for all $x, y, z \in X$:

1. $d(x, y) = 0$ if and only if $x = y$ (*identity of indiscernibles*).

2. $d(x, y) = d(y, x)$ (*symmetry*).

3. $d(x, y) \leq d(x, z) + d(z, y)$ (*triangle inequality*).

A.4   Normed Vector Spaces

A *normed vector space* consists of a *vector space* X and a norm $\|\cdot\|$ that maps elements of X to nonnegative real numbers such that for all scalars α and vectors $\mathbf{x}, \mathbf{y} \in X$:

1. $\|\mathbf{x}\| = 0$ if and only if $\mathbf{x} = \mathbf{0}$.

2. $\|\alpha\mathbf{x}\| = |\alpha|\|\mathbf{x}\|$ (*absolutely homogeneous*).

3. $\|\mathbf{x} + \mathbf{y}\| \leq \|\mathbf{x}\| + \|\mathbf{y}\|$ (*triangle inequality*).

The L_p norms are a commonly used set of norms parameterized by a scalar $p \geq 1$. The L_p norm of vector $\mathbf{x}$ is

$$\|\mathbf{x}\|_p = \lim_{\rho \to p} (|x_1|^\rho + |x_2|^\rho + \cdots + |x_n|^\rho)^{\frac{1}{\rho}} \tag{A.1}$$

where the limit is necessary for defining the infinity norm, L_∞. Several L_p norms are shown in figure A.1.

Norms can be used to induce distance metrics in vector spaces by defining the metric $d(\mathbf{x}, \mathbf{y}) = \|\mathbf{x} - \mathbf{y}\|$. We can then, for example, use an L_p norm to define distances.

L_1: $\|\mathbf{x}\|_1 = |x_1| + |x_2| + \cdots + |x_n|$

This metric is often referred to as the *taxicab norm*.

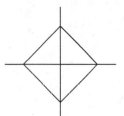

L_2: $\|\mathbf{x}\|_2 = \sqrt{x_1^2 + x_2^2 + \cdots + x_n^2}$

This metric is often referred to as the *Euclidean norm*.

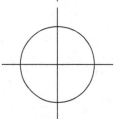

L_∞: $\|\mathbf{x}\|_\infty = \max(|x_1|, |x_2|, \cdots, |x_n|)$

This metric is often referred to as the *max norm*, *Chebyshev norm*, or *chessboard norm*. The latter name comes from the minimum number of moves that a king needs to move between two squares in chess.

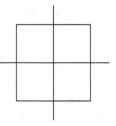

Figure A.1. Common L_p norms. The illustrations show the shape of the norm contours in two dimensions. All points on the contour are equidistant from the origin under that norm.

A.5   Positive Definiteness

A symmetric matrix $\mathbf{A}$ is *positive definite* if $\mathbf{x}^\top \mathbf{A}\mathbf{x}$ is positive for all points other than the origin. In other words, $\mathbf{x}^\top \mathbf{A}\mathbf{x} > 0$ for all $\mathbf{x} \neq \mathbf{0}$. A symmetric matrix $\mathbf{A}$ is *positive semidefinite* if $\mathbf{x}^\top \mathbf{A}\mathbf{x}$ is always nonnegative. In other words, $\mathbf{x}^\top \mathbf{A}\mathbf{x} \geq 0$ for all $\mathbf{x}$.

A.6   Convexity

A *convex combination* of two vectors $\mathbf{x}$ and $\mathbf{y}$ is the result of

$$\alpha \mathbf{x} + (1 - \alpha)\mathbf{y} \qquad \text{(A.2)}$$

for some $\alpha \in [0, 1]$. Convex combinations can be made from m vectors:

$$w_1 \mathbf{v}^{(1)} + w_2 \mathbf{v}^{(2)} + \cdots + w_m \mathbf{v}^{(m)} \qquad \text{(A.3)}$$

with nonnegative weights $\mathbf{w}$ that sum to 1.

A *convex set* is a set for which a line drawn between any two points in the set is entirely within the set. Mathematically, a set $\mathcal{S}$ is convex if we have

$$\alpha \mathbf{x} + (1 - \alpha)\mathbf{y} \in \mathcal{S} \qquad \text{(A.4)}$$

for all $\mathbf{x}, \mathbf{y}$ in $\mathcal{S}$ and for all α in $[0, 1]$. A convex and a nonconvex set are shown in figure A.2.

Figure A.2. Convex and nonconvex sets.

a convex set   a nonconvex set

A *convex function* is a *bowl-shaped* function whose domain is a convex set. By "bowl-shaped," we mean that it is a function such that any line drawn between two points in its domain does not lie below the function. A function f is convex over a convex set $\mathcal{S}$ if, for all $\mathbf{x}, \mathbf{y}$ in $\mathcal{S}$ and for all α in $[0, 1]$,

$$f(\alpha \mathbf{x} + (1 - \alpha)\mathbf{y}) \leq \alpha f(\mathbf{x}) + (1 - \alpha)f(\mathbf{y}) \qquad \text{(A.5)}$$

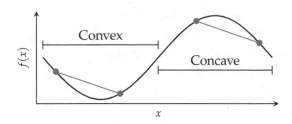

Figure A.3. Convex and nonconvex portions of a function.

Convex and concave regions of a function are shown in figure A.3.

A function f is *strictly convex* over a convex set $\mathcal{S}$ if, for all $\mathbf{x}, \mathbf{y}$ in $\mathcal{S}$ and α in $(0,1)$,

$$f(\alpha\mathbf{x} + (1-\alpha)\mathbf{y}) < \alpha f(\mathbf{x}) + (1-\alpha)f(\mathbf{y}) \tag{A.6}$$

Strictly convex functions have at most one minimum, whereas a convex function can have flat regions.[2] Examples of strict and nonstrict convexity are shown in figure A.4.

[2] Optimization of convex functions is the subject of the textbook by S. Boyd and L. Vandenberghe, *Convex Optimization*. Cambridge University Press, 2004.

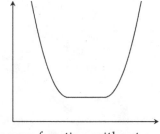

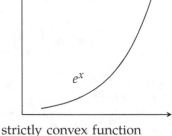

strictly convex function with one global minimum

convex function without a unique global minimum

strictly convex function without a global minimum

Figure A.4. Not all convex functions have single global minima.

A function f is *concave* if $-f$ is convex. Furthermore, f is *strictly concave* if $-f$ is strictly convex.

A.7 Information Content

If we have a discrete distribution that assigns probability $P(x)$ to value x, the *information content*[3] of observing x is given by

$$I(x) = -\log P(x) \tag{A.7}$$

[3] Sometimes information content is referred to as *Shannon information*, in honor of Claude Shannon, the founder of the field of information theory. C. E. Shannon, "A Mathematical Theory of Communication," *Bell System Technical Journal*, vol. 27, no. 4, pp. 623–656, 1948.

The unit of information content depends on the base of the logarithm. We generally assume natural logarithms (with base e), making the unit *nat*, which is short for *natural*. In information theoretic contexts, the base is often 2, making the unit *bit*. We can think of this quantity as the number of bits required to transmit the value x according to an optimal message encoding when the distribution over messages follows the specified distribution.

A.8   Entropy

Entropy is an information theoretic measure of uncertainty. The entropy associated with a discrete random variable X is the expected information content:

$$H(X) = \mathbb{E}_x[I(x)] = \sum_x P(x)I(x) = - \sum_x P(x) \log P(x) \qquad (A.8)$$

where $P(x)$ is the mass assigned to x.

For a continuous distribution where $p(x)$ is the density assigned to x, the *differential entropy* (also known as *continuous entropy*) is defined to be

$$h(X) = \int p(x)I(x)\,dx = - \int p(x) \log p(x)\,dx \qquad (A.9)$$

A.9   Cross Entropy

The *cross entropy* of one distribution relative to another can be defined in terms of expected information content. If we have one discrete distribution with mass function $P(x)$ and another with mass function $Q(x)$, then the cross entropy of P relative to Q is given by

$$H(P,Q) = - \mathbb{E}_{x \sim P}[\log Q(x)] = - \sum_x P(x) \log Q(x) \qquad (A.10)$$

For continuous distributions with density functions $p(x)$ and $q(x)$, we have

$$H(p,q) = - \int p(x) \log q(x)\,dx \qquad (A.11)$$

A.10   Relative Entropy

Relative entropy, also called the *Kullback-Leibler (KL) divergence*, is a measure of how one probability distribution is different from a reference distribution.[4] If $P(x)$ and $Q(x)$ are mass functions, then the KL divergence from Q to P is the expectation of the logarithmic differences, with the expectation using P:

$$D_{KL}(P \parallel Q) = \sum_x P(x) \log \frac{P(x)}{Q(x)} = -\sum_x P(x) \log \frac{Q(x)}{P(x)} \tag{A.12}$$

This quantity is defined only if the support of P is a subset of that of Q. The summation is over the support of P to avoid division by zero.

For continuous distributions with density functions $p(x)$ and $q(x)$, we have

$$D_{KL}(p \parallel q) = \int p(x) \log \frac{p(x)}{q(x)} \, dx = -\int p(x) \log \frac{q(x)}{p(x)} \, dx \tag{A.13}$$

Similarly, this quantity is defined only if the support of p is a subset of that of q. The integral is over the support of p to avoid division by zero.

[4] Named for the two American mathematicians who introduced this measure, Solomon Kullback (1907–1994) and Richard A. Leibler (1914–2003). S. Kullback and R. A. Leibler, "On Information and Sufficiency," *Annals of Mathematical Statistics*, vol. 22, no. 1, pp. 79–86, 1951. S. Kullback, *Information Theory and Statistics*. Wiley, 1959.

A.11   Gradient Ascent

Gradient ascent is a general approach for attempting to maximize a function $f(\mathbf{x})$ when f is a differentiable function. We begin at a point $\mathbf{x}$ and iteratively apply the following update rule:

$$\mathbf{x} \leftarrow \mathbf{x} + \alpha \nabla f(\mathbf{x}) \tag{A.14}$$

where $\alpha > 0$ is called a *step factor*. The idea of this optimization approach is that we take steps in the direction of the gradient until reaching a local maximum. There is no guarantee that we will find a global maximum using this method. Small values for α will generally require more iterations to come close to a local maximum. Large values for α will often result in bouncing around the local optimum without quite reaching it. If α is constant over iterations, it is sometimes called a *learning rate*. Many applications involve a *decaying step factor*, where, in addition to updating $\mathbf{x}$ at each iteration, we update α according to

$$\alpha \leftarrow \gamma \alpha \tag{A.15}$$

where $0 < \gamma < 1$ is the *decay factor*.

A.12   Taylor Expansion

The *Taylor expansion*,[5] also called the *Taylor series*, of a function is important to many approximations used in this book. From the *first fundamental theorem of calculus*,[6] we know that

$$f(x + h) = f(x) + \int_0^h f'(x + a)\, da \tag{A.16}$$

Nesting this definition produces the Taylor expansion of f about x:

$$f(x + h) = f(x) + \int_0^h \left(f'(x) + \int_0^a f''(x + b)\, db \right) da \tag{A.17}$$

$$= f(x) + f'(x)h + \int_0^h \int_0^a f''(x + b)\, db\, da \tag{A.18}$$

$$= f(x) + f'(x)h + \int_0^h \int_0^a \left(f''(x) + \int_0^b f'''(x + c)\, dc \right) db\, da \tag{A.19}$$

$$= f(x) + f'(x)h + \frac{f''(x)}{2!}h^2 + \int_0^h \int_0^a \int_0^b f'''(x + c)\, dc\, db\, da \tag{A.20}$$

$$\vdots \tag{A.21}$$

$$= f(x) + \frac{f'(x)}{1!}h + \frac{f''(x)}{2!}h^2 + \frac{f'''(x)}{3!}h^3 + \dots \tag{A.22}$$

$$= \sum_{n=0}^{\infty} \frac{f^{(n)}(x)}{n!}h^n \tag{A.23}$$

In the formulation given here, x is typically fixed and the function is evaluated in terms of h. It is often more convenient to write the Taylor expansion of $f(x)$ about a point a such that it remains a function of x:

$$f(x) = \sum_{n=0}^{\infty} \frac{f^{(n)}(a)}{n!}(x - a)^n \tag{A.24}$$

The Taylor expansion represents a function as an infinite sum of polynomial terms based on repeated derivatives at a single point. Any analytic function can be represented by its Taylor expansion within a local neighborhood.

A function can be locally approximated by using the first few terms of the Taylor expansion. Figure A.5 shows increasingly better approximations for $\cos(x)$ about $x = 1$. Including more terms increases the accuracy of the local approximation, but error still accumulates as one moves away from the expansion point.

[5] Named for the English mathematician Brook Taylor (1685–1731) who introduced the concept.

[6] The first fundamental theorem of calculus relates a function to the integral of its derivative:

$$f(b) - f(a) = \int_a^b f'(x)\, dx$$

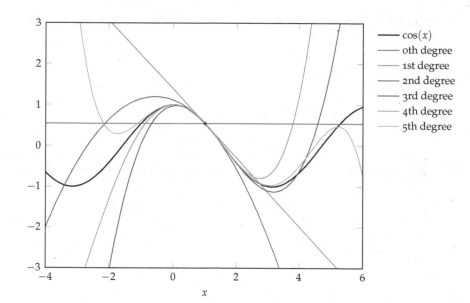

Figure A.5. Successive approximations of $\cos(x)$ about 1 based on the first n terms of the Taylor expansion.

A linear *Taylor approximation* uses the first two terms of the Taylor expansion:

$$f(x) \approx f(a) + f'(a)(x - a) \tag{A.25}$$

A quadratic Taylor approximation uses the first three terms:

$$f(x) \approx f(a) + f'(a)(x - a) + \frac{1}{2}f''(a)(x - a)^2 \tag{A.26}$$

and so on.

In multiple dimensions, the Taylor expansion about $\mathbf{a}$ generalizes to

$$f(\mathbf{x}) = f(\mathbf{a}) + \nabla f(\mathbf{a})^\top (\mathbf{x} - \mathbf{a}) + \frac{1}{2}(\mathbf{x} - \mathbf{a})^\top \nabla^2 f(\mathbf{a})(\mathbf{x} - \mathbf{a}) + \ldots \tag{A.27}$$

The first two terms form the tangent plane at $\mathbf{a}$. The third term incorporates local curvature. This book will use only the first three terms shown here.

A.13   Monte Carlo Estimation

Monte Carlo estimation allows us to evaluate the expectation of a function f when its input x follows a probability density function p:

$$\mathbb{E}_{x \sim p}[f(x)] = \int f(x)p(x)\,\mathrm{d}x \approx \frac{1}{n}\sum_i f(x^{(i)}) \tag{A.28}$$

where $x^{(1)}, \ldots, x^{(n)}$ are drawn from p. The variance of the estimate is equal to $\text{Var}_{x \sim p}[f(x)]/n$.

A.14   Importance Sampling

Importance sampling allows us to compute $\mathbb{E}_{x \sim p}[f(x)]$ from samples drawn from a different distribution q:

$$\mathbb{E}_{x \sim p}[f(x)] = \int f(x)p(x)\,dx \tag{A.29}$$

$$= \int f(x)p(x)\frac{q(x)}{q(x)}\,dx \tag{A.30}$$

$$= \int f(x)\frac{p(x)}{q(x)}q(x)\,dx \tag{A.31}$$

$$= \mathbb{E}_{x \sim q}\left[f(x)\frac{p(x)}{q(x)}\right] \tag{A.32}$$

The equation above can be approximated using samples $x^{(1)}, \ldots, x^{(n)}$ drawn from q:

$$\mathbb{E}_{x \sim p}[f(x)] = \mathbb{E}_{x \sim q}\left[f(x)\frac{p(x)}{q(x)}\right] \approx \frac{1}{n}\sum_i f(x^{(i)})\frac{p(x^{(i)})}{q(x^{(i)})} \tag{A.33}$$

A.15   Contraction Mappings

A *contraction mapping* f is defined with respect to a function over a metric space such that

$$d(f(x), f(y)) \leq \alpha d(x, y) \tag{A.34}$$

where d is the distance metric associated with the metric space and $0 \leq \alpha < 1$. A contraction mapping thus reduces the distance between any two members of a set. Such a function is sometimes referred to as a *contraction* or *contractor*.

A consequence of repeatedly applying a contraction mapping is that the distance between any two members of the set is driven to 0. The *contraction mapping theorem* or the *Banach fixed-point theorem*[7] states that every contraction mapping on a complete,[8] nonempty metric space has a unique fixed point. Furthermore, for any element x in that set, repeated application of a contraction mapping to that element results in convergence to that fixed point.

[7] Named for the Polish mathematician Stefan Banach (1892–1945) who first stated the theorem.

[8] A complete metric space is one where every Cauchy sequence in that space converges to a point in that space. A sequence $x_1, x_2, \ldots$ is Cauchy if, for every positive real number $\epsilon > 0$, there is a positive integer n such that for all positive integers $i, j > n$, we have $d(x_i, x_j) < \epsilon$.

Showing that a function f is a contraction mapping on a metric space is useful in various convergence proofs associated with the concepts presented earlier. For example, we can show that the Bellman operator is a contraction mapping on the space of value functions with the max-norm. Application of the contraction mapping theorem allows us to prove that repeated application of the Bellman operator results in convergence to a unique value function. Example A.1 shows a simple contraction mapping.

Consider the function $\mathbf{f}(\mathbf{x}) = [x_2/2 + 1, x_1/2 + 1/2]$. We can show that $\mathbf{f}$ is a contraction mapping for the set $\mathbb{R}^2$ and the Euclidean distance function:

$$
\begin{aligned}
d(\mathbf{f}(\mathbf{x}), \mathbf{f}(\mathbf{y})) &= \|\mathbf{f}(\mathbf{x}) - \mathbf{f}(\mathbf{y})\|_2 \\
&= \|[x_2/2 + 1, x_1/2 + 1/2] - [y_2/2 + 1, y_1/2 + 1/2]\|_2 \\
&= \|[\tfrac{1}{2}(x_2 - y_2), \tfrac{1}{2}(x_1 - y_1)]\|_2 \\
&= \tfrac{1}{2}\|[(x_2 - y_2), (x_1 - y_1)]\|_2 \\
&= \tfrac{1}{2}d(\mathbf{x}, \mathbf{y})
\end{aligned}
$$

We can plot the effect of repeated applications of $\mathbf{f}$ to points in $\mathbb{R}^2$ and show how they converge toward $[5/3, 4/3]$:

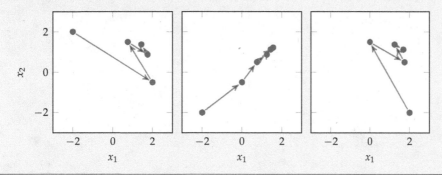

Example A.1. A contraction mapping for $\mathbb{R}^2$.

A.16   Graphs

A *graph* $G = (V, E)$ is defined by a set of *nodes* (also called *vertices*) V and *edges* E. Figure A.6 shows an example of a graph. An edge $e \in E$ is a pair of nodes (v_i, v_j). We focus primarily on *directed graphs*, where the edges are directed and define parent-child relationships. An edge $e = (v_i, v_j)$ is often represented graphically as an arrow from v_i to v_j with v_i as the *parent* and v_j as the *child*. If there is an edge connecting v_i and v_j, then we say that v_i and v_j are *neighbors*. The set of all parents of a node v_i is denoted as $\mathrm{Pa}(v_i)$.

A *path* from node v_i to node v_j is a sequence of edges connecting v_i to v_j. If this path can be followed from node to node along the direction of the edges, then we call it a *directed path*. An *undirected path* is a path without regard to the direction of the edges. A node v_j is a descendant of v_i if a directed path exists from v_i to v_j. A *cycle* is a directed path from a node to itself. If a graph does not contain any cycles, it is *acyclic*.

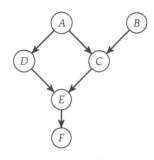

Figure A.6. An example of a graph. Here, $\mathrm{Pa}(C) = \{A, B\}$. The sequence (A, C, E, F) is a directed path, and (A, C, B) is an undirected path. Node A is a parent of C and D. Node E is a descendant of B. Neighbors of C include A, B, and E.

B   Probability Distributions

This appendix summarizes several families of probability distributions relevant to the topics introduced in this book.[1] The distributions are represented by either probability mass functions or probability density functions, and the relevant functions are provided, along with the parameters that govern each distribution. Plots show how the various parameters influence the distribution. The index includes page references to where these distributions are used in the body of the book. Some distributions are *univariate*, meaning that they are distributions over a scalar variable; others are *multivariate*, meaning that they are distributions over multiple variables.

[1] These distributions are implemented in Distributions.jl. M. Besançon, T. Papamarkou, D. Anthoff, A. Arslan, S. Byrne, D. Lin, and J. Pearson, "Distributions.jl: Definition and Modeling of Probability Distributions in the JuliaStats Ecosystem," 2019. arXiv: 1907.0861 1v1.

Name	Parameters		Distribution Function
Uniform $\mathcal{U}(a,b)$	a b	lower bound upper bound	$p(x) = \frac{1}{b-a}$ with $x \in [a,b]$

$$
\begin{aligned}
&a = -1, b = 1 \\
&a = 0, b = 3 \\
&a = -6, b = -5 \\
&a = 5, b = 8
\end{aligned}
$$

Name	Parameters		Distribution Function
Gaussian **(univariate)** $\mathcal{N}(\mu,\sigma^2)$	μ σ^2	mean variance	$p(x) = \frac{1}{\sigma}\phi\left(\frac{x-\mu}{\sigma}\right)$ where $\phi(x) = \frac{1}{\sqrt{2\pi}}\exp(-x^2/2)$ with $x \in \mathbb{R}$

$$
\begin{aligned}
&\mu = 0, \sigma = 1 \\
&\mu = 0, \sigma = 3 \\
&\mu = 5, \sigma = 4 \\
&\mu = -3, \sigma = 2
\end{aligned}
$$

Beta
Beta(α, β)

$\alpha > 0$	shape	
$\beta > 0$	shape	

$p(x) = \frac{\Gamma(\alpha+\beta)}{\Gamma(\alpha)\Gamma(\beta)} x^{\alpha-1}(1-x)^{\beta-1}$
with $x \in (0,1)$

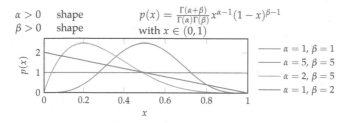

Gaussian
(multivariate)
$\mathcal{N}(\boldsymbol{\mu}, \boldsymbol{\Sigma})$

$\boldsymbol{\mu}$ mean
$\boldsymbol{\Sigma}$ covariance

$p(\mathbf{x}) = \frac{1}{(2\pi)^{n/2}|\boldsymbol{\Sigma}|^{1/2}} \exp\left(-\frac{1}{2}(\mathbf{x}-\boldsymbol{\mu})^\top \boldsymbol{\Sigma}^{-1}(\mathbf{x}-\boldsymbol{\mu})\right)$ where $n = \dim(\mathbf{x})$
with $\mathbf{x} \in \mathbb{R}^n$

$\boldsymbol{\mu} = [0,0], \boldsymbol{\Sigma} = [1\,0;\,0\,1]$ $\boldsymbol{\mu} = [0,5], \boldsymbol{\Sigma} = [3\,0;\,0\,3]$ $\boldsymbol{\mu} = [3,3], \boldsymbol{\Sigma} = [4\,2;\,2\,4]$

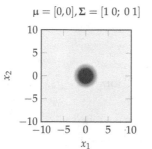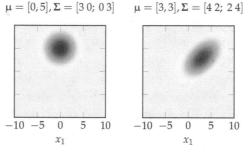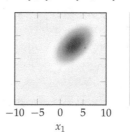

Dirichlet
Dir$(\boldsymbol{\alpha})$

$\boldsymbol{\alpha} > 0$ concentration

$p(\mathbf{x}) = \frac{\Gamma(\alpha_0)}{\prod_{i=1}^{n}\Gamma(\alpha_i)} \prod_{i=1}^{n} x_i^{\alpha_i-1}$ where $\alpha_0 = \sum_i \alpha_i$
with $x_i \in (0,1)$ and $\sum_i x_i = 1$

$\boldsymbol{\alpha} = [1,1,1]$ $\boldsymbol{\alpha} = [5,5,5]$ $\boldsymbol{\alpha} = [2,1,5]$

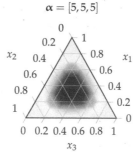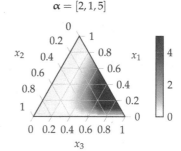

C   Computational Complexity

When discussing various algorithms, it is useful to analyze their *computational complexity*, which refers to the resources required to run them to completion.[1] We are generally interested in either time or space complexity. This appendix reviews asymptotic notation, which is what is generally used to characterize complexity. We then review a few of the complexity classes that are relevant to the algorithms in the book and discuss the problem of decidability.

[1] The analysis of algorithms represents a large field within computer science. For an introductory textbook, see O. Goldreich, *Computational Complexity: A Conceptual Perspective*. Cambridge University Press, 2008. A rigorous treatment requires the introduction of concepts and computational models, such as *Turing machines*, which we will bypass in our discussion here.

C.1   Asymptotic Notation

Asymptotic notation is often used to characterize the growth of a function. This notation is sometimes called *big-Oh notation*, since the letter O is used because the growth rate of a function is often called its *order*. This notation can be used to describe the error associated with a numerical method or the time or space complexity of an algorithm. This notation provides an upper bound on a function as its argument approaches a certain value.

Mathematically, if $f(x) = O(g(x))$ as $x \to a$, then the absolute value of $f(x)$ is bounded by the absolute value of $g(x)$ times some positive and finite c for values of x sufficiently close to a:

$$|f(x)| \leq c|g(x)| \quad \text{for } x \to a \tag{C.1}$$

Writing $f(x) = O(g(x))$ is a common abuse of the equal sign. For example, $x^2 = O(x^2)$ and $2x^2 = O(x^2)$, but, of course, $x^2 \neq 2x^2$. In some mathematical texts, $O(g(x))$ represents the set of all functions that do not grow faster than $g(x)$. For example, $5x^2 \in O(x^2)$. Example C.1 demonstrates asymptotic notation.

If $f(x)$ is a *linear combination*[2] of terms, then $O(f)$ corresponds to the order of the fastest-growing term. Example C.2 compares the orders of several terms.

[2] A linear combination is a weighted sum of terms. If the terms are in a vector $\mathbf{x}$, then the linear combination is $w_1 x_1 + w_2 x_2 + \cdots = \mathbf{w}^\top \mathbf{x}$.

Consider $f(x) = 10^6 e^x$ as $x \to \infty$. Here, f is a product of the constant 10^6 and e^x. The constant can simply be incorporated into the bounding constant c as follows:

$$|f(x)| \leq c|g(x)|$$
$$10^6|e^x| \leq c|g(x)|$$
$$|e^x| \leq c|g(x)|$$

Thus, $f = O(e^x)$ as $x \to \infty$.

Example C.1. Asymptotic notation for a constant times a function.

Consider $f(x) = \cos(x) + x + 10x^{3/2} + 3x^2$. Here, f is a linear combination of terms. The terms $\cos(x)$, x, $x^{3/2}$, x^2 are arranged in order of increasing value as x approaches infinity. We plot $f(x)$ along with $c|g(x)|$, where c has been chosen for each term such that $c|g(x = 2)|$ exceeds $f(x = 2)$.

Example C.2. Finding the order of a linear combination of terms.

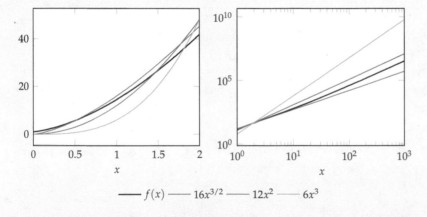

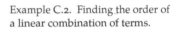

There is no constant c such that $f(x)$ is always less than $c|x^{3/2}|$ for sufficiently large values of x. The same is true for $\cos(x)$ and x.

We find that $f(x) = O(x^3)$, and in general, $f(x) = O(x^m)$ for $m \geq 2$, along with other function classes like $f(x) = e^x$. We typically discuss the order that provides the tightest upper bound. Thus, $f = O(x^2)$ as $x \to \infty$.

C.2   Time Complexity Classes

The difficulty of solving certain problems can be grouped into different time complexity classes. Important classes that appear frequently throughout this book include

- *P*: problems that can be solved in polynomial time,

- *NP*: problems whose solutions can be verified in polynomial time,

- *NP-hard*: problems that are at least as hard as the hardest problems in NP, and

- *NP-complete*: problems that are both NP-hard and in NP.

The formal definitions of these complexity classes are rather involved. It is generally believed that P $\neq$ NP, but it has not been proven and remains one of the most important open problems in mathematics. In fact, modern cryptography depends on the fact that there are no known efficient (i.e., polynomial time) algorithms for solving NP-hard problems. Figure C.1 illustrates the relationships among the complexity classes, under the assumption that P $\neq$ NP.

A common approach to proving whether a particular problem *Q* is NP-hard is to come up with a polynomial transformation from a known *NP-complete* problem[3] *Q'* to an instance of *Q*. The *3SAT* problem is the first known NP-complete problem and is discussed in example C.3.

C.3   Space Complexity Classes

Another set of complexity classes pertain to space, referring to the amount of memory required to execute an algorithm to completion. The complexity class *PSPACE* contains the set of all problems that can be solved with a polynomial amount of space, without any considerations about time. There is a fundamental difference between time and space complexity, in that time cannot be reused, but space can be. We know that P and NP are subsets of PSPACE. It is not yet known, but it is suspected, that PSPACE includes problems not in NP. Through polynomial time transformations, we can define *PSPACE-hard* and *PSPACE-complete* classes, just as we did with NP-hard and NP-complete classes.

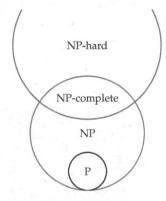

Figure C.1. Complexity classes.

[3] There are many well-known NP-complete problems, as surveyed by R. M. Karp, "Reducibility Among Combinatorial Problems," in *Complexity of Computer Computations*, R. E. Miller and J. W. Thatcher, eds., Plenum, 1972, pp. 85–103.

The problem of *Boolean satisfiability* involves determining whether a Boolean formula is *satisfiable*. The Boolean formula consists of conjunctions ($\wedge$), disjunctions ($\vee$), and negations ($\neg$) involving n Boolean variables $x_1, \ldots x_n$. A literal is a variable x_i or its negation $\neg x_i$. A 3SAT clause is a disjunction of up to three literals (e.g., $x_3 \vee \neg x_5 \vee x_6$). A 3SAT formula is a conjunction of 3SAT clauses like

$$
F(x_1, x_2, x_3, x_4) =
\begin{array}{cccccccc}
(& x_1 & \vee & x_2 & \vee & x_3 &) & \wedge \\
(& \neg x_1 & \vee & \neg x_2 & \vee & x_3 &) & \wedge \\
(& x_2 & \vee & \neg x_3 & \vee & x_4 &) &
\end{array}
$$

The challenge in 3SAT is to determine whether a possible assignment of truth values to variables exists that makes the formula true. In the formula above,

$$F(\text{true}, \text{false}, \text{false}, \text{true}) = \text{true}$$

Hence, the formula is satisfiable. Although a satisfying assignment can be easily found for some 3SAT problems, sometimes just by quick inspection, they are difficult to solve in general. One way to determine whether a satisfying assignment can be made is to enumerate the 2^n possible truth values of all the variables. Although determining whether a satisfying truth assignment exists is difficult, verification of whether a truth assignment leads to satisfaction can be done in linear time.

Example C.3. The 3SAT problem, which is the first known NP-complete problem.

C.4 Decidability

An *undecidable* problem cannot always be solved in finite time. Perhaps one of the most famous undecidable problems is the *halting problem*, which involves taking any program written in a sufficiently expressive language[4] as input and deciding whether it will terminate. It was proved that there is no algorithm that can perform such an analysis in general. Although algorithms exist that can correctly determine whether some programs terminate, there is no algorithm that can determine whether any arbitrary program will terminate.

[4] The technical requirement is that the language is *Turing complete* or *computationally universal*, meaning that it can be used to simulate any Turing machine.

D Neural Representations

Neural networks are parametric representations of nonlinear functions.[1] The function represented by a neural network is differentiable, allowing gradient-based optimization algorithms such as stochastic gradient descent to optimize their parameters to better approximate desired input-output relationships.[2] Neural representations can be helpful in a variety of contexts related to decision making, such as representing probabilistic models, utility functions, and decision policies. This appendix outlines several relevant architectures.

D.1 Neural Networks

A *neural network* is a differentiable function $\mathbf{y} = \mathbf{f}_\theta(\mathbf{x})$ that maps inputs $\mathbf{x}$ to produce outputs $\mathbf{y}$ and is parameterized by θ. Modern neural networks may have millions of parameters and can be used to convert inputs in the form of high-dimensional images or video into high-dimensional outputs like multidimensional classifications or speech.

The parameters of the network θ are generally tuned to minimize a scalar *loss function* $\ell(\mathbf{f}_\theta(\mathbf{x}), \mathbf{y})$ that is related to how far the network output is from the desired output. Both the loss function and the neural network are differentiable, allowing us to use the gradient of the loss function with respect to the parameterization $\nabla_\theta \ell$ to iteratively improve the parameterization. This process is often referred to as neural network *training* or *parameter tuning*. It is demonstrated in example D.1.

Neural networks are typically trained on a data set of input-output pairs $\mathbf{D}$. In this case, we tune the parameters to minimize the aggregate loss over the data set:

$$\arg\min_\theta \sum_{(\mathbf{x},\mathbf{y}) \in \mathbf{D}} \ell(\mathbf{f}_\theta(\mathbf{x}), \mathbf{y}) \tag{D.1}$$

[1] The name derives from the loose inspiration of networks of neurons in biological brains. We will not discuss these biological connections, but an overview and historical perspective is provided by B. Müller, J. Reinhardt, and M. T. Strickland, *Neural Networks*. Springer, 1995.

[2] This optimization process when applied to neural networks with many layers, as we will discuss shortly, is often called *deep learning*. Several textbooks are dedicated entirely to these techniques, including I. Goodfellow, Y. Bengio, and A. Courville, *Deep Learning*. MIT Press, 2016. The Julia package `Flux.jl` provides efficient implementations of various learning algorithms.

Consider a very simple neural network, $f_\theta(x) = \theta_1 + \theta_2 x$. We wish our neural network to take the square footage x of a home and predict its price y_{pred}. We want to minimize the square deviation between the predicted housing price and the true housing price by the loss function $\ell(y_{pred}, y_{true}) = (y_{pred} - y_{true})^2$. Given a training pair, we can compute the gradient:

$$\nabla_\theta \ell(f(x), y_{true}) = \nabla_\theta (\theta_1 + \theta_2 x - y_{true})^2$$
$$= \begin{bmatrix} 2(\theta_1 + \theta_2 x - y_{true}) \\ 2(\theta_1 + \theta_2 x - y_{true})x \end{bmatrix}$$

If our initial parameterization were $\theta = [10{,}000, 123]$ and we had the input-output pair $(x = 2{,}500, y_{true} = 360{,}000)$, then the loss gradient would be $\nabla_\theta \ell = [-85{,}000, -2.125 \times 10^8]$. We would take a small step in the opposite direction to improve our function approximation.

Example D.1. The fundamentals of neural networks and parameter tuning.

Data sets for modern problems tend to be very large, making the gradient of equation (D.1) expensive to evaluate. It is common to sample random subsets of the training data in each iteration, using these *batches* to compute the loss gradient. In addition to reducing computation, computing gradients with smaller batch sizes introduces some stochasticity to the gradient, which helps training to avoid getting stuck in local minima.

D.2   *Feedforward Networks*

Neural networks are typically constructed to pass the input through a series of layers.[3] Networks with many layers are often called *deep*. In *feedforward networks*, each layer applies an affine transform, followed by a nonlinear *activation function* applied elementwise:[4]

$$\mathbf{x}' = \phi.(\mathbf{Wx} + \mathbf{b}) \tag{D.2}$$

where matrix $\mathbf{W}$ and vector $\mathbf{b}$ are parameters associated with the layer. A fully connected layer is shown in figure D.1. The dimension of the output layer is different from that of the input layer when $\mathbf{W}$ is nonsquare. Figure D.2 shows a more compact depiction of the same network.

[3] A sufficiently large, single-layer neural network can, in theory, approximate any function. See A. Pinkus, "Approximation Theory of the MLP Model in Neural Networks," *Acta Numerica*, vol. 8, pp. 143–195, 1999.

[4] The nonlinearity introduced by the activation function provides something analogous to the activation behavior of biological neurons, in which input buildup eventually causes a neuron to fire. A. L. Hodgkin and A. F. Huxley, "A Quantitative Description of Membrane Current and Its Application to Conduction and Excitation in Nerve," *Journal of Physiology*, vol. 117, no. 4, pp. 500–544, 1952.

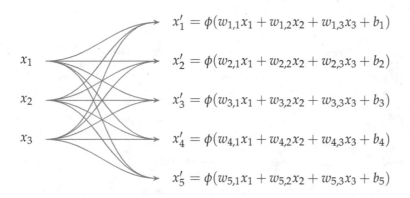

$$x'_1 = \phi(w_{1,1}x_1 + w_{1,2}x_2 + w_{1,3}x_3 + b_1)$$

$$x'_2 = \phi(w_{2,1}x_1 + w_{2,2}x_2 + w_{2,3}x_3 + b_2)$$

$$x'_3 = \phi(w_{3,1}x_1 + w_{3,2}x_2 + w_{3,3}x_3 + b_3)$$

$$x'_4 = \phi(w_{4,1}x_1 + w_{4,2}x_2 + w_{4,3}x_3 + b_4)$$

$$x'_5 = \phi(w_{5,1}x_1 + w_{5,2}x_2 + w_{5,3}x_3 + b_5)$$

Figure D.1. A fully connected layer with a three-component input and a five-component output.

If there are no activation functions between them, multiple successive affine transformations can be collapsed into a single, equivalent affine transform:

$$\mathbf{W}_2(\mathbf{W}_1\mathbf{x} + \mathbf{b}_1) + \mathbf{b}_2 = \mathbf{W}_2\mathbf{W}_1\mathbf{x} + (\mathbf{W}_2\mathbf{b}_1 + \mathbf{b}_2) \tag{D.3}$$

These nonlinearities are necessary to allow neural networks to adapt to fit arbitrary target functions. To illustrate, figure D.3 shows the output of a neural network trained to approximate a nonlinear function.

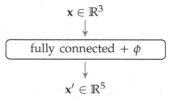

Figure D.2. A more compact depiction of figure D.1. Neural network layers are often represented as blocks or slices for simplicity.

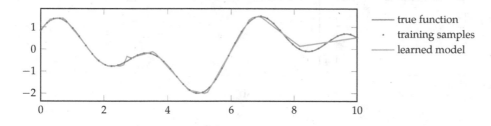

Figure D.3. A deep neural network fit to samples from a nonlinear function so as to minimize the squared error. This neural network has four affine layers, with 10 neurons in each intermediate representation.

There are many types of activation functions that are commonly used. Similar to their biological inspiration, they tend to be close to zero when their input is low and large when their input is high. Some common activation functions are shown in figure D.5.

Sometimes special layers are incorporated to achieve certain effects. For example, in figure D.4, we used a *softmax* layer at the end to force the output to represent a two-element categorical distribution. The softmax function applies

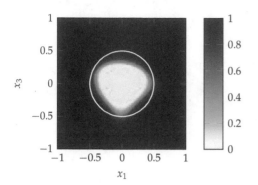

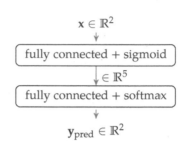

Figure D.4. A simple, two-layer, fully connected network trained to classify whether a given coordinate lies within a circle (shown in white). The nonlinearities allow neural networks to form complicated, nonlinear decision boundaries.

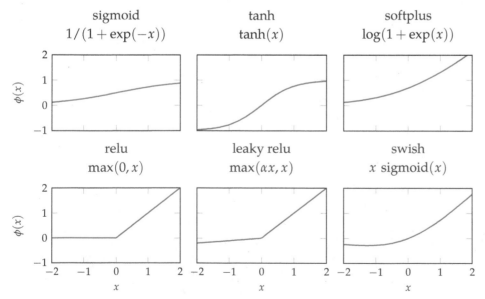

Figure D.5. Several common activation functions.

the exponential function to each element, which ensures that they are positive and then renormalizes the resulting values:

$$\text{softmax}(\mathbf{x})_i = \frac{\exp(x_i)}{\sum_j \exp(x_j)} \tag{D.4}$$

Gradients for neural networks are typically computed using *reverse accumulation*.[5] The method begins with a forward step, in which the neural network is evaluated using all input parameters. In the backward step, the gradient of each term of interest is computed working from the output back to the input. Reverse accumulation uses the chain rule for derivatives:

$$\frac{\partial \mathbf{f}(\mathbf{g}(\mathbf{h}(\mathbf{x})))}{\partial \mathbf{x}} = \frac{\partial \mathbf{f}(\mathbf{g}(\mathbf{h}))}{\partial \mathbf{h}} \frac{\partial \mathbf{h}(\mathbf{x})}{\partial \mathbf{x}} = \left(\frac{\partial \mathbf{f}(\mathbf{g})}{\partial \mathbf{g}} \frac{\partial \mathbf{g}(\mathbf{h})}{\partial \mathbf{h}} \right) \frac{\partial \mathbf{h}(\mathbf{x})}{\partial \mathbf{x}} \tag{D.5}$$

Example D.2 demonstrates this process. Many deep learning packages compute gradients using such automatic differentiation techniques.[6] Users rarely have to provide their own gradients.

D.3   Parameter Regularization

Neural networks are typically *underdetermined*, meaning that there are multiple parameter instantiations that can result in the same optimal training loss.[7] It is common to use *parameter regularization*, also called *weight regularization*, to introduce an additional term to the loss function that penalizes large parameter values. Regularization also helps prevent *overfitting*, which occurs when a network over-specializes to the training data but fails to generalize to unseen data.

Regularization often takes the form of an L_2-norm of the parameterization vector:

$$\arg\min_{\theta} \sum_{(x,y) \in \mathbf{D}} \ell(f_\theta(x), y) - \beta \|\theta\|^2 \tag{D.6}$$

where the positive scalar β controls the strength of the parameter regularization. The scalar is often quite small, with values as low as 10^{-6}, to minimize the degree to which matching the training set is sacrificed by introducing regularization.

[5] This process is commonly called *backpropagation*, which specifically refers to reverse accumulation applied to a scalar loss function. D. E. Rumelhart, G. E. Hinton, and R. J. Williams, "Learning Representations by Back-Propagating Errors," *Nature*, vol. 323, pp. 533–536, 1986.

[6] A. Griewank and A. Walther, *Evaluating Derivatives: Principles and Techniques of Algorithmic Differentiation*, 2nd ed. SIAM, 2008.

[7] For example, suppose that we have a neural network with a final softmax layer. The inputs to that layer can be scaled while producing the same output, and therefore the same loss.

Recall the neural network and loss function from example D.1. Here we have drawn the computational graph for the loss calculation:

Example D.2. How reverse accumulation is used to compute parameter gradients given training data.

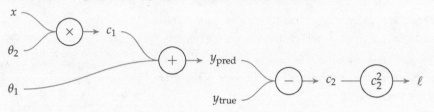

Reverse accumulation begins with a forward pass, in which the computational graph is evaluated. We will again use $\theta = [10{,}000, 123]$ and the input-output pair $(x = 2{,}500, y_{\text{true}} = 360{,}000)$ as follows:

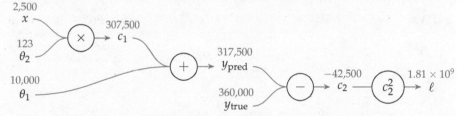

The gradient is then computed by working back up the tree:

Finally, we compute:

$$\frac{\partial \ell}{\partial \theta_1} = \frac{\partial \ell}{\partial c_2} \frac{\partial c_2}{\partial y_{\text{pred}}} \frac{\partial y_{\text{pred}}}{\partial \theta_1} = -85{,}000 \cdot 1 \cdot 1 = -85{,}000$$

$$\frac{\partial \ell}{\partial \theta_2} = \frac{\partial \ell}{\partial c_2} \frac{\partial c_2}{\partial y_{\text{pred}}} \frac{\partial y_{\text{pred}}}{\partial c_1} \frac{\partial c_1}{\partial \theta_2} = -85{,}000 \cdot 1 \cdot 1 \cdot 2500 = -2.125 \times 10^8$$

D.4 Convolutional Neural Networks

Neural networks may have images or other multidimensional structures such as lidar scans as inputs. Even a relatively small 256×256 RGB image (similar to figure D.6) has $256 \times 256 \times 3 = 196{,}608$ entries. Any fully connected layer taking an $m \times m \times 3$ image as input and producing a vector of n outputs would have a weight matrix with $3m^2n$ values. The large number of parameters to learn is not only computationally expensive, it is also wasteful. Information in images is typically translation-invariant; an object in an image that is shifted right by 1 pixel should produce a similar, if not identical, output.

Convolutional layers[8] both significantly reduce the amount of computation and support translation invariance by sliding a smaller, fully connected window to produce their output. Significantly fewer parameters need to be learned. These parameters tend to be receptive to local textures in much the same way that the neurons in the visual cortex respond to stimuli in their receptive fields.

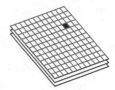

Figure D.6. Multidimensional inputs like images generalize vectors to tensors. Here, we show a three-layer RGB image. Such inputs can have very many entries.

[8] Y. LeCun, L. Bottou, Y. Bengio, and P. Haffner, "Gradient-Based Learning Applied to Document Recognition," *Proceedings of the IEEE*, vol. 86, no. 11, pp. 2278–2324, 1998.

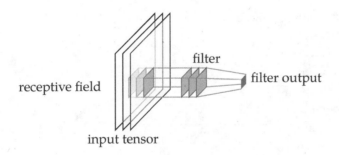

receptive field

filter

filter output

input tensor

Figure D.7. A convolutional layer repeatedly applies filters across an input tensor, such as an image, to produce an output tensor. This illustration shows how each application of the filter acts like a small, fully connected layer applied to a small receptive field to produce a single entry in the output tensor. Each filter is shifted across the input according to a prescribed stride. The resulting output has as many layers as there are filters.

The convolutional layer consists of a set of *features*, or *kernels*, each of which is equivalent to a fully connected layer into which one can input a smaller region of the input tensor. A single kernel is being applied once in figure D.7. These features have full depth, meaning that if an input tensor is $n \times m \times d$, the features will also have a third dimension of d. The features are applied many times by sliding them over the input in both the first and second dimensions. If the *stride* is 1×1, then all k filters are applied to every possible position and the output dimension will be $n \times m \times k$. If the stride is 2×2, then the filters are shifted by 2 in the first and second dimensions with every application, resulting in an output of size $n/2 \times m/2 \times k$. It is common for convolutional neural networks to increase in the third dimension and reduce in the first two dimensions with each layer.

Convolutional layers are translation-invariant because each filter behaves the same regardless of where in the input is applied. This property is especially useful in spatial processing because shifts in an input image can yield similar outputs, making it easier for neural networks to extract common features. Individual features tend to learn how to recognize local attributes such as colors and textures.

The MNIST data set contains handwritten digits in the form of 28×28 monochromatic images. It is a often used to test image classification networks. To the right, we have a sample convolutional neural network that takes an MNIST image as input and produces a categorical probability distribution over the 10 possible digits. Convolutional layers are used to efficiently extract features. The model shrinks in the first two dimensions and expands in the third dimension (the number of features) as the network depth increases. Eventually reaching a first and second dimension of 1 ensures that information from across the entire image can affect every feature. The flatten operation takes the $1 \times 1 \times 32$ input and flattens it into a 32-component output. Such operations are common when transitioning between convolutional and fully connected layers. This model has 19,722 parameters. The parameters can be tuned to maximize the likelihood of the training data.

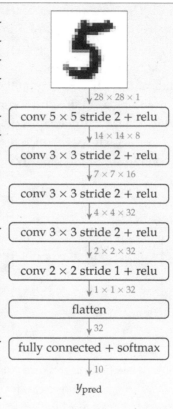

Example D.3. A convolutional neural network for the MNIST data set. Y. LeCun, L. Bottou, Y. Bengio, and P. Haffner, "Gradient-Based Learning Applied to Document Recognition," *Proceedings of the IEEE*, vol. 86, no. 11, pp. 2278–2324, 1998.

D.5 Recurrent Networks

The neural network architectures discussed so far are ill suited for temporal or sequential inputs. Operations on sequences occur when processing images from videos, when translating a sequence of words, or when tracking time-series data. In such cases, the outputs depend on more than just the most recent input. In addition, the neural network architectures discussed so far do not naturally produce variable-length outputs. For example, a neural network that writes an essay would be difficult to train using a conventional, fully connected neural network.

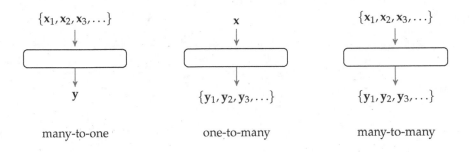

many-to-one   one-to-many   many-to-many

Figure D.8. Traditional neural networks do not naturally accept variable-length inputs or produce variable-length outputs.

When a neural network has sequential input, sequential output, or both (figure D.8), we can use a *recurrent neural network* to act over multiple iterations. These neural networks maintain a recurrent state $\mathbf{r}$, sometimes called its *memory*, to retain information over time. For example, in translation, a word used early in a sentence may be relevant to the proper translation of words later in the sentence. Figure D.9 shows the structure of a basic recurrent neural network and how the same neural network can be understood to be a larger network unrolled in time.

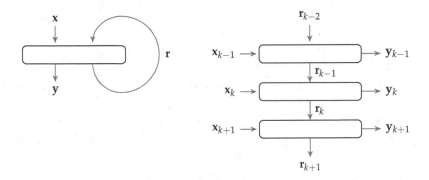

Figure D.9. A recurrent neural network (left) and the same recurrent neural network unrolled in time (right). These networks maintain a recurrent state $\mathbf{r}$ that allows the network to develop a sort of memory, transferring information across iterations.

This unrolled structure can be used to produce a rich diversity of sequential neural networks, as shown in figure D.10. Many-to-many structures come in multiple forms. In one form, the output sequence begins with the input sequence. In another form, the output sequence does not begin with the input sequence. When using variable-length outputs, the neural network output itself often indicates when a sequence begins or ends. The recurrent state is often initialized to zero, as are extra inputs after the input sequence has been passed in, but this need not be the case.

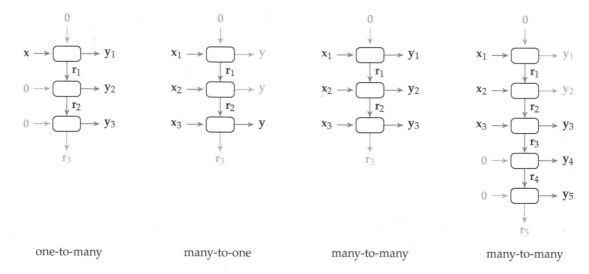

one-to-many   many-to-one   many-to-many   many-to-many

Recurrent neural networks with many layers, unrolled over multiple time steps, effectively produce a very deep neural network. During training, gradients are computed with respect to the loss function. The contribution of layers farther from the loss function tends to be smaller than that of layers close to the loss function. This leads to the *vanishing gradient* problem, in which deep neural networks have vanishingly small gradients in their upper layers. These small gradients slow training.

Very deep neural networks can also suffer from *exploding gradients*, in which successive gradient contributions through the layers combine to produce very large values. Such large values make learning unstable. Example D.4 shows both exploding and vanishing gradients.

Figure D.10. A recurrent neural network can be unrolled in time to produce different relationships. Unused or default inputs and outputs are grayed out.

To illustrate vanishing and exploding gradients, consider a deep neural network made of one-dimensional, fully connected layers with relu activations. For example, if the network has three layers, its output is

$$f_\theta(x) = \text{relu}(w_3 \, \text{relu}(w_2 \, \text{relu}(w_1 x_1 + b_1) + b_2) + b_3)$$

The gradient with respect to a loss function depends on the gradient of f_θ.

We can get vanishing gradients in the parameters of the first layer, w_1 and b_1, if the gradient contributions in successive layers are less than 1. For example, if any of the layers has a negative input to its relu function, the gradient of its inputs will be zero, so the gradient vanishes entirely. In a less extreme case, suppose that the weights are all $\mathbf{w} = 0.5 \, \mathbf{1}$, the offsets are all $\mathbf{b} = \mathbf{0}$, and the input x is positive. In this case, the gradient with respect to w_1 is

$$\frac{\partial f}{\partial w_1} = x_1 \cdot w_2 \cdot w_3 \cdot w_4 \cdot w_5 \ldots$$

The deeper the network, the smaller the gradient will be.

We can get exploding gradients in the parameters of the first layer if the gradient contributions in successive layers are greater than 1. If we merely increase our weights to $\mathbf{w} = 2 \, \mathbf{1}$, the very same gradient is suddenly doubling every layer.

Example D.4. A demonstration of how vanishing and exploding gradients arise in deep neural networks. This example uses a very simple neural network. In larger, fully connected layers, the same principles apply.

While exploding gradients can often be handled with gradient clipping, regularization, and initializing parameters to small values, these solutions merely shift the problem toward that of vanishing gradients. Recurrent neural networks often use layers specifically constructed to mitigate the vanishing gradients problem. They function by selectively choosing whether to retain memory, and these gates help regulate the memory and the gradient. Two common recurrent layers are *long short-term memory (LSTM)*[9] and *gated recurrent units (GRU)*.[10]

D.6   Autoencoder Networks

Neural networks are often used to process high-dimensional inputs such as images or point clouds. These high-dimensional inputs are often highly structured, with the actual information content being much lower-dimensional than the high-dimensional space in which it is presented. Pixels in images tend to be highly correlated with their neighbors, and point clouds often have many regions of continuity. Sometimes we wish to build an understanding of the information content of our data sets by converting them to a much smaller set of features, or an *embedding*. This compression, or *representation learning*, has many advantages.[11] Lower-dimensional representations can help facilitate the application of traditional machine learning techniques like Bayesian networks to what would have otherwise been intractable. The features can be inspected to develop an understanding of the information content of the data set, and these features can be used as inputs to other models.

An *autoencoder* is a neural network trained to discover a low-dimensional feature representation of a higher-level input. An autoencoder network takes in a high-dimensional input **x** and produces an output **x′** with the same dimensionality. We design the network architecture to pass through a lower-dimensional intermediate representation called a *bottleneck*. The activations **z** at this bottleneck are our low-dimensional features, which exist in a *latent space* that is not explicitly observed. Such an architecture is shown in figure D.11.

We train the autoencoder to reproduce its input. For example, to encourage the output **x′** to match **x** as closely as possible, we may simply minimize the L_2-norm,

$$\underset{\theta}{\text{minimize}} \quad \underset{\mathbf{x} \in \mathbf{D}}{\mathbb{E}}\left[\|f_\theta(\mathbf{x}) - \mathbf{x}\|_2\right] \tag{D.7}$$

[9] S. Hochreiter and J. Schmidhuber, "Long Short-Term Memory," *Neural Computation*, vol. 9, no. 8, pp. 1735–1780, 1997.

[10] K. Cho, B. van Merriënboer, C. Gulcehre, D. Bahdanau, F. Bougares, H. Schwenk, and Y. Bengio, "Learning Phrase Representations Using RNN Encoder-Decoder for Statistical Machine Translation," in *Conference on Empirical Methods in Natural Language Processing (EMNLP)*, 2014.

[11] Such dimensionality reduction can also be done using traditional machine learning techniques, such as principal component analysis. Neural models allow more flexibility and can handle nonlinear representations.

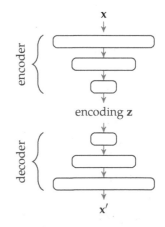

Figure D.11.   An autoencoder passes a high-dimensional input through a low-dimensional bottleneck and then reconstructs the original input. Minimizing reconstruction loss can result in an efficient low-dimensional encoding.

Noise is often added to the input to produce a more robust feature embedding:

$$\underset{\theta}{\text{minimize}} \quad \underset{\mathbf{x} \in \mathbf{D}}{\mathbb{E}}[\|f_\theta(\mathbf{x} + \boldsymbol{\epsilon}) - \mathbf{x}\|_2] \tag{D.8}$$

Training to minimize the reconstruction loss forces the autoencoder to find the most efficient low-dimensional encoding that is sufficient to accurately reconstruct the original input. Furthermore, training is *unsupervised*, in that we do not need to guide the training to a particular feature set.

After training, the upper portion of the autoencoder above the bottleneck can be used as an *encoder* that transforms an input into the feature representation. The lower portion of the autoencoder can be used as a *decoder* that transforms the feature representation into the input representation. Decoding is useful when training neural networks to generate images or other high-dimensional outputs. Example D.5 shows an embedding learned for handwritten digits.

A *variational autoencoder*, shown in figure D.12, extends the autoencoder framework to learn a probabilistic encoder.[12] Rather than outputting a deterministic sample, the encoder produces a distribution over the encoding, which allows the model to assign confidence to its encoding. Multivariate Gaussian distributions with diagonal covariance matrices are often used for their mathematical convenience. In such a case, the encoder outputs both an encoding mean and diagonal covariance matrix.

Variational autoencoders are trained to both minimize the expected reconstruction loss while keeping the encoding components close to unit Gaussian. The former is achieved by taking a single sample from the encoding distribution with each passthrough, $\mathbf{z} \sim \mathcal{N}(\boldsymbol{\mu}, \boldsymbol{\sigma}^\top \mathbf{I} \boldsymbol{\sigma})$. For backpropagation to work, we typically include random noise $\mathbf{w} \sim \mathcal{N}(\mathbf{0}, \mathbf{I})$ as an additional input to the neural network and obtain our sample according to $\mathbf{z} = \boldsymbol{\mu} + \mathbf{w} \odot \boldsymbol{\sigma}$.

The components are kept close to unit Gaussian by also minimizing the KL divergence (appendix A.10).[13] This objective encourages smooth latent space representations. The network is penalized for spreading out the latent representations (large values for $\|\boldsymbol{\mu}\|$) and for focusing each representation into a very small encoding space (small values for $\|\boldsymbol{\sigma}\|$), ensuring better coverage of the latent space. As a result, smooth variations into the decoder can result in smoothly varying outputs. This property allows decoders to be used as *generative models*, where samples from a unit multivariate Gaussian can be input to the decoder to

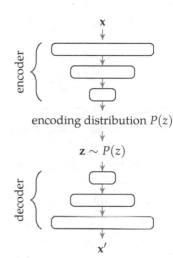

Figure D.12. A variational autoencoder passes a high-dimensional input through a low-dimensional bottleneck that produces a probability distribution over the encoding. The decoder reconstructs samples from this encoding to reconstruct the original input. Variational autoencoders can therefore assign confidence to each encoded feature. The decoder can thereafter be used as a generative model.

[12] D. Kingma and M. Welling, "Auto-Encoding Variational Bayes," in *International Conference on Learning Representations (ICLR)*, 2013.

[13] The KL divergence for two unit Gaussians is

$$\log\left(\frac{\sigma_2}{\sigma_1}\right) + \frac{\sigma_1^2 + (\mu_1 - \mu_2)^2}{2\sigma_2^2} - \frac{1}{2}$$

produce realistic samples in the original space. The combined loss function is

$$
\begin{aligned}
\underset{\theta}{\text{minimize}} \quad & \underset{\mathbf{x} \in \mathbf{D}}{\mathbb{E}} \left[\|\mathbf{x}' - \mathbf{x}\|_2 + c \sum_{i=1}^{|\boldsymbol{\mu}|} D_{\text{KL}} \left(\mathcal{N} \left(\mu_i, \sigma_i^2, \right) \middle\| \mathcal{N}(0,1) \right) \right] \\
\text{subject to} \quad & \boldsymbol{\mu}, \boldsymbol{\sigma} = \text{encoder}(\mathbf{x} + \boldsymbol{\epsilon}) \\
& \mathbf{x}' = \text{decoder}(\boldsymbol{\mu} + \mathbf{w} \odot \boldsymbol{\sigma})
\end{aligned}
\tag{D.9}
$$

where the trade-off between the two losses is tuned by the scalar $c > 0$. Example D.6 demonstrates this process on a latent space learned from handwritten digits.

Variational autoencoders are derived by representing the encoder as a conditional distribution $q(\mathbf{z} \mid \mathbf{x})$, where $\mathbf{x}$ belongs to the observed input space and $\mathbf{z}$ is in the unobserved embedding space. The decoder performs inference in the other direction, representing $p(\mathbf{x} \mid \mathbf{z})$, in which case it also outputs a probability distribution. We seek to minimize the KL divergence between $q(\mathbf{z} \mid \mathbf{x})$ and $p(\mathbf{z} \mid \mathbf{x})$, which is the same as minimizing $\mathbb{E}[\log p(\mathbf{x} \mid \mathbf{z})] - D_{\text{KL}}(q(\mathbf{z} \mid \mathbf{x}) \mid\mid p(\mathbf{z}))$, where $p(\mathbf{z})$ is our prior, the unit multivariate Gaussian to which we bias our encoding distribution. We thus obtain our reconstruction loss and our KL divergence.

D.7   Adversarial Networks

We often want to train neural networks to produce high-dimensional outputs, such as images or sequences of helicopter control inputs. When the output space is large, the training data may cover only a very small region of the state space. Hence, training purely on the available data can cause unrealistic results or overfitting. We generally want the neural network to produce plausible outputs. For example, when producing images, we want the images to look realistic. When mimicking human driving, such as in imitation learning (chapter 18), we want the vehicle to typically stay in its lane and to react appropriately to other vehicles.

We can use an autoencoder to train an embedding for the MNIST data set. In this example, we use an encoder similar to the convolutional network in example D.3, except with a two-dimensional output and no softmax layer. We construct a decoder that mirrors the encoder and train the full network to minimize the reconstruction loss. Here are the encodings for 10,000 images from the MNIST data set after training. Each encoding is colored according to the corresponding digit:

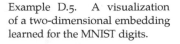

Example D.5. A visualization of a two-dimensional embedding learned for the MNIST digits.

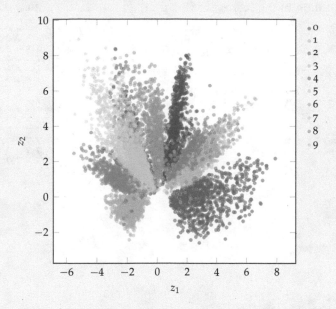

We find that the digits tend to be clustered into regions that are roughly radially distributed from the origin. Note how the encodings for 1 and 7 are similar, as the two digits look alike. Recall that training is unsupervised, and the network is not given any information about the digit values. Nevertheless, these clusterings are produced.

In example D.5, we trained an autoencoder on the MNIST data set. We can adapt the same network to produce two-dimensional mean and variance vectors at the bottleneck instead of a two-dimensional embedding, and then train it to minimize both the reconstruction loss and the KL divergence. Here, we show the mean encodings for the same 10,000 images for the MNIST data set. Each encoding is again colored according to the corresponding digit:

Example D.6. A visualization of a two-dimensional embedding learned using a variational autoencoder for the MNIST digits. Here, we show decoded outputs from inputs panned over the encoding space:

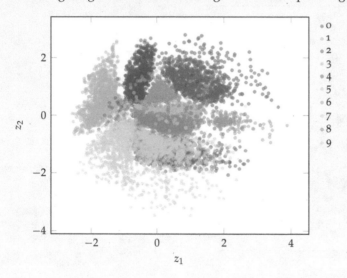

The variational autoencoder also produces clusters in the embedding space for each digit, but this time they are roughly distributed according to a zero-mean, unit variance Gaussian distribution. We again see how some encodings are similar, such as the significant overlap for 4 and 9.

One common approach to penalize off-nominal outputs or behavior is to use *adversarial learning* by including a discriminator, as shown in figure D.13.[14] A *discriminator* is a neural network that acts as a binary classifier that takes in neural network outputs and learns to distinguish between real outputs from the training set and the outputs from the primary neural network. The primary neural network, also called a *generator*, is then trained to deceive the discriminator, thereby naturally producing outputs that are more difficult to distinguish from the data set. The primary advantage of this technique is that we do not need to design special features to identify or quantify how the output fails to match the training data, but we can allow the discriminator to naturally learn such differences.

Learning is adversarial in the sense that we have two neural networks: the primary neural network that we would like to produce realistic outputs and the discriminator network that distinguishes between primary network outputs and real examples. They are each training to outperform the other. Training is an iterative process in which each network is improved in turn. It can sometimes be challenging to balance their relative performance; if one network becomes too good, the other can become stuck.

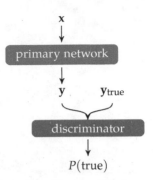

Figure D.13. A generative adversarial network causes a primary network's output to be more realistic by using a discriminator to force the primary network to produce more realistic output.

[14] These techniques were introduced by I. Goodfellow, J. Pouget-Abadie, M. Mirza, B. Xu, D. Warde-Farley, S. Ozair, A. Courville, and Y. Bengio, "Generative Adversarial Nets," in *Advances in Neural Information Processing Systems (NIPS)*, 2014.

E   Search Algorithms

A *search problem* is concerned with finding an appropriate sequence of actions to maximize the obtained reward over subsequent deterministic transitions. Search problems are Markov decision processes (covered in part II) with deterministic transition functions. Some well-known search problems include sliding tile puzzles, the Rubik's Cube, Sokoban, and finding the shortest path to a destination.

E.1   Search Problems

In a search problem, we choose action a_t at time t based on observing state s_t and then receive a reward r_t. The *action space* $\mathcal{A}$ is the set of possible actions, and the *state space* $\mathcal{S}$ is the set of possible states. Some of the algorithms assume that these sets are finite, but this is not required in general. The state evolves deterministically and depends only on the current state and action taken. We use $\mathcal{A}(s)$ to denote the set of valid actions from state s. When there are no valid actions, the state is considered to be *absorbing* and yields zero reward for all future time steps. Goal states, for example, are typically absorbing.

The deterministic state transition function $T(s, a)$ gives the successor state s'. The reward function $R(s, a)$ gives the reward received when executing action a from state s. Search problems typically do not include a discount factor γ that penalizes future rewards. The objective is to choose a sequence of actions that maximizes the sum of rewards, or *return*. Algorithm E.1 provides a data structure for representing search problems.

```
struct Search
    S  # state space
    A  # valid action function
    T  # transition function
    R  # reward function
end
```

Algorithm E.1. The search problem data structure.

E.2   Search Graphs

A search problem with finite state and action spaces can be represented as a *search graph*. The nodes correspond to states, and edges correspond to transitions between states. Associated with each edge from a source to a destination state are both an action that results in that state transition and the expected reward when taking that action from the source state. Figure E.1 depicts a subset of such a search graph for a 3×3 sliding tile puzzle.

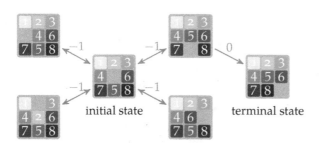

initial state   terminal state

Figure E.1. A few states in a sliding tile puzzle, portrayed as a graph. Two transitions can be taken from the initial state to arrive at the terminal solution state. The numbers on the edges represent rewards.

Many graph search algorithms conduct a search from an initial state and fan out from there. In so doing, these algorithms trace out a *search tree*. The initial state is the root node, and any time we transition from s to s' during search, an edge from s to a new node s' is added to the search tree. A search tree for the same sliding tile puzzle is shown in figure E.2.

E.3   Forward Search

Perhaps the simplest graph search algorithm is *forward search* (algorithm E.2), which determines the best action to take from an initial state s by looking at all possible action-state transitions up to a depth (or horizon) d. At depth d, the algorithm uses an estimate of the value of the state $U(s)$.[1] The algorithm calls

[1] The approximate value functions in this chapter are expected to return 0 when in a state with no available actions.

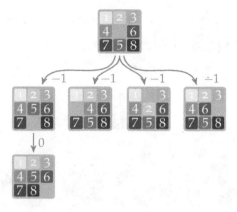

Figure E.2. The graph for the 3×3 sliding tile puzzle in figure E.1 can be represented as a tree search problem. The search begins at the root node and flows down the tree. In this case, a path can be traversed to the desired terminal state.

itself recursively in a depth-first manner, resulting in a search tree and returning a tuple with an optimal action a and its finite-horizon expected value u.

```
function forward_search(𝒫::Search, s, d, U)
    𝒜, T, R = 𝒫.𝒜(s), 𝒫.T, 𝒫.R
    if isempty(𝒜) || d ≤ 0
        return (a=nothing, u=U(s))
    end
    best = (a=nothing, u=-Inf)
    for a in 𝒜
        s' = T(s,a)
        u = R(s,a) + forward_search(𝒫, s', d-1, U).u
        if u > best.u
            best = (a=a, u=u)
        end
    end
    return best
end
```

Algorithm E.2. The forward search algorithm for finding an approximately optimal action for a discrete search problem $\mathcal{P}$ from a current state s. The search is performed to depth d, at which point the terminal value is estimated with an approximate value function U. The returned named tuple consists of the best action a and its finite-horizon expected value u.

Figure E.3 shows an example of a search tree obtained by running forward search on a sliding tile puzzle. Depth-first search can be wasteful; all reachable states for the given depth are visited. Searching to depth d will result in a search tree with $O(|\mathcal{A}|^d)$ nodes for a problem with $|\mathcal{A}|$ actions.

E.4   Branch and Bound

A general method known as *branch and bound* (algorithm E.3) can significantly reduce computation by using domain information about the upper and lower

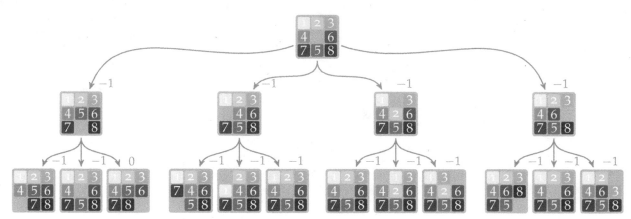

Figure E.3. A search tree arising from running forward search to depth 2 on a sliding tile puzzle. All states reachable in two steps are visited, and some are visited more than once. We find that there is one path to the terminal node. That path has a return of -1, whereas all other paths have a return of -2.

bounds on expected reward. The upper bound on the return from taking action a from state s is $\overline{Q}(s,a)$. The lower bound on the return from state s is $\underline{U}(s)$. Branch and bound follows the same procedure as depth-first-search, but it iterates over the actions according to their upper bound, and proceeds to a successor node only if the best possible value it could return is higher than what has already been discovered by following an earlier action. Branch and bound search is compared to forward search in example E.1.

```
function branch_and_bound(𝒫::Search, s, d, Ulo, Qhi)
    𝒜, T, R = 𝒫.𝒜(s), 𝒫.T, 𝒫.R
    if isempty(𝒜) || d ≤ 0
        return (a=nothing, u=Ulo(s))
    end
    best = (a=nothing, u=-Inf)
    for a in sort(𝒜, by=a→Qhi(s,a), rev=true)
        if Qhi(s,a) ≤ best.u
            return best # safe to prune
        end
        u = R(s,a) + branch_and_bound(𝒫,T(s,a),d-1,Ulo,Qhi).u
        if u > best.u
            best = (a=a, u=u)
        end
    end
    return best
end
```

Algorithm E.3. The branch and bound search algorithm for finding an approximately optimal action for a discrete search problem $\mathcal{P}$ from a current state s. The search is performed to depth d with a value function lower bound Ulo and an action value function upper bound Qhi. The returned named tuple consists of the best action a and its finite-horizon expected value u.

Consider using branch and bound on a hex world search problem. Actions in search problems cause deterministic transitions, so unlike the hex-world MDP, we always correctly transition between neighboring tiles when the corresponding action is taken.

The circle indicates the start state. All transitions incur a reward of -1. The blue tile is terminal and produces reward 5 when entered.

Here, we show the search trees for both forward search and branch and bound to depth 4. For branch and bound, we used a lower bound $\underline{U}(s) = -6$ and an upper bound $\overline{Q}(s,a) = 5 - \delta(T(s,a))$, where the function $\delta(s)$ is the minimum number of steps from the given state to the terminal reward state. The search tree of branch and bound is a subset of that of forward search because branch and bound can ignore portions it knows are not optimal.

Due to the upper bound, branch and bound evaluates moving right first, and because that happens to be optimal, it is able to immediately identify the optimal sequence of actions and avoid exploring other actions. If the start and goal states were reversed, the search tree would be larger. In the worst case, it can be as large as forward search.

Example E.1. A comparison of the savings that branch and bound can have over forward search. Branch and bound can be significantly more efficient with appropriate bounds.

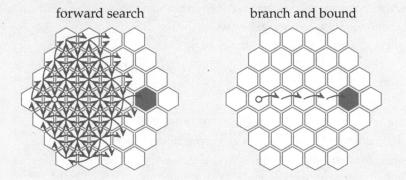

forward search   branch and bound

Branch and bound is not guaranteed to reduce computation over forward search. Both approaches have the same worst-case time complexity. The efficiency of the algorithm greatly depends on the heuristic.

E.5   Dynamic Programming

Neither forward search nor branch and bound remembers whether a state has been previously visited; each wastes computational resources by evaluating these states multiple times. *Dynamic programming* (algorithm E.4) avoids duplicate effort by remembering when a particular subproblem has been previously solved. Dynamic programming can be applied to problems in which an optimal solution can be constructed from optimal solutions of its subproblems, a property called *optimal substructure*. For example, if the optimal sequence of actions from s_1 to s_3 goes through s_2, then the subpaths from s_1 to s_2 and from s_2 to s_3 are also optimal. This substructure is shown in figure E.4.

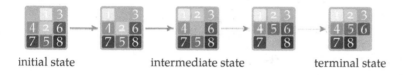

initial state   intermediate state   terminal state

Figure E.4. The sequence of states on the left form an optimal path from the initial state to the terminal state. Shortest path problems have optimal substructure, meaning that the sequence from the initial state to the intermediate state is also optimal, as is the sequence from the intermediate state to the terminal state.

In the case of graph search, when evaluating a state, we first check a *transposition table* to see whether the state has been previously visited, and if it has, we return its stored value.[2] Otherwise, we evaluate the state as normal and store the result in the transposition table. A comparison to forward search is shown in figure E.5.

[2] Caching the results of expensive computations so that they can be retrieved rather than being recomputed in the future is called *memoization*.

E.6   Heuristic Search

Heuristic search[3] (algorithm E.5) improves on branch and bound by ordering its actions based on a provided heuristic function $\overline{U}(s)$, which is an upper bound of the return. Like dynamic programming, heuristic search has a mechanism by which state evaluations can be cached to avoid redundant computation. Furthermore, heuristic search does not require the lower bound value function needed by branch and bound.[4]

[3] Heuristic search is also known as *informed search* or *best-first search*.

[4] Our implementation does use two value functions: the heuristic for guiding the search and an approximate value function for evaluating terminal states.

```
function dynamic_programming(𝒫::Search, s, d, U, M=Dict())
    if haskey(M, (d,s))
        return M[(d,s)]
    end
    𝒜, T, R = 𝒫.𝒜(s), 𝒫.T, 𝒫.R
    if isempty(𝒜) || d ≤ 0
        best = (a=nothing, u=U(s))
    else
        best = (a=first(𝒜), u=-Inf)
        for a in 𝒜
            s' = T(s,a)
            u = R(s,a) + dynamic_programming(𝒫, s', d-1, U, M).u
            if u > best.u
                best = (a=a, u=u)
            end
        end
    end
    M[(d,s)] = best
    return best
end
```

Algorithm E.4. Dynamic programming applied to forward search, which includes a transposition table M. Here, M is a dictionary that stores depth-state tuples from previous evaluations, allowing the method to return previously computed results. The search is performed to depth d, at which point the terminal value is estimated with an approximate value function U. The returned named tuple consists of the best action a and its finite-horizon expected value u.

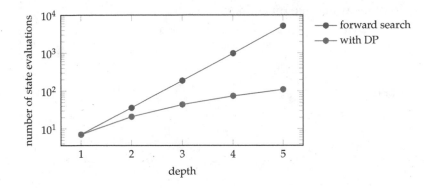

Figure E.5. A comparison of the number of state evaluations for pure forward search and forward search augmented with dynamic programming on the hex-world search problem of example E.1. Dynamic programming is able to avoid the exponential growth in state visitation by caching results.

```
function heuristic_search(𝒫::Search, s, d, Uhi, U, M)
    if haskey(M, (d,s))
        return M[(d,s)]
    end
    𝒜, T, R = 𝒫.𝒜(s), 𝒫.T, 𝒫.R
    if isempty(𝒜) || d ≤ 0
        best = (a=nothing, u=U(s))
    else
        best = (a=first(𝒜), u=-Inf)
        for a in sort(𝒜, by=a→R(s,a) + Uhi(T(s,a)), rev=true)
            if R(s,a) + Uhi(T(s,a)) ≤ best.u
                break
            end
            s' = T(s,a)
            u = R(s,a) + heuristic_search(𝒫, s', d-1, Uhi, U, M).u
            if u > best.u
                best = (a=a, u=u)
            end
        end
    end
    M[(d,s)] = best
    return best
end
```

Algorithm E.5.   The heuristic search algorithm for solving a search problem $\mathcal{P}$ starting from state s and searching to a maximum depth d. A heuristic Uhi is used to guide the search, the approximate value function U is evaluated at terminal states, and a transposition table M in the form of a dictionary containing depth-state tuples allows the algorithm to cache values from previously explored states.

Actions are sorted based on the immediate reward plus a heuristic estimate of the future return:

$$R(s,a) + \overline{U}(T(s,a)) \tag{E.1}$$

To guarantee optimality, the heuristic must be both *admissible* and *consistent*. An admissible heuristic is an upper bound of the true value function. A consistent heuristic is never less than the expected reward gained by transitioning to a neighboring state:

$$\overline{U}(s) \geq R(s,a) + \overline{U}(T(s,a)) \tag{E.2}$$

The method is compared to branch and bound search in example E.2.

We can apply heuristic search to the same hex world search problem as in example E.1. We use the heuristic $\overline{U}(s) = 5 - \delta(s)$, where $\delta(s)$ is the number of steps from the given state to the terminal reward state. Here, we show the number of states visited when running either branch and bound (left) or heuristic search (right) from each starting state. Branch and bound is just as efficient in states near and to the left of the goal state, whereas heuristic search is able to search efficiently from any initial state.

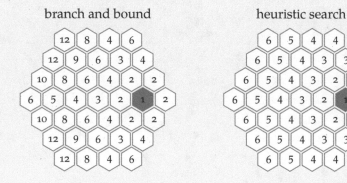

branch and bound   heuristic search

Example E.2. A comparison of the savings that heuristic search can have over branch and bound search. Heuristic search automatically orders actions according to their lookahead heuristic value.

F   Problems

This section covers some of the decision problems used throughout this book. Table F.1 summarizes some of the important properties of these problems.

Problem	$|\mathcal{I}|$	$|\mathcal{S}|$	$|\mathcal{A}|$	$|\mathcal{O}|$	γ
Hex world	—	varies	6	—	0.9
2048	—	∞	4	—	1
Cart-pole	—	$(\subset \mathbb{R}^4)$	2	—	1
Mountain car	—	$(\subset \mathbb{R}^2)$	3	—	1
Simple regulator	—	$(\subset \mathbb{R})$	$(\subset \mathbb{R})$	—	1 or 0.9
Aircraft collision avoidance	—	$(\subset \mathbb{R}^3)$	3	—	1
Crying baby	—	2	3	2	0.9
Machine replacement	—	3	4	2	1
Catch	—	4	10	2	0.9
Prisoner's dilemma	2	—	2 per agent	—	1
Rock-paper-scissors	2	—	3 per agent	—	1
Traveler's dilemma	2	—	99 per agent	—	1
Predator-prey hex world	varies	varies	6 per agent	—	0.9
Multicaregiver crying baby	2	2	3 per agent	2 per agent	0.9
Collaborative predator-prey hex world	varies	varies	6 per agent	2 per agent	0.9

Table F.1.   Problem summary. The `DecisionMakingProblems.jl` package implements these problems.

F.1   Hex World

The *hex world problem* is a simple MDP in which we must traverse a tile map to reach a goal state. Each cell in the tile map represents a state in the MDP. We can attempt to move in any of the six directions. The effects of these actions are stochastic. As shown in figure F.1, we move 1 step in the specified direction with a probability of 0.7, and we move 1 step in one of the neighboring directions, each with a probability of 0.15. If we bump against the outer border of the grid, then we do not move at all, at a cost of 1.0.

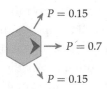

Figure F.1. Actions in the hex world problem have probabilistic effects.

Taking any action in certain cells gives us a specified reward and then transports us to a terminal state. No further reward is received in the terminal state. The total number of states in the hex world problem is thus the number of tiles plus 1, for the terminal state. Figure F.2 shows an optimal policy for two hex world problem configurations used throughout this book. We refer to the larger instance as "hex world" and to the smaller, simpler instance as "straight-line hex world."[1] The straight-line hex world formulation is used to illustrate how reward is propagated from its single reward-bearing state on the rightmost cell.

[1] The straight-line formulation is similar to the *hall problem*, a common benchmark MDP. See, for example, L. Baird, "Residual Algorithms: Reinforcement Learning with Function Approximation," in *International Conference on Machine Learning* (ICML), 1995.

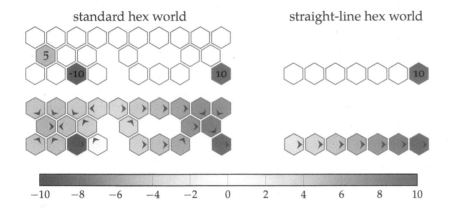

standard hex world   straight-line hex world

Figure F.2. The standard hex world and straight-line hex world problems. The top row shows the base problem setup and colors hexes that have terminal rewards. The bottom row shows an optimal policy for each problem, colored according to the expected value, with arrows indicating the action to take in each state.

F.2   2048

The *2048 problem* is based on a popular tile game played on a 4×4 board.[2] It has discrete state and action spaces. The board is initially empty except for two tiles, each of which can have value 2 or 4. A randomly selected starting state is shown in figure F.3.

The agent can move all tiles left, down, right, or up. Choosing a direction pushes all the tiles in that direction. A tile stops when it hits a wall or another tile of a different value. A tile that hits another tile of the same value merges with that tile, forming a new tile with their combined value. After shifting and merging, a new tile of value 2 or 4 is spawned in a random open space. This process is shown in figure F.4.

The game ends when we can no longer shift tiles to produce an empty space. Rewards are obtained only when merging two tiles, and they are equal to the

[2] This game was developed by Gabriele Cirulli in 2014.

Figure F.3. A random starting state in the 2048 problem consists of two tiles, each with value 2 or 4.

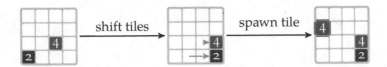

Figure F.4. An action in 2048 shifts all tiles in the chosen direction and then spawns a new tile in an empty space.

merged tile's value. An example state-action transition with a merge is shown in figure F.5.

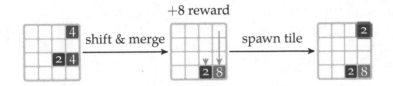

Figure F.5. Here, the **down** action is used to shift all tiles, resulting in the merging of two 4 tiles to produce an 8 tile and receive a reward of 8.

A common strategy is to choose a corner and alternate between the two actions that lead in that direction. This tends to stratify the tiles such that the larger-valued ones are in the corner and the newly spawned tiles are in the periphery.

F.3 Cart-Pole

The *cart-pole problem*,[3] also sometimes called the *pole balancing problem*, has the agent move a cart back and forth. As shown in figure F.6, this cart has a rigid pole attached to it by a swivel, so that as the cart moves back and forth, the pole begins to rotate. The objective is to keep the pole vertically balanced while keeping the cart within the allowed lateral bounds. As such, 1 reward is obtained each time step in which these conditions are met, and transition to a terminal zero-reward state occurs whenever they are not.

The actions are to either apply a left or right force F to the cart. The state space is defined by four continuous variables: the lateral position of the cart x, its lateral velocity v, the angle of the pole θ, and the pole's angular velocity ω. The problem involves a variety of parameters, including the mass of the cart m_{cart}, the mass of the pole m_{pole}, the pole length ℓ, the force magnitude $|F|$, gravitational acceleration g, the time step Δt, the maximum x deviation, the maximum angular deviation, and friction losses between the cart and the pole or between the cart and its track.[4]

[3] A. G. Barto, R. S. Sutton, and C. W. Anderson, "Neuronlike Adaptive Elements That Can Solve Difficult Learning Control Problems," *IEEE Transactions on Systems, Man, and Cybernetics*, vol. SMC-13, no. 5, pp. 834–846, 1983.

[4] We use the parameters implemented in the OpenAI Gym. G. Brockman, V. Cheung, L. Pettersson, J. Schneider, J. Schulman, J. Tang, and W. Zaremba, "OpenAI Gym," 2016. arXiv: 1606.01540v1.

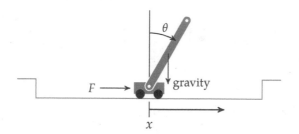

Figure F.6. In the cart-pole problem, a vehicle must alternate between accelerating left and right in order to balance a pole. The pole is not allowed to fall past a given angle, and the cart is not allowed to travel outside of given limits.

Given an input force F, the angular acceleration of the pole is

$$\alpha = \frac{g\sin(\theta) - \tau\cos(\theta)}{\frac{\ell}{2}\left(\frac{4}{3} - \frac{m_{\text{pole}}}{m_{\text{cart}} + m_{\text{pole}}}\cos(\theta)^2\right)} \tag{F.1}$$

where

$$\tau = \frac{F + \omega^2\ell\sin\theta/2}{m_{\text{cart}} + m_{\text{pole}}} \tag{F.2}$$

and the lateral cart acceleration is

$$a = \tau - \frac{\ell}{2}\alpha\cos(\theta)\frac{m_{\text{pole}}}{m_{\text{cart}} + m_{\text{pole}}} \tag{F.3}$$

The state is updated with Euler integration:

$$
\begin{aligned}
x &\leftarrow x + v\Delta t \\
v &\leftarrow v + a\Delta t \\
\theta &\leftarrow \theta + \omega\Delta t \\
\omega &\leftarrow \omega + \alpha\Delta t
\end{aligned}
\tag{F.4}
$$

The cart-pole problem is typically initialized with each random value drawn from $U(-0.05, 0.05)$. Rollouts are run until the lateral or angular deviations are exceeded.

F.4   Mountain Car

In the *mountain car problem*,[5] a vehicle must drive to the right, out of a valley. The valley walls are steep enough that blindly accelerating toward the goal with insufficient speed causes the vehicle to come to a halt and slide back down. The agent must learn to accelerate left first in order to gain enough momentum on the return to make it up the hill.

[5] This problem was introduced in A. Moore, "Efficient Memory-Based Learning for Robot Control," Ph.D. dissertation, University of Cambridge, 1990. Its popular, simpler form, with a discrete action space, was first given in S. P. Singh and R. S. Sutton, "Reinforcement Learning with Replacing Eligibility Traces," *Machine Learning*, vol. 22, pp. 123–158, 1996.

The state is the vehicle's horizontal position $x \in [-1.2, 0.6]$ and speed $v \in [-0.07, 0.07]$. At any given time step, the vehicle can accelerate left ($a = -1$), accelerate right ($a = 1$), or coast ($a = 0$). We receive -1 reward every turn, and terminate when the vehicle makes it up the right side of the valley past $x = 0.6$. A visualization of the problem is given in figure F.7.

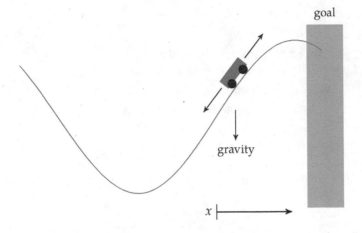

Figure F.7. In the mountain car problem, a vehicle must alternate between accelerating left and right in order to power itself up a hill. The goal region is shown in blue.

Transitions in the mountain car problem are deterministic:

$$v' \leftarrow v + 0.001a - 0.0025\cos(3x)$$
$$x' \leftarrow x + v'$$

The gravitational term in the speed update is what drives the underpowered vehicle back toward the valley floor. Transitions are clamped to the bounds of the state space.

The mountain car problem is a good example of a problem with delayed return. Many actions are required to get to the goal state, making it difficult for an untrained agent to receive anything other than consistent unit penalties. The best learning algorithms are able to efficiently propagate knowledge from trajectories that reach the goal back to the rest of the state space.

F.5   Simple Regulator

The *simple regulator problem* is a simple linear quadratic regulator problem with a single state. It is an MDP with a single real-valued state and a single real-valued

614   APPENDIX F. PROBLEMS

action. Transitions are linear Gaussian, such that a successor state s' is drawn from the Gaussian distribution $\mathcal{N}(s + a, 0.1^2)$. Rewards are quadratic, $R(s, a) = -s^2$, and do not depend on the action. The examples in this book use the initial state distribution $\mathcal{N}(0.3, 0.1^2)$.

Optimal finite horizon policies cannot be derived using the methods from section 7.8. In this case, $\mathbf{T}_s = [1]$, $\mathbf{T}_a = [1]$, $\mathbf{R}_s = [-1]$, $\mathbf{R}_a = [0]$, and w is drawn from $\mathcal{N}(0, 0.1^2)$. Applications of the Riccati equation require that $\mathbf{R}_a$ be negative definite, which it is not.

The optimal policy is $\pi(s) = -s$, resulting in a successor state distribution centered at the origin. In the policy gradient chapters, we learned parameterized policies of the form $\pi_\theta(s) = \mathcal{N}(\theta_1 s, \theta_2^2)$. In such cases, the optimal parameterization for the simple regulator problem is $\theta_1 = -1$ and θ_2 is asymptotically close to zero.

The optimal value function for the simple regulator problem is also centered about the origin, with reward decreasing quadratically:

$$U(s) = -s^2 + \frac{\gamma}{1-\gamma} \mathbb{E}_{s \sim \mathcal{N}(0, 0.1^2)} \left[-s^2 \right]$$
$$\approx -s^2 - 0.010 \frac{\gamma}{1-\gamma}$$

F.6   Aircraft Collision Avoidance

The *aircraft collision avoidance problem* involves deciding when to issue a climb or descend advisory to an aircraft to avoid an intruder aircraft.[6] There are three actions corresponding to no advisory, commanding a 5 m/s descend, and commanding a 5 m/s climb. The intruder is approaching us head on, with a constant horizontal closing speed. The state is specified by the altitude h of our aircraft measured relative to the intruder aircraft, our vertical rate $\dot{h}$, the previous action a_{prev}, and the time to potential collision t_{col}. Figure F.8 illustrates the problem scenario.

Given action a, the state variables are updated as follows:

$$h \leftarrow h + \dot{h}\Delta t \tag{F.5}$$
$$\dot{h} \leftarrow \dot{h} + (\ddot{h} + v)\Delta t \tag{F.6}$$
$$a_{prev} \leftarrow a \tag{F.7}$$
$$t_{col} \leftarrow t_{col} - \Delta t \tag{F.8}$$

[6] This formulation is a highly simplified version of the problem described by M. J. Kochenderfer and J. P. Chryssanthacopoulos, "Robust Airborne Collision Avoidance Through Dynamic Programming," Massachusetts Institute of Technology, Lincoln Laboratory, Project Report ATC-371, 2011.

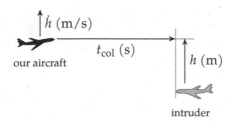

Figure F.8. State variables for the aircraft collision avoidance problem.

where $\Delta t = 1\,\text{s}$ and ν is selected from a discrete distribution over $-2, 0$, or $2\,\text{m}/\text{s}^2$ with associated probabilities 0.25, 0.5, and 0.25. The value $\ddot{h}$ is given by

$$\ddot{h} = \begin{cases} 0 & \text{if } a = \text{no advisory} \\ a/\Delta t & \text{if } |a - \dot{h}|/\Delta t < \ddot{h}_{\text{limit}} \\ \text{sign}(a - \dot{h})\ddot{h}_{\text{limit}} & \text{otherwise} \end{cases} \tag{F.9}$$

where $\ddot{h}_{\text{limit}} = 1\,\text{m}/\text{s}^2$.

The episode terminates when taking an action when $t_{\text{col}} < 0$. There is a penalty of 1 when the intruder comes within 50 m when $t_{\text{col}} = 0$, and there is a penalty of 0.01 when $a \neq a_{\text{prev}}$.

The aircraft collision avoidance problem can be efficiently solved over a discretized grid using backward induction value iteration (section 7.6) because the dynamics deterministically reduce t_{col}. Slices of the optimal value function and policy are depicted in figure F.9.

F.7 Crying Baby

The *crying baby problem*[7] is a simple POMDP with two states, three actions, and two observations. Our goal is to care for a baby, and we do so by choosing at each time step whether to feed the baby, sing to the baby, or ignore the baby.

The baby becomes hungry over time. We do not directly observe whether the baby is hungry; instead, we receive a noisy observation in the form of whether the baby is crying. The state, action, and observation spaces are as follows:

$$\mathcal{S} = \{\text{sated}, \text{hungry}\}$$
$$\mathcal{A} = \{\text{feed}, \text{sing}, \text{ignore}\}$$
$$\mathcal{O} = \{\text{crying}, \text{quiet}\}$$

[7] The version of the crying baby problem presented in this text is an extension of the original, simpler crying baby problem in M. J. Kochenderfer, *Decision Making Under Uncertainty: Theory and Application*. MIT Press, 2015.

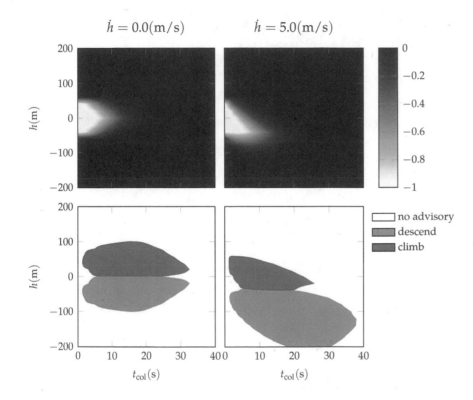

Figure F.9. Optimal value function slices (top) and policy slices (bottom) for the aircraft collision avoidance problem. The value function and policy are symmetric about 0 when the vertical separation rate is 0, but are skewed when the vertical separation rate is nonzero. Overall, our aircraft need not take action until the intruder aircraft is close.

Feeding will always sate the baby. Ignoring the baby risks a sated baby becoming hungry, and ensures that a hungry baby remains hungry. Singing to the baby is an information-gathering action with the same transition dynamics as ignoring, but without the potential for crying when sated (not hungry) and with an increased chance of crying when hungry.

The transition dynamics are as follows:

$$T(\text{sated} \mid \text{hungry}, \text{feed}) = 100\,\%$$
$$T(\text{hungry} \mid \text{hungry}, \text{sing}) = 100\,\%$$
$$T(\text{hungry} \mid \text{hungry}, \text{ignore}) = 100\,\%$$
$$T(\text{sated} \mid \text{sated}, \text{feed}) = 100\,\%$$
$$T(\text{hungry} \mid \text{sated}, \text{sing}) = 10\,\%$$
$$T(\text{hungry} \mid \text{sated}, \text{ignore}) = 10\,\%$$

The observation dynamics are as follows:

$$O(\text{cry} \mid \text{feed}, \text{hungry}) = 80\,\%$$
$$O(\text{cry} \mid \text{sing}, \text{hungry}) = 90\,\%$$
$$O(\text{cry} \mid \text{ignore}, \text{hungry}) = 80\,\%$$
$$O(\text{cry} \mid \text{feed}, \text{sated}) = 10\,\%$$
$$O(\text{cry} \mid \text{sing}, \text{sated}) = 0\,\%$$
$$O(\text{cry} \mid \text{ignore}, \text{sated}) = 10\,\%$$

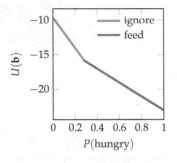

The reward function assigns -10 reward if the baby is hungry, independent of the action taken. The effort of feeding the baby adds a further -5 reward, whereas singing adds -0.5 reward. As baby caregivers, we seek the optimal infinite-horizon policy with discount factor $\gamma = 0.9$. Figure F.10 shows the optimal value function and associated policy.

Figure F.10. The optimal policy for the crying baby problem. This infinite horizon solution does not recommend singing for any belief state. As shown in figure 20.3, it is optimal to sing in some finite-horizon versions of this problem.

[8] R. D. Smallwood and E. J. Sondik, "The Optimal Control of Partially Observable Markov Processes over a Finite Horizon," *Operations Research*, vol. 21, no. 5, pp. 1071–1088, 1973. The original problem formulation includes *salvage values*, or *terminal rewards* that are equal to the number of working parts. We do not model terminal rewards separately in this book. Terminal rewards could be included in our framework by explicitly including the horizon in the problem state.

F.8 Machine Replacement

The *machine replacement problem* is a discrete POMDP in which we maintain a machine that creates products.[8] This problem is used for its relative simplicity and the varied size and shape of the optimal policy regions. The optimal policy for certain horizons even has disjoint regions in which the same action is optimal, as shown in figure F.11.

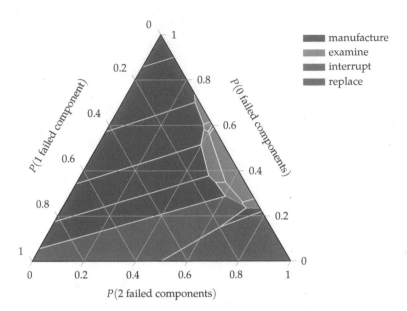

Figure F.11. The 14-step optimal policy for the machine replacement problem has disjoint regions where manufacturing is optimal. Each polygon corresponds to the region in which a particular alpha vector dominates.

The machine produces products for us when it is working properly. Over time, the two primary components in the machine may break down, together or individually, leading to defective products. We can indirectly observe whether the machine is faulty by examining the products, or by directly examining the components in the machine.

The problem has states $\mathcal{S} = \{0, 1, 2\}$, corresponding to the number of faulty internal components. There are four actions, used prior to each production cycle:

1. *manufacture*, manufacture product and do not examine the product,

2. *examine*, manufacture product and examine the product,

3. *interrupt*, interrupt production, inspect, and replace failed components, and

4. *replace*, replace both components after interrupting production.

When we examine the product, we can observe whether it is defective. All other actions observe only nondefective products.

The components in the machine independently have a 10 % chance of breaking down with each production cycle. Each failed component contributes a 50 % chance of creating a defective product. A nondefective product nets 1 reward, whereas a defective product nets 0 reward. The transition dynamics assume that component breakdown is determined before a product is made, so the manufacture action on a fully-functional machine does not have a 100 % chance of producing 1 reward.

The manufacture action incurs no penalty. Examining the product costs 0.25. Interrupting the line costs 0.5 to inspect the machine, causes no product to be made, and incurs a cost of 1 for each broken component. Simply replacing both components always incurs a cost of 2, but it does not have an inspection cost.

The transition, observation, and reward functions are given in table F.2. Optimal policies for increasing horizons are shown in figure F.12.

Action	$T(s' \mid s, a)$				$O(o \mid a, s')$			$R(s, a)$	
		s'				o			
manufacture	s	$\begin{bmatrix} 0.81 & 0.18 & 0.01 \\ 0 & 0.9 & 0.1 \\ 0 & 0 & 1 \end{bmatrix}$			s'	$\begin{bmatrix} 1 & 0 \\ 1 & 0 \\ 1 & 0 \end{bmatrix}$		s	$\begin{bmatrix} 0.9025 \\ 0.475 \\ 0.25 \end{bmatrix}$
examine	s	$\begin{bmatrix} 0.81 & 0.18 & 0.01 \\ 0 & 0.9 & 0.1 \\ 0 & 0 & 1 \end{bmatrix}$			s'	$\begin{bmatrix} 1 & 0 \\ 0.5 & 0.5 \\ 0.25 & 0.75 \end{bmatrix}$		s	$\begin{bmatrix} 0.6525 \\ 0.225 \\ 0 \end{bmatrix}$
interrupt	s	$\begin{bmatrix} 1 & 0 & 0 \\ 1 & 0 & 0 \\ 1 & 0 & 0 \end{bmatrix}$			s'	$\begin{bmatrix} 1 & 0 \\ 1 & 0 \\ 1 & 0 \end{bmatrix}$		s	$\begin{bmatrix} -0.5 \\ -1.5 \\ -2.5 \end{bmatrix}$
replace	s	$\begin{bmatrix} 1 & 0 & 0 \\ 1 & 0 & 0 \\ 1 & 0 & 0 \end{bmatrix}$			s'	$\begin{bmatrix} 1 & 0 \\ 1 & 0 \\ 1 & 0 \end{bmatrix}$		s	$\begin{bmatrix} -2 \\ -2 \\ -2 \end{bmatrix}$

Table F.2. The transition, observation, and reward functions for the machine replacement problem.

F.9 Catch

In the *catch problem*, Johnny would like to successfully catch throws from his father, and he prefers catching longer-distance throws. However, he is uncertain about the relationship between the distances of a throw and the probability of a successful catch. He does know that the probability of a successful catch is the same, regardless of whether he is throwing or catching; and he has a finite number of attempted catches to maximize his expected utility before he has to go home.

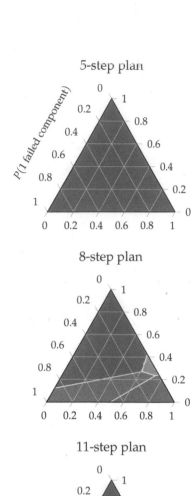

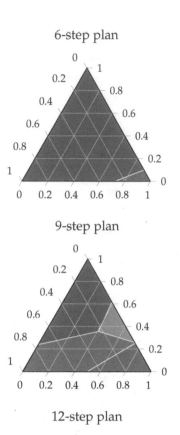

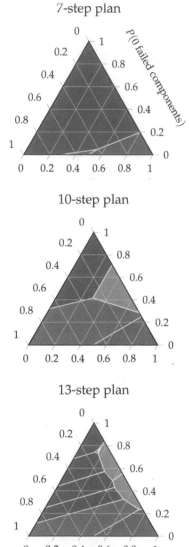

5-step plan

6-step plan

7-step plan

8-step plan

9-step plan

10-step plan

11-step plan

12-step plan

13-step plan

$P(2$ failed components$)$

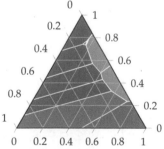

manufacture
examine
interrupt
replace

Figure F.12. Optimal policies for the machine replacement problem for increasing horizons. Each polygon corresponds to the region in which a particular alpha vector dominates.

As shown in figure F.13, Johnny models the probability of successfully catching a ball thrown a distance d as

$$P(\text{catch} \mid d) = 1 - \frac{1}{1 + \exp\left(-\frac{d-s}{15}\right)} \qquad \text{(F.10)}$$

where the proficiency s is unknown and does not change over time. To keep things manageable, he assumes that s belongs to the discrete set $\mathcal{S} = \{20, 40, 60, 80\}$.

The reward for a successful catch is equal to the distance. If the catch is unsuccessful, then the reward is zero. Johnny wants to maximize the reward over a finite number of attempted throws. With each throw, Johnny chooses a distance from a discrete set $\mathcal{A} = \{10, 20, \ldots, 100\}$. He begins with a uniform distribution over $\mathcal{S}$.

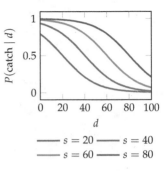

Figure F.13. The catch probability as a function of throw distance d for the four proficiencies in $\mathcal{S}$.

F.10   Prisoner's Dilemma

The *prisoner's dilemma* is a classic problem in game theory involving agents with conflicting objectives. There are two prisoners that are on trial. They can choose to cooperate, remaining silent about their shared crime, or defect, blaming the other for their crime. If they both cooperate, they both serve time for one year. If agent i cooperates and the other agent $-i$ defects, then i serves four years and $-i$ serves no time. If both defect, then they both serve three years.[9]

The game has two agents, $\mathcal{I} = \{1, 2\}$ and $\mathcal{A} = \mathcal{A}^1 \times \mathcal{A}^2$, with each $\mathcal{A}^i = \{\text{cooperate}, \text{defect}\}$. The table in figure F.14 expresses the individual rewards. Rows represent actions for agent 1. Columns represent actions for agent 2. The rewards for agent 1 and 2 are shown in each cell: $R^1(a^1, a^2), R^2(a^1, a^2)$. The game can be played once or repeated any number of times. In the infinite horizon case, we use a discount factor of $\gamma = 0.9$.

[9] A. W. Tucker gave the name to this game and formulated the story. It was based on the original problem formulation of Merrill Flood and Melvin Dresher at RAND in 1950. A history is provided by W. Poundstone, *Prisoner's Dilemma*. Doubleday, 1992.

F.11   Rock-Paper-Scissors

One common game played around the world is *rock-paper-scissors*. There are two agents who can each choose either rock, paper, or scissors. Rock beats scissors, resulting in a unit reward for the agent playing rock and a unit penalty for the agent playing scissors. Scissors beats paper, resulting in a unit reward for the agent playing scissors and a unit penalty for the agent playing paper. Finally,

		agent 2: cooperate	agent 2: defect
agent 1	cooperate	$-1, -1$	$-4, 0$
	defect	$0, -4$	$-3, -3$

Figure F.14. The rewards associated with the prisoner's dilemma.

paper beats rock, resulting in a unit reward for the agent playing paper and a unit penalty for the agent playing rock.

We have $\mathcal{I} = \{1, 2\}$ and $\mathcal{A} = \mathcal{A}^1 \times \mathcal{A}^2$ with each $\mathcal{A}^i = \{\text{rock}, \text{paper}, \text{scissors}\}$. Figure F.15 shows the rewards associated with the game, with each cell denoting $R^1(a^1, a^2), R^2(a^1, a^2)$. The game can be played once or repeated any number of times. In the infinite horizon case, we use a discount factor of $\gamma = 0.9$.

		agent 2: rock	agent 2: paper	agent 2: scissors
agent 1	rock	$0, 0$	$-1, 1$	$1, -1$
	paper	$1, -1$	$0, 0$	$-1, 1$
	scissors	$-1, 1$	$1, -1$	$0, 0$

Figure F.15. The rewards associated with the rock-paper-scissors game.

F.12 *Traveler's Dilemma*

The *traveler's dilemma* is a game where an airline loses two identical suitcases from two travelers.[10] The airline asks the travelers to write down the value of their suitcases, which can be between \$2 and \$100, inclusive. If both put down the

[10] K. Basu, "The Traveler's Dilemma: Paradoxes of Rationality in Game Theory," *American Economic Review*, vol. 84, no. 2, pp. 391–395, 1994.

same value, then they both get that value. Otherwise, the traveler with the lower value gets their value plus \$2 and the traveler with the higher value gets the lower value minus \$2. In other words, the reward function is as follows:

$$R_i(a_i, a_{-i}) = \begin{cases} a_i & \text{if } a_i = a_{-i} \\ a_i + 2 & \text{if } a_i < a_{-i} \\ a_{-i} - 2 & \text{otherwise} \end{cases} \tag{F.11}$$

Most people tend to put down between \$97 and \$100. However, somewhat counterintuitively, there is a unique Nash equilibrium of only \$2.

F.13 Predator-Prey Hex World

The *predator-prey hex world problem* expands the hex world dynamics to include multiple agents consisting of predators and prey. A predator tries to capture a prey as quickly as possible, and a prey tries to escape the predators as long as possible. The initial state of the hex world is shown in figure F.16. There are no terminal states in this game.

Figure F.16. The initial state in the predator-prey hex world. The predator is red and the prey is blue. The arrows indicate potential actions taken by the individual agents from their initial cells.

There is a set of predators $\mathcal{I}_{\text{pred}}$ and a set of prey $\mathcal{I}_{\text{prey}}$, with $\mathcal{I} = \mathcal{I}_{\text{pred}} \cup \mathcal{I}_{\text{prey}}$. The states contain the locations of each agent: $\mathcal{S} = \mathcal{S}^1 \times \cdots \times \mathcal{S}^{|\mathcal{I}|}$, with each $\mathcal{S}^i$ equal to all hex locations. The joint action space is $\mathcal{A} = \mathcal{A}^1 \times \cdots \times \mathcal{A}^{|\mathcal{I}|}$, where each $\mathcal{A}^i$ consists of all six hex directions of movement.

If a predator $i \in \mathcal{I}_{\text{pred}}$ and prey $j \in \mathcal{I}_{\text{prey}}$ share the same hex with $s_i = s_j$, then the prey is devoured. The prey j is then transported to a random hex cell, representing its offspring appearing in the world. Otherwise, the state transitions are independent and are as described in the original hex world.

One or more predators can capture one or more prey if they all happen to be in the same cell. If n predators and m prey all share the same cell, the predators receive a reward of m/n. For example, if two predators capture one prey together, they each get a reward of $1/2$. If three predators capture five prey together, they each get a reward of $5/3$. Moving predators receive unit penalty. Prey can move with no penalty, but they receive a penalty of 100 for being devoured.

F.14　Multicaregiver Crying Baby

The *multicaregiver crying baby problem* is a multiagent extension of the crying baby problem. For each caregiver $i \in \mathcal{I} = \{1,2\}$, the states, actions, and observations are as follows:

$$\mathcal{S} = \{\text{hungry}, \text{sated}\} \tag{F.12}$$

$$\mathcal{A}^i = \{\text{feed}, \text{sing}, \text{ignore}\} \tag{F.13}$$

$$\mathcal{O}^i = \{\text{crying}, \text{quiet}\} \tag{F.14}$$

The transition dynamics are similar to the original crying baby problem, except that either caregiver can feed to satisfy the baby:

$$T(\text{sated} \mid \text{hungry}, (\text{feed}, \star)) = T(\text{sated} \mid \text{hungry}, (\star, \text{feed})) = 100\,\% \tag{F.15}$$

where $\star$ indicates all possible other variable assignments. Otherwise, if the actions are not feed, then the baby transitions between sated to hungry as before:

$$T(\text{hungry} \mid \text{hungry}, (\star, \star)) = 100\,\% \tag{F.16}$$

$$T(\text{sated} \mid \text{sated}, (\star, \star)) = 50\,\% \tag{F.17}$$

The observation dynamics are also similar to the single-agent version, but the model ensures that both caregivers make the same observation of the baby, but not necessarily of each other's choice of caregiving action:

$$O((\text{cry}, \text{cry}) \mid (\text{sing}, \star), \text{hungry}) = O((\text{cry}, \text{cry}) \mid (\star, \text{sing}), \text{hungry}) = 90\,\% \tag{F.18}$$

$$O((\text{quiet}, \text{quiet}) \mid (\text{sing}, \star), \text{hungry}) = O((\text{quiet}, \text{quiet}) \mid (\star, \text{sing}), \text{hungry}) = 10\,\% \tag{F.19}$$

$$O((\text{cry}, \text{cry}) \mid (\text{sing}, \star), \text{sated}) = O((\text{cry}, \text{cry}) \mid (\star, \text{sing}), \text{sated}) = 0\,\% \tag{F.20}$$

If the actions are not to sing, then the observations are as follows:

$$O((\text{cry}, \text{cry}) \mid (\star, \star), \text{hungry}) = O((\text{cry}, \text{cry}) \mid (\star, \star), \text{hungry}) = 90\,\% \tag{F.21}$$

$$O((\text{quiet}, \text{quiet}) \mid (\star, \star), \text{hungry}) = O((\text{quiet}, \text{quiet}) \mid (\star, \star), \text{hungry}) = 10\,\% \tag{F.22}$$

$$O((\text{cry}, \text{cry}) \mid (\star, \star), \text{sated}) = O((\text{cry}, \text{cry}) \mid (\star, \star), \text{sated}) = 0\,\% \tag{F.23}$$

$$O((\text{quiet}, \text{quiet}) \mid (\star, \star), \text{sated}) = O((\text{quiet}, \text{quiet}) \mid (\star, \star), \text{sated}) = 100\,\% \tag{F.24}$$

Both caregivers want to help the baby when the baby is hungry, assigning the same penalty of -10.0 for both. However, the first caregiver favors feeding and the second caregiver favors singing. For feeding, the first caregiver receives an extra penalty of only -2.5, while the second caregiver receives an extra penalty of -5.0. For singing, the first caregiver is penalized by -0.5, while the second caregiver is penalized by only -0.25.

F.15 Collaborative Predator-Prey Hex World

The *collaborative predator-prey hex world* is a variant of the predator-prey hex world in which a team of predators chase a single, moving prey. The predators must work together to capture a prey. The prey moves randomly to a neighboring cell that is not occupied by a predator.

Predators also only make noisy local observations of the environment. Each predator i detects whether a prey is within a neighboring cell $\mathcal{O}^i = \{\text{prey}, \text{nothing}\}$. The predators are penalized with a -1 reward for movement. They receive a reward of 10 if one or more of them capture the prey, meaning that they are in the same cell as the prey. At this point, the prey is randomly assigned a new cell, signifying the arrival of a new prey for the predators to begin hunting again.

G Julia

Julia is a scientific programming language that is free and open source.[1] It is a relatively new language that borrows inspiration from languages like Python, MATLAB, and R. It was selected for use in this book because it is sufficiently high level[2] so that the algorithms can be compactly expressed and readable while also being fast. This book is compatible with Julia version 1.7. This appendix introduces the concepts necessary for understanding the included code, omitting many of the advanced features of the language.

[1] Julia may be obtained from http://julialang.org.

[2] In contrast with languages like C++, Julia does not require programmers to worry about memory management and other lower-level details, yet it allows low-level control when needed.

G.1 Types

Julia has a variety of basic types that can represent data given as truth values, numbers, strings, arrays, tuples, and dictionaries. Users can also define their own types. This section explains how to use some of the basic types and how to define new types.

G.1.1 Booleans

The *Boolean* type in Julia, written as `Bool`, includes the values `true` and `false`. We can assign these values to variables. Variable names can be any string of characters, including Unicode, with a few restrictions.

```
α = true
done = false
```

The variable name appears on the left side of the equal sign; the value that variable is to be assigned is on the right side.

We can make assignments in the Julia console. The console, or REPL (for read, eval, print, loop), will return a response to the expression being evaluated. The # symbol indicates that the rest of the line is a comment.

```julia
julia> x = true
true
julia> y = false; # semicolon suppresses the console output
julia> typeof(x)
Bool
julia> x == y # test for equality
false
```

The standard Boolean operators are supported:

```julia
julia> !x      # not
false
julia> x && y # and
false
julia> x || y # or
true
```

G.1.2   Numbers

Julia supports integer and floating-point numbers, as shown here:

```julia
julia> typeof(42)
Int64
julia> typeof(42.0)
Float64
```

Here, `Int64` denotes a 64-bit integer, and `Float64` denotes a 64-bit floating-point value.[3] We can perform the standard mathematical operations:

[3] On 32-bit machines, an integer literal like 42 is interpreted as an Int32.

```julia
julia> x = 4
4
julia> y = 2
2
julia> x + y
6
julia> x - y
2
julia> x * y
8
julia> x / y
2.0
```

```
julia> x ^ y # exponentiation
16
julia> x % y # remainder from division
0
julia> div(x, y) # truncated division returns an integer
2
```

Note that the result of x / y is a `Float64`, even when x and y are integers. We
can also perform these operations at the same time as an assignment. For example,
x += 1 is shorthand for x = x + 1.

We can also make comparisons:

```
julia> 3 > 4
false
julia> 3 >= 4
false
julia> 3 ≥ 4    # unicode also works, use \ge[tab] in console
false
julia> 3 < 4
true
julia> 3 <= 4
true
julia> 3 ≤ 4    # unicode also works, use \le[tab] in console
true
julia> 3 == 4
false
julia> 3 < 4 < 5
true
```

G.1.3 Strings

A *string* is an array of characters. Strings are not used very much in this textbook
except to report certain errors. An object of type `String` can be constructed using
" characters. For example:

```
julia> x = "optimal"
"optimal"
julia> typeof(x)
String
```

G.1.4   Symbols

A *symbol* represents an identifier. It can be written using the : operator or constructed from strings:

```julia
julia> :A
:A
julia> :Battery
:Battery
julia> Symbol("Failure")
:Failure
```

G.1.5   Vectors

A *vector* is a one-dimensional array that stores a sequence of values. We can construct a vector using square brackets, separating elements by commas:

```julia
julia> x = [];                       # empty vector
julia> x = trues(3);                 # Boolean vector containing three trues
julia> x = ones(3);                  # vector of three ones
julia> x = zeros(3);                 # vector of three zeros
julia> x = rand(3);                  # vector of three random numbers between 0 and 1
julia> x = [3, 1, 4];                # vector of integers
julia> x = [3.1415, 1.618, 2.7182];  # vector of floats
```

An *array comprehension* can be used to create vectors:

```julia
julia> [sin(x) for x in 1:5]
5-element Vector{Float64}:
  0.8414709848078965
  0.9092974268256817
  0.1411200080598672
 -0.7568024953079282
 -0.9589242746631385
```

We can inspect the type of a vector:

```julia
julia> typeof([3, 1, 4])              # 1-dimensional array of Int64s
Vector{Int64} (alias for Array{Int64, 1})
julia> typeof([3.1415, 1.618, 2.7182]) # 1-dimensional array of Float64s
Vector{Float64} (alias for Array{Float64, 1})
julia> Vector{Float64} # alias for a 1-dimensional array
Vector{Float64} (alias for Array{Float64, 1})
```

We index into vectors using square brackets:

```
julia> x[1]        # first element is indexed by 1
3.1415
julia> x[3]        # third element
2.7182
julia> x[end]      # use end to reference the end of the array
2.7182
julia> x[end-1]    # this returns the second to last element
1.618
```

We can pull out a range of elements from an array. Ranges are specified using a colon notation:

```
julia> x = [1, 2, 5, 3, 1]
5-element Vector{Int64}:
 1
 2
 5
 3
 1
julia> x[1:3]      # pull out the first three elements
3-element Vector{Int64}:
 1
 2
 5
julia> x[1:2:end]  # pull out every other element
3-element Vector{Int64}:
 1
 5
 1
julia> x[end:-1:1] # pull out all the elements in reverse order
5-element Vector{Int64}:
 1
 3
 5
 2
 1
```

We can perform a variety of operations on arrays. The exclamation mark at the end of function names is used to indicate that the function *mutates* (i.e., changes) the input:

```
julia> length(x)
5
julia> [x, x]                  # concatenation
2-element Vector{Vector{Int64}}:
```

```
  [1, 2, 5, 3, 1]
  [1, 2, 5, 3, 1]
julia> push!(x, -1)         # add an element to the end
6-element Vector{Int64}:
   1
   2
   5
   3
   1
  -1
julia> pop!(x)              # remove an element from the end
-1
julia> append!(x, [2, 3])   # append [2, 3] to the end of x
7-element Vector{Int64}:
  1
  2
  5
  3
  1
  2
  3
julia> sort!(x)             # sort the elements, altering the same vector
7-element Vector{Int64}:
  1
  1
  2
  2
  3
  3
  5
julia> sort(x);             # sort the elements as a new vector
julia> x[1] = 2; print(x)   # change the first element to 2
[2, 1, 2, 2, 3, 3, 5]
julia> x = [1, 2];
julia> y = [3, 4];
julia> x + y                # add vectors
2-element Vector{Int64}:
  4
  6
julia> 3x - [1, 2]          # multiply by a scalar and subtract
2-element Vector{Int64}:
  2
  4
julia> using LinearAlgebra
```

```
julia> dot(x, y)          # dot product available after using LinearAlgebra
11
julia> x·y                # dot product using unicode character, use \cdot[tab] in console
11
julia> prod(y)            # product of all the elements in y
12
```

It is often useful to apply various functions elementwise to vectors. This is a form of *broadcasting*. With infix operators (e.g., +, *, and ^), a dot is prefixed to indicate elementwise broadcasting. With functions like sqrt and sin, the dot is postfixed:

```
julia> x .* y   # elementwise multiplication
2-element Vector{Int64}:
 3
 8
julia> x .^ 2   # elementwise squaring
2-element Vector{Int64}:
 1
 4
julia> sin.(x)  # elementwise application of sin
2-element Vector{Float64}:
 0.8414709848078965
 0.9092974268256817
julia> sqrt.(x) # elementwise application of sqrt
2-element Vector{Float64}:
 1.0
 1.4142135623730951
```

G.1.6 Matrices

A *matrix* is a two-dimensional array. Like a vector, it is constructed using square brackets. We use spaces to delimit elements in the same row and semicolons to delimit rows. We can also index into the matrix and output submatrices using ranges:

```
julia> X = [1 2 3; 4 5 6; 7 8 9; 10 11 12];
julia> typeof(X)  # a 2-dimensional array of Int64s
Matrix{Int64} (alias for Array{Int64, 2})
julia> X[2]        # second element using column-major ordering
4
julia> X[3,2]     # element in third row and second column
8
```

```
julia> X[1,:]      # extract the first row
3-element Vector{Int64}:
 1
 2
 3
julia> X[:,2]      # extract the second column
4-element Vector{Int64}:
  2
  5
  8
 11
julia> X[:,1:2]   # extract the first two columns
4×2 Matrix{Int64}:
  1   2
  4   5
  7   8
 10  11
julia> X[1:2,1:2] # extract a 2x2 submatrix from the top left of x
2×2 Matrix{Int64}:
 1  2
 4  5
julia> Matrix{Float64} # alias for a 2-dimensional array
Matrix{Float64} (alias for Array{Float64, 2})
```

We can also construct a variety of special matrices and use array comprehensions:

```
julia> Matrix(1.0I, 3, 3)                # 3x3 identity matrix
3×3 Matrix{Float64}:
 1.0  0.0  0.0
 0.0  1.0  0.0
 0.0  0.0  1.0
julia> Matrix(Diagonal([3, 2, 1]))       # 3x3 diagonal matrix with 3, 2, 1 on diagonal
3×3 Matrix{Int64}:
 3  0  0
 0  2  0
 0  0  1
julia> zeros(3,2)                        # 3x2 matrix of zeros
3×2 Matrix{Float64}:
 0.0  0.0
 0.0  0.0
 0.0  0.0
julia> rand(3,2)                         # 3x2 random matrix
3×2 Matrix{Float64}:
 0.41794   0.881486
```

```
 0.14916   0.534639
 0.736357  0.850574
julia> [sin(x + y) for x in 1:3, y in 1:2] # array comprehension
3×2 Matrix{Float64}:
  0.909297   0.14112
  0.14112   -0.756802
 -0.756802  -0.958924
```

Matrix operations include the following:

```
julia> X'                 # complex conjugate transpose
3×4 adjoint(::Matrix{Int64}) with eltype Int64:
 1  4  7  10
 2  5  8  11
 3  6  9  12
julia> 3X .+ 2            # multiplying by scalar and adding scalar
4×3 Matrix{Int64}:
  5   8  11
 14  17  20
 23  26  29
 32  35  38
julia> X = [1 3; 3 1]; # create an invertible matrix
julia> inv(X)             # inversion
2×2 Matrix{Float64}:
 -0.125   0.375
  0.375  -0.125
julia> pinv(X)            # pseudoinverse (requires LinearAlgebra)
2×2 Matrix{Float64}:
 -0.125   0.375
  0.375  -0.125
julia> det(X)             # determinant (requires LinearAlgebra)
-8.0
julia> [X X]              # horizontal concatenation, same as hcat(X, X)
2×4 Matrix{Int64}:
 1  3  1  3
 3  1  3  1
julia> [X; X]             # vertical concatenation, same as vcat(X, X)
4×2 Matrix{Int64}:
 1  3
 3  1
 1  3
 3  1
julia> sin.(X)            # elementwise application of sin
2×2 Matrix{Float64}:
 0.841471  0.14112
```

```
 0.14112   0.841471
julia> map(sin, X)        # elementwise application of sin
2×2 Matrix{Float64}:
 0.841471  0.14112
 0.14112   0.841471
julia> vec(X)             # reshape an array as a vector
4-element Vector{Int64}:
 1
 3
 3
 1
```

G.1.7 *Tuples*

A *tuple* is an ordered list of values, potentially of different types. They are constructed with parentheses. They are similar to vectors, but they cannot be mutated:

```
julia> x = ()    # the empty tuple
()
julia> isempty(x)
true
julia> x = (1,) # tuples of one element need the trailing comma
(1,)
julia> typeof(x)
Tuple{Int64}
julia> x = (1, 0, [1, 2], 2.5029, 4.6692) # third element is a vector
(1, 0, [1, 2], 2.5029, 4.6692)
julia> typeof(x)
Tuple{Int64, Int64, Vector{Int64}, Float64, Float64}
julia> x[2]
0
julia> x[end]
4.6692
julia> x[4:end]
(2.5029, 4.6692)
julia> length(x)
5
julia> x = (1, 2)
(1, 2)
julia> a, b = x;
julia> a
1
julia> b
2
```

G.1.8   Named Tuples

A *named tuple* is like a tuple, but each entry has its own name:

```julia
julia> x = (a=1, b=-Inf)
(a = 1, b = -Inf)
julia> x isa NamedTuple
true
julia> x.a
1
julia> a, b = x;
julia> a
1
julia> (; :a⇒10)
(a = 10,)
julia> (; :a⇒10, :b⇒11)
(a = 10, b = 11)
julia> merge(x, (d=3, e=10))  # merge two named tuples
(a = 1, b = -Inf, d = 3, e = 10)
```

G.1.9   Dictionaries

A *dictionary* is a collection of key-value pairs. Key-value pairs are indicated with a double arrow operator =>. We can index into a dictionary using square brackets, just as with arrays and tuples:

```julia
julia> x = Dict(); # empty dictionary
julia> x[3] = 4 # associate key 3 with value 4
4
julia> x = Dict(3⇒4, 5⇒1) # create a dictionary with two key-value pairs
Dict{Int64, Int64} with 2 entries:
  5 ⇒ 1
  3 ⇒ 4
julia> x[5]          # return the value associated with key 5
1
julia> haskey(x, 3) # check whether dictionary has key 3
true
julia> haskey(x, 4) # check whether dictionary has key 4
false
```

G.1.10   Composite Types

A *composite type* is a collection of named fields. By default, an instance of a composite type is immutable (i.e., it cannot change). We use the `struct` keyword and then give the new type a name and list the names of the fields:

```
struct A
    a
    b
end
```

Adding the keyword `mutable` makes it so that an instance can change:

```
mutable struct B
    a
    b
end
```

Composite types are constructed using parentheses, between which we pass in values for each field:

```
x = A(1.414, 1.732)
```

The double-colon operator can be used to specify the type for any field:

```
struct A
    a::Int64
    b::Float64
end
```

These type annotations require that we pass in an `Int64` for the first field and a `Float64` for the second field. For compactness, this book does not use type annotations, but it is at the expense of performance. Type annotations allow Julia to improve runtime performance because the compiler can optimize the underlying code for specific types.

G.1.11   Abstract Types

So far we have discussed *concrete types*, which are types that we can construct. However, concrete types are only part of the type hierarchy. There are also *abstract types*, which are supertypes of concrete types and other abstract types.

We can explore the type hierarchy of the `Float64` type shown in figure G.1 using the `supertype` and `subtypes` functions:

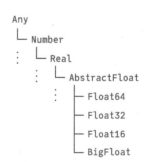

Figure G.1. The type hierarchy for the `Float64` type.

```
julia> supertype(Float64)
AbstractFloat
julia> supertype(AbstractFloat)
Real
julia> supertype(Real)
Number
julia> supertype(Number)
Any
julia> supertype(Any)          # Any is at the top of the hierarchy
Any
julia> using InteractiveUtils  # required for using subtypes in scripts
julia> subtypes(AbstractFloat) # different types of AbstractFloats
4-element Vector{Any}:
 BigFloat
 Float16
 Float32
 Float64
julia> subtypes(Float64)       # Float64 does not have any subtypes
Type[]
```

We can define our own abstract types:

```
abstract type C end
abstract type D <: C end # D is an abstract subtype of C
struct E <: D # E is a composite type that is a subtype of D
    a
end
```

G.1.12 *Parametric Types*

Julia supports *parametric types*, which are types that take parameters. The parameters to a parametric type are given within braces and delimited by commas. We have already seen a parametric type with our dictionary example:

```
julia> x = Dict(3⇒1.4, 1⇒5.9)
Dict{Int64, Float64} with 2 entries:
  3 ⇒ 1.4
  1 ⇒ 5.9
```

For dictionaries, the first parameter specifies the key type, and the second parameter specifies the value type. The example has Int64 keys and Float64 values, making the dictionary of type Dict{Int64,Float64}. Julia was able to infer these types based on the input, but we could have specified it explicitly:

```
julia> x = Dict{Int64,Float64}(3⟹1.4, 1⟹5.9);
```

While it is possible to define our own parametric types, we do not need to do so in this text.

G.2   Functions

A *function* maps its arguments, given as a tuple, to a result that is returned.

G.2.1   Named Functions

One way to define a *named function* is to use the `function` keyword, followed by the name of the function and a tuple of names of arguments:

```
function f(x, y)
    return x + y
end
```

We can also define functions compactly using assignment form:

```
julia> f(x, y) = x + y;
julia> f(3, 0.1415)
3.1415
```

G.2.2   Anonymous Functions

An *anonymous function* is not given a name, though it can be assigned to a named variable. One way to define an anonymous function is to use the arrow operator:

```
julia> h = x -> x^2 + 1 # assign anonymous function with input x to a variable h
#1 (generic function with 1 method)
julia> h(3)
10
julia> g(f, a, b) = [f(a), f(b)]; # applies function f to a and b and returns array
julia> g(h, 5, 10)
2-element Vector{Int64}:
  26
 101
julia> g(x->sin(x)+1, 10, 20)
2-element Vector{Float64}:
 0.4559788891106302
 1.9129452507276277
```

G.2.3   Callable Objects

We can define a type and associate functions with it, allowing objects of that type
to be *callable*:

```julia
julia> (x::A)() = x.a + x.b     # adding a zero-argument function to the type A defined earlier
julia> (x::A)(y) = y*x.a + x.b # adding a single-argument function
julia> x = A(22, 8);
julia> x()
30
julia> x(2)
52
```

G.2.4   Optional Arguments

We can assign a default value to an argument, making the specification of that
argument optional:

```julia
julia> f(x=10) = x^2;
julia> f()
100
julia> f(3)
9
julia> f(x, y, z=1) = x*y + z;
julia> f(1, 2, 3)
5
julia> f(1, 2)
3
```

G.2.5   Keyword Arguments

Functions may use *keyword arguments*, which are arguments that are named
when the function is called. Keyword arguments are given after all the positional
arguments. A semicolon is placed before any keywords, separating them from
the other arguments:

```julia
julia> f(; x = 0) = x + 1;
julia> f()
1
julia> f(x = 10)
11
julia> f(x, y = 10; z = 2) = (x + y)*z;
julia> f(1)
```

```
22
julia> f(2, z = 3)
36
julia> f(2, 3)
10
julia> f(2, 3, z = 1)
5
```

G.2.6   Dispatch

The types of the arguments passed to a function can be specified using the double colon operator. If multiple methods of the same function are provided, Julia will execute the appropriate method. The mechanism for choosing which method to execute is called *dispatch*:

```
julia> f(x::Int64) = x + 10;
julia> f(x::Float64) = x + 3.1415;
julia> f(1)
11
julia> f(1.0)
4.141500000000001
julia> f(1.3)
4.4415000000000004
```

The method with a type signature that best matches the types of the arguments given will be used:

```
julia> f(x) = 5;
julia> f(x::Float64) = 3.1415;
julia> f([3, 2, 1])
5
julia> f(0.00787499699)
3.1415
```

G.2.7   Splatting

It is often useful to *splat* the elements of a vector or a tuple into the arguments to a function using the ... operator:

```
julia> f(x,y,z) = x + y - z;
julia> a = [3, 1, 2];
julia> f(a...)
2
julia> b = (2, 2, 0);
julia> f(b...)
4
julia> c = ([0,0],[1,1]);
julia> f([2,2], c...)
2-element Vector{Int64}:
 1
 1
```

G.3   Control Flow

We can control the flow of our programs using conditional evaluation and loops. This section provides some of the syntax used in the book.

G.3.1   Conditional Evaluation

Conditional evaluation will check the value of a Boolean expression and then evaluate the appropriate block of code. One of the most common ways to do this is with an if statement:

```
if x < y
    # run this if x < y
elseif x > y
    # run this if x > y
else
    # run this if x == y
end
```

We can also use the *ternary operator* with its question mark and colon syntax. It checks the Boolean expression before the question mark. If the expression evaluates to true, then it returns what comes before the colon; otherwise, it returns what comes after the colon:

```
julia> f(x) = x > 0 ? x : 0;
julia> f(-10)
0
julia> f(10)
10
```

G.3.2 Loops

A *loop* allows for repeated evaluation of expressions. One type of loop is the while loop, which repeatedly evaluates a block of expressions until the specified condition after the `while` keyword is met. The following example sums the values in the array x:

```
X = [1, 2, 3, 4, 6, 8, 11, 13, 16, 18]
s = 0
while !isempty(X)
    s += pop!(X)
end
```

Another type of loop is the for loop, which uses the `for` keyword. The following example will also sum over the values in the array x but will not modify x:

```
X = [1, 2, 3, 4, 6, 8, 11, 13, 16, 18]
s = 0
for y in X
    s += y
end
```

The `in` keyword can be replaced by = or ∈. The following code block is equivalent:

```
X = [1, 2, 3, 4, 6, 8, 11, 13, 16, 18]
s = 0
for i = 1:length(X)
    s += X[i]
end
```

G.3.3 Iterators

We can iterate over collections in contexts such as for loops and array comprehensions. To demonstrate various iterators, we will use the `collect` function, which returns an array of all items generated by an iterator:

```
julia> X = ["feed", "sing", "ignore"];
julia> collect(enumerate(X)) # return the count and the element
3-element Vector{Tuple{Int64, String}}:
 (1, "feed")
 (2, "sing")
 (3, "ignore")
julia> collect(eachindex(X)) # equivalent to 1:length(X)
3-element Vector{Int64}:
```

```
 1
 2
 3
julia> Y = [-5, -0.5, 0];
julia> collect(zip(X, Y))    # iterate over multiple iterators simultaneously
3-element Vector{Tuple{String, Float64}}:
 ("feed", -5.0)
 ("sing", -0.5)
 ("ignore", 0.0)
julia> import IterTools: subsets
julia> collect(subsets(X))    # iterate over all subsets
8-element Vector{Vector{String}}:
 []
 ["feed"]
 ["sing"]
 ["feed", "sing"]
 ["ignore"]
 ["feed", "ignore"]
 ["sing", "ignore"]
 ["feed", "sing", "ignore"]
julia> collect(eachindex(X)) # iterate over indices into a collection
3-element Vector{Int64}:
 1
 2
 3
julia> Z = [1 2; 3 4; 5 6];
julia> import Base.Iterators: product
julia> collect(product(X,Y)) # iterate over Cartesian product of multiple iterators
3×3 Matrix{Tuple{String, Float64}}:
 ("feed", -5.0)    ("feed", -0.5)    ("feed", 0.0)
 ("sing", -5.0)    ("sing", -0.5)    ("sing", 0.0)
 ("ignore", -5.0)  ("ignore", -0.5)  ("ignore", 0.0)
```

G.4   Packages

A *package* is a collection of Julia code and possibly other external libraries that can be imported to provide additional functionality. This section briefly reviews a few of the key packages that we build upon in this book. To add a registered package like `Distributions.jl`, we can run

```
using Pkg
Pkg.add("Distributions")
```

To update packages, we use

```
Pkg.update()
```

To use a package, we use the keyword **using** as follows:

```
using Distributions
```

G.4.1 Graphs.jl

We use the `Graphs.jl` package (version 1.4) to represent graphs and perform operations on them:

```
julia> using Graphs
julia> G = SimpleDiGraph(3); # create a directed graph with three nodes
julia> add_edge!(G, 1, 3);   # add edge from node 1 to 3
julia> add_edge!(G, 1, 2);   # add edge from node 1 to 2
julia> rem_edge!(G, 1, 3);   # remove edge from node 1 to 3
julia> add_edge!(G, 2, 3);   # add edge from node 2 to 3
julia> typeof(G)
Graphs.SimpleGraphs.SimpleDiGraph{Int64}
julia> nv(G)                 # number of nodes (also called vertices)
3
julia> outneighbors(G, 1)    # list of outgoing neighbors for node 1
1-element Vector{Int64}:
 2
julia> inneighbors(G, 1)     # list of incoming neighbors for node 1
Int64[]
```

G.4.2 Distributions.jl

We use the `Distributions.jl` package (version 0.24) to represent, fit, and sample from probability distributions:

```
julia> using Distributions
julia> dist = Categorical([0.3, 0.5, 0.2]) # create a categorical distribution
Distributions.Categorical{Float64, Vector{Float64}}(support=Base.OneTo(3), p=[0.3, 0.5, 0.2])
julia> data = rand(dist)               # generate a sample
2
julia> data = rand(dist, 2)            # generate two samples
2-element Vector{Int64}:
 2
 3
julia> μ, σ = 5.0, 2.5;                # define parameters of a normal distribution
julia> dist = Normal(μ, σ)             # create a normal distribution
Distributions.Normal{Float64}(μ=5.0, σ=2.5)
```

```
julia> rand(dist)                     # sample from the distribution
3.173653920282897
julia> data = rand(dist, 3)           # generate three samples
3-element Vector{Float64}:
 10.860475998911657
  1.519358465527894
  3.0194180096515186
julia> data = rand(dist, 1000);       # generate many samples
julia> Distributions.fit(Normal, data) # fit a normal distribution to the samples
Distributions.Normal{Float64}(μ=5.085987626631449, σ=2.4766229761489367)
julia> μ = [1.0, 2.0];
julia> Σ = [1.0 0.5; 0.5 2.0];
julia> dist = MvNormal(μ, Σ)          # create a multivariate normal distribution
FullNormal(
dim: 2
μ: [1.0, 2.0]
Σ: [1.0 0.5; 0.5 2.0]
)
julia> rand(dist, 3)                  # generate three samples
2×3 Matrix{Float64}:
 0.834945  -0.527494  -0.098257
 1.25277   -0.246228   0.423922
julia> dist = Dirichlet(ones(3))      # create a Dirichlet distribution Dir(1,1,1)
Distributions.Dirichlet{Float64, Vector{Float64}, Float64}(alpha=[1.0, 1.0, 1.0])
julia> rand(dist)                     # sample from the distribution
3-element Vector{Float64}:
 0.19658106436589923
 0.6128478073834874
 0.1905711282506134
```

G.4.3   JuMP.jl

We use the `JuMP.jl` package (version 0.21) to specify optimization problems that we can then solve using a variety of solvers, such as those included in `GLPK.jl` and `Ipopt.jl`:

```
julia> using JuMP
julia> using GLPK
julia> model = Model(GLPK.Optimizer)          # create model and use GLPK as solver
A JuMP Model
Feasibility problem with:
Variables: 0
Model mode: AUTOMATIC
CachingOptimizer state: EMPTY_OPTIMIZER
```

```
Solver name: GLPK
julia> @variable(model, x[1:3])               # define variables x[1], x[2], and x[3]
3-element Vector{JuMP.VariableRef}:
 x[1]
 x[2]
 x[3]
julia> @objective(model, Max, sum(x) - x[2]) # define maximization objective
x[1] + 0 x[2] + x[3]
julia> @constraint(model, x[1] + x[2] ≤ 3)    # add constraint
x[1] + x[2] <= 3.0
julia> @constraint(model, x[2] + x[3] ≤ 2)    # add another constraint
x[2] + x[3] <= 2.0
julia> @constraint(model, x[2] ≥ 0)           # add another constraint
x[2] >= 0.0
julia> optimize!(model)                        # solve
julia> value.(x)                               # extract optimal values for elements in x
3-element Vector{Float64}:
 3.0
 0.0
 2.0
```

G.5   Convenience Functions

There are a few functions that allow us to specify the algorithms in this book more compactly. The following functions are useful when working with dictionaries and named tuples:

```
Base.Dict{Symbol,V}(a::NamedTuple) where V =
    Dict{Symbol,V}(n⟹v for (n,v) in zip(keys(a), values(a)))
Base.convert(::Type{Dict{Symbol,V}}, a::NamedTuple) where V =
    Dict{Symbol,V}(a)
Base.isequal(a::Dict{Symbol,<:Any}, nt::NamedTuple) =
    length(a) == length(nt) &&
    all(a[n] == v for (n,v) in zip(keys(nt), values(nt)))

julia> a = Dict{Symbol,Integer}((a=1, b=2, c=3))
Dict{Symbol, Integer} with 3 entries:
  :a ⟹ 1
  :b ⟹ 2
  :c ⟹ 3
julia> isequal(a, (a=1, b=2, c=3))
true
julia> isequal(a, (a=1, c=3, b=2))
true
```

```julia
julia> Dict{Dict{Symbol,Integer},Float64}((a=1, b=1)⟹0.2, (a=1, b=2)⟹0.8)
Dict{Dict{Symbol, Integer}, Float64} with 2 entries:
  Dict(:a⟹1, :b⟹1) ⟹ 0.2
  Dict(:a⟹1, :b⟹2) ⟹ 0.8
```

We define SetCategorical to represent distributions over discrete sets:

```julia
struct SetCategorical{S}
    elements::Vector{S} # Set elements (could be repeated)
    distr::Categorical # Categorical distribution over set elements

    function SetCategorical(elements::AbstractVector{S}) where S
        weights = ones(length(elements))
        return new{S}(elements, Categorical(normalize(weights, 1)))
    end

    function SetCategorical(
            elements::AbstractVector{S},
            weights::AbstractVector{Float64}
        ) where S

        ℓ₁ = norm(weights,1)
        if ℓ₁ < 1e-6 || isinf(ℓ₁)
            return SetCategorical(elements)
        end
        distr = Categorical(normalize(weights, 1))
        return new{S}(elements, distr)
    end
end

Distributions.rand(D::SetCategorical) = D.elements[rand(D.distr)]
Distributions.rand(D::SetCategorical, n::Int) = D.elements[rand(D.distr, n)]
function Distributions.pdf(D::SetCategorical, x)
    sum(e == x ? w : 0.0 for (e,w) in zip(D.elements, D.distr.p))
end
```

```
julia> D = SetCategorical(["up", "down", "left", "right"],[0.4, 0.2, 0.3, 0.1]);
julia> rand(D)
"up"
julia> rand(D, 5)
5-element Vector{String}:
 "left"
 "up"
 "down"
 "up"
 "left"
julia> pdf(D, "up")
0.3999999999999999
```

References

1. P. Abbeel and A. Y. Ng, "Apprenticeship Learning via Inverse Reinforcement Learning," in *International Conference on Machine Learning (ICML)*, 2004 (cit. on p. 361).

2. J. Agar, *Science in the 20th Century and Beyond*. Polity, 2012 (cit. on p. 10).

3. S. Amari, "Natural Gradient Works Efficiently in Learning," *Neural Computation*, vol. 10, no. 2, pp. 251–276, 1998 (cit. on p. 253).

4. C. Amato, D. S. Bernstein, and S. Zilberstein, "Optimizing Fixed-Size Stochastic Controllers for POMDPs and Decentralized POMDPs," *Autonomous Agents and Multi-Agent Systems*, vol. 21, no. 3, pp. 293–320, 2010 (cit. on pp. 478, 551).

5. D. Amodei, C. Olah, J. Steinhardt, P. Christiano, J. Schulman, and D. Mané, "Concrete Problems in AI Safety," 2016. arXiv: 1606.06565v2 (cit. on p. 13).

6. P. Anand, "Are the Preference Axioms Really Rational?" *Theory and Decision*, vol. 23, no. 2, pp. 189–214, 1987 (cit. on p. 112).

7. D. Ariely, *Predictably Irrational: The Hidden Forces That Shape Our Decisions*. Harper, 2008 (cit. on p. 122).

8. S. Arnborg, D. G. Corneil, and A. Proskurowski, "Complexity of Finding Embeddings in a *k*-Tree," *SIAM Journal on Algebraic Discrete Methods*, vol. 8, no. 2, pp. 277–284, 1987 (cit. on p. 52).

9. M. S. Arulampalam, S. Maskell, N. Gordon, and T. Clapp, "A Tutorial on Particle Filters for Online Nonlinear / Non-Gaussian Bayesian Tracking," *IEEE Transactions on Signal Processing*, vol. 50, no. 2, pp. 174–188, 2002 (cit. on p. 390).

10. K. J. Åström, "Optimal Control of Markov Processes with Incomplete State Information," *Journal of Mathematical Analysis and Applications*, vol. 10, no. 1, pp. 174–205, 1965 (cit. on p. 407).

11. P. Auer, N. Cesa-Bianchi, and P. Fischer, "Finite-Time Analysis of the Multiarmed Bandit Problem," *Machine Learning*, vol. 47, no. 2–3, pp. 235–256, 2002 (cit. on p. 187).

12.   T. Ayer, O. Alagoz, and N. K. Stout, "A POMDP Approach to Personalize Mammography Screening Decisions," *Operations Research*, vol. 60, no. 5, pp. 1019–1034, 2012 (cit. on p. 4).

13.   H. Bai, D. Hsu, W. S. Lee, and V. A. Ngo, "Monte Carlo Value Iteration for Continuous-State POMDPs," in *International Workshop on the Algorithmic Foundations of Robotics (WAFR)*, 2011 (cit. on p. 475).

14.   L. Baird, "Residual Algorithms: Reinforcement Learning with Function Approximation," in *International Conference on Machine Learning (ICML)*, 1995 (cit. on p. 610).

15.   Y. Bar-Shalom, X. R. Li, and T. Kirubarajan, *Estimation with Applications to Tracking and Navigation*. Wiley, 2001 (cit. on p. 383).

16.   D. Barber, *Bayesian Reasoning and Machine Learning*. Cambridge University Press, 2012 (cit. on p. 53).

17.   A. G. Barto, R. S. Sutton, and C. W. Anderson, "Neuronlike Adaptive Elements That Can Solve Difficult Learning Control Problems," *IEEE Transactions on Systems, Man, and Cybernetics*, vol. SMC-13, no. 5, pp. 834–846, 1983 (cit. on p. 611).

18.   A. G. Barto, S. J. Bradtke, and S. P. Singh, "Learning to Act Using Real-Time Dynamic Programming," *Artificial Intelligence*, vol. 72, no. 1–2, pp. 81–138, 1995 (cit. on p. 197).

19.   K. Basu, "The Traveler's Dilemma: Paradoxes of Rationality in Game Theory," *American Economic Review*, vol. 84, no. 2, pp. 391–395, 1994 (cit. on p. 622).

20.   R. Bellman, "Minimization Problem," *Bulletin of the American Mathematical Society*, vol. 62, no. 3, p. 270, 1956 (cit. on p. 399).

21.   R. Bellman, *Eye of the Hurricane: An Autobiography*. World Scientific, 1984 (cit. on p. 136).

22.   R. E. Bellman, *Dynamic Programming*. Princeton University Press, 1957 (cit. on pp. 133, 138).

23.   A. Bemporad and M. Morari, "Robust Model Predictive Control: A Survey," in *Robustness in Identification and Control*, A. Garulli, A. Tesi, and A. Vicino, eds., Springer, 1999, pp. 207–226 (cit. on p. 204).

24.   J. Bentham, *Theory of Legislation*. Trübner & Company, 1887 (cit. on p. 8).

25.   U. Berger, "Brown's Original Fictitious Play," *Journal of Economic Theory*, vol. 135, no. 1, pp. 572–578, 2007 (cit. on p. 507).

26.   D. Bernoulli, "Exposition of a New Theory on the Measurement of Risk," *Econometrica*, vol. 22, no. 1, pp. 23–36, 1954 (cit. on p. 112).

27.   D. S. Bernstein, R. Givan, N. Immerman, and S. Zilberstein, "The Complexity of Decentralized Control of Markov Decision Processes," *Mathematics of Operation Research*, vol. 27, no. 4, pp. 819–840, 2002 (cit. on pp. 545, 546).

28. D. P. Bertsekas, *Dynamic Programming and Optimal Control*. Athena Scientific, 2007 (cit. on p. 148).

29. D. P. Bertsekas, *Reinforcement Learning and Optimal Control*. Athena Scientific, 2019 (cit. on p. 335).

30. D. P. Bertsekas and J. N. Tsitsiklis, *Introduction to Probability*. Athena Scientific, 2002 (cit. on p. 20).

31. M. Besançon, T. Papamarkou, D. Anthoff, A. Arslan, S. Byrne, D. Lin, and J. Pearson, "Distributions.jl: Definition and Modeling of Probability Distributions in the JuliaStats Ecosystem," 2019. arXiv: 1907.08611v1 (cit. on p. 573).

32. W. M. Bolstad and J. M. Curran, *Introduction to Bayesian Statistics*. Wiley, 2016 (cit. on p. 11).

33. B. Bonet and H. Geffner, "Labeled RTDP: Improving the Convergence of Real-Time Dynamic Programming," in *International Conference on Automated Planning and Scheduling (ICAPS)*, 2003 (cit. on p. 197).

34. F. Borrelli, A. Bemporad, and M. Morari, *Predictive Control for Linear and Hybrid Systems*. Cambridge University Press, 2019 (cit. on p. 200).

35. M. Bouton, A. Nakhaei, K. Fujimura, and M. J. Kochenderfer, "Safe Reinforcement Learning with Scene Decomposition for Navigating Complex Urban Environments," in *IEEE Intelligent Vehicles Symposium (IV)*, 2019 (cit. on p. 3).

36. M. Bouton, J. Tumova, and M. J. Kochenderfer, "Point-Based Methods for Model Checking in Partially Observable Markov Decision Processes," in *AAAI Conference on Artificial Intelligence (AAAI)*, 2020 (cit. on p. 293).

37. M. Bowling, "Convergence and No-Regret in Multiagent Learning," in *Advances in Neural Information Processing Systems (NIPS)*, 2005 (cit. on p. 509).

38. M. Bowling and M. Veloso, "An Analysis of Stochastic Game Theory for Multiagent Reinforcement Learning," Carnegie Mellon University, Tech. Rep. CMU-CS-00-165, 2000 (cit. on p. 521).

39. S. Boyd and L. Vandenberghe, *Convex Optimization*. Cambridge University Press, 2004 (cit. on pp. 200, 565).

40. R. I. Brafman and M. Tennenholtz, "R-MAX—A General Polynomial Time Algorithm for Near-Optimal Reinforcement Learning," *Journal of Machine Learning Research*, vol. 3, pp. 213–231, 2002 (cit. on p. 323).

41. D. Brockhoff, A. Auger, N. Hansen, D. Arnold, and T. Hohm, "Mirrored Sampling and Sequential Selection for Evolution Strategies," in *International Conference on Parallel Problem Solving from Nature*, 2010 (cit. on p. 224).

42. G. Brockman, V. Cheung, L. Pettersson, J. Schneider, J. Schulman, J. Tang, and W. Zaremba, "OpenAI Gym," 2016. arXiv: 1606.01540v1 (cit. on p. 611).

43. G. W. Brown, "Iterative Solution of Games by Fictitious Play," *Activity Analysis of Production and Allocation*, vol. 13, no. 1, pp. 374–376, 1951 (cit. on p. 505).

44. C. B. Browne, E. Powley, D. Whitehouse, S. M. Lucas, P. I. Cowling, P. Rohlfshagen, S. Tavener, D. Perez, S. Samothrakis, and S. Colton, "A Survey of Monte Carlo Tree Search Methods," *IEEE Transactions on Computational Intelligence and AI in Games*, vol. 4, no. 1, pp. 1–43, 2012 (cit. on pp. 187, 276).

45. J. A. Bucklew, *Introduction to Rare Event Simulation*. Springer, 2004 (cit. on p. 287).

46. W. L. Buntine, "Theory Refinement on Bayesian Networks," in *Conference on Uncertainty in Artificial Intelligence (UAI)*, 1991 (cit. on p. 104).

47. C. F. Camerer, *Behavioral Game Theory: Experiments in Strategic Interaction*. Princeton University Press, 2003 (cit. on p. 504).

48. A. R. Cassandra, M. L. Littman, and N. L. Zhang, "Incremental Pruning: A Simple, Fast, Exact Method for Partially Observable Markov Decision Processes," in *Conference on Uncertainty in Artificial Intelligence (UAI)*, 1997 (cit. on p. 416).

49. J. Chakravorty and A. Mahajan, "Multi-Armed Bandits, Gittins Index, and Its Calculation," in *Methods and Applications of Statistics in Clinical Trials*, N. Balakrishnan, ed., vol. 2, Wiley, 2014, pp. 416–435 (cit. on p. 309).

50. D. M. Chickering, "Learning Bayesian Networks is NP-Complete," in *Learning from Data: Artificial Intelligence and Statistics V*, D. Fisher and H.-J. Lenz, eds., Springer, 1996, pp. 121–130 (cit. on p. 97).

51. D. M. Chickering, "Learning Equivalence Classes of Bayesian-Network Structures," *Journal of Machine Learning Research*, vol. 2, pp. 445–498, 2002 (cit. on p. 106).

52. D. M. Chickering, D. Heckerman, and C. Meek, "Large-Sample Learning of Bayesian Networks is NP-Hard," *Journal of Machine Learning Research*, vol. 5, pp. 1287–1330, 2004 (cit. on p. 97).

53. K. Cho, B. van Merriënboer, C. Gulcehre, D. Bahdanau, F. Bougares, H. Schwenk, and Y. Bengio, "Learning Phrase Representations Using RNN Encoder-Decoder for Statistical Machine Translation," in *Conference on Empirical Methods in Natural Language Processing (EMNLP)*, 2014 (cit. on p. 592).

54. E. K. P. Chong, R. L. Givan, and H. S. Chang, "A Framework for Simulation-Based Network Control via Hindsight Optimization," in *IEEE Conference on Decision and Control (CDC)*, 2000 (cit. on p. 207).

55. B. Christian, *The Alignment Problem*. Norton & Company, 2020 (cit. on p. 13).

56. G. F. Cooper, "The Computational Complexity of Probabilistic Inference Using Bayesian Belief Networks," *Artificial Intelligence*, vol. 42, no. 2–3, pp. 393–405, 1990 (cit. on p. 53).

57. G. F. Cooper and E. Herskovits, "A Bayesian Method for the Induction of Probabilistic Networks from Data," *Machine Learning*, vol. 4, no. 9, pp. 309–347, 1992 (cit. on pp. 97, 100).

58. T. H. Cormen, C. E. Leiserson, R. L. Rivest, and C. Stein, *Introduction to Algorithms*, 3rd ed. MIT Press, 2009 (cit. on p. 136).

59. A. Corso, R. J. Moss, M. Koren, R. Lee, and M. J. Kochenderfer, "A Survey of Algorithms for Black-Box Safety Validation," *Journal of Artificial Intelligence Research*, vol. 72, pp. 377–428, 2021 (cit. on p. 281).

60. A. Couëtoux, J.-B. Hoock, N. Sokolovska, O. Teytaud, and N. Bonnard, "Continuous Upper Confidence Trees," in *Learning and Intelligent Optimization (LION)*, 2011 (cit. on p. 197).

61. F. Cuzzolin, *The Geometry of Uncertainty*. Springer, 2021 (cit. on p. 19).

62. G. B. Dantzig, "Linear Programming," *Operations Research*, vol. 50, no. 1, pp. 42–47, 2002 (cit. on p. 8).

63. C. Daskalakis, P. W. Goldberg, and C. H. Papadimitriou, "The Complexity of Computing a Nash Equilibrium," *Communications of the ACM*, vol. 52, no. 2, pp. 89–97, 2009 (cit. on p. 498).

64. A. P. Dempster, N. M. Laird, and D. B. Rubin, "Maximum Likelihood from Incomplete Data via the EM Algorithm," *Journal of the Royal Statistical Society, Series B (Methodological)*, vol. 39, no. 1, pp. 1–38, 1977 (cit. on p. 87).

65. S. L. Dittmer and F. V. Jensen, "Myopic Value of Information in Influence Diagrams," in *Conference on Uncertainty in Artificial Intelligence (UAI)*, 1997 (cit. on p. 119).

66. J. Duchi, S. Shalev-Shwartz, Y. Singer, and T. Chandra, "Efficient Projections onto the ℓ_1-Ball for Learning in High Dimensions," in *International Conference on Machine Learning (ICML)*, 2008 (cit. on p. 485).

67. M. J. Dupré and F. J. Tipler, "New Axioms for Rigorous Bayesian Probability," *Bayesian Analysis*, vol. 4, no. 3, pp. 599–606, 2009 (cit. on p. 20).

68. M. Egorov, Z. N. Sunberg, E. Balaban, T. A. Wheeler, J. K. Gupta, and M. J. Kochenderfer, "POMDPs.jl: A Framework for Sequential Decision Making Under Uncertainty," *Journal of Machine Learning Research*, vol. 18, no. 26, pp. 1–5, 2017 (cit. on p. 381).

69. C. Elkan, "The Foundations of Cost-Sensitive Learning," in *International Joint Conference on Artificial Intelligence (IJCAI)*, 2001 (cit. on p. 373).

70. P. H. Farquhar, "Utility Assessment Methods," *Management Science*, vol. 30, no. 11, pp. 1283–1300, 1984 (cit. on p. 114).

71. J. A. Filar, T. A. Schultz, F. Thuijsman, and O. Vrieze, "Nonlinear Programming and Stationary Equilibria in Stochastic Games," *Mathematical Programming*, vol. 50, no. 1–3, pp. 227–237, 1991 (cit. on p. 521).

72. A. M. Fink, "Equilibrium in a Stochastic *n*-Person Game," *Journal of Science of the Hiroshima University, Series A-I*, vol. 28, no. 1, pp. 89–93, 1964 (cit. on p. 520).

73. C. Finn, S. Levine, and P. Abbeel, "Guided Cost Learning: Deep Inverse Optimal Control via Policy Optimization," in *International Conference on Machine Learning (ICML)*, 2016 (cit. on p. 368).

74. P. C. Fishburn, "Utility Theory," *Management Science*, vol. 14, no. 5, pp. 335–378, 1968 (cit. on p. 111).

75. P. C. Fishburn, "The Axioms of Subjective Probability," *Statistical Science*, vol. 1, no. 3, pp. 335–345, 1986 (cit. on p. 20).

76. H. Freudenthal, "Simplizialzerlegungen von Beschränkter Flachheit," *Annals of Mathematics*, vol. 43, pp. 580–582, 1942 (cit. on p. 445).

77. M. C. Fu, "Gradient Estimation," in *Simulation*, S. G. Henderson and B. L. Nelson, eds., Elsevier, 2006, pp. 575–616 (cit. on p. 231).

78. D. Fudenberg and D. Levine, "Consistency and Cautious Fictitious Play," *Journal of Economic Dynamics and Control*, vol. 19, no. 5–7, pp. 1065–1089, 1995 (cit. on p. 509).

79. D. Fudenberg and J. Tirole, *Game Theory*. MIT Press, 1991 (cit. on p. 493).

80. D. Gaines, G. Doran, M. Paton, B. Rothrock, J. Russino, R. Mackey, R. Anderson, R. Francis, C. Joswig, H. Justice, K. Kolcio, G. Rabideau, S. Schaffer, J. Sawoniewicz, A. Vasavada, V. Wong, K. Yu, and A.-a. Agha-mohammadi, "Self-Reliant Rovers for Increased Mission Productivity," *Journal of Field Robotics*, vol. 37, no. 7, pp. 1171–1196, 2020 (cit. on p. 5).

81. F. L. Gall, "Powers of Tensors and Fast Matrix Multiplication," in *International Symposium on Symbolic and Algebraic Computation (ISSAC)*, 2014 (cit. on p. 490).

82. S. Garatti and M. C. Campi, "Modulating Robustness in Control Design: Principles and Algorithms," *IEEE Control Systems Magazine*, vol. 33, no. 2, pp. 36–51, 2013 (cit. on p. 207).

83. A. Garivier, T. Lattimore, and E. Kaufmann, "On Explore-Then-Commit Strategies," in *Advances in Neural Information Processing Systems (NIPS)*, 2016 (cit. on p. 303).

84. A. Geramifard, T. J. Walsh, S. Tellex, G. Chowdhary, N. Roy, and J. P. How, "A Tutorial on Linear Function Approximators for Dynamic Programming and Reinforcement Learning," *Foundations and Trends in Machine Learning*, vol. 6, no. 4, pp. 375–451, 2013 (cit. on p. 162).

85. M. Ghavamzadeh, S. Mannor, J. Pineau, and A. Tamar, "Bayesian Reinforcement Learning: A Survey," *Foundations and Trends in Machine Learning*, vol. 8, no. 5–6, pp. 359–483, 2015 (cit. on p. 326).

86. S. B. Gillispie and M. D. Perlman, "The Size Distribution for Markov Equivalence Classes of Acyclic Digraph Models," *Artificial Intelligence*, vol. 141, no. 1–2, pp. 137–155, 2002 (cit. on p. 106).

87.   J. C. Gittins, "Bandit Processes and Dynamic Allocation Indices," *Journal of the Royal Statistical Society. Series B (Methodological)*, vol. 41, no. 2, pp. 148–177, 1979 (cit. on pp. 299, 309).

88.   J. Gittins, K. Glazebrook, and R. Weber, *Multi-Armed Bandit Allocation Indices*, 2nd ed. Wiley, 2011 (cit. on p. 309).

89.   P. W. Glynn, "Likelihood Ratio Gradient Estimation for Stochastic Systems," *Communications of the ACM*, vol. 33, no. 10, pp. 75–84, 1990 (cit. on p. 234).

90.   P. J. Gmytrasiewicz and P. Doshi, "A Framework for Sequential Planning in Multi-Agent Settings," *Journal of Artificial Intelligence Research*, vol. 24, no. 1, pp. 49–79, 2005 (cit. on p. 534).

91.   D. E. Goldberg and J. Richardson, "An Experimental Comparison of Localization Methods," in *International Conference on Genetic Algorithms*, 1987 (cit. on p. 394).

92.   D. E. Goldberg, *Genetic Algorithms in Search, Optimization, and Machine Learning*. Addison-Wesley, 1989 (cit. on p. 215).

93.   O. Goldreich, *Computational Complexity: A Conceptual Perspective*. Cambridge University Press, 2008 (cit. on p. 575).

94.   I. Goodfellow, Y. Bengio, and A. Courville, *Deep Learning*. MIT Press, 2016 (cit. on p. 581).

95.   I. Goodfellow, J. Pouget-Abadie, M. Mirza, B. Xu, D. Warde-Farley, S. Ozair, A. Courville, and Y. Bengio, "Generative Adversarial Nets," in *Advances in Neural Information Processing Systems (NIPS)*, 2014 (cit. on p. 597).

96.   L. Graesser and W. L. Keng, *Foundations of Deep Reinforcement Learning*. Addison Wesley, 2020 (cit. on p. 344).

97.   A. Greenwald and K. Hall, "Correlated Q-Learning," in *International Conference on Machine Learning (ICML)*, 2003 (cit. on p. 503).

98.   A. Griewank and A. Walther, *Evaluating Derivatives: Principles and Techniques of Algorithmic Differentiation*, 2nd ed. SIAM, 2008 (cit. on p. 585).

99.   E. A. Hansen, "Solving POMDPs by Searching in Policy Space," in *Conference on Uncertainty in Artificial Intelligence (UAI)*, 1998 (cit. on p. 475).

100.   E. A. Hansen, D. S. Bernstein, and S. Zilberstein, "Dynamic Programming for Partially Observable Stochastic Games," in *AAAI Conference on Artificial Intelligence (AAAI)*, 2004 (cit. on p. 533).

101.   N. Hansen and A. Ostermeier, "Adapting Arbitrary Normal Mutation Distributions in Evolution Strategies: The Covariance Matrix Adaptation," in *IEEE International Conference on Evolutionary Computation*, 1996 (cit. on p. 221).

102.   A. Harutyunyan, M. G. Bellemare, T. Stepleton, and R. Munos, "Q(λ) with Off-Policy Corrections," in *International Conference on Algorithmic Learning Theory (ALT)*, 2016 (cit. on p. 343).

103.   T. Hastie, R. Tibshirani, and J. Friedman, *The Elements of Statistical Learning: Data Mining, Inference, and Prediction*, 2nd ed. Springer Series in Statistics, 2001 (cit. on pp. 172, 174).

104.   M. Hauskrecht, "Value-Function Approximations for Partially Observable Markov Decision Processes," *Journal of Artificial Intelligence Research*, vol. 13, pp. 33–94, 2000 (cit. on pp. 427, 429, 436).

105.   D. Heckerman, D. Geiger, and D. M. Chickering, "Learning Bayesian Networks: The Combination of Knowledge and Statistical Data," *Machine Learning*, vol. 20, no. 3, pp. 197–243, 1995 (cit. on p. 104).

106.   F. S. Hillier, *Introduction to Operations Research*. McGraw-Hill, 2012 (cit. on p. 12).

107.   J. Ho and S. Ermon, "Generative Adversarial Imitation Learning," in *Advances in Neural Information Processing Systems (NIPS)*, 2016 (cit. on p. 369).

108.   S. Hochreiter and J. Schmidhuber, "Long Short-Term Memory," *Neural Computation*, vol. 9, no. 8, pp. 1735–1780, 1997 (cit. on p. 592).

109.   A. L. Hodgkin and A. F. Huxley, "A Quantitative Description of Membrane Current and Its Application to Conduction and Excitation in Nerve," *Journal of Physiology*, vol. 117, no. 4, pp. 500–544, 1952 (cit. on p. 582).

110.   R. Hooke and T. A. Jeeves, "Direct Search Solution of Numerical and Statistical Problems," *Journal of the ACM (JACM)*, vol. 8, no. 2, pp. 212–229, 1961 (cit. on p. 215).

111.   R. A. Howard, "Information Value Theory," *IEEE Transactions on Systems Science and Cybernetics*, vol. 2, no. 1, pp. 22–26, 1966 (cit. on p. 119).

112.   J. Hu and M. P. Wellman, "Nash Q-Learning for General-Sum Stochastic Games," *Journal of Machine Learning Research*, vol. 4, pp. 1039–1069, 2003 (cit. on p. 526).

113.   A. Hussein, M. M. Gaber, E. Elyan, and C. Jayne, "Imitation Learning: A Survey of Learning Methods," *ACM Computing Surveys*, vol. 50, no. 2, pp. 1–35, 2017 (cit. on p. 355).

114.   IEEE History Center Staff, "Proceedings of the IEEE Through 100 Years: 2000–2009," *Proceedings of the IEEE*, vol. 100, no. 11, pp. 3131–3145, 2012 (cit. on p. 387).

115.   J. E. Ingersoll, *Theory of Financial Decision Making*. Rowman and Littlefield Publishers, 1987 (cit. on p. 115).

116.   G. N. Iyengar, "Robust Dynamic Programming," *Mathematics of Operations Research*, vol. 30, no. 2, pp. 257–280, 2005 (cit. on p. 289).

117.   T. Jaakkola, M. I. Jordan, and S. P. Singh, "On the Convergence of Stochastic Iterative Dynamic Programming Algorithms," *Neural Computation*, vol. 6, no. 6, pp. 1185–1201, 1994 (cit. on p. 336).

118. E. T. Jaynes, "Information Theory and Statistical Mechanics," *Physical Review*, vol. 106, no. 4, pp. 620–630, 1957 (cit. on p. 368).

119. E. T. Jaynes, *Probability Theory: The Logic of Science*. Cambridge University Press, 2003 (cit. on pp. 19, 20).

120. F. V. Jensen and T. D. Nielsen, *Bayesian Networks and Decision Graphs*, 2nd ed. Springer, 2007 (cit. on p. 116).

121. I. L. Johansen and M. Rausand, "Foundations and Choice of Risk Metrics," *Safety Science*, vol. 62, pp. 386–399, 2014 (cit. on p. 281).

122. K. D. Julian and M. J. Kochenderfer, "Distributed Wildfire Surveillance with Autonomous Aircraft Using Deep Reinforcement Learning," *AIAA Journal of Guidance, Control, and Dynamics*, vol. 42, no. 8, pp. 1768–1778, 2019 (cit. on p. 4).

123. S. J. Julier and J. K. Uhlmann, "Unscented Filtering and Nonlinear Estimation," *Proceedings of the IEEE*, vol. 92, no. 3, pp. 401–422, 2004 (cit. on p. 387).

124. L. P. Kaelbling, M. L. Littman, and A. R. Cassandra, "Planning and Acting in Partially Observable Stochastic Domains," *Artificial Intelligence*, vol. 101, no. 1–2, pp. 99–134, 1998 (cit. on p. 407).

125. L. P. Kaelbling, *Learning in Embedded Systems*. MIT Press, 1993 (cit. on p. 305).

126. A. B. Kahn, "Topological Sorting of Large Networks," *Communications of the ACM*, vol. 5, no. 11, pp. 558–562, 1962 (cit. on p. 55).

127. D. Kahneman and A. Tversky, "Prospect Theory: An Analysis of Decision Under Risk," *Econometrica*, vol. 47, no. 2, pp. 263–292, 1979 (cit. on p. 122).

128. S. M. Kakade, "A Natural Policy Gradient," in *Advances in Neural Information Processing Systems (NIPS)*, 2001 (cit. on p. 254).

129. S. M. Kakade and J. Langford, "Approximately Optimal Approximate Reinforcement Learning," in *International Conference on Machine Learning (ICML)*, 2002 (cit. on p. 256).

130. R. E. Kálmán, "A New Approach to Linear Filtering and Prediction Problems," *ASME Journal of Basic Engineering*, vol. 82, pp. 35–45, 1960 (cit. on p. 383).

131. R. M. Karp, "Reducibility Among Combinatorial Problems," in *Complexity of Computer Computations*, R. E. Miller and J. W. Thatcher, eds., Plenum, 1972, pp. 85–103 (cit. on p. 577).

132. E. Kaufmann, "On Bayesian Index Policies for Sequential Resource Allocation," *Annals of Statistics*, vol. 46, no. 2, pp. 842–865, 2018 (cit. on p. 305).

133. M. Kearns and S. Singh, "Near-Optimal Reinforcement Learning in Polynomial Time," *Machine Learning*, vol. 49, no. 2/3, pp. 209–232, 2002 (cit. on p. 323).

134.   M. J. Kearns, Y. Mansour, and A. Y. Ng, "A Sparse Sampling Algorithm for Near-Optimal Planning in Large Markov Decision Processes," *Machine Learning*, vol. 49, no. 2–3, pp. 193–208, 2002 (cit. on p. 187).

135.   L. G. Khachiyan, "Polynomial Algorithms in Linear Programming," *USSR Computational Mathematics and Mathematical Physics*, vol. 20, no. 1, pp. 53–72, 1980 (cit. on p. 147).

136.   D. Kingma and M. Welling, "Auto-Encoding Variational Bayes," in *International Conference on Learning Representations (ICLR)*, 2013 (cit. on p. 593).

137.   D. E. Kirk, *Optimal Control Theory: An Introduction*. Prentice-Hall, 1970 (cit. on p. 2).

138.   M. J. Kochenderfer, *Decision Making Under Uncertainty: Theory and Application*. MIT Press, 2015 (cit. on pp. 3, 511, 615).

139.   M. J. Kochenderfer and T. A. Wheeler, *Algorithms for Optimization*. MIT Press, 2019 (cit. on pp. 102, 172, 213, 250).

140.   M. J. Kochenderfer and J. P. Chryssanthacopoulos, "Robust Airborne Collision Avoidance Through Dynamic Programming," Massachusetts Institute of Technology, Lincoln Laboratory, Project Report ATC-371, 2011 (cit. on p. 614).

141.   M. J. Kochenderfer, J. P. Chryssanthacopoulos, and P. Radecki, "Robustness of Optimized Collision Avoidance Logic to Modeling Errors," in *Digital Avionics Systems Conference (DASC)*, 2010 (cit. on p. 289).

142.   D. Koller and N. Friedman, *Probabilistic Graphical Models: Principles and Techniques*. MIT Press, 2009 (cit. on pp. 32, 36, 97).

143.   A. Kolmogorov, *Foundations of the Theory of Probability*, 2nd ed. Chelsea, 1956 (cit. on p. 562).

144.   H. Koontz, "The Management Theory Jungle," *Academy of Management Journal*, vol. 4, no. 3, pp. 174–188, 1961 (cit. on p. 12).

145.   B. O. Koopman, *Search and Screening: General Principles with Historical Applications*. Pergamon Press, 1980 (cit. on p. 11).

146.   F. Kschischang, B. Frey, and H.-A. Loeliger, "Factor Graphs and the Sum-Product Algorithm," *IEEE Transactions on Information Theory*, vol. 47, no. 2, pp. 498–519, 2001 (cit. on p. 53).

147.   A. Kuefler, J. Morton, T. A. Wheeler, and M. J. Kochenderfer, "Imitating Driver Behavior with Generative Adversarial Networks," in *IEEE Intelligent Vehicles Symposium (IV)*, 2017 (cit. on p. 375).

148.   H. Kuhn, "Extensive Games and the Problem of Information," in *Contributions to the Theory of Games II*, H. Kuhn and A. Tucker, eds., Princeton University Press, 1953, pp. 193–216 (cit. on p. 533).

149.   S. Kullback and R. A. Leibler, "On Information and Sufficiency," *Annals of Mathematical Statistics*, vol. 22, no. 1, pp. 79–86, 1951 (cit. on p. 567).

150.   S. Kullback, *Information Theory and Statistics*. Wiley, 1959 (cit. on p. 567).

151.   H. Kurniawati, D. Hsu, and W. S. Lee, "SARSOP: Efficient Point-Based POMDP Planning by Approximating Optimally Reachable Belief Spaces," in *Robotics: Science and Systems*, 2008 (cit. on pp. 440, 442).

152.   Y. LeCun, L. Bottou, Y. Bengio, and P. Haffner, "Gradient-Based Learning Applied to Document Recognition," *Proceedings of the IEEE*, vol. 86, no. 11, pp. 2278–2324, 1998 (cit. on pp. 587, 588).

153.   R. Lee, M. J. Kochenderfer, O. J. Mengshoel, G. P. Brat, and M. P. Owen, "Adaptive Stress Testing of Airborne Collision Avoidance Systems," in *Digital Avionics Systems Conference (DASC)*, 2015 (cit. on p. 294).

154.   J. Lehrer, *How We Decide*. Houghton Mifflin, 2009 (cit. on p. 122).

155.   T. P. Lillicrap, J. J. Hunt, A. Pritzel, N. Heess, T. Erez, Y. Tassa, D. Silver, and D. Wierstra, "Continuous Control with Deep Reinforcement Learning," in *International Conference on Learning Representations (ICLR)*, 2016. arXiv: 1509.02971v6 (cit. on p. 274).

156.   L.-J. Lin, "Reinforcement Learning for Robots Using Neural Networks," Ph.D. dissertation, Carnegie Mellon University, 1993 (cit. on p. 345).

157.   R. J. A. Little and D. B. Rubin, *Statistical Analysis with Missing Data*, 3rd ed. Wiley, 2020 (cit. on p. 84).

158.   M. L. Littman, "Markov Games as a Framework for Multi-Agent Reinforcement Learning," in *International Conference on Machine Learning (ICML)*, 1994 (cit. on p. 517).

159.   M. L. Littman, A. R. Cassandra, and L. P. Kaelbling, "Learning Policies for Partially Observable Environments: Scaling Up," in *International Conference on Machine Learning (ICML)*, 1995 (cit. on p. 427).

160.   W. S. Lovejoy, "Computationally Feasible Bounds for Partially Observed Markov Decision Processes," *Operations Research*, vol. 39, no. 1, pp. 162–175, 1991 (cit. on p. 445).

161.   O. Madani, S. Hanks, and A. Condon, "On the Undecidability of Probabilistic Planning and Related Stochastic Optimization Problems," *Artificial Intelligence*, vol. 147, no. 1–2, pp. 5–34, 2003 (cit. on p. 427).

162.   S. Mannor, R. Y. Rubinstein, and Y. Gat, "The Cross Entropy Method for Fast Policy Search," in *International Conference on Machine Learning (ICML)*, 2003 (cit. on p. 218).

163.   H. Markowitz, "The Utility of Wealth," *Journal of Political Economy*, vol. 60, no. 2, pp. 151–158, 1952 (cit. on p. 114).

164.   Mausam and A. Kolobov, *Planning with Markov Decision Processes: An AI Perspective.* Morgan & Claypool, 2012 (cit. on p. 197).

165.   S. B. McGrayne, *The Theory That Would Not Die.* Yale University Press, 2011 (cit. on p. 30).

166.   R. C. Merton, "Optimum Consumption and Portfolio Rules in a Continuous-Time Model," *Journal of Economic Theory*, vol. 3, no. 4, pp. 373–413, 1971 (cit. on p. 4).

167.   N. Meuleau, K.-E. Kim, L. P. Kaelbling, and A. R. Cassandra, "Solving POMDPs by Searching the Space of Finite Policies," in *Conference on Uncertainty in Artificial Intelligence (UAI)*, 1999 (cit. on p. 481).

168.   D. A. Mindell, *Between Human and Machine: Feedback, Control, and Computing Before Cybernetics.* JHU Press, 2002 (cit. on p. 11).

169.   V. Mnih, K. Kavukcuoglu, D. Silver, A. Graves, I. Antonoglou, D. Wierstra, and M. Riedmiller, "Playing Atari with Deep Reinforcement Learning," 2013. arXiv: 1312.5602v1 (cit. on p. 345).

170.   N. Moehle, E. Busseti, S. Boyd, and M. Wytock, "Dynamic Energy Management," in *Large Scale Optimization in Supply Chains and Smart Manufacturing*, Springer, 2019, pp. 69–126 (cit. on p. 208).

171.   G. Molenberghs, G. Fitzmaurice, M. G. Kenward, A. Tsiatis, and G. Verbeke, eds., *Handbook of Missing Data Methodology.* CRC Press, 2014 (cit. on p. 82).

172.   A. Moore, "Efficient Memory-Based Learning for Robot Control," Ph.D. dissertation, University of Cambridge, 1990 (cit. on p. 612).

173.   A. W. Moore, "Simplicial Mesh Generation with Applications," Ph.D. dissertation, Cornell University, 1992 (cit. on pp. 168, 170).

174.   A. W. Moore and C. G. Atkeson, "Prioritized Sweeping: Reinforcement Learning with Less Data and Less Time," *Machine Learning*, vol. 13, no. 1, pp. 103–130, 1993 (cit. on p. 321).

175.   G. E. Moore, "Cramming More Components onto Integrated Circuits," *Electronics*, vol. 38, no. 8, pp. 114–117, 1965 (cit. on p. 11).

176.   O. Morgenstern and J. von Neumann, *Theory of Games and Economic Behavior.* Princeton University Press, 1953 (cit. on p. 8).

177.   R. Motwani and P. Raghavan, *Randomized Algorithms.* Cambridge University Press, 1995 (cit. on p. 54).

178.   B. Müller, J. Reinhardt, and M. T. Strickland, *Neural Networks.* Springer, 1995 (cit. on p. 581).

179.   K. P. Murphy, *Probabilistic Machine Learning: An Introduction.* MIT Press, 2022 (cit. on p. 71).

180. R. B. Myerson, *Game Theory: Analysis of Conflict*. Harvard University Press, 1997 (cit. on p. 493).

181. R. Nair, M. Tambe, M. Yokoo, D. Pynadath, and S. Marsella, "Taming Decentralized POMDPs: Towards Efficient Policy Computation for Multiagent Settings," in *International Joint Conference on Artificial Intelligence (IJCAI)*, 2003 (cit. on p. 550).

182. J. Nash, "Non-Cooperative Games," *Annals of Mathematics*, pp. 286–295, 1951 (cit. on p. 498).

183. R. E. Neapolitan, *Learning Bayesian Networks*. Prentice Hall, 2003 (cit. on p. 97).

184. A. Y. Ng, D. Harada, and S. Russell, "Policy Invariance Under Reward Transformations: Theory and Application to Reward Shaping," in *International Conference on Machine Learning (ICML)*, 1999 (cit. on p. 343).

185. A. Y. Ng and M. Jordan, "A Policy Search Method for Large MDPs and POMDPs," in *Conference on Uncertainty in Artificial Intelligence (UAI)*, 2000 (cit. on p. 232).

186. N. J. Nilsson, *The Quest for Artificial Intelligence*. Cambridge University Press, 2009 (cit. on pp. 7, 9).

187. N. Nisan, T. Roughgarden, É. Tardos, and V. V. Vazirani, eds., *Algorithmic Game Theory*. Cambridge University Press, 2007 (cit. on p. 503).

188. F. A. Oliehoek and C. Amato, *A Concise Introduction to Decentralized POMDPs*. Springer, 2016 (cit. on p. 545).

189. C. Papadimitriou and J. Tsitsiklis, "The Complexity of Markov Decision Processes," *Mathematics of Operation Research*, vol. 12, no. 3, pp. 441–450, 1987 (cit. on pp. 427, 549).

190. J. Pearl, *Probabilistic Reasoning in Intelligent Systems: Networks of Plausible Inference*. Morgan Kaufmann, 1988 (cit. on p. 36).

191. J. Pearl, *Causality: Models, Reasoning, and Inference*, 2nd ed. Cambridge University Press, 2009 (cit. on p. 33).

192. J. Peng and R. J. Williams, "Incremental Multi-Step Q-Learning," *Machine Learning*, vol. 22, no. 1–3, pp. 283–290, 1996 (cit. on p. 341).

193. J. Peters and S. Schaal, "Reinforcement Learning of Motor Skills with Policy Gradients," *Neural Networks*, vol. 21, no. 4, pp. 682–697, 2008 (cit. on pp. 234, 243, 253).

194. M. Peterson, *An Introduction to Decision Theory*. Cambridge University Press, 2009 (cit. on p. 111).

195. A. Pinkus, "Approximation Theory of the MLP Model in Neural Networks," *Acta Numerica*, vol. 8, pp. 143–195, 1999 (cit. on p. 582).

196.   R. Platt Jr., R. Tedrake, L. P. Kaelbling, and T. Lozano-Pérez, "Belief Space Planning Assuming Maximum Likelihood Observations," in *Robotics: Science and Systems*, 2010 (cit. on p. 454).

197.   D. A. Pomerleau, "Efficient Training of Artificial Neural Networks for Autonomous Navigation," *Neural Computation*, vol. 3, no. 1, pp. 88–97, 1991 (cit. on p. 355).

198.   W. Poundstone, *Prisoner's Dilemma*. Doubleday, 1992 (cit. on p. 621).

199.   P. Poupart and C. Boutilier, "Bounded Finite State Controllers," in *Advances in Neural Information Processing Systems (NIPS)*, 2003 (cit. on p. 475).

200.   W. B. Powell, *Reinforcement Learning and Stochastic Optimization*. Wiley, 2022 (cit. on p. 161).

201.   W. B. Powell, *Approximate Dynamic Programming: Solving the Curses of Dimensionality*, 2nd ed. Wiley, 2011 (cit. on p. 161).

202.   M. L. Puterman, *Markov Decision Processes: Discrete Stochastic Dynamic Programming*. Wiley, 2005 (cit. on p. 133).

203.   M. L. Puterman and M. C. Shin, "Modified Policy Iteration Algorithms for Discounted Markov Decision Problems," *Management Science*, vol. 24, no. 11, pp. 1127–1137, 1978 (cit. on p. 141).

204.   J. Robinson, "An Iterative Method of Solving a Game," *Annals of Mathematics*, pp. 296–301, 1951 (cit. on p. 505).

205.   R. W. Robinson, "Counting Labeled Acyclic Digraphs," in *Ann Arbor Conference on Graph Theory*, 1973 (cit. on p. 99).

206.   S. Ross and J. A. Bagnell, "Efficient Reductions for Imitation Learning," in *International Conference on Artificial Intelligence and Statistics (AISTATS)*, 2010 (cit. on p. 358).

207.   S. Ross and B. Chaib-draa, "AEMS: An Anytime Online Search Algorithm for Approximate Policy Refinement in Large POMDPs," in *International Joint Conference on Artificial Intelligence (IJCAI)*, 2007 (cit. on p. 464).

208.   S. Ross, G. J. Gordon, and J. A. Bagnell, "A Reduction of Imitation Learning and Structured Prediction to No-Regret Online Learning," in *International Conference on Artificial Intelligence and Statistics (AISTATS)*, vol. 15, 2011 (cit. on p. 358).

209.   S. Ross, J. Pineau, S. Paquet, and B. Chaib-draa, "Online Planning Algorithms for POMDPs," *Journal of Artificial Intelligence Research*, vol. 32, pp. 663–704, 2008 (cit. on p. 453).

210.   D. E. Rumelhart, G. E. Hinton, and R. J. Williams, "Learning Representations by Back-Propagating Errors," *Nature*, vol. 323, pp. 533–536, 1986 (cit. on p. 585).

211.   G. A. Rummery and M. Niranjan, "On-Line Q-Learning Using Connectionist Systems," Cambridge University, Tech. Rep. CUED/F-INFENG/TR 166, 1994 (cit. on p. 338).

212. S. Russell and P. Norvig, *Artificial Intelligence: A Modern Approach*, 4th ed. Pearson, 2021 (cit. on pp. 2, 116).

213. D. Russo, B. V. Roy, A. Kazerouni, I. Osband, and Z. Wen, "A Tutorial on Thompson Sampling," *Foundations and Trends in Machine Learning*, vol. 11, no. 1, pp. 1–96, 2018 (cit. on p. 306).

214. A. Ruszczyński, "Risk-Averse Dynamic Programming for Markov Decision Processes," *Mathematical Programming*, vol. 125, no. 2, pp. 235–261, 2010 (cit. on p. 282).

215. T. Salimans, J. Ho, X. Chen, S. Sidor, and I. Sutskever, "Evolution Strategies as a Scalable Alternative to Reinforcement Learning," 2017. arXiv: 1703.03864v2 (cit. on p. 224).

216. T. Schaul, J. Quan, I. Antonoglou, and D. Silver, "Prioritized Experience Replay," in *International Conference on Learning Representations (ICLR)*, 2016 (cit. on p. 345).

217. P. J. H. Schoemaker, "The Expected Utility Model: Its Variants, Purposes, Evidence and Limitations," *Journal of Economic Literature*, vol. 20, no. 2, pp. 529–563, 1982 (cit. on p. 111).

218. J. Schulman, S. Levine, P. Moritz, M. Jordan, and P. Abbeel, "Trust Region Policy Optimization," in *International Conference on Machine Learning (ICML)*, 2015 (cit. on p. 254).

219. J. Schulman, P. Moritz, S. Levine, M. Jordan, and P. Abbeel, "High-Dimensional Continuous Control Using Generalized Advantage Estimation," in *International Conference on Learning Representations (ICLR)*, 2016. arXiv: 1506.02438v6 (cit. on p. 269).

220. J. Schulman, F. Wolski, P. Dhariwal, A. Radford, and O. Klimov, "Proximal Policy Optimization Algorithms," 2017. arXiv: 1707.06347v2 (cit. on p. 257).

221. S. Seuken and S. Zilberstein, "Memory-Bounded Dynamic Programming for Dec-POMDPs," in *International Joint Conference on Artificial Intelligence (IJCAI)*, 2007 (cit. on p. 550).

222. S. Seuken and S. Zilberstein, "Formal Models and Algorithms for Decentralized Decision Making Under Uncertainty," *Autonomous Agents and Multi-Agent Systems*, vol. 17, no. 2, pp. 190–250, 2008 (cit. on p. 549).

223. R. D. Shachter, "Evaluating Influence Diagrams," *Operations Research*, vol. 34, no. 6, pp. 871–882, 1986 (cit. on p. 119).

224. R. D. Shachter, "Probabilistic Inference and Influence Diagrams," *Operations Research*, vol. 36, no. 4, pp. 589–604, 1988 (cit. on p. 119).

225. R. D. Shachter, "Efficient Value of Information Computation," in *Conference on Uncertainty in Artificial Intelligence (UAI)*, 1999 (cit. on p. 119).

226.   A. Shaiju and I. R. Petersen, "Formulas for Discrete Time LQR, LQG, LEQG and Minimax LQG Optimal Control Problems," *IFAC Proceedings Volumes*, vol. 41, no. 2, pp. 8773–8778, 2008 (cit. on pp. 148, 149).

227.   G. Shani, J. Pineau, and R. Kaplow, "A Survey of Point-Based POMDP Solvers," *Autonomous Agents and Multi-Agent Systems*, vol. 27, pp. 1–51, 2012 (cit. on p. 432).

228.   C. E. Shannon, "A Mathematical Theory of Communication," *Bell System Technical Journal*, vol. 27, no. 4, pp. 623–656, 1948 (cit. on p. 565).

229.   L. S. Shapley, "Stochastic Games," *Proceedings of the National Academy of Sciences*, vol. 39, no. 10, pp. 1095–1100, 1953 (cit. on p. 517).

230.   Z. R. Shi, C. Wang, and F. Fang, "Artificial Intelligence for Social Good: A Survey," 2020. arXiv: 2001.01818v1 (cit. on p. 12).

231.   Y. Shoham and K. Leyton-Brown, *Multiagent Systems: Algorithmic, Game Theoretic, and Logical Foundations*. Cambridge University Press, 2009 (cit. on pp. 493, 515).

232.   D. Silver, G. Lever, N. Heess, T. Degris, D. Wierstra, and M. Riedmiller, "Deterministic Policy Gradient Algorithms," in *International Conference on Machine Learning (ICML)*, 2014 (cit. on p. 272).

233.   D. Silver, J. Schrittwieser, K. Simonyan, I. Antonoglou, A. Huang, A. Guez, T. Hubert, L. Baker, M. Lai, A. Bolton, et al., "Mastering the Game of Go Without Human Knowledge," *Nature*, vol. 550, pp. 354–359, 2017 (cit. on p. 276).

234.   D. Silver and J. Veness, "Monte-Carlo Planning in Large POMDPs," in *Advances in Neural Information Processing Systems (NIPS)*, 2010 (cit. on p. 457).

235.   S. Singh, M. Kearns, and Y. Mansour, "Nash Convergence of Gradient Dynamics in General-Sum Games," in *Conference on Uncertainty in Artificial Intelligence (UAI)*, 2000 (cit. on p. 509).

236.   S. P. Singh and R. S. Sutton, "Reinforcement Learning with Replacing Eligibility Traces," *Machine Learning*, vol. 22, pp. 123–158, 1996 (cit. on p. 612).

237.   S. P. Singh and R. C. Yee, "An Upper Bound on the Loss from Approximate Optimal-Value Functions," *Machine Learning*, vol. 16, no. 3, pp. 227–233, 1994 (cit. on p. 142).

238.   R. D. Smallwood and E. J. Sondik, "The Optimal Control of Partially Observable Markov Processes over a Finite Horizon," *Operations Research*, vol. 21, no. 5, pp. 1071–1088, 1973 (cit. on p. 617).

239.   T. Smith and R. G. Simmons, "Heuristic Search Value Iteration for POMDPs," in *Conference on Uncertainty in Artificial Intelligence (UAI)*, 2004 (cit. on p. 442).

240.   E. Sonu, Y. Chen, and P. Doshi, "Decision-Theoretic Planning Under Anonymity in Agent Populations," *Journal of Artificial Intelligence Research*, vol. 59, pp. 725–770, 2017 (cit. on p. 534).

241. M. T. J. Spaan and N. A. Vlassis, "Perseus: Randomized Point-Based Value Iteration for POMDPs," *Journal of Artificial Intelligence Research*, vol. 24, pp. 195–220, 2005 (cit. on p. 433).

242. J. C. Spall, *Introduction to Stochastic Search and Optimization*. Wiley, 2003 (cit. on p. 234).

243. D. O. Stahl and P. W. Wilson, "Experimental Evidence on Players' Models of Other Players," *Journal of Economic Behavior & Organization*, vol. 25, no. 3, pp. 309–327, 1994 (cit. on p. 504).

244. G. J. Stigler, "The Development of Utility Theory. I," *Journal of Political Economy*, vol. 58, no. 4, pp. 307–327, 1950 (cit. on p. 8).

245. M. J. A. Strens, "A Bayesian Framework for Reinforcement Learning," in *International Conference on Machine Learning (ICML)*, 2000 (cit. on p. 330).

246. F. P. Such, V. Madhavan, E. Conti, J. Lehman, K. O. Stanley, and J. Clune, "Deep Neuroevolution: Genetic Algorithms Are a Competitive Alternative for Training Deep Neural Networks for Reinforcement Learning," 2017. arXiv: 1712.06567v3 (cit. on p. 215).

247. Z. N. Sunberg and M. J. Kochenderfer, "Online Algorithms for POMDPs with Continuous State, Action, and Observation Spaces," in *International Conference on Automated Planning and Scheduling (ICAPS)*, 2018 (cit. on p. 457).

248. R. Sutton, "Learning to Predict by the Methods of Temporal Differences," *Machine Learning*, vol. 3, no. 1, pp. 9–44, 1988 (cit. on p. 341).

249. R. S. Sutton, "Dyna, an Integrated Architecture for Learning, Planning, and Reacting," *SIGART Bulletin*, vol. 2, no. 4, pp. 160–163, 1991 (cit. on p. 318).

250. R. S. Sutton and A. G. Barto, *Reinforcement Learning: An Introduction*, 2nd ed. MIT Press, 2018 (cit. on pp. 9, 335).

251. U. Syed and R. E. Schapire, "A Reduction from Apprenticeship Learning to Classification," in *Advances in Neural Information Processing Systems (NIPS)*, 2010 (cit. on p. 357).

252. C. Szepesvári and T. Lattimore, *Bandit Algorithms*. Cambridge University Press, 2020 (cit. on p. 299).

253. D. Szer, F. Charpillet, and S. Zilberstein, "MAA*: A Heuristic Search Algorithm for Solving Decentralized POMDPs," in *Conference on Uncertainty in Artificial Intelligence (UAI)*, 2005 (cit. on p. 550).

254. W. R. Thompson, "On the Likelihood That One Unknown Probability Exceeds Another in View of the Evidence of Two Samples," *Biometrika*, vol. 25, no. 3/4, pp. 285–294, 1933 (cit. on p. 306).

255. S. Thrun, "Probabilistic Robotics," *Communications of the ACM*, vol. 45, no. 3, pp. 52–57, 2002 (cit. on p. 10).

256.   S. Thrun, W. Burgard, and D. Fox, *Probabilistic Robotics*. MIT Press, 2006 (cit. on pp. 379, 385, 394).

257.   K. S. Trivedi and A. Bobbio, *Reliability and Availability Engineering*. Cambridge University Press, 2017 (cit. on p. 92).

258.   A. M. Turing, "Intelligent Machinery," National Physical Laboratory, Report, 1948 (cit. on p. 9).

259.   A. Tversky and D. Kahneman, "The Framing of Decisions and the Psychology of Choice," *Science*, vol. 211, no. 4481, pp. 453–458, 1981 (cit. on pp. 123, 124).

260.   W. Uther and M. Veloso, "Adversarial Reinforcement Learning," Carnegie Mellon University, Tech. Rep. CMU-CS-03-107, 1997 (cit. on p. 521).

261.   R. Vanderbei, *Linear Programming, Foundations and Extensions*, 4th ed. Springer, 2014 (cit. on p. 147).

262.   H. van Hasselt, "Double Q-Learning," in *Advances in Neural Information Processing Systems (NIPS)*, 2010 (cit. on p. 338).

263.   S. Vasileiadou, D. Kalligeropoulos, and N. Karcanias, "Systems, Modelling and Control in Ancient Greece: Part 1: Mythical Automata," *Measurement and Control*, vol. 36, no. 3, pp. 76–80, 2003 (cit. on p. 7).

264.   J. von Neumann and O. Morgenstern, *Theory of Games and Economic Behavior*. Princeton University Press, 1944 (cit. on p. 112).

265.   A. Wächter and L. T. Biegler, "On the Implementation of an Interior-Point Filter Line-Search Algorithm for Large-Scale Nonlinear Programming," *Mathematical Programming*, vol. 106, no. 1, pp. 25–57, 2005 (cit. on p. 205).

266.   C. J. C. H. Watkins, "Learning from Delayed Rewards," Ph.D. dissertation, University of Cambridge, 1989 (cit. on pp. 336, 341).

267.   D. J. White, "A Survey of Applications of Markov Decision Processes," *Journal of the Operational Research Society*, vol. 44, no. 11, pp. 1073–1096, 1993 (cit. on p. 134).

268.   M. Wiering and M. van Otterlo, eds., *Reinforcement Learning: State of the Art*. Springer, 2012 (cit. on p. 299).

269.   D. Wierstra, T. Schaul, T. Glasmachers, Y. Sun, J. Peters, and J. Schmidhuber, "Natural Evolution Strategies," *Journal of Machine Learning Research*, vol. 15, pp. 949–980, 2014 (cit. on pp. 219, 222).

270.   R. J. Williams, "Simple Statistical Gradient-Following Algorithms for Connectionist Reinforcement Learning," *Machine Learning*, vol. 8, pp. 229–256, 1992 (cit. on p. 245).

271.   B. Wong, "Points of View: Color Blindness," *Nature Methods*, vol. 8, no. 6, pp. 441–442, 2011 (cit. on p. xxi).

272.   J. R. Wright and K. Leyton-Brown, "Beyond Equilibrium: Predicting Human Behavior in Normal Form Games," in *AAAI Conference on Artificial Intelligence (AAAI)*, 2010 (cit. on p. 505).

273.   J. R. Wright and K. Leyton-Brown, "Behavioral Game Theoretic Models: A Bayesian Framework for Parameter Analysis," in *International Conference on Autonomous Agents and Multiagent Systems (AAMAS)*, 2012 (cit. on p. 505).

274.   N. Ye, A. Somani, D. Hsu, and W. S. Lee, "DESPOT: Online POMDP Planning with Regularization," *Journal of Artificial Intelligence Research*, vol. 58, pp. 231–266, 2017 (cit. on p. 459).

275.   B. D. Ziebart, A. Maas, J. A. Bagnell, and A. K. Dey, "Maximum Entropy Inverse Reinforcement Learning," in *AAAI Conference on Artificial Intelligence (AAAI)*, 2008 (cit. on p. 365).

276.   M. Zinkevich, "Online Convex Programming and Generalized Infinitesimal Gradient Ascent," in *International Conference on Machine Learning (ICML)*, 2003 (cit. on p. 509).

Index